Alaska

Also by Claus-M. Naske

An Interpretive History of Alaskan Statehood (Anchorage, 1973)

Alaska: A History of the 49th State, with Herman E. Slotnick (Grand Rapids, Mich., 1979; 2nd ed., 1987)

Edward Lewis "Bob" Bartlett of Alaska: A Life in Politics (Fairbanks, 1980)

Anchorage: A Pictorial History, with Ludwig J. Rowinski (Norfolk/Virginia Beach, Va., 1981)

Fairbanks: A Pictorial History, with Ludwig J. Rowinski (Norfolk/Virginia Beach, Va., 1981; rev. ed., 1995)

Alaska: A Pictorial History, with Ludwig J. Rowinski (Norfolk/Virginia Beach, Va., 1981)

Alaska, with Hans Blohm (Toronto, 1984)

A History of Alaska Statehood (Lanham, Md., 1985)

Paving Alaska's Trails: The Work of the Alaska Road Commission (Lanham, Md., 1986)

Alaska's Builders: Fifty Years of Construction in the 49th State, with Gail West (Anchorage, 1999)

Ernest Gruening: Alaska's Greatest Governor (Fairbanks, 2004)

49 at Last! The Battle for Alaska Statehood (Kenmore, Wash., 2009)

Alaska

A History

Claus-M. Naske and Herman E. Slotnick

UNIVERSITY OF OKLAHOMA PRESS : NORMAN

Library of Congress Cataloging-in-Publication Data

Naske, Claus-M.
Alaska : A History/ Claus-M. Naske and Herman E. Slotnick.
        p.   cm.
Includes bibliographical references and index.
ISBN 978-0-8061-4040-7 (pbk. : alk. paper)
1. Alaska—History.
I. Slotnick, Herman E., 1916–
II. Title.
F904.N37 2011
979.8—dc22
2010028186

The paper in this book meets the guidelines for permanence and durability of the Committee on Production Guidelines for Book Longevity of the Council on Library Resources, Inc. ∞

First edition copyright © 1979 by Wm. B. Eerdmans Publishing Co., Grand Rapids, Michigan. Second edition copyright © 1987 by the University of Oklahoma Press, Norman, Publishing Division of the University. Third edition copyright © 2011 by the University of Oklahoma Press. Manufactured in the U.S.A.

1 2 3 4 5 6 7 8 9 10

For Herman E. Slotnick, who guided me
on the path to becoming a historian.
In fond memory.

❦

Contents

Illustrations

Maps

Tables

Preface and Acknowledgments

The history of Alaska has attracted hundreds of authors over the years who have created a rich written record of the many facets of its varied geography, its diverse cultural complexities, and its ever-changing cast of dynamic and fascinating characters. Few books, however, have attempted to give a broad view of the entire sweep of Alaska's history, from its first inhabitants to the many challenges facing its citizens today. Herman E. Slotnick, my undergraduate mentor and friend at the University of Alaska, and I made such an attempt. William B. Eerdmans Publishing Company of Grand Rapids, Michigan, published the first edition in 1979. The University of Oklahoma Press published the second, slightly revised edition, in 1987. Since Slotnick's death at age eighty-five on January 6, 2002, in Seattle, it has been my task to prepare this new edition. I miss Herman E. Slotnick's collaboration.

Even a casual survey of the available literature is overwhelming. There are, for example, the accounts of the Russian, English, American, French, German, and Spanish explorers; primary and secondary accounts dealing with Russian America; and many, many volumes dealing with various aspects of Alaska as an American possession, acquired in 1867. Voluminous federal government reports examine everything from the number of salmon and reindeer to the conditions of the aborigines. The literature of the Klondike Gold Rush into Canada's Yukon Territory is vast, and eager writers in all fields have added substantially to this body of written work as it played out in Alaska.

I have consulted the works, both lengthy and authoritative, of many specialists; the holdings of the University of Alaska Fairbanks library were particularly useful. But I have not attempted to survey all of the available literature. This book presents a narrative account of Alaska's major developmental strands from early times to the present, including a brief survey of the Russian background, with an emphasis on developments in the twentieth century. Upon its initial publication the public received it well, and the hope is that this will be the case with this third edition.

I am grateful to several colleagues at the University of Alaska Fairbanks (UAF) and the University of Alaska Anchorage (UAA) who, over the years, read various drafts of parts of the manuscript and critically and helpfully commented. These include the late Richard A. Pierce, the preeminent authority on Russian America; Thomas A. Morehouse, since retired from the Institute of Social and Economic Research at UAA; Gerald A. McBeath of the Department of Political Science at UAF; my son, Nathaniel-M. N. Naske, who helped edit the manuscript, and above all my good friend and skillful editor, Terrence Cole, director of the Office of Public History at UAF.

Special thanks go to Julia Parzick, the ever-cheerful former administrative assistant of the Department of History and Northern Studies at UAF and now administrative coordinator for the Experimental Program to Stimulate Competitive Research (EPSCoR) at UAF. For years she has typed my handwritten scholarly papers as well as book chapters. Along the way, she corrected misspellings, caught missing footnotes, and transformed obscure paragraphs into clear English. I continue to be grateful for all her help. Finally, I would like to express my gratitude to Patricia Heinicke, my gifted editor, who helped shape this volume.

CLAUS-M. NASKE

Fairbanks, Alaska

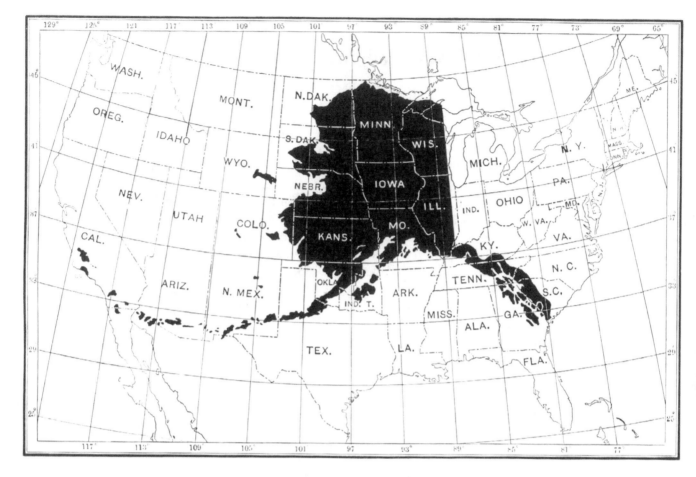

Alaska Compared in Size to the Lower Forty-eight.

The bay and the mountains at Seward, 2008. The little fishing town of Millers Landing, away from the action of Seward, has become a resort for people wanting to take fishing and wildlife tours. The cruise ships dock here as well.

(Photo by David Bjornsgaard, used with permission.)

Introduction
Looking Backward and Forward

The First Alaskans

Anthropologists and archaeologists still vigorously debate the origins of the First Americans. Into the early 1990s the belief that Native Americans are one people, descendants of North Asians, remained the prevalent view. But the First American debate heated considerably in 1996 with the discovery of, first, a skull, and then a nearly complete skeleton near Kennewick, Washington, on the Columbia River. James C. Chatters, an archaeologist and paleoecologist, dated the skeleton at about 8,400 radiocarbon years, or around 9,500 calendar years. If it was of "European" origins, as the evidence suggested, then all theories about who was living in North America 8,000 years ago would become questionable. So would "the prevailing ideas of how, and by what route or routes, people might have migrated here." If

Chatter's initial identification of the skeletal remains stands, it would support the emerging hypothesis that our continent was settled over millennia by different competing peoples from scattered parts of the world.[1]

What is clear is that for thousands of years the progenitors of the Indians, Aleuts, and Eskimos made Alaska their home. They used the resources of this subcontinent to sustain themselves and successfully adapted to the varied climates of the North. Then came the Europeans, who brought modern technology as well as diseases. As elsewhere, upon contact with whites, thousands of Alaska's indigenous inhabitants died, most from unfamiliar European maladies.

Nabesna Glacier sweeps off high ice fields in the Wrangell Mountains in the Wrangell–Saint Elias National Park Preserve.

(Courtesy of the National Park Service.)

"The Inside of a House in Oonalashka."

(Author's collection.)

The Russian Presence in Alaska

The Russians came first. Russian Cossacks and *promyshlenniks* (fur hunters) first reached the Pacific in 1639. By the end of the century, the Russians began their eastward thrust via Kamchatka. Peter I (1682–1725), called Peter the Great, took the greatest steps in consolidating and expanding the Russian empire. He supplied the energy and vision behind the voyages of Vitus Bering, a Dane in Russian service. Bering undertook the first (1728) and second (1741) expeditions of discovery, and when the survivors returned from the second voyage they brought news of a "great land" across the Eastern Ocean (the Pacific). More importantly, they brought numerous samples of sea otter pelts, which were to prove even more valuable than the Siberian sable skins. This discovery prompted a rush across the Bering Sea via the Aleutian Islands, giving the Russians a half-century head start on foreign competitors who were not alerted to the discovery until the publication of Captain James Cook's third voyage (1776–1779).

The Russian entrepreneurs rushed into what was to become known as Russian America. It comprised mainland Alaska, the Aleutian, Pribilof, Commander, and Kuril islands, as well as temporary settlements in northern California and Hawaii and eventually also the island of Sakhalin. These areas were peripheral not only to the expanding Russian empire but also to North America's emerging nations, the United States, Canada, and Mexico. Nevertheless, between 1790 and 1840, Russia vied for control of the resources of America's northwest coast with Great Britain, Spain, and the United States.

The early Russian entrepreneurs, with little supervision from the government in Saint Petersburg, reduced the Aleuts, the Native people with whom they first came into contact, into submission. By the end of the century the private traders had been replaced by a government-sponsored monopoly, the Russian-American Company. Aleksander Baranov, the outstanding personality of Russian America, came to Alaska in 1790 and capably managed the company. He departed in 1818, and his successors

Interior of a Tlingit dwelling.

(Courtesy of Alaska and Polar Regions Department, Elmer E. Rasmuson Library, University of Alaska Fairbanks.)

Habitants d'ounalacheka avec leurs canots (Iles Aleutiennes) [Inhabitants of Unalaska with Their Canoes].

(Courtesy of Alaska and Polar Regions Department, Elmer E. Rasmuson Library, University of Alaska Fairbanks.)

were naval men. They were better educated, and among them were some explorers of note. They attempted to increase Russian influence among the Natives by establishing schools, improving their livelihood, and encouraging the evangelizing efforts of the Russian Orthodox Church. Father Ioann Veniaminov, a cleric of the church, devised an alphabet and gave the Aleuts a written language. The Russians established New Archangel (later Sitka) as the Pacific coast's largest town, though it was by no means a metropolitan center.

By the middle of the nineteenth century, however, the Russian-American Company was in a precarious position, subsisting on government favors and subsidies. Russia's leaders believed that the country could not both defend Russian America and carry out an imperialistic policy in Asia. In 1867 they decided to sell their possession to the United States for $7,200,000.

The Russians had never colonized their possession. There never were more than eight hundred Russians who inhabited the region, and they were limited to the islands and the coastal areas. They left the vast interior almost untouched. Even the Panhandle region, south of what is today Juneau, the Russians had leased to the Hudson's Bay Company. What remains of the Russian presence upon the landscape today are Russian names among the Aleuts and many Tlingits and the Russian Orthodox Church.

A New U.S. Possession

American rule brought little change to the North, now called Alaska, for the United States in 1867 was not much better prepared than Russia to govern the subcontinent. The Civil War had just ended, and the problems of Alaska held little interest. With no precedence to guide it in the administration of noncontiguous territories, Congress took the easiest course and turned Alaska over to the military. For the next seventeen years the army, and then the navy, ruled the region. But even if the quality of the American statesmanship had been greater and more thought been given to Alaska, there was little incentive for Americans to move north.

The population declined when the Russian-American Company left Alaska. Most Russians and those individuals of mixed blood who had been given the option to remain in Alaska under the treaty of purchase went either to Russia, or to Canada, or to other parts of the United States, where they felt they had better prospects. A few Americans rushed to preempt land in Sitka, but they soon departed when the boom they hoped for failed to materialize.

It is not clear whether the Alaskan Natives preferred the Russian or the American presence. Some altercations between U.S. soldiers and the aboriginal population took place, but no great wars such as occurred in the American West ever developed in Alaska.

Skagway's Main Street (to the north) in the Klondike Gold Rush National Historical Park.

(Courtesy of the National Park Service.)

Alaska's great size, remoteness, and formidable climate seemed to discourage small businesses and favored those possessing substantial capital. One thriving organization, the Alaska Commercial Company, apparently had some political influence and was given the monopoly of the fur seal harvest of the Pribilof Islands. The Yukon Valley was opened for the fur trade under the auspices of this company. The exploitation of the valuable salmon fisheries began, but with virtually no benefit to Alaska or Alaskans, since large salmon-packing firms from the contiguous states provided the needed capital for the industry. They paid few taxes and brought in not only the fishermen but also the crews to work in the canneries.

By the 1880s, only a few adventurous tourists came to Alaska. The trip was long and expensive, and so tourists did not come in great numbers. Eventually it was the lure of gold that drew Americans north. Gold discoveries in the Gastineau Channel led to the founding of Juneau, the first town established under American rule. Prospectors also found gold on the American segment of the Yukon River at Fortymile and then Birch Creek. Far more

important, however, were the great discoveries on the Canadian segment of the Yukon River near the banks of one of its tributaries, the Throndiuck, or Klondike. Alaska benefited greatly. Skagway, a port on Lynn Canal, became the gateway to the Klondike, and the Canadian boom stimulated the search for gold in Alaska. Nome, on the Seward Peninsula, where twenty thousand men worked its "golden sands," was the scene of Alaska's greatest gold rush, followed by Fairbanks and a host of others, including Iditarod, Chandalar, and Livengood.

The gold rush marked a new discovery of Alaska. Business looked to the territory as a place for investment, and several government agencies began work in Alaska. For example, in 1905 Congress created the Board of Road Commissioners for Alaska, making road building a reality. The U.S. Geological Survey undertook geographical exploration and geological and mineral resource investigations. Congress, for the first time, granted Alaska's citizens limited rights of political self-government. Towns were permitted to incorporate and their citizens were enabled to elect their own officials. In 1906 Alaskans received permission to send a delegate to Congress. In 1912 Congress granted a legislature to the territory, although it retained for the federal government control over Alaska's lands and resources.

By 1910 Alaska's population had stabilized at about 60,000, dropping a little during World War I and increasing slightly to a high of 72,000 just before the United States entered World War II in 1941. After the war, population growth accelerated, reaching 138,000 in 1950 and 228,000 in 1960. Soon fisheries became the most important industry, putting minerals into second place.

The First Half of the Twentieth Century

Generalizations about Alaska's population abound: its people were highly transient, and men outnumbered women five to one. Few brought their families with them. Once they made their "stake," they returned home. But many came to love Alaska—the "Great Land," as they called it—and many wrote affectionately about it. Henry W. Elliott championed the conservation of the fur seals and was a noted water colorist and author. William Healy Dall summarized in one volume, published in 1870, the most important knowledge of Alaska known to that time. John Muir was fascinated by Alaska's great beauty, and Rev. Sheldon Jackson saw it as a place for saving Native souls.

Like residents of other territories before them, Alaskans complained constantly that the federal government ignored and neglected their interests. Although neither Congress nor successive administrations ever made Alaskan concerns a priority, several presidents did pay some attention. Early in the twentieth century, the federal government made a determined effort to keep Canadians from poaching fur seals bound for the Pribilof Islands in the Bering Sea. Theodore Roosevelt adamantly countered Canadian claims to part of the Alaska Panhandle. He also closed Alaska's coal fields to further entry and asked Congress to reclassify coal lands and enact laws making coal mining workable in Alaska. Roosevelt had acted for good reasons, but many Alaskans criticized him harshly for this action.

In his first presidential message, Woodrow Wilson asked Congress to pay heed to Alaska's needs, and Congress responded, passing legislation that allowed the leasing of coal lands and authorized the construction of a railroad with federal funds. It did not, however, change Alaska's governmental system. Warren G. Harding, the first president to visit Alaska, drove the golden spike in Nenana that symbolized the completion of the Alaska Railroad. He traveled widely and promised much, but the only important piece of legislation to emerge from his corrupt and ineffective administration dealt with Alaska's fisheries. During the New Deal era of President Franklin D. Roosevelt, the federal government for the first and only time attempted to bring people to Alaska, in the 1935 settlement program for the Matanuska Valley.

World War II revolutionized Alaska. The territory's strategic location made it a key component in America's defense program. Thousands of troops were rushed north while army and navy bases were built in locations ranging from Unalaska to Kodiak Island, and from Sitka to Anchorage and Fairbanks. In the summer of 1942, Japanese forces invaded the Aleutian chain. America's pride was hurt, and American armed forces began intensive efforts to oust the enemy. Fearing Japanese disruption of the sea-lanes to Alaska, the United States began work in the spring of 1942 on the Alaska-Canada Military Highway, also called the Alaska Highway, to link the territory with the contiguous states. The 1,671-mile highway was completed speedily and opened to military traffic in November of that same year.

By the fall of 1943 the enemy had been expelled from Alaska. Ground forces were reduced from a high of 150,000 in November 1943 to 50,000 by March 1945. Forts were closed, bases dismantled, and military airfields turned over to the Civil Aeronautics Administration.

The military presence irrevocably altered the pace and tenor of Alaskan life. The residual benefits to the civilian economy and the development of Alaska were tremendous. In addition to the influx of well over $1 billion in the territory between 1941 and 1945, Alaskans also benefited from the modernization of the Alaska Railroad and the expansion of airfields and the construction of roads.

Federal activities declined sharply after 1945, but the outbreak of the Cold War in the late 1940s once again caused the federal government to spend million of dollars in defense-related activities. Federal projects became the primary base of the Alaska economy. Within two decades the population of Alaska more than tripled. Anchorage and Fairbanks—especially the former—became the new population centers. Political demands of the "new" Alaska led to the achievement of statehood in 1958 and Alaska's admission into the Union as the 49th State in 1959.

Statehood, Oil, and Native Claims

The new state assumed its responsibilities vigorously, but its finances and budgets soon became major concerns. Alaskans quickly realized that it was expensive to provide the amenities of modern life to their sprawling subcontinent. Additionally, military expenditures declined in the 1960s. But a modest oil strike on the Kenai National Moose Range in 1957, a growing forest industry, and developments in the fisheries made up for some of the losses in federal spending. The discovery of North America's largest oil field on Alaska public lands in 1968 finally gave reason to believe that Alaska's economy would become more stable.

In 1971 Congress passed and President Richard M. Nixon signed into law the Alaska Native Claims Settlement Act (ANCSA), which compensated the state's original inhabitants for losses suffered over many years. With land (including subsurface rights) and money, Native Alaskans rapidly became influential in state politics and business. At the same time, the construction of the Trans-Alaska Pipeline created a boom, bringing prosperity as well as many problems to the state. After oil began flowing in the summer of 1977, the state treasury and with it all Alaskans gained some financial stability and security.

In the latter part of 1985 and during the first two months of 1986, world oil prices tumbled. Falling oil prices hurt producing states, such as Alaska, which in 1985 received 84 percent of its unrestricted general fund revenues from petroleum royalties and taxes (and so it has remained). On February 17, 1986, a spokesman for Sohio, which owned about one half of the 1.5 million barrels of oil pumped from Prudhoe Bay each day, confirmed that the company's negotiated contract price of crude oil from the North Slope fell four dollars a barrel retroactive to February 1, 1986. Officials of the State of Alaska Department of Revenue had stated that every one-dollar drop in the price of oil cost the state $150 million a year in lost revenues.[2] Sohio's Alaska crude had sold for twenty dollars a barrel on the West Coast and twenty-one dollars a barrel on the Gulf Coast earlier in the year; by the summer, oil prices dropped below ten dollars a barrel and Alaska's economy plunged, bankruptcies abounded, and many panicked and left the state.

The precipitous drop in oil prices hurt Alaska as well as other oil-producing states. Oil companies, faced with declining revenues, deferred exploratory activities. For example, Conoco, Inc., announced in February 1986 that it had suspended drilling operations at its Milne Point oil field on the North Slope because of plunging oil prices. A spokesman for the company stated that if crude oil prices continued to fall, it would also shut down production from the field.

Obviously the declining crude oil prices and the state's heavy reliance on oil-generated revenues worried many northern residents. Alternative sources of revenues had to be found. Unfortunately, at a time of high crude oil prices and record revenues for the state, the legislature decided to abandon Alaska's state income tax system. Many cautioned the lawmakers to suspend rather than abolish the tax. But with prospects of ever-rising oil revenues, those warnings were not heeded, and the legislature abolished it. No one seemed to remember that territorial governor Ernest Gruening had struggled for ten years, from 1939 to 1949, to have the legislature fashion and adopt a modern tax system. It took only one day to abolish what had taken a decade to create. Then Governor Jay S. Hammond failed to veto the tax abolition, convinced that his veto would be overridden, and today reimposing the tax still remains a political impossibility.

Voters created the Alaska Permanent Fund via constitutional amendment in 1976. The original goal was to place part of the one-time oil wealth beyond the reach of day-to-day government spending. Governor Jay S. Hammond, among others, favored direct distribution of a portion of the oil revenues, thus giving each citizen a personal stake in the oil revenues and protecting the Permanent Fund from possible raids by legislators. In 1980 the legislature passed a Permanent Fund distribution measure. In the summer of 1982 the computer in the Juneau State Office Building began printing the first oversized blue and gold one-thousand-dollar checks, which were mailed to more than four hundred thousand Alaska residents. The program works much like a company sharing profits with shareholders. In this case the stockholders of the invested Permanent Fund include everyone who has lived in Alaska for more than one year. Dividend payments over the years have fluctuated, reflecting the earnings of the Permanent Fund. In 2007 the Permanent Fund's values stood at about $39 billion, but as of 2009, the fund was worth about $30 billion, putting it $9 billion underwater.

There has been continuous discussion of whether or not the distribution of Permanent Fund dividends represents the best use of these dollars. Suggestions have been made to discontinue the dividend program and use the income, after inflation proofing, to support the state budget as

Alaska's oil revenues continue to decline. Each such suggestion is greeted with outrage on the part of the majority of the shareholders. Alaskans have come to consider the Permanent Fund dividend program a birthright. The debate will continue.

Non-oil Resources

Alaska has also attempted to diversify its economy, an effort going back to the days of Russian America. It has not been crowned with overwhelming success. The timber industry in southeastern Alaska is in the doldrums. Oversupply and soft markets plagued it for a number of years, and the pulp mills in Sitka and Ketchikan shut down permanently.

Mining has been more successful. Cominco and NANA Regional Corporation, the latter based at Kotzebue in northwestern Alaska, together developed the Red Dog lead and zinc mine, located about 120 miles north of NANA headquarters. The state legislature appropriated about $200 million to build a road and port facilities to ship ore to the smelters, and the developers then repaid the state. In 2005 the mine recorded a $325 million operating profit, and during the first half of 2006, it earned a $240 million profit.[3]

In 2009 Alaska had five large mines, including the oldest, Usibelli Coal Mine, with sixty-six years in operation. Many large international companies are engaged in exploratory and drilling work throughout Alaska. The mining industry had become a business in excess of $1 billion annually.

The state government has carefully managed the salmon stocks since it assumed control of this resource in 1960. Nearly ruined under federal mismanagement, the salmon runs increased substantially over the years, reaching record levels in the 1970s and 1980s. The state and various nonprofit organizations developed a vigorous hatchery program that contributed to the revival of the salmon runs, and Alaska salmon fishers made a good living. But in the 1990s the salmon fishery weakened for several reasons. One was the increasing competition from lower-cost salmon farms in Canada, Chile, and Scandinavia; in addition there was a down cycle in the salmon runs and less demand from the traditional Japanese market. The fisheries' decline

Ketchikan, with a 2002 population of 7,845, is located on the southern coast of Revillagigedo Island, on the north shore of Tongass Narrows in the Alexander Archipelago. A port of entry, Ketchikan grew as a fishing town around a cannery established in 1887. The town became a supply center during the Gold Rush period in the late 1890s. The town was named after Ketchikan Creek, a corruption of the Tlingit name Kitschkhin. The photograph shows the town probably in the 1940s.

(Courtesy of Machetanz Collection, Alaska and Polar Regions Department, Elmer E. Rasmuson Library, University of Alaska Fairbanks.)

prompted the governor at the time, Tony Knowles, to urge the Alaska legislature to provide relief funding for western Alaska villages dependent on income from this source. A long-range marketing effort got under way to distinguish the high-quality wild Alaska salmon from its inferior, pen-raised cousin.

When the federal government claimed a two-hundred-mile economic zone off the coasts in 1976, the plan was to have American rather than foreign fishers harvest the bountiful bottomfish, such as pollock and haddock in the eastern Bering Sea. Over the years foreign harvest quotas have been completely eliminated. The Bering Sea/Aleutian Islands pollock fishery, a mid-water trawl fishery, is the world's largest whitefish fishery, with annual average landings over the last twenty years of about 1.1 million metric tons. It accounts for approximately 30 percent of all fish landed in the United States by weight. The North Pacific Fishery Management Council develops management measures for the fishery, including recommending acceptable biological catch (ABC) and total allowable catch (TAC). The U.S. Secretary of Commerce receives and approves the council's recommendations.

Japan, the United States, and Europe are the primary markets for Alaska pollock products. Surimi (or minced fish) and roe products go to Japan, while fillet-type products are sold in the United States and Europe. Surimi is used for imitation crab and similar products. In their totality, Alaska fishery resources produce revenue of about a $1 billion a year for fishermen at the vessel level, and almost $2 billion a year in fish wholesale value. Secondary economic benefits extend to businesses that support commercial fishing and seafood processing in the state. State government and local communities collect millions of dollars in fish taxes. Economic studies performed as recently as 2003 estimate that the seafood industry provides more direct jobs than oil and gas, mining, agriculture, and forestry combined. Total direct sales within Alaska are about $3 billion, and $4.6 billion nationwide. Major components of the industry include salmon, crab, sablefish, halibut, Pacific cod, pollock, herring, and other miscellaneous bottomfish, and shellfish, species. The fishery encompasses a vast geographical area, from the Bering Sea/Aleutian Islands to the Gulf of Alaska and southeast Alaska.[4]

In 2006, the Alaska salmon harvest totaled 141 million fish, the fifteenth largest harvest since Alaska took over the management of its salmon fisheries from the federal government in 1960. Preliminary prices for all species but sockeye salmon were higher than in 2005. An estimate of the 2006 vessel value of the salmon harvest is $308 million, above the most recent ten-year average of $279 million.[5]

Estimates of Alaska's coal resources have varied through the years. In 1967, Farrell Barnes, a U.S. Geological Survey geologist, quantified Alaska's coal resources at 120 billion short tons, but more recent and speculative estimates put the numbers at 1,800 to 5,000 billion tons. Whatever the exact magnitude, Alaska's coal resources are huge. Extensive coal fields lie in the Cook Inlet region and on the North Slope, and there are other fields of substantial size. Despite these mammoth reserves, in 2007 there existed only one fairly large operating mine, the Usibelli Coal Mine at Healy, about ninety miles southwest of Fairbanks.

The scarcity of successful coal mines is not due to ignorance. Eskimos began using coal on the North Slope in the nineteenth century after the whalers showed them how to utilize it. The Russian-American Company opened its first Alaska coal mine in 1855 at Port Graham, in Kachemak Bay, and over the years many other mines have operated. But all except the Usibelli Coal Mine failed. Usibelli supplies fuel for the Healy coal-fired generating plant of the Fairbanks-based Golden Valley Electric Association and the University of Alaska Fairbanks power plant, and the mine also exports coal to South Korea and ships some to Chile. The Alaska Railroad transports the coal to Seward, where a modern loading facility transfers it onto freighters.

The visitor industry has increased every year since statehood. The number of out-of-state visitors to Alaska between May and September of 2008 came to just over 1.7 million, having dropped by 0.4 percent since the summer of 2007. About half of these visitors (49 percent) exited the state via cruise ships; 47 percent by air; 4 percent via the highway; and 1 percent by state ferry.[6] There is a high interest in Alaska as a unique wilderness destination, and the weak dollar has made the North attractive to European visitors. The cruise ship industry has grown, and behemoth vessels ply the inland passage to Alaska between Seattle and Vancouver, British Columbia, in total making hundreds of trips each season.[7]

Agriculture plays but a minimal role in Alaska's economy. The 1935 Matanuska Valley Colony did not meet expectations. The Jay Hammond administration expended substantial state dollars to develop the Delta area, about ninety-eight miles south of Fairbanks. The plan was to grow barley for export to Asia, but it never materialized. The weather refused to cooperate fully, a buffalo herd at Delta grazed in the barley fields every fall, and the farmers were undercapitalized and heavily indebted to the state. The more recent and modest plan produces feed barley for cattle and domesticated buffalo and supplies red meat to the interior market. A dairy development project at Point McKenzie, near Anchorage, totally failed after considerable state expenditures.

The Effects of ANCSA

The legal status of Alaska Natives involves many complicated, controversial, and often emotional issues. The relevant history is extensive and dates back to a time before the United States purchased Alaska from Russia in 1867. Unfortunately, many of these issues have not yet been resolved to the satisfaction of all concerned. Often there is a state, a federal, and one or more Native positions on any specific question.

In part because of this complexity, many Alaska Natives have become disillusioned with the Alaska Native Claims Settlement Act (ANCSA) of 1971, which created thirteen regional corporations to administer Native land and financial claims. Perhaps William "Spud" Williams, president of the Tanana Chiefs Conference in 1981, put it best when he stated, "I get tired of these newspaper articles [that say] they gave us 44 million acres and a billion dollars. They didn't give us shit. They stole it [from us], and the only time they were interested in settling it [the land claims] was when they found a few barrels of oil. And now they're trying to steal our identities."[8] Many Natives had become disappointed with the structure of the regional corporations. Many also wanted Congress to amend ANCSA to protect their stock and lands. Congress complied in 1988 when it passed an extensive set of ANCSA amendments that virtually restructured the act.

One unforeseen result of competing claims under ANCSA was that between 1973 and 1993, the regional corporations lost approximately $760 million of the $962.5 million originally received for the extinguishment of aboriginal claims in 1971. In response, U.S. Senator Ted Stevens had Congress insert into the Internal Revenue Code a provision that allowed ANCSA corporations to sell their accumulated financial losses. These net operating losses, or NOLs, could be sold to profitable corporations for the value of the tax write-off given to those

A Sitka pulp mill.

(Photo by Claus-M. Naske.)

A halibut boat in the Kenai Fjords National Park sets its line in Wildcat Pass between Ragged and Rabbit islands in 1980. The pass swirls with tidal chop. Spruce and hemlock blanket Rabbit Island in the Pye Island group on Nuka Bay.

(Photograph by M. Woodbridge Williams; courtesy of the National Park Service.)

profitable corporations. Within a short few years, these NOLs had generated more than $1 billion in new capital, in effect refinancing ANCSA. Congress closed this tax loophole in 1988.

The Alaska National Interest Lands Conservation Act of 1980 (ANILCA) divided Alaska among the various federal agencies. The jurisdictional disputes over boundaries between the federal and state governments and Native regional corporations will probably take several generations to resolve.

Alaska's Dependence on Federal Revenue and Oil

Most every year, the state legislature has appropriated more money than flows into the general fund, mostly from royalties and taxes on the oil industry. Alaska has considerable financial reserves to draw on, most importantly the Permanent Fund. State-wide debates and frequent forums have dealt with the fiscal gap—all with the same result, namely, "Do not touch the sacred Permanent Fund dividend check" that each resident shareholder receives each year. Alaskans have thus looked to the congressional delegation to bring home the cash. Long incumbency has given them seniority and clout in the appropriation process. Alaskans have never asked their lone congressman or their two U.S. senators to play major roles as shapers of important national legislation—just to bring home the bacon. They have obliged, and with few exceptions, such as the Magnuson-Stevens Fishery Conservation and Management Act, have not played a major role on the national scene.

Alaska license plates proclaim this "The Last Frontier," but a good four-fifths of residents live in urban areas well equipped with all the comforts of modern life, including box stores and espresso bars. And Alaskans enjoy rich subsidies. Citizens Against Government Waste, a watchdog group, has calculated that Alaska receives more pork per head than any other state. The federal largesse is partially understandable. It supports a sizable military presence, it owns and must manage 60 percent of Alaska's lands, and also has an obligation to Alaska's indigenous population.

Politics in Alaska primarily deal with two major issues, namely, how to extract the maximum funds out of Washington, D.C., and how to suck more fossil fuels out of the ground. At the former task Alaska's congressional delegation is very adept. The latter involves continuing negotiations with the energy firms. Alaskans also have been attempting to persuade the American public that drilling in the coastal plain of the Arctic National Wildlife Refuge (ANWR) will not cause too much damage. Most Alaskans hope that ANWR will be opened to drilling, precipitating another boom and keeping oil flowing through the Trans-Alaska Pipeline System. Congress, however, has to approve the opening of ANWR to oil drilling, and despite the best efforts of Alaska's congressional delegation over the last twenty-nine years and the support of the George W. Bush administration, Congress has refused to do so. The Alaska Coalition and the Alaska Conservation Foundation, together with a coalition of conservation, labor, religious, and other citizen groups representing millions of Americans, all believe that ANWR should remain wild, unspoiled, and free of oil rigs. They argue that drilling in ANWR won't solve America's energy problem. The U.S. Geological Survey estimates that ANWR may hold less oil than the United States consumes in a year.

Perhaps the resolve of the lawmakers was also reinforced by the 2001 report the National Research Council of the National Academies issued at the request of Congress. Titled *Cumulative Environmental Effects of Oil and Gas Activities on Alaska's North Slope*, the report pointed out that industrial activity on the North Slope had grown from a single operational oil field at Prudhoe Bay to an industrial complex of developed oil fields and their interconnecting roads, pipelines, and power lines that stretches from the Alpine oil field in the west to Badami in the east. In short, the North Slope has developed into a large industrial complex that has disrupted and negatively affected natural processes, interfered with subsistence activities, and changed the North Slope landscape in ways that have had accumulating aesthetic, cultural, and spiritual consequences. Development, however, also has brought wealth to the North Slope Borough, and made possible the economic success of the Arctic Slope Regional Corporation.[9]

The development-minded Alaskan public too often will encourage projects that create jobs for the twenty- to thirty-year life of a mine in exchange for the permanent damage inflicted on the renewable resources. An example of this is the proposed Pebble Mine in southwest Alaska. There, the Canadian-owned Northern Dynasty Mines, Inc., wants to develop the largest open-pit gold/copper mine in North America. It is a sprawling undertaking, including a mine pit two and a half miles wide and a fifteen-square-mile tailings pond that would be visible from outer space. The mining process would involve the use of highly toxic chemicals, such as cyanide, that could spill into the surrounding Bristol Bay watershed. The exposed mine pit could leach acid into the watershed for centuries if not millennia to come. Bristol Bay is home to the world's most productive commercial sockeye salmon fishery. Alaska's and perhaps the world's largest Chinook run occurs in the Nushagak-Mulchatna river system, downstream of the proposed mine site. The area is also world famous among sport fishermen who support numerous fishing lodges and guide, outfitter, and transporter services that add about $50 million annually to Alaska's economy. Development of the Pebble Project could ruin Bristol Bay's world famous fishery. Already proponents and opponents are squaring off on the project.

English artist Frederick Whymper depicted this Tanana Indian in 1868. The man is wearing a decorated moosehide shirt. His curved-handled knife is worn in a sheath in front.

(From Whymper, *Travel and Adventure in the Territory of Alaska, 1868*. Courtesy of Alaska and Polar Regions Department, Elmer E. Rasmuson Library, University of Alaska Fairbanks.)

Looking Ahead

It is exciting to live in the largest and only arctic and subarctic state in the Union, embracing fully one-fifth the land area of the forty-eight contiguous states combined. Alaska claims a unique Russian heritage, shared only by California, where the Russians maintained a toehold for a few decades in the early part of the nineteenth century. Alaska's early economy was based on the utilization of its abundant natural resources: furs, minerals, and fish. It served a long political apprenticeship, first as a district and then a territory, gaining statehood in 1959. A major actor in overcoming congressional opposition to statehood had been the realization, gained during World War II, that Alaska's location was of prime strategic importance in the modern air age. The Cold War merely reinforced that realization.

The discovery of North America's largest oil field at Prudhoe Bay on the state's North Slope made Alaska an oil-rich state. It was in Alaska that Congress tackled the Native claims question with the passage of the innovative ANCSA in 1971. In 1980, ANILCA divided 60 percent of Alaska's land area among various federal agencies. The dust has not yet settled from that division. Indeed, it is exciting to be living in a state where every major issue is still in the process of being settled.

PART I

The Great Land
and Its Native Peoples

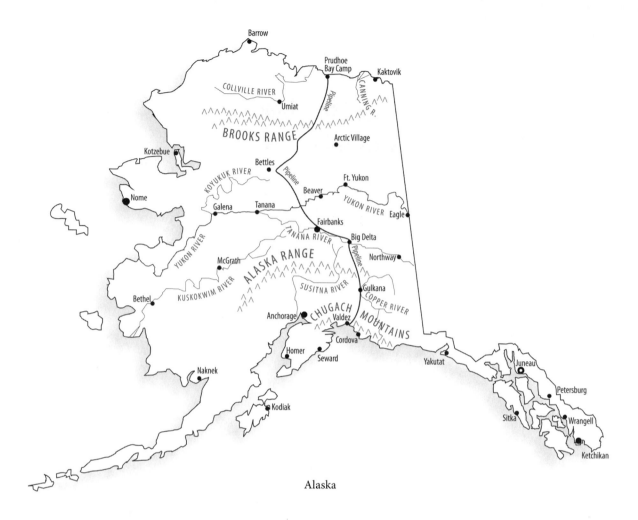

Alaska

Chapter 1

Alaska's Prehistory

THE LAND AND THE FIRST AMERICANS DEBATE

Geologists, cartographers, and geographers have worked in Alaska since the latter part of the nineteenth century. The relatively rapid development of the region after the discovery of gold attracted public attention and led to demands for government-sponsored and financed explorations, surveys, and other investigations. Within a few years both public and private enterprise combined to produce a great amount of material on the geography, geology, and mineral resources of Alaska.[1] Despite continuing effort, this huge landmass remains relatively unknown geologically. Geological mapping thus far has been done only at a reconnaissance level; complete geological mapping on a scale of one mile to the inch, comparable to that done in much of the lower forty-eight contiguous states, would require more than a century of intensive work and substantial expense.

Similarly, relatively little is known about the identity and origin of the first Americans, even though speculation on this topic probably dates back several generations. More is learned with each archeological discovery, but much about the 49th State's distant past in still shrouded in mystery. This chapter attempts to survey what we know at present.

The Geological History of Alaska

Not surprisingly, theories about Alaska's early geological history are in a state of flux. The geology of Alaska was once thought to be simple, based on its great regions of ancient rocks and ancient shallow seas. But the data from research begun in the early 1970s are revealing the complex forces at work and leading geologists to rethink old concepts. Scientists now consider the region key to understanding the geological relationships around the northern Pacific and the geology of the circumarctic areas. The study of Alaska's continental margins is crucial in evaluating the ancient histories of the Arctic and northern Pacific oceans. The region also serves for the testing of various theories of continental drift and seafloor spreading in the Arctic.[2]

Present knowledge indicates that the Alaskan subcontinent is made up of many fragments of continental and oceanic materials that were rafted from the Pacific area on the backs of the major crustal plates and coalesced to form the terrain we see today. (Appropriately, the Aleuts called the Alaskan subcontinent "Alaxsxag," which literally means "the object toward which the action of the sea is directed."[3]) An agglomeration of geologically different fragments would explain many of the dramatic variations in rock type across Alaska. It is not known when the various fragments became joined to each other and to ancestral Alaska, but it appears certain that the process is continuing, for the evidence indicates that one fragment, known as the Yakutat block, is now in the process of "docking," or joining with, the North American continent. Just as the major earthquakes in the Gulf of Alaska and the Yakutat region testify to movements of the earth's crust in our time, so do the very high, very young mountains of the Wrangell–Saint Elias Range bear mute testimony to earlier arrivals.

The other mountain ranges of Alaska are also thought to have resulted from collisions brought about by the movement of the major plates and of the geological flotsam they carried. The Brooks Range is perhaps the oldest of these mountain ranges, having been uplifted in the late Jurassic or early Cretaceous period, about 140 million years ago. Parts of today's Alaska Range were still basins as recently as the Miocene epoch, about 5 to 24 million years ago, and parts of the Chugach and southernmost ranges have arisen since then.

The Regions and Climates of Alaska

The Russians called their American possession "Bolshaya Zemlya," the Great Land, and justifiably so.[4] Sweeping across four time zones, it encompasses 591,004 square miles, or 378,242,560 acres, about 2.2 times the area of Texas, the largest of the lower forty-eight states. (Surrounded by fellow Americans from the Southwest working on the Trans-Alaska Pipeline, Alaskans often countered Texans' boastings about the size of Texas by threatening to "split in two and make you third in size.")

Alaska extends from 51° to 71°25' north latitude and from longitude 129°58' west to longitude 172°22' east, thus occupying both the Western and the Eastern hemispheres. A map of Alaska superimposed on a map of the contiguous United States would touch the Atlantic and Pacific oceans and the Canadian and Mexican borders; Barrow, Alaska's northernmost settlement, would be situated near Lake of the Woods in northern Minnesota, while Ketchikan, Alaska's southernmost city, would be situated in the vicinity of Charleston, South Carolina. Alaska measures about 1,420 miles from north to south and about 2,400 miles from east to west. The Aleutian Islands reach westward toward the Commander Islands of Russia, forming the stepping-stones from Kamchatka that the Russian fur hunters followed in their quest for the sea otter.

The geographic diversity of this lonely and lovely subcontinent is as incredible as its size. Alaska possesses arctic plains, great forests, swamps, glaciers, ice fields, broad valleys and fjords, the highest mountain of North America, active volcanoes, twelve major river systems, 3 million lakes, and countless islands. Alaska boasts 50 percent more seacoast than all the contiguous states combined—about 33,900 miles—and its coasts are washed by two oceans and three major seas. Yet the entire state has only about 710,231 people (2010 U.S. Census estimate), fewer residents than San Francisco.

Geographically Alaska has six regions—the Panhandle, south-central, southwestern, western, and interior Alaska, and the Arctic—each with a distinctive topography and climate. The climates range from temperate to frigid and from desertlike aridity to almost continuous rainfall and much snow. Barrow, Alaska's northernmost settlement, is not as cold as Fairbanks, in the interior, though it is only a comparatively short distance from the arctic ice pack and the North Pole. Alaska's southernmost point in the Aleutians is at about the same latitude as London and has a similar climate.

Approaching Alaska from Seattle by ship, the traveler enters the so-called Panhandle, a narrow, four-hundred-mile strip of land that crowds closely against the coast of British Columbia. It is cut off from the main body of the Alaskan landmass by the great Saint Elias Mountains. Juneau, Alaska's capital, is in the Panhandle, as is Ketchikan, self-proclaimed "Salmon Capital of the World." Sitka, the former capital of Russian America, is situated on the west side of Baranof Island amid forested mountains overlooking Sitka Sound. At the upper end of the Panhandle lies Skagway, where thousands of argonauts disembarked in 1898 for their difficult climb over Chilkoot Pass and their subsequent journey down the Yukon River to the Dawson gold fields.

Many islands, steep valleys, and rugged peaks ranging to ten thousand feet stretch all along the Panhandle, and the seashores teem with marine life. At the head of the Panhandle towers Mount Saint Elias, at 18,008 feet. The climate is moderate, with warmer temperatures than those found in most of the rest of Alaska and with a good deal of rain and cloudiness. Temperatures seldom dip below ten degrees and often climb to the sixties and seventies during the summer. Annual rainfall varies from 25 to 155 inches, which produces lush forest growth. As a result, the region contains most of the state's commercially marketable timber, western hemlock and Sitka spruce being the two major species.

The southern side of Alaska confronts the Pacific Ocean in a wide-sweeping arc of about seven hundred miles, flanking some of the highest mountains in North America. Within this arc lies the Gulf of Alaska. One of the arms of the arc is formed by the Alaska Peninsula, while the other is formed by the Panhandle and the coast of British Columbia. At the very center of this geographical formation lies the Kenai Peninsula, where Alaska's modern oil boom began in the mid-1950s. Set off from the mainland by Cook Inlet, this peninsula is mountainous, dotted with lakes, and indented with fjords. Resurrection Bay, on the peninsula's east side, is long, deep, and completely sheltered. At the head of the bay lies Seward, the starting point of the Alaska Railroad and for many years the shipping and rail terminus for cargo coming into Alaska from the "outside." In recent years Seward has been superseded in importance by the port of Anchorage. Since the 1950s, Anchorage has been the economic and social center of south-central Alaska. It also has become Alaska's largest city, with an estimated population of 286,174 in 2009. Situated on Cook Inlet, Anchorage began its existence as a tent city in 1915 when construction of the Alaska Railroad began.

Cordova, on Prince William Sound, southeast of Anchorage, is today a small fishing town, but it was once the terminus of the Copper River and Northwestern Railway, which carried copper ore two hundred miles from the Alaska Syndicate mine in the Chitina Valley to tidewater. In one corner of Prince William Sound lies Valdez, the second shipping terminal for goods and passengers arriving from the contiguous states. Completely devastated in the Good Friday earthquake of 1964, Valdez was relocated on stable ground. It has since become famous as the terminus of the 798-mile Trans-Alaska Pipeline originating at Prudhoe Bay, on Alaska's North Slope.

Kodiak Island, lying southwest of the Kenai Peninsula, is a mountainous region within the rich fishing waters of the northern Pacific. Home of the gigantic Kodiak brown bear, it is also where seafood manufacturers process millions of pounds of king and tanner crabs, as well as shrimp, halibut, and salmon.

Southwestern Alaska includes the Alaska Peninsula, the Katmai National Monument, and the great sweeping arc of the Aleutian Islands. It is a region of contrasts, stretching southwest from the lightly wooded hillsides and rugged mountains of the Alaska Peninsula and then curving westward through the barren and volcanic Aleutians, almost to Siberia. The Aleutians form the dividing line between the Pacific and the Bering Sea. The distance from Mount Katmai, at the head of the Alaska Peninsula, to Attu, westernmost of the Aleutians, is nearly 1,500 miles. The international date line makes a sharp angle to the west to take in the last of the Aleutian Islands and to keep all of Alaska within the same day. There are actually only a few large islands in the Aleutian chain; in order from east to west along the chain they are Unimak, Unalaska, Umnak, Atka, Adak, and Attu. Thousands of rocks and islets dot the ocean between Unimak and Attu.

The Russian anthropologist Vladimir Jochelson described the Aleutian Islands in 1928:

> All of the islands are of volcanic origin and covered with high mountains, among which are both active and extinct volcanoes. The shoreline is irregular, the rocky mountains sloping abruptly to the sea. The bays are shallow, full of reefs, and dangerous for navigation. The vegetation is luxurious though limited to grasses, berry-bearing shrubs, creeping [plants], and varieties of low willows.
>
> Alpine mosses and lichens cover the mountain slopes, while in the narrow valleys between the mountain ridges and on the low isthmuses with insufficient drainage are fresh-water lakes with hummocky shores. . . . [T]he absence of arboreal vegetation is due not to climate, which is comparatively mild, but to the constant gales, and fogs and mists that are encountered in Aleutian waters, and that deprive the plants of much sunlight.[5]

The foggy Aleutians are stormy and rainy, swept alternately by the cold winds of the Arctic and the humid winds of the Pacific. On the eastern side of the Bering Sea lies the relatively shallow continental shelf, while on the south the extremely deep Aleutian Trench under the Pacific parallels the islands. The upwelling of nutrients where these shallow Bering Sea waters meet those of the deep Pacific Ocean creates one of the richest marine environments in the world. Close to the Aleutian Islands flows the Japan Current, which brings a warm front from the south into conflict with the cold winds from the north and accounts for the continuous fog, rain, and snow of the region. "There are only two seasons, " wrote Jochelson, "a long autumn and a short, mild winter. Both the incessant winds and gales cause the slightest cold to be felt and, in summer particularly, the constant fogs hide the sun."[6] Temperatures rarely drop below zero degrees Fahrenheit in winter or rise above fifty-five degrees Fahrenheit in summer, but the climate is characterized by "frequent, often violent cyclonic storms and high winds, countered by dense fogs and eerie stillness."[7] Spread along the Aleutians are a number of military installations, weather stations, airports, and fish-processing and supply settlements.

The heart of Western Alaska, also referred to as the Bering Sea coast region, is a broad lowland where the Yukon and Kuskokwim rivers flow the last two hundred miles to the Bering Sea. To the north the region extends across high hills and low mountains to the Seward Peninsula. To the south it covers the Ahklun and Kilbuck mountains and the southwestern extensions of the Kuskokwim Mountains and extends across the Nushagak River to Bristol Bay and the lowlands on the western side of the Alaska Peninsula. Cool, rainy, and foggy weather with temperatures in the fifties and low sixties characterizes the summers. Winter temperature readings average around zero degrees Fahrenheit, but the windchill factor temperatures are much lower. Annual snowfall in the lowland areas ranges from forty to ninety inches; annual precipitation totals about twenty inches. Much of the Bering Sea coast is treeless tundra underlain by permafrost, and the region contains thousands of lakes, ponds, and sloughs and almost unmoving rivers, such as the muddy mouths of the Kuskokwim and Yukon rivers.

Alaska's interior lies south of the Brooks Range and generally north of the Alaska Range and extends west from the Canadian border to an imaginary north-south line a distance of forty to two hundred miles from the coast of the Bering Sea. On the north and west lie the low mountains of the Tanana-Yukon upland and the Kuskokwim Mountains. The Tanana, Yukon, and Kuskokwim rivers flow in the heart of the wide-open spaces of the interior. The Yukon is the longest river in Alaska, at 1,875 miles. Approximately 1,400 of these flow westward the entire breadth of Alaska into the Bering Sea; the remainder flow in Canada. Along this river and its tributaries are situated most of the settlements and towns of interior Alaska. The Fairbanks North Star Borough has a population of 98,660 (2009 estimate). The city itself, with a population of 35,252 (2009 estimate), has been the metropolis and supply center for interior and northwest Alaska, particularly since the 1970s and the North Slope oil boom.

Temperatures in the interior often drop to fifty to sixty degrees below zero Fahrenheit, and ice fog hovers over Fairbanks and some other populated and low-lying areas when the temperatures fall below twenty degrees below zero. Winters are cold and clear, and summers are generally hot and dry, with light rainfall of approximately twelve to fourteen inches a year. Because of the extreme cold, snowfall often consists of dry, powdery flakes that blow and drift easily. Fairbanks, however, has much fairer weather and enjoys long hours of splendid daylight during the spring and summer months, reaching temperatures in the eighties, which balances the dark and grimly short winter days.

The Arctic extends from the southern flanks of the Brooks Range, which rises to over nine thousand feet in the east and forms a mighty barrier between the interior and the Arctic Slope. It extends from Kotzebue, north of the Seward Peninsula, to the Canadian border. The slope, about 750 miles long and 250 miles wide, consists of large areas of rolling uplands and coastal plains that stretch northward from the Brooks Range. The whole Arctic Slope region is devoid of timber except for the occasional dense thickets of alder, willow, and resin birch in many river valleys. Tundra stretches across

A Dangerous Land

Americans became aware of Alaska's great natural resources as early as the 1840s, when New England whalers ventured into the Bering Sea in pursuit of their prey. After the United States acquired Alaska from Russia in 1867, the restless and adventurous went north in search of fortune. They soon found gold, and by 1890 Alaska's mineral production was valued at nearly eight hundred thousand dollars. By 1904 gold production exceeded $9 million in value. In short, Americans were becoming aware of Alaska's land and natural resources. Yet even as they found that the hardy could reap fabulous wealth from Alaska, they also discovered that the land itself was dangerous.

Alaskans were harshly reminded of the danger on June 6, 1912, when snow-covered, glaciered, and seemingly dormant Mount Katmai, on the Alaska Peninsula, blew up in a series of violent explosions that threw more than five and a half cubic miles of debris into the air. For hundreds of square miles around, the eruptions destroyed the country. The city of Kodiak, one hundred miles away, was plunged into total darkness for sixty hours while volcanic ash covered everything to a depth of several feet. The accompanying thunder and lightning convinced the terrified residents that the end of the world had come. In Juneau, about 750 miles away, the explosive sounds of the erupting mountain were plainly heard. In Seattle and Port Townsend, Washington, over two thousand miles from Katmai, cloth fabrics disintegrated from the effects of sulfuric acid rain, which fell for days.

Alaskans were again reminded of the geologically unstable nature of their land on Good Friday, March 27, 1964, when one of the greatest earthquakes of all time struck south-central Alaska. Measuring 9.2 on the moment magnitude scale, it released at least twice as much energy as the 1906 earthquake that destroyed San Francisco, and it was felt over almost one half million square miles. The motions lasted longer than those for most other recorded earthquakes, and more land surface was vertically and horizontally dislocated than had been moved by any previous known tremor. Not only was the land surface tilted, but an enormous mass of land and seafloor moved several tens of feet toward the Gulf of Alaska.

The earthquake left 114 people dead or missing, and Alaska's governor estimated property damages at between one-half and three-quarters of a billion dollars. A compilation by geophysicist T. Neil Davis, a retired professor at the Geophysical Institute at the University of Alaska Fairbanks, shows that between July 1788 and August 1961, about 880 earthquakes measuring five points or more on the Richter scale occurred in Alaska. It is obvious that Alaska's geological setting, while promising great wealth in mineral resources, also holds great danger.

Sources: Bernard R. Hubbard, S.J., *Mush, You Malemutes* (New York: American Press, 1943), 70–71; Arthur Grantz, et al., *Alaska's Good Friday Earthquake, March 27, 1964,* Geological Survey Circular no. 491 (Washington, DC: Department of the Interior, 1964), 1; Edwin B. Eckel, *The Alaska Earthquake, March 27, 1964: Lessons and Conclusions,* Geological Survey Professional Paper no. 546 (Washington, DC: Government Printing Office, 1970), 1; T. Neil Davis and Carol Echols, *A Table of Alaskan Earthquakes, 1788–1961,* Geophysical Research Report no. 8 (College: University of Alaska, 1962).

most of the area, and during the short summer months the profusion of flowering plants makes the Arctic a place of beauty. Its summers are nightless; its winters, sunless. Temperatures are low because of the prevailing northerly winds during all seasons of the year. The average July temperature at Barrow is forty degrees Fahrenheit, while the average January temperature is seventeen degrees below zero Fahrenheit. Total annual precipitation averages about five inches, making the area a desert. For much of the year, the shores of the Arctic are ice locked. In 1968 the Arctic Slope achieved sudden fame when several oil companies discovered vast oil and gas deposits at Prudhoe Bay. The oil fields lie alongside the Sagavanirktok River delta, about seventy miles west of the Arctic National Wildlife Refuge. The slope has now become potentially the wealthiest region in the state.[8]

Alaska Prehistory

Today the overwhelming majority of Alaskans are urban dwellers. According to 2009 estimates, more than 286,000 Alaskans live in the town of Anchorage, and more than 98,000 reside in the Fairbanks North Star Borough. The rest live in small urban centers from Ketchikan to Barrow and from Seward to Kodiak and in the approximately 220 villages scattered throughout the state. Thus most of Alaska's current inhabitants are urbanites. Newcomers from the contiguous states settle mostly in the urban centers, and many Natives are leaving their villages for the towns as well. On the other hand, many Natives, disillusioned with urban life, are returning to their villages. High birthrates among the Native population also keep the village populations fairly stable.

Much less is known about the region's earliest human inhabitants. No one knows just when human beings entered the Americas—experts are still debating how long human beings have inhabited the Americas, and how they came here. It is accepted, however, that no hominids ancestral to modern humans entered the Americas. Skeletons of *Homo erectus,* the primate from whom we are supposedly descended, have been found in Africa and Asia, but no *erectus* remains have ever been discovered in the Western Hemisphere. Perhaps it can be safely

stated that long after humankind had settled the continents of Asia, Africa, Australia, and Europe, America was unknown to any people.

Scholars debate the origins of the first Americans anew with each unearthing of skulls, bones, burial sites, hunting camps, and utensils. Some experts have suggested that Egyptians first saw America, while others supported the various claims of the Greeks, Etruscans, Hindus, Chinese, Buddhists, Japanese, and Irish. The Spanish scholar and writer Fray Jose de Acosta, in his 1589 volume *Historia natural moral de las Indias,* hypothesized that the first people who saw what today is called America were following Ice Age mammals migrating east from Siberia into present-day Alaska in search of food. Acosta and others postulated that in time these hunters and gatherers, still following the game, wandered into the woodlands and grasslands of western and interior America, then east to the Atlantic shores of Canada and south across the deserts, through Central America, and finally down the spine of the Andean highlands to the tip of South America, reaching Tierra del Fuego more than twelve thousand years ago.

These early hunters and gatherers may well have entered Alaska via the so-called Bering Land Bridge, about one thousand miles wide, when Pleistocene glacial ice sheets locked up much of the earth's supply of water and lowered the sea levels. As the ice receded, the sea levels rose again until, about 14,500 years ago, Alaska and Siberia were again parted by the waters. Today, fifty-six miles of stormy water separate Siberia's Chukchi Peninsula from the Seward Peninsula of Alaska at the point where the United States and Russia meet each other most closely. The Bering Land Bridge hypothesis remains prevalent, supported by widely accepted evidence from molecular and genetic studies that Native Americans are one people, descendants of North Asians.[9] Most scientists agree that it was twenty to thirty thousand years ago that the first humans arrived in the Americas. Excavations elsewhere in the Americas have confirmed this approximate date.

The "First American debate" heated up considerably in 1996, when a pair of college students in search of a good vantage point from which to watch the annual hydroplane races in Kennewick,

Washington, found a human skull at the edges of the Columbia River. Suspecting foul play, the Benton County coroner called James C. Chatters, an archaeologist and paleoecologist specializing in forensic and archaeological consulting.[10]

Chatters's initial report characterized the skull and face as having "Caucasoid" features, namely, a long, narrow skull, receding cheek bones, and a high chin. Chatters quickly collected a nearly complete skeleton near the site where the skull had been found. He ordered a CAT scan, which revealed a healed wound in the pelvis caused by a stone projectile, still embedded in the bone. He sent bone samples to be radiocarbon dated. The age was about 8,400 radiocarbon years, or around 9,500 calendar years. Kennewick Man, as the remains became known, was ancient, and he quickly became a news sensation.

If Kennewick Man was of "Caucasian" origins, all theories of who was living in North America eight thousand years ago would become questionable, as had "the prevailing ideas of who, and by what route or routes, people might have migrated here." Could it be that European-looking people had come to the New World long before the Vikings, and that they been among the first to colonize the Americas? If so, how might that affect the moral and legal status of the Native Americans presumed to be the continent's first inhabitants?[11]

The Umatillas and other local Indian tribes called Kennewick Man their sacred ancestor and demanded the return of the bones for reburial. The U.S. Army Corps of Engineers wanted to placate the Indians and decided to return the remains to them. In the ensuing controversy the U.S. government locked Kennewick Man's bones, unexamined, into the University of Washington's Burke Museum. Bruce Babbitt, the secretary of the interior, insisted that Indian tribes enjoyed the right to Kennewick Man's remains because according to Indian oral histories, "the tribes have occupied 'for millennia' the area in Washington where Kennewick Man was found." Scientists pointed out that if the remains were returned to the Indians, North American archaeology "would be compromised to indulge multicultural sensitivities who have vested interest in doing just that—compromising archeology to head off the belief that Indians arrived in the Americas as a single, related group."[12] Eight prominent anthropologists, including one from the Smithsonian Institution, sued for and won the right to study the bones.

Speculation about the origins of Kennewick Man comes at a time when scientists are reconsidering the origins of the First Americans. Researchers now think it possible that the continent's earliest arrivals may have come by boat or some other route instead of walking across the land bridge from Asia, as the Bering Land Bridge theory holds. If Chatters's sinitial identification of the skeletal remains stands, it would support the emerging hypothesis that our continent was settled over many years by different competing peoples from scattered parts of the world.

Archaeologists now argue that some nomads almost certainly came by way of the land bridge some 13,500 years ago. Their culture has been named "Clovis" for its distinctive weapons, found nationwide in excavations. But according to the newest theory, the continent's first inhabitants may have crossed the Atlantic more than 18,000 years ago from the Iberian Peninsula. Researchers argue that these earliest arrivals, belonging to a group known as the Solutreans, settled the eastern seaboard, and that over the next six millennia their hunting and gathering culture may have spread as far as the American deserts and Canadian tundra, and perhaps even into South America. These and other researchers who believe that the Clovis and Bering Land Bridge theories are outdated refer to sites at Monte Verde, Chile, as well as Pennsylvania, Virginia, and South Carolina as having been settled in 12,500 B.C. to 16,000 B.C.[13]

The debate about the First Americans will certainly continue. In the meantime, much can be learned about the people who were living in Alaska when the Europeans arrived: the coastal Indians, the Athapaskans, the Aleuts, and the Eskimos.

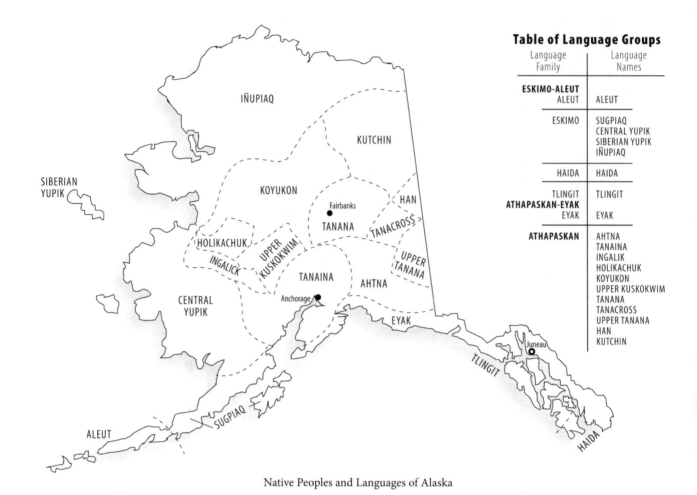

Table of Language Groups

Language Family	Language Names
ESKIMO-ALEUT	
ALEUT	ALEUT
ESKIMO	SUGPIAQ
	CENTRAL YUPIK
	SIBERIAN YUPIK
	IÑUPIAQ
HAIDA	HAIDA
TLINGIT	TLINGIT
ATHAPASKAN-EYAK	
EYAK	EYAK
ATHAPASKAN	AHTNA
	TANAINA
	INGALIK
	HOLIKACHUK
	KOYUKON
	UPPER KUSKOKWIM
	TANANA
	TANACROSS
	UPPER TANANA
	HAN
	KUTCHIN

Map labels: IÑUPIAQ, KUTCHIN, SIBERIAN YUPIK, KOYUKON, HAN, Fairbanks, TANANA, TANACROSS, HOLIKACHUK, UPPER KUSKOKWIM, INGALICK, UPPER TANANA, TANAINA, AHTNA, Anchorage, CENTRAL YUPIK, EYAK, TLINGIT, Juneau, SUGPIAQ, ALEUT, HAIDA

Native Peoples and Languages of Alaska

Chapter 2

Alaska's Ancestral Native Peoples

Throughout prehistoric times there were countless and mostly unknowable population shifts within the area that is now Alaska. It follows that the Alaskan Native groups that are known today were the latest wave of perhaps hundreds or even thousands of groups that occupied the area at one time or another from prehistoric times onward. In historic times, for example, Eskimos were extending their control inland along rivers flowing into the Bering Sea and the western Arctic Ocean and in the process were acculturating and assimilating Indian groups. On the southern fringe, in turn, the Aleuts successfully encroached on the peninsular Eskimos from the west.

Consequently, the Native groups of Alaska are many and varied, and their ancestral cultures developed unique ways of living in this diverse landscape. Many of their early beliefs and practices either are no longer carried out or have changed greatly.[1] But our attempt to describe the state's Native cultures as they existed before the arrival of the Europeans is aided by archeological data and the recorded observations and memories of both Europeans and Native peoples. For purposes of this survey, Alaska's ancestral peoples are divided into four groups: the coastal Indians, the Athapaskans, the Aleuts, and the Eskimos.[2]

The Coastal Indians

Three distinct native groups—the Tlingits, Haidas, and Tsimshians—occupied an area in Alaska that lies approximately between Yakutat Bay in the north and Prince Rupert in British Columbia in the south. The ancestral Tlingits, the most numerous, were scattered throughout the region in many permanent villages. They spoke a language that is believed to be related to the Athapaskan language of the interior of the continent. Tradition has it that the Tlingits originally migrated north to Alaska from the Skeena River, in western British Columbia, while other Athapaskan-speaking groups, following the Stikine River, moved from the interior to the coast. Consisting of some fourteen tribal divisions, the Tlingits had been pressing westward just before making limited contact with the Russians in 1741, and ongoing contact with Europeans continued after Captain James Cook's visit in 1777. The Yakutat Tlingits had probably driven the Chugachmiut Eskimos off Kayak Island, and they, or some related tribe, established an outpost among the perhaps linguistically related Eyaks at the mouth of the Copper River.[3]

The ancestral Haidas inhabited the Queen Charlotte Islands in what is today British Columbia and the southern part of Prince of Wales Island off the

Panhandle. Tradition has it that the Alaska Haidas were moving north in the 1700s, in the process driving out some of the Tlingit tribes.

The ancestral Tsimshians, divided into three major subdivisions, lived on the mainland and the islands south of southeastern Alaska. Some Tsimshian tribes wintered in villages along Metlakatla Pass, near the modern town of Prince Rupert; after the Hudson's Bay Company built Fort Simpson in 1834, they shifted their quarters there. In 1887 a large group, primarily from Fort Simpson, led by the energetic Anglican missionary William Duncan, moved to Annette Island after some church-related disagreements.

The Tlingits, Haidas, and Tsimshians all adapted themselves extremely well to coastal life. They used fish traps, nets, and dip nets for fishing, and for both fishing and hunting sea mammals they employed harpoons with detachable heads connected to the shaft with a short line. They also utilized hooks for angling, particularly for cod and halibut. All three groups constructed fine canoes of various sizes for different purposes. For land hunting, the bow and arrow were standard equipment, but snares and deadfalls were used as well.

The coastal Indians used wood as a primary material for most of their manufactures, which were distinguished by fine workmanship and elaborately carved and painted decorations. The cutting blades of their tools were made from stone and shell, while tough, hard, bright-green nephrite stones were used for adze blades. They built large, rectangular, gable-roofed houses in which the individual timbers were carefully joined, and several families occupied each house.

The social framework among the Tlingits, Haidas, and Tsimshians was matrilineal, with descent traced exclusively through the maternal line. Each of the Tlingit and Haida tribes had two major moieties, or subdivisions, and each individual had to marry a member of the other moiety. In some tribes, such as the Tlingits, the moieties were composed of clans—smaller unilateral social divisions whose members traced their relationship from a legendary common ancestor.

All these matrilineal societies, however, were built up around lineages, or families, consisting of a nucleus of males related through females: a group of brothers and some male maternal cousins, their sisters' sons, and the sons of the sisters of the second generation. This social unit was usually politically independent; it claimed fishing, hunting, and berrying grounds, it had its own houses and chiefs, and it operated socially—and usually ceremonially as well—as an independent unit. Each lineage also had its own crest, personal names, and songs and dances for ceremonial occasions. Warfare between lineages was a well-established practice aimed at driving out or even exterminating another lineage to acquire its lands and material possessions. The Tlingits would prove especially skilled in later conflicts with the Russians. These matrilineal societies were also organized by status, with individuals identified as chiefs, nobles, commoners, and slaves. It was a flexible system, however, with a good deal of mobility among levels.

Religious belief played an important part in everyday life. Coastal Indian religion included a value notion of a disinterested supreme being or beings, the immortality of certain economically important animals together with ritual practices designed to ensure the return of these creatures, and the possibility of lifelong assistance from a personal guardian spirit. The religions did not include a systematization of beliefs in creation, cosmology, and deities.

The term "potlatch" as used among Indians along the North Pacific coast of North America refers to a highly competitive redistribution celebration. This institutionalized redistribution of goods played an important part in the Tlingits' economic lives. Gift exchanges linked the various interdependent units of society in diverse ways. The Tlingits distinguished numerous exchange forms, beginning with barter, then gift exchange, food gifts, feasts, the ceremonial exchange of labor, and finally ceremonial gifts or potlatches, which had as their purpose the giving and acquisition of property. Slaves were the most important of potlatch goods; sometimes they were killed, but most often they were freed. Second, plates of native copper pounded into shield-like form were a means of concentrating wealth. These coppers were exchanged intact, cut into sections as mementos for guests, or thrown into the sea to validate one's wealth. Finally, blankets and ceremonial robes were given whole or torn into sections and distributed to guests to commemorate a potlatch. There was a constant effort to give greater potlatches than one's rivals. Therefore, the production and accumulation of these goods was emphasized.[4]

The elaborately carved totem poles of the coastal Indians, actually comparable to European crests or coats of arms, would become their trademark among non-Indians. There were several varieties of totems, with different functions. Memorial poles were usually erected by the heir of a deceased chief as part of the process of assuming his predecessor's titles and prerogatives. Mortuary poles and house-portal poles were also constructed. All portrayed symbols that belonged to a particular lineage or family and referred to events in its past.[5]

The Athapaskans

While the coastal Indians enjoyed nature's bounty, the Athapaskan Indians occupied the difficult and demanding expanse of the arctic and subarctic lands stretching across the northern edge of the American continent. This vast area, greatly varied in topography, is not richly endowed with sustenance for life, and the Athapaskans had to search diligently for the resources they needed for survival.

The archaeological evidence indicates that the ancestral Athapaskans crossed the Bering Land Bridge into Alaska about ten thousand years ago, near the end of the last great glacial period. As the glaciers receded, some of these people (later called the southern Athapaskans) moved east and south through what became the Yukon Territory and interior British Columbia and on into many of the present-day western states. The northern Athapaskans inhabited the drainages of the Yukon River just short of where it empties into the Bering Sea and also those parts of northern Canada drained by the Mackenzie River and as far east as Hudson Bay.[6] Much of this huge area is mountainous and for the most part covered by northern coniferous forests, home to moose, caribou, black and grizzly bears, sheep, and a variety of small game and fish. This region has great environmental contrasts and imposed many natural barriers between tribal groups. Long, cold winters and short, warm summers characterize the region.

Resourceful hunters and gatherers, the Athapaskans relied on fish and caribou as staples for their survival. Depending on the area, they fished for salmon with dip nets and basket-shaped traps; they also caught other fish, such as trout, whitefish, and pike, employing a variety of fishing methods. Caribou, abundant at certain times of the year, were driven between two long converging rows of wooden sticks that led to a large enclosure of branches where the hunters had set up snares of partly tanned moose or caribou hide; once caught, the animals were easily killed with bows and arrows. The hunters also employed water drives; herded into a lake or stream, the animals were quickly killed with lances or stabbed with knives. The Athapaskans also hunted moose, which were tracked down and shot or sometimes caught in deadfall traps. Bears, wolverines, and smaller fur-bearing animals were also caught in deadfalls, shot with bow and arrows, or captured in rawhide nets. Snares sufficed for hares and ptarmigans (grouse). Spruce hens, ducks, geese, and roots and berries supplemented the Athapaskan diet. Periods of starvation were not uncommon, however, because of the cyclicity of some of the major animal species on which they relied for food.

During the ancestral period all winter hunting was done on foot, since dogs were not yet used for pulling sledges or toboggans. Snowshoes were therefore important, and many northern Athapaskans made two types. Hunting snowshoes were long and rounded in front for walking over fresh snow, while travel snowshoes were shorter, with pointed and sharply upturned front ends.

The Tanaina Indians in the Cook Inlet–Susitna River basin were the only Athapaskans who lived on the seacoast. Influenced by their Eskimo neighbors, they became sea mammal hunters, borrowing the necessary material-culture traits required for coastal life. Their low population density suggests, however, that they never became as skillful as the Eskimos in hunting sea mammals.

The more mobile a particular group of Athapaskans, the simpler its dwellings; conversely, sedentary groups employed more complex forms of construction. The shelter reflected the subsistence activities characteristic not only of particular times of the year but also of climatic variations. There were many differences among the dwellings constructed, but all were built with the same basic materials. Athapaskans of every group built log or pole houses of various sizes covered with animal hides. The more sedentary groups, such as the Ingalik, in the Yukon and Kuskokwim basins, occupied permanent villages in the winter and temporary fishing camps in the summer. Living near Eskimos, they built winter houses that closely resembled the semi-subterranean, earth-covered Eskimo houses of southwestern Alaska.

Unlike the coastal Indians, the Athapaskan bands had simple organizational structures. Anthropologists have therefore described northern Athapaskan culture as continuous, carried on by a series of interlocking bands whose lifeways differed in only minor details from those of their immediate neighbors. Most ancestral northern Athapaskans spent most of the year in small bands consisting of a few nuclear families. If resources permitted, small groups came together and combined into a regional band for some specific purpose—to hunt caribou, for example. Adult males made decisions together, and leaders often emerged who attained prestige and influence by demonstrating their superior abilities, particularly as hunters. The northern Athapaskans engaged in both offensive and defensive warfare, often producing a war leader who demonstrated great physical strength. Generally, then, leadership was not hereditary but acquired, and once a leader lost his special abilities, he ceased to exert any special influence.

As in all other Alaskan groups, the nuclear family constituted the basic unit of social organization among Athapaskans. Furthermore, Athapaskan extended kinship was characterized by the matrilineal sib organization. These sibs were held together by reciprocal social obligations, and a member generally had to find a mate outside his or her sib.

An important feature of many Native Alaskan cultures was the potlatch, a ceremonial feast in which gifts were given in a demonstration of wealth and generosity. Among many Athapaskans the potlatch was given for a variety of reasons and constituted an important feature of social organization. When someone died, a potlatch was given so that the living would socially forget the death, and it also

helped assuage grief. It was also given to mark the killing of the first game of each kind by a child; to mark a deed or an unusual accomplishment; to celebrate the return, recovery, or rescue of a relative or friend; and to pay for an offense or a transgression of some rule.[7]

One potlatch could be given for several reasons, and two or several men or women might join to give a potlatch for the same person. A small potlatch could include just the members of the band, but depending on the wealth of the giver, invitations to a larger potlatch might be sent to other villages. The larger the potlatch, the more ceremonial it was, and the number and quality of the ritual elements were directly related to the amount of wealth expended or the number of guests. Often less wealthy people took advantage of the occasion to give away a few blankets while most of the other expenses were paid by the main host. The contributions each individual made, like the money given away, the amount of food contributed, and the number and kinds of gifts, were all recorded. Each giver had his or her own pile of blankets or other gifts, and long speeches were made to specify exactly who gave what.

Giving potlatches was a means of achieving prestige within one's own group as well as in neighboring areas. For example, a man was expected to potlatch at least one and preferably three times before he married. If he aspired to leadership, he had to celebrate whenever possible, and the death of even a distant relative provided an excuse. It was necessary for him to have a sufficient supply of food, rifles, calico, blankets, and other items to give away on these occasions. The individual who gave such large potlatches had to give away all the property he owned and could not accept aid from anyone for one year following the ceremony.

Some authorities believe that the Athapaskans borrowed the potlatch directly from the more elaborate ceremonies among the tribes of the American Northwest, and Tlingit influences are seen in the ceremony as the Upper Tanana perform it.[8] Recent studies of Athapaskan culture have revealed that some of these shared elements are common among the twelve Athapaskan groups in Alaska. Therefore, it is possible that many of the cultural elements common to the western Athapaskans and the Tlingits originated in earlier times when the people of both areas shared more cultural traits.[9] The western Athapaskans, however, transformed the potlatch from the community rite it was among the Tlingit and other northwest coast groups to an essentially individualistic one. Perhaps this was related to the limited availability of surplus food.

The Athapaskans' belief in human reincarnation in animal form blurred their distinction between animals and human beings and stressed the importance of placating animal spirits to enable the people to continue using the natural environment. The religion of the northern Athapaskans also emphasized individual rather than community rites, because the survival of hunters depended largely on individual skills. Their complex mythology provided answers to most of the questions concerning the origin of the world and humanity; they lived in a many-spirited world which they believed influenced every aspect of their lives and destinies.[10] Shamans—the individuals with the greatest personal power in the culture—were the only religious practitioners. They used certain magical-religious rites to control the spirit world, prevent and cure disease, bring game to hunters, predict the weather, and foretell the future. In fact, Athapaskan leaders and shamans were co-equal but on a different level.[11]

The Aleuts

The Aleuts adapted themselves superbly to life in the harsh marine environment of the Aleutian Islands. The ancestors of the Aleuts, relatives of the Eskimos, settled on the fog-shrouded and windswept islands nearly ten thousand years ago. They developed a rich culture and secured a well-balanced livelihood from the rich fauna of the sea.

The ancestral Aleut population has been estimated to have been as high as fifteen to twenty-five thousand, although no exact demographic information exists. But neither their culture nor their livelihood long survived the arrival of the Russians in the 1740s. The late American anthropologist Margaret Lantis has concluded that at least 80 percent of the Aleut population was lost in the first two generations of Russian-Aleutian contact: "A few were taken to southeast Alaska and California; most, however,

were not merely lost to their homeland, they were totally lost.[12] Smallpox, measles, tuberculosis, venereal diseases, and pneumonia—as well as Russian guns—drastically reduced the Native population to 2,247 in 1834 and to 1,400 in 1848. In 1848 a smallpox epidemic struck, further reducing the number of Aleuts to approximately 900. By 1864, following the advent of intermarriage with the Russians, the population had increased to 2,005, but the 1890 census indicated a decline to 1,702 persons—968 Aleuts and 734 mixed bloods.[13]

The many explorers who visited the Aleutians provided an adequate picture of Aleut home life but told little about the social structure. According to these observers, a typical Aleut house was large and built underground, containing several related nuclear families. Villages were composed of related individuals. Large villages might have as many as four such dwellings occupied at any one time. These were the permanent settlements, usually situated on the northern, Bering Sea side of the island because of the more abundant fish resources and larger supplies of driftwood there.[14]

Households usually included a man and his wife or wives, older married sons and their families, and sometimes a younger brother and his family. The adolescent sons of the household head were sent to their mother's village to be reared by her older brother or brothers. Women owned the houses. Although anthropologists have been unable to determine the Aleuts' rule of descent, many assume matrilineal descent. Aleut society, according to its eighteenth- and early-nineteenth-century observers, was divided into three classes: honorables, common people, and slaves. At the death of a highly honored person, often a whaler, the body was mummified, and slaves were occasionally killed to show the grief of the principal survivor. Aleuts were generally permissive regarding sexual relations and marriage, but incest was well defined and prohibited.[15]

The Aleuts, living in an ice-free maritime region, developed sophisticated open-sea hunting techniques that enabled them to harvest the sea otter, hair seal, sea lion, and seasonally, the migrating fur seals and whales. They encountered walruses only rarely, but different species of whales were especially abundant in the area from Unimak Island eastward to Kodiak, as were fur seals and other sea mammals. Therefore, it was there that most of the population resided.[16]

The Aleuts shared with the southern Eskimos a great number of subsistence tools, such as the kayak and bone and antler tools, but in place of the toggling harpoon used by the Eskimos for large sea mammals, the Aleuts used a multibarbed harpoon head. The Aleuts also fished for cod and halibut with hook and line, fastening bone hooks to braided strips of the stalks of giant kelp. They also caught salmon in nets or traps as the fish ascended the streams to spawn.[17]

The Aleuts derived a major portion of their diet from the shoreline itself. Women, old men, and children shared in the food-gathering activities. They took clams and other mollusks and also collected huge quantities of green spiny sea urchins. Gathering the sea urchins at low tide, they rubbed off the spines and broke the shells. Inside were clumps of bright-yellow eggs, which they ate raw or steamed. They also ate several species of kelp and seaweed found along the coast. The Aleuts also gathered large amounts of salmonberries, blueberries, crowberries, and roots, which contributed to their diet.[18]

Birds and their eggs also furnished much food. During the summers, millions of birds nest in the Aleutians. The Aleuts hunted cormorants, murres, ducks, geese, loons, ptarmigans, gulls, and several other waterfowl. In fact, more than 140 species of birds are found in the islands, and it is not surprising that the people not only used the birds for their meat and eggs but also utilized their skins for parkas and for decorations. On the ground the Aleuts captured birds in nets or with snares, and in flight they caught them with bolas. The bola consisted of four to six strings about three feet long and tied together at one end; to the free ends were attached small stones for weight. As birds flew over, the hunter twirled the bola and threw it into the flock, each string swinging out like a spoke on a wheel. The lines wrapped around a bird and brought it down.[19]

The Aleuts also perfected the art of using the atlatl, a long, narrow board with one end carved to fit the hand and with a small peg inserted at the other end to hold the butt of a spear shaft. The throwing spear or dart was laid on the board and then cast. The device extended the length of the arm, thereby giving more power and distance to the cast. On Unimak Island and farther east along the tip of the Alaska Peninsula, some bear and caribou were killed with spears or atlatls.

Lantis observed that the Aleut and Pacific Eskimo cultures were related and the Aleuts shared with the Tlingits their regard for wealth and status. There may also have been cultural links with various Siberian groups.[20] However, the cultural and historical place of the Aleuts among the peoples of their region is still not clearly understood.

It is clear that the Aleuts, over thousands of years, developed a functional society that enabled them to wrest a very adequate living from their difficult environment. The ancestral culture was threatened with rapid extinction under the Russians; however, individuals as well as parts of the old culture survived, and with the help of the Russian Orthodox Church the Aleuts began to develop a new culture.

The Eskimos

Much has been written about the Eskimos, particularly the Greenland and Canadian Eskimos, because of their adaptations to the far-north arctic environment. But not all Alaskan Eskimos faced the same rigors. They inhabited a great diversity of environments, and contrary to popular conception, many did not live in a bleak, dark, snow-driven landscape in igloos (snow houses), eating only blubber and muktuk (whale fat and skin).

Today many experts agree that the progenitors of the Eskimos and the Aleuts as well as of various Paleo-Siberian groups (called Arctic-Mongoloid peoples) arrived in the Bering Sea area approximately ten thousand years ago.[21] Eskimo culture developed in western Alaska, and it was also in Alaska that the division into Eskimo and Aleut stocks occurred. In time, the Eskimos developed techniques that allowed them to exploit the arctic seas. The so-called arctic small-tool tradition, reaching back to Siberia, represents the technological base for Eskimo culture. It crystallized in Alaska and spread across the

Arctic from Alaska to Greenland about four thousand years ago.

Proto-Eskimo is the ancestor of all Eskimo languages. About two thousand years ago the proto-Yupik and proto-Iñupiaq languages replaced all intermediate dialects. Eventually the Alaskan Yupik speakers became separated from Siberia when Iñupiaq speakers occupied the Seward Peninsula, and in time the Yupik languages developed into Sugpik, Central Yupik, and Siberian Yupik.[22]

Unfortunately, ancestral Eskimo culture no longer exists. Anthropologists have painstakingly tried to reconstruct it and point out that Eskimos and Aleuts form a cultural unit. The Danish anthropologist Kaj Birket-Smith identified a difference in some basic points between the Aleuts and the Pacific Eskimos, on the one hand, and all remaining Eskimo groups, on the other, with the inhabitants of Bristol Bay and the Yukon-Kuskokwim Delta occupying an intermediate position. This difference expressed itself in articles of clothing, in the shape of the blubber lamp, in the preference for the spear instead of the harpoon for whaling, and in the mummification of bodies, which were interred in caves in a crouched position. In fact, the Yukon formed a cultural dividing line.[23] So far this dualism in Eskimo culture has not been explained satisfactorily.

There were other differences as well. For example, the Central Eskimo culture in Arctic Canada occupied a special position in relationship to the Western and Eastern Eskimos—in Alaska and Greenland, respectively. In the coastal areas and Arctic Archipelago between Alaska and Greenland, which form the central regions, certain cultural elements were lacking that were present in the western and eastern parts of the Eskimo area. They include the *umiak* (a large skin boat), the seal net, and gut-skin frocks. They were found rarely in the central regions, and then in a modified form. Other elements were widely disseminated, particularly throughout the central area; examples are the special tools used for harpooning seals through breathing holes in the ice.[24]

From Alaska's north coast to Greenland, the ancestral Eskimos hunted large sea mammals—whales, walruses, and seals. There were, however, some small groups whose lifeways had a markedly inland character and for whom caribou hunting provided the mainstay of their existence. These groups included the Caribou Eskimos in the Barren Grounds west of Hudson Bay and smaller groups along the Colville and Noatak rivers in northern Alaska and in the Yukon-Kuskokwim Delta. In addition, certain Eskimo cultural features were the result of varying degrees of influence of Indian and Siberian peoples. In return the Eskimos influenced other groups.[25]

Iñupiat Eskimo culture became fairly uniform about one thousand years ago, when the Thule culture spread from Alaska all the way to Greenland. Researchers believe that the original Thule Eskimos were a maritime people of Alaskan origin. The late anthropologist James W. VanStone showed that the modern Central Eskimo culture probably was a direct outgrowth of Thule.[26]

Eskimo social life centered around the nuclear family as the primary unit. But in a culture with an overwhelming emphasis on subsistence activities, men were obligated not only to their households and kindred but also to voluntary associations such as organized whale-hunting crews. Among the Yupiks the *kashgees* (ceremonial houses for men) were very important in the individual lives of all males; consequently, the *kashgees* were patricentric, while the households were matricentric. Adult males taught traditional skills to the boys in the *kashgee*, while mothers taught their daughters in the homes. Most people chose marriage partners from within the community.[27]

Physical survival depended on the hunters' ability to take game and fish. These animals, therefore, occupied an important place in tribal religions, and Eskimo supernaturalism was based to a great extent on charms that aided individuals. For example, an *umelik,* or whaling captain, had a special wooden container whose top included the figure of a whale in relief. The charms in the container might include a beetle, the hair of a famous whaler who had died, a stuffed raven skin, or baleen carvings of seals and whales. These charms might be inherited or obtained from an independent shaman or the whaling crew's spiritual advisor. Their purpose was to get a whale to swim near an *umiak,* to prevent the loss of a whale, or to prevent disaster.[28]

Family charms were passed down a patrilineal line among some groups, and among Pacific Eskimos, the knowledge required to hunt whales was similarly transmitted. There were also many taboos, such as the prohibition against combining land and sea products. The Bering Sea Eskimos developed an intense involvement with the species taken, and this was evident in their religious practice. The so-called bladder feast was the most complex of the various cults and focused primarily on the seals. The arctic hunters and fishermen, on the other hand, did not develop rituals as complex as those of the Bering Sea peoples or the whalers.[29]

In short, Eskimos displayed many traits that were also found among other peoples. In Alaska the term "Eskimo" therefore stands for much subcultural diversity. Like other ancestral inhabitants of Alaska, the Eskimos evolved ingenious and highly flexible techniques and lifeways, which enabled them to live in a rugged arctic and subarctic environment.

Conclusion

Little is known about the early migrants who traveled eastward across the Bering Land Bridge from Asia in prehistoric times. Evidence of human occupation in Alaska is not as ancient as elsewhere on the American continent and dates back only about twelve thousand years. More than 2,700 archaeological sites have been identified in Alaska, but the age of only a few of them has been determined because of the high cost of fieldwork and analysis in these remote regions.[30]

What is clear is that Alaska's Eskimos, Indians, and Aleuts developed widely varying lifeways that were superbly adapted to their respective environments. Living in harmony with the land and seas, they flourished, despite occasional famines among various groups brought about by the cyclicity of game animals, until they encountered the industrial and technological culture of the Europeans. A long decline ensued, and today only fragments of their once-rich cultures remain.

PART II

Аляска

Russian Alaska

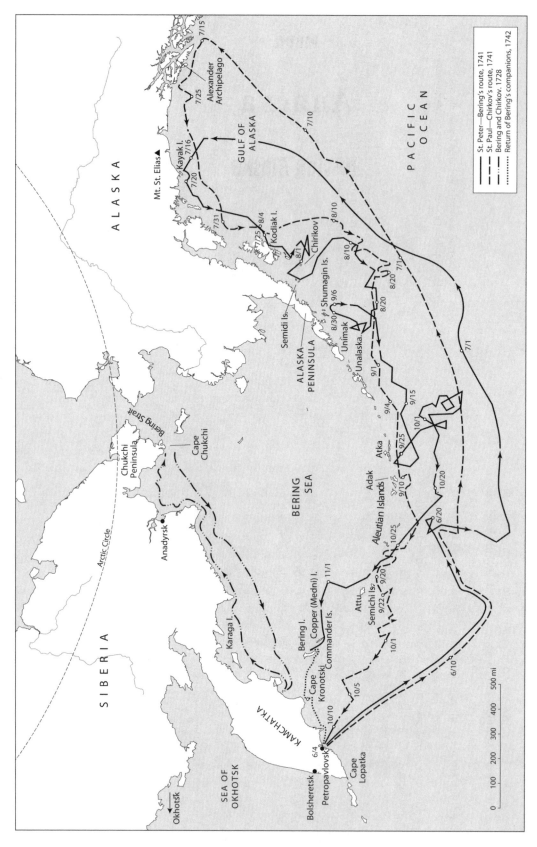

Area of Russian Exploration in the Bering Sea and America. Dates are in Old Style.

Chapter 3

Russian Expansion into Siberia and Exploration of North America

The Native peoples of Alaska met the outside world through Russia, whose penetration and settlement of Siberia and Asia all the way to the Pacific Ocean was a spectacular achievement. Although the Russian government supported this expansion, the driving forces behind it were hunters, trappers, and traders who sought to increase the fur trade, assisted by the seminomadic Cossacks. By the mid-seventeenth century, Russia's presence far into Siberia allowed it to become the first European state to establish itself on the Pacific. Then, on a historic voyage in 1741, the Danish navigator Vitus Bering, serving Russia, made Alaska known to the rest of the world.

Russian Expansion in Siberia

In January 1547, Ivan IV (Ivan the Terrible) became the first Russian grand prince to formally assume the title of czar. Ivan faced a multitude of problems in creating an autocratic empire. Yet Russia's peculiar geographic features—a huge, mostly level plain bounded by a network of natural river roads—enabled a single prince to politically unify the region while the economy remained at a subsistence level. As part of his efforts to establish an absolute Russian monarchy, Ivan IV brought more land under Russian control. During the last years of his reign, Russian expansion reached Siberia, a huge subcontinent that encompasses 5 million square miles. This expansion would bring Russia to the Pacific, and finally, to America.

The expansion started as a defensive measure. During the long Livonian War (1557–81), Ivan IV's government entrusted the defense of its eastern frontier and the Urals region to a single entrepreneurial family. The Stroganovs were traders and financiers who had accumulated a great fortune, founded on salt, ore, grain, and furs, through skillful dealings over a couple of centuries from Ustyug and Vologda to Kaluga and Ryazan. The Stroganovs traded with the English and the Dutch on the Kola Peninsula and also had established commercial links with Central Asia. They employed foreign agents who traveled and dealt on their behalf as far away as Antwerp and Paris.

In 1581 the Stroganovs in turn hired an armed group of 840 Don Cossack men under the leadership of Vasily (Yermak) Timofeyovich, a third-generation bandit and the most notorious Volga River pirate of his day, to protect their operations against raids by the Khan of western Siberia. Turning defense into attack, Yermak succeeded in 1581–82 in conquering the Khan's capital on the lower Irtysh River. That opened the way across Siberia, which was populated by indigenous people who were loosely organized, without state structures, and who did not put up much of a fight. The Cossacks reached the Pacific Ocean in 1639 and founded the harbor of Okhotsk in 1649.

Semyon Ivanov Dezhnyov (Dezhev; 1605–73?), an Iakutsk Cossack *ataman,* or Arctic seafarer, was the first to round the northeast cape, later named Cape Dezhnev. Between 1647 and 1649, he passed through Bering Strait and discovered the Anadyr (Bering) Sea. In the summer of 1649, Dezhnyov and his men ascended the Anadyr River and established the post of Anadyrsk. Soviet writers called Dezhnyov the "discoverer" of the strait separating Asia and North America, but he probably had no knowledge of North America, nor of doing anything other than following the coast, a remarkable feat in itself. For a time some scholars questioned whether or not Dezhnyov made the voyage at all, but Soviet scholars uncovered documents that made his achievement a certainty.[1]

The Russians dominated the territory in only a fragmentary fashion. Freebooters, hunters, trappers, and traders came first, lured by the region's fabled wealth. Subsequently, the government sent soldiers, clergy, officials, and a few peasants to thinly colonize the region. China prevented further advance southward and also exercised a stabilizing influence. After a period of indecisive conflict, in 1689 the Russians signed the Treaty of Nerchinsk with the Chinese, which settled the mutual border for almost two hundred years. Further north, no such power existed to restrain the Russians—not even the Pacific Ocean—so Russian expansion continued into North America.

Peter the Great

The first sponsor of Russian exploration into the North Pacific was the great Westernizing czar, Peter the Great. The period from 1694 to 1699 reflected both Peter's interest in military development and his intent to exercise a strong, expansionist foreign policy, which eventually included the Russian path to Alaska.

When Peter and his half brother, Ivan V, came to the throne as co-rulers of Russia in 1682, many Europeans viewed Russia as a backwater of civilization, more Asiatic than Western. Its ruler was absolute, the administration of the government and judicial system was haphazard, and the armed forces reportedly were undisciplined. In contrast to the population of the West, where serfdom had almost died out, over half of the Russian population was in a state of bondage. Historians have given various explanations for Russia's differences from the West: its heritage was Byzantine, not Roman; its Christianity had been imported from Constantinople; the Tartar invasion and conquest had shut Russia off from the West for two centuries and stunted its development; and Russia had not experienced either the Renaissance or the Reformation.[2]

Even before coming to the throne, Peter had experienced some Western influence. His interest in the West had been stimulated through contact with foreigners in what the Russians called "the German quarter" of Moscow. From them he had learned that Europeans looked on Russia as inferior in its development and regarded the Russian people as almost barbarians. After coming of age and assuming personal rule, in 1697–98, Peter traveled in central and western Europe, learning the rudiments of several artisan trades, including shipbuilding and dentistry. He made a poor impression upon European leaders, but Peter had gone to the West not to shine in high society but rather to learn. He visited shipyards, factories, museums, and hospitals and even had the opportunity to work as a common carpenter in the shipyards of the Dutch East India Company.

During his trip to Europe, Peter had hired more than seven hundred European experts—military officers, mathematics teachers, engineers, and seamen—who now helped in his early efforts to westernize Russia. Within a week of his return to the Kremlin on August 25, 1698, Peter ordered his courtiers to shave their beards (which violated the dictates of the Russian Orthodox Church) and insisted they exchange their flowing kaftans for Western clothing. Peter then spent the next decade in frenzied activities, westernizing every aspect of Old Russia's economic, social, and political life.

The symbol of all these changes was Peter's abandonment of Moscow as his capital and the construction of a new one, Saint Petersburg, near where the Neva River flowed into the Gulf of Finland. He used his new city as means of westernizing Russia, making Saint Petersburg a center of trade and government, which diminished such activity in the older Russian cities. He required merchants, for example, to shift their trade routes from the northern port of Archangel to Saint Petersburg.

After Peter became involved in the Great Northern War (1700–21), he made substantial changes to the Russian military, including compulsory military service for most of the Russian male population. Peter also introduced modern firearms and artillery and promotion on the basis of merit. In 1725, Russia had a permanent army two hundred thousand strong, the largest force in Europe. Long interested in ships and naval affairs, Peter created the Russian navy on the Baltic Sea and started a Russian shipbuilding industry. At the end of his reign, Russia possessed almost fifty major war vessels and its navy counted almost thirty thousand men.

Peter also made many changes to Russian government and society. He imposed increasingly heavy taxes on the Russian populace, reorganized the church to bring it under government control, regulated government and military service, encouraged upper-class women to be take more prominent social roles, and encouraged familiarity with foreign ideas and literature among the elite. In 1711 he created the Senate, which supervised the important operations of the government (administration, court, and finances) in the name of the czar; drafted laws for the czar; and became the country's supreme court. Beginning in 1717 Peter established administrative colleges—modern government departments to deal with specific branches of government work, such as the War College and Foreign Affairs College.

There is no question that Peter the Great created a more centralized and efficient government system, but its chief weakness was that it required a ruler as capable and energetic as Peter. During his absence on military campaigns, the Senate and administrative colleges did not function effectively. Provincial and local governments had to deal with a series of reorganizations during his reign as well, as Peter divided and redivided Russian territory into provinces, counties, and districts. This caused difficulties, particularly in collecting taxes. Many opposed Peter's reforms, and resistance took form in popular upheavals and plots connected to conservative members of the monarch's family, including his own son, Alexis (1690–1718). Many traditional Russians found Western ways offensive, and the peasants objected to the heavy burdens now placed on them.

Peter, like other European leaders, pursued a mercantilist economic policy that called for government aid to build industry, promote economic self-sufficiency, and expand exports. Between 1700 and 1725, entrepreneurs (often merchants) founded about two hundred new industrial enterprises. Government aid consisted of protective tariffs, tax exemptions, and direct subsidies. After the Great Northern War started, the most important task was to produce weapons. The government established weapons factories and then handed them over to private entrepreneurs, who included middle-class industrialists and members of the nobility.

Peter westernized education by sending Russian noblemen to schools in Europe, and he built schools like those found in the advanced western societies. These included the School of Mathematical and Navigational Sciences, established in 1701, and the Naval Academy, founded in 1715. Peter was especially interested in the promotion of science, particularly geography and geology, which had practical implications. A visit to the Royal Society at London had fascinated him, and he seriously considered the founding of a Russian Academy of Sciences. He established it on paper in 1724, and its members met for the first time after his death.

The problem confronting the czar as he aged was his succession. Much to Peter's sorrow, his wife Catherine's two sons, Peter and Paul, died in infancy. There remained only one male heir, his grandson, Peter. There were four possible female heirs. In 1722 Peter arrogated to himself the right to freely choose a successor as emperor, but he never named one. In 1724 he complicated the succession problem by the formal coronation of his peasant wife, Catherine, as empress. As he lay on his deathbed in January 1725, Peter was persuaded to express his wishes but could go no further than "Give everything. . . ." Thus Peter's reign ended with the succession question unsettled. But before he died, Peter made one appointment that directly affects our story.

The Goals of Vitus Bering's First Voyage

On December 29, 1724, Peter the Great appointed Captain Vitus Jonassen Bering commander of the First Kamchatka Expedition to explore the Russian Pacific. Born and trained in Denmark, Bering had served as an officer in the Russian naval service for twenty years. Bering's lieutenants were Martin Spangberg (also spelled "Spanberg" and "Spangsberg") and Aleksey Chirikov. Spangberg was a fellow Dane known for his toughness, tenacity, and seamanship. Chirikov was trained in mathematics and navigation and had taught at the new Naval Academy in Saint Petersburg.[3]

Peter had envisioned the expedition to consist of about twenty men. By January 8, 1725, thirty-four men had been selected, drawn mostly from Russia's Baltic fleet, including thirteen sailors and nine artisans. The expedition was to carry only essential equipment and supplies probably not available in Siberia. These included anchors of about 360 pounds each, eight cannon, twenty-four guns, compasses, sounding leads, hourglasses, rigging sail, canvas, and a truck of medications.[4]

Peter's death on January 28, 1725, ended decisive leadership and firm control and direction of Russian domestic and foreign policies. Catherine, who had been at Peter's bedside throughout January as he lay dying, promised as empress to continue Peter's projects.[5] However, as a result of the transfer of power, Peter's original intention for Bering's mission remains an open question. Historians long believed that Peter instructed Bering to determine whether the Asian and American continents were joined or separated, whether a northeast passage to Asia was feasible.

But in recent years, several Russian and particularly one American scholar, Raymond H. Fisher, have re-examined the documentation about the purposes of the First Kamchatka Expedition. Was it Peter's intent that Bering map the route to Kamchatka and Asia's northeast extremity? Was Bering to look for a land bridge between Asia and America? Was it Peter's intent that Bering find America and describe whatever he could find out about the continent? The answers to such questions have varied and produced different judgments. What is clear is that most scholars who have written about the first expedition criticize Bering for insufficient accomplishments.[6]

We do know that Peter's orders from Empress Catherine instructed him "to build one or two ships with decks" in Kamchatka or someplace else. He was to sail "along land, which lies to the north," and finally he was "to search for the place where that land might be joined to America, and from there proceed to some settlement belonging to a European power." If he encountered a European ship, he was to "find out from it what the coast was called, and write it down." Then he was to "go ashore, obtain accurate information, locate it on a map" and return to Saint Petersburg.[7] The second and third tasks were vague enough, and Peter did not order Bering to find America.

Voyage to Kamchatka

Chirikov left Saint Petersburg in January 1725 with twenty-six men and five horse-drawn sledges for Vologda, a distance of 411 miles. Bering and Spangberg remained behind to receive the Admiralty College's precise instruction, the Senate's orders to Siberia's governor to render all needed assistance, and the emperor's orders. They left Saint Petersburg on February 6, 1725, with six men and eight sledges and joined Chirikov eight days later at Vologda. On March 16, the two groups reached Tobolsk, having traveled 1,763 miles over a low pass in the Ural Mountains. They had averaged about forty-five miles per day, the easiest part of the journey. Winter and good roads ended, and Bering now needed boats instead of horses.

The ice on the Irtysh River broke on April 23, 1725, and Bering needed to add additional personnel to build the boats and portage goods. But he did not hire as many men as he needed, the four flat-bottomed riverboats were not ready until May 14, and his travel funds did not arrive until May 12.[8] They were off to a late start.

Bering's expedition followed a century-old and well-established river highway. Major rivers flowing north to the Bering Sea had tributaries that, with portages, connected the river systems. Forts along the way could resupply small groups of travelers. Bering's problem was that he needed to recruit large numbers of men to accomplish his tasks. At Yeniseisk, Bering finally got the men he requested, but unfortunately many were physically unable to perform the required jobs. The expedition reached Yakutsk in June 1725. Here nothing was prepared. The government had instructed the Yakutsk district governor to prepare for Bering's arrival, but there were no horses and not enough men. After an appeal, the governor sent only fifty workers to help manage the boats. Bering was furious, and only after threatening the governor with responsibility for the expedition's failure did he get sixty-nine more workers, together with 660 horses and drivers from among the Yakut native Siberian villages. It was the middle of August when most of the expedition finally left town. Chirikov was left behind with the task of getting as much flour as he could and following the next spring. The rest of the party experienced a very difficult winter journey. Men died and deserted, but the group finally arrived in Okhotsk in the spring of 1726. An advance party of Chirikov's group reached the settlement in early June and saved the main group from starvation.[9]

In Okhotsk the men built the single-masted *Fortuna* within a month and repaired another ship, the *Vostok,* which was badly damaged. Spangberg took the shipbuilder, named Kozlov, along with carpenters, blacksmiths, soldiers, and sailors, forty-eight men in all, and sailed the 630 nautical miles across the sea to Kamchatka on the *Vostok* so he could build a ship in the spring of 1727. When the two ships returned to Okhotsk, Chirikov had arrived with additional supplies. Finally, on August 22, 1726, the expedition sailed for Kamchatka and finally reached the Lower Kamchatka Post in 1727. Bering's expedition had completed an astounding overland journey of some six thousand convoluted miles from Saint Petersburg to the Lower Kamchatka Post.[10]

Exploration by Sea

In the spring of 1728, Kozlov and his men built the sixty-foot-long, two-masted *Archangel Gabriel.* It carried three cannons, was loaded with provisions for forty-four men for one year, and set sail on July 14. Once around Cape Kamchatka, the ship followed the land in a northeastern direction. Bering cautiously kept the Asian shore within sight to his portside for much of the voyage. When land appeared off the starboard quarter with dwellings similar to those they saw along the continental shore, they named the island Saint Lawrence in honor of the saint of the day. Bering approached the island and got within five miles but decided not to land there. Approaching latitude 65° north, they found the sea still open to the north. Unknown to Bering, he now sailed northward past Cape Dezhnev and through the strait that England's Captain James Cook was to name for Bering fifty years later. Eventually the land turned away to the west, and the ship was in danger of meeting the pack ice.[11]

Bering conferred with his two lieutenants on August 13. He read Peter's instructions to them and asked them if it was not clear that with the Asian shore turning westward, Asia was separated from America by sea. The commander mistakenly believed, as his question implied, that Cape Chukotsk was Asia's most easterly point and that there was no reason to go much farther. Chirikov suggested that they continue until August 25, either as far as the mouth of the Kolyma River or to the ice pack farther north. Maybe they would find a place to spend the winter, perhaps opposite Cape Chukotsk, where forested land was said to exist. Spangberg suggested that the *Archangel Gabriel* continue northward until August 16 and then return to the Kamchatka River before winter for the safety of both men and ship.[12]

Bering, however, was correct to fear being locked into the ice. The safe navigation season in those high latitudes was almost over. Critics are correct that Bering did not sail far enough to the north to prove conclusively that no land bridge existed between Asia and America. It might also be said, however, that no matter how far north he had gone, short of the North Pole, an isthmus might have existed. Historian Frost writes that it would have been impossible for Bering to satisfy all later critics, whether he had gone "west to the Kolyma River, north to the Pole, or east to America . . . imprudent under the circumstances and . . . beyond his instructions."[13]

Bering gave his opinion in writing. Staying in these northern regions any longer was dangerous. The ship was in poor condition, with leeboards and keelboards broken, which made it difficult to search for a safe wintering place. It was therefore better to return and search in Kamchatka for a harbor where they could spend the winter. In the end, Bering continued to sail northward for several more days. On August 14 they saw an island to the south. On August 15, the ship had reached latitude 67°24' north and had gone a little more than 30° longitude east of the mouth of the Kamchatka River. Bering ordered the return trip. When they saw again the island they had seen a couple of days earlier, they named it Saint Diomede. On August 18 the ship again passed Saint Lawrence Island. On September 1, 1728, the ship reached Cape Kamchatka and the next day entered the mouth of the Kamchatka River. The voyage had taken fifty days, thirty-three outbound and seventeen on the return.[14]

Bering reached Okhotsk on July 24, 1729, and Saint Petersburg on February 28, 1730. He submitted his final reports within two weeks, and in December 1731 he received promotion to the rank of captain-commander and the government awarded him one thousand rubles. Spangberg and Chirikov were promoted to captain. The cost of the First Kamchatka Expedition had been high. Fifteen men died, many deserted, and most of the 660 horses died, which left their owners, the Yakut native Siberians, poverty stricken. The commandeering of dogs, sledges, and drivers also severely disrupted the life of the native Itelmen and contributed to their decline.[15]

Bering and his lieutenants had searched for a nonexistent land connection. In the process, they first charted the Asian side of the Bering Sea and Bering Strait and named two islands they sighted. Russia gained a new map of its Siberian territories, chiefly the work of Aleksei Chirikov and naval cadet Peter Chaplin, a member of Bering's expedition, who used modern, west European charting technology to make fairly precise latitude and longitude observations. The Russians shared Bering's map with western European governments, which gave Russia prestige. The map showed how much more extensive than previously imagined were Russia's claims to landholdings in northeast Asia. The map showed the enormous distance from Tobolsk to Kamchatka and also showed the easternmost extremity of Siberia for the first time.[16]

Bering returned to Saint Petersburg during a difficult time for the government. A struggle over succession had left Anna Ivanovna, Peter the Great's niece, in power. Anna's accession and subsequent actions produced significant turmoil in the capital, and because of all these changes, it took Bering some time to gain a hearing for his new proposal. He wanted to return to Kamchatka and build larger seaworthy ships with which to find America.[17]

Chapter 4

The Second Kamchatka Expedition

Bering's second voyage toward North America in the 1740s was plagued with troubles. The two ships in the expedition were separated near the beginning of their voyage; the crews were decimated by illness; and Bering himself did not survive the journey. But the Second Kamchatka Expedition[1] was significant for its discoveries, including the Aleutians, the southeastern coast of Alaska, and Alexander Archipelago, and for providing the earliest European descriptions of the Alaskan landscape and people.

The Expedition: Proposals and Preparations

In 1730, Vitus Bering presented to the Admiralty College two proposals regarding Siberian affairs and a return to Kamchatka. The first suggested improvement in the administration of the easternmost regions of Siberia and the utilization of the region's natural resources.[2] More precisely, the proposed expedition was to inventory the peoples, flora, fauna, and minerals of Siberia and initiate metallurgical industry and agriculture. It was to build new ports on the Pacific Ocean and find a new southern route from Irkutsk to that ocean as well as establish a reliable postal service east of the Ural Moutains.[3]

The second proposal suggested that voyages be launched eastward to America and southward to Japan in order to open trade with each. The Arctic coast of Siberia between the Ob and Lena Rivers was to be charted. Bering also indicated that he was willing to sail to America, as were Chirikov and Spangberg.

The Senate received the proposals favorably in December 1730, and in the next twenty-seven months it issued numerous orders putting them into effect. By April 17, 1732, an imperial order, or *ukaz*, ordered Bering to Kamchatka for the second time. On May 2, the Senate issued two ukases: the first one contained instructions for preparing the Second Kamchatka Expedition and its materials, equipment, support personnel, provisions, and numerous supporting activities. It also laid out the responsibilities of the central agencies and local authorities and ordered the exploration of the Arctic coast from the Ob to the Lena Rivers and Kamchatka. The second ukaz ordered the construction of vessels in Kamchatka to be used to look for lands between Kamchatka and America and for islands south of Kamchatka, to visit the Shantar Islands located near the mouth of the Amur River, and to explore a sea passage to the Japanese Islands.[4]

Early that summer the Senate added a contingent of professors to accompany Bering as far as Kamchatka, where they were to learn everything of scientific interest. The Academy of Sciences appointed George Gmelin to study natural history, Louis Delisle de La Croyere to make astronomical observations, and Gerhard Friedrich Müller to study the Native peoples.[5]

Bering's original proposals had been so enlarged

that this expedition promised to become a logistical nightmare. Wives and children would accompany naval officers, and the three professors would together have sixteen assistants. Several thousand other individuals composed the support staff en route, such as soldiers, boatmen, carpenters, and general laborers. Supplying such a large group of people in such inhospitable regions called for supplies to be delivered by sea. To this end, Count Nikolay F. Golovin, who in 1733 was appointed president of the Admiralty College, proposed to the empress in the late fall of 1732 that two frigates and a transport vessel be sent to Kamchatka each year by way of Cape Horn. That proposal, however, was not approved.[6]

In October 1732, the Admiralty College instructed Bering to build a couple of two-masted ships on the Kamchatka River. He was to command one and Chirikov the other, and they were to sail as far north as 67° north to search, within a single sailing season, for the American coast. Each commander was to keep a journal describing coasts, islands, channels, and other information in order to make an accurate map.

The Empress Anna Ivanovna approved the plans for the Second Kamchatka Expedition at the end of 1732. Spangberg left Saint Petersburg in February 1733, together with a small group of men. He was bound for Okhotsk, and his group carried some of the heaviest equipment needed for shipbuilding. In April the main expedition left the capital, consisting of Chirikov, eight lieutenants, and the officers' wives and children, about five hundred individuals altogether. Later there were added about five hundred soldiers and two thousand workers to help transport the freight. Bering, his wife Anna, and their two youngest children, a two-year-old boy and a one-year-old girl, left the capital at the end of April.[7] In the middle of May, Bering and his family caught up with the expedition. It had traveled to the Volga by horses and continued on boats on the Volga and Kama Rivers. Late in the fall it would use sledges to reach Tobolsk. The three professors and their staffs left Saint Petersburg in early August and arrived separately in Tobolsk near the end of January 1734.[8]

Ships, Provisions, and Initial Voyages

The expedition struggled along over incredibly difficult terrain for several years. By 1737, Spangberg's carpenters in Okhotsk had refitted the *Archangel Gabriel* from Bering's first expedition and also built two new ships, the brig *Archangel Michael* and the double sloop *Nadezhda*. Bering arrived in the summer of 1737 with enough provisions to supply the three ships for their voyage toward Japan in 1738.[9]

The government had promised Bering to facilitate transportation in Siberia. Everything was to be ready for him: riverboats, horses, munitions, provisions, and workers. In return, the Russian government expected Bering to mount multiple voyages along the Arctic coastline, along the Kuril Islands toward Japan, and from Kamchatka to North America. Bering was instructed to buy and transport supplies without much effort or expense. He was to find an easier and shorter route to Kamchatka. The imperial government expected that all the objectives of the Second Kamchatka Expedition could be accomplished in no more than four years. Also, it was to cost no more than twelve thousand rubles, apart from salaries and freight. Yet Bering was still in Yakutsk after four years. Nothing had been ready when he arrived, and the local officials instructed to aid his efforts had failed. After five years he was still in Okhotsk, and expenses had mounted to over three hundred thousand rubles.[10]

Expedition members and Siberia's inhabitants suffered great privations because of the demands the expedition placed on them. Lack of food and timber slowed the construction of the two ships for the American voyage. The government had been forced to extend the expedition from four to eight years, to 1741, and as an expression of its dissatisfaction with Bering's lack of progress, the Admiralty College had cut his salary in half in 1737. In fact, in 1738 the government had considered terminating the expedition altogether.[11]

Spangberg finally departed for Japan in 1738 but had little success. The three ships became separated in the foggy and stormy Kuril Islands. The crews saw about thirty islands, and all three ships returned to Bolsheretsk by the fall of 1738. They had not landed anywhere, nor had they seen Hokkaidō or Honshū. A second expedition in 1739 was very successful. Four ships left Okhotsk on June 1, 1739, and again became separated. Spangberg, commanding the sloop *Bolsheretsk,* sighted the northeast coast of Honshū on June 27 and traded with two Japanese junks. He left, however, when seventy-nine Japanese boats appeared around him. Spangberg's report described the Japanese boats and the stature and physiognomy of the Japanese. Four Japanese men visited his cabin and told him that their nation called itself Nippon, not Japan, as shown on his chart or globe.[12]

Bering and his men left for Okhotsk in 1737 to begin the construction of the *Saint Peter* and the *Saint Paul,* the oceangoing vessels that were to carry him to America. The job was completed in 1740. The ships were ninety feet long, twenty-three feet wide, and nine and a half feet high. Each displaced 211 tons and had fourteen mounted cannon and a fairly good-sized captain's cabin, where a dozen officers could meet. Altogether, each ship accommodated seventy-seven, and they were provisioned for six months. Together with ballast, firewood, one hundred barrels of water, and artillery, the cargo weighed 106 tons. Each had two shore boats, one ten-oared longboat nineteen feet long, and a six-oared yawl, each with a mast and rigging.[13] After wintering in Kamchatka at Avatcha Bay, the two ships sailed into the Pacific Ocean from the tiny port of Petropavlovsk on June 4, 1741.

Finally at Sea

Bering commanded the *Saint Peter* and Chirikov the *Saint Paul,* both with seventy-six men aboard. Accompanying Bering was the German physician and scientist Georg Wilhelm Steller. Trained in the natural sciences, Steller had traveled to Saint Petersburg, where he made the acquaintance of individuals in the Academy of Sciences and learned of the aims of the Second Kamchatka Expedition. The Academy of Sciences sent Steller to Kamchatka in 1738 to investigate plants, animals, and minerals. Bering learned about Steller and his self-described "insatiable desire to visit foreign lands and to investigate their conditions and curiosities," which convinced Bering to recruit him for his voyage.[14] Steller's journals would provide an invaluable first-hand account of the journey.

Professor of astronomy Deslisle de La Croyere was on board Captain Chirikov's *Saint Paul.* A French scientist, he came from a notable family that included the historian Simon-Claude Deslisle and the geographer Guillaume Deslisle. Deslisle de La Croyere joined the Academy of Sciences in 1732 and received an assignment to the Second Kamchatka Expedition.[15]

Steller reported that on June 12, the crew "saw the first considerable signs of land lying to the south or southeast. In totally calm waters, we suddenly saw many different sea plants . . . floating around our vessel. We also saw gulls, terns, and ducks, which are all land birds not usually seen on the sea or very far from land." Steller was convinced that if they continued on their "initial course," they would soon reach land. Instead, the officers turned north, and the ship experienced its "first little storm" and also the first calamity. In the fog and drizzle, wrote Steller, "we lost the *St. Paul* . . . under Captain Chirikov's command. We never saw it again." It was near midnight on June 20. The *Saint Peter* searched several days in vain for the lost *Saint Paul.* Bering eventually gave up the search.[16]

The two ships had sailed across what are today called the Emperor Seamounts. The nearest land was the westernmost Aleutians, Near and Rat islands, about four hundred nautical miles away in an arc from north to northeast. Had the ships continued southeast by east indefinitely, they might eventually have reached, with luck, Midway Island or the Hawaiian Islands after crossing more than one thousand nautical miles of open sea.[17]

The Voyage of the *Saint Paul*

Until July 13 the *Saint Peter* was three to five days behind the *Saint Paul* as both ships entered the Gulf of Alaska. Neither one had seen any land since leaving Kamchatka. On July 15 Chirikov and his crew on the *Saint Paul* sighted land. Chirikov took compass bearings of Cape Bartolomè on Baker Island, southeast Alaska, west of today's Ketchikan, and of northeast Cape Addington, on Noyes Island. He marked three projections on Baker Island: Cape Chirikov, Granite Point, and Outer Point. Judging by the maps in his possession, Chirikov assumed that his ship was not far from Spanish America. These maps, however, reflected Spanish claims rather than an established Spanish presence north of San Francisco Bay.

The next day, Chirikov sent a boat toward shore to investigate Windy Bay on Coronation Island. On July 18, he sent Fleetmaster Avram Dementiev and ten armed men in a longboat into Takanis Bay on Yacobi Island, northwest of today's Sitka, to go ashore if possible. When on land, they were to fire a rocket, distribute gifts to Native Americans if any were found, sketch the harbor, identify trees and any precious metals, and fill two empty water barrels. No one saw the longboat land, no rocket was fired, and for five days there was not a sign of the longboat.[18]

On July 23 the fog lifted and Chirikov saw a fire on the beach where he thought his men had landed. He fired a gun several times to signal that the men ashore should return to the ship, but no boat appeared. The next day, Chirikov and his officers decided to send the yawl ashore with a carpenter, a caulker, and tools to repair the longboat if it had been damaged. A boatswain and a sailor volunteered to go along. They were to leave the repair crew ashore and return with Dementiev and a few others in the yawl, which held six to seven men.

The yawl made no signal and failed to return to the ship. In the evening the ship fired a cannon to summon the men back to the ship. The crew of the ship saw a fire intermittently on the beach. The next day, two boats came out of the bay, one small and one large. When they came closer, Chirikov realized that they were not his, for one had a sharp bow and those in it were paddling instead of rowing. Chirikov saw four persons. One stood in the stern and the others paddled. Suddenly the four stood up in their canoe, shouted "Agai, Agai" twice, waved their hands, and returned to shore. The two boats quickly disappeared in the bay. Chirikov and his officers were convinced that misfortune had befallen their fifteen men and that the Native Americans had killed or imprisoned them. The *Saint Paul* continued to hover near the opening of the bay.[19]

The most common assumption among historians is that the boats were swamped in riptides, common at narrow mouths of bays and straits along the American coast, and that the men were drowned. "Agai" may have been the Tlingit word "agon," which means "come here" and was probably a friendly invitation, perhaps to investigate any flotsam from the two boats that had broken up.[20] In any case, the *Saint Paul* had no more boats to send ashore to investigate, and on July 27 a sea council convened and decided that the *ship* should return directly to Avatcha Bay. There were only forty-five barrels of fresh water left. The *Saint Paul* started on its homeward journey.

By September 9, the *Saint Paul* was anchored in a fog only one hundred yards from shore opposite Adak Island. When the fog lifted, the crew saw two men walking on the beach. The Russians eventually traded knives, an ax, and some sea biscuits for some of the islanders' water, a hat, and several other items. The wind suddenly rose in the afternoon, putting the ship in danger of being driven onto the rocks, so Chirikov had the anchor cable cut and they narrowly escaped disaster.

The *Saint Paul* sighted Agattu Island on September 21, entered Avatcha Bay on October 10, and landed two days later at the port of Saint Peter and Saint Paul. Chirikov had lost six men to scurvy. Both Chirikov and his mate, Ivan Yelagin, were gravely ill and reached port none too soon.[21]

The *Saint Peter* Sights America and Exploration Begins

Meanwhile, on July 16, 1741, Captain-Commander Bering and his crew of seventy-six saw a huge, snow-topped mountain range topped by a volcanic peak. Later named the Saint Elias Mountain Range, its highest peak, Mount Saint Elias, rises to 18,008 feet. The sighting represented the official discovery of northwestern America by the Russians.[22] The officers and crew were jubilant, but Bering, according to Steller, was indifferent. Later he told Steller and Surveyor Friedrich Plenisner that he feared many difficulties and hardships lay ahead. They were far from home, and accidents might very well come up and prevent a return home. Above all, they did not know the land, and existing provisions would not last through the winter.[23]

On July 20 the *Saint Peter* anchored among a

group of islands near Kayak Island. Everyone agreed to take on fresh water, which prompted Steller to remark, "We have come only to take American water to Asia." After some pleading, Bering allowed Steller to go ashore with the water carriers, but, as Steller complained in his journal, "without giving me the least help or a single person other than the Cossack Thoma Lepekhin, whom I myself had brought along."[24]

Steller knew that time was precious, and he made the best of the situation. He and Lepekhin quickly headed for the mainland "to discover people and habitations." Before long he found a camp, suddenly deserted, where people had cooked meat and "bones lay scattered, some with meat remaining." He thought the bones came from reindeer, and he also found dried fish, various kinds of mussels, and sweet grass lying in bowls over which the Natives had poured water to extract the sweetness.[25] In the rain forest they found a fourteen-by-twenty-one-foot-long "dug-out cellar," a large underground cache filled with smoked red salmon stored in bark containers. The Eskimos had gathered the food and household items and hidden them. In the fall they would return with their goods to islands in Prince William Sound.

Somewhere along the way, Steller sent Lepekhin to the landing site to take cultural artifacts back to the ship and to warn the men hauling water not to feel too safe. Lepekhin again asked Bering for the use of two or three men. Bering refused, but he instructed Lepekhin and a group of men to go to the cache and obtain salmon, leaving in return various trinkets, such as kettles, knives, and glass beads, among other items.

Hiking along the island's beach, Steller collected botanical specimens and one bird, a jay. In his few hours on shore he compiled an extensive record of island flora, took notes on magpies, ravens, foxes, seals, sea otter, whales, salmon, and jay, and made careful ethnological notes about the local diet, food preparation, and crafting of implements. He did not see any Native Americans but speculated that they resembled the Itelmen and could have Asian origins.[26]

A Troubled Return

After an inauspicious beginning, the return voyage went from bad to worse. On July 21 Bering ordered to weigh anchor. His officers refused to return to Kamchatka the way they had come, instead opting to follow the contours of the land. Historian Frost writes that Bering's hands were virtually tied because of the institution of the sea council, where every officer had an equal voice. The *Saint Peter* was doomed in stages because of time lost, the beginnings of scurvy, and terrible storms. Bering no longer effectively controlled the ship, and therefore it was almost helpless.

It all began as the *Saint Peter* got under way again. The ship dodged various reefs, shoals, and islands. On August 10 Bering called Lieutenant Sven Waxell, Mate Andreas Hesselberg, and Fleetmaster Safron Khitrovo to his cabin. They talked about the May 4 agreement, specifically that the ship should return to Avatcha Bay in Petropavlovsk in the last days of September. They agreed that approaching the land was unsafe because of the many obstructions, heavy fog, and violent storms. They decided to forego any further exploration of America and return to their harbor in Kamchatka, sailing along the 53rd parallel of latitude as the winds permitted.[27]

Unbeknownst to Bering and his crew was the fact that the *Saint Paul* was two days' sailing behind and bearing down on the *Saint Peter*. Chirikov had started on the homeward voyage on July 27, and since he had lost both of his shore boats he was not tempted to explore. The *Saint Paul* soon passed its sister ship without seeing it.

Another reason for the decision to return was the onset of scurvy. Sixteen men were already sick. On August 30 the *Saint Peter* anchored midway between Nagai and Little Near Island in the Shumagin Islands. Steller accompanied a party to shore to obtain some water. During two days the larger boat landed perhaps as many as eight times to fill water barrels and take the sick ashore. Unfortunately, the water taken on was slightly salty and so not conducive to good health. Steller advised that they take on fresh water. His advice would have prevented much of the suffering that occurred later, but it was ignored. In the evening of August 30 the first man sick with

This monument—a cross and an engraved plaque—honors Vitus Jonassen Bering, commander of a Russian expedition to the New World and the man for whom the Bering Strait is named.

(Photo by Claus-M. Naske.)

Getting Bering Straight:
Modern Forensics Finally Show Us What the Great Russian Explorer Really Looked Like

On September 16, 1992, six coffins with a uniformed guard of honor arrived in Commander Bay on the Russian Coast Guard frigate *Kedrov*. Two days earlier a military ceremony had been held in Lenin Square, with the coffins paraded on gun carriages. Present were officers of the Russian Pacific fleet, the governor of Kamchatka, a delegation from Denmark, and the Danish ambassador to Russia. The coffins were lowered into a compact grave site on the slope of a bluff several hundred yards above the site of Vitus Bering's 1741–42 camp and cemetery.

Five wooden panels set just above ground level listed the names of the fourteen men who died during the Bering expedition. The Bering Monument—a high, steel Latin cross above a cast-iron plaque set in the ground decades earlier—bears the inscription:

1681–1741
To the Great Navigator
Captain-Commander Vitus Bering
From the Residents of Kamchatka
June 1966

The memorial to Bering and the others is not the only recent recognition of the man and his contribution to Alaskan history. Now for the first time we know what Vitus Bering really looked like. The long-accepted image of Bering shows a man with puffy cheeks and perhaps jowls and a double chin—an obese individual from an eighteenth-century oil painting. That was not Bering.

On August 2, 1991, the small, Russian-Danish "Bering '91 Archaeological Expedition" arrived at Commander Bay on Bering Island. The Danes were four archaeologists, an interpreter, a photojournalist, a television producer, a geographer, and a representative of descendants of the Bering family living in Denmark. There were twenty-two Russians, including the expedition leader and a forensic physician along with numerous scientific specialists and their assistants.

The aim was to locate Bering's grave, which the Russians thought might take a long time. The Danes, however, knew that Georg W. Steller, Bering's naturalist, had written in his journal that the commander was buried close to the 1741–42 winter camp. On the first day, they went

This was for many years the accepted image of Vitus Bering. Recent research suggests this is his great-uncle, Vitus Pederson Bering, the royal historiographer in Denmark.

(Courtesy of Wikimedia Commons.)

This three-dimensional image, based upon skeletal remains and modern forensic science, is probably very close to what Bering actually looked like.

(Author's collection.)

directly to a spot next to the camp's house-pit sites, dug a short trench, pulled back the turf, and found a small unmarked cemetery. It had been there for 250 years, relatively undisturbed. Among the six skeletal remains recovered were those of Vitus Bering.

Reconstruction of Bering's appearance from his skeletal remains revealed a man resembling a world-champion weight lifter. He had been so muscular that the principal Russian forensic physician concluded that Bering, even late in life, "could not but distinguish himself among those around him by his obvious physical strength." His weight, about 168 pounds, was ideal for his height of five feet six inches.

Historians had written that Bering had died of scurvy, but his teeth were intact and in good condition, ruling out a disease in which lost teeth are a sure indication. The immediate cause of death was heart failure. What is clear today is that the forensically reconstructed image is probably Bering's. The portrait used so far used may have been that of the commander's great-uncle, Vitus Pederson Bering, the royal historiographer in Denmark.

Source: Orcutt Frost, *Bering: The Russian Discovery of America* (New Haven, Conn.: Yale University Press, 2003).

scurvy died, the sailor Nikita Shumagin. He was the first European to be buried on America's northwest coast. Later, Shumagin's name was bestowed upon the entire archipelago of fifty islands.[28]

In the meantime, Bering had sent Khitrovo in the smaller boat to investigate a fire on an island. Unfortunately, Khitrovo and his crew were flung up on a sandy beach. The water stop of two days had to be extended by six more days to rescue the men. Thereafter, the crew of the *Saint Peter* attempted to gain the open ocean, but on September 4 they were going nowhere. They were finding nothing.

Since it had left Kayak Island six weeks earlier, the ship had covered only one-fourth of the distance home, and it was still 1,277 nautical miles from port. The crew had made no progress during the last couple of weeks. One man had died, they had abandoned the small yawl, taken on bad water, and wasted good winds.[29] The autumn equinox was six days away, and winter was close behind. Time and provisions were running out. There was one hopeful event, namely, almost all of the scurvy on the ship had suddenly disappeared, thanks to Steller's ministrations. He had fed the crew with lingonberries and crowberries with scurvy grass, sourcok, gentian, and other cresslike plants.[30]

On Bird Island in the Shumagins the crew finally met their first Americans, a group of Aleuts who came out in two kayaks. Bering dispatched Waxell, Steller, and ten others, including the Koryak interpreter, to the island. They briefly met with the group of Aleuts and quickly returned to the ship. On September 5 the ship moved to a more sheltered spot and anchored, and once again Aleut kayaks came out to meet the ship, this time seven in number. The Russians exchanged some trade items for two Aleut hats and a five-foot-long rod with many different kinds of feathers attached.[31]

On September 6 the *Saint Peter* weighed anchor and sailed into the sea. A storm came up on the next day. Steller observed that it "stormed furiously all night. . . . [G]iven these conditions, the late fall season and the great distance from Avacha, the officers as well as the crew suddenly became discouraged" and "began to express doubts about reaching home."[32] The ship made good progress and on September 23 it was two-fifths of the way home from the Shumagin Islands, but everyone feared the return of scurvy. Steller's supply of antiscorbutic plants was soon exhausted. On that same day Grenadier Andrei Tretyakov died of scurvy. On September 24 the ship came upon numerous islands and was in danger of running onto one of them, so it turned east, back into the sea.[33]

Thereafter the *Saint Peter* encountered violent storms, one after the other. By October 24 Steller reported that "danger and death suddenly got the upper hand on our ship to such extent that not only were the sick dying but also men claiming to be healthy, who, on being relieved at their posts, dropped dead from exhaustion." Not much happened between October 31 and November 3 "except that our sick were suddenly dying off very quickly and numerously, and we could hardly manage the ship any more or make alterations in the sails."[34] On November 6 a sea council, over Bering's objections, decided to enter a bay in sight and land there. The ship anchored close to shore, and Steller and several men went onshore on November 7. The officers and crew were convinced they had reached Kamchatka, but Steller was not. On November 10 a number of sick men, among them an exhausted Bering, went ashore.

Stranded

Steller and his companions built a crude dugout for a shelter. As others arrived on shore, they followed suit. On November 12 many sick men arrived, and some died "as soon as they came into the air, others in the boat on the crossing over."[35] On November 15, all the remaining sick were brought on shore. The dying continued on land. Then, during the night of November 28, a violent storm severed the anchor cables and beached the ship near the bank of a small river below camp. The ship sank and filled with saltwater, ruining the remaining gunpowder and partially destroying five tons of rye flour.[36]

Bering sent a search party on December 1 to go southwest and look for forests and to determine whether they had landed on the Asian continent. Gone for four weeks, the party found no forests and concluded that the land was an island. Bering's crew, in fact, had anchored in a broad channel between

Copper and Bering islands called the Commander Islands, the last distant link between America and Asia.[37]

On the island eventually named for him, Bering died on December 8, according to Steller "more from hunger, cold, thirst, vermin, and grief than from disease." He probably died of heart failure. Steller was convinced that he would have lived had the ship reached Kamchatka and he "could have had the benefit of a warm room and fresh food." The men tied Bering's body to a plank and buried him next to Andreas Hesselberg, the navigator, who had died earlier. Sven Waxell, the new commander, led a brief service.[38]

Gradually most of the sick began to recover because Steller lightly cooked fresh meats in soups. In December six men died and in January two. The last to die was ensign Ivan Lagunov on January 8, 1842. That was the fourteenth burial on the island. Thereafter there were no more deaths, thanks chiefly to the labors of Steller.[39]

Under the able leadership of Waxell and Steller, the survivors set about to survive the winter. They lived in five underground dwellings located side by side. They killed sea mammals for the meat, and because of good management, "from the beginning to the end, we were no day totally without bread." The flour, which had been stored firmly pressed in leather sacks for several years, had gotten totally wet when the ship ran aground and sank. Steller wrote that lying in saltwater for a lengthy time, the flour "became a tincture of all kinds of materials contained in the ship-gunpowder and other trash." Until they got used to it, "it caused such gas that our stomachs swelled like drums."[40]

Steller wrote that the men and officers passed the time playing cards, gambling for money and sea otter pelts. The "gambling addiction" was so bad "that no one bore our deliverance much in mind anymore." The construction of new ship from the wreck of the *Saint Peter* "proceeded sleepily." Eventually, in June, "several upright petty officers" stopped the gambling. The crew succeeded in killing more than seven hundred sea otters between November 1741 and August 1742. They eventually took the pelts with them to Kamchatka.[41]

By mid-July 1742, "the ship stood ready on the stocks" and the men spent their days making "rigging, spars, and masts, in blacksmithing, in the tedious burning to tar from old ropes, and in erecting a platform for launching the ship." On August 13 all boarded the ship, and the next morning they weighed anchor and were under way.[42] On August 26, "after using the oars 24 hours without a break," the ship at night arrived at the entrance to Avatcha Bay and anchored on August 27 in the harbor of Petropavlovsk. Steller bade everyone farewell and hiked the thirty miles to the Bolshaya River "to reach my own longed-for people."[43]

Home at Last

During their first hours ashore, the survivors learned that Chirikov's *Saint Paul* had returned to the harbor on October 12, 1741. In the spring of 1742 Chirikov and his crew had left Avatcha Bay to search for Bering and his ship. They were, of course, unsuccessful, but they did sight Bering Island, which they named Saint Julian. In July, Chirikov and others had begun the long voyage to Yeniseisk in Siberia, and from there several years later back to St. Petersburg.[44]

Aleksey Ivanov, a special courier, delivered Sven Waxell's report about the voyage to America to the Admiralty College on November 15, 1742. The report, and news of Bering's death, caused the Senate to terminate the Second Kamchatka Expedition on September 25, 1743. It also ordered the return of all participants.[45]

Bering's reputation slid into virtual obscurity for 250 years after his death, for several reasons. The Russian government was secretive about the results of the Second Kamchatka Expedition, wanting to protect its imperial interests in the North Pacific Ocean. Not until 1748 did a brief factual report on Bering's voyage to America appear, written anonymously and published in both German and Russian. Gerhard Friedrich Müller produced the first official map, completed in 1754, and completed a history of the expedition that was published in Saint Petersburg in German in 1758, and in 1761 in an English translation.[46]

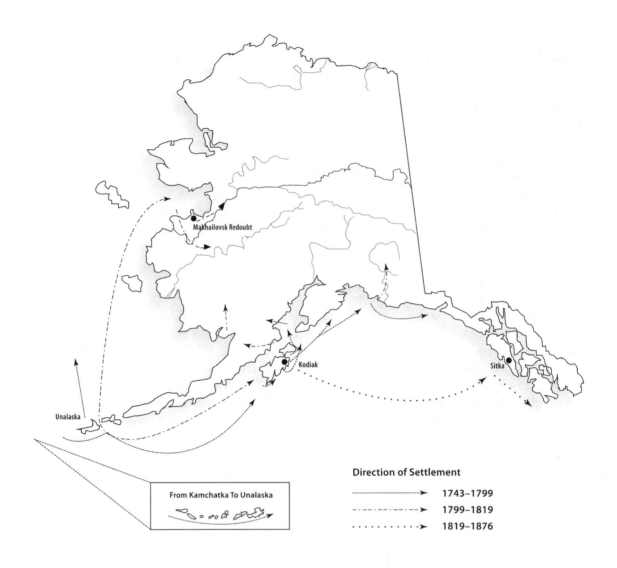

Makhailovsk Redoubt

Kodiak

Sitka

Unalaska

Direction of Settlement

- —————————▶ 1743–1799
- —·—·—·—·—▶ 1799–1819
- ··········▶ 1819–1876

From Kamchatka To Unalaska

Routes and Times of Settlement of Alaska by the Russians

Chapter 5

The Early Russian Fur Trade

The Second Kamchatka Expedition, also called the Great Northern Expedition, was complex in its various operations. Vitus Bering's primary interest lay in finding America, but he also recognized that the expedition might enable Russia to find a route to Japan from Kamchatka by way of the Kuril Islands. The expedition also contributed immensely to natural and geographic knowledge. Expedition members spent a decade mapping the entire Russian Arctic coast, they inventoried Siberia's flora, fauna, minerals, and peoples, and they took steps to strengthen commercial and diplomatic relations with China.[1]

The return of the expedition's survivors in 1741–42 generated local excitement because they brought back furs. The returnees reported that they had encountered an abundance of marine mammals such as whales, walrus, sea lions, dolphins, and most importantly the highly marketable fur seals and sea otters. Small entrepreneurs had hunted fur-bearing sea mammals, particularly the sea otter, in Kamchatka and the Kuril Islands for decades. They had also obtained fur seals in the Shantar Islands. The newly discovered region promised great riches, and the rush to the new islands began soon after the return of Bering's men.[2]

The First Promyshlenniks

Sergeant Emelian Basov of the Nizhne-Kamchatsk garrison was the first documented entrepreneur to explore the area after the Great Northern Expedition. In 1743, his vessel, the forty-two-foot *Saint Apostle Peter*, sailed as far as Bering Island. A second voyage, in 1745–46, brought back 1,600 sea otter, 2,000 fur seal, and many blue fox pelts. Basov's voyages demonstrated to his countrymen that riches could be gained in the unknown islands.[3] About one hundred expeditions followed Basov's pioneering voyage, most organized by merchants from the various towns of the central and northern regions of Russia and from Siberia. These wealthy merchants organized and equipped the expeditions, for the most part leaving the dangerous voyages to lesser merchants.

The partners in such voyages agreed contractually on the share numbers and their owners; recruitment of the *promyshlenniks,* or fur hunters; appointment of a skipper and a foreman and their duties; and the number of workers for each share, among other issues. The shares were distributed among the principal partners, usually merchants who had participated in building and outfitting the vessel. The individual who held the majority of shares was considered the company's head, and it was named after him.

After the basic shares had been created, a small number of shares were established that, unlike the basic shares, were not covered by workers. One of these was usually reserved for the benefit of the church; the second, for the skipper; the third, for

49

his mate—the foreman of the company and the one responsible for collecting the furs. In addition, the number of "on landing" shares had to be determined. These shares were sold to people who did not participate in building and equipping the vessel. The owners of these shares usually were working people who had a right only to a portion of the profits generated directly from fur gathering. They could not interfere in any of the company affairs, except in fur gathering.[4] Other shares might be distributed among the crew members.

Each participant in the company had to supply one worker per share. Many one-share owners could not afford to hire a laborer and therefore had to work themselves. Often the companies hired Itelmen (also called Kamchadals), who, having been raised in a severe climate, bore the rigor of these voyages more easily than their Russian counterparts. The Itelmen were paid between fifty and seventy rubles annually, but they always had to ask their master to give them salary advances to take care of their families. Thus these workers immediately became indebted to the companies, often for years on end. Other workers received their pay in kind, that is, in furs.[5]

It was the promyshlenniks, the fur hunters, who performed the labor on these voyages. The promyshlenniks were a varied and colorful lot. Most were former peasants and townsmen, and only rarely intellectuals not belonging to the gentry; emigrants from various towns in European Russia also became fur hunters. Many had emigrated to escape Russia's confining and arbitrary social structure or to seek entrepreneurial freedom. Once they reached Okhotsk or Kamchatka they hired themselves out on the vessels sailing for furs. Among the peasants were those who possessed passports and sought work in order to purchase their freedom (a payment called an *obrok*). There also were fugitives without passports and, finally, exiled peasants who had been sent to Siberia for settlement or hard labor.[6]

After the vessel was outfitted and manned, the way was clear to sail into what the Russians called the Eastern Sea. The companies' official aim was to discover new islands, to bring their inhabitants under Russian rule, and to trade with them and collect furs from sea and land animals.[7] If the vessel returned with a profitable cargo of furs, the company usually decided to send it out again. Then all the participants in the venture had to pay the expenses of equipping it in proportion to their ownership shares. Partners and workers joined in the construction of the vessels using timber available at the construction site, usually the shores of the rivers Kamchatka, Bolshaya, Urak, or Okhota. Called *shitiks*, these early vessels were bound together, or sewn, with whale bone or thongs, and sometimes even willow twigs.[8]

In 1757 the merchants began building boats (*boty*) or barks (*barki*) that used wooden ribs. To distinguish them from the shitiks, they were called *gvozdenniks*, held together with nails or pegs. Although simple craft, they were expensive to build because all the necessary materials, except wood, had to be transported over long distances at great expense. In addition, equipping such a vessel for a fur-collecting voyage cost anywhere from four to ten thousand rubles.[9]

The promyshlenniks exterminated the fur animals on the islands closest to Kamchatka fairly rapidly, requiring the ships and crews to sail ever farther to the east and making the voyages more expensive. This forced the merchant companies to request aid from the Kamchatka and Okhotsk administrations, which granted loans to be repaid with interest after the return of the vessels.[10]

Taxation and Profits from the China Trade

Local authorities, usually the commandants of the ports of debarkation, had to grant permission to the merchant companies to sail. The authorities also assigned a tax (*iasak*) collector to each vessel. The Russian historian R. V. Makarova wrote that the merchant companies were less than eager to collect the tax; their interest lay in personal gain. But they had to observe the legalities. Companies strove to avoid having a government representative on board, and whenever possible they assigned to the foreman of the fur-gathering party the task of collecting the tax from Russia's new subjects, the islanders. Back in port, and after having delivered the tax, the companies paid a "tenth" tax on all other furs taken from the islands. Between 1744 and 1775, the state treasury received from the fur trade a "tenth" tax of 51,396 rubles, and iasak of 74,145 rubles.[11]

The promyshlenniks who had served as crew members also squared their obligations with the treasury. The peasants had to pay a soul tax, the Kamchadals paid an iasak, and merchants of the third guild who because of straitened financial circumstances had been forced to hire on as promyshlenniks paid "capital" money. Thereafter, the company partners divided the furs according to shares owned and then paid the promyshlenniks. Depending on the success of the voyage, promyshlenniks could materially improve their condition in life. For example, the *Vladimir* arrived in Okhotsk with a cargo of furs valued at over three hundred thousand rubles. Promyshlenniks received between one thousand and fifteen hundred rubles apiece. If unsuccessful, they received nothing, were in debt because of advances taken out, and had to hire out again on another voyage.[12]

The partners usually sold their furs to wholesalers, who transported them to the Chinese market where there was a lively demand for them. The Russian-Chinese trade had started at the end of the seventeenth century, with Russian caravans of furs going first to Beijing, China's capital, and later to locations in Manchuria and elsewhere. As a government monopoly, crown caravans, about ten in the first half of the eighteenth century, carried goods (mostly furs) to Beijing until 1762. Eventually, however, clandestine private trade made this crown undertaking unprofitable. The crown relinquished its monopoly in 1762 and opened the trade to private enterprise.[13]

This date coincided with the particularly intensive exploitation of the fur wealth of the Aleutian and other northeast Pacific islands. The end of the government monopoly helped the fur trade and contributed to the trade between Russia and China. China remained the main market for Russian furs throughout the eighteenth century; fur exports to China between 1780 and 1784 constituted 85 percent of the goods carried to China, and income to the czarist treasury from the China trade in the second half of the eighteenth century amounted to 20 to 38 percent of all customs revenue collected. Not surprisingly, the Russians supported good relations with China.[14]

Unfortunately, a major political conflict with China from 1763 to 1768 interrupted the fur trade, and it did not recover until 1780. In the meantime, in the second half of the eighteenth century, small Russian merchant companies had completed over one hundred fur-hunting expeditions in the North Pacific Ocean. In the process, Russian captains discovered the entire Aleutian Island chain and reached North American shores.[15]

Shelekhov and Eastward Expansion

By the early 1780s the merchant companies were forced to extend their operations ever farther eastward because the promyshlenniks had hunted out the fur-bearing animals on the nearer islands. They now gathered furs primarily on islands off the North American coast or on the coast itself. This led to new geographic discoveries. In the spring of 1786, the navigator Gavril L. Pribylov discovered an island that hosted large fur seal rookeries, which he named Saint George. In 1787 he found another island that had even larger rookeries. The two islands, Saint George and Saint Paul, are collectively known as the Pribilof Islands, named in honor of their discoverer.[16]

As the fur business further developed from the 1770s to the 1790s, the increasing operational costs of ever-longer voyages squeezed out the small operators. In the late 1770s, two men with long experience in the fur trade, Ivan Larionovich Golikov and his associate, Grigory Ivanovich Shelekhov, planned to organize the Aleutian Islands fur trade by obtaining a monopoly for their company and establishing a permanent settlement. In 1781 the two traveled to Saint Petersburg, probably to secure government permission for their plans as well as ships and support. In any event, on their return from the city the two men, together with Golikov's nephew, Captain M. S. Golikov, established the American, Northeastern, Northern, and Kurile Company, better known as the Shelekhov-Golikov Company and later as the Russian-American Company. Its main purpose was to reap the fur wealth of the American coast, but the company also planned to establish permanent settlements on land that Russia annexed. The capitalization of seventy thousand rubles was to be

Conflict with the Aleuts

It was inevitable that the Russians would eventually provoke the Aleuts to defend themselves against the invader's transgressions. Ivan Bechevin was an Irkutsk merchant and early trader in the Aleutian Islands who, together with his crew, wintered on the Alaska Peninsula in 1761–62. There they committed "unspeakable and apparently unprovoked atrocities" against the Aleuts (Black, *Russians in Alaska,* 89). The latter retaliated against the Russians and caused the loss of four vessels: one on Umnak Island, two on Unalaska, and one on Unimak. Of the over two hundred crew members, only twelve survived from the two ships, anchored in different locations on Unalaska Island. They were saved only when Stepan G. Glotov, who had wintered on Kodiak Island, and Ivan Solov'iev from Kamchatka arrived just in time in the summer of 1764.

Inhabitants of Unalaska.

(Courtesy of Alaska and Polar Regions Department, Elmer E. Rasmuson Library, University of Alaska Fairbanks.)

Glotov gave only token support to the ensuing conflict, knowing that the government forbade revenge. But Solov'iev convinced himself that a preventive strike was necessary in order to ensure the safety of his crew. Several times in the summer of 1764 and through the next year, Solov'iev or his lieutenant, Grigory Korenev, attacked Aleut villages in different locations. The late anthropologist and historian Lydia T. Black has concluded that these events became part of Aleutian folk memory, recalled as a time of destruction and the ending of Aleut independence. Solov'iev became the symbol of this destructive force. Most violence the Russians committed thereafter has been blamed on Solov'iev.

Solov'iev reported that between forty to sixty Aleut men were killed during the hostilities. Whatever the numbers, this was traumatic for the Aleut villages because it deprived them of their providers, without whom they could not survive. The most efficient way to subdue the Aleuts, Solov'iev believed, was to destroy their ability to conduct war. Therefore, he systematically destroyed all their weapons and their kayaks and large skin boats. These actions incapacitated the islanders.

Source: Lydia T. Black, *Russians in America, 1732–1867* (Fairbanks: University of Alaska Press, 2004), 87, 89.

Saint Paul Russian Orthodox Church, Pribilof Islands.

(Courtesy of Alaska and Polar Regions Department, Elmer E. Rasmuson Library, University of Alaska Fairbanks.)

used to build three ships and dispatch them "to the land of Alaska, which is called America, to islands known and unknown, in order to trade in furs, to make explorations, and to arrange voluntary trade with the natives." Shelekhov was to command the expedition and establish forts and colonies on the American coasts and islands. He planned to build the first settlement on Kodiak Island.[17]

The expedition sailed on August 16, 1783. There were 192 officers and others aboard, including Shelekhov, his wife, Natalia, their two children, and several relatives, as well as his partner, Captain M. S. Golikov. One ship disappeared; the remaining two wintered on Bering Island and arrived at Unalaska on June 12, 1784. Shelekhov made repairs, filled up with fresh water, and took along two Fox Island Aleuts as interpreters and two more as workers.

The two ships reached Kykhtak or, as it became known, Kad'iak (Kodiak) on August 3. According to Shelekhov, the Koniags had driven off previous

Russian landing attempts in 1761 and 1776, but he had at his disposal 130 armed Russians. Eventually, he claimed, he defeated a group of about four thousand Natives on Sakhlidak Island, but the number was most likely no more than four hundred. During the battle, some drowned, and Shelekhov took many more prisoners and had some leaders killed. He kept a number of children as hostages and released the remainder. Shelekhov stated that he built a school for twenty-five boys who were taught to read and write Russian and to garden. He claimed that he subjugated fifty thousand islanders, but again, it could not have been more than five thousand.[18]

In the spring of 1776, Shelekhov returned to Okhotsk for supplies and reinforcement. He left Konstantin A. Samoilov in charge of the settlement, with lengthy instructions that included the establishment of additional settlements in the Kenai and Chugach regions and southward along the coast "toward California," to latitude 40°. Samoilov was to bury copper plates at various locations to indicate Russian ownership.[19]

Shelekhov left Three Saints Bay in May 1786, accompanied by his family, other passengers, and some forty Natives—adults and children, some prisoners, and others who were on board of their own free will. One third were to be sent to the court of Empress Catherine II, another third were to be taught useful skills in Siberia, and the rest were to return to Kodiak after they had observed domestic life in Okhotsk. Shelekhov eventually traveled to Irkutsk, where he reported to Governor-General Ivan Iakobii and submitted lengthy written reports, also requesting one hundred soldiers, a number of specialists, two priests, and a deacon. He asked permission to conduct further trade with the British and held out the hope for profitable future commerce with Japan, Korea, China, India, and the Philippine Islands, as well as the Spanish and the Americans (American Indians). He requested that his company be allowed to establish businesses on any island it discovered, bringing it under Russian rule. He also asked for a loan of five hundred thousand rubles for twenty years and the use of one of the government ships at Okhotsk. Iakobii approved Shelekhov's proposals.[20]

In February 1788, Shelekhov and Ivan Golikov arrived in Saint Petersburg. Governor-General Iakobi's favorable report about the Shelekhov-Golikov Company activities had arrived at court before they did. The two men petitioned Catherine II directly, asking her to approve a loan of two hundred thousand rubles, to give them a monopoly of the fur trade, and to send one hundred soldiers to protect their settlements on Kodiak and Afognak islands. They also asked Catherine II to "take note of their services to the fatherland."[21]

Iakobii's report had been given to the Commission on Commerce for examination, and in March 1788 the commission recommended giving the company a monopoly for no more than twenty years, granting the loan, and sending the requested military detachment. But the empress refused all of these recommendations. Specifically, she did not believe in the viability of trade monopolies. Also, she was a cautious ruler and did not want to offend rival powers. She wrote that "to trade is one thing, to take possession is another." Despite her negative reaction, the empress awarded Shelekhov and Golikov gold medals, silver sabers, and citations in recognition of their services to the fatherland.[22]

Technical Advances and International Interest in Pacific Exploration

When Shelekhov left for Russia from his settlement at Three Saints Bay in 1786, he had two other forts under construction: one on Afognak Island and Fort Aleksandrovsk on the American mainland, on the southwest tip of the Kenai Peninsula at the entrance to Kenai Bay. Shelekhov's settlements were different from those the Russians had established on Unalaska. First, their base was on Kodiak Island. Siberia supplied it with workers, tools, weapons, and other necessities. There was to be agriculture as well as the fur trade. The plan, postponed at least by Catherine II, was to study and utilize natural resources, to build ships, and to trade with various nations.[23]

Indeed, Russia was not the only nation engaged in Pacific exploration. New technologies came into use that made the winds and currents and the vast size and remoteness of the North Pacific less daunting for all. With improved sails, and more of them, sailors were able to harness the full energy of shifting winds. Ship designs changed as well, and flat decks and shallow-draft hulls sheathed in copper or studded with nails replaced the high castles and deep keels of baroque ships. The new designs reduced drag and discouraged the attachment of barnacles. The horizontal tiller, which required several men to operate, gave way to the yoke-and-drum system, which enabled a single helmsman to steer the rudder using a wheel. Finally, the American Benjamin Franklin had invented the lightning rod in 1752 , which almost totally eliminated lightening-caused fire at sea.[24]

Another improvement involved the prevention and treatment of scurvy, a lack of vitamin C, which had killed countless seafarers. In 1747 naval surgeon James Lind treated twelve scurvy-stricken seamen and fed them all the same diets but gave some of them oranges and lemons as well. These patients recovered within a week. By 1795 the British Admiralty was issuing lemon juice to its naval personnel.[25]

Cook in Alaska

Famed British navigator Captain James Cook set out on his third and last epic voyage in 1776. His instructions were to search for the Northwest Passage at 65° north. Two Russian maps lay behind that number. In 1754 Gerhardt Müller had drawn one that fairly accurately outlined Kamchatka and Siberia, but it was blank for most of northwest North America. In 1774, the Russian Academy of Sciences had published another map, drawn by Jacob von Stählin. Reputedly based on new discoveries, it showed "Alaschka" as an island separated from America by a wide strait at 65° north, 140° west. Cook was to round the Cape of Good Hope, winter in Tahiti, steer for New Albion at 45° north, and then sail to 65° north and search for Stählin's strait. Cook sailed on July 12, 1776.

Cook's flagship, *Resolution*, and the *Discovery*, which Charles Clerke commanded, arrived in Tahiti in August 1777. On January 18, 1778, Cook "discovered" the Sandwich, or Hawaiian, Islands. The ships eventually proceeded northward to 65° but never found Stählin's strait. Cook navigated Bering Strait as far north as 70°. There, in August, he encountered twelve-foot-tall walls of ice. He turned around and on the way south stopped at Unalaska Island, where he encountered Russians. He showed them Stählin's map and found that they were as perplexed as he had been. Cook concluded that Stählin was a fraud and finished his work for the season. He headed straight south to the Sandwich Islands, and in January 1779 the Polynesians killed Cook in Kealakekua Bay on the island of Hawaii. Meanwhile, Commander Clerke, deathly ill with consumption, passed through Bering Strait until ice forced the ships back. He died two days before the ships reached Kamchatka. After undergoing repairs, the two ships circled Asia and Africa and anchored in the Thames River in London in October 1780.

Captain James Cook. His voyage of discovery brought him to America's northwest coast and Alaska in 1778. He mapped much of the coast and named many familiar features (including naming Cook Inlet for himself).

(Author's collection.)

The Northwest Passage proved elusive. Still, Cook's voyage can be said to have opened Alaska to non-Russians. Two years before his death, Cook's crew members had acquired some sea otter pelts at Nootka. The ship stopped at Macao on the way home, where the handful of pelts sold for two thousand pounds. The news set off a rush of private, mostly British and American, ships to the North Pacific. There they broke the Russian fur monopoly. Cook had shown the route in his third voyage and discovered Hawaii in the process, a perfect place of call on the way to Nootka, Alaska, or the Far East.

Source: Walter A. McDonugall, *Let the Sea Make a Noise . . . : A History of the North Pacific from Magellan to MacArthur* (New York: Basic Books, 1993), 85–89.

Navigation improved when quadrants, used for sighting the sun at noon and calculating latitude, were refined and calibrated to one minute of arc; new sextants for sighting the moon and stars were accurate to seconds of arc. Charts, maps, almanacs, and tide and current tables improved. Most important was John Harrison's marine chronometer in 1759, a spring-driven clock that was both accurate and impervious to the ship's motions. Now figuring longitude was easy, as long as one knew what time it was. All of these inventions came together so that circumnavigation in the half century after 1763 became routine.[26]

The North Pacific became a focus of international rivalries after 1779. British and American traders, many arriving North via Cape Horn and passing the Spanish California coast, were searching for furs. The Spanish were particularly interested in Russian activities in the North Pacific, and the Spanish ministers in Saint Petersburg kept their home government informed about Russian moves in the region. As early as 1768 the Spanish government alerted José de Gálvez, visitador general of Spanish Mexico, to watch for Russians on the coast. The *Sonora*, under the command of Juan de Bodega y Quadra, sailed as far north as 58°, within sight of Mount Edgecumbe, and then returned south. In 1779, Don Ignacio Arteaga, accompanied by Bodega y Quadra, sailed to almost 60° and saw Mount Saint Elias. The Spaniards stopped at various points along the coast and took possession of the land for Spain. They overlapped Russian explorations but reported seeing no Europeans.[27]

In 1788, a new Spanish expedition sailed from San Blas to learn everything about the Russian settlements. The frigate *Princess* and the packet boat *San Carlos* visited Prince William Sound, Kodiak, and Unalaska, among other places. Evstrat I. Delarov, the chief manager of the Northeastern Company, supplied the Spaniards with most of the information about the number of Russian settlements when they met him at Kodiak. The largest was on Unalaska, numbering 120 Russians and one galiot. There were about seven Russian settlements with 462 promyshlenniks between Unalaska and Prince William Sound. On Unalaska, the Spanish met the navigator P. K. Zaikov, who indicated that there were about five hundred Russians in the islands and on the mainland coast. It is possible that the Spanish missed a few other Russian settlements.[28]

Shelekhov's Vision

Shelekhov's activities expanded every year. He sent vessels to explore and study the coast of northwest America, and he developed agriculture, gardening, animal husbandry, and metallurgy on the mainland and on the Kuril Islands. At his request, navigators left imperial emblems along the American mainland from Kodiak and beyond Cape Saint Elias to California. Shelekhov reported to the governor-general of Irkutsk, I. A. Pil', that during 1788–1789 about thirty foreign vessels had been seen north of Kodiak and Afognak Islands and south toward California. Shelekhov suspected that they claimed suzerainty over the Native peoples of this region. Consequently, Pil' thought that Russia should assert to the European courts its rights on the Pacific Islands and on the west coast of North America. Russia needed to create a Far East naval force and replace Okhotsk with a new port needed for such a fleet. He reported to Saint Petersburg that only a strong company of merchant-promyshlenniks would be able to hold back the foreign fur traders, particularly the British. Pil' directed the government's attention to this aspect of the Shelekhov-Golikov Company. It did not matter that during 1789 the treasury had received only 3,500 rubles from the company. What was most important was that as a result of its activities "the right of the Russian state to the American mainland and to the islands of the Pacific Ocean is confirmed."[29]

Pil' proposed to the imperial court that the Shelekhov-Golikov Company merge with the other Russian fur enterprises, as had been the dream of Shelekhov and Golikov. The goal of an amalgamated organization was not only to preserve the company's profits but also to halt the intrusion of foreigners who were boldly "plundering . . . the treasures that belong to Russia alone."[30] Pil's proposals caught the interest of Russia's ruling circles in the merchant companies active in the North Pacific Ocean.

Shelekhov continued to expand his enterprises. He used Native men not only as hunters for the company but also as fighters in areas other than their own. For example, Delarov, his chief manager, used the Kodiak islanders from the Pacific side in fighting the Native settlements in Shelikof Strait. In this process, intertribal and local hostilities were used skillfully. Shelekhov also realized that force would not suffice in the long run to establish and maintain Russian settlements. Thus acts of brutality and intimidation were followed by gifts, unanticipated fairness, and sometimes kindnesses. For example, he told Konstantin A. Samoilov, one of his associates, to impress the Natives with the power of the Russian state and the empress and to assure them that Russia would annihilate any who raised against it. But at the same time he also directed that all hostages, and also those used for labor, be treated fairly and be well fed and clothed, and that Samoilov's men not be allowed to exploit women. Any violation was to result in severe penalties. Shelekhov also instructed his managers to conduct a full census and suggested that young Russian bachelors be married to Native women. Shelekhov also introduced Christianity to the Kodiak islanders, and he and his partners financed the construction of the first Orthodox church on Kodiak Island.[31]

Shelekhov wanted to develop Russian America into a settled and developed country. To this end he introduced various crafts, such as blacksmithing, carpentry, joinery, fine metal smithing, and others. To start agriculture, he sent seeds and farm animals to the colony. In 1794 he instructed that shipbuilding facilities be created immediately. In short, he was a man with a vision, endowed with a keen intellect and a will of steel. In 1790, he found and hired a man who seemed to share his dreams—Aleksandr A. Baranov, a native of the Russian north who had for some time been a merchant with a trading post among the Chukchi. Baranov was destined to build Russia's empire in America, remaining in the colonies for twenty-eight years. Shelekhov's selection of Baranov was perhaps his most enduring legacy.[32]

Aleksandr Andreyevich Baranov.

(Courtesy of Alaska and Polar Regions Department, Elmer E. Rasmuson Library, University of Alaska Fairbanks.)

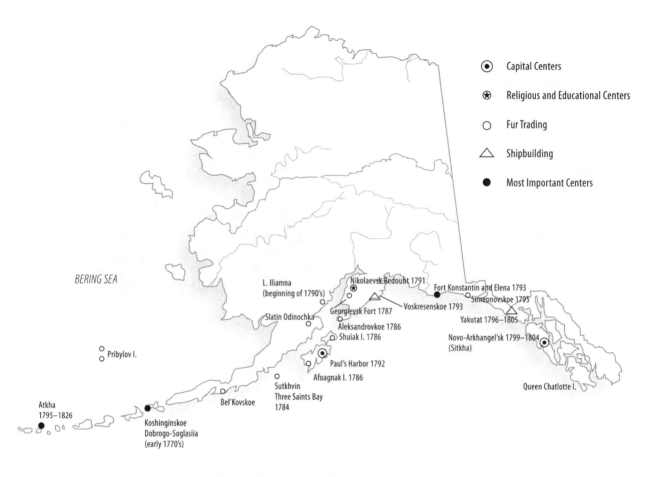

Legend:

- ⊙ Capital Centers
- ✹ Religious and Educational Centers
- ○ Fur Trading
- △ Shipbuilding
- ● Most Important Centers

BERING SEA

L. Iliamna
(beginning of 1790's)

Nikolaevsk Redoubt 1791

Fort Konstantin and Elena 1793

Simeonovskoe 1795

Georgievsk Fort 1787

Voskresenskoe 1793

Slatin Odinochka

Aleksandrovkoe 1786

Yakutat 1796–1805

Shuiak I. 1786

Novo-Arkhangel'sk 1799–1804
(Sitkha)

Pribylov I.

Paul's Harbor 1792

Afoagnak I. 1786

Sutkhvin
Three Saints Bay
1784

Queen Chatlotte I.

Atkha
1795–1826

Bel'Kovskoe

Koshinginskoe
Dobrogo-Soglasiia
(early 1770's)

Russian Settlements in Alaska, 1770–1800

Chapter 6

The Age of Alexander A. Baranov, 1790–1818

Alexander A. Baranov must be credited with the creation of Russian America. He was Shelekhov's chief manager from 1790 to 1799 and then was the chief manager of the Russian-American Company's eastern area from 1799 to 1818. Under his management, Russian America expanded eastward and southward, establishing friendly relations with King Kamehameha the Great of Hawaii, with the Spanish in California, and with British and American fur traders. He embodied Russian America for twenty-eight years.

Baranov Comes to Alaska

Baranov was born in 1746 in Kargopol' in Russia's north. Despite his lack of a formal education, he gained entry into the mercantile classes in Saint Petersburg and Moscow. Around 1780 he moved to Irkutsk, where he managed a glass factory. He soon established another glass factory, founded a distillery, collected taxes for a fee, and together with his brother Petr, established a trading post on Krugovor main, an arm of the Anadyr River, to trade with the Chukchi. In 1787 he was elected to the Free Economic Society for the part he had played in developing the glass industry in Siberia.

In about 1790 Baranov experienced serious business losses when Chukchi raiders destroyed his trading post. Baranov left his brother to conclude their business affairs in Siberia and readied himself to return to Kargopol', but Shelekhov asked him to instead go to Russian America to develop his enterprises.[1] Shelekhov had apparently offered him the same job a couple of times before but Baranov had refused the opportunity. With his fortune now practically gone, however, Baranov signed a detailed contract with Shelekhov on August 15, 1790. Shelekhov needed a strong manager and thought he had found his man in Baranov.[2] The contract gave Baranov the title of chief manager, shares in the company, and wide discretion in his actions in the colony.

In the 1780s and 1790s British and American merchants had entered Russian American territory. James Strange, an Englishman, had formed a company in India, and two of his ships sailed along the coasts of what are now British Columbia and Alaska. His men symbolically buried evidence of British presence and formally took possession for the British crown. As we have seen, the Russian government had quickly become aware of these activities. When Baranov sailed for Kodiak in the fall of 1790, the Russian government issued him five numbered possession plates and crests, the latter to be displayed and the former buried.[3]

At the end of September 1790, on Baranov's voyage to Russian America to assume his duties, his vessel was wrecked in a storm, and Baranov, the crew, and other passengers had to seek refuge at the Unalaska settlement. During the winter there

Baranov took a census of the local population and had three *baidarkas,* or sea kayaks, built. In the spring of 1791 he sent two baidarkas to search for new hunting areas and set out for Kodiak in the third. His party experienced a difficult voyage but finally arrived in late June at Three Saints Bay on Kodiak Island, then the company center. Baranov examined numerous localities and in 1792 moved his headquarters to Paul's Harbor on Chiniak Bay, the site of present-day Kodiak. He set to work establishing other settlements and developing the sea otter trade. He sent Aleut parties to Kenai Bay and along the Alaska Peninsula. In June 1792, while returning from a trip to Chugatsk Bay, his party camped at Montague Island, where it fought off a night attack by the Yakutat Tlingit (Kolosh) and the Ugaliagmiuts from Cape Saint Elias.[4]

Baranov established a settlement on Resurrection Bay, the site of present-day Seward. James Shields, a British shipbuilder and naval officer and an employee of Shelekhov's company, started working on the first ship built in Russian America, the three-masted *Phoenix.* In 1794, Baranov sent two promyshlenniks, Egor Purtov and Demid I. Kulikalov, to reconnoiter Yakutat Bay for a possible settlement site. The chief manager was back in Kodiak at the end of September 1794 with Archimandrite Ioasaf and ten clerics, who were to establish a spiritual mission in Russian America. A month later he greeted the *Saint Ekaterina,* which carried 130 promyshlenniks and 30 settlers, together with their families, sent by the government at Shelekhov's request.[5]

Russia's "Native Subjects"

The missionaries soon claimed that they had converted thousands among the local population to the Russian Orthodox faith. Although these "conversions" were probably at first superficial, they demonstrated a willingness among the Natives to accept change and laid the basis of the more lasting subsequent work of the Orthodox clergy. Nonetheless, Baranov resented the monks' criticism of his personal life (he was known as a womanizer) and their interference on behalf of Natives.[6]

In the meantime, Baranov carried out Shelekhov's labor policies, which aimed at using the Native population as a labor base and incorporating it into the political and economic system Shelekhov wanted to establish. Labor had become scarce in Russia, and there were but few skilled seafarers, shipwrights, fur hunters, and trappers who hired themselves out for work in Russian America. Shelekhov and his heirs, with governmental help, hired navigators and ships' commanders who were serving in the navy and a few old voyagers like Gerasim G. Izmailov, Dmitrii I. Bocharov, and Gavril L. Pribylov, who were near retirement. But for the most part, the company had to depend on the few available Russians and on Native workers, all of whom had to learn on the job.[7] So after his return from Russian America in 1787, Shelekhov asked Governor-General Iakobii to grant permission to use Natives as laborers. The governor-general granted it with the caveat that they be paid fair wages for their work, which would inspire them "to be subjects under the Russian scepter."[8]

As a consequence, Baranov recruited Native laborers on a large scale soon after his arrival in Russian America. Each Native settlement under Russian control had to furnish several male and female laborers. The Russians called this class of laborers *kaiury,* a Kamchatkan term used to identify hired dog team drivers. Aleut war captives and their descendants added to this labor force. Baranov also impressed Native hunters into forced labor and used them, like the Russian laborers, as warriors when needed. These practices violated government orders that Natives be paid fair wages for labor performed and were stopped immediately after Baranov's dismissal in 1818.[9]

The Russians took large numbers of young, able-bodied Native people, particularly males, away from their home settlements. This had dire consequences for the remaining old men, women, and children, who were robbed of those who provided subsistence and defended the settlements, and the resulting hunger and hardship negatively affected the Aleut population of the islands. Lydia Black wrote that it is uncertain how destructive the Russian presence was to the Aleut population because nobody really knew what the size of the original population was. However, the first official census of the Aleut population in the central and eastern part of the island chain, which took place in 1791–92, although incomplete, provided a basis for a reasonable estimate and shows a total population for the census area of about 4,796 to 5,995.[10]

The Russian ethnographer Roza G. Liapunova analyzed the population data from the earliest Russian sources, not including the 1791 census. She concluded that at the time of contact, the entire Aleutian archipelago, from Attu Island to the Shumagins, was home to an estimated maximum of 7,500 to 9,500 Aleuts. Black reasoned that this number should be somewhat increased because many able-bodied males were absent at the time of the census and the Shumagin Islands had not been included. During the time when the promyshlenniks controlled the region, the Aleut population diminished somewhat, and it decreased significantly during the Baranov era, due at least in part to his use of forced labor. In 1834 Father Ioann Veniaminov reported a total population of slightly over 2,000 for the eastern and central Aleutians combined.[11] This represents an eventual decline of about 75 percent.

Expansion under the New Monopoly

In 1795, Baranov instructed James Shields to construct two vessels, thirty-five to forty feet in keel length, on Spruce Island near Kodiak. They were named the *Dolphin* and the *Olga*. In 1796 the Russians established a settlement at Yakutat, which they called New Russia. In 1797, Baranov traveled to Konstantinovsk (Nuchek), where employees of the competing Lebedev-Lastochkin Company had been working. Baranov persuaded most of the group to switch employment to the Shelekhov Company. Those who refused returned to Okhotsk. Baranov had thus secured the whole Chugatsk Bay area for his company.[12]

While Baranov had been reconnoitering the resources of the region for his company, its founder, Grigory I. Shelekhov, died suddenly in Irkutsk on July 20, 1795. A number of changes soon occurred. On July 20, 1797, the Shelekhov and Mylnikov companies merged. On August 3, 1798, an imperial ukaz put most of the fur companies, including the Shelekhov Company, under the United American

Company. The company's main office was located in Irkutsk.[13]

Empress Catherine II, who had consistently refused to grant Shelekhov a trading monopoly in Russian America, had died in 1796. Her son, Paul I, succeeded her. In this turbulent period various merchants attempted to wrest control of the company from Natalia Shelekhova, the founder's widow. Fortunately, Shelekhov's daughter Anna had married Nikolay P. Rezanov (1764–1807), court chamberlain, government official, and ambassador to Japan.

Rezanov was well connected at court. In 1794 or 1795 he was sent to Irkutsk, where he became acquainted with the Shelekhov family. He listened to Shelekhov's tales of the fur trade and Russian settlements and married his daughter, Anna, then about fifteen years old. After Shelekhov's death, Rezanov became the protector of the family interests.

The czar was disgusted by reports of the abuses the Shelekhov Company had heaped on the Natives

Nikolay Petrovich Rezanov.

(Courtesy of Alaska and Polar Regions Department, Elmer E. Rasmuson Library, University of Alaska Fairbanks.)

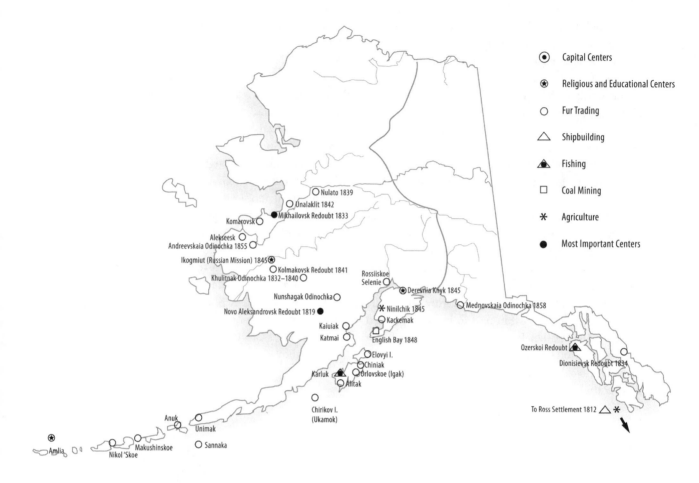

Legend:
- ◉ Capital Centers
- ✴ Religious and Educational Centers
- ○ Fur Trading
- △ Shipbuilding
- ▲ Fishing
- □ Coal Mining
- ✳ Agriculture
- ● Most Important Centers

Map labels:
- Nulato 1839
- Unalaklit 1842
- Mikhailovsk Redoubt 1833
- Komarovsk
- Alekseesk
- Andreevskaia Odinochka 1855
- Ikogmiut (Russian Mission) 1845
- Kolmakovsk Redoubt 1841
- Khulitnak Odinochka 1832–1840
- Rossiiskoe Selenie
- Derevnia Knyk 1845
- Nunshagak Odinochka
- Ninilchik 1845
- Mednovskaia Odinochka 1858
- Novo Aleksandrovsk Redoubt 1819
- Kackemak
- Kaiuiak
- English Bay 1848
- Katmai
- Ozerskoi Redoubt
- Elovyi I.
- Chiniak
- Orlovskoe (Igak)
- Dionisievsk Redoubt 1834
- Karluk
- Alitak
- Chirikov I. (Ukamok)
- To Ross Settlement 1812
- Anuk
- Unimak
- Amlia
- Makushinskoe
- Nikol'Skoe
- Sannaka

Russian Settlements in Alaska, 1800–1867

The government storehouse at Sitka.

(Courtesy of Alaska and Polar Regions Department, Elmer E. Rasmuson Library, University of Alaska Fairbanks.)

of the Aleutian Islands, and he was about to abolish the company's privileges. But Natal'ia's determination and Rezanov's influence saved the day. Rezanov persuaded Paul I to grant a monopoly, which became a reality on June 8, 1799, with an imperial decree creating the Russian-American Company (RAC). Built on Shelekhov's foundation, the new company survived, even prospered, for nearly seventy years.[14]

Baranov was unaware of the changes that had occurred in Saint Petersburg. He continued to send out hunting parties, including one in the spring of 1796 that consisted of 450 baidarkas and traveled as far as Lituya Bay. At the end of June 1796, Baranov arrived in Yakutat Bay together with a group of colonists, and they spent two months building a fort and settlement. This was the first European colony on Tlingit land.[15]

About eighty Russians remained in Yakutat during the 1796–97 winter, which brought death to many. Thirteen promyshlenniks died of scurvy, as did seven colonists and several women and children. During this winter the Russians abused the Yakutat Natives, which engendered much bitter feeling. Baranov took eleven hostages from among the Tlingit in Yakutat. The leader of the colonists, named Polomoshnyi, behaved violently toward the Natives and treated them coarsely, as did some of the promyshlenniks.[16]

Baranov abandoned his plans for an agricultural colony at the location because cereal crops did not ripen at 60° north latitude, and the relations with the Tlingits were too problematic. He had few hopes of developing any trade with the various Tlingit groups because the Russians had only a limited supply of cheap Chinese cotton fabrics to offer them in return. He decided, therefore, to merely maintain a storage depot and a resting place for the sea otter hunting parties en route to the straits of the Alexander Archipelago. So Yakutat became a transshipment place, and Baranov distributed several guns to the long-range hunting groups in Yakutat for defense against possible Tlingit attacks.[17]

Establishment of a Base at Sitka

From 1797 the baidarka flotilla began regular trips to the Sitka Island region, where sea otters were plentiful. Baranov selected Sitka Island for the establishment of a new base south of Yakutat in the Alexander Archipelago. A new colony was necessary to secure the region the Russians had explored earlier. Rumors that a new English trading company had been founded for the northwest coast trade motivated Baranov to act quickly.[18]

Therefore, in the spring of 1799 Baranov sent a large flotilla of five hundred baidarkas and two ships to the Sitka region with necessary materials and

Attack on Fort Mikhailovskii

Baranov left Sitka in the spring of 1800 in the knowledge that relations between the Russians and Tlingits that winter had been tense. In the summer of 1802, the Tlingits, with firearms from the English, attacked the fort, reduced it to ashes, and killed its people. It was now necessary to rescue the surviving Russians and Kodiak islanders, who were described to Baranov as "wandering through the forests and exhausted by hunger."

Several days after the attack, the English brig *Unicorn,* commanded by Captain Henry Barber, arrived at Sitka Bay, followed by two American ships. One of the few Russian survivors of the attack escaped to the *Unicorn.* The English then picked up another Russian and several Kodiak islanders, who had hidden on the island's shore. Several days later two Tlingit chiefs came onboard the *Unicorn* to trade. Barber seized both and demanded that the Natives accompanying them return all captives and furs taken from the demolished fort or he would hang both chiefs. Barber and the American skippers then sank some of the Indian canoes with case shot and cannon balls, and many Natives were killed or drowned. The Tlingits, thereupon, returned almost all the captives and furs seized from the fort. Barber appropriated the furs and then took the former captives to Kodiak, where he demanded fifty-thousand rubles for their rescue and maintenance. After lengthy arguments with Baranov, he released the former captives for ten thousand rubles.

Sources: Svetlana G. Fedorova, *The Russian Population in Alaska and California: Late 18th Century–1867* (Kingston, Ontario: The Limestone Press, 1973), 134; Andrei Val'Terovich Grinev, *The Tlingit Indians in Russian America, 1741–1867* (Lincoln: University of Nebraska Press, 2005), 120–21.

people to found a new colony.[19] Baranov himself arrived in Sitka in early July and found a small outpost, led by Vasily Medvednikov. He negotiated with the Sitka chiefs and for "a notable sum" in goods, acquired the parcel of land on which the outpost had been built. That same month the Russians started the construction of Fort Mikhailovskii, some six miles north of the present-day town of Sitka. With construction incomplete in the fall, Baranov, together with twenty-five Russians, fifty-five Koniag men, and twelve Koniag women, wintered at the new fort. Among the women was Baranov's Native wife, Anna Grigor'evna.[20]

The establishment of Fort Mikhailovskii was a step in the company's advance southward to the fertile lands of the Columbia River basin and Califor-

nia. The most important waymark on this route was Sitka Island, where for more than ten years English and American merchants had traded freely with the Tlingits. In these transactions the Natives had obtained firearms, among other items.

Baranov also wanted to extend Russian rule to Nootka, forestalling the occupation of that coast by other nations. The Spanish had established a settlement in the Nootka Sound region on Vancouver Island in 1789 but abandoned it shortly thereafter, and by the late eighteenth and early nineteenth centuries the English and Americans dominated the area. They took furs from Nootka and the Charlotte Islands and undermined the Russia-China trade by taking the furs directly to Canton.[21]

In 1802 several ships arrived in Kodiak from

Russia carrying much needed trade goods, as well as news. The directors of the RAC had appointed Baranov the chief manager of the colonies in America, in charge of Unalaska and the other districts in recognition of his hard work and leadership.[22] There had been other changes in the RAC as well. Rezanov had became a member of the Finland Commission, and at his urging the new emperor, Alexander I, and many members of the imperial household became shareholders in the RAC. By the end of 1802, the number of shareholders had risen from seventeen to four hundred.[23] Company policies now enjoyed imperial sanction.

By 1804, Baranov was ready to establish a second settlement in the face of Tlingit resistance. He dispatched three hundred kayaks and three ships, which were joined in Sitka Sound by a navy frigate, the *Neva*. The Russians stormed the Tlingit stronghold, and the defenders repulsed them. Complicated negotiations began, but on the night of October 7 the Tlingits abandoned their camp, "having killed babies and dogs to avoid alerting the enemy," according to historian Black. Later, formal peace negotiations established a modus vivendi, which lasted to the end of Russian America in 1867, with few interruptions and only one short-lived armed revolt, at Sitka in the 1850s. Baranov now set about rebuilding the settlement in a new location, about five miles from Fort Mikhailovskii. Called New Archangel, it became the capital of Russian America as well as an international port.[24]

In the fall of 1805 the Eskimo-Ugalakhmiuts, who inhabited the Pacific coast between the mouth of the Copper River and Yakutat Bay, destroyed the Russian settlement there. Forty inhabitants escaped, and thirteen were taken prisoner. These events slowed but did not stop the Russian advance to the south.[25]

Rezanov in Alaska

Meanwhile, Nikolay Rezanov's wife, Anna, had died shortly after giving birth to their second child, a daughter, in October 1802. Rezanov was grief stricken, and a planned voyage around the world to the American colony came as a welcome diversion. Ships were always in short supply, and the ship-building capabilities of Okhotsk, Kamchatka, and Russian America were inadequate to furnish an adequate number to satisfy the needs of the RAC. All supplies, equipment, and foodstuffs for the RAC, the Okhotsk flotilla, and all settlements on the Pacific Ocean came overland from Russia through roadless Siberia to Okhotsk, a route that was hugely expensive. Important items, such as ship's anchors and cables, were cut into manageable pieces for transport to Okhotsk and there rejoined and loaded on ships for delivery to Russian America.

For these reasons it was necessary to organize the first Russian round-the-world expedition. The vessels chosen were the *Nadezhda* and the *Neva,* under the commands of Iurri F. Lisianskii and Adam Johann von Krusenstern.[26] The *Neva* was to sail to Russian America, and the *Nadezhda* to Kamchatka. On June 10, 1803, one month before the ships were to sail, the emperor awarded Rezanov the Order of Saint Anna, first degree, and gave him the title of chamberlain of the imperial court. The emperor assigned him to sail on the *Nadezhda* as ambassador to Japan.[27]

The two vessels left Kronshtadt, on the Baltic Sea, on July 16, 1803. The *Nadezhda* arrived in Nagasaki, Japan, on September 26, 1804. The Japanese did not welcome Rezanov and instead held him under house arrest. He was not released until April 6, 1805, after which he returned to Kamchatka. Rezanov and his German physician, Georg Heinrich von Langsdorff, boarded the RAC vessel *Saint Maria Magdalena* in Petropavlovsk, bound for America. The ship arrived in New Archangel on August 26 of that year. They found Baranov supervising the construction of the fort.

Rezanov was a keen observer of activities in the colony. He was an imperialist, and as a director of the RAC he wanted to advance Russia's interest in the Pacific. He differed in this respect from Baranov, whose main concern was to make a profit. Rezanov wanted to increase the colony's population and make it an outpost for further Russian expansion. He recommended that recruitment be given priority and that the living and working conditions of the colonists be improved, thereby attracting others to come and settle permanently. He urged his fellow directors to petition the czar to approve freedom of emigration to Russian America and to require prospective settlers to undergo physical exams to determine their suitability to live in the colony. He abolished the practice of paying colonists with shares in the company and instead replaced this with an annual wage, offering generous bonuses to workers who had done their tasks well as a means of raising living standards. He also believed that efficient management would result in lower prices at the company stores.[28]

Rezanov's reform zeal ranged widely. He scolded the clergy for its interference in government affairs, its lack of missionary zeal, and especially its failure to learn the Native languages, which he believed would make preaching more effective. He himself collected Native words and gave these to the board of directors, requesting they be printed and sold to those sailing to Russian America. He also endeavored to improve the colony's morals by restraining men from immoderate drinking because he believed it contributed to their poverty. Rezanov proposed to establish homes for the aged, hospitals, schools for children, and a people's court to deal with minor offenses.[29] He also wanted the colony to broaden its economic base and warned against overhunting because that inevitably led to the extinction of the furbearing animals, the colony's economic mainstay.

Rezanov admired Baranov and valued many of his policies. He praised the chief manager for his selfless devotion and concern for the colony's welfare. He admitted that the RAC directors had not always been well informed on conditions in the colonies, and he promised to stop abuses that had crept into company operations. Baranov had maintained that trade with foreigners was absolutely necessary in order to supply the colonies. Rezanov agreed, but he advised Baranov to buy ships from the Americans because they were superior to Russian vessels. He gave Baranov a letter of credit enabling him to purchase ships enabling colonists to trade where and when they wanted.[30]

Efforts to Supply the Colonies

Rezanov had arrived in New Archangel in late August 1805 and had seen the consequences of the colony's dependence on others for their supplies. The settlement of 192 Russians and an undetermined number of Natives was suffering a severe food shortage. There had been no Russian supply ship for three years, and the cargoes of the few American ships had been inadequate. Von Langsdorff reported that the settlement was "in need of almost all the necessities of life." The laborers were in such poor shape that "all work was in danger of being stopped." Bread was rationed to one pound a week, and even this meager allotment might end by the first of October, when the grain supplies would be gone. The hostile Tlingits controlled the coast and prevented the Russians from fishing. Only the dried meat of fish, sea lions, and seals were available in the settlement. The men supplemented their short rations by eating anything they could shoot or find. Those afflicted with scurvy received millet with molasses and pine cone beer.[31] In this dire situation Rezanov decided to travel to San Francisco, where he would attempt to convince the Spanish to enter into trade with the Russians, currently forbidden by Spanish law.

Rezanov's ship, the *Juno,* entered San Francisco harbor on April 8, 1806. Acting commandant Luis Argüello received the Rezanov party and introduced them to his family, including his oldest daughter, Maria de la Concepción Marcela. For a week Rezanov waited for the return of Commandant José Dario Argüello and the visit of Governor José Arillaga. With the help and advice of Concepción, Rezanov befriended the padres of the Mission of Saint Francis of Assisi (Dolores). He also met padres from San Jose and Santa Clara missions, as well as the ladies of the Presidio. Rezanov gave valuable presents to each person and thereby gained allies. After the commandant and the governor arrived, they accepted Rezanov's credentials and entertained his party.[32]

For several weeks Rezanov attempted to persuade the officials to permit trade. His allies interceded with the commandant and the governor. During these weeks Rezanov also proposed marriage to Concepción, and she accepted. When Rezanov formally asked Commandant Argüello for Concepción's hand in marriage, the man was utterly surprised. He was not too bothered by the age difference—Rezanov was forty-two years of age in 1806 and Concepción fifteen years old—the problem was that Rezanov was Russian Orthodox and Concep-

La Beata

José Argüello became commander of the Presidio of Santa Barbara in 1806, and Concepción and the rest of his family accompanied him there. When Argüello became governor of Baja California at Loreto, she again moved with her parents, staying with them until they died. Suitors called during this period, but Concepción gave them only friendship. She probably learned of Rezanov's death in 1807.

Concepción returned to Monterey in 1830 and served California's poor for about nineteen years. She became a member of the Third (Secular) Order of Saint Francis, fully dedicated to the religious life. The communities she served bestowed on her the title "La Beata," the blessed one. When Mother Mary Goemaere established the first convent in California, Concepción received permission to become a Dominican novice. In 1851 she took vows and so became California's first native-born nun. She taught at Saint Catherine's Academy in Monterey and later helped Mother Mary to move both the school and the convent north to Benicia. She died at the convent on December 23, 1857.

Source: Richard A. Pierce, ed., *The Romance of Nikolai Rezanov and Concepcion Argüello: A Literary Legend and Its Effect on California History,* by Eve Iverson, and *The Concha Argüello Story: Memory Visits with Old Vinnie,* by Father Maurice M. O'Moore, O.P. (Kingston, Ontario and Fairbanks, Alaska: The Limestone Press, 1998).

ción was Roman Catholic. Such a "mixed marriage" needed a dispensation from the church. The padres decided to allow a betrothal and a marriage contract was drawn up, but there was to be no wedding until the pope and the king of Spain had given their permission.[33]

After the betrothal Rezanov became a member of the Argüello family and a trading method was worked out. The governor sent Rezanov's proposed trade treaty to the viceroy in Mexico City, urging favorable consideration. Rezanov promised to return within two years with the necessary marriage permissions, and Concepción vowed to marry Rezanov or no one.[34]

Rezanov left California on May 8, 1806, on the *Juno,* which was loaded with wheat, flour, barley, peas, beans, lard, slat, and a small quantity of dried meat. He delivered the cargo in New Archangel in early June. In his absence, scurvy had killed seventeen Russians, and sixty others had been nearly immobilized. Fortunately, herring appeared at the end of March and health began to improve. Rezanov did not linger but returned to Siberia. In Petropavlovsk he did not wait for winter and easy sleigh travel but attempted to ride back to Saint Petersburg. He rode horses in relays and fell ill at least twice, probably with pneumonia. Each time he did not wait long enough to recover. He then contracted a fever and died in March 1807 at Krasnoyarsk. With him died his far-reaching plans for the colony.

Before his death, Rezanov had sent his report to the RAC headquarters, along with a proposal to establish a Russian colony north of San Francisco. Baranov responded to the proposal and in 1807 sent Ivan A. Kuskov to locate a site with ample hunting grounds that could provide a reliable food supply for Russia's American colony. Kuskov located a suitable location on Bodega Bay, and with permission of the Spanish government, he began construction of Fort Ross on the banks of the San Sebastian River. In a short time the colony grew to eight hundred persons, and in 1815 colonists started several farms, where they raised crops and cattle. In 1827, the Spanish built Santa Rosa Mission, six miles from the Russian colony. Although Spain did not approve of Russian expansion in the region, relations between the Russians and Spaniards remained friendly.[35]

In 1840, Fort Ross produced 2,500 Spanish bushels of rye, which were exported to the Russian-American colony to the north. The colony, however, never prospered. Annual deficits continued, while hopes for acquiring more fertile lands were dashed by the Mexican government's opposition. The RAC saw no further advantage in maintaining Fort Ross, and the czar approved of the colony's disposal on April 15, 1839. Late in 1839 or in early 1840 the RAC concluded a contract with the Hudson's Bay Company for annual deliveries of foodstuffs to New Archangel, removing any reason for keeping Fort Ross. In early September 1841, Captain John A. Sutter purchased the Russian properties for $30,000.[36] The Russian expansion into California had ended.

In May 1806, Baranov sent Sysoi Slobodchikov to head a party of Aleuts with fifty baidarkas south on an American vessel under the command of Jonathan Winship. Previously, in 1803 and 1804, RAC employees Shvetsov and Tarakanov had sailed as far as San Diego Bay in baidarkas. Now Slobodchikov and his party were to stay and hunt for a period of ten to fourteen months. They hunted sea otters along the shore and then crossed to Seros Island, latitude 28°2' south and longitude 115°2' west.

There Slobodchikov disagreed with some of Winship's demands, bought a small schooner from an American for 150 sea otter pelts, and hired two Americans and three men from the Sandwich Islands. Then he sailed there, the first Russian from the New World that Hawaiians had seen. He wintered in the islands, living, according to the Russian writer S. N. Mrakov, in this land of perpetual summer "as in a fairy tale, among palm and mimosa, at the palace of a giant-king." After hunger in Russian America, "he ate coconuts and pork."

Slobodchikov entered into a trade agreement with Hawaii's ruler, and Baranov had the opportunity to buy breadfruit, sandalwood, and pearls from the king. King Kamehameha the Great gave Slobodchikov a priceless cloak make from the feathers of tropical birds as a gift for Baranov. The kings and great nobles of Hawaii wore such garb.[37] Thus Slobodchikov established friendly relations between Russian America and the Hawaiian Islands. Kamehameha the Great valued his friendship with the Russians and exchanged letters and gifts with Baranov on a regular basis. Slobodchikov and his men returned to New Archangel in August 1807, and Winship, in September.[38]

Labor Unrest and Tlingit Resistance

In the meantime several problems required Baranov's immediate attention in the colonies, including labor unrest in New Archangel, the hostility of the Tlingits, and the continuing problem of supplying the colony. The company administration admitted that the Russians recruited for the colony were far from ideal. They drank too much, were given to debauchery, and were savage in character. Their pay was low, their food was inadequate, and they lived in squalor. Discipline was severe; Baranov punished workers for the slightest infraction with gaskets and cat-o'-nine-tails, or deportation to some thinly populated island where no supplies reached those thus punished.[39]

There had been worker unrest in the past: as early as 1795 workers had refused to take orders from the administration, presented lists of demands, and attempted to dispose of the colonial authorities altogether. Some of these uprisings had been fairly well organized, including a secret agreement among the workers and the election of leaders.[40]

In 1809 poor conditions led the fur hunter Vasily Naplakov to lead a group of plotters in an attempt to murder Baranov, all those close to him, and the Tlingit chiefs who collaborated with him. The plan was to take all sympathizers and the best furs, load them on the new company vessel *Ot-krytie,* and sail to some remote place in the South Pacific. Their model was the Polish count Moritz August Beniowski, who had successfully mutinied in Kamchatka in 1771. Three of Naplakov's group, however, informed Baranov of the plan on July 26. Baranov took a group of armed men and raided the meeting place. He ordered Naplakov and five of his colleagues be kept in irons under guard until they could be sent to Kamchatka for trial.[41]

Kyrill T. Khlebnikov, an official of the RAC, questioned the leaders of the plot. Recognizing that their main motivation had been hunger, overwork, and cruel treatment, he warned the directors that if Naplakov and his accomplices were tried in some government office they could "reveal truths which could harm and shame the company." He advised that the whole affair be forgotten. The company directors disagreed and ordered the plotters tried before a court. The case dragged on for years. Some of the accused died, and others received long prison terms.[42]

The Tlingit posed a greater threat to the Russians. They had destroyed Fort Mikhailovskii in 1802 and Yakutat in 1805. As a result, men in New Archangel slept with arms at their sides and never went out alone. Baranov had the little settlement surrounded by a high palisade. In 1806 the situation was so tense that no hunting party went out to sea. Those who sailed in the next few years endured much harassment. Yet during Baranov's years as chief manager the Tlingits were allowed to come into New Archangel from time to time to trade furs, fish, and vegetables they had raised for Russian goods.[43]

The RAC and American Traders

Baranov worked closely with Americans after 1812 because he could depend on them to furnish needed supplies. The relationship also enabled him to conduct joint hunting on half shares along the California coast, and to hire the ship's captains to carry company furs to sell in Canton, the dominant market for the China trade. (The Russians were barred from Canton, but the Americans were free to enter the port.) There were drawbacks to this relationship. Americans cruised, hunted, and traded in waters the Russians regarded as their exclusive domain. The Americans traded directly with Natives, bought their furs, and sold them not only liquor but also arms and ammunition, which, the Russians charged, the Natives used against them. The czar's representatives in Washington, D.C., protested this "illicit traffic," but the American government contended that its citizens were free to come and go as they pleased. Baranov did not have the manpower to keep the Americans out, and the czar's government offered no help. Baranov was certainly unhappy with this reality but also did not want to terminate the relationship that had so reliably supplied the colony and gained so many customers for the Russian furs.[44]

John Jacob Astor, the head of the American Fur Company of Astoria, Oregon, worked out an agreement in May of 1812 to resolve the differences between the Russians and the Americans and to define their respective spheres of interest on the Pacific coast. According to the terms of the agreement, Astor recognized the Russians' exclusive rights to hunt and trade with Natives in the area north of 55° north latitude. The Americans were to have the same privileges south of the line. Both parties promised not to sell liquor, arms, or ammunition to the Natives. They agreed to work together and do what was necessary to keep rivals out of the territory. In addition Astor agreed to supply the Russians with all the goods they needed, while the Russians designated him their sole agent to take their furs to Canton and sell on a commission basis. The agreement was to be for four years, renewable for a similar term unless an unforeseen contingency arose and called for modifications. The advantage for the Russians would be better quality provisions at cheaper prices and on a regular basis.

The outbreak of war between the United States and Great Britain in 1812 terminated the agreement. Astor sold his holdings to the British-owned Northwest Company in order to save them from seizure by the British Navy.[45] Baranov was not disappointed to see the termination of the Astor-RAC association. Although the relationship had been short, Baranov had quickly become dissatisfied with the prices charged and the quality of the goods received. Astor ships had been unreliable as well, never arriving when promised or bringing much of what he had ordered. In 1813, having accumulated supplies acquired from previous dealings with other American traders to last him for several years, he was in a good position to make new arrangements.[46]

Baranov's Final Years

In 1813 Baranov found that Napoleon's 1812 invasion of Russia had increased his already significant isolation from the mother country. He also found that the War of 1812 had turned to his advantage. After the British had taken over Astoria, American ships sailed north to New Archangel to avoid capture. Baranov bought several American vessels, leased others, and registered all under the Russian flag, which made them safe from British seizure since the latter had become the czar's allies in the war against Napoleon. American seamen were much more efficient than the Russian crews, and Baranov used them widely. For the next two years RAC profits soared because of the lively commerce between Russian America and China, Hawaii, and California. There was one major inconvenience: ships flying the Russian flag could no longer sell their furs in Canton but instead were forced to make the long overland journey to Kiakhta, with its much inferior trading facilities. Still, in 1814 RAC profits came to nearly 1 million silver rubles, resulting in extra dividends for the shareholders. Times were good for Baranov.[47]

In the meantime, however, naval officers like Vasily M. Golovnin, known as one of the best officers in the imperial navy, and Iurii F. Lisianskii, also a naval officer and explorer who had visited and reported on Russian America, had asserted that the navy should represent the imperial state in the far North East and East and on the Pacific Coast. In November 1813, one of these officers, Lieutenant Mikhail P. Lazarev, in command of the RAC vessel *Suvorov*, arrived in New Archangel with a cargo of goods. Baranov welcomed him and the news that the Napoleonic empire had collapsed.

But soon Lazarev clashed with the chief manager. Lazarev refused to recognize Baranov's civilian authority over the *Suvorov* or the chief manager's prerogative to use the vessel as he chose while it remained in Russian American waters. Temperamental incompatibilities between the two principals

sharpened what both understood to be a basic clash over who was to represent the state and govern the region—the RAC or the imperial navy? Lazarev continued to defy Baranov, and when he left New Archangel in 1815 (in the middle of the night against Baranov's wishes), Baranov sent an angry report to Saint Petersburg charging Lazarev with damaging the RAC's Pacific interest.[48]

Lazarev left behind imperialist-minded, intelligent, but quarrelsome Dr. Georg Anton Schaeffer. A trained physician of German birth, Schaeffer had entered Russian service in 1808, and in 1813 he signed on with the RAC on the *Suvorov* under Lazarev's command. After Lazarev's departure, Baranov asked Schaeffer to go to Hawaii to obtain Kamehameha's help in the return of the fur cargo of the ship *Bering*, which the local king of Kauai, Kaumualii, had appropriated when it was wrecked on the island in January 1815.

Schaeffer arrived in Hawaii in November 1815. He failed to accomplish his goal and antagonized Kamehameha. So he went instead to Kauai in May 1816 and gained King Kaumualii's confidence. Schaeffer persuaded him to restore what remained of the *Bering*'s cargo and to pledge allegiance to the czar. He also convinced the king to trade exclusively with the RAC and to allow the company to establish factories on the island in exchange for protection against his enemies. Under this agreement, Schaeffer built two forts with Native labor, established plantations, and bought a good American ship for Kaumualii.[49]

All of this goodwill lasted for one year, until the king expelled Schaeffer in the face of war with Kamehameha the Great. Schaeffer had no other choice but to sail to Honolulu, Kamehameha's capital. There the king had his ship disarmed, but he was allowed to sail to Canton on an American ship in July 1817. In December 1818, Schaeffer arrived in Saint Petersburg, where he tried, unsuccessfully, to obtain military assistance to reassert Russian rights in Hawaii. The RAC had already sustained substantial losses from Schaeffer's actions and did not wish to add to them. He returned to Germany in 1821, and after many other adventures failed to return from an expedition to the interior of Brazil.[50]

The Saint Petersburg office of the RAC knew

nothing as yet of the Schaeffer affair when it dispatched two vessels, the *Kutuzov* and the *Suvorov*, to the colony. The main office of the RAC had finally decided to retire Baranov, who had requested several times to be relieved of his duties. The company had sent replacements twice before, but both men died before reaching their destination. Now Captain-Lieutenant Leontii A. Hagemeister was designated Baranov's replacement, and he was to carry the order from the RAC, issued in Saint Petersburg in 1816, directly to Baranov in New Archangel. Baranov was "to hand over his post, the capital and business in an orderly manner to Mr. Hagemeister."[51] All employees were to obey the newly appointed head of the territories. As it happened, the Schaeffer affair had troubled Baranov and affected his health, and he was doubtless more than ready to retire.

The *Suvorov* arrived in New Archangel in November 1817, but Hagemeister did not inform Baranov of his replacement until two months later. In the meantime Lieutenant Semen I. Ianovskii, a member of Hagemeister's ship, proposed to Baranov's daughter, Irina. Hagemeister replaced Baranov with Ianovskii in January 1818 and a few days later the two were married.[52]

Now seventy-two years old, Baranov was undecided about where he wanted to go. He thought about Kodiak, but the isolation, damp climate, and boredom made the place unattractive. He had thought occasionally of finishing his days with his brother in Izhiga, Russia. At other times he had dreamed of moving to the Hawaiian Islands, where King Kamehameha the Great had invited him. Eventually Golovnin advised him to return to Russia, where the RAC, obligated to him for decades of faithful and effective service, "would undoubtedly undertake to provide him with all the perquisites of a peaceful and pleasant life." So he decided to leave New Archangel in November on the *Kutuzov*. After passing the Hawaiian Islands and landing on Guam for fresh supplies, the ship then proceeded to Batavia, where it remained for thirty-six days. Baranov lived ashore for that time and the tropical climate proved to be fatal to his failing health. The ship left Batavia on March 12, 1819, and Baranov died in the Straits of Sunda on April 16. The following day there was a funeral service for him off Prince Island and he was buried at sea.[53]

Baranov had spent twenty-eight years in the colony. His vision, leadership, and drive had expanded the Russian toehold in Kodiak to North America's mainland as far as Lake Iliamna. He took over the Kenai Bay area from a competing company and occupied the whole of Chugatsk Bay to the mouth of the Copper River. He established many settlements, including Yakutat, New Archangel, and Fort Ross in Spanish California. Kirill Khlebnikov, an RAC official and historian who became one of Baranov's greatest admirers, concluded that he had "always acted in the best interest of the company and the state." He had been a tough taskmaster and sometimes been guilty of brutality. But he also was an inspiring leader who inculcated deep loyalty. He never avoided danger or hard work and endured hardship with fortitude. His was a life well lived.[54]

Chapter 7

Russian Naval Rule, 1818–67

In the years before Baranov's retirement it had become apparent that the imperial government was assuming ever greater control of company operations. The RAC's political activities were now overseen by a new council, the State Council, which became a permanent part of the company's governing board in 1813. Further, officers in the Navy Department assumed many colonial positions, particularly in the company's fleet. Czarist expansionist plans necessitated that ships of considerable tonnage be officered and manned by qualified personnel. Because of a lack of qualified crews, in 1802, the czar encouraged the release of sailors, naval officers, and navigators for company service. The government paid one-half of the salaries, and those released to RAC duty preserved all the rights and privileges of those serving on active duty.[1] In short, naval officers came to play an increasingly important part in resupplying the colony. As we have seen, not a few refused to obey Baranov's orders, and after his retirement the imperial government concentrated the whole colonial administration in the hands of naval officers who received appointments as governors of the Russian colony in America.[2]

The navy had won its campaign to oust the merchants from control of the RAC. However, naval rule coincided with a decline in the populations of fur-bearing animals, and naval officers had little interest in business affairs. They instead concentrated on administrative improvements that resulted in a considerable enlargement of the bureaucracy. Some of the governors, who usually served for five years, were noted explorers. Others concerned themselves with the welfare of the Natives. None had any fur trade experience. The Soviet historian Semen B. Okun wrote that there was "more order and less peltry" in the new regime.[3]

The Second Charter

American financier and fur trader John Jacob Astor had not been idle in the meantime. He and his allies in Washington, D.C., believed that the 1818 Convention between the United States and Great Britain, which provided that the territory west of the Rocky Mountains remain "free and open to the vessels, citizens, and subjects of both" for ten years, had betrayed American interests, and they lobbied for federal occupation of Oregon and the establishment of an American fur company.[4]

The Russians had taken note of the 1818 Convention and concluded that it would increase Yankee business interest in the Russian possessions. Captain Vasily M. Golovnin, who had written an extensive report on conditions in the colony, advised the Russian government to act quickly to save Russian America from the dangers of a possible American takeover. He suggested the dispatch of warships to patrol the waters along the northwest coast that Russia claimed. In the future,

Fort Ross should supply all foodstuffs to Russian America, while round-the-world voyages from Russia should supply all other needed commodities.[5] Golovnin went so far as to charge that the United States supplied the Natives with arms to be used in an alliance against Russia.[6]

Golovin's recommendations and Russian diplomatic reports, as well as history, convinced many that the time to act had come. This was at a time when the imperial government had become increasingly active and conservative in international affairs. Czar Alexander I, who had ascended the throne in 1801 after the assassination of his father, Paul I, had played an important role in defeating Napoleon, and he had been the chief architect of the Holy Alliance (1815) between Russia, Austria, and Prussia.[7]

The czar's government was disturbed about reports on the activities of foreigners in Russian America, particularly the Americans, who had appropriated a disproportionate share of the colonial fur market. The Yankees also profited from supplies they sold to the Russians. Russian officials were also alarmed by the views of some American members of Congress, who were calling on their government to prevent further Russian expansion in North America and asking that American traders in Russian America be protected from harassment.[8]

Captain Matvei I. Murav'ev, appointed in September 1820 as governor of the colony, received instructions to prepare for a total trade ban with the United States. Vasily Golovnin, in charge of the company headquarters in Saint Petersburg, proposed that the southern boundary of the company's charter be changed from 55° to 51° north latitude. The Russian Senate ratified this measure in September 1821, and the government simultaneously sent three Russian war sloops to patrol the waters north of 51°.[9]

In September 1821 the czar issued two ukases. By the first, Russia claimed sovereignty over territory in America from 55° down to 51° north, extending to 115 miles offshore on both the North American and Asian sides of the Pacific Ocean. The second renewed the RAC charter, granting all fur-hunting, fishing, whaling, and other commercial interests in the regions to the company for another twenty years. Both the British and American governments were quick to protest the exclusion of their nationals from these Russian economic activities, and the Hudson's Bay Company decided to push its own activities far north and westward of the Fraser River valley to keep the Russians at a distance.[10]

Each government reminded the imperial regime that the territory it claimed south of the 55th parallel lay within the Oregon country, which both countries claimed and jointly occupied under the terms of the October 20, 1818, convention between Great Britain and the United States, renewed in 1827. Stratford Canning, the British foreign secretary, proposed that the two nations act together in warning the Holy Alliance, especially Russia, against further provocation. On the advice of Secretary of State John Quincy Adams, President James Monroe issued the Monroe Doctrine on December 2, 1823, stating that the New World was no longer open for further colonization.

The Russian government, however, had realized that its North American colonial policy was a failure even before the Monroe Doctrine's proclamation. The Russian policy of prohibiting trade with the Americans had deplorable results. Russian furs previously marketed in the United States could not be sold after the ban. They could not readily be sold in Russia, either, so many simply rotted in the warehouses. Neither Fort Ross nor Spanish California were able to provide enough grain for colonial needs, and as a result, many Russian settlers went hungry. Russian goods shipped from the Baltic port of Kronshtadt around the world to the colony usually arrived late and often in poor condition. They cost more than double what the Americans had charged. This resulted in smaller RAC profits. Chief Manager Murav'ev criticized the ban on trading with foreigners, requested the company directors to send more supplies, and also dispatched a ship to Hawaii to obtain food.[11]

The 1824 Convention

By 1823 the imperial government faced its failing policies in the colony. It was unwilling to reduce its commitment to playing European power politics and was therefore unable to help its Russian-American colony. It was also unable to challenge the world's greatest naval power, England. Russia was ready to compromise.

In 1824, the czar charged Ernest Louis Leopold, the Baron de Tuyll, the new Russian ambassador to the United States, to resolve the difficulties caused by the two ukases, which had been suspended pending the outcome of negotiation. The talks took place in Saint Petersburg. After more than six conferences, articles satisfactory to both sides were finally drawn up, and the northwest coast border treaty between Russia and the United States was signed on April 17, 1824. Its eight articles granted to U.S. citizens the right of free access, for ten years, along the northwest coast for fishing and trading with the Natives but excluded alcohol and firearms. The convention recognized Russian America's boundaries as extending to 54°40′ north latitude.

More complex negotiations between the Russians and the British continued thereafter, and the two powers finally signed a convention on February 28, 1825, in which Great Britain confirmed the American-Russian Convention of 1824.[12] Great Britain was less interested in acquiring land than in the commercial aspects of the treaty. Like the Americans, the British were given the right to trade along the coast of Russian America for a ten-year period. Also, British ships received the freedom to navigate the rivers flowing through the Russian territory in the interior into the Pacific Ocean.

A wide spectrum of Russian literate society protested the two conventions. One critic, for example, suggested that unless citizens of the United States were completely barred from the northwest coast the RAC might as well abandon New Archangel completely. Another stated that permitting foreigners free navigation of the rivers in perpetuity made them the real owners of the land, leaving Russia with only a meaningless title of possession.[13]

In essence, the two conventions spelled the beginning of the end of Russian America. The international community for the first time recognized that Russia owned not only the Aleutian Islands but also a defined territory on the American continent. Yet the conventions deprived the RAC from expanding its activities even within the borders of the territories that it formally owned.[14]

The United States and Great Britain together had acted to check Russia's advance into North America. But as a result of the conventions, the colony's economic stability improved, and as it turned out, the 1830s were the high point of Russia's American possession. And even though Russian expansion in North America had formally ended, trade and trading rights continued to be major issues. The British-owned Hudson's Bay Company was prepared to challenge the RAC for control of the fur trade.

The Unbeatable Hudson's Bay Company

The Hudson's Bay Company (HBC) was far more efficient than the Russians. It had built a chain of trading posts at two-hundred-mile intervals, reaching the southern boundaries of Russian America by 1833. Its agents were educated men who did not hunt or trap themselves but had goods to sell or barter for furs. They sold their high-quality goods at low prices, even at a loss if necessary, and paid more for furs than the Russians. This enabled the "Honorable Company," as it often was called, to drive out of business smaller American firms in the interior. The Russians, for their part, had also decided to rid their territory of competition from small traders. The RAC completed the ouster of the Americans by informing them that the ten-year period allowing them to trade in Russian territory had elapsed and that they must move.[15]

With the Americans gone, the HBC now took on the Russians. George Simpson, the North American head of the HBC, decided to dispatch Peter Skene Ogden, one of his toughest traders, to establish a post up the Stikine River in 1834. Baron Ferdinand Petrovich von Wrangel, a charismatic naval officer and explorer, had been appointed governor (as the chief managers now were called), of Russian America in 1830.[16]

Aware that the British would establish a post up the Stikine River, Wrangel hastily set up a blockade at the river mouth, fortifying a nearby Indian village that he renamed Redoubt Saint Dionysius. He anchored the fourteen-gun *Chichagov*, under the command of Captain-Lieutenant Dionisii F. Zarembo, at a strategic turn in the channel. When Ogden appeared aboard his little brig, the *Dryad*, Zarembo fired a shot across her bow and ordered the HBC ship back into the Pacific Ocean. Ogden

In 1839 the Russians leased their redoubt, Saint Dionysius, to the British, who renamed it Fort Stikine. In 1867 the Americans established Fort Wrangel here but abandoned it in 1877. The post office in the remaining community was called Fort Wrangel and was renamed Wrangel in 1902. It survived as a supply point for fur traders and miners. This is an 1878 view.

(Courtesy of Alaska Historical Library.)

and Zarembo argued their respective positions for eleven days, and eventually Ogden retreated.[17]

To resolve the touchy situation, Simpson and John Pelly, the British governor of the HBC, left London in 1838 for Saint Petersburg. There Simpson met Wrangel, and the two signed an agreement in 1839.[18] Under the agreement, the Russians leased to the British the mainland of their territory south of Cape Spencer for ten years at annual payments of two thousand land-otter skins. Additionally, the HBC promised to sell the Russians two thousand or more otters at twenty-three shillings per pelt and three thousand other animal skins at thirty-two

shillings per pelt. Most important, the HBC obligated itself to supply not only Russian America but Kamchatka as well with provisions and manufactured goods at stipulated prices.[19]

The Russians benefited by this arrangement. The dispute on the Stikine had been peacefully resolved, and Russia would receive income from an unoccupied area. A supply of furs and provisions were assured, and the closing of Redoubt Saint Dionysius resulted in savings. For almost thirty years the HBC occupied a part of the Russian colony, subject only to the nominal jurisdiction of the RAC.[20]

The HBC and Trading Posts

There was little friction between the two companies, but HBC officials disagreed among themselves about how the leased territory should be organized and administered. John McLoughlin, the company's chief factor on the Pacific, advocated the use of trading posts. He built Fort Durham, usually referred to as Fort Taku, on the Taku River some twenty-five miles south of present-day Juneau. On the Stikine River he replaced the Russian Redoubt Saint Dionysius with Fort Stikine. Sir George Simpson, the overseas governor of the company, reasoned that the high operation and maintenance costs of the two posts could not justify their continued existence, especially since the furs brought to them came mostly from the British-held interior. When Indians attacked Fort Stikine and killed McLoughlin's son, Simpson believed that only the timely arrival of the Russians had prevented more British from being killed.

The senior McLoughlin strongly disagreed with Simpson. He argued that once the posts had been abandoned, British influence over the Natives would decline: the Indians would go directly to the Russians for needed articles rather than waiting for the British to come to them. Simpson's views, however, prevailed; Fort Taku closed in 1842 and Fort Stikine in 1847. For the remainder of the HBC's stay in the coastal strip, it conducted its trade on the steamer *Beaver*.

Sources: John S. Gilbraith, The Hudson's Bay Company as an Imperial Factor (Berkeley and Los Angeles: University of California Press, 1957), 157–58; Sir George Simpson, Narrative of a Journey Round the World during the Years 1841 and 1842 (London: Henry Colborn, 1847), 2: 182, 200–13.

A Profitable Arrangement

Both companies apparently were very pleased with their new relationship, although as part of the bargaining process each pretended otherwise in order to secure the most beneficial changes to the lease. Together they agreed on new prices to be paid the Natives for their furs, prices considerably lower than those they had paid when competing with one another.[21] The farms of the Puget Sound Agricultural Company, an HBC subsidiary, had become so productive that the parent organization was able to sell the Russians an additional ten thousand bushels of wheat. The Russian colony had an abundance of foodstuffs for the first time, and the grain was said to be superior to that California previously had supplied. The Russians discovered that British goods were of the highest quality and much cheaper than those they had obtained from the Americans. British ships carried all goods to the colony, freeing the vessels of the RAC for other purposes. All in all, the Russians felt that they had gained the most from the deal, especially since the leased area had yielded but few furs.[22]

The HBC also profited considerably from the agreement. Grain sales from the Puget Sound Agricultural Company and the farmers of the Willamette Valley in the Oregon Country brought in about $3,125 a year. Earnings from freighting amounted to almost $8,000 in 1844. The income from furs ranged from $8,000 to $10,000 a year.[23]

When the lease lapsed in 1849, the parties renewed it for another ten years, albeit with substantial changes. The Russians refused to lower the rental fee, but they recognized that changing conditions made it almost impossible for the British to provide exactly the same services as in the past. The HBC had lost some of its most productive farms because the United States had annexed Oregon in 1846, and there was a labor shortage because many of its workers had defected to the California gold fields in 1849. Therefore the British were no longer required to ship foodstuffs to Russian America and Kamchatka. The Russians also found it advantageous to do business with others and not be dependent on a single supplier. By dealing directly with European firms, the RAC could buy manufactured goods more cheaply. The Russians lowered transportation costs by chartering vessels to carry goods to Russian America.[24] Since fur-bearing animals had become scarce, the new contract did not mention that the HBC had to sell furs to the Russians.

In 1854 the Crimean War pitted Great Britain and France against Russia. The foreign offices of Great Britain and Russia agreed to abide by the wishes of the HBC and the RAC, both of which desired that the northern territory remain neutral in the war. The Russians felt that they benefited the most because the British controlled the seas and could have readily attacked their North American settlements. In 1859 the two companies agreed to a new accord to continue their association. This time, however, it was to be for only three years, and the rental payment was to be rendered in cash. The Russians reserved to themselves the right to use the ice, timber, coal, and fish found in the area as they saw fit. Thereafter the two companies renewed the lease for periods of one to two years until the United States purchased Russian America in 1867.[25]

Changes in the RAC

In the meantime, significant changes had been taking place in Russian America. The naval officers who served as governors made important alterations in the Baranov management style and direction of business affairs. These new governors, most of whom belonged to the aristocracy, set themselves apart from the Natives and the company workers, replacing the rough equalitarian system of the Baranov era with one in which rank and class standing were important. Government became more formal and the administrative staff grew, including additional accountants and staff to deal with employee problems. A new position, that of assistant chief manager, was created to help manage the colonies and allow the governor to leave New Archangel from time to time to inspect the outlying settlements.

Colonial expenses increased with the construction of new buildings to house personnel, provide a home for the governor, install fortifications, and erect barracks. Captain-Lieutenant Murav'ev, who served as governor from 1820 to 1825, was a great builder; in fact, Murav'ev was reputed to have added more buildings to the company's stations than any subsequent governor. In the winter of 1820–21, which saw severe weather and heavy snowfall, the governor kept the laborers at New Archangel busy cutting timber, burning charcoal, building new vessels, and repairing old ones. He had the town's fortifications and the outlying settlements repaired, and new buildings were erected where needed. In March 1821 Murav'ev started construction on a new house for himself and his successors on the height overlooking the settlement, replacing the seedy building from Baranov's time.[26]

In 1821 Murav'ev visited all the stations in the colony except Atka and Attu. As a result of his tour, he divided the colony into districts to improve the administration.[27] Murav'ev also reversed Baranov's policy and allowed the Tlingits to come into New Archangel, subject to certain restrictions. During his administration, explorations continued, and naval officers made a detailed survey of the coast from Bristol Bay westward to the mouth of the Kuskokwim River. Nunivak Island was discovered, and Norton Sound was explored along its eastern and northern coasts. The explorers also accurately located many prominent points with the help of astronomical observations.

Murav'ev's health had deteriorated during his tenure of office, and he left New Archangel in July 1825 in command of the *Elena,* which had brought his replacement, Lieutenant Petr E. Chistiakov.[28] The new governor encouraged commercial expansion of the RAC. He requested the board of directors of the RAC to dispatch an experienced whaler to the

An early view (about 1828) of New Archangel, which later became Sitka. Baranov established the settlement as his headquarters in 1804. The fortified "castle" on the hill commanded the harbor and the area in which the town developed.

(Courtesy of Alaska and Polar Regions Department, Elmer E. Rasmuson Library, University of Alaska Fairbanks.)

colony in order to develop this industry in Russian American waters. In 1828 he organized a trading post on Atka Island, and in the same year he secured the southern Kurils for Russia, establishing a permanent fur hunting post on the island of Urup. He sent a small expedition from Bristol Bay up the Nushagak River and over to the Kuskokwim River. Here they discovered new fur hunting grounds, which led to the establishment of a post on the Kuskokwim.[29]

During Chistiakov's administration, arctic foxes from the Pribilof Islands and black and silver foxes from the American mainland were transplanted to the central Aleutians and Rat Islands for fox farming, which lasted until World War II. Company vessels also explored Native trade possibilities in the north and considered participation in the trad-ing rendezvous on the Buckland River in Kotzebue Sound. The Russians shipped whale blubber from Kodiak Island for trade with the Iñupiats. The RAC was interested in the flow of furs through Native trade networks from the Yukon River via the Koyukuk River to the North Slope's Iñupiat and from there to the Chukchi and Siberian markets. The RAC also was interested in acquiring beaver pelts and castor, the dried perineal glands of the beaver, in great demand by perfume manufacturers, as well as the furs of other land animals.[30]

Wrangel's Tenure as Governor

Chistiakov's successor, Baron Ferdinand von Wrangel, turned out to be one of the ablest governors in the history of the colony. Under his administration, relations with the Tlingit steadily improved. He also established a system, started in small steps by Baranov and then more systematically under Chistiakov, to put marine fur-bearing harvests on a sustainable yield basis. Wrangel also made the colonial administration more efficient and worked to remove unfit employees and priests. He also asked the main office to transfer the talented Father Ioann Veniaminov, who later became the famous Bishop Innokentii, from Unalaska to New Archangel to Kodiak; and to assign a new priest to Unalaska to continue Father Veniaminov's work.[31]

An experienced explorer, Wrangel traveled extensively in the colony and collected much geographical and ethnographical material, which he published as a book in 1839. Wrangel and his successors supported the scientific studies and expeditions of naval officers and merchant marine navigators. Their accurate observations and maps supplanted the crude information Baranov had obtained from the hunters and the Natives. Perhaps these governors wanted to increase knowledge about Russian America, but probably they also wanted to find new areas suitable for trading posts and forts and to promote the fur trade. For example, in later years, Lieutenant Lavrenty A. Zagoskin transferred from the navy to the RAC because of his interest in exploration. The late anthropologist James VanStone wrote that Zagoskin's travels between 1842 and 1844, which took him as far as the Tanana River, "represented the outstanding Russian achievement in interior Alaskan exploration. His contributions were a fitting culmination to the efforts of Wrangell to foster the pursuit of scientific interest in Russia's American possessions."[32]

Wrangel had schools built and hospitals and other facilities established, and he provided better working conditions for company employees. He ordered the construction of a new church in New Archangel as a replacement for the old church, which was not repairable. He established a sawmill at Ozerskoi Redoubt in 1833.[33]

Russian ship-building efforts in the colony had been uneconomical, so in 1834 Wrangel ordered that all colonial shipyards, except the one at New Archangel, were to be closed. A Creole master shipwright, Osip Netsvetov, served for thirty-two years in the New Archangel shipyard, where he constructed two company vessels and retimbered others.[34]

Wrangel was the first governor to bring his Russian wife to the New World. The young baroness, Elizabeth, transformed the town's life. The old chief residence now witnessed formal dinners and balls. Company men and local women who had lived in casual relationships were now married. Apparently all loved the baroness, the rough Russian hunters above all. The elders of the local tribe, Hootze, Anahootz, and Navshkete, praised her virtues, and she moved easily among the Natives. But the loneliness and monotony of life in the frontier town weighed heavily on her, and she looked forward to their return to Russia. The Wrangels left New Archangel in November 1835 and arrived in Kronshtadt in June 1836.[35]

The Problem of Labor

From Baranov's tenure onward, RAC governors had to spend much of their time dealing with a difficult labor problem. There were never enough men to perform the various necessary tasks such as skilled work, hunting, trading, and common labor or to defend the colony in a proper fashion. It was the responsibility of the chief manager (or, after 1818, the governor) to determine how to use the available manpower most efficiently—which jobs to assign to whom and which settlements most needed their services.

As the nineteenth century progressed, Creoles became a more significant factor in colonial life, furnishing much of the needed labor, especially skilled labor, and much of the exploratory work in the interior. Persons who could demonstrate descent from a Russian ancestor in the male line were assigned to this class. (Anthropologist and historian Lydia Black wrote, however, that "theoretically and in law, descendants of [Russian] females could also make such a claim." It was possible for Russian women to marry Native men, but it happened seldom, particularly since there were so few Russian women in the colonies.) The RAC had cultivated this class of mixed-race people by providing it with special privileges and, in some cases, education. The intent was to create from among this group a reliable and loyal permanent labor pool. Many Creoles achieved important positions in colonial society and contributed greatly to its stability.[36]

Still, Russian America always had a labor shortage. Part of the problem lay with the colony's purpose: settling people and establishing communities on the land was not the primary goal. The RAC's main objective was to provide support for fur-hunting activities, trade with the Natives, and the marketing of trade goods. The government had no plan to establish a permanent Russian population in North America; in fact, its regulations prohibited Russian settlement for its own sake.[37]

Company critics recognized the difficulty of bringing men to America but pointed out that the company did little recruitment. Soviet historians later pointed out that the company brought serfs to the colony only once because it was reluctant to pay the high transportation costs or to train the men.[38] Captain Pavel N. Golovin would write in an 1862 report that if the company wanted to attract skilled labor, it would have to raise its wage scale. Men could easily make at home as much as the company offered in America, and therefore prospective employees had little motivation to move to a far-off and little-known land. He thought that the company could do more to encourage foreigners to come to the colony because emigrants did not have to be of the Orthodox faith.[39]

In its second charter of 1821 the company had striven to keep those already in the colony from leaving. This charter had eliminated much of the complicated procedure the government had hitherto required of those who wanted to remain in the colony after their term of employment ended. The second charter also granted company employees the same privileges enjoyed by those in state service, although this concession mainly benefited men in the upper ranks.

The new charter also dealt with employee rights. For example, the RAC was required to provide healthy and convenient winter and summer quarters, as well as sufficient food and clothing. It also was to maintain enough church personnel and buildings to serve the needs of believers. The charter also recognized Creoles as imperial subjects on the same basis as all other Russian citizens. In short, the czar extended the company's exclusive right to utilize the colonial resources, but he also obligated it to provide a wide range of social services to its employees, and restrictions on the use of Native labor had expanded considerably.[40]

Of great interest to most employees was the 1835 creation of the class known as "colonial citizens," which included workers who had been in the company's service for at least twenty years, widows of company employees, and those who because of poor health or for other reasons were no longer able to work. Colonial citizenship bestowed benefits of some importance: namely a guaranteed pension, the right to a small piece of land, and the right to sell the products of the land as well as whatever was obtained in hunting, fishing, or trapping.[41]

It is uncertain how many workers became colonial citizens, but certainly it was not enough to establish a large permanent population. According to Captain Pavel N. Golovin, colonial citizens were more of a burden than an asset and contributed little to the well-being of the colony. In any case, the Russian population of the colony never counted many more than seven hundred souls.[42]

The RAC and Native Alaskans

Partly in response to the colony's labor shortage, the naval governors after Baranov developed new policies in their dealings with the Native peoples. They hoped to improve a relationship that retained many aspects of a truce, especially with the Tlingits, who were never conquered. When Murav'ev arrived as the governor of the colony in 1820, he invited the Tlingits to come back to Baranof Island, from which Baranov had banished them in 1804. Yet he restricted them to a village just outside New Archangel, where they could be easily observed. He permitted them in town only during daylight hours. Spies in the village regularly reported on their activities.

Captain Arvid A. Etholen had served in the colony for many years before he was promoted to governor in 1840. He was convinced that he would have to employ new policies to deal with the Tlingits. In 1841, he invited them to a fair in New Archangel, providing entertainment and a place to exchange their furs, fish, and vegetables for Russian goods.

Miners and "muckers" at Evans Jones Coal Company mine at Jonesville.

(Author's collection.)

The governor also started to hire Tlingits to work in the town and at the harbor. The RAC board commended him for his efforts and encouraged him to make the fair an annual event. Still, the détente was short-lived, and the Russians continued to mistrust the Tlingits.[43] Captain Mikhail I. Rosenberg, one of Etholen's successors, who served as governor from 1850 until 1853, ended the employment of Tlingits in the town. Two years later, in 1855, the Tlingits attacked New Archangel but the Russians repulsed them.

Russian relations with the Aleuts can be conveniently divided into three phases: the era of the promyshlenniks, Baranov's rule, and the era of the naval officers. Almost totally free of government supervision, the promyshlenniks destroyed many Aleut settlements and caused misery or death for several thousand indigenous inhabitants. During Baranov's tenure as chief manager, Aleut living conditions improved slightly, but Baranov was said to have a low opinion of the Aleuts, and during his administration they lost their last vestiges of freedom. He had many forcibly removed from the Aleutian Islands and resettled at Kodiak and New Archangel and on the mainland as far south as the Fort Ross colony. Aleuts were required to participate

Ice and Other Enterprises

Mikhail I. Rosenberg's relatively short tenure as RAC governor coincided with the peak of the company's ambitions as a commercial enterprise. For example, the 1849 California Gold Rush had energized the trade between Russian America and California. The company sent Petr S. Kostromitinov to San Francisco in 1852 to function as agent and Russian vice consul. Kostromitinov was concerned with the ice trade, which promised to generate new revenue for the company.

Later that year the RAC signed a three-year contract with the new American-Russian Commercial Company, based in San Francisco, to supply at least 1,200 tons of ice per year at twenty to twenty-five dollars per ton. In order to fill its part of the contract, the RAC built an ice house in New Archangel large enough to store up to 1,500 tons of ice. In 1853, the Russians built another ice storage facility capable of holding 2,000 tons.

Rosenberg also oversaw the completion of a two-story house for employees in 1852 and a small foundry for producing copper and iron vessels and machine parts. Work also continued on a large stone barn for fish salting, and construction began on a flat-bottomed boat some eighty-five feet long and thirty-two feet wide, which was to carry a sawmill from place to place where needed.

Source: P. A. Tikhmenev, *A History of the Russian-American Company*, trans. and ed. Richard A. Pierce and Alton S. Donnelly (Seattle: University of Washington Press, 1978), 32.

---

in warfare and in expeditions to hunt sea otters as far south as California.[44] This harsh treatment and the spread of diseases among the Aleuts, which the Russians were accused of having brought, resulted in a steady decline of the population that continued until 1840.

A paternalistic spirit guided the naval officers who came to the colony to serve as governor. They were a well-educated group of men, intent on doing their best for the people they ruled. The company established schools and hospitals for the Aleuts and employed many. Some of the Aleuts learned trades, many were taught the rudiments of gardening, and a few became priests.[45]

The Russians regarded the Aleuts as imperial subjects and thus protected by Russian law against arbitrary action. They had the right of self-government, but this was mainly limited to the authority granted their elders, or *toyons,* as the Russians called them, to settle disputes among the people. Aleuts lacked freedom of movement; none were permitted to leave their place of residency without permission from the authorities. All males between the ages of eighteen and fifty were required to participate in company-organized expeditions for sea otter hunting. But unlike the arbitrary demands of the Baranov years, after 1820 the government placed a limit on the number of baidarkas the Aleuts were required to send out in a year. It also restricted the company from drafting more than 50 percent of the eligible males for duty on the hunt.

The company derived many of its profits from the sale of sea otter skins, and so its profits could be seen to depend on Native cooperation in the enforced hunts. Yet the company justified the hunts on the basis that they also benefited the Aleuts. The Russians portrayed the Aleuts as good-natured but inherently lazy people who worked only enough to satisfy immediate needs without any concerns for the future. They were also described as lacking the will to organize the large-scale expeditions needed to hunt successfully. Captain Pavel N. Golovin wrote that "in forcing the Alleuts [*sic*] to work, the company not only provides them with the basic necessities but also gives them the opportunity of improving their condition and way of life, and almost completely prevents them from starving to death."[46]

Sergei Alexandrovich Kostlivtsev, a state councilor who accompanied Golovin on his inspection trip, disagreed with the captain. He accused the company of evading the government's restrictions on Aleut employment by using more than the allowable quota of men. He noted that the Aleuts "spend the best part of the year hunting sea otters and return home when all of the periodic fish have gone out to sea," and they "have no opportunity to lay in sufficient provisions for their families for the winter, which provisions consisted chiefly of dried or sun-dried fish."[47] What the government and the company probably did not want to remember was that the Aleuts, before Russian contact, had lived perfectly self-sufficient lives for thousands of years.

Bishop Innokentii

It was among the Aleuts that the Russian Orthodox church made its greatest progress in converting Natives to Christianity. The greatest credit belongs to Ioann Veniaminov (1797–1879), priest, archbishop; metropolitan, and savant. Trained at the Irkutsk Theological Seminary, he was also versed in mechanics and in various crafts, including clock-making.[48]

In 1817, before he had finished his studies, Ioann married Ekaterina Ivanovna, the daughter of a priest. He graduated from the seminary in 1820 and was ordained as a priest in 1821. In 1823, the Holy Synod asked the bishop of Irkutsk to send a priest to the island of Unalaska in Russian America. Veniaminov volunteered for the assignment and started out for faraway Russian America with his family in May 1823, and after an arduous journey they arrived in New Archangel in October. Veniaminov stayed the winter in town and took the opportunity to learn the Aleut language from Aleut company employees.[49]

In 1824 Veniaminov and his family embarked for Unalaska, where he built a rectory and home for his family and taught the Native workmen to be carpenters, joiners, locksmiths, blacksmiths, brick makers, and stone masons. He built the furniture for his home. As soon as enough workmen had been trained, he employed them to build a new chapel, which was consecrated in June 1826.[50]

Veniaminov continued to study the Aleut language and soon ministered to parishioners and made converts. In March 1825 he opened an elementary school for boys, convinced that good Christians must be able to read and write. He soon was proficient in Aleut, and with the aid of Ivan Pan'lov he devised an alphabet for the language and translated the Russian Short Catechism and the Gospel of Saint Matthew into Aleut. He summarized Christian doctrine in "The Way to the Heavenly Kingdom," written in Aleut and later translated into Russian. Before his death it had gone through forty editions, including translations in English and other languages. Also, during his seven years in Unalaska he kept daily weather records, a first in Russian America.[51]

Veniaminov remained in Unalaska until 1834, when Governor Wrangel secured his transfer to New Archangel. There he established a workshop where he made and repaired furniture and clocks and constructed an organ. He learned Tlingit and made notes on their customs and language for inclusion as a supplement to his Unalaska district book. It was not until the smallpox epidemic of 1836 and 1837 that the Tlingits asked the Russians for vaccinations and also became more receptive to Christianity. Veniaminov had a special church built in New Archangel for the Tlingits.[52] Four toyons, or headmen, of Inuit tribes on the Bering Sea coast north of Nushagak visited him in New Archangel and asked him to baptize them, opening a new region to missionary activity. In September 1837, one Captain Edward with the British survey vessel HMS *Sulphur* visited New Archangel and left this description of Veniaminov: "The padre, who officiated in his splendid robes, was a very powerful athletic man, about forty-five years of age, and standing in his boots (which appear to be a part of his costume) about six feet three inches; quite Herculean, and very clever."[53]

Russian Orthodox church and school, Unalaska, about 1910.

(Author's collection.)

In 1838 Veniaminov received a leave of absence and returned to Russia to get his translations and his book about the Aleutian Islands published. He arrived in Saint Petersburg in June 1839. He proposed the creation of a bishopric of Kamchatka and the Aleutian Islands, wrote articles, lectured, and gave interviews to raise funds for the American mission. In 1840, the RAC paid for the publication of his major work, *Notes on the Islands of the Unalashka District*. His grammar on the Aleut language was published in 1846. While still in the capital, he learned that his wife had died in Irkutsk in November 1839. At the urging of Filaret, the metropolitan of Moscow, the Holy Synod advised Veniaminov to become a monk. In November 1840 he took monastic vows with the rank of archimandrite and was renamed Innokentii.

As a result of an audience with Czar Nicholas I and discussions between the Holy Synod and the emperor, a new Diocese of Kamchatka, the Kuril Islands, and the Aleutians was created. Innokentii became its first bishop in 1840 and was back in New Archangel in September 1841 to administer his new diocese on two continents. In 1850, while in Ayan, he received news that the Holy Synod had promoted him to the rank of archbishop as a reward for his successful missionary work. From 1852 to 1862, Innokentii traveled almost constantly to the various parts of his archbishopric in Kamchatka, the Chukchi country, Iakutsk, and later the Amur region. In fact, in 1858, Innokentii accompanied the governor-general of Eastern Siberia, N. N. Murav'ev, down the Amur River for negotiations with the Chinese, which resulted in the May 1858 Treaty of Aigun by which China ceded the Amur Valley to Russia.[54]

In 1865 Innokentii was appointed to membership in the Holy Synod and thereafter resided in European Russia. In January of 1868, after the death of Metropolitan Filaret, Czar Alexander II appointed Innokentii to fill the highest position in the Russian Orthodox Church, metropolitan of Kolomna and Moscow. He died in March 1879. His work as a missionary, church administrator, and scholar was outstanding. He brought the Natives of Russian America and Siberia into the worldwide Christian community, which eased their entry into the modern world.[55]

Unfortunately Veniaminov was very much the exception among the Russian clergy who came to America. Only a few were well educated. Captain Pavel N. Golovin complained, as Rezanov had earlier, about those clergy who had come as missionaries but had not bothered to learn the Native languages. Golovin agreed that the missionaries could claim some success in converting the Natives, but he criticized them for failing miserably "to spread Christian teachings among the savages, and to set a fine example—by word and deed to modify their customs, and to help them in need, to heal them of bodily and spiritual ills, and systematically to teach them to adjust to settled and industrious lives, and primarily to influence the upbringing of their children, and finally to bring about a condition wherein the savages themselves will desire to be converted."[56]

Social Gains and Decline in Trade

Following the Baranov era, life in Russian America, particularly in New Archangel, became more refined, as the little town became used to a more orderly social life. Baroness Wrangel and her husband had started the custom of giving balls, and later governors and their wives continued this tradition. Colonial visitors expressed their pleasure at how much attention they received and how well they were entertained. Some, however, like Sir George Simpson, the overseas governor of the HBC, noted the great disparity in living conditions, especially between the well-furnished quarters of company officials and the hovels of the common people. Simpson called it the most miserable place he had ever visited.[57] Nonetheless, New Archangel did possess structures of merit, notably the cathedral, which had been rebuilt during Wrangel's tenure, as well as the governor's mansion, known as "Baranov's Castle" because it was built on the site of the old chief manager's abode.

New Archangel also could boast of a few schools, one of which gave boys some training in mathematics and navigation. Before he was governor of the colony, Lieutenant Etholen had been the director of the school and it improved greatly under his leadership. His wife founded a finishing school for girls. The church assumed responsibility for educating Natives and established schools at New Archangel, Kodiak, and Unalaska. Unfortunately, with the notable exception of Veniaminov, most members of the clergy tended to regard learning as secondary to their mission, the saving of souls. In addition to schools, the RAC established infirmaries in New Archangel and Kodiak to care for the sick.

As the colony underwent a social transformation, the Russian fur trade changed considerably. Overhunting, mainly before 1820, had greatly reduced the number of animals, particularly the highly valued sea otters. China had been the chief market for the company's furs, but demand declined sharply after 1830 because conflicts with Western powers severely weakened Chinese power and wealth. The Russians were inept in the art of fur processing and therefore found themselves disadvantaged in the competition for new customers in Europe and the United States because the Americans, British, and Canadians all supplied high-quality furs for the market.[58]

The second charter expired in 1841. Czar Nicholas I, who insisted on personally reviewing all matters pertaining to administration, had delayed its renewal for three years before extending the RAC's authority for another twenty years. The real issue for the czar and his government centered on the question of the existence of the company and the role it should have in the future. The third charter, signed in 1844, stressed the government's role in administration and colonization, slighting the company's commercial character in the process.[59]

The RAC continued to try and a make a profit in the American colony, and company officials initiated several new business ventures, including coal mining and whaling. But only the ice trade prospered. In the 1860s the fur trade had declined and the other company enterprises had either faded or failed, so the Russians had little choice but to leave.[60]

Chapter 8

The Sale of Russian America

The Russian-American Company (RAC) had represented Russia in North America since it received its first monopoly charter in 1799. It had been profitable until the last few years of Baranov's leadership, and profits again increased under the governors who followed. But even though it was a private company, the RAC came under close scrutiny from the czar's administration, which expected the company to develop the colony and utilize its natural resources of furs, fisheries, and minerals, often without adequate support from the government.

The RAC faced too many obstacles to prosper and cement the Russian foothold in North America: the distance from the mother country made transportation costs prohibitive, settlers could not be supplied regularly, and colonial management was not up to the task. By the middle of the nineteenth century there were many indications that the company was declining. The fur trade decreased, and unfortunately so did the trade in fish, ice, timber, and coal. From the end of the 1840s American expansion in the northern part of the Pacific increased sharply. The RAC was unable to contain its foreign rivals without government aid.[1] All of these factors came into focus in the latter half of the nineteenth century, eventually convincing both Russia and the United States that a sale of the colony would benefit them both.

The Idea of a Sale

Even before the outbreak of the Crimean War in 1853, a number of Russia's political and social leaders realized their country's need to strengthen its position in Asia. This could, in part, be accomplished by maintaining and expanding friendly relations with the United States as a counterweight to Great Britain.

In the spring of 1853, Eastern Siberia's governor-general, N. N. Murav'ev-Amurskii, presented a memorandum to Czar Nicholas I in which he argued that the United States was destined to occupy the whole of North America, forcing Russia to cede its North American possession. Maintaining good relations with the United States would act as a counterweight to Great Britain and aid Russia's quest to rule over the whole Asian coast of the Eastern Ocean.[2] The RAC administration was also aware of the threat to its North American colony in the case of war with England and France.[3] Fearing that the British fleet might attack New Archangel, the RAC reached an agreement with the Hudson's Bay Company in 1854 for the "mutual neutralization of possessions and vessels." The British government agreed with the proviso that it "not extend to the open sea." The Russian government agreed to observe the neutrality of the HBC possessions in America.[4]

The news about this agreement did not reach Russian America until the fall of 1854. In the meantime, fearing a British attack, the colonial administration had concluded a fictitious sale of the company's property and possessions to the American-Russian Commercial Company in San Francisco. E. A. Stoeckl, the Russian representative in Washington, D.C., had originally proposed the idea, and although he eventually vetoed it as impractical, the false sale was carried out. Rumors of the transaction resulted in reports in American newspapers that there was talk about selling Russian America. Thereupon, U.S. Secretary of State William L. Marcy, thinking that Russia wanted to sell its colony, contacted Stoeckl, who flatly denied the rumor. Stoeckl wrote Chancellor and Minister of Foreign Affairs Prince Aleksander Mikhailovich Gorchakov that he was certain that the Americans would not forget the incident.

Stoeckl, who eventually managed the negotiations for the sale of Russian America to the United States, was an experienced diplomat and a seasoned observer of the Washington, D.C., scene, and with an American wife he had a good grasp of American viewpoints. The czar instructed him to use his own judgment in American affairs.[5]

The outbreak of the Crimean War in 1853 placed the Russian possessions in North America in a difficult position. The Russian government faced a united front of the major European powers and Turkey. In essence, Russia was attempting to change the Turkish core area into a Russian protectorate and project Russian naval power from the Black Sea into the Mediterranean. This the major European powers were determined to prevent. Even Prussia and Austria, traditional Russian allies, did not support Czar Nicholas I. Under these conditions, American attitudes were important.

Relations between the two countries continued to be friendly. The czar met Thomas H. Seymour, the new American envoy to Saint Petersburg, in March 1854 and expressed the hope that the United States would take the Russian side and that trade between the two countries would continue. In July 1854, Russia and the United States signed an official convention of maritime neutrality.[6] The United States maintained an active neutrality during the Crimean War. Both countries realized that Great Britain was the common rival.

In the meantime, however, France and Great Britain were victorious in the war. Russia was forced to sue for peace, and the Treaty of Paris of 1856 ended the conflict. At a stroke, Russia ceased to be a major military power.

Czar Alexander II (1855–1881) had succeeded Czar Nicholas I in 1855. The Crimean War had convinced the Russian government that it could not develop a modern industrial nation based on serfdom. Alexander II, therefore, liberated the serfs in 1861, one in a number of monumental decisions and reforms that deeply affected Russia's domestic and foreign policies. Reforms of the press, schools, local self-government, towns, courts, and the military followed, starting a new era in Russian history. The most important steps in Alexander's foreign policy consisted of Russian annexation of large parts of central Asia, the Amur basin, the Maritime Province, and Sakhalin Island.[7] In historical perspective, the sale of Russian America to the United States turned out to be the most highly charged of these decisions. It removed Russia from the North American continent and placed the United States in firm control of the North Pacific littoral.

Russia Considers a Sale

The younger brother of Czar Alexander II, Grand Duke Konstantin Nikolaevich, had first proposed the sale of Russian America to the United States in the spring of 1857. He reasoned that the United States would dominate the North American continent and simply take the Russian colony, and that Russia would not have a chance to regain it. Furthermore, the colony brought but little profit, and its loss would not be greatly felt.

The RAC, of course, would need to be compensated. To arrive at a fair value, Konstantin recommended the opinions of the former governors: Admiral Baron von Wrangel, Rear Admiral Mikhail D. Teben'kov, and retired Rear Admiral Etholin. The Grand Duke asked Prince Gorchakov, the minister of foreign affairs, to discuss these considerations with the czar.[8]

The czar wrote that the idea was worth considering. Gorchakov consulted Wrangel, who was knowledgeable about the colony's natural resources, and concluded that the imperial government should charge the United States 7,442,800 silver rubles. This price, he argued, was reasonable in view of the colony's rich coal deposits, ice, construction timber, fish, and excellent naval ports, which offered the United States "enormous advantages." Wrangel cautioned that the strictest secrecy had to be preserved. Wrangel went further in the spring of 1857, writing that "beyond all doubt 20 million silver rubles could not be considered full recompense for the loss of possessions" promising significant industrial activity in the future.[9]

The Ministry of Foreign Affairs incorporated the various opinions for Czar Alexander II in a memorandum, which supported Grand Duke Konstantin's recommendation to cede the colony to the United States. The memo recommended, however, that the proposal not be hastened and that above all the strictest secrecy be observed. Stoeckl was to ascertain the views of the American government on the matter. The transfer should take place no later than 1862, when the charter of the RAC expired.[10] Discussions among government officials continued, and with the czar's approval Prince Gorchakov continued his policy of delay. In 1858, Gorchakov told Stoeckl not to take any initiative and to inform him only if the United States made a proposal.[11]

In the winter of 1859–60, Stoeckl, U.S. Senator William McKendree Gwin of California, and Assistant Secretary of State John Appleton talked about the Russian colony and its possible sale. The two Americans told Stoeckl that President James Buchanan favored the acquisition of Russian America but did not desire to formalize the talks. If the imperial government accepted the American proposal to purchase the Russian colony, Buchanan would consult Congress and his Cabinet to decide how to accomplish the purchase. Gwin mentioned US$5 million as a possible price for the Russian colony.[12]

Stoeckl told Gorchakov that he doubted that the United States would pay more than US$5 million, or 6.5 million rubles, for Russia's colony. Such a sum would yield an annual income of about 300,000 ru-

bles. He doubted that the colonies would ever bring an annual income of that magnitude. Stoeckl sent a report on these discussions to the czar and to the Ministry of Foreign Affairs. The czar let it be known that he had not yet reached a final decision on the matter.[13] Despite the arguments favoring a sale, Gorchakov remained unconvinced that it would benefit Russia to give up her colony except if there was a great financial advantage to sell, and US$5 million came not close to "the real value of our colonies."[14]

In the meantime, Stoeckl told Appleton and Gwin that the imperial government did not outright reject the American proposal but wanted to postpone the matter until a more opportune time, at least until the charter of the RAC expired in 1862. In the meantime, Americans elected Abraham Lincoln president in 1860, and in April 1861 the Civil War began. That put an end to any negotiations concerning the sale of Russian America.[15]

The Third Charter

Meanwhile, a general meeting of the RAC shareholders elected a special committee. Together with the company's main office, the committee prepared a new draft RAC charter, along with accompanying memoranda. The company management forwarded the draft to the minister of finance in July 1860, petitioning for an extension of the RAC's charter for another twenty years, until January 1, 1882. Russian historian N. N. Bolkhovitinov wrote that the RAC management "poorly understood the general situation in the country on the eve of the reforms of 1861 and the clouds that were gathering over the company." The administration did not renounce monopoly rights and privileges, but instead insisted on broadening them. It wished to retain for another twenty years its exclusive right "to utilize all objects and advantages which industry and trade can extract, both on the surface and in the bowels of the earth."[16] It also insisted on monopoly fishing and whaling in the waters of Russian America. The new draft, thereupon, was sent to all interested ministries and departments with a request to submit comments on those items within their sphere of activity.

The various departments delayed their responses.

The Western Union Telegraph Extension Project

While the fate of the RAC was being discussed in Russia, the idea of tying the American and Asian continents by telegraph cable was also being worked out. Telegraphic communication had developed into an ever-expanding network in the United States and Europe. Attempts to link North America and Europe via submarine cable had failed in 1857 and again in 1858. In 1860, the U.S. commercial agent in Russia, Perry Collins, proposed to Congress that North America, Asia, and Europe be connected via telegraph across the fifty-six miles of water separating America and Europe through Asia on the Pacific side. A transcontinental line was to be completed to California in 1861 and would stretch north to Oregon. All that needed to be done was to extend the line north. Hiram Sibley, founder and president of the Western Union Telegraph Company, thought that Collins's idea had merit, and it also found support in Congress.

The United States was embroiled in its Civil War, but Congress twice recommended appropriations for such an undertaking. Although no money was budgeted, Congress approved a right-of-way grant across public lands and U.S. Navy help in building the line. The enormous engineering and construction project started in 1865. The line was to go north from Vancouver, British Columbia, to the headwaters of the Yukon River. From there it was to follow the Yukon to Nulato, north to the Seward Peninsula, across Bering Strait, and south across Siberia to meet the Russian line from Europe at the mouth of the Amur River. The five-thousand-mile line was estimated to cost about $1.5 million, or $300 per mile. The Western Union Telegraph Company organized the Western Union Telegraph Extension Company (WUTE) and distributed stock.

Three separate divisions were to perform the work in British Columbia, Russian America, and Siberia. By the spring of 1867, a telegraph line operated as far as Fort Stager in central British Columbia. The Siberian division built a fifty-mile line near Okhotsk and also constructed forty telegraph stations. But the Russian-American division did not perform nearly as well as the others. The crew built fifty miles of line north and west of Saint Michael; another party, working south from Port Clarence, strung another thirty miles. Finally, the men raised a few poles on January 21, 1867, at Unalakleet. That, however, was about the extent of the Western Union

---

The 1859–60 period was one characterized by revolutionary fervor in Russia, and critics railed against the exploitation of the Aleuts in the colonies as well as the company's monopolistic activities. Eventually this forced the czarist government to form a special committee in 1860 to examine the organization of Russia's American colony. This resulted in the dispatch of two inspectors there, Sergei A. Kostlivtsev from the Ministry of Finances and Captain Pavel N. Golovin from the Naval Ministry. The two returned in 1861 and presented their reports to their respective ministries.[17]

Kostlivtsev apparently was a competent but nondescript bureaucrat who left no trace in the literature other than his report.[18] Golovin, on the other hand, was a career naval officer, descended from two old and distinguished Russian noble families who had served the empire for generations in many capacities. He was a disciplined officer who meticulously carried out every assignment, culminating in his report.[19]

Both men submitted full and detailed accounts. Golovin's report, published in February 1862, consists of four sections. The first examines the found-

A painting (artist unknown) depicts a field camp for men engaged in the construction of a telegraph line to connect North America with eastern Asia and Europe across the Bering Strait. The project, called the Western Union Telegraph Extension, was abandoned in 1866 after the successful completion of an Atlantic submarine cable between North America and Europe.

(Courtesy of Alaska and Polar Regions Department, Elmer E. Rasmuson Library, University of Alaska Fairbanks.)

Telegraph in Russian America. On June 24, 1867, news that the trans-Pacific telegraph project had been terminated reached the Russian-American party. The reason was the success of the Atlantic submarine cable.

Together with the news of the project's termination, the men learned that the United States had bought Russian America for US$7 million from the Russian government. Frank Smith, a member of the Russian American division, wrote: "Torrents of news left us almost speechless." The effort had cost the WUTE $3 million.

Source: N. N. Bolkhovitinov, *Russian-American Relations and the Sale of Alaska, 1843–1867* (Kingston, Ontario: The Limestone Press, 1996), 160–67.

ing, early activities, and problems of the RAC. The second analyzes the climate, resources, and the subjugated and hostile Native populations of the region. The third critically reviews the educational, religious, industrial, and commercial activities of the company and its trade with California and China. The final part submits his recommendations. These, if implemented, would put the entire region on a sound economic and administrative basis freed from bureaucratic interference. Golovin was particularly concerned for the well-being of the Native population. He was also well aware of the region's abundant natural resources and its potential to supply the Asiatic portion of the Russian Empire.

Golovin's criticisms of the company's activities only emboldened those individuals already opposed to the RAC. One of the most outspoken of these was Aleksandr F. Kashevarov, a Creole who had been educated in Saint Petersburg at the Kronshtadt Navigation College and had served the company in the colony as a navigator and cartographer. At the time Golovin's report appeared, Kashevarov lived in Saint Petersburg, where he was working on an atlas of the Pacific Ocean. He wrote a highly critical response to Golovin's report in which he described the company's treatment of Natives. He revealed abuses that had never before been made public. But before his report could be published, Golovin, just returned from his North American voyage, died at the age of thirty-nine.[20]

Kashevarov did not want to criticize a dead man so harshly and rewrote his report. At this point, former governor Wrangel entered the debate and declared that he regarded the company more highly than did Kashevarov, but he conceded that the latter's accusations were based on fact. Wrangel's opinions carried great weight and subsequently became very critical in view of Kashevarov's revelations.[21]

The czar's government now referred the question of what to do about Russia's North American colony to a committee of fourteen individuals, including government officials, scientists, and members of the RAC. The committee members consulted previous reports, such as that by Petr A. Tikhmenev, a naval officer and historian for the RAC who had recently written a history of the company. Published in two dispassionate volumes, it details information on the company and its personnel from the 1790s to the 1860s. Together with the Golovin and Kashevarov reports and the opinions of former company governors Wrangel, Etholin, Teben'kov, and Johan Hampus Furuhelm, the committee published its deliberations in two volumes, titled *On the Organization of the Russian-American Colonies in 1863*.[22]

Although somewhat critical of the RAC, the committee recognized its achievements and advocated that it be preserved. It recommended state oversight of the colony, freeing the Native population from compulsory labor, limiting the company's monopoly rights and privileges, and extending a more limited charter for twelve years. The RAC was unhappy with the recommendations and filed its objection.

Finally, in June 1865 the czarist government published its directives for the future of the colony and a new RAC charter, which was to run for twenty years, until January 1882. The government was to appoint the governor, and the company was to be transferred from the jurisdiction of the Ministry of Finance to that of the navy. In April 1866, after discussion among the affected departments and the RAC, the czar approved and Grand Duke

Konstantin signed the last State Council decision on the matter.[23] The RAC's future seemed to be secure, and although the prolonged discussion had exposed the colony's weaknesses, few could predict that the days of the colony were numbered.

The Sale of Russian America

In the meantime, relations between Russia and the United States had become increasingly friendly. A major contributing factor had been an unsuccessful attempt on the life of Czar Alexander II in 1866. As soon as the news became known, Secretary of State William Henry Seward instructed Ambassador Cassius Clay to congratulate the emperor in the name of President Andrew Johnson on the happy outcome of the matter. He was also to assure the czar of "the sincere esteem and friendship of the American people." Congress unanimously adopted a joint resolution, expressing the lawmakers' deep regret on the assassination attempt "by an enemy of emancipation" and congratulating the Russian serfs that their emancipator had escaped death. The United States sent an embassy to Russia to give special significance to the congressional resolution.[24] After they had fulfilled their official mission to Saint Petersburg, the American embassy toured the country, visiting Moscow, Nizhnii Novgorod, Kostroma, Tver' and elsewhere in Central Russia. Everywhere they were received with lavish Russian hospitality.[25]

A number of factors contributed to the Russian decision to sell its North American colony. One was the exhaustion of the Russian treasury. The Russian minister of finance wrote that even if state expenditures were cut to the bone, it would still be necessary to acquire some 45 million rubles in foreign loans over the next three years to meet Russia's barest needs. Meanwhile, Stoeckl met with his immediate superiors, Grand Duke Konstantin, and Finance Minister Mikhail K. Reitern to discuss the cession of the colony. Grand Duke Konstantin identified three main reasons for selling the colony: The RAC was in poor shape and had to be supported with treasury funds; the development of the Amur regions needed attention; and continued close relations with the United States were important.[26]

Thereupon, Prince Gorchakov, Grand Duke Konstantin, Finance Minister Reitern, the head of the Naval Academy, N. K. Krabbe, Stoeckl, and the czar met in December 1856 in the Ministry of Foreign Affairs. All agreed to sell the colony to the United States after considering all relevant diplomatic and financial aspects. The czar asked Stoeckl to return to the United States and conclude the deal. The grand duke gave him a map on which the frontiers were traced, and Reitern told him not to take less than $5 million.[27]

Upon Stoeckl's arrival in New York in February 1867, he contacted Secretary of State Seward.[28] A former senator, governor of New York, and presidential candidate, Seward had served as secretary of state in the Cabinets of presidents Abraham Lincoln and Andrew Johnson. He had long been a believer in America's "Manifest Destiny." Russian historian Bolkhovitinov has asserted that Seward was not so much an advocate of unlimited American territorial expansion in the Western Hemisphere as a proponent for a worldwide American trade hegemony. He therefore considered it important to annex strategically important regions that would help the United States to control the sea lanes.[29] The acquisition of Russian America fit Seward's plans.

Negotiations between Stoeckl and Seward began in early March. It took the men more than two weeks to draft the treaty and agree on its text.[30] Stoeckl provided detailed reports about the progress of the negotiations to his superiors in Saint Petersburg. In a draft of his notes on the proposed treaty, Seward suggested "that Russia cede and convey to the U.S. [h]er possessions on the North American continent and the adjacent Aleutian islands, the line to be drawn through the center of Bhering straits and include all the islands East of and [i]ncluding Attoo." After some negotiation, Seward specified a price of US$7 million in gold.[31]

On March 12 President Johnson officially authorized Seward to conclude the treaty. Soon thereafter, the two men agreed on the draft outline and the purchase price of US$7 million. Stoeckl made certain to include Articles III and IV of the Russian-English Convention of February 28, 1825, which had determined the boundary between the Russian and British possessions in northwest America. On March 19, Seward presented the agreed-upon treaty text to his colleagues in the Cabinet. All agreed to the treaty. A few days later, on March 23, Seward sent a note to Stoeckl in which he insisted that the cession was "to be free and unencumbered by any reservations, privileges, franchises, grants or possessions," for which he was willing to pay an additional US$2 million with the approval of the president. On the same day Stoeckl sent a coded cable to his government, summarizing the treaty. On March 26, the imperial government sent its reply, which gave Stoeckl a free hand to sign the treaty. He received it on March 29 and immediately set out for Seward's home.[32]

Seward's son Frederick left an account of what followed. His father was playing whist with some family members when Stoeckl arrived. Stoeckl told the secretary that the czar had approved the cession and suggested that he would come to the State Department in the morning to sign the treaty. Seward instead insisted they sign it that very night, despite Stoeckl's objection that the department was closed and the clerks and secretaries had gone home for the day. Seward stated that if Stoeckl could muster his delegation before midnight, he would find Seward at the department, "open and ready for business." In less than two hours the Russians and Americans were at work at the State Department, and "by four o'clock on Saturday morning [March 30] the treaty was engrossed, signed, sealed, and ready for transmission by the President to the Senate."[33]

Seward, however, had on March 29 written a note to Senator Charles Sumner of Massachusetts, asking him to come to his house that evening because he had "a matter of public business" to discuss with him. As chairman of the Senate Committee on Foreign Relations, Sumner would play a major role in the ratification of the treaty, and Seward did not want to keep him any longer in the dark. When Sumner arrived at Seward's house late that evening, Frederick Seward and Stoeckl greeted him; Seward had already departed for the State Department. Stoeckl informed Sumner of the Treaty of Cession and the boundaries of the territory. Sumner did not express his own views and returned home at midnight.[34]

The treaty reached the Senate at 10:00 A.M. on March 30. Seward arrived at the Capitol earlier to

Sitka in about 1898, when a few tourists were beginning to arrive. The Sitka Trading Company (right) occupied one of the old Russian buildings. Just beyond is a small establishment advertising "general merchandise and photographs by E. de Groff." The sign on the roof to the right of the church advertises "Alaska Views, Curios." The Cathedral of Saint Michael, which dominates the town, was begun in 1844 and dedicated in 1848. The building burned in 1966 but the Russian Orthodox Church built a fireproof replica. Icons and furnishings that had been saved from the fire were reinstalled.

(Courtesy of Alaska and Polar Regions Department, Elmer E. Rasmuson Library, University of Alaska Fairbanks.)

meet with the Cabinet and then lobbied senators to vote for ratification. After President Johnson had submitted the treaty, it went to the Committee on Foreign Relations, which was to debate it in executive session the following Monday.[35]

For the next several days, Seward lobbied hard for ratification, both in person and through the press. Most newspapers endorsed the treaty; only Horace Greeley's *New York Tribune* strongly opposed it, but even the *Tribune* softened its opposition within a month. Several ranking military officers endorsed the purchase, as did many outside the military. Senator Sumner held the key to approval, and at the beginning he did not favor the treaty. After debates within the committee, however, Sumner presented

the treaty to the full Senate together with a three-hour speech defending it on April 8, 1867, ten days after Stoeckl and Seward had signed it. Historian Ronald J. Jensen has called the speech "a masterpiece of nineteenth-century oratory." The Senate approved the cession by a vote of 73–2 on April 9, 1867.[36]

The United States in Alaska

The United States was to take possession of Russian America immediately following ratification, although it had ten months to pay Russia the purchase price. The czar accepted the Treaty of Cession and rewarded Stoeckl with an honorarium worth almost

$19,000. The Russian government completed the ratification of the treaty by the middle of May 1867, but many Russians attacked it because they opposed any land cessions to foreigners and thought the price was too low. Eventually press censorship silenced further criticism.[37]

Seward appointed Brigadier General Lovell H. Rousseau commissioner to effect the transfer. He accompanied captains Alexis Peschurov, the Russian commissioner, and Karl Alexander Theodor von Koskull, the agent, to act for the RAC at the transfer ceremonies.[38] The three men were on board the *Ossippee,* which arrived in Sitka Harbor on October 18, 1867, preceded by several other U.S. Navy vessels. Brevet Brigadier General Jefferson C. Davis had been designated commander of the Alaska Military District. It was suggested that the name "Alaska" be used to designate the new military district.[39]

The transfer ceremony took place in New Archangel, now Sitka, on the afternoon of October 18. Two hundred fifty American troops drew up in front of Baranov's Castle, the governor's two-story residence overlooking Sitka harbor. A company from a Siberian line battalion drew up opposite the American soldiers; between them stood Prince Dmitrii Maksutov, the governor of the RAC, and his wife, the Princess Maria Alexandrovich Maksutova. Also present were the two commissioners and agent Koskull as well as a handful of residents, including some Tlingit Indians.

As the Russian flag was lowered, the *Ossippee* fired salutes from its nine-inch guns, which the Russian battery answered in return. While descending, the Russian flag got caught in the ropes. The soldier lowering it tugged harder, tearing its border and winding the cloth tightly around the pole. A pulley rig hoisted a soldier up the ninety-foot pine staff to detach the flag, which dropped onto the bayonets of the Russian troops below. Thereupon Princess Maksutova fainted. Then the American flag went up and the transfer ceremony ended.[40]

On October 26 representatives signed the official protocol, which transferred Alaska to the United States. Also included were the colonial archives, the fortifications, and Sitka's public buildings, including the governor's house, wharves, storehouses, bar-

Princess Maksutova, wife of Dmittrii Maksutov, the last governor of the Russian-American Company. Under the naval governors some efforts were made to establish settlements and missions and to provide education for some of the population.

(Courtesy of Alaska and Polar Regions Department, Elmer E. Rasmuson Library, University of Alaska Fairbanks.)

racks, batteries, the hospital, and the school. The churches and clergy residences remained the property of the parishioners. About twenty individuals received ownership certificates to their houses and land, and all other house owners received title to their houses without the land. Company property on Kodiak Island was transferred to the United States.[41]

Russian governmental authority had ended, and American rule had begun.

PART III

U.S. Territorial Alaska

Chapter 9

American Settlement of Alaska

THE ARMY, TREASURY DEPARTMENT, AND NAVY PHASE, 1867–84

The United States was not much better prepared to administer the new acquisition, now called Alaska, than the Russians had been. Little in the American past provided the wisdom and experience needed to guide the destinies of a land so distant and remote. The Civil War had just recently ended, and Americans and their political leaders focused on the problems emanating from that conflict. Americans were also generally far too enthused about the great prospects opening at home in both industry and agriculture to give much thought to Alaska.

Although residents referred to Alaska as a "territory," it was not a territory and did not become one until the twentieth century. Congress had instead made Alaska a military district and a U.S. customs district. In his final State of the Union address, President Andrew Johnson had devoted but a single sentence to the new possession, namely that "the acquisition of Alaska was made with the view of extending national jurisdiction and republican principles in the American hemisphere."[1] Nobody really knew what that meant for the future. Thus the region moved through three jurisdictions in its early years: governance by the U.S. Army, by the U.S. Treasury Department, and by the U.S. Navy.

Liquidating RAC Properties

In the meantime, in Sitka (the former New Archangel) Prince Maksutov, the governor of the RAC,

oversaw the liquidation of the company as well as the affairs of the Russian government in America. Maksutov was the only chief representative of the RAC after the transfer ceremony on October 18, 1867. Shortly after the transfer, Brigadier General Jefferson Davis ordered the Russian citizenry to vacate their homes to make room for the U.S. soldiers. The Russians complained to Maksutov, stating that the houses belonged to the RAC, but he was powerless to help and merely advised them to find other shelter. Some, thereupon, moved onto the company ships out in the harbor. General Davis next had the battery placed in the company's warehouse and stationed sentries at either end of the building. He forbade Russians entry without special permission. The American authorities clearly mistreated the Russians.[2]

The treaty stipulated that those Russians who wanted to remain in Alaska would acquire "all the rights, advantages and immunities of citizens of the United States" within a three-year period. For the majority of these people, most of them Creoles, individuals of mixed Native and Russian ancestry, the prospect of American citizenship and acculturation did not appeal. They dispersed, some to British Columbia, some to California and most to Russia.[3]

In 1867 the U.S. military and recently arrived civilian personnel probably totaled no more than nine hundred. In Sitka, the number of former RAC employees varied. Added to the several hundred "old

Sitkans" were Russians who had come to the capital from outlying posts across Alaska. They soon left Alaska, however, and the Native population of the subcontinent probably did not exceed thirty thousand.[4]

While the United States had gained possession of Russia's public properties, this did not include commercial goods—such as the warehouses in Sitka filled with furs and trade goods, including eighty thousand fur seal skins and thirty thousand gallons of liquor—or the company ships and trading posts, scattered along the coast, out to the Aleutian Islands and up to Saint Michael on the Yukon River. Maksutov's job was to sell these on behalf of company stockholders. The Treaty of Cession, however, was vague on distinguishing government property from private property. This led to repeated misunderstandings later.[5]

It is unknown what orders Maksutov received from the RAC regarding the sale of its properties, nor is much known about the sequence in which the sales occurred nor to whom a number of items were sold. What is known is that by early June 1867, some four months before the formal transfer, adventurers, mostly from Pacific Slope communities, had begun to arrive in Sitka. They were not pioneers hoping to acquire a homestead suitable for farming, but rather folks hoping to build stores, get rich through appreciating urban real estate, seek minerals, stake out city lots, and buy up RAC goods.[6]

Maksutov, in one of the first of these transactions, sold 160 acres in Ozerskoi Redoubt near Sitka to the American-Russian Commercial Company of San Francisco for $15,000. Financier Joseph Mora Moss, who headed the firm, apparently was interested in the red salmon fishery there and also may have planned to ship ice to San Francisco from what today is known as Redoubt Lake. There also is some evidence that Moss considered purchasing other RAC holdings. At about the same time, Leopold Boscowitz, a British Columbia fur merchant, asked Maksutov if any furs were for sale. To his surprise the prince told him that he could buy all those stored in the company's Sitka storehouse. The price was a low forty cents apiece, the price the company had been receiving. Boscowitz bought sixteen thousand fur seal skins, shipped them to Victoria, and

Brevet Major General Jefferson Columbus Davis, Twenty-third Infantry, commanded troops that occupied the first noncontiguous dependency of the United States. When Davis was stationed in Alaska, he commanded a few hundred soldiers and several forts.

(Courtesy of Alaska and Polar Regions Department, Elmer E. Rasmuson Library, University of Alaska Fairbanks.)

there sold them for two to three dollars apiece. After that windfall he tried to buy the remainder, but by that time Maksutov had received orders not to sell any more.[7]

Rumors soon circulated that the San Francisco firm of Louis Sloss and Company were prepared to acquire the RAC's extensive fur-trading network. In 1868 Louis Sloss combined forces with the successful wartime business promoter, Hayward M. Hutchinson, and steamboat captain William Kohl and created the Alaska Commercial Company. Hutchinson went directly to Maksutov and bought everything the RAC owned, such as steamers, fishing boats, wharves, salt, furs, and facilities in such varied places as Sitka, Kodiak, and Unalaska, as well as the remote northwest trading posts.[8]

Boom and Bust

The adventurers who had landed in Sitka believed that in a dozen or so years the town would be home to thousands of residents. They built competing stores and erected saloons and ten-pin alleys. Promoters squatted over the whole town and its vicinity and, according to a California newspaper, even "preempted the Governor's house."[9] The surviving RAC buildings in 1867 in Sitka, built of large, hewn logs, included the governor's residence, the saw-house, the hospital, barracks and warehouses, and also the Russian Orthodox Cathedral of Saint Michael. The Russians had built a stockade dividing the town from the Indian quarter, called the Ranche, which now was rather dilapidated. Even though the Sitka Natives had not tried to drive out the invaders, the Americans took no chances and had soldiers on regular patrol along the stockade.[10]

Soon after the ratification of the treaty, President Johnson recommended that since Alaska had become a part of the United States, Congress act to provide for its occupation and government. Unfortunately, Johnson was unpopular and narrowly missed removal from office. He wielded no influence with the legislators, and Congress spent little time on Alaska. It did, however, extend American laws governing commerce and navigation and prohibited the importation, manufacture, and sale of liquor.

In the spring of 1868 the District of Alaska became the Department of Alaska under the military Division of the Pacific. The same year also witnessed the arrival of four artillery batteries and the establishment of several new posts: at Fort Tongass, on a small island at the mouth of Portland Canal; at Fort Wrangel, also in southeastern Alaska; and at Fort Kodiak, at Saint Paul Harbor, Kodiak Island. In 1869 the army built another establishment at the old Russian post Fort Saint Nicholas, one hundred miles up Cook Inlet, and called it Fort Kenay (Kenai). It also sent troops to the Pribilof Islands to help the Treasury Department regulate the fur seal harvest. From 1870 until the army left Alaska in 1877, troops and post commanders were rotated about every two years.

During its ten-year tour of duty in the north, the army had but a vague concept of what it was supposed to accomplish. What it did, in essence, was prevent difficulties between arriving Americans and the Indians and enforce the provision of the Indian trade laws, which consisted in the main of enforcing the prohibition against importing liquor.[11] General Davis, who commanded the army troops stationed at Sitka, Fort Wrangell, Fort Kodiak, Fort Tongass, and Fort Kenai, virtually ruled Alaska, but the interior had no army presence, and the posts at Kodiak, Tongass, and Kenai were soon closed. Nothing was done to create a civil government, and for the next seventeen years Alaska remained under military rule. There were numerous proposals to change Alaska's status. One would have made the area a county of Washington Territory. Another one was the suggestion that Alaska become a penal colony.[12]

In the meantime, the town's residents, with the blessing of General Davis, drew up a charter, elected a governing council, and elected William S. Dodge, Alaska's first special agent of the Treasury Department, as mayor. Thomas Murphy started the town's first newspaper, and since he did not have a press available, he handwrote copies of the *Sitka Times*. The council even hired a teacher at seventy-five dollars per month. Unfortunately, the town's prosperity soon vanished as the port's commerce steadily declined. There were not enough Natives or soldiers to sustain the merchants. People started to move out, and the city council held its last meeting in the summer of 1873.[13]

Many who came and then left Alaska blamed the federal government for Sitka's decline and the district's misfortunes. Congress had failed to provide a long list of needed services. There was no regular mail delivery, and no lighthouses had been built to guide navigators in Alaska's dangerous waters. There had been no land surveys, and people were unable to obtain title to land. They lacked any assurance that their hard work would not be in vain. In fact, General Davis had used his troops to evict individuals who had tried to preempt lots for themselves. In his first edition of the *Sitka Times*, Murphy lambasted military rule. He wrote that only when Alaska had a civil government could the region "expect to hear of rich minerals having been fully developed by our latent industry but not before."[14] It is here that the myth of federal neglect of Alaska's needs was born, one that many historians subsequently used to explain the north's lack of rapid development.

The Limits of Military Rule

William Henry Seward visited Sitka soon after his retirement as secretary of state. He told his audience that civil government must come "because our political system rejects alike anarchy and executive absolutism," but he cautioned that, since fewer than two thousand whites lived among twenty-five thousand Natives, "a display of military force was needed."[15]

But was that really necessary? Alaska never experienced the wars between Native tribes and white settlers that had been characteristic of much of early American history. Personal incidents rather than unending conflict characterized the Native-white relations in Alaska. Both army officers and enlisted men behaved in a deplorable fashion, and many a night Russians and Natives alike asked to be protected from drunken military personnel. Misunderstandings were frequent because Americans did not understand or appreciate Native culture, while the Natives had difficulties understanding the new American rules and regulations.[16]

The army's task to govern Alaska was difficult because of the complete lack of laws, general orders, or any guidelines to sanction and direct the military's actions. The law never authorized the military regime, except for a statute that liquor be kept out of Indian hands. No legislation gave the garrison the necessary civil powers or defined the extent of its authority. Aside from the statutes governing foreign commerce, coastwise trade, and customs collections, no laws were in force in Alaska. Civil courts had no jurisdiction except in cases arising from a violation of those few statutes. The treaty of purchase or the general orders that established the occupation gave no more than the haziest guidelines.[17]

General Halleck, the commander of the Military Division of the Pacific, advised Brevet Major General Jefferson C. Davis only to respect the rights of the Russian subjects remaining in Alaska and protect their civil rights and liberties. He suggested that Davis thoroughly familiarize himself with the principles of international, constitutional, and municipal law so as to avoid mistakes in advising, warning, and governing the settlers. Davis handed these instructions unchanged to his successor, and they remained the only general guidelines the War Department or any other Washington authority issued as long as the military regime lasted.[18]

No courts or other agencies of civil government existed, so commanders created substitute machinery of their own. Military orders provided ordinances and laws for Alaska's small civil society. The staff of headquarters served as the administrative bureaucracy, military guards also performed police functions, boards of officers acted as civil courts, and commanders and staff officers performed duties normally allotted to governors and legislatures and mayors and councils. The responsible officers attempted to act fairly, resolve problems justly, and avoid the hardships associated with martial law and authoritarianism.[19]

Army surgeons and military hospitals provided the only medical care available in Alaska. At every port, physicians and hospital stewards took care of ailing civilians and made hospital and dispensary facilities available whenever time and space permitted. Citizens who could afford it paid for the care, and those who were too poor received free care and drugs.[20] For a time the army even provided food and clothing for many former employees of the RAC who had been left behind destitute, numbering about 375 in 1869. But the secretary of war, who approved this program in 1871, ordered that the rations "be as small as possible and only to prevent starvation." That forced the commanders to trim the relief rolls severely each year, and this assistance ended in 1873.[21]

Scientific Contributions of the U.S. Army

Despite the army's difficulties, it did make significant strides in exploring the territory, many of these made by the U.S. Army Signal Service, which remained active there until the 1880s. The Signal Service made meteorological observations in the Yukon-Kuskokwim deltas, cooperating closely with the Smithsonian Institution, which nominated meteorological observers who also were trained naturalists. Lucien McShan Turner of the service arrived

Nuklukayet trading camp and settlement near the junction of the Tananon and Yukon rivers.

(Reproduced from the *Report from an Expedition* by Lieutenant Henry T. Allen, 1887.)

at Saint Michael in May 1874. Before long he had assembled a striking ethnological collection, one of the best ever contributed to the Smithsonian.

In 1877 Private Edward W. Nelson replaced Turner at Saint Michael. Coming to the Yukon Delta region by way of Chicago and the Smithsonian Institution, he was instructed to obtain an unbroken series of weather observations in Alaska and to gather data on the geography, ethnology, and zoology of the area surrounding his station. Nelson achieved spectacular results in each category of his assignment. His collections were even larger than those of his predecessor, and since ornithology was his private forte, he sent over two thousand bird skins and fifteen hundred egg specimens to the Smithsonian. Through cooperation with the Yukon trader Leroy Napoleon McQuesten, Nelson obtained rare mammalian species from upriver, including types of mountain sheep, which he named after the dean of Alaska science, William Healey Dall.

Nelson devoted the bulk of his published report

to ornithology. Volume three of the Signal Service's Arctic series, handsomely illustrated with color plates, contained an appendix consisting of joint articles on mammals, fishes, and diurnal Lepidoptera, making it by far the most valuable contribution to Alaskan natural history up to that point. Turner returned to Alaska in the summer of 1878, this time to the Aleutians, where he trained voluntary observers and traveled widely collecting additional specimens until relieved in 1881.[22]

General Nelson A. Miles, the commandant of the Northwestern Department of the Columbia, Division of the Pacific, initiated a number of army explorations of Alaska between 1883 and 1885 in the face of opposition from a Congress reluctant to spend taxpayer money in a region with a miniscule white population, vociferous proponents of civilian as opposed to military science, the rival ambitions of federal scientific bureaus, and the deliberate obstructionism from the War Department and his own superiors. One of these explorations was led by

Left to right: Private Fickett, Lieutenant Allen, Sergeant Robertson.

(Author's collection.)

Lieutenant W. K. Abercrombie of the Second U.S. Infantry attempted to explore the Copper River Basin in 1884. He was thwarted by high water, ice, and glaciers in the Valdez area. As a captain he returned to the area and established Fort Liscum.

(Author's collection.)

Lieutenant Henry Turman Allen, a West Point graduate, in the spring and summer of 1885. Allen, with two other army men and two prospectors, ascended the Copper River, crossed the Alaska Range, and descended the Tanana River, reaching the Yukon River on June 25. After exploring the Koyukuk River, he began a return trip on August 9, intersecting the Yukon on August 21. The party then drifted down the Yukon beyond Nulato and reached the Unalakleet River portage to Saint Michael on Norton Sound, where they took a ship to the states.[23]

Allen had completed an original exploration of about fifteen hundred miles, traveling from below the 61st parallel, crossing the Alaska Range, and venturing to the Arctic Circle. He had charted three major river systems for the first time. Historian Morgan Sherwood concluded that "it was an incredible achievement that deserves to be ranked with the great explorations of North America."[24]

About one month before the outbreak of the Spanish-American War in 1898, the army organized three expeditions to explore Alaska. Specific orders stated that the expeditions were to collect "all the information valuable to the development of the country regarding topographical features, available routes of travel, feasible routes for railroad construction, appropriate and available sites for military posts, mineral resources, timber, fuel, products, capability of sustaining stock of any kind, animals, etc. . . . to give the Department information on which to base its action, and the public as full an understanding as possible of the resources of . . . this country."[25] Both military and civilian agencies benefited from the knowledge gained by the explorations of 1898. Others followed, and in 1899 the army began construction of a military road from Valdez to Copper Center, whence it was to go by the most direct route to Eagle City.[26]

Early American Mission Work

While the army had shown little interest in education during its ten-year rule, on an inspection tour of southeastern Alaska in 1875 General Oliver Otis Howard had found many Tlingits who wanted teachers in their midst. Commandant of the Department of the Columbia, Howard was a famous Civil War hero, popularly called the "Christian General" because of his religious and educational endeavors.[27] He returned to Portland supporting Tlingit desires for education, and if the federal government did not provide it, then he suggested Christian denominations should. In early 1877 a group of Christian Indians came to Fort Wrangell to cut firewood for the garrison. Post Commander Captain Stephen P. Jocelyn provided them room for services and hymnals and protected the worshipping Natives from interruptions. In September of that year the Christian Indians, aided by Jocelyn, established a rudimentary school. It attracted some tribespeople who wanted to learn to read and write. Jocelyn was impressed and recommended that a missionary society should be found to continue the work and that the federal government should grant it title to some land.[28]

Shortly before the army evacuated Fort Wrangel in 1877, a private of the garrison who had been impressed by the Natives' efforts to educate themselves wrote to General Howard and asked him to foster missionary work in Alaska. Howard gave the letter to Rev. A. L. Lindsey, his neighbor, who had become interested in undertaking missionary work in Alaska. The letter eventually came into the hands of Rev. Sheldon Jackson, the superintendent of the Presbyterian Missions in the Territories. Impressed by the soldier's letter, Jackson visited Alaska a few months after the army withdrew its troops. He was appalled by the conditions he found, and by his return he had become determined to commit his church to educate and Christianize the Natives there. Jackson recognized that the Natives would have to be educated to cope with the settlers' way of life before evangelization could succeed. He persuaded Amanda McFarland, widow of a Presbyterian missionary, to lead the school in Wrangell.[29]

Jackson had found his life's work, and the "Apostle of Alaska" committed himself to it fully. While Amanda McFarland stayed at Wrangel and labored under difficult conditions and without salary to expand Christianity, Jackson drummed up denominational support and recruited missionaries for the new field. McFarland publicized the Natives' plight, especially those of young girls sold as concubines to degenerate whites. Jackson published McFarland's letters to advertise the urgent need for Alaska mission work and to solicit support for such work, especially McFarland's goal of establishing a home for Indian girls to save them from concubinage.[30]

Jackson persuaded the skeptical Presbyterian Board of Home Missions to work on education and evangelization in Alaska and to recruit new missionaries. Jackson sent north Rev. John G. Brady and Fannie Kellog, niece of Rev. Lindsey of Portland, to open a school at Sitka. He also persuaded Samuel Hall Young, a recent theological seminary graduate, to help McFarland with her work at Wrangel. Young enthusiastically devoted himself to education and postponed the establishment of a new church until August 1879 in order to train elders, deacons, and members. Brady and Kellog opened a school in Sitka. It succeeded for a time, but then Kellog left to marry Young, Brady lost his enthusiasm, and the school closed in December 1878.[31]

Brady apparently was disenchanted with teaching in such a limited and crude school. He returned to the contiguous states and lobbied to establish an industrial school to train the Tlingits for assimilation into American society. The Board of Home Missions did not encourage him because it was reluctant to spend its limited monies in a new field. Jackson urged him to obtain federal funding, but discussions with the commissioner of education, Secretary of the Interior Carl Schurz, and President Rutherford. B. Hayes were fruitless. Brady returned to Sitka after he had ended his ties with the Board of Home Missions and started a career as a lawyer, merchant, and eventually territorial governor, reasoning that he could do more to Christianize and assimilate the Natives in these roles than as a preacher.[32]

The early work of Jackson and the Presbyterian missionaries laid the groundwork for the church-federal school system that developed in Alaska. Missionary work helped blunt the most destructive effects of American civilization and helped

A dead beluga (white whale).

(Author's collection.)

the Natives to adapt to change. McFarland's home for Indian girls was built, as was Brady's industrial school, which eventually evolved into the modern-day Sheldon Jackson College.[33] The mission workers also provided new leadership in southeastern Alaska, where the former leadership had departed in the economic depression of the late 1860s and early 1870s, and they also added a certain amount of social stability to society. In the early 1880s the missionaries also took part in the struggle for a civil government.[34]

Early American Whaling and Fishing and Their Effects on Alaska Natives

The efforts of American missionaries were complicated by the negative effects of American resource exploitation. Along the Arctic coast, Yankee whale hunters had moved into the Bering Sea by 1848 either by way of the Sea of Okhotsk or by passage through the Aleutian Islands. Soon as many as 250 vessels cruised along the edge of the ice pack in pursuit of the bowhead whale. In 1848 the first American ship, the *Superior*, of Sag Harbor, New York, passed through Bering Strait and entered the Arctic

Ocean. Others soon followed, and when whale hunters found the bowhead in short supply, they often hunted the walrus for its oil and tusks

The presence of American whalers had a disastrous effect on the lives of Natives who lived along the shores they frequented. Drunkenness and diseases soon ravaged the population. Ivan Petroff, Alaska's first census taker, reported the devastation of Saint Lawrence Island Eskimos that occurred in 1874, when four hundred or more people succumbed to famine and disease. Petroff observed that "living directly in the track of vessels bound for the Arctic for the purpose of whaling and trading, this situation has been a curse to them; for as long as the rum lasts they do nothing but drink and fight among themselves." John Murdock, an American scientist, and Captain Michael A. ("Hell Roaring Mike") Healy, of the Revenue Marine Service, called attention to yet another problem stemming from whaling activities. In the course of trade with whalers, Natives acquired modern firearms, which immensely increased their hunting efficiency and probably helped deplete the vast caribou herds. In addition, American whalers and Eskimos competed for the bowhead and walrus, soon resulting in reduced numbers and famine for the Eskimos. It has been estimated that approximately two hundred thousand walrus were killed between 1860 and 1880.[35]

By 1878 the Tlingits and Haidas were experiencing the encroachment of white commercial fishers on their traditional fishing grounds. The various Pacific salmon species, one of the most important food resources for various Native groups, were soon harvested commercially. In 1878 canneries were established at Klawock and Old Sitka. The salmon-canning industry spread rapidly northward and westward into central and western Alaska between 1882 and 1884, affecting Eskimos and Aleuts as well. From an initial pack of 8,159 cases of forty-eight one-pound cans, annual production quickly rose to approximately 2,500,000 cases at the turn of the century and averaged 4,800,000 cases during the 1920s.[36]

Whereas Natives had always caught salmon for their immediate and winter needs as well as for some trade, commercial packers caught as many as could be processed and sold. Using a variety of deadly efficient gear, such as stationary fish traps and mobile seines, they soon overfished the salmon stocks. In short, the story was the same as that of Alaska's other natural resources. Intense and often wasteful exploitation of the sea mammal, fish, and fur resources of Alaska soon resulted in severe damage to the economic base of the North's varied Native cultures.

Despite the paper assurances of both the Treaty of Cession of Russian America and the First Organic Act of 1884, which declared that "the Indians or other persons in said district shall not be disturbed in the possession of any lands actually in their use or occupation or now claimed by them, but the terms under which such persons may acquire title to such lands is reserved for future legislation by Congress," there was little actual regard for the rights of Natives to their land and resources.[37]

Enforcing the Law

The army's most important functions in Alaska were to control the Natives, promote amiable relations between them and the Americans, and to protect set-tlers from attack. Washington army planners knew little about Alaska's aboriginal groups but thought they were similar to those encountered in the American West. Officials feared trouble, especially in the early years when settlers would be especially isolated and exposed to danger. The army had sole responsibility for shaping Indian relations as long as it remained in Alaska. Treasury officers helped occasionally, but since Congress had not extended to Alaska the jurisdiction of the Department of the Interior's Bureau of Indian Affairs, its civil Indian service and agency and reservation system never became a part of Alaska's institutions. As it turned out, among the army's responsibilities and its greatest headache became liquor control and arms traffic, which proved an impossible assignment. Aside from that, there were no major confrontations between Natives and Americans, and there were no wars between the groups.[38]

Law enforcement duty proved frustrating because the garrisons exercised effective control only in the immediate environs of their posts. After all other garrisons were withdrawn in 1870 (Fort Wrangel was reoccupied from 1874–77), only Sitka's neighborhood was controlled. The troops were isolated on an island and had neither ships nor launches to give them mobility, so they could rarely preserve order or enforce law on the mainland or even on islands but a few miles from their posts. Occasionally the Revenue Marine Service or naval vessels provided transportation. A few customs agents and other federal officers, scattered throughout Alaska, helped spread federal influence. For the most part, however, the troops were marooned.[39]

Within this limited jurisdiction, the army dealt with some unusual crimes. For example, Fort Kodiak's commander twice investigated complaints lodged by two Natives, Squatzoff and Vaschrichoff. Someone had stolen the dead whales that they had caught and beached for future butchering. A military guard apprehended the thieves in both cases and retrieved the animals. The commander imposed a ten-dollar fine on one culprit, while the other spent twenty days at hard labor working for his victim.

On another occasion, in May 1869, thieves entered the Cathedral of Saint Michael in Sitka and stole a bible encrusted with gems, some crosses, and other jewels reportedly worth about $20,000. The case quickly became famous. The Russians and Creoles were greatly upset about the violation of their church, and the long-standing antagonism between them and the American community surfaced.

General Davis ordered a thorough investigation, and after almost two months guards arrested four men: Seldon Hall, a civilian; William Harrington, a former soldier of the Sitka garrison who had received a dishonorable discharge for stealing; and privates William B. Bird and Henry Brockway. The army confined the four in Sitka's guardhouse. A three-man officer board tried the men, concluding that Harrington and Brockway had committed the robbery but that the stolen items were worth only $1,236. Davis eventually exiled both men from Alaska after keeping them confined for several months.[40]

Murders, apparently rare in Alaska, posed problems of how to punish the guilty party. Commanders convened a hearing before a board of officers, which served both as a coroner's jury and a criminal court. That was the case when one Jacob Risenberger from Belleville, Illinois, stabbed a member of his prospecting party, one George Hoffman. The army immediately put Risenberger into the guardhouse. When Hoffman died a few days later, the incident became a murder case. The board decided that Risenberger had committed "unjustifiable homicide" and ordered the murderer confined in the military guardhouse at Sitka until proper authorities could handle the case. Risenberger, however, never came to trial. After he spent eleven months in the guardhouse, General Davis released the man, reluctantly, because there was no civil court in Alaska competent to investigate and dispose of the case. Risenberger promptly left Sitka.[41]

Military officers were also kept busy with various other civil problems. The army served subpoenas for local and federal courts in the contiguous states and took affidavits under oath for use as testimony in these proceedings. The military also took affidavits of citizenship, issued documents certifying nationality, registered property claims and deeds, notarized various documents requiring certification by a government agency, and processed naturalization applications. Boards of officers and post surgeons also held sanity hearings into alleged mental disorders among civilians and sent those adjudged insane under guard to a California sanitorium. Officers also served as probate judges to clear accounts, settle debts, and dispose of the belongings of deceased soldiers and civilians.[42]

If this was not enough, many troops behaved badly, especially so during the first few years after Alaska's transfer to the United States. The enlisted men were a hardened lot who drank excessively, brawled, fought, and occasionally mistreated women. Adding to the problem, in Alaska the soldiers and civilians lived cheek to jowl because the forts were not separated from the civilian communities. Life was monotonous and boring. It rained much, and there really was not much to do but to drink, gamble, and visit the dance halls and brothels.[43]

Consequently, Sitka's guardhouse was almost always full. Between December 1874 and January 1875, half of the Sitka command was court-martialed for a variety of offenses. By late 1875 and early 1876, however, the situation had much improved. Captain Joseph B. Campbell reported in March 1876 that only a few men under his command were guilty of bad conduct, and those were all "hard and well-known cases."[44]

The Army Leaves Alaska

The army had never felt comfortable performing its Alaskan duties. Over the years its disenchantment and discouragement had increased steadily, for several reasons: the army's inability to control the illicit liquor and arms trade, the lack of clear-cut authority, the uncertainty of Alaska's legal status, and the army's limited ability to provide law and order. Several years before 1877, many staff officers had concluded that the army should abandon Alaska at the first possible opportunity and turn its duties over to the Treasury Department or to a local civil government. Reduction in manpower and appropriations and increasing demands for troops elsewhere in the West also led many to believe the army should withdraw.

The situation was particularly serious by late 1876 because the War Department not only had to garrison the defeated South during Reconstruction but also had to field troops throughout the contiguous West to protect settlers from Indian attacks. In the twenty-five years following the Civil War, starting in 1868–69, the army fought eleven separate Indian wars.[45] In 1874, Congress cut the army to 25,000 from a strength of 30,000 authorized in 1870, and in 1876 all recruiting was stopped. Congress also long delayed the military appropriations bill for the 1876–77 fiscal year, which severely impacted War Department planning. With further cutbacks, the military had only 20,610 officers and men by the end of 1876. These cutbacks particularly impacted the Department of the Columbia, where troop strength fell from 1,194 in 1872 to 1,134 in 1876.

On June 25, 1876, the Sioux and Cheyenne Indians killed General George Armstrong Custer and his troops at the Battle of the Little Bighorn. The defeat stunned the nation, and General Philip Sheridan, who commanded the Division of the Missouri where the battle had occurred, pulled all available troops from both coasts to supplement his own forces. Pacific forces not diverted to fight for Sheridan fought Indians in Arizona and were tied down by a series of Mexican border troubles. All demanded more manpower.[46]

As troop strength and money dwindled and demands increased, the War Department increasingly questioned the usefulness of maintaining the Alaska garrison. Never enthusiastic about the northern duties, it considered abandoning the Sitka and Wrangel garrisons and turning the army's duties over to the Treasury Department's Revenue Marine Service. When a fire destroyed four sets of officers quarters at Sitka near midnight on February 9, 1877, it furnished the army with a reason to abandon its Alaskan assignment. Replacing the buildings at a cost of approximately $15,000 was out of the question. The expense of maintaining the one hundred–odd men in the remote garrisons was extremely high in view of the small population. All agreed the troops and money could be used better elsewhere, particularly since shortly after the fire General Howard had been forced to take many troops from his own and other departments to wage a long and costly campaign against Chief Joseph and his band of Nez Perce Indians.[47]

Upon the recommendation of the officers of the Division of the Pacific, the new secretary of war, George W. McCrary, formally asked Secretary of the Treasury John Sherman on March 17, 1877, to take control of Alaska, and Sherman accepted a week later. On April 10 the secretary of war ordered the removal of all troops from both Sitka and Wrangel. The troops formally left these posts on June 14 and 15, 1877, and sailed for Portland, Oregon, on the mail steamer *California* to assume duties elsewhere. Military control over Alaska had ended.[48]

Treasury Rule and the Alcohol Problem

The Treasury Department officially assumed control on June 14, 1877. M. P. Berry, the Sitka customs collector, his deputies at other ports, and other customs service employees were the only officials capable of exercising federal authority. They were to exercise control, augmented, as necessary, with occasional yet brief revenue steamer visits. When absolutely necessary, a cutter could be dispatched to meet emergencies. The Departments of War and Treasuries anticipated a smooth transition without any troubles.[49]

After the troops departed, Sitka practically became a ghost town, with almost no Americans, Europeans, or Creoles left. The handful remaining were panicked, fearing that the Tlingits would soon overrun them. They asked that an armed vessel be stationed nearby in order to ensure their safety. And trouble began soon. The Sitka Tlingits soon took advantage of the situation and informed the residents that since there was no gunboat or soldiers, they no longer had any fear. And even before the *California*, filled with the departing troops, left the dock, the Natives, helped by a few Creoles, took over the empty government buildings, almost completely emptied the hospital, and also started tearing down the stockade and blockhouses.

Collector Berry complained to his superiors in the Treasury Department that they had been misled to believe that there would be no trouble. He feared that if the government did not quickly send a vessel there was a good chance that the Tlingits would massacre Sitka's remaining residents. Others echoed these fears, including William Gouverneur Morris, special agent of the U.S. Treasury Department. The *California*'s captain, Charles Thorne, had told Morris that the Sitka Tlingits had become overbearing and that their chief had said that Alaska and all in it belonged to them. In response, the Treasury Department sent the cutter *Oliver Wolcott* to Sitka and Fort Wrangel in early September. It stayed only a short time, but its captain told the Natives that there would be reprisals should they cause trouble.[50]

Despite the dire warnings and fears the citizen expressed, Deputy Collector Isaac C. Dennis reported from Wrangel that most Indians were law abiding and that threats of retaliation kept most of the rest orderly. It was alcohol that made for trouble. Dennis knew that illicit distilling caused most disorders, so he raided and smashed at least eighteen stills. He also assembled a small vigilante group of Christian Indians to help in maintaining order. He also fined Indians blankets when they were caught distilling or bringing liquor into Wrangel. However, it was the transients—American miners and others who caroused through Wrangel—who made trouble, and Dennis had no control over them. These troublemakers also encouraged the local Indians to defy Dennis. The cutter *Oliver Wolcott* arrived in April 1878 and eased tensions, but Dennis resigned his position, disgusted with the state of affairs.[51]

Sitka, with a population of only three hundred white people, had fifty-one stills operating, according to one press account. In addition, many other stills operated in the Indian village. "Hoochinoo" sold for a quarter a quart on the street. Drunkenness abounded, and Collector Henry C. DeAhna reported that he was helpless to restore order. The Revenue Marine Service had only three steam cutters to patrol the entire Pacific coast and could spare cutters only for sporadic visits. In July 1878, for example, the *Richard Rush* stopped for a couple of days in Sitka on its way to western Alaska. But these occasional visits only temporarily brought order to the hoochinoo-fueled chaos.[52]

In short, the Treasury Department was in a worse position than the army had been. The Act of July 27, 1868, relating to the laws of customs, commerce, and navigation, as amended by the Act of March 3, 1873, prohibiting distilleries and placing control of wines and spirits under the War Department, was the only law in force in Alaska over which a court had jurisdiction. Since the War Department no longer had authority over Alaska, it did not issue permits for the importation of alcoholic beverages. The Treasury Department believed that this only encouraged illicit distilling. However, the import of molasses, the basis for hoochinoo, was legal, and between August and November 1878 Portland merchants sold and shipped 4,889 gallons of the stuff to Sitka and another 1,635 gallons to Wrangel.[53]

By the end of 1878 the Treasury Department's failure in administering Alaska became evident in the region's first lynching. Miner John Boyd, wintering in Wrangel, shot and killed another man in a fight over an Indian woman. Deputy Collector R. D. Crittenden, who had replaced Dennis, claimed he had no jurisdiction and refused to take charge of Boyd. Thereupon the miners constituted a court, tried Boyd, found him guilty of murder, and hanged him forthwith. Clearly the government had failed to maintain law and order, and problems in the region only accelerated in late 1878 and early 1879.

Then in the summer of 1878, five of six members of the trading schooner *San Diego*, all Indians, drowned in the Bering Sea when their canoe capsized. The lone survivor eventually returned to Sitka. There he and the relatives of the drowned men demanded wages of $1,400 and compensation for the five deaths. Customs Collector Mottrom D. Ball refused to meet their demand for compensation but promised that he would try to obtain the wages. Then in early January 1879 a miner who wintered in Sitka discovered that one Thomas Brown had disappeared. He suspected Brown had been murdered. Indians confirmed his suspicion, identified two Kiksadi clan members as the killers, and offered to apprehend them for a reward, which Sitka residents put up. The Indians selected Annahootz, chief of the Kokwanton clan, to get the murderers, who were then put into the military guardhouse.[54]

The young leader of the Kiksadi clan, Katlean, now saw an example of American justice that was unjust to his way of thinking. First, five members of his clan had perished without compensation paid or retribution taken. Then one American man had died, and two Indians were now prisoners in the military guardhouse. Katlean once again demanded compensation for the five drowned men. Refused, he allegedly threatened to kill five men selected from Sitka's merchants.

This alarmed many residents. On the night of February 6, 1879, several Kiksadis became drunk and rowdy in the Indian village, and word spread that the Natives were going to enter town and take vengeance. Sitka's white residents barricaded their houses and prepared their guns and ammunition. Twenty-five Creole families sought refuge at the home of the Russian priest. Annahootz and several of his clan members stopped the drunken Kiksadis from entering the town.

The next morning, Sitka's residents formed a safety committee, organized a guard to patrol Sitka at night, and formulated emergency defense plans. The merchants pledged not to sell powder, shot, and sugar, the last used to make hoochinoo. On February 9, 1879, the mail steamer *California* arrived at Sitka. After some discussion, the Americans and the Russian priest decided to appeal to the British Royal Navy at Esquimault, Victoria, British Columbia, for protection. Meanwhile, Collector Ball reported the Sitka situation to Treasury Secretary Sherman and requested army assistance.[55]

After checking with American officials, the captain of the HMS *Osprey,* Commander H. Holmes à Court, sailed the *Osprey* to Sitka to protect American lives on American soil. That same day Secretary Sherman ordered the cutter *Oliver Wolcott* to Sitka. The *Osprey* arrived on March 1, 1879, and the town's residents relaxed. Night patrols stopped, and the sale of alcohol resumed. On March 2 the *Oliver Wolcott* anchored in Sitka, which led the former patrolmen to get thoroughly drunk. The two commanders conferred, and à Court decided to remain in Sitka until the United States sent further assistance.[56]

HMS *Osprey* remained in Sitka for over a month, and the humiliation of having a foreign war ship, particularly a British one, protecting American citizens in a U.S. possession forced quick federal governmental action. The American press reacted angrily, claiming that the federal government had left American pioneers at the mercy of the Alaskan "savages" and concluding that the United States had disgraced itself "before the civilized world." It now was up to the U.S. Navy to erase the humiliation. On March 13, 1879, Robert W. Thompson, the secretary of the navy, ordered the USS *Alaska*, a twelve-gun steam sloop, to be ready to sail to Sitka. Captain George Brown proceeded to Sitka and arrived there on April 3. Secretary Thompson undoubtedly was unaware that he had committed the navy to ruling southeastern Alaska for the next five years.[57]

Early Commercial Endeavors

In the meantime, the Cassiar region, in British Columbia, had attracted miners north, but as its yields declined, the miners started to prospect the islands and mainland of the Alaskan Panhandle. Prospectors had made minor discoveries there almost from the time of transfer. In the mid-1870s gold discoveries near Sitka led to the incorporation of the Alaska Gold and Silver Mining Company in 1877. Major James Stewart, Sitka's former post commander, was the leading shareholder. In 1879 the company built a ten-stamp mill, but its revenue never even met expenses. Nevertheless, the presence of that and other small mines, along with the knowledge that southeastern Alaska contained mineral wealth, attracted mine workers, prospectors, and mining engineers, creating a basis for one of Alaska's industries.[58]

The marine resources had largely sustained a sizable Native population in the region for thousands of years. It was no surprise, then, that the abundant salmon runs attracted the interest of American settlers, especially after the canning process for preserving salmon was perfected. Treasury agent William Morris reported in December 1877 that a canning company had asked to temporarily use a government building at Fort Kenay while building its own facility. Morris recommended approval, and soon another company made a similar request at Sitka. The North Pacific Trading and Packing Company constructed a cannery on Prince of Wales Island in 1878. The Cutting Packing Company built a facility at the site of the original Sitka settlement on Baranof Island that same year. By 1900 there were almost fifty canneries in operation.

But the industry did not experience its great growth until after the turn of the century. As the late economist Richard Cooley wrote of the salmon business, "in the early years isolation of the fishing areas and the primitiveness of Alaska with its sparse population necessitated the importation of fishermen, cannery laborers, and supplies from the major population center in the south." San Francisco and later Seattle were "the main outfitting, employment, and financial centers for the Alaskan salmon industry." These cities, not Alaska, benefited most from the fisheries.[59]

The Alaska Commercial Company

In the minds of many Alaskans in these early years, the real power in Alaskan affairs was not the military or the treasury, but the Alaska Commercial Company. An outgrowth of the firm of Hutchinson and Kohl, the Alaska Commercial Company in 1870 bid and acquired a twenty-year lease from the government, giving it exclusive rights to harvest seals on their breeding grounds, the Pribilof Islands. Within a short time the company had extended its commercial empire to the Aleutians, Kodiak Island, and the Yukon River valley, having taken over the Hudson's Bay Company's post at Fort Yukon after the British had been ordered to leave American territory. A most efficient organization, the Alaska Commercial Company alone possessed the capital to build and maintain the ships needed to bring labor and supplies to the different parts of the vast territory.

As the company's economic power grew, so too did its role in the political and social affairs of Alaska. It provided schools and medical services in some communities and even took responsibility for the maintenance of what little law and order existed, especially in the interior. Alaska Natives were said to have received better treatment from the company than from petty traders, who could be expected only to look after immediate profit. The explorers and scientists who came to Alaska appreciated the company's help, and officials of the Smithsonian Institution were grateful for the many services the company rendered to its agents without asking for any compensation.[60]

The company's critics, however, were legion. They claimed that the organization was motivated solely by considerations of self-interest and held it responsible for much of Alaska's backwardness and for its failure to obtain self-government. According to the first census in Alaska, in 1880, there were only 430 American men living in Alaska; many attributed the decline mostly to the company's power in stifling individual initiative and discouraging people from settling the territory. There is no question that the company, because of its predominant interest in the fur trade, naturally enough desired the preservation of the wilderness and was generally opposed to settlement.[61]

The company was equally adverse to government regulations and the payment of taxes, and it made its voice known whenever there was talk of extending government services to Alaska or organizing it as a territory. There was much muttering and protest in 1870, when the company was awarded the monopoly for exploiting the fur seal trade of the Pribilof Islands even though it had been the high bidder. In 1867 the naturalist William Healey Dall accused its officers of seeking to crush all opposition and of not having "hesitated at force, fraud, and corruption" to attain these ends.[62] A congressional committee called on to investigate these and other charges absolved the company of abusing its authority, conducting unethical practices against its competitors, showing a lack of concern for the Natives, and using its political connections to obtain favors. Complaints against the company continued, however, long after the committee issued its report.

In 1880 the Alaska Commercial Company paid a 100 percent dividend to its stockholders.[63] The company's profit, much of which came from the exploitation of the fur seal monopoly of the Pribilof Islands, clearly indicated that the fur trade was still lucrative in Alaska. But changes could be seen in the Alaskan economy in 1880. People were engaged in various enterprises, some of which eventually surpassed the fur trade in importance for the Alaskan economy. For example, the timber industry, which was not to experience its period of great expansion until the middle of the twentieth century, produced primarily for local needs in southeastern Alaska. Along with the development of mining and fishing, entrepreneurs built new mills, and logging increased to meet the demands of these industries for lumber.[64]

Gold Is Discovered

It was mining that gave the impetus to Alaska's first population boom. After the 1849 California gold discovery, prospectors worked their way up the Pacific Coast in search of new eldorados as the older mining centers played out. They moved into British Columbia in 1859 to work deposits near the Fraser River. They moved into the Stikine River area and from there to the Cassiar region, and gold was probably first found in Alaska at Wyndham Bay in 1869 on a tributary of the Schuck River, about seventy miles south of present-day Juneau. Quartz veins containing gold had been discovered a few years earlier at Sitka. The 1880 census listed 82 residents of Sitka as miners, out of a total of 721.[65]

In 1880 George Pilz, a German-born mining school graduate who had been working in Sitka, grubstaked two men, Joe Juneau and Richard Harris, to search for gold. In the course of prospecting in the vicinity of Gastineau Channel, they found placer gold in a stream they called Gold Creek, and also at Silver Bow Basin at the head of the creek. Since only shovels and relatively inexpensive equipment were needed for this type of mining, the area soon attracted hundreds of gold seekers. Historian Robert De Armond has stated that no mining district in the western United States and Canada was "so easy to reach at such an early date."[66]

After about the end of March 1881, there was a monthly boat available from either Portland or Victoria to the Harris mining district, so named after Richard Harris. The town that grew up in the area was given the name Harrisburg; it was next called Rockford for a brief period, in honor of a naval officer who had assisted in organizing the district. Finally, the miners themselves decided upon the name Juneau. According to De Armond, Juneau was the only mining district in the United States that was developed under the auspices of the navy.[67]

The Juneau area would probably have gone the way of most other mining districts after the placers had been exhausted if it had not been for the discovery of lode, or hard rock deposits, which required expensive machinery to mine. John Treadwell, a California promoter, purchased a claim, called the Paris Lode, on Douglas Island from a prospector known as "French Pete" for somewhere between five and forty dollars, depending on one's source of information. According to the geologist Alfred Brooks, the site was worthless to French Pete, for he had "neither the experience nor the capital to develop a large body of low-grade ore." Treadwell recognized the area's potential, and by taking advantage of cheap ocean freight, the water-power sites, the abundance of timber, and a favorable climate, he succeeded in developing the Paris Lode—situated in the great pit known as the "Glory Hole," which eventually covered thirteen acres—into a very profitable enterprise.[68] The Treadwell Mine, as it was formally called, provided year-round employment, and Treadwell's Alaska Mill and Mining Company gave Juneau its economic base.

In 1890, Juneau had a population of 1,251, of whom 671 were Americans. It was a typically American town, with its variety of privately owned mercantile establishments, schools, and a hospital supported almost entirely by private subscription—and possessing, despite the edict of Alaskan prohibition, nine saloons and two breweries. It had thus grown from a small mining community whose inhabitants' chief interest in 1882, next to the staking of claims, had been "buying, swapping, [and] selling claims," as historian De Armond has observed.[69]

In 1886, as at other places on the Pacific coast, the area was swept with anti-Chinese riots. In 1884, Treadwell had begun hiring Chinese laborers to work in the mines. The American miners' antipathy to the Chinese, the late historian Ted Hinckley tells us, was not simply a dislike of the color of their skin. What the Americans resented most was the docility of the Chinese, whose hard work and willingness to accept lower wages than those paid to the Americans had made possible the wealth and great success of the Treadwell group, while the American miners suffered from hard times. It must be pointed out, however, that the miners were not interested in employment at the mill and spurned jobs offered by Treadwell. They disliked quartz mining and were interested only in placer mining.

A house in which some Chinese were living was blown up by jealous American miners in January,

THE GREAT TREADWELL GOLD MINE.— LARGEST IN THE WORLD. 59-804/95

The Great Treadwell Gold Mine, the largest in the world.

(Courtesy of Alaska and Polar Regions Department, Elmer E. Rasmuson Library, University of Alaska Fairbanks.)

and when the Chinese still did not leave Juneau, they were herded to the beach by American miners in August, put on two sailing vessels, and sent on their way. Upon hearing the news, Alfred P. Swineford, by then governor of Alaska, attempted, unsuccessfully, to persuade the officer in charge of the one small naval vessel on the coast of Alaska to bring the men back. The officer claimed that he lacked the force to "cope with the situation." Treadwell subsequently refused to press charges, and the matter was dropped. Asian labor was never again employed in the mines in Juneau.[70]

In 1889, Treadwell sold his interest, which by then included four mines: the Treadwell, the 700, the Mexican, and the Ready Bullion. By the following year this group of mines had yielded more than $3 million in gold.

The Yukon Valley was opened up to mining largely through the efforts of Leroy "Jack" McQuesten, Arthur Harper, and Al Mayo, agents of the Alaska Commercial Company. Though primarily interested in the fur trade, these men did some prospecting on their own, furnished supplies needed by the gold seekers, and even grubstaked a few of the prospectors. Mining on the Yukon had been confined almost entirely to the Canadian side of the border until 1886, when discoveries of gold near one of its tributaries, the Fortymile River, in American territory, triggered a new rush. Men left their Stewart River diggings and came to the Fortymile, as did a few individuals from Juneau.[71]

In 1893, two men who had been grubstaked by McQuesten found gold in the Birch Creek area, which subsequently became the gold-mining center of the Yukon and the most important mining camp there until the Canadian Klondike discoveries of 1896 and 1897. Circle City grew up as the supply point for the area. Its population of five hundred made it the largest town on the Yukon. The settlement had an "opera house," where stage performances were given.[72] A decade after the discovery of gold in the Fortymile region, the value of mining from the Alaska Yukon increased from thirty thousand dollars in 1887 to eight hundred thousand dollars in 1896. On the coast, mining at Juneau and elsewhere had raised the annual value of gold production along the coast from twenty thousand dollars in 1880 to $2 million in 1896. And since 1880 the American population of Alaska had increased from fewer than five hundred to eight thousand, most of whom were miners. Of these about one thousand were in the Yukon Valley.[73]

The Clamor for Self-Government during Naval Rule

In the absence of a formal government structure, the miners of Juneau and the interior, like their counterparts in western America, drafted their own form of frontier democracy, known as the miners' code. In their initial meetings they decided upon the boundaries for their mining district, drew up the rules for the staking of claims, and elected an official, known as the recorder, to register the site staked out by each prospector. They then prescribed the rules of conduct for the community: fines for minor offenses, banishment for stealing, and hanging for murder. A court composed of the miners themselves would sit in judgment and mete out the penalties.

In the meantime, the arrival of the USS *Alaska* in Sitka on April 3, 1879, marked the beginning of naval rule. Secretary of the Treasury Sherman still considered Alaska his department's responsibility, and so he appointed three of his Washington assistants, the chiefs of the Customs Department, the Revenue Marine Service, and the Special Agents Division, to act as a board and submit a plan for the government of Alaska. In late May 1879, the board reported that it had found no laws that permitted the appointment of local officials, and so even if they were appointed, their acts would be invalid. The board recommended that the laws of Oregon relating to the powers of justices of the peace and constables be adopted for Alaska to avoid the expense of drawing up a code of laws. The board submitted a draft to that effect and Secretary Sherman forwarded the

proposed legislation to Congress—which, however, ignored the matter.[74]

At the end of the Civil War the U.S. Navy had a fleet of nearly seven hundred commissioned ships, the largest navy in the world. By 1878 it had fewer than one hundred fifty vessels, and only thirty-three were seagoing steamers. Only five ships, including the USS *Alaska*, had been built since the Civil War. The navy, like the army, now performed its peacetime duties, namely exploration, hydrographic research and survey, protection of commerce, and general police duty on the seas. Old and obsolete ships were adequate for these tasks. Like the army, the navy had little experience in civil and Alaska Native affairs before its assignment to Alaska.[75]

The *Alaska*'s stay in Sitka was temporary, and the USS *Jamestown* relieved it in June 1879. Built in 1843, the sailing sloop was to be captained by forty-three-old Commander Lester A. Beardslee, who had already served twenty-nine years in the navy. Secretary of the Navy Thompson personally briefed Beardslee on his new duties. He was to study Alaskan conditions and try to restore and permanently establish harmonious relations between Americans and Natives. Since there existed no governing power nor a code of laws, he was to "use [his] own discretion in all emergencies that might arise."[76]

Upon his arrival in Sitka, Beardslee found a decaying little village with a population of 360 souls, all American citizens: 34 by birth, 79 by naturalization or statement, and the rest under the provisions of the Treaty of Cession. The commander divided Sitka's population into three classes: "a very few respectable people worth saving; a large number of Russians and half-breeds, miserable, poverty-stricken creatures not worth much effort except for our pledge to Russia," and a few unprincipled white men, mostly discharged soldiers (or deserters) "who make what little money they can by any scheme, however nefarious." Beardslee was surprised that despite its tiny population, Sitka had seven general stores and numerous service occupations, including four tinsmiths. The population apparently subsisted by "taking in each other's laundry."[77]

Beardslee believed that hoochinoo was Alaska's major problem. To prohibit or restrict the importation of molasses, the raw material for its production, would, he stated, be the "first and only step by which Alaska can ever be saved or developed." A *Jamestown* raiding party subsequently found three stills and much molasses and liquor in the town and thirty-eight stills and 150 gallons of hoochinoo and as much mash in the Indian village. Liquor, however, was only a symptom of Alaska's problems, namely, the absence of law and government. How to govern a mixed community, and numerous troublemakers, with no code of laws but the Revised Statutes of the United States, the United States Naval Regulations, and the Treaty of Cession presented major problems. Beardslee knew that neither his commission nor his broad instructions gave him the right to arrest citizens or inflict punishment, for that would leave him personally liable to civil proceedings. Yet he also knew that the navy's presence would be useless unless he exercised civil authority. He used his small brig space aboard ship to confine miscreants, and reopened the old army guardhouse. He sent marines ashore to act as jailers.[78]

However, Beardslee also wanted to gain the support of the people he was to govern. He therefore called a citizens' meeting on July 9, 1879, to discuss the formation of a local government with sufficient authority to restrain disorder and control the liquor traffic. Sitka's voters, after a couple of false starts, elected Mottrom D. Ball, the collector of customs, as chief magistrate, and the Russian priest, two merchants, and a salmon canner as city council members. These men adopted a preamble that "organized, adopted, and established . . . 'The Provisional Government of the Town and District of Sitka, Alaska.'"[79]

Beardslee had accomplished much within three months, having brought order, if not law, to Sitka. The secretary of the navy praised his efforts. The *Jamestown* remained at anchor in Sitka Harbor until August 1881. Beardslee used steam launches to reach beyond Sitka, and he was the virtual governor of southeastern Alaska until September 1880, when Commander Henry Glass relieved him. Beardslee earned the navy's praise and rose to rear admiral, the highest rank in the navy at the time, and took command of the North Pacific Squadron before he retired in 1898.[80]

Commander Glass and his successors were equally capable. The *Jamestown* was, in turn, succeeded by the USS *Wachusett* in 1881, followed by the *Adams* in 1882. Their captains patrolled the Panhandle, maintaining peace among Indians and Americans and aiding miners and missionaries, until August 1884, the end of naval rule in Alaska.[81]

The navy certainly was more popular than the army had been, but the clamor for civil government became more articulate as Alaska's white population increased. In 1881 the miners of southeastern Alaska met and elected as their "delegate to the congress" Mottrom Ball, the former customs collector and chief magistrate of Sitka. Ball never received official recognition, although the U.S. House of Representatives voted to pay his expenses. While in the nation's capital, he condemned the American neglect of Alaska and warned the House members that Alaska would not advance in civilization or population until they passed laws to protect the rights of persons and property.[82]

Ball's views were contradicted by Henry Elliott, who had been a member of the Western Union's scientific project and was considered by many congressmen as an authority on Alaska. A fervent champion of the Natives and of conserving the seals, Elliot saw no need for territorial government and its attendant services. He asserted in an article written for *Harper's Weekly* that agriculture would never thrive in Alaska and that the population would always remain small.[83] Elliott's colleague on the expedition, William Healey Dall, while enthusiastically extolling the potential riches of Alaska's mineral wealth, remained dubious about the advisability of immediate territorial government.

Most influential of all the spokesmen on Alaska affairs was Rev. Sheldon Jackson. Although he never became a resident of Alaska, he quickly established himself as the authority on the northern territory and spoke to hundreds of groups, primarily in the northeastern part of the United States. He appealed for their aid in his crusade against the evil influence of those Americans who corrupted the Native men with drink and ravished the Native women. In Washington he was well known among members of Congress, being the intimate friend and fellow churchman of Benjamin Harrison, later president of the United States and author of the

First Organic Act, which established civil government in Alaska.[84]

The Establishment of Civil Government: The Organic Act

Dr. Sheldon Jackson became the catalyst who prodded Congress to pay attention to Alaska. He lobbied Congress on behalf of the district, maintaining extensive contacts with federal officials in Washington, D.C., and corresponding with key leaders in Congress. In these efforts he eventually won the backing of Republican Benjamin Harrison, whom Indiana citizens had elected to the U.S. Senate in 1880. By 1882 Alaska bills were introduced in both houses of Congress, but as before, they died in committees.

When Representative J. T. Updegraff introduced a measure to provide schools for Alaska, Jackson, who appeared before the Committee on Education, was greatly encouraged. Although lawmakers again defeated the legislation, Harrison at least had developed an interest in Alaska's problems. As a member of the Committee on Territories, he had become acutely aware of Alaska's legal and governmental deficiencies. Jackson quickly recognized the senator's interest and linked it to his own proposals for an educational system. Consequently, the measures calling for federal support for education in the district became closely related to those calling for an adequate civil government.[85]

Between 1883 and 1884 there was much popular interest in Alaska. Jackson worked hard to take advantage of it by approaching all the leading Protestant denominations and by soliciting the support of the National Education Association and other teachers' organizations. When Congress convened in December 1883, the lawmakers were swamped with petitions from more than twenty-five states. Prospects for Alaska legislation, therefore, were bright, and by December 11 representatives had introduced four civil government measures in the House. On December 4, 1884, Harrison introduced his own measure (Senate Bill 153), and after extended debate, both houses passed the senator's measure, and President Chester A. Arthur signed the Organic Act into law on May 7, 1884.[86]

The act contained fourteen sections. It provided for a governor, judge, attorney, clerk of court, marshal, four deputy marshals, and four commissioners, who were to function as justices of the peace. The president was to appoint these officers and the Senate to confirm them for four-year terms of office. The act also declared that the general laws of Oregon "now in force are hereby declared to be the law in said district, so far as the same may be applicable and not in conflict with the provisions of this act or the laws of the United States."[87]

Senator Harrison perhaps best stated the intent of his committee when drafting the measure. When asked by a colleague whether or not the Constitution and laws of the United States were operative in the North without having been specifically extended by legislation, he replied that his committee had been able "to devise this simple frame of government for Alaska without meeting any constitutional stumps. We provided for the extension of such laws as we thought the few inhabitants, the scattered population, of that Territory needed."[88]

In his 1887–88 annual report to the Congress, Secretary of the Interior Samuel J. Kirkwood described Alaska's conditions in its civil relations as "anomalous and exceptional." He referred to the Organic Act as "an imperfect and crude piece of legislation" because it provided only "the shadow of civil government, without the right to legislate or raise revenue." It had not extended the general land laws of the United States to Alaska, but it declared the mining laws to be fully operational. There was no mechanism to incorporate towns and villages, and this deprived district residents of the benefits and protection of municipal law. It had created a single tribunal "with many of the powers of a Federal and State court, having a more extensive territorial jurisdiction than any similar court in the United States, but without providing the means of serving its process or enforcing its decrees." In fact, the Organic Act had well been described as a "legislative fungus, without precedent or parallel in the history of American legislation." Perhaps historian Jeannette P. Nichols put it best when she wrote that Alaska's Organic Act "evolved from a composite of honest intentions, ignorance, stupidity, indifference, and quasi-expediency."[89]

Many Alaskans protested that the act gave them

no rights of self-government and dealt only super-
ficially with their problems. No provision had been
made for law enforcement in the interior. The act
acknowledged that Alaska constituted a land district
and should be governed by the mining laws of the
United States, but as Kirkwood pointed out, it cat-
egorically denied that the American land laws extended to the region. It made no provisions for private ownership of property except for allowing the
mission stations to retain up to 640 acres of land.
Again, the Natives were not to be disturbed in their
occupancy or use of land, but Congress reserved
to itself the ultimate settlement of Native claims to
ownership of the land. Prohibition was retained.
Congress appropriated $25,000 for the education of
all children, Native and American, but this was not
enough to erect the school buildings or to pay the
salaries of more than a few instructors.

Clearly, the Organic Act of 1884 was far from
perfect. However, a beginning had been made in
bringing civil government to Alaska. The act ended
Alaska's uncertain status and made it a civil and judicial district, with the capital city located at Sitka.

Early Political Debates: Alcohol and the
Treatment of Native Peoples

President Arthur, a Republican, appointed John
Kinkead, a former Alaska resident then living in
Nevada, as governor, and named Samuel Ward
McAllister of California and E. W. Haskett of Iowa
as judge and district attorney, respectively. Almost
immediately a conflict broke out between the officeholders and Rev. Dr. Jackson, who had been
appointed general agent of education for Alaska.
Jackson and the missionaries who sided with him
championed the cause of the Natives, who, they
declared, were being exploited and corrupted by the
Americans. Kinkead, like Jackson a Republican and
a Presbyterian, was no enemy of the Natives, but he
strongly supported the Americans in their determination to develop Alaska. His opposition to Prohibition aroused the resentment of the newcomers and
of Jackson, who denounced him and the other presidential appointees as high-living, hard-drinking
men whose interest in the Natives was minimal.

In turn, Rev. Jackson's political enemies accused
him of using the money entrusted to him as the
general agent of education for Alaska solely for
the benefit of the Natives and his church. Haskett,
the district attorney, ordered Jackson's arrest on
charges of attempting to convert a public road into
the private property of the Sitka Industrial School,
of which he was a sponsor, but soon dropped the
case. When Grover Cleveland was inaugurated as
president, Rev. Jackson persuaded him to replace
the Alaskan officeholders. The president complied,
naming Alfred Swineford, a Democrat, as governor.[90] Swineford, a vigorous champion of self-
government, became the inveterate foe of the Alaska
Commercial Company, which he accused of wanting to control the territory—and, like Kinkead, he
also won the enmity of Rev. Jackson.

The controversy between the governors and Rev.
Jackson was essentially a struggle for influence in
the nation's capital over who should be consulted on
Alaska legislation and political appointments. More
specifically, the two were at odds over the liquor
question and its control. Jackson was a strict prohi-
bitionist for whom alcohol was an evil and largely
responsible for the depressed condition of the Alaska Natives. In Swineford's judgment, on the other
hand, Prohibition could not be enforced in Alaska,
as it "served only to flood the territory with liquors
most vile and poisonous to the enrichment of a few
who have been engaged in their illegal importation."
In his opinion the only way to control the liquor
traffic was to limit the number of businesses allowed
to sell liquor by requiring them to be licensed—
and to establish rules, strictly enforced, for selling
beverages.[91] Jackson was the immediate victor in
the struggle. Prohibition continued in Alaska until
almost the turn of the century, when a system of licensing along the lines advocated by Swineford was
adopted.

Jackson and Swineford also clashed on the issue
of education. Swineford, according to historian
Hinckley, "[did] not realize the appropriateness of
a Christian leader as General Agent of Education;"
rather, he believed that Rev. Jackson was interested
in foisting a system of education upon Alaska in
which religious organizations would be dominant.[92]

In the meantime, leaders also had different solutions to the "Native problem." The coming of the Americans was affecting the Native peoples more than the Russians had. For one, the Americans had penetrated not only the interior but also the Arctic regions. Their aggressive exploitation of Alaskan resources threatened the Native food supply in some areas.

Whalers, who had been present even during the Russian days, eventually decimated the whales. They then began hunting walruses for their highly valued ivory tusks and for their blubber, which was rendered into oil; the bodies were usually left to rot. Some Eskimos, having become enchanted with the goods that could be obtained from a commercial economy, soon took part in this reckless destruction, discarding their age-old practice of killing only those animals needed for food. Eventually whole villages were threatened with starvation.[93] In the southeast, Natives complained that the Americans were taking over the salmon runs and endangering the Indian economy.

While some missionaries, like Jackson, believed that education and conversion to Christianity were the answers to Native problems, Rev. William Duncan sought to lead the way by creating a model community. In 1887 he had brought to Annette Island one thousand Tsimshian followers from Metlakatla (Fort Simpson), in British Columbia, where his superiors in the Church of England had condemned his views on theology. There, on land obtained through a congressional grant, he built a new Metlakatla, designed to make the Natives self-sufficient. They were taught trades such as carpentry, seamanship, boat building, and other crafts. They built their own sawmills and cannery and engaged in other enterprises. But despite their prosperity, the younger Tsimshians in particular became restless under Duncan's authoritarian rule and in 1912 successfully petitioned the government for a school, which he opposed.[94]

Rev. Jackson also threw great energy into finding an answer to the Natives' economic problems so that they would not be dependent on charity or public assistance. His friend Captain Michael Healy, of the Revenue Marine Service, suggested that the

Pacific walrus hauled out on ice floe.

(Courtesy of Alaska Department of Fish and Game.)

Eskimos might be taught the cultivation of the reindeer, which was the basis of livelihood for the Natives of the nearby Chukotski Peninsula, just across the Bering Strait. Rev. Jackson, very much taken with the idea, immediately began a campaign of public subscription and obtained enough money to bring a small herd and instructors in 1891 to train the Eskimos in their care. Subsequently he secured a congressional appropriation to further the work. This began a new enterprise in Alaska, which, according to geologist Alfred Brooks, prospered despite Jackson's mismanagement.[95]

Alaska in 1896

By 1896, the year of the Great Klondike gold discoveries, Alaska's Americanization had proceeded apace. What had survived of the Russian heritage? Certainly, the Russian Orthodox Church, which Native villagers cherished and Native leaders, clergymen, and their wives fostered. Many Russian place-names on Alaska's map reminded its residents of the region's early Russian heritage. Particularly

Father Duncan's Metlakatla Christian Church, on Annette Island.

(Courtesy of Alaska and Polar Regions Department, Elmer E. Rasmuson Library, University of Alaska Fairbanks.)

Early Efforts at Resource Conservation

American concern over another industry—the seal fisheries and in particular the hunting of seals on the high seas—brought about a diplomatic controversy with Great Britain. Each spring the seals made their way from southern waters to the Pribilof Islands to mate. There the Alaska Commercial Company, the lessee of the islands, designed a conservation program to keep the seal population stable. Since an adult bull has his own harem and keeps the younger males away from the females, the company killed only the three-year-old "bachelors."

But other sealers made no distinction between male and female, young and old, and hunted them on the seas, where many seals drowned after having been shot. To stop this wanton slaughter, the United States declared the Bering Sea an American waterway on March 2, 1889, and prohibited all hunting of seals. American warships seized Canadian vessels and crews that refused to heed the edict, and Great Britain protested on behalf of its Canadian subjects. An arbitration tribunal, meeting in Paris, awarded damages of slightly less than half a million dollars to the Canadians, but the two governments agreed to limit the number of seals taken in a single year.

Source: Thomas A. Bailey, *A Diplomatic History of the American People* (New York: Appleton-Century-Crofts, 1950), 446–49.

Sitka as seen from a steamer in 1890, showing the Russian ward house in the foreground and Baranov's Castle in back.

(Courtesy of Alaska and Polar Regions Department, Elmer E. Rasmuson Library, University of Alaska Fairbanks.)

on the Aleutian Islands, many residents had Russian surnames. Although most Russian architectural landmarks had disappeared, those that remained, especially in Sitka, attracted out-of-state and foreign visitors. And last but not least, traces of Russian folktales were found in the folklore of some Alaska Native groups.

Americans who migrated north quickly spread far beyond the area the Russians had controlled. Since the end of the Russian period, the American population of Alaska had increased tenfold. These migrants had established new communities, and most of these newcomers either became independent miners or found employment in the industry.

Before 1884, in the absence of civil government, the miners had established their own codes to regulate affairs. After 1884, the miners' code continued to operate because the First Organic Act left much to be desired. Alaskans had a right to complain because the act had not granted them self-government and they still could not obtain title to land, nor could they tax themselves to organize the services they needed. Alaskans knew the framework of American politics. They had sent delegates to Washington, D.C., and participated in the 1888 national party conventions—but to little avail. The federal government and the Congress knew little and cared less about far-off Alaska.

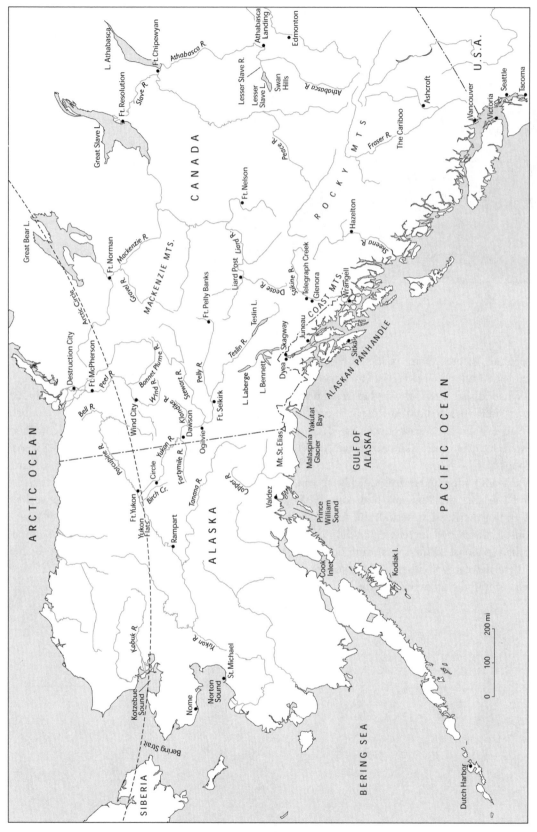

The Gold Rush in Alaska

Chapter 10

The Great Gold Rush and Its Aftermath

The Gold Rush has a prominent role in the history of Alaska, marking for some the beginnings of the modern era. It was indeed a time of great excitement. Thousands from all walks of life went to the territory for gold and adventure. With the new towns that sprang up came the first semblances of self-government, and Alaskans felt that they were beginning to receive the recognition that was their due. But the Gold Rush essentially remains an episode in Alaskan life and development, acting more as a stimulant than as a instrument of change. While it drew more people to the territory and resulted in a population that was to remain numerically stable until the great increase following World War II, those who came usually remained only a few years. But interest had been kindled, and indeed there was optimism concerning Alaska and its potential as the twentieth century opened.

Early Yukon Explorers

In the years after the Russians sold Alaska to the United States, adventurers were curious to discover what lay beyond Alaska's coastal mountains. The trail there led across Chilkoot Pass, a closely guarded property of the Tlingit Indians. "Chilkoot Jack" Benson, as the Tlingit named Kayich was known to white men, described in 1914 to a reporter the groups of white men he had led over the Chilkoot Pass in the 1870s and 1880s. On his first trip, in 1873, he guided the first American to cross the pass, prospector and adventurer George Holt. They reached Lake Teslin and the Hootalinqua River, crossing the headwaters of the Yukon River. Although the local Indians were hostile to any attempts by outsiders to cross the pass, the two men apparently slipped across undiscovered. When Benson attempted to take a large group of prospectors from Sitka across the pass in 1878, the local Chilkat Indians forced the party to give up its attempt and return to Sitka. Benson tried again in 1880 with a group of some twenty prospectors, headed by one Edmund Bean. The group successfully crossed the pass with the help of several U.S. Marines equipped with a Gatling gun, who negotiated an agreement with the Chilkats. The signed agreement stipulated that the miners would not trade with the interior Indians.[1]

Europeans had known the Yukon River for many years. The Russian-American Company had established posts for trade with the Indians along the river as far as Nulato and also traded with the Indians upriver. In 1847 Alexander H. Murray of the Hudson's Bay Company built Fort Yukon within the Arctic Circle in Russian territory. In 1869, Captain Charles W. Raymond of the U.S. Army steamed up the river to Fort Yukon and raised the American flag over the post, whereupon the HBC withdrew.

Despite much activity along the river, its upper course was not well charted. The U.S. Army dispatched Lieutenant Frederick Schwatka in 1883 to follow the entire length of the river. He did so successfully. Schwatka and his party scaled the Chilkoot Pass and at Lake Lindemann built a raft. On the passage down the river they noted gold in the river bar sands and met two bedraggled American prospectors, precursors to the thousands of men who would pour over the Chilkoot Pass in 1897–98.[2]

After 1880 small groups of prospectors reached the upper Yukon via the Chilkoot Pass. They tested the bars along the headwaters, but the main river was all but untraveled for 1,800 miles. Only Natives and an occasional free trader working on a commission for the Alaska Commercial Company traveled the river. One of these was Arthur Harper. Unsuccessful in seeking gold in the sands of the tributary creeks, he had become a trader, bartering tea and flour for furs. Along with his partners, Al Mayo and "Jack" McQuesten, Harper helped to open the Yukon Valley for prospectors who followed.

The three were pretty much alone for more than fifteen years, not seeing another American. They all took Indian wives, but they did not live like Indians. They and their families lived in substantial square-cut log homes with vegetable gardens in the backyard. Their wives were truly their partners, and they sent their children to be educated in private schools in the contiguous states. In fact, years later McQuesten retired to California, where his wife, Katherine, became the mistress of a large home in Berkeley. Upon his death in 1921, she managed their estate and headed the family.[3]

In 1874 the trio established their first post, Fort Reliance, which became the focus for future river settlements. A number of tributaries derived their names from their distance from the post: the Twelvemile River and the Fortymile River were so named because they flowed into the Yukon twelve and forty miles downstream from Fort Reliance, respectively, and the Sixtymile joined the Yukon sixty miles upstream from the fort. Later towns established at the mouths of these tributaries took the names of the rivers.

These three men and a fourth, Joseph Ladue, who arrived a decade later, were instrumental in the series of events that led to the Klondike discovery.

They extended generous credits to the prospectors and sent them off to promising sections of the country. They followed each substantial discovery by laying out a town site and building a general store. Their little steamboat, the New Racket, was their connection to the outside world. They maintained a casual relationship with the Alaska Commercial Company in San Francisco. In the early years they were on its payroll but free to prospect if they so desired. Later they bought their supplies from the company but were independent contractors who traded on their own. Other traders who worked along the river had similar arrangements with the company, but Harper, McQuesten, and Mayo were most responsible for the Yukon's mining development.[4]

A number of smaller gold rushes into the Yukon Valley occurred before the Klondike stampede, and several mining camps developed along the river. Placer, or "free gold"—that gold which geological forces had ground into dust and nuggets—attracted the first miners. Any man with a strong back, a shovel, and a pan could mine it, unlike gold found in veins in hardrock, which required capital and machinery to mine.[5]

By 1886 about two hundred miners had passed across the Chilkoot Pass and worked their way three hundred miles down the river to the mouth of the Stewart River. On that river's sandbars they mined one hundred thousand dollars worth of fine placer gold in a single year. Harper and the others quickly built a trading post at the Stewart's mouth, and McQuesten left for San Francisco for more supplies because the partners expected the flow of prospectors to increase.[6]

Harper persuaded a couple of prospectors to try the Fortymile River, which flowed into the Yukon one hundred miles farther downriver. There they found the gold that Harper had failed to discover years earlier. It was coarse gold, nuggets—the kind miners sought. As soon as the news reached the Stewart, the miners deserted the area and rushed to the new strike. Harper suspected that as soon as the news of the new strike reached the outside world, hundreds of men would come over the Chilkoot Pass down to the new diggings. The provisions in the country were insufficient to feed the expected hordes, and he had to notify McQuesten in San

Francisco to increase his orders or there would be starvation. But winter had come and sealed off the region. George Williams, a steamboat man, and his Indian companion volunteered to take the message to McQuesten. The two suffered incredible hardships. They made it to Dyea Inlet, where Williams died at John J. Healy's trading post in March 1887. His dying message, which his Indian companion relayed, was that gold had been discovered.[7]

As a result of William's message, a little settlement took shape at the junction of the Fortymile and Yukon Rivers. The men of this little community were a mixed lot, including Civil War veterans, Indian fighters, English "remittance men," and prospectors from the far west.[8] Although the community of Fortymile was on Canadian territory, it was initially an American town. Its supplies came from the United States without custom duties, and miners sent out mail franked with American stamps. This ended with the arrival in 1894 of Inspector Charles Constantine of the Northwest Mounted Police, who was joined by a detachment of twenty men a year later. Shortly thereafter, the inspector abolished the miners' meeting, an American institution with the force of law that had settled disputes until then.[9]

In 1894, Circle City developed further downstream from Fortymile, on American territory. For several years McQuesten and Harper had grubstaked miners to search the region for so-called Preacher's Creek, on which a missionary had once seen gold in abundance. Finally, in 1893, two Russian Creoles found the creek in the headwaters of Birch Creek near the Arctic Circle. Within a year the district produced $400,000 in gold.

Circle City was McQuesten's town; by this time his former partners had dispersed.[10] By 1896, Circle City had a population of 1,200. Known as "the Paris of Alaska," it had acquired a two-story trading post, a music hall, two theaters, eight dance halls, and twenty-eight saloons. The North American Trading Company opened a store in competition with McQuesten's Alaska Commercial Company store. The Episcopal Church purchased land on which to build a hospital, and the *Chicago Daily Record* sent a foreign correspondent into town, which now called itself "the largest log town in the world."[11]

One of the prospectors was Robert Henderson, a Nova Scotian who had searched for gold all over the world for practically all his life and not found it. He and his two companions drifted on the Yukon River until they reached the mouth of the Sixtymile, whose tributaries meandered back toward the headwaters of the Fortymile. On an island they saw a small collection of cabins and tents, the trading post of Harper and Ladue. The little community bore the name of Ogilvie after William Ogilvie, the Canadian who had surveyed the Alaska–British Northwest Territories boundary.

Ogilvie was located about one hundred miles upstream from Fortymile. Between these two settlements, two rivers joined the Yukon from the right (looking downstream): the Indian River, about thirty miles downstream from Ogilvie, and the Thron-diuck River, another thirty miles farther down. Ladue had explored the latter some years earlier but had found no gold. He now believed that the Indian River region contained gold, and he extolled its promises to every prospector who stopped at the post. He persuaded Henderson, whose companions had left the north, to try his hand once again.

For the next two years Henderson searched the Indian River and its tributaries for gold—finding a little, but never enough for him. Eventually he climbed a rounded mountain that rose above the other hills. At the summit he saw hill upon hill, valley after valley, gulch after gulch, as far as he could see. Creeks radiated out from the summit, likened by Gold Rush historian Pierre Burton to "the spokes of a wheel, with [Henderson] at the hub, three falling off toward the Indian River and three more, on the far side, running to some unknown stream." Henderson did not know that these were six of the richest gold creeks in the world. He panned in a little creek near the dome, and recovered about eight cents of gold in his pan. That was good enough for him. He returned over the divide to the Indian River, where he found twenty men panning for gold. He persuaded three to come with him to the creek, which he named Gold Bottom. By the midsummer of 1896, the four men had recovered $750 in gold. Henderson, thereupon, returned to Ogilvie for supplies and on the way told each man he met about the V-shaped valley in the back of the hills.[12]

Henderson got his supplies and drifted down the Yukon toward the Thron-diuck, known as one of the best salmon streams in the Yukon. Its name in the local language meant "Hammer-water," so called because the Natives drove stakes across its shallow mouth where they anchored their nets. The Americans called it the Klondike. There, among the smell of drying fish, Henderson met George Washington Carmack, called "McCormick." He was known as a "squawman"—that is, he wanted to be an Indian in a land where most everyone else wanted to be a miner. His wife, Kate, was the daughter of a Tagish chief. Carmack spoke both the Chilkoot and Tagish dialects and had worked with other Indians as a packer on the Chilkoot Pass. By the time he and his wife moved into the interior with her two brothers, the couple had three or four children.[13]

Henderson told Carmack about the strike at Gold Bottom and suggested that he probably could stake a claim there. Henderson made it clear, however, that he did not "want any damn Siwashes[14] staking on the creek." That last remark rankled Carmack and his brothers-in-law, called Skookum Jim and Tagish Charlie. In any event, Carmack and his family moved on to the fork of Rabbit Creek and soon made camp for the night. The next day was August 16, a day still celebrated as a holiday in the Yukon Territory today. Who found the first nugget is unclear, as Carmack, Kate, Skookum Jim, and Tagish Charlie all claimed the honor. At any rate, they found much gold. A panful yielded a quarter of an ounce, worth about one dollar. A ten-cent pan had always been an excellent prospect, so this was an incredible find.

After the discovery, Carmack became a miner, and he and his brothers-in-law staked claims on Rabbit Creek, soon renamed Bonanza Creek. Under Canadian mining law, no one may stake more than one claim in any mining district except the discoverer, who can stake two. The three men did not tell Henderson, who was waiting for news on the far side of the hill, because he had alienated them with his anti-Indian views. Carmack told four Nova Scotians he met struggling up the Thron-diuck about his discovery and gave them directions to his claim. On his way to Fortymile to record his claim, he told everyone he met about his strike. Soon Fortymile

emptied, and as the news spread up and down the Yukon Valley the little camps emptied and men rushed to the Klondike.[15]

Getting to the Gold

The rush was on, and by the end of August all of Bonanza Creek had been staked. Prospectors spread out across the Klondike watershed and staked claims. By the spring of 1897 a tent town had sprung up along the Yukon's margins near the Klondike's mouth, called Dawson. That summer the *Portus B. Ware* and the *Alice* steamed down the Yukon. More than eighty prospectors had taken passage on the two boats, loaded with gold. At Saint Michael the passengers transferred to the ocean-going vessels *Portland*, destined for Seattle, and the Alaska Commercial Company's *Excelsior*, bound for San Francisco. The *Portland* arrived in Seattle on the morning of July 17, 1897. Some five thousand people greeted the ship because the *Excelsior* had arrived in San Francisco on July 15. The Klondike stampede started instantly.[16]

Men flocked from all parts of the globe to one of the world's greatest gold rushes, which eventually yielded more than $150 million worth of the yellow metal. Americans clamored for information about Alaska and the north, unaware that the Klondike was in Canada's Yukon territory. The hardships of the prospectors, many of whom were Americans, became front-page news stories for the "yellow press," then in its infancy. Since Alaska was the gateway to the Klondike, it prospered. New settlements developed, and businesses sprang up to meet the needs of those going to the new El Dorado. Alfred Brooks, the U.S. Geological Survey geologist who first came to Alaska in 1898 and later became chief Alaskan geologist, credited miners from the Klondike with advancing the opening of Alaska's gold fields by many years.[17]

Although it was possible to make the journey to the Klondike entirely through Canadian territory, most of the gold seekers preferred the more accessible routes from Alaskan ports. Some went entirely by water, departing by ship from San Francisco or Seattle to Saint Michael, on Norton Sound, and there transferring to a river craft going up the

Soapy Smith

Almost overnight, Skagway, the supply center for the Yukon, burgeoned into Alaska's largest town. For those finding employment there, Skagway was the end of the journey, while others waited sometimes for months on end for favorable weather to leave for Dawson or for a ship to take them home. The town achieved a great deal of notoriety, largely as a result of the activities of Jefferson C. Smith and his gang. In the autumn of 1897, because of the virtual nonexistence of formal government authority, "Soapy," as he was called, was able to make himself master of Skagway and terrorize its inhabitants.

Smith's men, stationed along Seattle's waterfront, advised travelers where to go and whom to see in Skagway. Upon arriving in town, the travelers would be met by other members of the gang, taken under Soapy's protection, and very often fleeced of their money, either at gunpoint or in crooked gambling games. Returnees from Dawson might be treated in similar fashion. Newcomers to Skagway were encouraged to send telegrams to their loved ones announcing their safe arrival. Not long afterward they would be asked to pay an additional five dollars for return messages that had been sent "collect." The only problem was that no telegraph line existed in Skagway. Like a Mafia godfather, Smith was regarded by some as a great public benefactor, for as the head of the local welfare agency he was most generous to those in Skagway who found themselves destitute. A patriot, Smith organized volunteers for service in the war against Spain. The secretary of war, however, politely declined their help.

Smith's rule came to an end in July 1898. Under the leadership of Frank Reid, a surveyor, angry townspeople formed a vigilante group to rid Skagway of the outlaws. Reid himself, at the head of the posse, challenged Smith. They exchanged shots, and Smith died instantly. Reid died a few hours later, a martyr in defense of law and order.

Source: William R. Hunt, *North of 53°: The Wild Days of the Alaska-Yukon Mining Frontier, 1870–1914* (New York: Macmillan Publishers, 1974), 37–43.

Yukon to Dawson, the metropolis of the Klondike. This was the easiest but also the longest in distance and most expensive route, and late in the season it was threatened by a freeze-up of the river that could leave passengers stranded until the spring thaws. The most celebrated route was the Trail of '98 from the head of Lynn Canal, in the Alaska Panhandle, across the White Pass or the Chilkoot Pass. The Chilkoot, accessible from Dyea, today a ghost town, was shorter but steeper. The White Pass, out of Skagway, had the advantage that animals could be used for transporting supplies. Hun-dreds of horses, frequently overloaded by incompetent or brutal masters, slid to their deaths on the slippery, boulder-strewn trail.

After crossing the passes, the thousands of gold seekers built boats and rafts along the headwaters of the Yukon River. They launched their home-made crafts, navigated across Lake Bennett, and proceeded down the Yukon to their destination. For many, the most difficult part of the journey was the climb to the summit of the passes. The Canadian government required that each man have at least one year's supply of food. The food, together

Moore's Wharf, Skagway.

(Courtesy of Alaska and Polar Regions Department, Elmer E. Rasmuson Library, University of Alaska Fairbanks.)

with other necessities, such as medical supplies, tools, and camping equipment, might weigh several tons. It was common for two men to form a team, push part of their cargo on sleds, and carry as much as 150 pounds on their backs to the summit of the pass. Then, after reaching the top, one man might go back for another load while the other stood guard, and so they would alternate until they had brought up all their possessions. The climb was dangerous as well as arduous. On April 3, 1898, a great snowslide took the lives of forty-three persons near Chilkoot Pass.

The Gold Strike at Nome

Alaska soon experienced its own gold rush on the Seward Peninsula, the tip of which is only sixty miles from Siberia. Daniel Libby, who had worked on the Western Union Telegraph Extension (see chapter 8), had found gold there in 1866, but it was not until 1897 that he returned to the area. Libby and three partners left San Francisco on August 18, 1897, on board the steamer *North Fork* bound for Golovin Bay. The four organized the first mining district on the peninsula at Council City. Then on September 22, 1898, three prospectors, Jafet Linde-

Freight and supplies being landed on the Nome beach, 1900.

(Courtesy of Mulligan Album, Alaska and Polar Regions Archives, Elmer E. Rasmuson Library, University of Alaska Fairbanks.)

berg, Jon Brynteson, and Eric Lindblom, made their great strike at Anvil Creek, and the Nome mining district came into existence.

No great stampede followed immediately. Prospectors had become leery of new El Dorados. Some of the newcomers came from Kotzebue, where they had pursued riches in vain. Others, returning from the Klondike by way of the Yukon River, decided after their arrival at Saint Michael that they had little to lose and made the one-hundred-mile crossing to Nome to try their luck again. But after the ice had gone out in the spring of 1899 and ships arrived in Seattle laden with treasure from the peninsula, the rush was on. By October more than three thousand men were working at Nome.

Life at Nome was much different from that in the Klondike. Although the place was more readily accessible, living conditions in Nome were more difficult. Most of the Seward Peninsula is barren of trees. Aside from driftwood, all lumber had to be imported, and it was almost impossible for miners to build cabins for themselves or to secure fuel for heating. There was little game on the Seward Peninsula. Climatic conditions made vegetable growing

Members of the U.S. Signal Corps become a hunting detail to replenish the food cache at Seward, Alaska, June 10, 1927. (Courtesy of the National Archives.)

impossible. A person unable to obtain lodging at Nome or its vicinity in winter had no choice but to leave.[18]

In the words of geologist Brooks, Nome in the summer of 1899 "was anything but a contented community."[19] Its problems were complicated by a general air of lawlessness combined with numerous instances of claim jumping. Professional claim takers, armed with powers of attorney, had been busy filing claims for themselves and others, a practice contrary to American law since no gold had been found at the time they made their applications. Their claims, as well as those held by foreigners, were challenged by newcomers who were incensed to find that all the gold-bearing areas had apparently been staked.

Mining had come almost to a standstill, and Nome appeared to be on the verge of civil war.

But within a few days the discovery that Nome's beaches contained gold pushed these controversies into the background. Beach mining is easier than creek mining, for there is never any frozen material to thaw and the equipment needed is minimal. Access to the beaches was apparently open to all, though a mining company with adjacent claims tried to collect royalties. When the miners refused to pay, an attempt was made to evict them from the beaches, but the opposition was too great. By the summer of 1900, Nome was a tent city with more than twenty thousand men working its "golden sands."[20]

Judge James Wickersham feeds a moose.

(Courtesy of Alaska and Polar Regions Department, Elmer E. Rasmuson Library, University of Alaska Fairbanks.)

Law Comes to the Gold Country

Nome was wide open, condemned by moralists as comparable only to Skagway in its flouting of the law and disregard of convention. "Shootouts, muggings, and saloon brawls," according to historian William R. Hunt, "made life insecure." Brooks reported that in all his years of travel throughout Alaska and the Yukon, Nome was the only place where he carried a gun or felt any apprehension of being robbed. In 1900 the town was filled with pimps, prostitutes, conmen, and gamblers. It had fifty saloons, and that figure soon doubled.[21]

Therefore C. S. Johnson, the judge for the District Court of Alaska, headquartered in Sitka, decided to hold court in the various new Gold Rush communities. In the summer of 1899 Judge Johnson, accompanied by A. J. Daly, the U.S. attorney, and Governor John G. Brady, headed for Dawson and from there traveled down the Yukon River, holding terms of court at settlements along the river. They stopped at Saint Michael, went to Nome, and then returned by way of Dutch Harbor, stopping at various places on the return trip to administer the laws of the land.

It was a long circuit, spanning approximately seven thousand miles and taking almost all summer to complete.

There was not enough time to deal with the many complicated cases. Johnson appointed Alonzo Rawson as U.S. commissioner and told him not to try any title cases because his jurisdiction did not extend to this sort of litigation. The judge, decked out in long rubber boots and a yellow rain slicker, held court in a leaky but spacious tent. Historian Edward S. Harrison described the first session of the court as follows: "The judge instructed a bailiff to convene court, and the 'Hear ye! Hear ye!' was punctuated by the patter of rain on the roof. The litigants and attorneys sat upon improvised chairs and boxes and the spectators uncovered and remained standing, and for the first time in Nome the Federal Court of the District of Alaska was in session."[22]

In response to the gold discoveries, Congress passed and President William McKinley signed into law on June 6, 1900, a measure "making further provisions for a civil government for Alaska." Section 4 of the act divided Alaska into three judicial districts and provided for the appointment of three district court judges, each presiding over a court "of general jurisdiction in civil, criminal, equity, and admiralty cases" in the "district to which they may be respectively assigned by the President."[23]

President McKinley appointed James Wickersham, an attorney from Tacoma, Washington, to fill the bench at Eagle on the Yukon River in the third judicial division; Melville C. Brown of Wyoming to the bench in the first judicial division headquartered in Juneau; and Arthur H. Noyes, a lawyer who had practiced in Grand Forks, North Dakota, and Minneapolis, Minnesota, to the judgeship in the second judicial division at Nome. Noyes was to become infamous in the so-called Nome gold conspiracy.[24]

While the argonauts headed for Nome in great numbers, the U.S. Senate debated a civil code for Alaska, partially designed to remedy the Nome situation. The Nome gold rush figured prominently in the congressional debates about the civil code and dominated discussions in the Senate. What few senators seemed to realize was that the 1900 civil code was put together in the middle of a conspiracy designed to steal the richest claims in the Nome district. In fact, framing the civil code was part of the contemplated fraud.[25]

The Nome Gold Conspiracy

In 1900 Alexander McKenzie, a longtime member of the Republican National Committee from North Dakota, almost succeeded in pulling off one of the most spectacular frauds in American legal history. He started by manipulating the Alaska Civil Code in Congress. The basis for his scheme was the uncertainty over whether aliens could legally stake mining claims; that was the issue that had agitated the miners in the Nome district since Lindeberg, Lindblom, and Brynteson had made their rich strike.

Many prospectors believed, or wanted to believe, that it was legal to restake, or "jump," any claim located by an alien. However, according to American law and Supreme Court rulings, only the government had the right to raise the question of alienage at the time the claim came up for patent. Claim jumpers continued to insist that they were in the right. By 1900 many of the original alien claim-

ants had sold their property, mostly to American citizens, who now incurred the anger of the claim jumpers. Charles D. Lane, a mining entrepreneur who early on had realized the mineral potential of the Nome region, purchased many mining claims from the Lapp reindeer herders and Scandinavian miners.[26]

Among the claims Lane had purchased was No. 10, Above Discovery, on Anvil Creek, which John S. Tornanses, a Lapp reindeer herder, had staked on October 19, 1898. In the spring of 1899 a miner jumped the Tornanses claim because he alleged that the reindeer herder was an alien and therefore could not locate a mining claim. When he refused to drop his claim, the miner was arrested and jailed.

The claim jumper continued to maintain that he and his two companions were the lawful owners of the No. 10 Above Discovery. They argued that since Tornanses, as an alien, had no right to stake the claim in the first place, he could not sell it to Lane, and the three men decided to contest Lane's title in court. They hired as their attorneys Oliver P. Hubbard and William T. Hume of the law firm of Hubbard, Beeman, and Hume, which represented many of the claim jumpers in Nome.[27]

Hubbard came to Alaska in the spring of 1898 and, together with his partners, Edwin Beeman and William Hume, agreed to represent anyone with a jumper's title in exchange for contingency interest in the contested claim. Thus the attorneys became partners with their clients, and eventually the three gained an interest in approximately one hundred jumper's titles.[28]

During the winter of 1899–1900 Hubbard tried to gain the interest of investors in Chicago, New York, Washington, D.C., and London who were willing to gamble that the alien claims in Nome would be invalidated. These potential investors included Senator Alexander McKenzie, a member of the Republican National Committee from North Dakota who was most adept in the art of bribery and influence buying. From North Dakota's admission to statehood in 1899 until the Progressive "Revolution of 1906," the McKenzie ring controlled most of the elected officials in the state and influenced the election of nearly every senator during North Dakota's first twenty-four years in the Union. When Hubbard and McKenzie met in January 1900, the North Dakota political boss recognized a chance to make a fortune out of the turbulent conditions in Nome.

With the help of several key senators he could influence, McKenzie planned to attach an amendment to the Alaska Code that would retroactively nullify any mining claims in Alaska staked by aliens. If he was successful, the jumpers' titles could be worth millions of dollars. McKenzie and Hubbard apparently agreed upon a strategy to follow, and McKenzie formed the Alaska Gold Mining Company, a phony syndicate with a paper capitalization of $15 million. McKenzie exchanged stock in his paper corporation for about one hundred jumpers' titles to alien claims in the Nome district and other areas in Alaska as well. He paid Hubbard, Beeman, and Hume $750,000 in Alaska Gold Mining Company stock for their interest in the titles, and made Hubbard secretary of the company. McKenzie hoped to gain control of the richest mines in Nome for one season, enabling his company to take out millions of dollars worth of gold. At freeze-up, he hoped to sell the company's worthless stock on Wall Street, bilking an unwary public.[29]

Alexander McKenzie did not put anything in writing, and it therefore has been impossible to identify all of his backers. The Ninth Circuit Court of Appeals perceptively observed that McKenzie obviously put the stock of his company in the hands of those who could help him the most. These included U.S. Senators Thomas H. Carter of Montana, the sponsor of the Alaska Civil Code, and Henry C. Hansbrough of North Dakota. A lawyer and an expert in the incredibly complex mining laws of the United States, Carter was then chair of the Senate Committee on Territories and was set to steer the Alaska Civil Code, subsequently known as the Carter Code, to passage.

On March 5, 1900, Carter reported the measure out of his committee. The Alaska Civil Code was basically a modification of the Oregon Code, in force in Alaska since 1884. Very little was controversial in the bill, and the senator urged his colleagues to pass it quickly in order to give Alaskans a system of law

and order, made necessary by the Gold Rush population boom.[30] As it emerged from Carter's committee, the Alaska Civil Code clearly stated that aliens had the right to acquire mining property, and that a title "shall not be questioned nor in any manner affected by reason of the alienage of any person from or through whom such title may have been derived." This provision obviously protected the right of those aliens who had staked claims, and others who had bought mining ground from them.[31]

Circumstantial evidence and Carter's clever maneuvers on the Senate floor suggest that the chairman and Hansbrough were in collusion with McKenzie. The record of the debates, however, still contains the most incriminating evidence. For on the floor of the Senate, Carter argued that the alien provision in the Alaska Civil Code had to be stricken to prevent the confirmation of "shady, or doubtful titles" and the bestowing of "rights where none existed under the law," namely, on aliens. He told his colleagues that numerous aliens had illegally and immorally taken the richest claims in Nome, and that therefore the Alaska Civil Code had to be amended to protect the rights of American citizens. The chairman warned that "it will be a dark and evil day for this country when the badge of American citizenship will not be at least as good a cloak for protection as the ancient citizenship of Rome was in the days of that Republic."[32]

Carter offered a solution to the dilemma. Senator Hansbrough just happened to have drafted an amendment to the original code, "moved by a high sense of duty to a distant body of his fellow-countrymen, men on an ice-bound coast 8,000 miles away," which would have invalidated the title to any claims purchased from an alien locator and would haven given courts the right to inquire into a locator's citizenship. Another proviso in Hansbrough's amendment stated that unless an alien had filed his declaration of becoming a U.S. citizen before staking his claim, the title would not be valid.[33]

Senator Carter warned of dire consequences to the nation if the Hansbrough amendment failed. He claimed that the aliens he feared most were not the Swedes and Lapps, but rather those from China, Russia, Korea, and Japan. Should the government notify the Japanese people that they "may proceed to Cape Nome and Cape York and on the whole of that Alaskan coast and there participate like our own citizens in the benefits which accrue to the locator of mining claims"? He answered his own question by stating that this "would be equivalent to turning Alaska over to the aliens."[34]

Despite the valiant efforts of Senators Hansbrough and Carter and McKenzie's other friends in Washington, the "Hansbrough amendment" to the Alaska Civil Code was defeated, thanks in part to the opposition of Charles D. Lane and others. McKenzie, however, did not give up easily and decided to have a friendly judge appointed in Nome. Using his connections with financiers and leading Republican politicians, he pushed through the appointment of Arthur H. Noyes, an undistinguished Minnesota attorney and longtime McKenzie friend, as judge for the new Second Judicial Division of Alaska, which included the Nome gold fields.[35]

Judge Noyes and his party, including McKenzie, arrived at Nome in mid-July 1900, and the new judge did nothing to establish law and order in that city. In fact, his arrival in Nome marked the beginning of the reign of "the Spoilers," as novelist Rex Beach called the judge and his gang in a book by the same name.

Within four days after their arrival, Alexander McKenzie controlled the richest placer mining claims of Nome. Judge Noyes had appointed McKenzie as receiver to administer the mining claims while they were in litigation. Customarily, a receiver holds such disputed property in trust so that its value cannot be dissipated before judicial determination has been made. The best way to preserve the value of the claims was to leave the gold in the ground. Instead, McKenzie hired every able-bodied male he could find to work the claims.

McKenzie was not shy in pressuring others to acquiesce to his scheme. Hume later testified that McKenzie had advised him and Beeman to cooperate with him, as Hubbard had done. If they did, they would make a "large and ample fortune." If they did not cooperate, McKenzie threatened to ruin them and make certain that they would win "no suits in the District Court for the District of Alaska, Second Division, as he controlled the Judge" of that court.[36]

McKenzie also demanded that he and U.S. Attorney Joseph Wood receive a one-quarter interest in the profits of the law firm. Hume understood that McKenzie would hold his one-quarter share of the business "in trust" for Judge Noyes. The new partners signed an agreement on July 22, 1900. McKenzie thereupon instructed his partners immediately to prepare applications for the appointment of receivers for the contested claims on Anvil Creek. Hume took the legal documents to the judge, who signed them without reading them, enabling McKenzie to take over five of the richest placer mining claims, including four on Anvil Creek.[37]

McKenzie immediately rushed out to Anvil Creek with the court orders forcing the owners to give him "immediate possession, control, and management." The miners were caught off guard by these bizarre events, or they might have resisted by force. Most of Nome's citizens assumed that everything was in order because the judge had approved it and because they did not understand that the claim jumpers' suits depended on the alien ownership argument and had only very weak cases, at best. Additionally, the military forces in Nome were prepared to back up the receiver's authority and the orders of the district court.[38]

The attorneys for Lane and Lindeberg, the chief opponents of the McKenzie forces, protested the receivership to Judge Noyes but got no response. The judge continued to deny the defendants' motions, and they had no choice but to appeal directly to San Francisco.[39]

In the meantime C. S. A. Frost, the investigator for the attorney general in Nome in 1900, summed up his impressions for his chief on August 16. He gave Judge Noyes a clean bill of health and criticized the defendants who "have undertaken to force an appeal to the appellate court in San Francisco." In conclusion, Frost observed that law officials who came into the Nome area took "their lives in their hands. An upright Judge needs . . . encouragement that your confidence can furnish, and Judge Noyes merits it."[40]

The attorneys for Charles Lane's Wild Goose Mining and Trading Company and the Pioneer Mining

Company traveled by steamship the nearly three thousand miles to San Francisco to deliver their petitions and applications for appeal to Judge William Morrow of the Ninth Circuit Court of Appeals. The judge reviewed the applications in late August and ruled that Judge Noyes "had grossly abused the judgment and discretion vested in him by law" and allowed the appeals. He issued a writ of supersedeas, ordering the judge to halt his proceedings and McKenzie "to forthwith turn back and deliver to the defendants all the property of every kind and character taken by him" under the order appointing him receiver. Morrow also directed the defendants to furnish a supersedeas bond of thirty-five thousand dollars. This they did.[41]

On September 14, 1900, Morrow's orders were served upon Judge Noyes, the plaintiff, and Alexander McKenzie. Nome's citizens welcomed the news that Noyes and McKenzie had been overruled, but jubilations were premature because the receiver decided to ignore the orders of the Circuit Court, claiming they were invalid. Judge Noyes stayed out of sight, pretending to be sick, and stated that he was powerless to make McKenzie return property because the Ninth Circuit Court of Appeals had usurped his jurisdiction in the case. Once more lawyers traveled to San Francisco to complain. At this point, armed men from the Pioneer Mining Company chased McKenzie's men from several claims on Anvil Creek. McKenzie complained, and both sides asked the army for help. Major John Van Orsdale, the officer in command and a North Dakotan friendly to McKenzie, arranged a conference between the receiver and William H. Metson, the principal attorney for the Pioneer Mining Company. At the meeting the two men almost shot each other but were disarmed by soldiers before any harm had been done. Judge Noyes came out of seclusion long enough to order the army to ignore the writs from California.[42]

There were those in Nome who feared that McKenzie, who had deposited about a quarter of a million dollars in Anvil Creek gold in the Alaska Banking and Safe Deposit Company, would grab the fortune and run. After a nearly violent encounter at the bank between McKenzie and the armed men representing the defendants, McKenzie agreed that the gold should stay at the bank and nobody should take it out. Armed soldiers thereafter guarded the fortune, and both sides waited for the arrival of new instructions from the Ninth Circuit Court of Appeals. Finally, on October 15, 1900, two deputy U.S. marshals from California landed in Nome with orders to enforce the writs of the circuit court. They also carried a warrant for the arrest of Alexander McKenzie, who was sentenced to one year in the Oakland, California, jail. The marshals took the receiver back to California for trial, where he was convicted of contempt of court in February 1901. On the day of McKenzie's arrest, the mine owners and operators at Anvil Creek fired their guns in the air, celebrating the end of the receiver's three-month rule.[43]

President William McKinley, one of McKenzie's personal friends, pardoned him after he had served only a few months in jail, declaring that McKenzie was in poor health and probably would die in prison. Instead, McKenzie died some twenty years later in 1922 and took most of the secrets of the gold conspiracy to his grave. Neither McKenzie nor anybody else was ever charged with conspiracy because, it has been suggested, top officials in the Department of Justice had participated in the plot.[44]

Judge Arthur Noyes never went to prison. He remained judge of the Second Judicial Division until convicted of contempt of court and fined one thousand dollars, after which then-president Theodore Roosevelt removed him from office. U.S Attorney Joseph K. Wood, also convicted of contempt of court, was sentenced to four months in jail. C. S. A. Frost, the investigator for the Department of Justice, was found to have "grossly betrayed the interests of the United States which were intrusted to his care." He received a one-year jail sentence for his contempt conviction.[45]

The thousands of pages of documents gathered in the various contempt proceedings still do not answer the question of whether or not there was a conspiracy, but Judge Morrow of the Ninth Circuit Court of Appeals stated that the evidence showed "beyond any reasonable doubt" that a conspiracy did exist.[46] Many were annoyed that the "Spoilers"

Felix Pedro, who discovered gold in the Tanana Valley near the site of present-day Fairbanks, on July 22, 1902.

(Courtesy of Alaska and Polar Regions Department, Elmer E. Rasmuson Library, University of Alaska Fairbanks.)

got off so easily and that conspiracy charges were never brought against the chief actors. This failure perhaps was not a cover-up, for even Judge Wickersham, sent to clean up the judicial mess in Nome, resisted efforts to get a grand jury indictment, arguing that "the quicker the people of Nome, and the court forgot those black days the better it would be for the administration of justice in that district."[47]

The Birth of Fairbanks

All the troubles in Nome failed to keep the restless miners from searching for the next El Dorado. Several prospectors searching the Tanana Valley had found good placer prospects. Felix "Pedroni" Pedro, an Italian coal miner, had prospected the north for years. He and his partner, Tom Gilmore, doggedly searched on tributaries of the Tanana River and eventually found gold at Fish Creek and Goldstream. Just as Pedro was ready to hike to Circle City

for provisions, on August 26, 1901, he saw smoke on the horizon. He stood on a hill overlooking the valley, later named Ester Dome, and watched as the *Lavelle Young*, a small river steamer owned by E. T. Barnette, slowly moved up the Chena River and docked. When Pedro and Gilmore reached the boat, they told Barnette that there were other prospectors in the area. Barnette sold winter outfits to the two miners and christened his post "Chenoa City."[48]

Soon a minor stampede occurred, and on September 27, 1902, the miners held a meeting and elected Barnette recorder of the district. Barnette, who had originally intended to establish his post at Tanana Crossing, thus became the founding father of Fairbanks, named at the request of Judge Wickersham after Senator Charles W. Fairbanks, the senior senator from Indiana who would become vice president in 1904. In return, the judge promised to do everything in his power to help Captain Barnette succeed, no small promise from the most powerful

Fairbanks, 1904.

(Courtesy of Alaska and Polar Regions Department, Elmer E. Rasmuson Library, University of Alaska Fairbanks.)

government official within three hundred thousand square miles. Barnette later explained that both he and the judge thought the name Fairbanks was a good idea because should they ever need assistance in the nation's capital, they were assured of the senator's friendship.

Barnette was eager to advertise the gold discovery in the Tanana Valley, and he invited friends to come to share in the good fortune even before there was much evidence of a great supply of the precious metal. Just before Christmas 1902, he sent his cook, Jujiro Wada, to Dawson with a load of furs to sell. Upon his arrival there, Wada gave an interview to the *Yukon Sun* and told of the wonderful riches in the Tanana area. About eight hundred men were said to have left Dawson for the Tanana Valley in the dead of winter when the temperature hovered about fifty degrees below zero Fahrenheit. Before their arrival, other men had come from the Rampart diggings.

Many of the prospectors came to the new town

of Chena, started on the Tanana River near the mouth of the Chena River. In 1901, George Belt and Nathan Hendricks had established a trading post below Bates Rapids on the Tanana. They had been in the area longer than Barnette and maintained that sternwheelers would be unable to ascend the Chena River to Fairbanks in the spring. The *Lavelle Young* had trouble in 1901, and the *Isabelle* had made it only halfway to Fairbanks in 1902 before it was stranded on a sandbar. Belt and Hendricks thus believed that the town of Fairbanks would soon be high and dry and would disappear with the snow. In the spring of 1903, the two men began to move their trading post across the Tanana River, next to the mouth of the Chena.

Speculators from Rampart staked most of the town lots, and the settlement, first named Tanana City and then simply Chena, was established. Everyone wanted to have the biggest and most valuable property, resulting in bedlam. Claim jumpers were

A native's fish wheel at Copper River, Alaska. The gold rush stampeders introduced the fish wheel.

(Courtesy of Alaska and Polar Regions Department, Elmer E. Rasmuson Library, University of Alaska Fairbanks.)

stopped with a rifle. Fairbanks, in the meantime, was well organized and town site lots could be had for a $2.50 recording fee. The competition between Chena and Fairbanks, only seven miles apart, grew increasingly bitter.

But no great boom developed in either town. For a time the area was threatened with starvation; supplies of food were dangerously low. There were threats to lynch Wada. By June 1903, it seemed that "the bottom had fallen out of the stampede." Good town lots in Fairbanks were selling for ten dollars. What many miners did not realize was that conditions in Fairbanks made mining more difficult than in the Klondike. The gold was buried much deeper in the ground, some of it a few hundred feet down.[49]

Within a few months, three great discoveries had been made near the town, at Cleary Creek, Fairbanks Creek, and Ester Creek. Miners slowly came back. By Christmas 1903, fifteen to eighteen hundred were in the Tanana Valley, most of them employed by others at five dollars a day. Since expensive machinery and equipment were needed to thaw the ground and extract the metal from it, the individual prospector in time became a rarity, and the valley was dotted with a number of small companies.

Fairbanks was now well on its way to becoming the metropolis of interior Alaska. It called itself "the largest log cabin town in the world." Barnette had succeeded in persuading the Northern Commercial Company, formerly the Alaska Commercial Company and the largest firm in Alaska, to buy a two-thirds interest in his store, which was soon converted into total ownership.[50] In 1904, after the ice went out, boats had come from Dawson bringing half the population with them. Construction work had begun on the Tanana Valley Railroad, a narrow-gauge line to connect Fairbanks and Chena with the mining camps and towns in the Tanana Valley. For years, Fairbanks and Chena competed with each other to be the leading town of the district. Fairbanks won out, aided in part by Judge Wickersham, who moved the headquarters of the Third Judicial District Court to Fairbanks. All government buildings in the area—the courthouse, post office, and jail—were built in Fairbanks. Most people coming to the Tanana Valley chose to live in Fairbanks rather than Chena, where lots were more expensive. By 1915, Chena was almost deserted, and the Tanana River washed away most of the town site; today only a marker indicates where the town once stood.

Many of the men who chose to settle in Fairbanks sent for their families to join them. As a consequence, the town acquired some domestic institutions such as schools, churches, and a hospital. Although churches thrived in this frontier town, they had to compete for the miners' money with saloons, open twenty-four hours a day and offering wide-open gambling. Miners in from the diggings for a day or a week could find entertainment and solace on the "line," a section of the town set aside for prostitutes who wanted their share of Alaska gold. By 1905 the population had grown to five thousand. That Fairbanks was still primarily a mining community is emphasized by the statistics on gold production. In 1906 production reached more than $6 million, in contrast to the 1903 take of only $40,000.

Gold throughout Alaska

Once the Klondike boom peaked, interest in Alaskan gold grew. Of the thousands who had gone to Dawson, many crossed the border to try their luck in Alaska, some prospecting for new strikes and others joining established camps at Nome, Fairbanks, or more remote sites. Mining had begun at Rampart in 1893 but did not move into full swing until about four years later. At its height, the town had about two thousand people, many of whom had been at Dawson. North of the Arctic Circle, gold had been found in the vicinity of the Chandalar and Koyukuk rivers, where two towns, Coldfoot and Wiseman, came into existence. In the area of the Kuskokwim and Innoko rivers, Iditarod, McGrath, Bethel, Flat, and Ophir were communities of some size that had developed from mining camps.[51]

Valdez and Eagle, although not mining towns, were very much affected by the activities of the miners. Eagle, on the Yukon River only a few miles from the border, served as the port of entry for those coming from Canada. At its height Eagle provided services to more mining camps than any other American town along the Yukon.[52] Men from the camps around the Seventymile, Nation, Charley, Tatonduk, and Fortymile rivers came to trade. Eagle became the terminus for a telegraph line from Valdez. Fort Egbert, the headquarters for the army in northern Alaska, was in Eagle, as was the seat for the Third Judicial District before its transfer to Fairbanks.

In 1898 prospectors on the way to the Klondike came to Valdez and crossed the Valdez Glacier. But most of those who used the trail to the interior went to the Copper River country, which had a good many mining camps, or to Eagle. Valdez, an ice-free port, became increasingly more important with the development of Fairbanks. A trail built to connect the two towns became a wagon road after 1905.

The Effects of the Gold Rush

The Gold Rush focused attention on Alaska as nothing else had. Alaska and things Alaskan became front-page news. When rumors circulated that Americans in the Klondike and on the Alaska trails to the Klondike faced starvation, Congress appropriated two hundred thousand dollars for relief. Rev. Sheldon Jackson was sent to Norway to purchase reindeer for transporting the supplies to the stricken miners. These "government pets," as critics of the

Wilford B. Hoggatt, *left front,* was the first governor of Alaska to use Juneau as the capital, in September 1906. U. G. Myers, *right front,* was his U.S. commissioner. The back row, *left to right,* finds Lieutenant C. C. Herman, Dr. John M. Mosley, Major Wilds P. Richardson, president of the newly formed Alaska Road Commission, and C. L. Andrews of the U.S. Customs Service.

(Author's collection.)

expedition called the reindeer, were shipped to New York, then overland to San Francisco, and from there by boat to Skagway. Many of the animals perished before reaching their destination, and more died as they passed over the White Pass trail. As it turned out, the relief expedition was unnecessary; food had been provided by the Canadian government almost as soon as cries for help had been made, and no one went hungry.[53]

Undeterred by the reindeer fiasco, Congress, for the first time since the purchase of Alaska, went on to deal more seriously with Alaskan problems. It appropriated money for the U.S. Geological Survey to begin work on the survey and exploration of Alaska, and it extended the coal-mining laws of the United States to the district. The U.S. Army built posts at Eagle, Nome, Haines, and Tanana, at the junction of the Yukon and Tanana rivers. The Department of Agriculture received money to examine the potential of farming in Alaska.

The U.S. Army presence was also affected by the Gold Rush; the temporary nature of the mining camps necessitated much flexibility, and the army established and discontinued posts as circumstances required. In 1897 the army established Fort Saint Michael on Norton Sound; followed in 1899 by Fort Gibbons, on the north bank of the Yukon River opposite and a little below the mouth of the Tanana River; and at Fort Egbert, at the mouth of Mission Creek near Eagle City on the Yukon. In the meantime, in February 1898, the army also created the Lynn Canal Military District, headquartered at Camp Dyea.[54]

Then at the turn of the century the War Department reorganized the army in the north, creating the Department of Alaska, with headquarters at Fort Saint Michael. Only one company was still stationed at Skagway, and the Lynn Canal Military District had been discontinued some time earlier. In the meantime, in response to the rush to the Nome gold fields, a detachment of troops had been stationed at Anvil City (Nome) to keep order. In 1900 construction began on Fort Davis, about two miles outside the tent city of Nome, and troops also built Fort Liscum, across the bay from the port of Valdez. Finally, on September 15, 1901, the War Department announced the abolition of the Department of Alaska and once again attached the district to the Department of the Columbia.[55]

Also in response to the Gold Rush, Congress made the first changes in the Organic Act of 1884, enacting three pieces of legislation dealing with the economy and the Alaska political system. The first, passed in 1898, made it possible for railroad builders to obtain a right-of-way and gave settlers their first opportunity to receive title to land by extending the Homestead Act to Alaska. Then in 1899, Congress recognized that Alaska had unique problems and enacted a few changes to make the criminal code portion of the Organic Act more responsive to Alaskan conditions. At the same time, taxes were levied on businesses, and the revenues collected went into the treasury of the United States, presumably to pay the costs of government in Alaska. Canneries were assessed four cents for each case of salmon packed (a case contained forty-eight one-pound cans). Railroads were taxed one hundred dollars for each mile of operation even before the lines were completed. Companies had to pay license fees for the privilege of doing business in Alaska, the charge varying with the nature of the enterprise; that for liquor was highest of all. The sale of liquor was legalized despite the objections of Rev. Jackson. Even John Brady, Alaska's governor, who was a staunch temperance advocate, recognized that the government's liquor policy had been a failure. He admitted that effective regulation of liquor could be achieved only through the payment of a high license fee that would limit the number of establishments engaged in the trade.[56]

In 1900, Congress revised the civil code and turned its attention to the government of Alaska. Commensurate with the increase in population, Congress added two new judicial districts. Saint Michael and then Nome served as the headquarters for the newly created northern division, while in the interior, first Eagle and then Fairbanks served as the seat of the judiciary. Congress also decreed that the capital was to be moved from Sitka to Juneau, a larger town, whenever "suitable grounds and buildings" were obtained; this move was not accomplished until a few years later.

Congress also gave Alaska an initial taste of self-government when it provided for the incorporation of towns. Once a community had met the requirements of incorporation, it could elect a council of seven, one of whom served as mayor. The council had the power to furnish various services, such as street improvements and police and fire protection, and to provide for a school system. Towns were limited in their sources of revenue, however, as borrowing was expressly prohibited, and taxes on real and personal property were restricted to 1 percent of assessed valuation. The municipalities were permitted to impose license fees on businesses; half the money collected was to be used in support of education. Businesses thereupon protested that they were subject to a duplicate set of license fees. Congress responded by rescinding the authority of municipalities to impose license fees, and all revenues the federal government collected from this source were turned over to the towns.[57]

The Alaska-Canada Boundary Dispute

The era of the Gold Rush brought to a head the Alaska boundary dispute with Canada that had long been festering. It was generally agreed that the portion of the treaty of 1825 that had sought to define the limits of the Russian and British possessions south of 60° north latitude was ambiguous. On several occasions after the United States took possession of Alaska, disputes arose and suggestions were made, chiefly by the Canadians, to settle the controversy. Neither side, however, seemed to be willing to undertake the cost of a survey.

By 1897 the dispute had been made acute by the discovery of gold in Canada's Yukon Territory and the subsequent influx of argonauts. Consequently, troops of the U.S. Fourteenth Infantry were stationed at Dyea, Fort Wrangell, and Skagway in 1897.[58] By 1898 the Canadian case extended the claims of ownership to Skagway and Dyea, which, if recognized, would give Canadians in the Yukon direct access to the sea without having to pass through American territory. Theodore Roosevelt, who had succeeded McKinley as president following the latter's assassination in 1901, proposed that a tribunal of six impartial jurists, three from each side, be constituted to examine the merits of the controversy.

For the American delegation Roosevelt named Henry Cabot Lodge, the ultranationalistic senator from Massachusetts; Elihu Root, secretary of war; and Senator George Turner of the state of Washington, who knew that the trade of the city of Seattle would be affected if the Canadian claims to Skagway and Dyea were upheld. None of them could be called impartial. The British-Canadian delegation

"On the way to Dawson" on the Canyon Dyea Trail, 1898.

(Author's collection.)

included Lord Alverstone, the lord chief justice of England; Sir Louis Jette, a former member of the Canadian Supreme Court; and Allen B. Aylesworth, a distinguished member of the Canadian bar.

By a vote of four to two, the tribunal, with Lord Chief Justice Alverstone siding with the Americans, rejected the Canadian claims except for two small islands in Portland Canal. The Canadians accused Alverstone of having sold out their interests in behalf of British-American relations. The Alaska boundary was now clearly defined, but relations between the United States and Canada were long embittered by this dispute and its settlement.[59]

The Gold Rush Impact on Native Alaska

The discovery of gold also led to the first large-scale migration to Alaska, and this influx of Americans had many unforeseen consequences for the territory's Native people. Population figures illustrate the changes that occurred. When in the early part of October 1880, Joe Juneau and Richard Harris discovered gold in Silver Bow Basin near what later became Juneau, Alaska's population consisted of an estimated 430 non-Natives and some 32,996 Natives. By 1890 the number of non-Natives had grown to 4,298, while that of the Natives had declined to 25,354. In 1900 non-Natives outnumbered Natives for the first time, with 30,450 of the former and 29,542 of the latter.[60] Soon the Eskimos of western Alaska and the Athapaskans of the interior experienced the impact of white fortune seekers. Alaska Natives began to organize.

The primary goal of the first Native organization to be formed on a more than local basis was the winning of citizenship. The Alaska Native Brotherhood (ANB), founded by nine Tlingits and one Tsimshian in Sitka in 1912, was followed in 1915 by a woman's organization, the Alaska Native Sisterhood, and within a decade chapters, called camps,

The people of Fort Yukon in a photograph taken in the early 1900s. All members of the group are in western clothing except the older man in the right front, who wears a shirt of small skins that resembles the traditional garment.

(Courtesy of Alaska and Polar Regions Department, Elmer E. Rasmuson Library, University of Alaska Fairbanks.)

existed in most towns and villages of southeastern Alaska.[61]

Along with the intention of winning citizenship, the ANB also concerned itself with Indian education and the abandonment of aboriginal customs considered "uncivilized" by whites. The latter concern was prompted by one of the provisions of the General Allotment Act of 1887, which provided for acquisition of citizenship by Indians who had "severed tribal relationship and adopted the habits of civilization."[62]

In part through ANB efforts, the 1915 Alaska territorial legislature passed an act enabling Indians to become citizens. To do so they had to demonstrate that they had given up their tribal ways and adopted the habits of "civilized" life. Despite the complicated qualifying procedures, increasing numbers of Natives used the territorial law to become citizens. In 1924, Congress followed suit when it made citizens of all American Indians.[63]

The founders of the Alaska Native Brotherhood, formed in 1911, include, *left to right,* Paul Liberty, James Watson, Ralph Young, Eli Katinook, Peter Simpson, Frank Mercer, James C. Johnson, Chester Worthington, George Field, William Hobson, and Frank Price.

(Author's collection.)

Athapaskan chiefs of the villages in the Tanana Valley gathered in Fairbanks in 1915 to discuss the problems of their people with James Wickersham, Alaska's delegate to Congress. *Bottom row, left to right:* Chief Alexander of Tolovana, Chief Thomas of Nenana, Chief Evan of Koschasat, and Chief Alexander William of Tanana. *Top row, left to right:* Chief William of Tanana, Paul Williams of Tanana, and Chief Charlie of Minto. For this picture they posed in their chiefs' jackets of moose hide decorated with beadwork and beaver fur. Note the *dentalium* and bead decorations at the necks and supporting the sheaths, which held their curved-handle knives.

(Courtesy of Charles E. Bunnell Collection, Alaska and Polar Regions Department, Elmer E. Rasmuson Library, University of Alaska Fairbanks.)

In the meantime, on July 5 and 6, 1915, a number of Athapaskan chiefs and headmen met at the Thomas Memorial Library, in Fairbanks, with James Wickersham, now Alaska's delegate to Congress, and various officials, among them C. W. Richie and H. J. Atwell, the acting registrar and the receiver of the U.S. Land Office at Fairbanks, and the Reverend Guy H. Madara, minister in charge of all Episcopal missions in the Tanana Valley. Delegate Wickersham told the assembled leaders that he expected that increasing homesteading activity would soon take up all the good land, and "when all the good land is gone . . . the Indians are going to have to move over." The delegate offered two alternatives: 160-acre homesteads or reservations.

In 1906 the passage of the Native Allotment Act had enabled Alaska Natives to obtain legal title to 160-acre homesteads to be selected from the vacant, unappropriated, and unreserved public domain.[64] Although it enabled Natives to gain title to land, it was a regressive piece of legislation since it endeavored to turn hunters and food-gatherers into home-

Hoonah, in southeast Alaska, 1959, was typical of the small coastal Tlingit villages where fishing was the economic mainstay.

(Photo by Claus-M. Naske.)

steaders, and Alaska lands for the most part were not suitable for agricultural pursuits. Only eighty allotments, and most of these in southeastern Alaska, were issued under the act between 1906 and 1960.

Homesteads, the Indians argued, were incompatible with their seminomadic lifestyle. Chief Ivan of Crossjacket probably best expressed Indian opposition to reservations by stating, "[We] wish to stay perfectly free just as we are now and go about just the same as now. . . . We feel as if we had always gone as we pleased and the way they all feel is the same." Chief Joe of Salchaket said: "We want to be left alone. As the whole continent was made for you, God made Alaska for the Indian people, and all we

hope is to be able to live here all the time." Paul Williams, the interpreter, eloquently summarized their plight:

Just as soon as you take us from the wild country and put us on reservations . . . we would soon all die off like rabbits. In times past our people did not wear cotton clothes and clothes like the white man wears, but we wore skins from the caribou. We lived on fish, the wild game, moose and caribou, and blueberries and roots. That is what we are made to live on—not vegetables, cattle and things like the white people eat. As soon as we are made to leave our customs and wild life, we will all get sick and soon

The Fairbanks-Valdez Stage, run by Ed. S. Orr and Company, carried passengers and freight along the Richardson Road (later the Richardson Highway), named for the first president of the Board of Road Commissioners for Alaska. The approximately 360-mile trip was easiest in the winter after the mud of the trail and the creeks and rivers had frozen. Along the trail were many roadhouses of varying quality. In 1913, Robert E. (Bobby) Sheldon made the first trip by automobile between Valdez and Fairbanks, and soon "motor stages" took over. The roadhouses continued to operate because it was still a long, arduous journey.

(Courtesy Archie Lewis Collection, Alaska and Polar Regions Archives, Elmer E. Rasmuson Library, University of Alaska Fairbanks.)

die. We have moved into cabins. There is no such thing now as the underground living and as soon as we have done this the Natives begin to catch cold. You used to never hear nothing of consumption or tuberculosis. The majority of people say that whiskey brings tuberculosis to the Indians, but this is not true. It is because we have changed our mode of living and are trying to live like the white man does.[65]

Delegate Wickersham promised to report the chiefs' opposition to reservations to Washington, though he himself disagreed with them: "I think that a reservation is excellent and the best thing that can be done for the Indians." The meeting adjourned with the delegate admonishing the Indians that "as soon as . . . [you] have established homes and live like the white men and assume the habits of civilization…[you] can have a vote."[66]

Wickersham no doubt did report the sentiments of the Athapaskans to the secretary of the interior, but that is where the matter rested. A few years later, in 1926, Congress amended the Townsite Act, which enabled Alaska Natives to receive restricted deeds to surveyed town lots. The legislation also exempted

The Alaska Central Railway unloading one of its engines in Seward in 1904.

(Courtesy of Rorl, Alaska Railroad Collection; Anchorage Museum. Loan from the Alaska Railroad Corporation [BL79.2.4813].)

Indians and Eskimos of full or mixed blood from all forms of taxation on lots occupied and claimed by them. Between 1926 and 1971 the federal government surveyed only 28 of more than 175 Native villages and issued restricted deeds to their inhabitants.[67]

Developing Alaska's Agriculture and Transportation

As Alaska's population grew, schemes were afoot to make the area less dependent on the outside for food. The Russians had considered the possibilities of farming and planted some vegetable gardens. During the American era, travelers to the Yukon River valley had come back with tales of the tremendous cabbages grown there. But it was not until the advent of the Gold Rush and the expectations of an increased population that Alaskan agriculture could no longer be considered a "fascinating oddity," in the words of historian Orlando Miller. In 1897 the U.S. Department of Agriculture sent three special agents to southeastern Alaska, the south-central region, Kodiak, the Alaska Peninsula, and the Yukon Valley. After mentioning the difficulties involved in farming in the north, they nevertheless indicated that a "variety of crops" could be grown and noted that cattle raising and vegetable gardening were already being undertaken. One of the investigators recommended encouraging people to settle on small plots and "engage in mixed fishing, lumbering and farming." He believed that this would result in "settling the country with a hardy race of fishermen and others used to the water, from which we may secure seamen for the merchant marine and navy, and at the same time . . . develop other resources" and thus establish in Alaska "a great civilization."[68]

Acting on the agents' recommendations, the federal government established several agricultural experiment stations, first at Sitka in 1898 and then at Kenai, Kodiak, Rampart, Copper Center, Fairbanks, and finally Matanuska in 1917. Danish-born Charles G. Georgeson, appointed to head the station at Sitka, was an ardent promoter of Alaska agriculture. His constant refrain was that "the hope for the natives and the development of the territory [lies] in a prosperous agriculture, for it stands to reason that if the means to support life exist within the boundaries of the territory all other resources will become more valuable."[69]

More immediate to the pressing needs of Alaska was a good system of transportation. Use of the inland waterways had been considerably improved in the Klondike era with the increase in the number of steamboats plying the Yukon and later the Tanana. Dogsleds were of importance almost everywhere, but there were few roads or trails. Although Congress had authorized private individuals to build and collect tolls on roads and bridges in 1898, few ventured to take advantage of such opportunities. It was not until the passage of the Nelson Act in 1905 and the establishment of the Board of Road Commissioners for Alaska in the same year that road building in Alaska became a reality.

The Nelson Act created the Alaska Fund, decreeing that 70 percent of all monies collected from license fees outside incorporated towns were to be used for road building, 25 percent for education, and the remaining 5 percent for the care of the insane. Congress appropriated additional road-building funds annually. By 1920 about 4,890 miles of roads and trails, 1,031 miles of which were wagon roads, had been built; the most notable of these was the Richardson Road (now Richardson Highway), which connected Valdez and Fairbanks.

While private companies had little interest in building Alaska roads, the lure of adventure in constructing lines in the Far North and the prospect of fabulous profits did attract railway companies to Alaska. Among these, the Alaska Syndicate was to become famous, or infamous, depending on the sources consulted, in Alaska's economics and politics. Historian William H. Wilson has told of its involvement in railroads, copper, and coal. The syndicate was organized in 1906 by the Guggenheim mining family, J. P. Morgan and Company, and others initially to provide development capital for copper claims along the Copper River. To move the copper ore to the Guggenheim smelter at Tacoma, Washington, the syndicate bought steamship and lighterage companies, which it consolidated under the Alaska Steamship Company. It also bought and sold canneries, creating various corporations.

The syndicate was also building the Copper River and Northwestern Railway from Cordova toward the interior. That railroad had not crossed the mountains into the Tanana Valley, but its backers had decided that no other railroad would traverse the mountains. When the time came, the Alaska Syndicate would extend its mining operations into the interior along with its railroad.[70]

The syndicate used various means to discourage competing railways. Though violence was the least necessary and politically most damaging means, syndicate employees used it on two occasions. In one instance Copper River construction crews drove another railroad's workers from the Cordova area. On the more famous occasion the deputized leader of an armed band shot and fatally wounded a worker for a rival railroad, the Alaska Home Railroad, which was attempting to build through the Keystone Canyon near Valdez. The event was particularly unfortunate because the Alaska Home Railroad, which was never built, was a promotional line attempting a route the Alaska Syndicate had already surrendered in all but title. During the subsequent trial of the deputy, the syndicate lost much face as charges of bribery and other irregularities were aired.

While several small narrow-gauge railroads served the needs of local inhabitants on the Seward Peninsula and in the Tanana Valley, only two of the larger lines prospered: the White Pass and Yukon Route railway, built by Close Brothers of London, connecting Skagway, in Alaska, with Whitehorse, in Canada's Yukon Territory, and the 195-mile Copper River and Northwestern Railway, connecting the Kennecott mines with the port of Cordova.

Unfortunately for promoters, their interest in building railroads in Alaska came at a time when railroads in the United States, accused of having violated the public trust, were highly unpopular. Railroads had received large tracts of land from federal, state, and local governments; had been lent money at low rates of interest; and had been given other subsidies. Critics accused them of abusing their privileges by charging exorbitant rates, corrupting politics, and giving poor service. In Alaska the struggling companies faced tremendous problems of building in a rugged terrain and were hampered by severe climatic conditions. The federal government, however, not only refused aid but penalized the operators by imposing a tax of one hundred dollars for each mile the railroad had in operation, even though the construction of the line had not been completed.

When President Roosevelt closed the coal fields of Alaska to further entry in 1906, railroad builders felt that they had been struck another blow by being deprived of a cheap source of fuel. Roosevelt, the first American president to become vitally interested in the conservation of America's resources, claimed that the existing laws limiting investors to 160 acres were unworkable and conducive to fraud. He asked Congress to enact legislation that would enable prospective coal-mine operators to obtain enough land to make mining profitable yet prevent any individual or group from securing a monopoly. The Alaska Coal Act, passed on May 28, 1908, permitted the consolidation of claims up to 2,560 acres. The act did not contain a leasing system, but it prevented the monopolization of Alaska coal lands and eliminated the use of dummy entrymen, that is, individuals who claimed lands with the intention of conveying them to someone else.

Roosevelt further recommended that the United States should aid in building a railroad from the Gulf of Alaska to the Yukon. He also repeated an earlier proposal: that Alaska be allowed to send a delegate to Congress who would be entitled to a seat in the House of Representatives with all the emoluments of a member of that body. The delegate could introduce measures of concern to himself and his constituents and take part in the debates but could not vote. Some believed that once Alaska had secured such a delegate, he would be listened to as an authority on Alaska affairs and would be able to influence Congress on the proper legislation for Alaska.

Early Oil Exploration

Gold was not the only sought-after resource in Alaska. In the late nineteenth century, oil prospectors directed their energies to finding the source of the oil seeps in the more accessible areas in the Gulf of Alaska. Various companies, such as Alaska Petroleum Company, Alaska Oil Company, Pacific Oil and Commercial Company, and Chilkat Oil Company, among others, were the first to sink wells in Alaska. There were also reports of oil seeps in lakes and near riverbeds. The abundance of oil on the surface made the area attractive to wildcatters. These men did not know, however, that seeps more often than not were not an accurate indicator of subsurface petroleum reservoirs.[71]

In 1892, a prospector named Edelman staked claims to the oil-and-gas seeps on the western shore of Cook Inlet, near the Iniskin Peninsula. In 1896 oil seepages were also noted in the Katalla and Yakataga areas of the Gulf of Alaska.[72] Edelman abandoned his claims for unknown reasons, but in 1896 prospectors again staked claims on the Iniskin Peninsula and also in the Katalla and Yakataga districts. Operators began drilling for oil in the Iniskin area and in 1898 brought in a wildcat well at Oil Bay. The operators reported an oil flow of fifty barrels a day at seven hundred feet. After probing to one thousand feet, the drill tapped a sea water stratum that choked off the oil flow.

In 1902 the Alaska Oil Company drilled a wildcat

well at Puale Bay, on the east coast of the Alaska Peninsula. At about the same time the Chilkat Oil Company drilled another well in the Katalla district on the coast east of the mouth of the Copper River. Although both were unsuccessful, the operators had found enough encouragement to continue testing. In 1904 the Alaska Oil Company had drilled two more dry holes at Cold Bay. The Chilkat Oil Company was luckier at the time and found oil in the Katalla district. Between 1902 and 1931 it drilled thirty-six wells, eighteen of which produced oil. This was the first commercial oil production in Alaska, although oil flow was low, ranging to twenty barrels a day.

In 1911 the Chilkat Oil Company built a small topping plant at Katalla Slough. It began operating in 1912 and sold its products in Cordova. Katalla prospered, and its main street was lined with hotels, restaurants, and saloons. As many as ten thousand people may have called Katalla home during the boom year of 1907, but the number declined gradually. Late in 1933 a fire destroyed the boiler house at the topping plant, and the company abandoned the entire operation. Katalla soon became a ghost town.[73] During the twenty-nine years of its production history, the Katalla field produced only a modest 154,000 barrels of oil—not enough to supply even local needs. The Katalla wells had been shallow, most not over one thousand feet deep and none more than two thousand feet deep.[74]

For all practical purposes oil exploration ended in 1904 because operators had failed to find oil in commercial quantities, exploration costs had been high, and it had been difficult to obtain title to oil lands under the placer-mining laws then in effect. Furthermore, oil discoveries and developments elsewhere, particularly in California, supplied demands at reasonable prices. The federal government withdrew Alaska lands from oil and gas leasing in 1910.

The Push for Home Rule and the Ballinger-Pinchot Affair

A curious chain of circumstances enabled Alaska to secure a congressional delegate. In a Supreme Court case involving a Mrs. Rasmussen, who had been convicted by a six-man jury of running a house of ill fame in Fairbanks, the high court ruled that when the United States purchased Alaska it had guaranteed to the white inhabitants and persons of mixed blood the rights, privileges, and immunities of American citizens. As an Alaska inhabitant, therefore, Mrs. Rasmussen was a resident of an incorporated territory and entitled to the full protection of the Constitution. Her conviction by a six-man jury violated the Sixth Amendment and was therefore void. Congress reacted quickly to the Court's views on the status of Alaska and changed the official designation from "district" to "territory." It also enacted the measure that gave Alaska a delegate to Congress.[75]

In 1909, the newly inaugurated president, William Howard Taft, attended the Alaska-Yukon Exposition in Seattle, where Alaskans greeted him warmly and made him a member of the Arctic Brotherhood, a fraternal organization of Alaska pioneers. While he was in Seattle, Taft advocated the creation of a legislative commission to deal with Alaska problems, with members appointed by the president. This was the system that he had administered while he was governor-general of the Philippines, and it would, he thought, be most suitable for Alaska, which lacked the population and resources for a legislature. However, Taft's remarks were greeted with cries of "No, no," and were generally interpreted by Alaskans as insulting. The president, they felt, thought they were not fit for self-government.[76]

Undoubtedly Taft would have been happier if he had never heard of Alaska and had not become involved in northern affairs. His administration was plagued by an Alaska issue that had far more serious consequences for him than the question of a territorial legislature. Two members of his administration—Richard Ballinger, secretary of the interior, and Chief Forester Gifford Pinchot—became embroiled in a controversy that quickly became known as the Ballinger-Pinchot Affair. To understand the origins of the affair and its consequences for the Alaska home-rule movement, it is necessary to return to Roosevelt's withdrawal of the coal lands in 1906.

Among those who had attempted to obtain coal lands in Alaska before Roosevelt withdrew them were thirty-two persons who had given land agent and attorney Clarence Cunningham the power of attorney to make selections for them. Acting on their behalf, Cunningham had taken an option on 5,280 acres of land in the Bering River area, which Roosevelt incorporated in 1908 into the newly established Chugach National Forest. Cunningham's efforts to obtain patents for the land, hindered by repeated delays, were followed by rumors that the group had never intended to mine the coal themselves, as the law required, but that they had formed their association precisely for the purpose of transferring their claims to the Alaska Syndicate.

Richard Ballinger had been the commissioner of the General Land Office when Cunningham first applied for patent on behalf of his clients. Following his resignation from government service, as a private attorney Ballinger had advised the Cunningham group on the procedures to follow in processing their claims. Louis Glavis, an agent of the Department of the Interior sent to Alaska to examine the Cunningham claims, soon became convinced that Ballinger was preparing to validate their transfer to the syndicate. Glavis consulted Gifford Pinchot, an ardent conservationist, friend of Roosevelt, and head of the Bureau of Forestry. Pinchot advised Glavis to submit his findings to the president, which Glavis did. Taft, after reading Glavis's report, ordered Ballinger, who by then was secretary of the interior, to dismiss him "for filing a disingenuous statement unjustly impeaching the integrity of his superior officers." Pinchot himself was later fired on charges of insubordination for having written a letter to Senator Jonathan P. Dolliver highly critical of Taft's handling of the affair and his support of Ballinger. To the embarrassment of the administration, Dolliver read the letter on the floor of the Senate.

A joint congressional committee was formed to investigate the Department of the Interior for its handling of the Cunningham claims. The committee was also to examine the accusations made by Ballinger against some officials of the Bureau of Forestry, who, he complained, "had inspired the charges against his department." Voting on strictly party lines, the majority, composed of stalwart Republicans, exonerated Ballinger of any wrong-doing, while the Democrats and one progressive Republican found him guilty of violating his trust. Ballinger resigned in the summer of 1911. His successor as secretary of the interior, Walter Fisher, vice president of the National Conservation Association, soon afterward invalidated the Cunningham claims.[77]

Alaskans reveled in the publicity of the Ballinger-Pinchot Affair, which accelerated the movement for home rule in the territory. Its disclosures confirmed what proponents of home rule had been saying all along—that federal control had frustrated Alaska's development and that only Alaskans sitting in a legislature of their own could deal effectively with territorial problems. Supporters of the drive for a territorial legislature resented the total exclusion of Alaskans from matters of concern to them and were hardly mollified by the recent changes in the First Organic Act. Nor would they agree that a delegate to Congress could be an effective representative for Alaska. Such a delegate, they argued, was only one voice among many with interests in Alaskan affairs. A minority of Alaskans, chiefly representing mining and fishing interests, were satisfied with Alaska government as it was. They argued that Alaska's population was too small and unstable to afford a legislature and feared that if such a body were constituted it would undoubtedly destroy existing Alaska industries by excessive taxation.[78]

James Wickersham and the Second Organic Act

James Wickersham, the former judge of the third judicial district who had been elected as Alaska's delegate to Congress in 1908, took the leadership in the fight for a territorial legislature. Wickersham had portrayed himself in his election campaigns as the enemy of the trusts and monopolies, particularly the Guggenheim family (the "Guggs"), whom he denounced as enemies of Alaska self-government who wanted to bring all the resources of Alaska under their control. Wickersham's enemies made much of a letter that had come to light revealing that the self-professed "trustbuster" had once applied for a position with the syndicate and had been turned down. His enemies regarded his opposition to the

The first Alaska territorial House of Representatives, First Legislature, 1913.

(Courtesy of Historical Photograph Collection, Alaska and Polar Regions Archives, Elmer E. Rasmuson Library, University of Alaska Fairbanks.)

syndicate as sour grapes, and his recent conversion to home rule as equally opportunistic and insincere.

Wickersham used his influence to help defeat a bill, sponsored by Senator Albert J. Beveridge of Indiana, that embodied Taft's recommendations for a legislative commission to govern Alaska. He was unsuccessful in his early attempts to have the House approve any proposals for a territorial legislature for Alaska. But by 1911 the political climate had changed considerably. President Taft, an adamant opponent of a territorial legislature, had lost control of Congress in the mid-term elections of 1910. But formidable opposition to home rule for Alaska

remained. Wickersham was very much aware that he would have to make substantial concessions to different groups to get congressional approval for his bill and avoid a veto by the president. Although progressives were ideologically committed to home rule, there was fear among the conservationists that an Alaska legislature would be dominated by developers. Business groups, notably representatives of fishing and mining interests, opposed the idea that a territorial legislature would regulate the industries. These interests also feared the high taxes that a legislature might impose. Crusaders for moral reform heard Wickersham branded a tool of the liquor and gambling interests by his enemies, and they questioned whether Alaskans were capable of undertaking the responsibilities of self-government.[79]

Wickersham's campaign had mixed results. On August 24, 1912, President Taft signed the Second Organic Act, which created a new government for Alaska. The territory now had a legislature, but so many restrictions had been placed upon that body that Wickersham's many critics, including some who had opposed home rule, complained bitterly that he had sold out Alaska. The federal government still retained control of the use of Alaska's resources. The Alaskan Lobby, as the representatives of the mining and fishing interests were called, had succeeded in putting a clause in the Second Organic Act that expressly forbade the Alaska legislature "to alter, amend, modify and repeal measures relating to fish and game, or to interfere with the primary disposal of the soil." Congress retained for itself the exclusive right to legislate on matters relating to divorce, gambling, the sale of liquor, and the incorporation of towns, and it required that its approval be obtained before the Alaska legislature could set up a form of county government. Strict limitations were placed on the fiscal authority of the new government. The territory was forbidden to borrow money; its taxing power was restricted to 1 percent of the assessed valuation of property, except for towns, which were allowed 2 percent. Alaska's governor was a presidential appointee whose veto power extended to line items in appropriation bills.[80]

The Second Organic Act provided that the Alaska legislature was to consist of two houses: a senate of eight members and a house of representatives of sixteen members. Since Alaska had no political subdivisions, members of the Alaska legislature were selected in accordance with the judicial districts. Each district, regardless of population, elected four members to the House and two to the Senate. Alaska was still unique among territories in not having a judiciary of its own; the U.S. president appointed the judges, whose numbers had been increased to four in 1900. Although the judges were federal appointees, their jurisdiction included both federal and territorial affairs. Congress agreed to pay the salaries of the legislators and the expenses of administration.

Following the passage of the Second Organic Act, Alaskans held an election and organized the legislature. Most of the legislators regarded themselves as independents; party organization was still very weak. Although severely limited by the restrictions of the act, the early legislature dealt with a wide variety of subjects. Lawmakers made substantial changes to bring civil and criminal codes more in conformity with the Alaska environment. Labor legislation included establishing an eight-hour work day, defining conditions of employment in the mines, and providing for a system of pensions. Alaska women were granted the right to vote. Native villages in southeastern Alaska were accorded some rights of self-government. Education received much attention. A territorial board was formed to coordinate the school system and give aid to schools.[81] Segregation of school children by race, introduced with the passage of the Nelson Act of 1905, continued. Apologists for the dual system argued that putting Natives with poorer backgrounds in schools with Americans not only would place them at a serious disadvantage but also would result in lowering educational standards for all.

President Woodrow Wilson and Alaska

When Democrat Woodrow Wilson was elected to the presidency in 1912, he promised that Alaska's problems would receive the utmost consideration in his administration. Wilson was an activist, and his legislative program contemplated substantial reforms in the United States. On the subject of Alaska he was explicit. In his State of the Union address to Congress in 1913 (the first delivered in person by a president since the days of Thomas Jefferson), he emphasized that "a duty faces us with regard to Alaska," a duty that he found "very pressing and very imperative"—in effect a "double duty," for it concerned "both the political and material development of the territory." He urged that Alaska be given "full territorial government" Although he did not elaborate, he undoubtedly was calling attention to the deficiencies in the Alaska system, for its people did not have the right to elect their governor and choose their judges, as the citizens of other territories did. He wanted the resources of Alaska unlocked and made available for use, but he counseled that they should not be "destroyed or wasted," for the "abiding interests of communities" must be placed above any "narrow idea of individual rights" that could bring about monopoly. A railroad should be built in Alaska and administered by the federal government "for the service and development of the country and its people.[82]

Although Congress refused to make changes in the Alaska system of government, it did pass the Mondell Act, which reopened the Alaska coal lands to entry. In line with Wilson's suggestion, it instituted a method of leasing rather than outright ownership that could lead to monopoly. Prospective coal-mine operators were given the opportunity to obtain up to 2,560 acres of land, for which they paid a rental fee ranging from twenty-five cents an acre for the first year of operation to one dollar after the fifth year. For each ton of coal mined, a royalty of two cents was paid. Alaskan coal thus could be available for use by the railroad recently authorized by Congress.

Even before Wilson took office as president, the groundwork had been laid for the federal government's sponsorship of a railroad in Alaska. So now, largely owing to the influence of Wickersham, regarded as an authority on Alaska affairs, the president was given the authority to choose the route of the railroad. Surveys of alternate sites had already been made by the Alaska Engineering Commission, established during the preceding administration. After some study and discussion, Wilson directed that the line should run from Seward, at tidewater, to Fairbanks, in the interior. Congress appropriated $35 million for the project. Construction began in April 1915, but the project was not finished until 1923 because the difficulties in construction were formidable. Work was carried on sporadically and was marked by innumerable delays. Also Congress followed the practice of annual appropriations, allotting only a certain amount of money for each year's operation; when funds ran out, work stopped. During World War I the use of labor and materials was drastically curtailed.

The immediate effect of the railroad construction was a boom in Alaska. More than 2,000 workers were employed in construction in 1914, their numbers rising to a high of 4,500. Although the pay was only thirty-seven and a half cents an hour in the early years, the number of applicants for jobs far exceeded demand. Anchorage, now Alaska's largest city, owes its beginnings to the railroad. Begun as a construction site, it won out in competition with Seward to become the headquarters of the Alaska Engineering Commission. The commission built Anchorage, installing water, electrical, sewage, and telephone facilities; putting in streets; and providing firefighting services as well as a hospital and a school for the children of its employees. An official of the railroad was named the town site manager.

While the American government was building a railroad to improve Alaska's transportation system, Congress passed legislation that placed new restrictions on Alaska's commerce. The Maritime Act, usually called the Jones Act after its sponsor, Washington senator Wesley Jones, was intended to build up the American merchant marine, and it mandated that all ships engaged in commerce between American ports be American-owned and built in the United States. The act gave shippers the option of using either American- or Canadian-owned vessels to carry goods from a port in the United States to its destination somewhere in the Atlantic or the Pacific—with the exception of Alaska. Merchandise coming into or exported from Alaska had to be carried on American ships. American vessels had to be used even if shippers to Alaska could obtain better rates from Canadians.

Alaskans protested that this discrimination violated the commerce clause of the Constitution. They brought suit to have the portion of the act singling out Alaska declared null and void. Justice James Clark McReynolds, speaking for the Supreme Court, acknowledged that the act discriminated against Alaska commerce but pointed out that the Constitution clearly states that "no preference shall be given any regulation or commerce or revenue to the ports of one state over those of another."[83] Since Alaska was a territory, not a state, Congress had the power to discriminate if it so chose. That the act might be beneficial to Seattle, the chief port of Senator Jones's state, Washington, was not for the courts to decide.

Alaska Enters a New Era

In 1920, Alaska had a population of slightly more than fifty-five thousand, a loss of more than 14 percent during the previous decade. When the United States entered World War I, many residents had left Alaska to enter the armed services or to work in war industries. Following the war, the United States experienced an economic boom, and many felt little inducement to return to Alaska, where the opportunities appeared to be more limited. The Alaska economy was still centered on the exploitation of its natural resources. Mining and fishing far outdistanced the fur trade, Alaska's mainstay in the Russian era. But the fisheries provided little employment for territorial residents, since the salmon packers brought their crews with them from the outside. The era of the great Gold Rush was over, and the primitive mining methods of the prospector had given way to the use of machinery. Dredges were now recovering the gold buried deep in the ground. Copper mining had come to rival gold but provided jobs for several hundred at most. Alaska agriculture had not flourished. In 1923, Alaska's chief agricultural regions, Fairbanks and Anchorage-Matanuska, had only ninety farmers, and they held 22,167 acres of land, only 11,421 of which were cultivated.

Alaska was still very much a colony of the United States. It had been given a limited form of home rule, but control of its resources remained in the hands of Congress. The Alaska economy was colonial; the territory supplied raw materials to the mother country, from which it obtained most of its finished goods and the capital needed for investment in its enterprises. While Congress had finally appropriated money to build a railroad in Alaska, American lawmakers more often than not ignored Alaska's problems or passed laws that were ill advised. Alaska's coal fields had been closed to entry for eight years because of congressional inaction. How much harm was done to Alaska commerce by the Jones Act is uncertain, but there is no doubt about the discriminatory nature of the legislation.

President Warren G. Harding speaking in Fairbanks, Alaska, July 1923.

(Courtesy of Alaska and Polar Regions Department, Elmer E. Rasmuson Library, University of Alaska Fairbanks.)

Chapter 11

Normalcy, the Depression, and the New Deal

Warren G. Harding succeeded Wilson as president of the United States in 1921. An exponent of the contemporary reaction, he repudiated the idealism of his predecessor, denounced the League of Nations, and declared in his inaugural address that it was a time for "normalcy and not nostrums." His brief tenure as president was an unhappy time for him, and his administration was plagued with scandals. He referred to the presidency as "this damned job," complained about the multiplicity of problems that he so little understood, and confessed his inability to make choices from conflicting advice, especially that of economists.

On the subject of Alaska, Harding was much more positive. The first president to visit the territory, he went to Nenana in 1923 to drive the golden spike symbolizing the completion of the Alaska Railroad. He spoke with feeling about Alaska, remarking that "if the Finns owned Alaska they would in three generations make it one of the foremost states of the Union." He urged that Alaska's resources should be used to benefit settlers and not for the advantage of outside speculators. He promised that his administration would work to the utmost to help develop Alaska. Unfortunately, on his return trip to Washington he became ill, and he died shortly thereafter. With his death, wrote Ernest Gruening, governor of Alaska in the New Deal era and later elected U.S. senator from the new state, Alaska "lost a great friend at court."[1]

It was during Harding's administration that the federal government made its only serious attempt to deal with the problem of the Alaska salmon fisheries. In the years that followed, this issue, among others, brought to light the territory's ambiguous relationship with Washington, D.C., and its dependence on external factors for its growth and development. The Depression brought the New Deal to Alaska in unique ways, and brought it to the brink of its "coming of age" in World War II.

Alaska's Salmon: The Problem

The salmon industry was dominated early by firms from outside the territory. There was little capital available in Alaska to make the heavy investments necessary for building canneries and carrying on fishing operations. The fishing grounds were usually in isolated areas, where the population was small and scattered. It was much easier for the great packers with headquarters in Seattle and San Francisco to bring their own crews to Alaska than to recruit labor in the territory.[2]

Even before the turn of the century, warnings were given that overfishing and reckless exploitation endangered the salmon supply. Government regulation, when it came, was sporadic and generally ineffective. In 1889, Congress passed a law that forbade the damming of streams to catch fish on their way to the spawning beds. Three years passed

An aerial view of salmon traps in various stages of construction at Sunny Point, near Ketchikan.

(Courtesy of Lulu Fairbanks Collection, Alaska and Polar Regions Department, Elmer E. Rasmuson Library, University of Alaska Fairbanks.)

before the lawmakers appropriated the funds to hire an inspector and an assistant to see that the law was enforced. And since no commercial transportation existed, the inspectors had to depend on the ships of the packers whose activities they sought to regulate.[3]

In the 1890s several scientists of the U.S. Fish Commission became convinced that artificial propagation was the answer to the dwindling salmon runs. Little was done, however, until 1903, when the control of the Alaska fisheries was transferred from the U.S. Treasury Department to the newly created Department of Commerce and Labor, and the duties involved in regulating the fishing industry were

entrusted to the department's Bureau of Fisheries. In 1905 the bureau succeeded in getting appropriations for the construction of two hatcheries in Alaska but met with great opposition from the packers when it attempted to gain greater regulatory powers from Congress. The bill "for the protection and regulation of fisheries in Alaska," which became law in 1906, gave the secretary of commerce the authority to regulate fishing only within five hundred yards of the mouths of rivers and streams instead of within the three miles that the bureau desired.[4]

The problem of overfishing was exacerbated by the introduction of traps. By the turn of the century many Alaskans were fishing as a means of livelihood or to supplement their income, and the bargaining over prices was spirited. In 1912, when a major strike of fishermen took place, many packers decided to use more traps for catching fish as a way of bypassing the independent fishermen altogether. A trap was a huge, permanent installation of log piles and netting that extended out from the shore for about a half mile across the paths fish travel on their way to spawning grounds in rivers and streams. In the fall the trap was dismantled, and it had to be rebuilt anew for each fishing season. The cost of construction was high, but it was easy to maintain; usually only a single watchman was employed to load the fish into a scow and guard against theft.

Traps were the most efficient method of catching fish, but their employment touched off the great political debate that ended only after Alaska achieved statehood and the legislature made their use illegal. Although traps were blamed for having brought about the depletion of the salmon, the controversy surrounding the use of the traps, according to economist Richard Cooley, was basically an issue between labor and capital, and between resident and nonresident groups, about who should benefit from the exploitation of Alaska's salmon resources. Alaskans who wanted the fisheries used primarily to afford more people the opportunity of earning a livelihood and thus to encourage settlement feared that traps would give the packers complete control of the industry and drive independent fishermen out of business. In contrast, an article in the *Pacific Fisherman*, the packers' trade journal, asserted that the trap was "the best and only friend the canners have in Alaska" and went on to say that "if this method of catching fish is prohibited it will mean almost the entire dissolution of the industry."[5]

The Bureau of Fisheries ignored the social aspects of the conflict, instead supporting the use of traps as part of the competitive system on which the nation's economy was based. The packers praised the Bureau of Fisheries and preferred federal to local regulation—at least in Alaska. Hearings on the fisheries were usually held in Washington, and though few Alaska fishermen could afford the trip there, the representatives of the packers never missed a meeting. Further, when the bureau established a Pacific branch in Seattle in 1917, the office was conveniently housed in a building where twenty of the major salmon companies were located. The *Pacific Fisherman* was pleased by the continued federal control of the fisheries and following the passage of the Second Organic Act, it openly gloated that Alaskans had been given "a toy legislature to play with."[6]

Both the Bureau of Fisheries and the Department of Commerce and Labor strongly resisted any suggestions that the territory be given a voice in the management of the salmon fisheries. William C. Redfield, secretary of commerce in President Wilson's cabinet, had feared that the territory would destroy the industry through high taxes and license fees. E. Lester Jones, deputy commissioner of the Bureau of Fisheries, insisted that "any idea of transferring jurisdiction to the Territory or any other agency should be completely dismissed."[7]

When Hugh Smith, a scientist, became commissioner of the fisheries in 1915, he stated that there was no cause for alarm concerning the depletion of Alaska salmon. He claimed that by expanding the program of artificial propagation through the fish hatcheries, "the perpetuation of the Alaska salmon fisheries can be achieved . . . without any general or material curtailment of fishing operations or reduction of output." Economist Cooley points out that this was something the packers "wanted to hear," and Smith was hailed for his intelligence and practical wisdom. Artificial propagation was accepted as an act of faith, but no studies were carried out to see whether Smith's optimism had any validity.

Congress appropriated more money for the hatchery program than for any other aspect of the bureau's work. Only a pittance, however, was made available for its scientific studies and regulatory functions. Warnings from Alaska fishermen and territorial officials that salmon were declining in great numbers went unheeded as long as the demand, accelerated by wartime government orders, continued. But with the conclusion of the war, not only were fish no longer needed in large quantities, but other countries were also selling their surplus salmon stocks on the open market. Prices for salmon declined drastically. Spokesmen for the packers now admitted that overfishing had been taking place and that the need for conservation was manifest. "Even before Dr. Smith took office," an editorial writer in the *Pacific Fisherman* stated, "the approaching danger to the salmon fishery and the need of accurate knowledge were apparent to anyone interested in its future."[8] Smith resigned under a cloud in 1921. Three years later, his successor as commissioner of fisheries, Henry O'Malley, told a congressional committee that artificial propagation was not the solution to the problem of conservation of Alaska's salmon.

The Fishery Reserves and the White Act

In view of the emergency, Herbert Hoover, secretary of commerce in the Harding administration, took personal charge and held lengthy hearings on the plight of the salmon industry. When he was unable to secure the legislation from Congress that he felt was necessary to restore the health of the salmon fisheries, Hoover recommended that President Harding issue an extensive order temporarily establishing the Alaska Peninsula Reserve, where fishing was to be by permit only. The executive order was issued on February 17, 1922. Several months later, another executive order created the Southwestern Fishery Reservation, which included the Kodiak and Bristol Bay areas. Supporters of reservations maintained that the only way to halt overfishing was to limit the number of people allowed to fish. This restriction of the use of the fisheries was indeed a revolutionary development, for it marked a break in the American tradition of a fishery generally free and open to all.[9]

Opposition to the reservations came quickly. Dan Sutherland, the Alaska delegate to Congress, charged that only employees of the large companies, and no Alaskans, were able to secure fishing places. He accused the administration of hypocrisy and declared that the government had never been interested in conservation, as it now claimed, but was really interested only in establishing a monopoly for the salmon packers. Several newspapers echoed his cry. The administration, stung by the force of the criticism, sought to involve Congress in finding a solution to the problem of the salmon fisheries.[10]

In 1923, Secretary Hoover accompanied President Harding to Alaska for the ceremonies marking the completion of the Alaska Railroad. While they were there, Hoover held hearings in several towns to hear firsthand about fishery conditions in Alaska. Congress passed bills based largely on his recommendations, and Harding's successor, President Calvin Coolidge, signed the measure known as the White Act in 1924.

The White Act was very much the product of compromise. Two controversial items that had been proposed—the fishery reservations and the outlawing of fish traps—were deleted. The act gave the secretary of commerce the authority "to limit or prohibit fishing in all territorial waters of Alaska" and allowed him to fix the size and character, but not the amount, of fishing gear. To achieve the desired goal of conservation, Congress directed that at least 50 percent of the fish be allowed to escape to their spawning grounds. Nothing, however, was done to see that this objective was attained.

Secretary Hoover spoke with pride of his achievement in getting Congress to approve the measure, and shortly after it was signed, he announced that fish had become so plentiful that foreign vessels were invading the Alaska fishing grounds. By 1925 the demand for salmon had increased significantly, and as the price rose, the salmon catch increased correspondingly. The packers hailed Hoover as the savior of the salmon industry, and as long as the total output continued to increase year after year, they considered the government's conservation program successful.[11]

The Alaska Railroad and the Growth of Aviation

While Secretary Hoover was holding hearings in Alaska to save the salmon industry, Alaskans, especially those from the interior, hailed President Harding as he drove the golden spike at Nenana symbolizing the completion of the Alaska Railroad. The railroad, the first great construction project the federal government had initiated in Alaska, stimulated the Alaska economy by providing hundreds of jobs. Its construction was proclaimed as the advent of a new era of prosperity that would open up the interior for settlement and development.

Completed in 1923, the Alaska Railroad cost

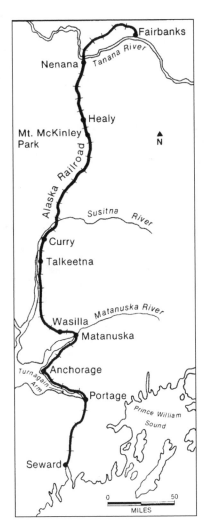

Route of the Alaska Railroad from
Seward to Fairbanks

A car with sled runners attached to the front wheels and chains on the
rear drive wheels at Valdez in the 1920s.

(Author's collection.)

$65 million, almost twice the amount originally earmarked for its construction; successive managers of the railroad blamed the poor condition of the roadbed and the low quality of the equipment for the unusually high operations costs. Soon after service began, Congress appropriated an additional $17 million for improvements, but much more was needed to make the railroad efficient. In its early years the Alaska Railroad seemed to be almost constantly under attack. The anticipated boom following its completion did not materialize. According to George Rogers, an authority on northern areas, "When the railroad was new, three out of four people one met along the Yukon maintained

that the railway to Fairbanks had done harm to the Interior by competing with river traffic just enough to ruin the steamboat companies without supplying an alternative service more adequate to take their place."[12]

The railroad was plagued by almost continuous deficits. The cost of maintenance was high and the number of passengers few, since the population of the rail belt remained small. While the mines benefited from the railroad, an export trade in coal failed to develop as the railroad planners had anticipated. This meant lower freight loads and not enough business to make the railroad a success. In Congress there was almost constant criticism of the railroad as an expensive luxury, and several members demanded that the line be closed. Then, in 1928, Colonel Otto F. Ohlsen, a veteran railroad man with twenty-seven years' experience with the Northern Pacific Railroad, became general manager of the Alaska Railroad. Under his direction the line experienced its first profitable year in 1938.[13]

Of much greater consequence for Alaska than the building of the Alaska Railroad was the beginning of the air age in the 1920s. Of all forms of transportation, air travel was the most readily adaptable to the northern environment. Alaska's great size, rugged terrain, and severe climatic conditions, together with the vast distances between communities, made the building and maintenance of roads and railroads

High trestle and construction camp, Mile 49, 1907. A trestle of the Alaska Central Railroad, demonstrating the engineering expertise needed in the harsh terrain.

(Author's collection.)

extremely expensive. Before World War II there were only 2,500 miles of road in Alaska, and only a single highway, the Richardson, connected Valdez to Fairbanks. Apart from the Alaska Railroad, only 22.4 miles of the White Pass and Yukon Route railroad, which ran from Skagway to Whitehorse, passed through Alaska. Service on the Copper River and Northwest Railway was discontinued in 1938.

The airplane made it possible for previously isolated communities such as Nome to have year-round contact with the outside world. Bush pilots were able to fly into villages that previously had been accessible only by dogsled. Supplies could be taken into remote areas as needed by miners, fishermen, loggers, traders, and trappers. Thanks to the airplane, it became possible to bring the sick and the injured swiftly to hospitals in towns, or doctors and nurses could be sent into the field where help was

urgently needed. Government agencies were able to use the airplane to great advantage. In the summer of 1929, navy fliers undertook an aerial survey in southeastern Alaska, mapping ten thousand miles of territory. Weather observations by plane were first made in 1930 and 1931. The Bureau of Fisheries also used planes to check for violations of regulations.

By the 1930s planes were being used extensively in Alaska. Airmail service, which had been used intermittently for a number of years, was established in 1937 on a regular basis for many communities. That year planes carried almost five hundred thousand pounds of mail, and the U.S. Post Office ceased using dogsleds in many areas. Before World War II, "Alaska had 116 times as many planes, which flew 70 times as many miles, carried 23 times as many passengers, carried 1,034 times as much freight and express and 48 times as much mail as the United States on a per capita basis." A report compiled in 1937 listed ninety-seven civilian airfields in Alaska, most built with money appropriated by the territorial legislature. The federal government spent only a pittance in support of Alaska aviation; most of the money appropriated for transportation in Alaska went to the Alaska Railroad.[14]

The "Twilit Twenties"

Calvin Coolidge, who succeeded Harding as president of the United States, never exhibited his predecessor's interest in the welfare and development of Alaska. A firm believer in the dogma that "the business of America is business," Coolidge's chief concern regarding Alaska seemed to be that the money spent there appeared to be "far out of proportion to the number of its inhabitants and the amount of production,"[15] and he whittled away at appropriations for the territory.

Although the Harding-Coolidge era was a period of prosperity for the United States, Alaska, which was not in the mainstream of American life, was little affected by the great advances made in manufacturing and commerce. The Alaska population remained almost static, growing by only a few thousand during the decade one writer has called "the twilit twenties." Aside from the building of the Alaska Railroad, which employed hundreds, Alaska's colonial economy followed with consistent "regularity . . . the seasonal harvesting of fish, canning of salmon, trapping of fur bearers and the mining of gold."[16]

Mining production was lower because the great demand for copper of the war years had ended. In 1930, the fifteenth census listed 4,800 persons working in the mines, and it was estimated that an equal number were engaged in supplying and servicing the industry. After the postwar slump, the demand for salmon increased again, attaining a new high in 1926 when more than 6.5 million cans were packed. Almost six thousand Alaskans operated as independent fishermen, but they were only a small percentage of the workforce employed in the industry. The value of furs taken in Alaska, slightly more than

Recovering the bodies of Will Rogers and Wiley Post from the tail of the plane in which they died, Point Barrow, August 1935. The famous comedian and film star was also a great booster of aviation and undertook a flight around the world with a fellow Oklahoman, world-renowned aviator Wiley Post, in the summer of 1935. Post's plane, an experimental and nose-heavy hybrid of Lockheed Explorer and Orion, crashed south of Barrow, Alaska, on August 15, 1935, when its engine failed on takeoff, killing both men.

(Courtesy of the National Archives.)

Salmon drying racks at the village of Aniakchak.

(Courtesy of the National Park Service.)

$2 million, was small compared to that of mining or fishing. But trapping provided most or all of the cash income for many Alaskans, especially Natives, and many Alaskans lived off the land by hunting, fishing, and trapping.

Alaska's timber resources were gradually being put to use. In 1913 the territory imported 84 percent of its timber; by 1925 this percentage had been reversed. Two years earlier a mill at Ketchikan had begun exporting to Seattle spruce, which exporters then shipped to the United Kingdom and Australia. But with the onset of the Great Depression, the plans that had been made to build two pulp mills in southeastern Alaska were abandoned.[17]

The federal government had withdrawn lands from oil and gas leasing in 1910, but in 1920, the Oil and Gas Leasing Act was passed. This legislation once again spurred activities in Alaska that centered on the known oil-bearing areas of south-central Alaska, but prospectors also examined new regions, such as the Chignik district on the Alaska Peninsula; the vicinity of Anchorage; the Cook In-let–Susitna Valley area; and a location near Killis-noo, on Admiralty Island, in southeastern Alaska. Major companies drilled in the Kanatak district, on the Alaska Peninsula, between 1923 and 1926, and the first test well in the Yakataga district was drilled during 1926 and 1927. In 1920 entrepreneurs drilled a well to a shallow depth on the outskirts of Anchorage, an event recorded in the name of Oil Well Road. From 1926 to 1930 a test well was drilled near Chickaloon in the Matanuska Valley, and between 1938 and 1940 operators sank two deep test wells, one on the Iniskin Peninsula and the other in the Kanatak district. Neither produced oil in commercial quantities. This, and the advent of World War II, with its restrictions and withdrawals of public lands for leasing, temporarily ended oil explorations.[18]

The Teapot Dome Scandal

Despite failures, geologist Alfred Brooks maintained his optimism regarding territorial oil. In June 1922, the press quoted him as telling a Seattle group that he was confident that "oil will be found in Alaska, and the probabilities are that there are extensive [oil] areas in the Territory." Perhaps President Harding was influenced by Brook's optimism when he created Naval Petroleum Reserve No. 4 (NPR-4) by executive order on February 27, 1923. The reserved area on the North Slope comprised approximately thirty-seven thousand square miles, a large area surrounding the oil seeps at Cape Simpson and extending to the Colville River on the east and south to the crest of the Brooks Range.

NPR-4 was the last reserve an executive order created. NPR-1, Elk Hills, had been created on September 2, 1912; NPR-2, Buena Vista Hills, on December 13, 1912; and NPR-3, Teapot Dome, on April 30, 1915. These executive orders did not vest in the Navy Department any specific jurisdiction over the reserves or authorize it to "perform any acts" within the reserves. Neither did any legislation give the Navy Department any power over the reserves; the Department of the Interior maintained general jurisdiction over the land in the reserves. On June 4, 1920, legislation directed the secretary of the navy to take possession of government property in the naval petroleum reserves. It authorized him to conserve, develop, use, and operate the reserves and to use, store, exchange, or sell the oil and gas from the reserves. Despite this broad authority, the Navy Department decided on a policy of preserving the reserves intact, permitting drilling only when

necessary to offset protection against drainage from oil wells on adjacent lands.

On May 31, 1921, the naval reserves were transferred to the Department of the Interior. Subsequently, the Department of the Interior leased all the government land in NPR-1, the Elk Hills reserve, to the interests of oilman Edward L. Doheny. The department also leased the entire NPR-3, Teapot Dome, which consisted entirely of federal land, to another oilman, Harry F. Sinclair. Contractual arrangements provided for the disposal of the government's royalty oil to the Doheny and Sinclair interests. Circumstances surrounding the Sinclair leases led the Walsh Committee of the U.S. Senate to conduct an investigation. It resulted in litigation and the 1927 cancellation of the Doheny and Sinclair leases and contracts because the act of June 4, 1920, had not authorized these transactions and because the leases and contracts had been obtained fraudulently.

On March 17, 1927, the executive order that had transferred the naval petroleum reserves to Interior was revoked and jurisdiction returned to the navy. The Department of the Interior, however, continued the actual administration of all leases in the reserves in accordance with an interdepartmental agreement signed on July 9, 1927, and revised on February 1, 1934. On December 31, 1927, after the return of the reserves to the navy, all producing wells in NPR-3 were shut down. Individuals who produced oil from nearby lands outside the reserve entered into compensatory royalty agreements to compensate the government for loss suffered through drainage. To prevent rapid development of NPR-2 by government lessees under leases issued when Interior had jurisdiction, a plan for cooperative development was adopted on October 1, 1935. This agreement controlled the rate of prospecting and development and the quantity and rate of production on government land in and outside the reserve but on the same geologic structure.

The Standard Oil Company owned a checkerboard pattern of lands outside NPR-1 that endangered the reserve. The navy asked Congress to protect the reserve. The act of June, 30, 1938, amended the act of June 4, 1920. It authorized the secretary of the navy, with presidential approval, to contract with the private owners of lands within the exterior

President Franklin D. Roosevelt in a mess hall on the Aleutian Islands, August 3, 1944.

(Courtesy of Franklin D. Roosevelt Library, Hyde Park, New York.)

boundaries of reserves to conserve oil in the ground, and to make exchanges in order to acquire privately owned lands in NPR-1. In accordance with this act, the Navy Department and Standard Oil Company signed an agreement on November 20, 1943. Under its terms Standard Oil Company conveyed its lands to the United States in return for the right to operate the combined properties in the reserve and to receive its full share of production from the reserve. The U.S. attorney general, however, found that the agreement was inconsistent with the 1938 one, and thus it was rescinded on September 8, 1943. The act was basically revived, however, on June 17, 1944,

when Congress amended the 1938 act further so as to broaden and clarify the Navy Department's authority to operate the reserves.[19]

Alaska in the Great Depression

Because Alaska had not shared in the American prosperity of the 1920s, it suffered less from the traumas of the 1930s, but the Great Depression did have some effects upon the territorial economy. Employment in the mines declined; the number of copper miners decreased from 570 to 143. The value of salmon fell with the drop in commodity prices, and wages were cut. The expansion of the lumbering industry halted. Federal appropriations for agencies in Alaska, which had never been very high, were cut. Because of its perennial deficits, the Alaska Railroad came increasingly under attack. As the depression deepened in the 1930s, some Americans looked to Alaska as a place to escape from their economic woes. After all, there were plenty of moose, caribou, and salmon, and land, they believed, could be had for the asking.

In the heart of the depression, the American people turned to Franklin Delano Roosevelt as their new leader. When Roosevelt took office, more than 13 million Americans were unemployed, and many of those with jobs were not much better off. Wages ranged from twenty to thirty cents an hour in many basic industries, and it was not uncommon for men and women to receive less than two dollars for ten hours of labor. Although Roosevelt had been much opposed to an extensive public works program, he reluctantly came to the conclusion that increased intervention by the federal government was necessary. In essence, the New Deal was a composite of relief and reform programs that at times seemed to be working at cross purposes with one another. Alaskans shared in the New Deal, but since Alaska was a territory and not a state, its share was often small or even nonexistent.

Several actions of the Roosevelt administration benefited the territory, however. The president's decision to devalue the dollar by raising the price of gold stimulated an industry that had played a leading role in the development of Alaska. Beginning in

1936, gold production increased annually. The value of the mined ore rose from $10,209,000 in 1932 to $26,178,000 in 1940, and more workers were being employed in the mines as the production of gold rose.

Some New Deal agencies were active in Alaska, and direct relief payments made by the federal government were of some help in aiding the economy. The Work Projects Administration (WPA) gave employment to people on the relief rolls, paying them slightly more than the welfare grants they had been receiving but less than the prevailing wage. Another agency, the Public Works Administration (PWA), sponsored public undertakings in which private contractors employed men and women at the prevailing community wage rates. The federal government, through the National Youth Administration (NYA), helped young people remain in school by making part-time jobs available to them. As a result of these efforts, a number of public buildings, roads, airfields, docks, and bridges were constructed in the territory; a guidebook to Alaska was published; improvements were made to harbors; and a hotel was established at Mount McKinley National Park. Governor Ernest Gruening and Anthony J. Dimond, Alaska's delegate to Congress, were unsuccessful in their efforts to have some of the money received from the WPA used for undertakings they considered more appropriate to Alaska conditions. Dimond, however, was able to get a bill through Congress authorizing the town of Skagway to issue bonds of up to $40,000 so that it could obtain an equal grant or loan from the PWA to renovate its water system.[20]

Of all the New Deal agencies active in Alaska, the most innovative was the Civilian Conservation Corps (CCC). The CCC, established for young men eighteen to twenty-three years of age without regular employment, provided work on projects to "conserve, protect and renew natural resources." In Alaska, the U.S. Forest Service was put in charge of the CCC camps, and age restrictions were eliminated, since in Alaska most of the unemployed were middle-aged men rather than youths. A requirement of one year's residence in Alaska was instituted for enrollees. The CCC's work in Alaska took on many aspects: Men were used to build forest roads

Anthony J. Dimond

(Courtesy of the Dimond Collections, Alaska and Polar Regions Archives, Elmer E. Rasmuson Library, University of Alaska Fairbanks.)

and trails, bridges, warehouses, small-boat facilities, a trout hatchery at Ketchikan, a dock and small boat harbor at Cordova, drainage ditches, community wells, and landing fields. Houses were erected for the Bureau of Fisheries, along with shelter cabins, floats, a salmon weir, and a fifteen-room biological laboratory.

A good part of the work of the CCC was devoted to planning and building recreational areas. CCC workers helped excavate and restore Old Sitka, the site of a fort that Baranov had built in 1799. One of the most impressive projects was the restoration of totem poles. Historian Lawrence Rakestraw has stated that "nowhere was the work of the CCC more appreciated than in the isolated Native villages and missions in the Interior." There employees of the CCC built a musk ox corral on Nunivak Island; razed the army barracks at Saint Michael; helped clear land at Galena that had suffered extensive flood damage; built a telegraph line between Nulato and Unalakleet; and erected community houses and installed sanitation projects in many villages. Missionaries and teachers sent letters to the regional forester, expressing their appreciation for the projects.[21]

New Fisheries Problems

The New Deal not only created new agencies of government but also attempted to use old ones in its effort to bring the nation out of the depression. Frank Bell, in 1933 the newly appointed commissioner of the Bureau of Fisheries, emphasized that the bureau not only intended to maintain the salmon resource but also was very much interested in bringing its policies into line with the social and economic objectives of the New Deal, especially the goal of spreading employment. He recommended a program that involved reducing the number of fish traps and restricting their use so that local and independent fishermen could gain a larger share of the catch. However, Commissioner Bell ran into considerable opposition when he attempted to put his program into operation. As general market conditions improved in 1934 and 1935, more fish were caught, and the packers were successful not only in having most of Bell's program nullified but also in having Congress kill a bill proposed by Delegate Dimond to abolish the use of traps.[22]

A conflict also developed between resident and nonresident independent fishermen about who should benefit from the use of the Alaska salmon fisheries. Both groups were organized in the Alaska Fishermen's Union, headquartered in San Francisco. The union insisted that packers should pay the nonresident fishermen four cents more per fish than they paid the residents, and that nonresidents should receive most of the available fishing jobs. George Lane, the union's secretary, declared, "if the Alaska Fishermen's Union is expected to permit Alaskan residents to usurp their just proportion of jobs from the men in the States, we will refuse to permit any fishing in the area." Alaskans' attempt to organize their own union was unsuccessful because they were unable to secure recognition from the packers. According to economist Cooley, the resulting hostility that many Alaskans felt toward the outside forces of labor, capital, and government did much to hasten the drive for statehood for Alaska.[23]

In 1939, Bell resigned as commissioner of fisheries. His policies had come under attack from all quarters. The packers felt that he had gone too far in emphasizing the social responsibilities of the bureau, while the Alaska fishermen considered him ineffective. The Bureau of Fisheries was transferred from the Department of Commerce, which had always been more interested in promoting the sale of salmon than in their conservation and regulation, to the Department of the Interior, where it was merged with the Bureau of Biological Survey, an agency concerned with wildlife preservation, to become the Fish and Wildlife Service.

In the same year Delegate Dimond succeeded in having the House of Representatives agree to make an investigation of the administration of the Alaskan salmon fisheries. A subcommittee of the House Merchant Marine and Fisheries Committee, together with a joint committee of both houses of the Alaska legislature, traveled more than 3,700 miles and heard testimony both in Alaska and in the contiguous states before making its report. The subcommittee strongly recommended that "the fisheries of Alaska should be administered by the United States not solely for the purpose of conservation as contended by some, but also as an Alaska resource to be administered, controlled, regulated and operated in the interest of and for the benefit of the Alaskan people."[24]

But World War II once again increased demand for canned salmon. The canned salmon industry, based outside of the territory, had been at odds with Alaskan fishermen over the regulation of the territorial fisheries. With strong demand and rising prices for canned salmon, the adversaries jettisoned their disagreements and attempted only to gain the biggest slice of the salmon fishery for their respective groups. "Groups that normally were at each other's throats on certain issues frequently found no difficulty in making expedient alignments in opposition to government proposals which might reduce their respective cuts of the pie."[25] Regulation of the salmon became virtually a dead letter after 1940.

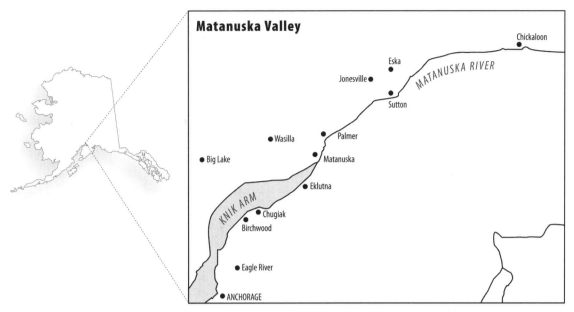

Matanuska Valley

Chickaloon

Eska

Jonesville

MATANUSKA RIVER

Sutton

Wasilla • Palmer

Big Lake • • Matanuska

• Eklutna

KNIK ARM

• Chugiak
Birchwood

• Eagle River

• ANCHORAGE

Matanuska Valley colonists drawing farm plots, 1936.

(Courtesy of Alaska and Polar Regions Department, Elmer E. Rasmuson Library, University of Alaska Fairbanks.)

The Matanuska Valley Colony

Of all the New Deal activities in Alaska, the Matanuska Valley Colony excited the greatest interest, extending far beyond the boundaries of the territory. As originally conceived, the colony was just one of the many resettlement projects the Roosevelt administration designed to take people away from rural districts in which poverty had long been prevalent and move them to places where they might lead more productive lives. But no other settlement approached Matanuska in the publicity it received, and in no other were the expectations so high.

The idea of creating a community in the wilderness stirred the imagination. Sponsors of the Alaskan colony included many who were not interested in relief and resettlement. Officials of the Alaska Railroad, who had long sponsored the movement of people to Alaska, were delighted, for the colony meant more passengers and freight, which would help make the line self-supporting. For Alaskans, the Matanuska project meant that the government was doing something for Alaska. There was a widespread belief that the colony would clearly demonstrate that farming was feasible in Alaska, and a successful agricultural industry would help to free Alaska from dependence on outside sources for food supplies.[26]

The Matanuska Valley is in the railbelt area of south-central Alaska. Its leading settlement, Palmer, is about forty miles from Anchorage. Before the colony was established, there was homesteading in the valley, but few settlers had made farming their principal means of livelihood. The climate of the valley is much milder than the latitude might indicate. It is warmer there in winter than in many areas of the northern part of the United States, although it is much cooler in the summer. Rainfall averages about sixteen inches a year. The quality of the soils of the valley varies considerably.

President Roosevelt opened the way for the new settlement on February 4, 1935, when he issued an executive order banning further homesteading in the valley and reserving all remaining land for the colonists. The Alaska Relief and Rehabilitation Corporation, then a part of the Federal Emergency Relief Administration, later the WPA, was formed to manage the colony. Surveys were made, and the land was divided into 208 plots ranging from forty to eighty acres, depending on the quality of the soil. Prices for these plots varied, and settlers were to make payments over a thirty-year period. The federal government agreed to build the houses and barns and pay for transporting families and up to two thousand pounds of their household goods to Alaska. Farm machinery, equipment, and livestock were made available by the corporation to the colonists for purchase or lease, and supplies could be obtained as needed at cost until the colonists became self-supporting. Educational, cultural, recreational, and health services were to be provided by the corporation, while the colonists agreed to observe the directives issued by the corporation relating to farm management and other colony affairs.

Colonists, 201 families in all, were to be selected for a place in the colony, all from northern counties of Michigan, Minnesota, and Wisconsin. It was believed that these people of northern European stock, coming from an area where climatic conditions presumably most closely resembled those of the Matanuska Valley, would make the best colonists.

Relief workers were given the task of selecting the colonists. Most of them worked hard to find suitable candidates for the colony and did not, as alleged, foist their most difficult cases on the Matanuska project. But they were limited in their selections. Successful farmers were not interested in going to Alaska and could not go even if they wanted to; only people receiving welfare payments were eligible to be chosen. As it turned out, few of those who went to Matanuska had any farming experience.[27]

Great fanfare attended the movement of the colonists. As they traveled by train across the country, newspaper reporters interviewed them and reported on their activities. In San Francisco and Seattle they were entertained with dinners and speeches. Upon their arrival in Alaska, they were greeted at the port of Seward. At Anchorage a half-day holiday was declared in their honor. Don Irwin, manager of the Matanuska Agricultural Experiment Station, warned them of the difficulties that lay ahead. Indeed it was raining the day they arrived in May 1935, and during the next few weeks the rainfall was heavier than usual. Because their homes were not ready, the colonists lived in tents, surrounded at times by a sea of mud. Some waited several months before their homes were ready for occupancy.[28]

Discontent was soon high. Nine families left Alaska in July, and they were followed by others. But some of the colony's severest critics among the settlers in the early days changed their minds after a few months in Alaska. One announced that she was now "having the time of my life." When rumors began circulating that the colony might be disbanded, none of the remaining settlers appeared to be very happy with the prospect of being sent home.[29]

Of all the government resettlement projects, Matanuska was by far the most expensive. Almost everything needed—equipment, materials, and supplies—had to be imported into Alaska at great expense. "Above all," writes historian Miller, "the Matanuska project had to provide almost every facility that a new community would need." The project "built and equipped a general store or trading post, warehouses, shops, garage, community hall, dormitory, offices, staff houses, power plant, cannery, creamery, hatchery, hospital and school." If all the expenditures relating to the colony are taken into account, the total cost would be over $5 million.[30]

Yet Matanuska has been considered a qualified success. With the advent of World War II and the building of military facilities in the Anchorage area, a ready market became available for the colony's products. About 31 percent of the original settlers and 43 percent of the replacements were still living in the colony in 1948. Many who left found jobs or established businesses for themselves elsewhere in Alaska. Palmer benefited substantially from the founding of the colony, since the town also attracted people who were not members of the agricultural experiment.

Alaskans had mixed feelings about the Matanuska Colony. The support of the government was undoubtedly a major factor in the Matanuska story, and there was some appreciation that the federal government was at last doing something for Alaska. But some of the old-timers resented the special treatment and benefits conferred on outsiders who had never experienced the real problems of life in Alaska. And not all Alaskans were convinced that the Matanuska colony was a success.

Although many Alaskans spoke of the need to settle Alaska, they were usually reluctant, if not hostile, whenever there was any discussion of founding new settlements in the territory. There was a great outcry of opposition in the territory when a bill was introduced in Congress that called for the settlement of unemployed Americans and refugees from Nazi persecution in Alaska. There also was little enthusiasm for another proposal to bring Finns to Alaska after the Russo-Finnish War. Opposition was based in part on the practical grounds of the difficulty involved in assimilating urban groups who did not have skills they needed to fit into the Alaska environment, but at least in the case of the congressional bill, it was also mixed with some feelings of xenophobia and anti-Semitism.[31]

The "New Deal" for Native Peoples

While attention centered on the newest settlers in Matanuska, the Roosevelt administration prom-ised a "New Deal" for Alaska's Native people, too. Although Alaska never experienced the extensive warfare that had marked relations between whites and Indians in the United States, the coming of the Europeans had seriously disrupted, and in some cases destroyed, the Native economy. The Natives' standard of living was much lower, they were subjected to social discrimination, and a separate school system had been established for their children.

On June 18, 1934, Congress passed far-reaching legislation known as the Indian Reorganization Act, or the Howard-Wheeler Act. Its intent was to improve the lot of Native Americans in keeping with the spirit of the New Deal. In 1936, Congress extended the Indian Reorganization Act to Alaska's Indian peoples, Eskimos, and Aleuts, including the authority to create reservations if approved by a majority vote of not less than 30 percent of the Natives involved. Both Secretary of the Interior Harold L. Ickes and his commissioner of Indian affairs, John Collier, firmly believed that the revival and preservation of American Indian culture required the establishment of reservations.[32]

Alaska's inclusion in the provisions of the Indian Reorganization Act enabled several Native American communities to incorporate and to draw up constitutions for self-government. Loans extended to a number of villages allowed them to set up canneries. Individual fishermen borrowed money to purchase boats and gear for themselves, while two of the Native canneries established businesses on a territory-wide basis. In 1938 the secretary of the interior was authorized to withdraw up to 640 acres of land for the use of the territory's schools and hospitals and for other purposes he might deem advisable.

Yet the act soon became embroiled in territory-wide controversy. The most controversial aspect of the program was the one that contemplated the creation of reservations and a system of communal land tenure. Its sponsors regarded this as the means of implementing the provisions of the First Organic Act of 1884 that "the Indians or other persons in the said District shall not be disturbed in the possession of any lands actually in their use or occupation or now claimed by them." But opposition to the reservations was most vehement. Both Natives

Tlingit Land Claims

Reservations were not the only avenue for safeguarding Native land rights. After years of efforts by various of its members, Congress enacted the Tlingit and Haida Jurisdictional Act of June 15, 1935, which Alaska's Delegate to Congress, Anthony J. Dimond, had introduced. The measure authorized the Tlingit and Haida Indians of southeastern Alaska to bring suit in the U.S. Court of Claims for any claims they might have against the United States. The Tlingits filed a suit against the United States demanding $35 million "for the value of the land, hunting and fishing rights taken without compensation." The court of claims, however, dismissed the case in 1944 because the Tlingit-selected attorneys had not been approved by the secretary of the interior as the act required. Several times the deadline for filing claims expired, only to be extended by Congress.

After two such extensions, the Tlingits and Haidas filed a claim for compensation for tribal property rights expropriated by the United States in southeastern Alaska. In a 1959 decision, the Court of Claims decided that the Tlingits and Haidas had established aboriginal Indian title to six designated areas in southeastern Alaska. After the case dragged through the courts for another nine years, the Court of Claims awarded $7,546,053.80 to the Tlingits and Haidas on January 9, 1969. The court also found that, except for eight small parcels for which patents were granted, Indian title to an area of 2,634,744 acres had not been extinguished.

Sources: Ernest Gruening, *The State of Alaska*, 2nd ed. (New York: Random House, 1968), 370; U.S. Congress, Senate, *Alaska Native Claims Settlement Act of 1971*, 93.

and whites objected to particular features, the latter fearful that even more land would be closed to them, preventing the development of resources and therefore hampering economic growth. Natives feared that the reservations would repeat the miserable pattern seen in the "Lower 48." Reservations were condemned by some Natives and the majority of Alaska's citizens as alien to the Native way of life, and their introduction was termed a step backward; the need of the people, it was said, was equality, not wardship. The very word "reservation," indicating restriction on the use of land, has always aroused strong feelings in Alaska.

What especially startled Alaskans was the announcement that there would be approximately one hundred reservations from which all but local Native residents would be excluded. This announcement was coupled with the creation of the large Venetie Reservation just north of the Arctic Circle. If 1.4 million acres were to be withdrawn for the benefit of some twenty-five Athapaskan families, many reasoned, then perhaps as much as one-third to one-half of Alaska would eventually be enclosed within the one hundred reserves. Land given to the Natives, it was feared, would be taken from the majority population, and any large withdrawals for reservations would thwart Alaska's development. Many Natives feared that they might be confined to small areas with limited resources.

Despite the controversy, however, by 1946 the secretary of the interior had added seven villages in seven reservations. The Venetie Reservation, the largest, included the villages of Venetie, Arctic Village, Kachik, and Christian Village, while Unalakleet Reservation, the smallest, contained a mere 870 acres. The secretary established the other reservations at Akutan, Little Diomede, Hydaburg, Karluk, and Wales.[33] Many other villages prepared petitions for reservations, and three villages voted against them.

Following many protests, the plan for reservations was eventually withdrawn, and after 1946 no others were created under the act, leaving some twenty in existence.[34] Not until 1971, more than a quarter of a century after the era of the New Deal, did Congress finally settle the Alaskan Native land claims.[35] While Natives asserted their claims to the federal government, they also were determined to make political gains in Alaska. As early as 1924, Tlingit attorney William L. Paul won election to the territorial house of representatives. Twenty years later, in 1944, Frank Peratrovich of Klawock and Andrew Hope of Sitka won house seats; Frank G. Johnson of Kake was elected to the house and Peratrovich to the senate in 1946. In the legislative session beginning in 1952, seven Natives held seats.[36] From then on, Native political gains were slow but steady.

Alaska on the Brink of War

President Roosevelt had shown greater interest in Alaska than had any of his predecessors, with the possible exception of Harding. The New Deal spent more money on Alaska, though not much, and even provided the territory with a new settlement. But Alaska was never central to the New Deal, and its effect on Alaska was not profound. A long-awaited congressional study on Alaska, issued in 1937, concluded that "an appraisal of the national interests indicates that there is no clear need to speed the development of Alaska." Secretary of the Interior Harold Ickes, whose department was most concerned with Alaska, observed that "Alaska ought to do more for itself than running to Washington for everything."[37]

Ernest Gruening recalls in his memoirs that, just before he left Washington to take up his duties as governor of Alaska in 1939, Roosevelt told him that Alaska had "lost touch with the federal government" and that a "lot of the New Deal . . . hasn't come to Alaska."[38] But only a few months earlier, in January, Roosevelt had announced that in view of the threatening world situation, the reform program of the New Deal was over. "Dr. New Deal" was giving way to "Dr. Win-the-War." It was not the New Deal but the war that broke out in September 1939 that profoundly changed Alaska.

Chilkoot Barracks is located four-tenths of a mile south of Haines, on Portage Cove, Chilkoot Inlet, and seventeen miles south-southwest of Skagway in southeastern Alaska. In 1904 the U.S. War Department established a military post here, called Fort William H. Seward in honor of the man who negotiated the purchase of Alaska. In 1922, the name was changed to Chilkoot Barracks, after the Chilkoot tribe of Tlingit Indians living in this area. The post was abandoned in 1943. Private citizens purchased the land and buildings and named the "new" settlement "Port Chilkoot." It had a population of 125 in 1950.

(Courtesy of Machetanz Collection, Alaska and Polar Regions Department, Elmer E. Rasmuson Library, University of Alaska Fairbanks.)

Chapter 12

Alaska's Strategic Role in World War II

The 1930s were a troubled period for the United States. On October 24 and 29, 1929, Wall Street stock market prices plummeted, and by November 13 of that year about $30 billion in the market value of listed stocks had been obliterated. The "great crash" triggered the worldwide Great Depression. By the middle of 1932 market losses had mounted to approximately $75 billion. By 1933 about 15 million Americans had lost their jobs. America found itself in a desperate situation.

Europe and Asia did not fare well, either. In Germany, Adolf Hitler had taken power, while in Italy, Fascist dictator Benito Mussolini was riding high. After a bloody and bitterly fought civil war that lasted three years, the fascist dictatorship of General Francisco Franco replaced Spain's republican government in 1939. Russia boasted of a "dictatorship of the proletariat," which made the tyranny of the czars seem benevolent by comparison. Since 1931 economic penetration and military intervention had enabled the Japanese to bring a widening area of China under their control, and in September 1940, Japanese forces occupied Indochina.

By 1939 war clouds rose ominously across the Atlantic and Pacific, and on September 1 of that year, Hitler's armies, led by dive bombers and tanks, invaded Poland. Europe's major powers were soon embroiled in World War II. When the United States entered the conflict in 1941, Alaska would come to play a strategic part in the nation's war effort. The war in the Aleutians may have been a turning point in the larger conflict, and it turned the nation's attention to Alaska's role as guardian of the north.

Alaska's Strategic Position—Early Warnings

Despite a wide range of activities, U.S. military interest in Alaska had declined during the first thirty-five years of the twentieth century. At the outbreak of World War II, only a token garrison remained, at Chilkoot Barracks, located at Haines near the head of Lynn Canal in southeastern Alaska. An infantry post dating back to the Gold Rush days, Chilkoot Barracks was situated where it could observe traffic bound inland over the Dalton Trail and three other historic trails—the Chilkoot, Chilkat, and White passes. Eleven officers and approximately three hundred men armed with Springfield rifles manned the post. The installation did not have a single anti-aircraft gun. The troops' only means of transportation was the venerable tug Fornance, whose engines were so feeble that, while returning from Juneau in December 1939, it encountered a thirty-knot headwind, was unable to advance, and had to be rescued by the Coast Guard.[1] In essence, the territory was indefensible.

However, there had been voices reminding the United States of Alaska's strategic importance. As early as 1931 the territorial governor, George A. Parks, had reminded the secretary of the interior

The U.S. revenue cutter *Bear*, "the Queen of the Arctic," about 1900. The *Bear* was built in 1873 in Dundee, Scotland, for use in the Arctic sealing trade. In 1883 it was called upon to rescue the Greely Expedition, lost in the Arctic. The *Bear* subsequently spent forty years along the Alaska coasts. It was the first vessel to go north each spring, taking mail, medical services, and news and dispensing law and order. The U.S. Navy decommissioned the *Bear* in 1944, whereupon she was purchased by a private company in Nova Scotia and sat at anchor in Halifax Harbor until 1962. In that year a U.S. investor purchased the *Bear* for use as a floating restaurant in Philadelphia. As the ship was being towed to Philadelphia, a storm came up, and the *Bear* sank on March 19, 1963, at an unmarked spot in the North Atlantic.

(Courtesy of Historical Photograph Collection, Alaska and Polar Regions Archives, Elmer E. Rasmuson Library, University of Alaska Fairbanks.)

of Alaska's strategic position as the feasible air route to Asia. The governor recommended that the U.S. Army Air Corps station planes in Alaska, if only to train pilots in flying conditions as they existed in northern latitudes. The pleas fell on deaf ears.[2]

In December 1934, Japan denounced the five-power naval treaty of February 6, 1922. Under its terms the United States had agreed—among other things—not to fortify the Aleutians. Japan's action prompted Alaska's delegate to Congress, Anthony Dimond, to plead for bases at Anchorage or Fairbanks, and also in the Aleutians: "I say to you, defend the United States by defending Alaska." The

delegate pointed out that the shortest distance between the United States and Asia was the great circle route, located 2,000 miles north of fortified Hawaii but only 276 miles south of the undefended Aleutians. Delegate Dimond reminded his colleagues that these geographical factors would invite an enemy of the United States, moving across the Pacific, to invade Alaska first. Dimond's measure provided $10 million for an air base and another $10 million for a naval base, but it died quietly in the House Military Committee and the Naval Affairs Committee, respectively.[3]

Early in 1935, however, Congress named Alaska

as one of six strategic areas in which there would be an army air corps base. In subsequent congressional testimony, military witnesses unfailingly supported an Alaskan base both for defensive-offensive purposes and for providing training in cold-weather aviation. In his testimony, Brigadier General William Mitchell, an advocate of air power, dramatically declared that Japan was America's most dangerous enemy in the Pacific. "They will come right here to Alaska . . . (which) is the most central place in the world for aircraft. . . . I believe in the future he who holds Alaska will hold the world, and I think it is the most important strategic place in the world."[4] It was to no avail; Congress did not appropriate the necessary funds.

Congressional inaction did not deter Alaska's Dimond. Year after year he warned his colleagues of the potential danger from Japan. In 1937 he pointed out that some Japanese, ostensibly fishing off Alaska's coast, were actually disguised military personnel seeking information on the depths, defenses, and landmarks of Alaska's harbors. At the same time, he attempted to secure a $2 million appropriation to begin construction of the air base near Fairbanks that had been authorized in 1935. At the very least, he urged, army air corps pilots should be trained in cold-weather flying. Congress refused the necessary funds. In time, however, Dimond made converts, most importantly General George C. Marshall, the army chief of staff, and Major General Henry H. Arnold, head of the army air corps.[5]

In 1940 an appropriation of $4 million allowed construction to begin near Fairbanks on a cold-weather testing station for airplanes. One year earlier, a naval air station at Sitka was authorized, and now the navy was proceeding with the construction in a leisurely fashion. Delegate Dimond apprehensively declared: "We are starting defensive measures too late and proceeding with them too feebly."[6]

Washington Finally Listens

Included in the army's budget for fiscal year 1941 was a request for a base near Anchorage. When the defense budget reached the full appropriations committee, however, the entire funds for the Anchorage

William "Billy" Mitchell (right) stands by an SE-5, the type of plane he used in his famous demonstrations of the vulnerability of ship to air attack.

(Courtesy of Alaska and Polar Regions Department, Elmer E. Rasmuson Library, University of Alaska Fairbanks.)

base had been eliminated, and the House refused to reconsider its decision on April 4, 1940.[7] A few days later, on April 9, Hitler's armies invaded and occupied Norway and Denmark. Now, for the first time, many legislators realized that the Scandinavian peninsula was just over the top of the earth from Alaska and that bombers able to fly such a distance existed. Both Generals Marshall and Arnold appeared before the Subcommittee on the War Department of the Senate Appropriations Committee on April 30 and once again asked for restoration of the Anchorage base. Then in May 1940, the German air force bombed Rotterdam

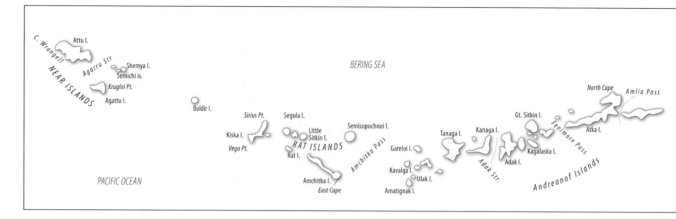

The central and western Aleutian Islands

without provocation or warning, while the German army seized the Netherlands. The Senate restored the Anchorage base, and the House concurred.[8]

Construction of bases had been under way at various locations, among them bases for seaplanes and submarines on Kodiak and Dutch Harbor that had been commissioned as naval air stations and could even handle submarines. The Civil Aeronautics Administration and the army engineers supplemented naval efforts by building a series of staging fields, north from Puget Sound inland, and out to Cold Bay on the Alaska Peninsula. Then on February 4, 1941 the U.S. Army redesignated the Alaskan Defense Force as the Alaskan Defense Command under Colonel, soon to be Brigadier General, Simon Bolivar Buckner, Jr. The navy quickly followed with the creation of an Alaskan sector under the Thirteenth Naval District headquartered at Seattle and appointed Captain Ralph C. Parker to the command.[9]

Yet, when the Japanese struck Pearl Harbor without warning on December 7, 1941, Alaska was hopelessly unprepared for war. Major General Buckner exclaimed in exasperation, "We're not even the second team up here—we're a sandlot club." There were a few tiny army garrisons, a scattering of airfields guarded by a few bombers and fighters, and a navy fleet of outmoded World War I vintage destroyers and wooden "Yippee" boats, which, in the opinion of their commander, Carl "Squeaky" Anderson, "would sink if they got rammed by a barnacle."[10]

As early as May 5, 1942, Japanese imperial headquarters ordered that the "Commander-in-Chief combined fleet will, in cooperation with the Army, invade and occupy strategic points in the Western Aleutians and Midway Island."[11]

The Japanese Attack

On the night of June 2, 1942, a Japanese force of two aircraft carriers with eighty-two planes, two heavy cruisers, three destroyers, and an oiler steamed through the foggy North Pacific toward Dutch Harbor (in the Eastern Aleutians). Supporting the task group not far to the west cruised the ships of Vice Admiral Boshiro Hosogaya's northern force, including four cruisers, nine destroyers, and three transports carrying 2,500 Japanese army invasion troops. Submarines screened the fleet. The planes were to strike a paralyzing blow at Dutch Harbor while troops were to land on and occupy the islands of Adak, Kiska, and Attu.

The Japanese carrier force had turned into a foggy, cold-weather front earlier in the day, after Rear Admiral Kakuji Kakuta, the task force commander, had been alerted by the sighting of a patrol plane in the clouds overhead. The Japanese were uncertain whether it was an American or a Russian plane. Not wanting to lose the element of surprise, the task force stayed with the leading edge of the storm.[12] On the morning of June 3, the carriers *Junyo* and *Rynjo*

Dutch Harbor, June 16, 1943. A submarine approaches the dock at the naval air station in the Aleutians. The base serviced subs and provided an air field—one of the first recognitions of Alaska's strategic importance. The Japanese attacked it—twice—on June 3 and 4, 1942, resulting in fifty-two American deaths or injuries

(Author's collection.)

launched their planes for the attack on Dutch Harbor, less than 170 miles away. Unknown to the Japanese, however, their element of surprise had been lost. The flying boat Admiral Kakuta had seen the previous day had been an American patrol plane.

When the planes of the carrier *Junyo* attacked Dutch Harbor early on the morning of June 3, 1942, they were met by the blazing anti-aircraft guns of the alerted American base. The attack planes of the carrier *Rynjo* had lost their bearings in the dense fog and had turned back (though they would return on June 4). From the very beginning both American and Japanese forces realized that despite all human courage and mechanical genius, the forces of nature called the shots in the Aleutians. The two attacks on Dutch Harbor did not last very long, and the American defenders soon discovered that the base had weathered the opening skirmish of the Aleutian campaign without much physical damage or defense impairment.[13]

Although the attack on Dutch Harbor has been recorded in history as merely an "incident," it nevertheless powerfully influenced the course of the war. The Japanese assault on the Aleutians was designed to divert massive American naval forces north toward Alaska. According to the plan, the main body of Admiral Isoroku Yamamoto's combined imperial fleet was to intercept and destroy the American fleet at Midway Island on June 4, 1942. But because the Dutch Harbor attack diverted Japanese forces needed at the rendezvous, Japan lost the balance of power at Midway, a major battle, and perhaps even the war.[14]

After regrouping and some indecisiveness, early on June 5, 1942, Vice Admiral Boshiro Hosogaya ordered Rear Admiral Sentaro Omori, commander of the Adak-Attu Occupation Force, who was then some 225 miles southwest of Adak, to turn back and proceed to Attu. On the morning of June 7, 1942, Omori landed his 1,200 troops on Holtz Bay, from where they marched overland through snow to Chichagof Harbor. The main part of the troops got

Three Vega Venturas—the U.S. Navy's PV-1 attack bombers—speed past the four-thousand-foot high Kiska volcano to aid Allied forces, which had taken over the Aleutian Island on August 15, 1943. The Japanese, unbeknownst to the Americans, had abandoned Kiska before the Allies landed.

(Courtesy of the National Archives.)

lost and arrived at Massacre Bay by mistake. The remaining troops attacked the little settlement of Chichagof and made prisoners of its entire population of thirty-nine Aleuts and one teacher, a Mrs. Jones, and her husband. The Kiska Occupation Force also made its landing on June 7 without opposition from the ten members of the temporary U.S. weather station.[15]

Subsequently, it has become clear that the Japanese had no intention of capturing anything east of Adak, that they had no plans to invade the Alaskan mainland, Canada, or the United States. Apart from its diversionary aspect, the Aleutian operation was principally defensive, designed to prevent an American invasion of Japan. Because of the loss at Midway, Kiska essentially had become worthless as the northern anchor of the new defense chain. Nevertheless, the Japanese high command decided to keep the island and develop it as an air base, partly to block a possible invasion and partly for nuisance and the effect on morale.[16]

Stalemate

The American command did not discover the occupation until June 10, when a Catalina amphibious plane reported four ships in Kiska. This initiated a new phase of the war, with the Japanese attempting to hold what they had and the Americans trying to blast them out. The war in the Aleutians essentially became a contest of air power in which both sides were hampered by the foul weather.[17] Nobody won fame or fortune, and none of the operations accomplished anything important or had any noticeable effect on the outcome of the conflict. American and probably Japanese sailors, soldiers, and aviators regarded stationing in this area of almost perpetual winds, fogs, and snow as little better than punishment. Distance and weather constantly impeded both American and Japanese operations.

Vice Admiral Hosogaya, commander in chief of the Northern Area Force, was responsible for maintaining and defending Attu and Kiska. On the American side, Rear Admiral Robert A. "Fuzzy" Theobald, commander of the North Pacific Force, had been instructed by Admiral Chester W. Nimitz to keep pounding the two islands until forces could be spared to recover them.

Admiral Theobald had established his headquarters at Kodiak. Rear Admiral William W. Smith commanded a cruiser task force, while Brigadier General William O. Butler commanded the Eleventh Army Air Force, consisting of medium

Wreck of the *Mazio Maru,*
Kiska Harbor.

(Photo by Claus-M. Naske.)

Major General Simon Bolivar Buckner, Alaska Defense Command, U.S. Army, views the Stars and Stripes on June 2, 1943, flying over a former Japanese headquarters at Attu.

(Author's collection.)

American Defense Efforts

In the meantime, Major General Buckner's Alaska Defense Command had grown to 150,000 troops. With the help of two army reserve officers, Captain Carl Schreibner and Major (later Lt. Col.) M. R. Marston, Governor Gruening had organized the Territorial Guard, a security force primarily composed of Natives instructed to guard the long coastline and pass intelligence to the armed forces in the absence of the National Guard.

Dutch Harbor, the assembly point of the Aleutian theater of war, handled approximately four hundred thousand tons of shipping a month. Alaskan coal production had increased tenfold in 1942. And the army constructed the four-inch-wide Canol Pipeline to carry crude oil from Norman Wells on the Mackenzie River in Canada's Northwest Territories to a refinery in White-horse. From there a three-inch pipeline was to carry the various petroleum products to Alaska. Alaska's population had mushroomed under the stimulus of the military construction boom. And under the protection of the U.S. Navy and Coast Guard, Alaskan fishing fleets made record catches, most for export to the lower forty-eight states.

A road connecting the contiguous United States with Alaska had been in the talking stage since the 1930s, and the long awaited opening of Alaska-Canada Military Highway (called AL-CAN) on November 20, 1942, represented a major engineering achievement. Built to connect

Start of the Alaska Military Highway.

(Courtesy of Machetanz Collection, Alaska and Polar Regions Department, Elmer E. Rasmuson Library, University of Alaska Fairbanks.)

many of the landing fields on the air route to Alaska—Great Falls, Montana; Lethbridge, Calgary, Edmonton, and Grand Prairie, Alberta; Fort Saint John and Fort Nelson, British Columbia; Watson Lake and Whitehorse, Yukon Territory; and Northway, Tanacross, Big Delta, Mile 26, and Ladd Field at Fairbanks, Alaska—the 1,420-mile pioneer road wound its way through the wilderness. Seven engineer regiments, aided by forty-seven contractors employed by the Public Roads Administration, worked toward each other from various points along the route, under often harsh weather conditions over extremely difficult terrain. They finished the pioneer road exactly nine months and six days after the start of construction. Although the road was crude, by December of 1942 army convoys crawled north to Alaska with supplies and materials for the Alaskan command and for the Soviet Union as well.

Sources: U.S. Army, Alaska, *The Army's Role in the Building of Alaska,* Pamphlet 360-5, April 1, 1959 (Headquarters, U.S. Army, Alaska, 1969), 90; Brian Garfield, *The Thousand-Mile War: World War II in Alaska and the Aleutians* (Garden City, N.Y.: Doubleday, 1969), 150–51; Claus-M. Naske, "The Alcan: Its Impact on Alaska," *Northern Engineer* 8, no. 1 (Spring, 1976): 12–18.

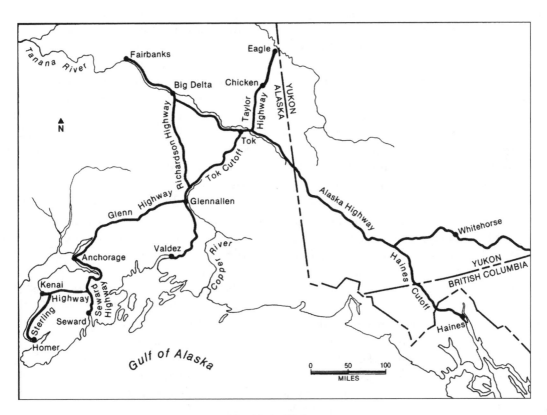

The Alaska Highway

bombers and fighters, a few Flying Fortresses, and a growing group of PBYs. Major General Buckner was the army commander of the Alaskan sector with a token garrison at Fort Morrow at the base of the Alaska Peninsula. Fort Glenn on Umnak Island, 536 miles east of Kiska by air and 660 miles by sea, was the westernmost American airfield. The only American naval and seaplane base in the Aleutians, inadequate and also damaged by the June 4 raid, was Dutch Harbor, about sixty miles eastward on Unalaska Island. Fort Randall at Cold Bay on the Alaska Peninsula possessed a good army airfield but was located another 155 miles eastward by air or 185 miles by sea. Alaska's main advanced military and naval base was on Kodiak Island, some 373 miles east of Cold Bay by air and 505 miles by sea. All needed supplies for the American armed forces had to come from Seattle, which meant a flight of 1,742 miles or a sea voyage of 1,957 miles to get reinforcements and material to Umnak.[18]

The Japanese also had a difficult time. Hosogaya's base at Paramushiro in the Kuril Islands lay 1,200 miles north of Tokyo and 650 miles west of Attu. Ships bound for Kiska faced another 378 miles of steaming through reef-filled waters.[19] On July 7 and 8, 1942, Admiral Yamamoto withdrew four carriers and other capital ships southward. This left Vice Admiral Hosogaya with an insufficient Northern Area Force for offensive operations. He therefore decided to build airstrips on Attu and Kiska from which land-based bombers could defend the Japanese Aleutians. Because of the lack of construction equipment capable of dealing with the spongy muskeg and the underlying frozen volcanic ash, work proceeded very slowly. For all practical purposes, Japanese offensive bombing in the Aleutian campaign ceased after a high-altitude attack on the morning of July 20, 1942.[20]

American forces, however, went on the offensive. Admiral Theobald ordered the construction of an airfield on Adak within fighter-plane distance of Kiska so that bombers could be escorted on the round trip. Construction crews found an almost ready-made airfield in the form of a flooded tidal basin. Army engineers drained and filled it and within ten days finished their job. On September 14, 1942, the first Kiska-bound fighter-bomber strike took off from Adak.[21]

The island of Kiska, with its massive antiaircraft emplacements and network of underground bunkers, had become virtually impervious. Only its supply line remained vulnerable. In the fall of 1942, American forces landed only forty miles from Kiska on Amchitka Island, where they built a forward air base that became operational in February 1943.[22]

Lend Lease and Intensive Warfare

The Alaska-Siberia Lend Lease Route (called AL-SIB) originated on March 11, 1941, when Congress passed the Lend-Lease Act, which was designed to help hard-pressed Great Britain and any other nation at war with Nazi Germany. When Germany invaded the Soviet Union on June 22, 1941, the USSR soon became a lend-lease participant. As early as September 1941, the United States suggested that lend-lease aircraft be delivered to Siberia via Alaska, using American pilots and crews. The Russians declined initially because they considered the route too dangerous.

The exigencies of the war finally made the use of ALSIB imperative, and from September 1942 until the fall of 1945, some 7,926 combat and transport aircraft were delivered in Fairbanks to the Russians, who then flew them to Nome and Siberia. ALSIB cut the travel distance from thirteen thousand miles via the Middle East to less than three thousand miles. In addition, the Russians took over lend-lease destroyers and other ships at Cold Bay. Cargo shipped from West Coast ports by the U.S. and Canadian navies was escorted through the Aleutians and on to Vladivostok, a major Russian seaport.[23]

At the same time, American planes kept bombing the Japanese installations. The winter of 1942–43 turned into the worst in thirty-four years. Fairbanks temperatures dipped to sixty-seven degrees below zero Fahrenheit in December, and in the Aleutians it took crews two hours to ice off airplane wings, while blowtorches were used to thaw engines before they would start. Yet despite these handicaps, the bombers dropped more than a half-million pounds of explosives on enemy bases during the last three months of 1942.[24] Early in January 1943, Rear Admiral Thomas C. Kinkaid arrived to replace Rear Admiral Theobald as commander of the North Pacific Force, and Rear Admiral Charles H. McMorries relieved Rear Admiral William W. Smith as commander of the cruiser-destroyer group. With the arrival of these two men, the Aleutian campaign went into high gear.[25]

On March 26, 1943, Admiral Hosogaya, who had decided to run the American blockade and resupply Attu, encountered a small task group under Rear Admiral McMorries. In the subsequent engagement, named the Battle of the Commander Islands, McMorries fought a retiring action against Hosogaya's forces, twice as large as his own and with double the firepower. The battle lasted continuously for three and a half hours, and the opponents shot at each other at ranges of eight to twelve miles. No planes or submarines intruded, and neither side did the other great harm. The Japanese finally broke off the battle when Admiral Hosogaya became convinced that he was under air attack. What had happened was that the heavy cruiser *Salt Lake City*, having run out of armor-piercing shells, started shooting high explosives with white phosphor splashes that looked exactly like bombs dropping through the overcast sky.[26] The battle was decisive, because after Hosogaya turned back, no further Japanese convoys were to reach the Aleutians.

On May 11, 1943, American troops landed on Attu, a forbidding, mountainous island some thirty-five miles long and fifteen miles wide. Bitter fighting raged for nearly three weeks. On May 28, Colonel Yasuyo Yamasaki took stock of his situation. Of the 2,600 men he had started with on May 11, fewer than 800 fighting men remained. Some 600 were wounded. He estimated American strength at 14,000 men. There would be no evacuation because the fleet of large transport submarines, called I-boats, had been turned back by the American destroyer screen. The colonel, therefore, decided to attack, in the remote hope of raiding American supplies. That evening he sent his last radio message to Japan, burned his records, and prepared his soldiers for the assault. Lieutenant Nebu Tatsuguchi returned to his post that evening and made his last diary entry: "At 2000 we assembled in front of

headquarters. The last assault is to be carried out. All patients in the hospital are to commit Suicide. . . . Gave 400 shots of morphine to severely wounded, and killed them. . . . Finished all the patients with grenades. . . . Only 33 years of living and I am to die here. I have no regrets. Banzai to the Emperor . . . . Goodbye Tasuko, my beloved wife."[27]

On the morning of May 29, Yamasaki made a banzai charge with his remaining men. The Japanese came close to taking back what the Americans had gained in bitter and bloody fighting. Individual Japanese soldiers held out in the hills; some were not flushed out until three months later. When finally cornered, every Japanese soldier chose to commit suicide.[28]

It had been an expensive battle. In proportion to the numbers of troops involved, it would rank as the second most costly American battle in the Pacific Theater, second only to Iwo Jima. Landing Force Attu had suffered 3,829 casualties: 549 killed, 1,148 wounded, 1,200 injuries due to the severe cold; 614 disease casualties, including exposure; 318 other casualties, which included self-inflicted wounds, psychiatric breakdowns, drownings, and accidents. The Japanese were practically annihilated. Only twenty-eight prisoners were taken, not one officer among them, and the American burial parties counted 2,351 Japanese bodies; several hundred more dead were presumed to have been buried in the hills by the Japanese during the three days of battle.[29]

Anticlimax at Kiska

American attention next turned to Kiska. From June 1 until August 15, army pilots flew 1,454 sorties and dropped 1,255 tons of bombs on Kiska. In addition, the navy bombarded Kiska from its cruisers and destroyers. Unknown to the Americans, however, the Japanese had decided to evacuate the Kiska garrison. At first, thirteen big I-boat transport submarines were to be used, but seven of these were lost or crippled while only 820 men were evacuated. On July 28 and 29 the Japanese, under the cover of fog, skillfully brought a surface fleet into Kiska Harbor. Within fifty-five minutes, Rear Admiral Shozo Akiyama, officers, enlisted men, and civilians, numbering 5,183, crowded on board two cruisers

At recaptured Attu on June 4, 1943, are, *from left,* Ernest Gruening, governor; Brigadier General Archibald V. Arnold (in charge of the garrison at Attu); and General A. M. Landrum, commanding general, U.S. forces in Alaska, June 4, 1943.

(Author's collection.)

carrying 1,200 each and six destroyers averaging 470 passengers each. The ships left undetected and safely reached Paramushir Island on August 1, 1943.[30]

Before the evacuation of Kiska, on July 23, the radar of a Catalina amphibious plane had contacted what was believed to be seven vessels some two hundred miles southwest of Attu. The American command believed that these ships were a Japanese reinforcement convoy bound for Kiska. American warships rushed to the scene, and on July 26 the American fleet made radar contact and fought what was to become known as the Battle of the Pips. After expending 1,005 rounds, Rear Admiral R. C. Griffen gave the order to cease firing and at dawn circled back to the scene of the "battle." An observer plane found no debris, no wreckage—nothing but the gray waves of the North Pacific. Apparently return echoes from the mountains of Amchitka and other islands had shown up on radar some 100 to 150 miles distant.[31]

On August 14 the Kiska invasion proceeded on a colossal scale. Two days later the American troops reached the enemy's main camp and discovered all the signs of hasty departure, with food, stores, and weapons only partially destroyed. Yet the Americans still suffered casualties. Patrols occasionally shot fellow Americans by mistake. Some twenty-five soldiers died and thirty-one suffered wounds from these errors. In addition, the navy lost seventy men dead or missing and forty-seven wounded.[32]

The War's Effect on the North

After the Aleutians had been secured, military activities in the North declined sharply. From 152,000 members of the armed forces in Alaska in 1943, the number declined to 60,000 in 1945 and to a mere 19,000 in 1946. In November 1943, the army renamed the Alaska Defense Command as the Alaskan Department. Yet the war had a profound and lasting impact on the territory. It irrevocably altered the pace and tenor of Alaskan life. The residual benefits to the civilian economy and the development of Alaska were tremendous. Between 1941 and 1945 the federal government spent about $3 billion in Alaska.[33]

The modernization of the Alaska Railroad and the expansion of airfields and construction of roads benefited the civilian population as well as the war effort. Many of the docks, wharves, and breakwaters built along the coast for the use of the U.S. Navy, the Coast Guard, and the Army Transport Service were turned over to the territory after the war. Thousands

Dutch Harbor thirty years later.

(Courtesy of *Fairbanks Daily News-Miner.*)

of soldiers and construction workers had come north, and as reflected in population statistics, many decided to make Alaska their home at the end of the hostilities. Between 1940 and 1950 the territory's civilian population increased from approximately 73,000 to over 128,600.[34] This influx put a tremendous strain on Alaska's already inadequate social services, such as schools, hospitals, housing, and local government.

In short, the war was the biggest boom Alaska ever experienced, bigger than any of the gold rushes of the past. Yet with the curtailment of defense spending at war's end, Alaskans once again were confronted with the problems of a seasonal economy. With the end of the war, the closure, abandonment, transfer, or change to caretaker status of many military stations in Alaska began. For example, Fort Greely on Kodiak Island (the first Fort Greely), Fort Morrow at the base of the Alaska Peninsula, and forts at Cold Bay, Randall, Ray, and Raymond were discontinued or placed in caretaker status as early as 1944. The other forts, with the exception of Richardson, closed in 1945. The federal government transferred many army airfields and emergency strips to the Civil Aeronautics Administration; it transported supplies and equipment, where feasible and economically practicable, from the Aleutian Islands and used them in areas where the conflict still raged, and put the remainder into reserve stocks. Also, a detachment of Navy Seabees that had been surveying potential petroleum lands and drilling test wells near Point Barrow since August 1944 closed down in March 1946.[35] In short, the United States was in the process of demobilization and attempted to return to peace after the victorious conclusion of World War II.

But there was to be no return to the world that had existed before World War II. During 1946, American and Russian military forces confronted one another in Manchuria, Iran, Turkey, and Europe. Several times they were near the flashpoint. The Cold War had begun.

Alaskan Natives (likely Bering Sea Eskimos) row their kayak out to the side of a U.S. Coast Guard flying patrol boat to greet the American flyers as they land in Aleutian waters during a patrol flight, 1943.

(Courtesy of the National Archives.)

Chapter 13
Ramifications of War

EVACUATIONS AND CENSORSHIP

World War II brought to the northern territory many cataclysmic changes that had far-reaching repercussions altering the social, economic, and political patterns of life in Alaska. The impact of military construction and the associated influx of military personnel and construction workers totally disrupted the rhythm of life in the Aleutian Islands. U.S. Army troops moved to newly constructed Fort Glenn on Umnak Island starting in January 1942. By the end of the war, 176 officers and 4,450 enlisted men were stationed there. Nikolski, some sixty miles from Fort Glenn and one of the most ancient occupied sites in Alaska, became a subpost of Fort Glenn and witnessed the arrival of 5 officers and 141 enlisted men. Never before had Umnak Island been occupied by so many people.

But it was the town of Unalaska on neighboring Unalaska Island that experienced the brunt of military development. Construction workers had flooded the area to build Fort Mears and the navy's Dutch Harbor installations even before the military arrived. Beginning in September 1940, Dutch Harbor was transformed into an Aleutian defense center. By June 1941, both the army and navy facilities were operational. Civilian and military personnel encountered Unalaska's Aleuts, and frictions developed between the newcomers and the longtime residents. The existing infrastructure, such as schools, recreational facilities, electrical generating capacity, sewage and garbage disposal, and fire and police protection, were totally inadequate. Neither the federal nor territorial governments offered to pay for such facilities. In response to these pressures and a rumor that Unalaska might be placed in a "naval reserve" enabling a proclamation of "martial law," Unalaska incorporated as a first-class city in December 1941.[1]

But the most far-reaching wartime impact can be seen in the evacuation of Alaskans from their homes and the censorship of media entering and leaving the territory. Both of these policies targeted Alaskan residents on a greater scale than stateside residents, highlighting the fact that because Alaska was a territory, its people were without all the protections enjoyed by other U.S. citizens.

Executive Order 9066

During the early months of 1942, the Japanese inflicted stinging defeats on the Allies. During those long weeks of military setbacks, President Roosevelt ratified an action that was widely accepted at the time but later viewed as one of the sorriest episodes in American history. On February 19, 1942, he signed Executive Order 9066, which gave the army, through the secretary of war, the authority to designate certain military areas from which persons were to be evacuated. Then the army was to provide for such persons "transportation, food, shelter, and other accommodations as may be necessary . . . until

Landing at Attu, Aleutian Island, May 11, 1943.

(Courtesy of Alaska and Polar Regions Department, Elmer E. Rasmuson Library, University of Alaska Fairbanks.)

other arrangements are made." Aleuts, Japanese, and Japanese Americans were not specifically named in the order, although they, and they alone, were to be affected. While some historians dismiss these evacuations as a "wartime mistake," others assert that the excuse of military necessity was used to cover "a particular variant of American racism." Roger Daniels, the foremost scholar on the evacuation, wrote that "the legal atrocity . . . committed against the Japanese Americans [and Aleuts] was the logical outgrowth of over three centuries of American experience that taught white citizens that the United States was a country in which non-whites had no inviolable rights."[2]

In March 1942, Secretary of War Henry Stimson extended his authority under Executive Order 9066 to Major General Simon Bolivar Buckner, Jr., who commanded the army in Alaska. Buckner acted quickly, and between April 7 and June 30, 1942, he issued four public proclamations. In the first he ordered the removal of Japanese, German, and Italian aliens, in addition to Japanese American citizens. About 230 Alaskan Japanese, over half of them American citizens, were sent to stateside internment camps. Second, he empowered military commanders to exclude from their areas any "undesirable person" who might "imperil or impede military defense or other military operations." Next was the creation of a system to register and issue "certificates of identification" for "citizens and subjects of foreign countries at war." In the final proclamation, Buckner then restricted civilian travel and transportation to, from, and within Alaska. All these measures Buckner regarded to be necessary wartime precautions.[3]

Women and children dependents of armed services personnel and construction workers were also removed, a process that had been under way since shortly after the Japanese attack on Pearl Harbor on December 7, 1941. Hundreds of military dependents were evacuated as quickly as transportation was available, with, for example, 250 departing from Dutch Harbor and 700 from Kodiak. All women were removed from Unalaska except one hospital patient.

After Pearl Harbor, Territorial Governor Ernest Gruening was inundated with requests for the government's evacuation plans by civil defense directors. His government did not have any such plans, and he opposed them anyway because a mandatory civilian evacuation would wreck Alaska's economy.[4] Nonetheless, many Alaskan residents were forcibly removed.

Evacuation of the Aleutians

The first Aleuts to be evacuated were residents of Atka. After the Japanese occupation of Kiska, some six hundred miles to the west, the navy decided to use Atka's Nazan Bay for landing, refueling, rearming, and repairing seaplanes. In addition, navy PBY patrol planes, stationed at Dutch Harbor, began offensive strikes against Kiska, and thus Nazan Bay became a strategic way station for the Kiska targets. Seaplane and PBY crews and support staff came to the island; Atka's eighty-three Aleuts had never seen so many military personnel or planes before, and they had certainly never seen so much offensive military action. The so-called Kiska Blitz lasted only forty-eight hours. Fearing Japanese retaliation, the navy ordered the Aleuts to leave Atka village, which it then made off-limits. The villagers went to campsites elsewhere on the island for their summer fishing activities. The navy ordered them to camouflage their tents.[5]

The military had no clue what plans the Japanese had for the Aleutian Islands, and many feared they would move eastward along the chain toward the Alaska mainland. Also there was apprehension that the Japanese were about to besiege Atka. On June 12, 1942, navy Lieutenant Commander J. P. Heath, the captain of the USS *Gillis*, ordered that Atka village be burned to the ground so as to deprive the Japanese of shelter. Late that night and early the next day, a number of Atka's Aleuts were rounded up and then boarded the *Hulbert*. Sixty-two Aleuts left the naval ship in the evening of June 13 at Nikolski, leaving twenty-one still on Atka Island. The arrivals stayed at Nikolski for three days with little more than the clothing they wore. The navy failed to either feed or house the evacuees, but this the Nikolski Aleuts did. On June 16 these people were taken to Dutch Harbor on an army transport, put in military barracks, and reunited with the twenty-one other Atkans, who had been flown to Dutch Harbor the day before.[6]

A few days after the Atka evacuation, General Buckner ordered the evacuation of Saint Paul Island. The USS *Oriole*, joined by the U.S. Army Transport *Delarof*, anchored off Saint Paul, and loading began on the afternoon of June 15. The Orthodox priest, his wife, and thirteen Fish and Wildlife Service employees joined 294 Aleuts on the transport. On June 16 the *Delarof* sailed south and took on board six Fish and Wildlife personnel, one Orthodox priest, and Saint George's 183 Aleuts. On June 17 the *Delarof* picked up the Atkans who had been evacuated to Dutch Harbor, adding to the ship's overcrowding. It now carried 83 Atka Aleuts and 477 from the Pribilofs, plus 22 non-Indians—a total of 582 men, women, and children. The ship could accommodate 376 passengers. It left on June 18 for an unknown destination. Rumor had it that it was either Seattle, Alaska's Cook Inlet, or Wrangell village in southeast Alaska.[7]

It soon became clear that at best there had been very little planning for the evacuation. The late historian of the Aleut relocation, Dean Kohlhoff, has written that "what followed this military action became a quagmire of events so confusing and contradictory that it is extremely difficult to clarify them." The question that had to be settled was what Alaskan port should be used first for the evacuees

A 1907 view of the Tlinket Packing Company's Cannery at Funter Bay on the west coast of Mansfield Peninsula, nineteen miles southwest of Juneau in the Alexander Archipelago. In 1942, the United States government resettled Aleuts here from Saint Paul and Saint George, in the Pribilof Islands. The Japanese had invaded the Aleutian Islands and the move was designed to save the Aleuts from danger. Close to three hundred Aleuts and Fish and Wildlife Service personnel occupied miserable quarters. Many Aleuts died.

(Courtesy of Lulu Fairbanks Collection, Alaska and Polar Regions Department, Elmer E. Rasmuson Library, University of Alaska Fairbanks.)

from Atka and the Pribilofs. Neither the armed forces nor the Department of the Interior had any clear ideas. Finally, on June 16, the Department of the Interior directed that Aleuts aboard should be kept in southeastern Alaska. Interior personnel decided that it would be best to put each village separately into inoperable canneries. By the end of July, Akutan, Biorka, Kashega, Makushin, Nikolski, and Unalaska Aleuts were removed and relocated to southeast Alaska.[8]

Most of the Pribilofians were settled into an abandoned cannery site and an adjoining mining camp at Funter Bay on Admiralty Island. The conditions at the camps were terrible. The sanitary system consisted of outhouses located on pilings just above the high water mark. Each high tide flushed the facilities. There was inadequate heating, and the water system froze in the winter.

Atkan families were brought to Killisnoo on the southern end of Admiralty Island. They were dumped off with only their clothes on their backs and told to shelter themselves in old cannery buildings, never meant for winter living. Another 122 Aleuts from Unalaska found themselves at a burned-out cannery location at Burnett Inlet on Etolin Island, southwest of Wrangell Island, while many from the smaller villages wound up at an old CCC camp at Ward Lake, eight miles from Ketchikan. It was the most attractive of the resettlement camps, yet here also the evacuees were crowded in unhealthy conditions. The Aleuts suffered from inadequate food, lack of medical help, deplorable shelter conditions, depression, and homesickness. Despite all of this, some Aleut men enlisted in the armed services of the United States.[9]

At first the official policy had been to restrict Aleuts to the camps, but that was soon lifted. Within the first six months, 135 Pribilofians found work outside Funter Bay, mostly in Juneau, and a year later almost 200 did, nearly one-half of the evacuees. In the spring of 1943, about 150 Aleuts and government employees were allowed back to the Pribilofs to prune the fur seal herds, but there was no full Aleut sealing crew in the summer of 1943. The Fish and Wildlife Service, which had hoped to resettle Saint George in 1943, had to postpone its plans until 1944.[10]

In all, the military evacuated 881 Aleuts. Most of these remained in their dismal camps at Funter Bay, Killisnoo, Burnett Inlet, and Ward Lake until 1945, when they returned to their island homes, only to find nothing intact. Many of their homes had been burned or leveled, their possessions looted. It is unlikely that white Americans would have been treated in a similar fashion, and it took a generation before the U.S. Congress made reparations to the Aleuts as a part of the claims of Japanese Americans who had been relocated and interned.

The Aleuts of Attu village experienced the worst fate of all the evacuees, at the hands of the Japanese. The Japanese did not treat the villagers harshly at first, but it was eventually decided that they be removed from the island. The occupiers had several motives. Fearing a harsh winter, the Japanese had contemplated a withdrawal, and if the villagers had been left behind they would have been able to give invaluable intelligence to the Americans. The Japanese decided to stay, and then reasoned that the Aleuts might conduct guerilla operations in case of an American attack. So in the end the Japanese removed the Attuans. They were loaded on a Japanese merchant ship on September 12, 1942, and unloaded at the city of Otaru on the island of Hokkaidō.

The Attuans were Japanese prisoners for three years, and twenty-four died in the harsh conditions of their captivity.[11]

Alaska's Japanese Americans

It took the U.S. government about one month to get the relocation machinery ready for evacuating Japanese Americans. Eventually, about 112,000 men, women, and children—practically the entire Japanese American population of Washington, Oregon, and California—were shipped to War Relocation Authority camps in the interior—semi-permanent establishments surrounded with barbed wire and guarded by small military detachments.[12]

Included in the removal order were 230 Japanese Americans in Alaska. They belonged to four categories: the Issei, immigrants who had lived in Alaska for a long time but were ineligible for naturalization because of the Naturalization Act of 1870; the Nisei, persons of alien immigrant parentage, born in Alaska, and therefore American citizens; the offspring of Japanese-American and Japanese-Native unions, who were thus citizens by birth; and Japanese nationals, such as members of ships' crews, who were just passing through Alaska.[13]

Japanese immigrants had begun arriving in Alaska in the 1890s. Predominantly single males, they worked in the fishing industry and settled along the coast and the Inside Passage of southeastern Alaska. The northern and interior regions attracted a few Japanese individuals as well, best exemplified by Jujiro Wada. He was a long distance runner who had shipped aboard a whaler and jumped ship in northern Alaska, where he lived with the Eskimos. He gained a reputation as being unbeatable in a fifty-mile race, and his dog-mushing exploits were legendary. He also was a good cook, and in 1902 he worked for E. T. Barnette, the founder of Fairbanks. He played an important part in establishing the gold camps in the Tanana Valley (see chapter 10).[14]

Like many other Asian immigrants to the United States, Japanese rarely brought their wives, at least initially. Most married within Alaska's Native population or arranged to marry someone from home. These immigrants established themselves in Alaska and often founded small businesses and gained social acceptance in both Native and American communities in the territory.[15]

Japanese residents of Alaska felt vulnerable, however, and on December 8, 1941, one day after the Japanese attack on Pearl Harbor, W. H. Fukuyama, who operated the laundry in Juneau and had lived in the city for thirty-six years, felt it necessary to explain that he had no sympathy for Japan. In fact, he stated, he sometimes felt "more American than my children who were born here and are American citizens." As many Juneau residents knew, he "would have become an American citizen if the law permitted." On December 9, J. K. Tatsuda of Ketchikan expressed the sentiment of the town's forty-two Japanese residents when he stated that "this is our country, we want to help." Tatsuda and his wife, operators of a grocery story, had two sons in the U.S. Army who were both stationed at Chilkoot Barracks.[16]

Similarly, the Kimura family of Anchorage placed an advertisement in that town's newspaper, publicly reaffirming their loyalty "to the country of our adoption and of our birth." Frank Kimura had some forty years before been an employee of the U.S. Navy aboard the USS *Albany*. In 1916 he and his small family had moved to Anchorage and "to a small degree, prospered." All his children were native born and "proud citizens," and his son George was a soldier in the U.S. Army stationed at nearby Fort Richardson.[17]

The editor of the *Anchorage Daily Times* addressed the problem of what to do with the Japanese in an editorial titled "Our Enemy Aliens." He conceded that many Asians were probably loyal to the United States. However, he concluded, race was "involved in this war and special attention must be given any Japanese." The United States was "compelled to regard the Japanese population as a potential 'fifth column'" and to protect itself against subversive activities. He concluded that this, no doubt, would work hardships "on many who deserve nothing but the best," but the nation had to do what was best for America's defense. Nowhere did he mention the U.S. Constitution or any defense of civil liberties.[18]

Some Alaskans did not share the general hysteria. On January 16, 1942, the *Anchorage Daily Times* published a letter by a reader who was ashamed about what was to be done with the individual evacuees and with the property they owned. And Governor Gruening also warned against singling out an entire population. When a cannery operator asked him what he should do about his Japanese employees, the governor advised that "aliens who behave themselves should be treated like citizens."[19]

By early January 1942, several Japanese Alaskans had been rounded up and interned at Fort Richardson. Among them was Harry Kawabe, who had come to the territory in 1908 and had settled in Seward in 1916. There he had bought a steam laundry, which eventually became the cornerstone of many enterprises, including a fur store, a gift shop, a hardware store, a hotel, a restaurant, a bar and liquor store, gold mining operations, and an investment firm. Kawabe, like many others, had no choice but to abandon his property. Soon the army ordered all "enemy aliens" in Ketchikan to turn in all firearms, radios, and photo equipment and warned them not to leave the community.[20]

At first the army was to be responsible for enemy alien property, but Major General Buckner protested that he had no means to operate established businesses or take care of physical possessions. The U.S. Treasury Department thereupon allowed the governor's office to issue licenses to individuals, permitting them to operate Japanese businesses. Buckner also suggested the appointment of an alien property custodian to relieve the army of all responsibilities.

As it turned out, however, the license system did not work well. For example, Harry Kawabe's laundry and hardware stores in Seward continued to operate under makeshift arrangements. Two different parties claimed to have Kawabe's permission to manage his property, but he refused to grant full power of attorney to anyone. Alaska's acting governor (during Gruening's absence), Bob Bartlett, suggested that "those anxious to act for Kawabe may be thinking more of personal gain than protection of property interests." This, of course, proved to be true everywhere. After much back and forth, the Federal Reserve Bank of San Francisco agreed, if necessary, to provide two men who would handle the properties of Alaskan evacuees as part of that agency's program for the entire Western Defense Command (WDC).[21]

On April 17 the governor's office announced that "each adult Japanese evacuating Alaska . . . will be permitted to take 1,000 pounds of baggage." For those living in isolated places, the army would provide their transportation to the nearest military installation. The evacuation began on April 25, and before their departure many expressed their feelings. Although they hated to leave their homes and friends, some, like Frank Kimura of Anchorage, feared that if they stayed they "might be blamed for overt acts of sabotage. If a mysterious fire should break out, or some act of treason should occur, we, and other persons of Japanese blood who are loyal to the United States might be blamed." In Petersburg, workers at the Alaska Glacier Sea Food Company, where many Japanese adults had been employed, sponsored a farewell party at the Presbyterian church for the evacuees. About sixty townspeople attended, and various speakers voiced their regrets over their departure, wished them well, and hoped they could return soon.[22]

Major General Buckner's order created many hardships. A notable case was that of Henry Hope, a Japanese Eskimo boy of seventeen living in Wiseman, in the southern foothills of the Brooks Range. Lucie and Sammy Hope, the former an Athapaskan Indian and the latter an Eskimo, had adopted Henry when he was a baby. Henry helped support his adoptive parents but was evacuated nevertheless. A Fairbanks friend of the Hopes appealed to Governor Gruening, who in turn appealed the case to Lieutenant General John L. DeWitt at the WDC in San Francisco. The general's answer: Sorry, "no exceptions can be made."[23]

On May 2, 1942, Governor Gruening visited the assembly center at Puyallup, Washington, and "expressed pleasure at the treatment Alaskan and Washington evacuees are receiving and at their happy frame of mind." Gruening was no fool and knew that people uprooted from their homes and jobs could scarcely be in a "happy frame of mind." His observation to the newspapers obviously was designed to make the best out of a sorry situation. Furthermore, the Japanese internees, with their *shigata ganai* (it cannot be helped) philosophy and their reluctance to complain before *hakujin* (white folks), might well have put a good face on their misery as well. In any case, reports soon reached Alaska from evacuees at Puyallup. Howard Suziki wrote to Ketchikan friends that his family's quarters consisted of rooms unfurnished except for beds, mattresses, and a stove. All other furniture had to be built with tools and wood the government furnished. Conditions were primitive.[24]

By late fall 1942 most Alaskan evacuees had been transferred from the Puyallup Assembly Center to the War Relocation Authority camp in Idaho. In October more than 120 Alaskans of mixed and pure Japanese descent, of whom 50 were minors, lived at Minidoka, Idaho. Not a single head of household was with his respective family, complained one of the evacuees, because "of the mass indiscriminate internment of all first generation male Japanese in Alaska, regardless of their past record." Mike Hagiwara complained to the governor that every first-generation Japanese man, except for four very feeble individuals, had been shipped directly to Camp Lewis, Washington, and from there to Fort Sam Houston, Texas, and then to Lordsburg, New Mexico, or another camp elsewhere. Apparently they were to be separated from their families for the duration. Governor Gruening merely passed the complaint up the chain of command, and there the matter rested.[25]

As the months wore on, Alaska's Japanese evacuees languished. By 1943 many had become worried about properties left behind, and Ralph J. Moore, the project attorney at Minidoka, met with a number to discuss these matters. To his amazement he discovered that forty families had left behind tangible and intangible properties worth over $2 million. Since the evacuation had been so sudden, they had been unable to arrange for the proper management and care of their assets. Moore was astounded that a large number of the Japanese had been very important persons in their communities. On a per capita basis, he marveled, the Alaskan Japanese had acquired more wealth than evacuees from the states; they all seemed to be pretty well off.[26]

In 1943 various Alaskan evacuees, after much paperwork, were allowed to leave Minidoka. For example, Grace Hagiwara and Alice Togo, awarded scholarships to Hobart and William Smith Colleges and Vassar College, were released to attend school.

Finally, on January 3, 1945, the army terminated its exclusion order, permitting Japanese Americans to return home. Bureaucracy and mountainous paperwork, however, considerably slowed the journey. Not until March 1945 was a procedure for the return to Alaska worked out, and it was difficult, time-consuming, and cumbersome. Even after all the papers had been generated and approved, it was still difficult for evacuees to return to Alaska because it was almost impossible to obtain reservations on ships northbound out of Seattle. Getting home was a long and arduous process.[27]

Reparations

The army finally revoked in full its exclusion orders for persons of Japanese ancestry from West Coast areas on September 4, 1945. This also applied to Alaska, and thereafter most of the Alaskan evacuees returned to the North. But they remained on parole. The Commanding General, Alaskan Department finally removed all remaining restrictions on returning Alaskan Japanese in November 1945.[28]

The expulsion of the Japanese and the Aleutians has long been recognized as a black mark against America's record of basic fairness and devotion to human rights. In the bicentennial year an executive order was issued symbolically on February 19, 1976, the thirty-fourth anniversary of President Roosevelt's edict, and President Gerald R. Ford both publicly apologized and revoked Executive Order 9066. In 1980 Congress established a commission to investigate wartime relocation and internment of civilians. The commission was to review the facts and circumstances surrounding Executive Order 9066 and its impact on American citizens and permanent resident aliens and to recommend appropriate remedies. In 1981, the commission held hearings in various cities in the contiguous states and Alaska.[29]

Japanese Americans were determined to be compensated for the hardships they had suffered during relocation, and they invited Aleuts, who shared these grievances, to join them in requesting compensation. Alaska's congressional delegation successfully steered an amendment to the measure that had created the review commission through Congress that included the Aleuts. President Jimmy Carter signed this measure, the Commission on Wartime Relocation and Internment of Civilians Act, Public Law 96-317, into law on July 31, 1980. The commission was to investigate Japanese American internment and Aleut evacuation.[30]

Funds needed to investigate, gather, and document the Aleut claims were not available, but eventually the Alaska state legislature appropriated $165,000 for the project and Governor Jay S. Hammond signed the measure into law. After more political wrangling and maneuvering, President Ronald Reagan signed Public Law 100-383 on August 10, 1988. Under its provision, eligible Aleuts were each paid twelve thousand dollars and eligible Alaskan Japanese and their West Coast counterparts were paid $20,000 each. These payments were excluded from income and resources for purposes of public aid eligibility.[31]

The Attuans clearly had suffered the most. In October 1945 the Department of the Interior filed claims against the Japanese government through the Department of State. Attuans claimed a total of $294,425, which included destruction of the fox breeding stock and loss of income and human life. The Department of the Interior temporarily lost the Attuan claims, but eventually they were filed with the War Claims Commission on July 3, 1951. Alfred Prokopioff, Jr., the only survivor born in Japan, received $19.99, the minimum, while those older than eighteen received a maximum of $2,358. In total the Attuans received just over $52,000, rather than the $294,425 they had requested. The funds came from money realized from the sale of enemy property that the Office of Alien Property, Department of Justice, had retained.[32]

Censorship in Alaska

Along with selflessness, bravery, devotion to duty, and loss of life, liberty, and property, the war also brought many absurdities. One of these involved censorship in many different forms, enforced by the Civilian Office of Censorship in Washington, D.C. In addition, the military had devised, and vigorously enforced, its own form of censorship.

Many news dispatches disseminated freely throughout the contiguous states, and the army and navy maintained that anything published in the contiguous states could be sent to Alaska. But the Seattle office of the Civilian Office of Censorship thought otherwise and tampered with printed materials. Most galling to many was the clipping of newspapers and magazines. Governor Gruening protested that copies of the *Washington Post* and *Newsweek* addressed to him arrived with whole sections the Seattle censors had excised. This was happening to all Alaskan subscribers to national publications. All letters to and from Alaska were also subject to the prying eyes of the Seattle censors.

Likewise, color films, which had to be sent to Eastman Kodak Company in Rochester, New York, or Los Angeles, California, to be developed, did not escape scrutiny, even though spies would certainly have used black and white film, which could be developed and printed at home, something impossible with color at that time. And although there existed no such censorship of photographs for anyone in the contiguous states, Alaska photographs thought to have some military aspect were not returned to the senders. Even General Buckner was among the indignant victims of this censorship. Censors had removed a photo of a sled from one of his orders, presumably on the assumption that if such a picture fell into enemy hands it might reveal the use of sleds in Alaska.[33]

The army and navy controlled outgoing news and dispatches. During the first six months of the war, the military had blocked out any news dealing with Alaska. It also had prevented regular journalists from sending out any stories and generally tried to keep northern residents in the dark as to events concerning Alaska that were being published openly elsewhere in the contiguous states.[34] It also forbade news organizations from identifying aliens arrested in Alaska for possible internment, a practice unheard of in the contiguous states.[35]

Soon after the start of the war, and when it had become evident that Alaska might become a theater of war, various newspapers had requested permission to send correspondents to the territory, only to be denied by the Department of War and the WDC in San Francisco. In fact, the latter requested that no material should be released to or approved for the correspondents already in Alaska for transmission

to the states. Instead, material deemed suitable for release to the press outside the territory was to be sent to headquarters in San Francisco to be screened and then made available.[36]

The WDC also initially refused to allow numerous reporters to work in Alaska. Journalist Edwin E. Dowell had come to Alaska in January 1942, but Lieutenant General DeWitt refused to allow him to work, barring him from everywhere the army had jurisdiction. United Press officials protested, but to no avail. In fact, on January 20, Alaskan military authorities interpreted yet another stringent directive from DeWitt to mean that Dowell and others like him could not file either military or nonmilitary news because they were special representatives and not longtime territorial residents. As an immediate consequence, the Alaskan Defense Command refused to let Dowell file a story on a civilian airplane crash at Cordova on January 19, 1942. Dowell managed to clear the story only over the signature of William Wagner, a veteran Alaskan and local part-time United Press representative. United Press officials, not unreasonably, accused DeWitt of high-handedness and recalled that the general had told the *San Francisco Chronicle* during the first air raid alarm on the West Coast that certain information sought by reporters was "none of the public's damned business." They speculated that perhaps DeWitt had extended the scope of that peculiar interpretation of public relations to Alaska on the theory that this was his personal war.[37]

Within a few months after the outbreak of the war, the WDC moderated its policies and reached workable agreements with the correspondents. But no such accords were reached with Byron Price, the director of censorship, a respected former Associated Press editor. As early as February 1942, Governor Gruening had complained to Price about the maze of conflicting censorship practices and asked that there be some coordination between the armed forces regulations and those that Price's office issued because many were totally unnecessary and "distinctly detrimental to moral[e]." Price quickly agreed that the press censorship regulations were unwarranted and blamed the Department of War. After all, even in peace time the department had controlled cable and radio communications between Alaska and Seattle, and it had always exercised a broad supervision over the transmission of news. This practice had intensified after Pearl Harbor. Price pointed out that the Department of War had not notified his office of these practices, and it could not act in any event since the statute authorizing international censorship omitted any authority over communications between the states and outlying territories.[38]

After armed forces regulations were relaxed, censorship from Price's office continued unabated. Magazines such as *Time* and *Newsweek*, already circulating in millions of copies in the contiguous states, continued to be delivered to Alaskan subscribers with whole pages missing. Bulk copies of these publications coming to Alaska, however, escaped unscathed, and subscribers simply had to go to the neighborhood drugstore to find what had been cut. Residents faithfully listened to the radio to get the uncensored news. Private and official correspondence between Alaska and the contiguous states continued to be opened in Seattle on a random basis. Worse yet, the governor discovered, the excised materials, called "intercepts," were collected and made available to a wide range of federal agencies, even including foreign governments. Although objectionable, Gruening found it amusing as well in the case of one of the intercepts he read. Taken from the letter of a Juneau resident to her husband in the contiguous states, it referred to the governor as "that s.o.b."—an attitude, he dryly observed, "she had never showed when we met socially or otherwise."[39]

Others objected to censorship as well. In October 1942, Ruth Gruber, a special field representative for Secretary of the Interior Harold Ickes, toured Alaska. She reported that continued "censorship is dealing a body-blow to Alaskan morale." Mail, newspapers, and magazines sent north continued to be "heavily censored. A whole staff of ex-bank clerks sits in Seattle doing nothing but boldly snipping articles out the *Seattle Post-Intelligencer*, *Newsweek*, and other periodicals." Seattle had a complex censorship system, she explained, which included postal, navy, army, radio, and other communication forms. She thought some of the censorship wise and necessary, "but some of it is asinine." She recommended that the most offensive censorship of news-

papers and magazines bound for Alaska be lifted.[40]

Gruber's recommendation and a similar one by Assistant Attorney General Norman M. Littell fell on deaf ears in the Civilian Office of Censorship. Littell had recently toured Alaska and reported that the residents everywhere he went complained about censorship. It caused bad public relations between the federal government and northern residents. He had heard of many examples of ridiculous censorship cases. For example, a letter was returned because a father had written to his little daughter in the contiguous states that he had passed the Matanuska Valley and stated that he "wished she could see it under the snow." This was a reference to weather conditions, which the censor had found objectionable. Then there was the Fairbanks Selective Service Board registrant who had left the territory for a job in the contiguous states. Required to keep in touch with his board, he had informed it that he had moved again and that thereafter mail should be sent to him in care of the United States Engineers, but the censor had excised the new address. Thus the Fairbanks Board lost track of a potential soldier.[41]

Another absurdity involved a schoolteacher who carried a copy of Robert Service's *The Spell of the Yukon* on his departure south. Since the army early in the war had prohibited photographing or mentioning of any shore lines, towns, and rivers, a military policeman confiscated the volume because it mentioned a river. The aftermath of this episode was even more bizarre. Robert B. Atwood, the publisher and editor of the *Anchorage Daily Times*, wrote a humorous editorial about the incident. The local chief censor, one "Duke" Myers, suppressed it. Myer's preparation for his important job had been a stint as a book reviewer for a small-town California weekly and teaching journalism at a college in that state. Myers had arrived in Alaska with the rank of lieutenant and was successively promoted until he reached the rank of lieutenant colonel. Shortly after he had suppressed the Atwood editorial, the army found the man insane and retired its chief Anchorage censor. Gruening reported that Alaskans had reached the same verdict, only much earlier.[42]

Price finally met with the governor, Delegate to Congress Anthony J. Dimond, and Ben W. Thoron, the director of the U.S. Division of Territories and Island Possessions, in November 1942 to discuss the censorship situation. All the familiar complaints were voiced, and Price was "most pleasant and very vague," alleging a lack of knowledge about the situation. He explained that the Japanese invasion necessitated the careful scrutiny of all communications between the territory and the contiguous states. But since the war situation had changed for the better in recent months, Price stated, he had issued instructions to discontinue clipping from American newspapers and magazines, and mail inspection had been reduced to the very minimum. His office still supervised cable and radio communication in order to protect Alaskan shipping. He asked the conferees for sympathy and understanding, and admitted "that mistakes had been made by individual censors. We must depend on human judgment which is sometimes in error."[43]

The governor particularly objected to the differential treatment Alaska received in the censorship matter, and at the end of the conference he remarked to Price that there was no legal authority to treat Alaska differently. Price maintained he had that authority. Subsequently Gruening discovered that a measure giving Price that authority had passed both the House and the Senate. The governor, thereupon, prevailed upon sympathetic senators to use a parliamentary maneuver to recall the measure. Senators called Gruening to testify on the matter, and he did so skillfully, particularly citing intercepts from Alaskan residents written to their senator, which made members of the Senate Judiciary Committee angry.[44]

The Senate Judiciary Committee called Price to testify and criticized him sharply. But he defended himself and stated that the matter affected not only Alaska but all the territories, including the Panama Canal Zone. Soon thereafter Secretary Ickes informed the governor that Stephen Early, President Roosevelt's secretary, had called him and told him to relay to Gruening that "the president wanted [Gruening] to lay off Byron Price." Early and Price were good friends, and the latter apparently had appealed to the White House for help. He had been successful, and in the end the Senate Judiciary Committee sustained Price. In Alaska, meanwhile, censorship was lessened.[45] Finally, the end of the war in 1945 made censorship superfluous.

The Alaska communication system, April 2, 1947.

(Courtesy of the Signal Corps, U.S. Army.)

Chapter 14
The Cold War

The development of tensions between the United States and the Soviet Union after World War II, resulting in the Cold War, rescued Alaska from economic depression and obscurity. The territory's geographic position astride the northern great circle route from Asia to the United States gave it a strategic importance in the free world, an importance that once again was to bring thousands of troops and the expenditure of millions of dollars.

Changes in military technology buttressed the territory's strategic role. These changes included long-range planes, atomic weapons, and guided missiles that increased the importance of the transpolar routes. Soon after the war, defense strategists envisioned a defense line from Okinawa, across Alaska and northern Canada, to Greenland and Iceland. The importance of aerial warfare in any future conflict highlighted Alaska's importance and ensured the positioning of large U.S. air bases with ground troop support in the territory.[1]

In the immediate postwar period, the military's most important job in the north consisted of deterring any possible aggression from the Soviet Union. Alaska also offered an excellent environment for training troops in arctic warfare.

Arguing for Alaska's Continued Strategic Role

As early as August 1945, members of the House Committee on Territories toured Alaska to investigate several military installations and conduct hearings into the territory's conditions. In its report to the House of Representatives, the committee wrote that World War II had "focused national attention on the Territory as at no time since the period of the gold rushes." As a result of the war, the nation had recognized it "as one of the important strategic areas of the world." Consequently the continued defense of Alaska and the active encouragement of the territory's economic development had become vitally important to the United States.[2]

On December 14, 1949, President Harry S. Truman approved a unified command plan, designed by the Joint Chiefs of Staff, to reorganize the military in Alaska. The structure created the Alaskan Command, composed of the Alaskan Air Command and the Office of the Commander in Chief, Alaska. In 1947, the air force became a separate force, coequal with the army and navy. By late 1947, additional reorganization created the U.S. Army Alaska and the Alaskan Sea Frontier, which together with the Alaskan Air Command comprised the unified command. The commander in chief, Alaska, with headquarters at Fort Richardson, reported directly to the Joint Chiefs of Staff.[3]

In October 1948, *Foreign Affairs* published an article by Captain John J. Teal. Like others before him, Teal wrote that Alaska's defense necessitated its economic development. The federal government could promote economic stability in Alaska while

A Ballistic Missile Early Warning System (BMEWS) station at Clear, Alaska. Three detection antennae, capable of "seeing" an object three thousand miles out in space, were 165 feet high and 400 feet long. They were able to resist 180-mile-per-hour winds and earthquakes. The $60 million project was built in 1959–60 by the Army Corps of Engineers.

(Author's collection.)

fortifying America's top shield, for "we can do what we wish" in Alaska, "and the extent to which we develop its possibilities will to a considerable extent determine our security."[4]

Teal pointed out that Soviet leaders had long ago recognized the strategic value of the Arctic and had actively promoted industrial development and population growth in the Soviet Union's northern regions. Thus, the Soviets were far ahead of the United States in preparing for warfare under arctic conditions. Teal also wrote that Alaska's weak defenses unnecessarily tempted Soviet military planners to threaten an offensive move against the United States through its northern territory.[5]

Ernest Gruening, Alaska's territorial governor, argued that expanding military capacity in the North, promoting economic development, and granting statehood together would create an adequate defense for both Alaska and the contiguous United States. The governor envisioned Alaska both as a western bastion of defense and as a "fortress of the American way of life."[6]

Postwar Expansion of the Military

Military construction between 1946 and 1949 concentrated on building housing, improving existing facilities, erecting hangars at the military installations near Anchorage and Fairbanks, and extending runways. The Joint Chiefs of Staff had decided to discontinue the maintenance of most air bases located along the Aleutian Islands and the coast and instead developed the so-called heartland concept of Alaskan defense. This involved a massive strengthening of the military bases near Fairbanks and Anchorage. The new concept coincided with a general realignment in the overall strategic emphasis from the Pacific to the Atlantic.[7] *Time* magazine reported that this theory reflected the view of military strategists that rather than "make U.S. airplanes vulnerable by scattering them through the wilderness [of the territory] . . . let them range from bases in the heartland."[8]

At both Fort Richardson near Anchorage and Ladd Field near Fairbanks, the military built housing for officers, enlisted men, families, and civilians, in addition to mess halls, warehouses, fuel storage facilities, and general utilities. At both bases the hospitals were improved. Additionally, rebuilding and expansion took place at Fort Greely near Big Delta; Fort Kodiak; Shemya and Adak in the Aleutian Island Chain; and smaller bases and stations elsewhere.[9]

By 1947 construction had commenced on what was then the largest airfield in the world, Eielson Air Force Base, twenty-six miles south of Fairbanks. Long-range bombers were to use this facility. The rebuilding and expansion of other major defense facilities proceeded apace at Fort Richardson and Elmendorf Air Force Base, Fort Greely, and facilities on Kodiak and Shemya Islands. Adak Naval Station and smaller bases and stations elsewhere got under way as well.

By 1949 military planners had become worried about Russian activities in Siberia and speculated that Soviet aircraft stationed on the Chukotski Peninsula could theoretically attack the atomic bomb plant at Hanford, Washington, and return to their bases. A limited radar network existed, but much had to be done to upgrade Alaska's defenses effectively. The construction and equipping of the electronic Distant Early Warning Line resulted, soon to be followed by the White Alice system, a tropospheric scatter radio communications network.

Challenges to the Heartland Approach

Before Alaska could be well defended, however, massive problems had to be overcome. The territory was a region of magnificent distances, lethal cold, forbidding terrain, and a still totally inadequate system of communication and transportation. As on previous occasions, the territory challenged American technical imagination and ingenuity. For despite the intensive construction activity during the war, Alaska was still a primitive frontier that lacked housing and possessed no modern economic and social infrastructure to support the defense effort.

Supplies still came mostly by sea from Seattle to the ports of Seward, Whittier, Anchorage, or Valdez, each one insufficient in one way or another. The best was probably Seward, although wood worms had done severe damage to the docks, which required frequent replacements. Whittier was plagued by high winds and almost continuous rain and snowfall, in addition to inadequate docking and unloading facilities. With a glacier behind it, the sea in front of it, and thirty to fifty feet of snow on top of it in the winter, Whittier was isolated, had no recreational facilities, and appeared to be the end of nowhere for army personnel unfortunate enough to serve there. Large floating ice cakes and thirty-six-foot tides plagued Anchorage.[10]

The Alaska Railroad, which carried freight from the ports, was antiquated. Completed in 1923, the railroad's average daily capacity of some 1,500 tons was insufficient even for normal civilian requirements. It had inadequate rolling stock and poor grades and roadbed. In the so-called loop area between Seward and Portage, the trains had to traverse a high ravine in nearly a full circle; the tracks were supported on high wooden trestles that were quite shaky by 1949. In addition, heavy snows and occasional avalanches between Seward and Anchorage often interrupted train service.[11]

The Alaska Highway connected the territory with the contiguous United States. Although open year round, it had a maximum capacity of only 1,000 to 1,500 tons daily. Alaska's 2,500-mile road system was primitive, and not one road from any of the ports was consistently open all winter. The

Building the Alaska Highway—the "Pioneer Road."

(Author's collection.)

territory's communication system was similarly primitive. Only one land line existed, running along the Alaska Railroad. The Alaska Communications System, which the Army Signal Corps ran, relied on radio transmission, which ionospheric interference often blocked.[12]

Housing was abysmal throughout the territory, particularly for military personnel, thereby severely undercutting morale and causing an almost negligible reenlistment rate for the territory. Many of the single men among the twenty to thirty thousand troops lived in overcrowded barracks and dark Quonset huts. Family quarters were scarce and sub-

standard, and rents were exorbitant. Packing-case houses, open walls, and outdoor privies predominated. Construction costs, two and one-half to three times above those in the contiguous United States, severely limited new housing starts, while exceedingly high prices for food, appliances, and services stretched already modest budgets to their limits. Compounding the problems was the lack of adequate recreational and social activities.[13]

In order to achieve the "heartland" concept of defense in Alaska, the military realized that vast expenditures would be needed to provide basic facilities. The Defense Department asked Congress for funding, and military expenditures approached $100 million in 1949, starting the territory's postwar economic boom.[14]

The Postwar Defense Construction Boom

By June of 1950 it had become apparent that some $250 million worth of construction would be undertaken. Despite a strike among craft unions, workers had been flocking to the territory from the contiguous states since early spring, hoping for quick employment at high wages. Their resources were slim, and many suffered hardships because of the prolonged strike.

The influx of defense spending made prices soar. Housing in Fairbanks, always insufficient and mostly substandard, now fetched premium prices. Cabins without electricity or water rented for $150 per month. In Anchorage, hotel rooms were even worse because rooms were scarce and prices were 10 to 20 percent higher than in Fairbanks.

After the strike ended, workers earned big money, and they worked a good deal of overtime. Building mechanics, for example, received weekly paychecks that often exceeded $200, in addition to free board and room. The basic daily wage of a waitress amounted to $8.60; that of a cook, $18. Craft unions such as those for plumbers and steamfitters, electricians, carpenters, and painters all made over $3.00 per hour. But prices corresponded to wages. The prices of fruits and vegetables, all airborne, were exorbitant. But despite the prices, business boomed.

Population, like prices, had also skyrocketed. In 1940 the territory had about 73,000 residents, of whom some 1,000 were military personnel. By 1950 Alaska's population had jumped to 129,000, of whom 26,000 belonged to the military services.[15] Anchorage had been a sleepy railroad town of 3,495 in 1940; in 1950 it had an estimated 11,060 residents, not including several outlying suburbs that would have brought the population to approximately 20,000. Also not included were the transients and military personnel stationed at the bases. The population of Fairbanks jumped from approximately 5,600 in 1940 to 11,700 in 1950, and that of Seward from 949 to 2,063 during the same decade.[16]

While contractors hurried to complete military construction, the influx of job-seekers severely taxed Alaska's housing and social services. Transients clogged the cities, and although there was no spectacular increase in major crimes in Fairbanks, Anchorage police reported half a dozen murders during the first half of 1950. Police blamed an increase in robberies in both cities on the boom conditions. Gambling flourished in the construction centers, and although it was against territorial laws, officials overlooked the games "so long as these are carried on in an orderly and gentlemanly fashion." Certainly the municipal taxes from these activities had something to do with official leniency. Prostitution flourished despite the fact that red-light districts in both cities had been closed some years earlier. Prostitutes now cautiously walked the streets or operated outside the city limits. Cab drivers often acted as steerers, directing customers to prostitutes for a fee.[17] Both Anchorage and Fairbanks suffered from a lack of school facilities, and Fairbanks was in dire need of a sewage disposal system.

Despite the many problems, Alaskans ultimately stood to profit from the turmoil of the boom. The massive infusion of military dollars stimulated tertiary growth, and the private business sector flourished. In Fairbanks the number of bank deposits doubled between 1949 and 1952, while car registration in Anchorage increased 1,390 percent in a decade and school attendance increased nearly 1,000 percent within the same period. The population of the greater Anchorage area increased 52.1 percent between April 1, 1950, and December 31, 1951.

Civilian construction grew apace: modern hotels and office buildings sprang up, in addition to new residential areas. In Fairbanks, the Community Savings Bank of Rochester, New York, financed the 270-family Fairview Manor development with about $3,080,000. In Anchorage, the Government Hill Apartments, designed for 696 families, took shape at a cost of $10 million, and the Brady-Smalling Construction Company built two 132-unit housing developments at a cost of $3 million. In both Anchorage and Fairbanks large and small modern houses supported by Federal Housing Authority guarantees were built in new subdivisions. The Anchorage suburb of Spenard numbered three thousand residents, and a modern shopping center was built on a tract that had been part of Alaska's wilderness only five years earlier. However, these modern subdivisions were often next door to unattractive slum areas containing shacks and wanigans, largely the result of slipshod regulations and hurry-up building.

Air transportation expanded vastly, with new commercial airports and connections to most points in Alaska and to many international destinations. Considerable sums also went into the expansion of the small highway network and Alaska Railroad extensions and improvements.[18] New radio stations gained permission to operate, and increased demands stimulated the professional and business communities to expand services, as Alaska offered opportunities to young professionals for the first time.

In short, Alaska coped with its problems. In this period of growth and transition, fewer and fewer people fled when the weather turned cold. The territory slowly built up a backlog of social overhead that made living easier and more comfortable. Despite worries within Alaska's business community, the defense boom continued unabated.

By 1954 the territory had passed the peak of military construction. Military housing needs had largely been met, and Alaska's defenses were nearly completed, with a network of radar defenses and massive military bases. The gains had been great. Within the five-year period from 1949 to 1954, the territory had become habitable on a year-round basis for a vastly increased population. Expenditures for defense and civilian construction combined had been approximately $250 million per year from 1949 to 1954.[19]

Alaska's road system had more than doubled, from a prewar mileage of 2,400 miles of dirt and gravel roads to 5,196 miles of high-grade, paved highways and gravel roads in 1958. The Alaska Highway and the Haines Cutoff had become all-year links. Highway construction received massive funding and was transferred to civilian program direction with the inclusion of Alaska in the federal aid-to-highways program in 1956.[20]

The DEW Line

In the meantime, between 1949 and 1953, the Soviet Union had attained nuclear capability, exploding its first atomic bomb in 1949 and its first hydrogen bomb in 1953. Additionally, the Soviets rapidly developed long-range bombers for the delivery of nuclear weapons, and they also quickly tested ballistic missiles with a range of eight hundred miles. In June 1955 the Soviets downed a U.S. Navy patrol plane near Saint Lawrence Island in the Bering Sea, dramatizing the possibility that the Cold War could quickly turn hot. Although the Soviets acknowledged responsibility, apologized, and compensated the United States with a payment of $700,000 for the loss, Americans felt threatened.[21]

American defense planners had worried about a Soviet invasion of Alaska in the postwar period, but by the early 1950s the development of strategic bomber fleets and intercontinental missile systems altered the nature of any future armed conflict. By 1950 warnings of an attack were reduced from hours to minutes. This placed priority on the construction of detection and early warning facilities.

As early as April 1948 James Killian, president of the Massachusetts Institute of Technology, had published a scientific paper in which he proposed that an Arctic radar detection system could give the United States advanced warning of a massed surprise attack from Soviet bomber fleets. In 1949, President Truman authorized, and MIT conducted, a series of top-secret projects. Two years of research confirmed that a Distant Early Warning (DEW) Line to detect Russian bombers was feasible. New vacuum-tube computer technology could be linked to command centers and fighter-interceptor squadrons to engage Soviet bomber penetration over the Arctic en route to American targets.[22]

Although scientists warned that the imminent advent of ballistic missiles would make such an early detection system obsolete, President Dwight D. Eisenhower authorized the DEW system in 1952. The United States and Canada also concluded agreements for reciprocal continental defense and warning systems for their joint defense.[23]

A Native "cleaning crew" on the Gulkana-Chisana Road, 1931.

(Author's collection.)

Construction of the DEW Line, a chain of radar stations located roughly along the seventieth parallel at the top the North American continent, got under way in 1953. It stretched from the far west coast of Alaska to the east coast of Greenland. Originally, there were sixty-one sites, barrack-like buildings topped with giant white domes, about one every fifty miles.[24] Western Electric, the primary contractor, finished the first phase in 1957 at a total cost of about $600 million. In that year, the military had the DEW Line extended to the Aleutian Islands with six additional radar stations, termed "Operation Stretchout." Another chief component of the warning system, built between 1950 and 1960, consisted of two rings of Air Control and Warning radar stations, one along the coast of Alaska and the other in the interior.[25]

The DEW Line tied into the North Atlantic radio system via Iceland as well as the North American Aerospace Defense Command (NORAD) system near Colorado Springs, Colorado. Backed by radar systems and later on by satellites, computers, fighter jets, and communication links, the network could detect and track bomber and missile launches throughout the world while following every satellite and object, even one as small as a baseball, circling in space.[26]

In August 1957 Howard La Fay, a staff member of the *National Geographic* magazine, visited the DEW Line. He reported to the magazine's readers that "the elaborate electronic fence across the roof of North America may one day spell the difference between life and death for the United States and Canada."[27] La Fay noted that each of the DEW Line's six sectors covered about five hundred miles. Each main station was manned by about forty civilians, in addition to a U.S. Air Force complement charged with evaluating radar findings. At approximately one-hundred-mile intervals between main sites stood the smaller, auxiliary stations, each manned by about twenty technicians and mechanics. The DEW Line could not cope with intercontinental ballistic missiles, but La Fay wrote that researchers were already working on a long-range radar system adapted to the missile age.[28]

Scientists overcame formidable obstacles in devising the DEW Line. The main problem consisted of perfecting an absolutely reliable communications network, requisite for an effective warning line. The Arctic had been a communications no-man's-land because of violent storms and various magnetic disturbances. Static often blotted out conventional radio signals, delaying vital messages for days. Scientists solved this problem with a new form of ultra–high frequency radio, called "forward propagation tropospheric scatter," which had a range of up to four hundred miles. The signal was then relayed still farther and was immune to almost all known atmospheric phenomena.[29]

The physical obstacles the contractor dealt with were phenomenal, consisting of permafrost, wind-driven snow that packed like concrete and could bury buildings, unrelenting cold in the winter, and a brief summer where the top of the ground thawed into a liquid marsh that all but prevented cross-country travel. DEW Line builders placed a bed of gravel beneath most stations and placed the structures on pilings. The gravel and pilings insulated the permafrost from the heated buildings and also kept it from melting in the summer.[30]

Despite all the difficulties encountered, Western Electric turned the completed DEW Line over to the air force on July 31, 1957. The air force, in turn, immediately transferred custody of the three-thousand-mile line, stretching from western Alaska to Baffin Bay, to Federal Electric, the service division of the International Telephone and Telegraph Corporation.[31]

Here's how the system worked: the radar systems across Canada's middle were to confirm the DEW Line's preliminary alert, while the Pinetree radar system at a lower latitude, operational since 1955, was to provide data on height, speed, and direction of enemy bombers. Radar-equipped ships and airplanes completed the warning chain encircling North America. Information from any link in the fifteen-thousand-mile land-sea-air warning chain was relayed to centers where computers digested the facts and issued combat instructions.[32] By the early 1960s, however, changing technology had made the DEW Line all but obsolete, and the military decommissioned many of the sites.

Then in the late 1980s, the deployment of air-launched cruise missiles mounted on Soviet Backfire and Bear H bombers precipitated a renewed interest in the DEW Line. On March 18, 1985, the United States and Canada signed a military agreement governing the renovation, upgrading, and modernization of the DEW Line, renamed the North Warning System (NWS). Between 1987 and 1992 contractors finished the project, which included about fifty-two sites along the 70th parallel. Jointly financed, the NWS is tied into NORAD and the underground command center at nearby Cheyenne Mountain. The NWS is also linked to operation control centers at Elmendorf Air Force Base near Anchorage and at North Bay, Canada. Additionally, long-range over-the-horizon backscatter radars located on the east and west coasts of the United States supplement the NWS through coverage of the eastern and western approaches to the North American Arctic. The United States and Iceland also built two radar stations in Iceland to monitor air and sea traffic in the Arctic. The United States and Canada further devised a new North American Air Defense Master Plan that intended to put at least six additional Airborne Warning and Control System aircraft in service for the northern defense and envisioned the development of Arctic air-intercept capabilities and also the construction of ground-based warning systems to counter the threat of air-launched cruise missiles in the Arctic region.[33]

BMEWS and White Alice

Soviet ICBM capabilities improved in the late 1950s, leading to the development of another air defense system, the Ballistic Missile Early Warning System, or BMEWS, since the DEW Line was of no value against these new weapons. Construction soon began on three BMEWS sites: at Clear Air Force Station near Nenana in Alaska's interior; at Thule, Greenland; and at Fylingdales, Yorkshire, United Kingdom. These three sites were to give at least fifteen-minute warning of a missile attack.[34]

Construction on the BMEWS at Clear Air Force Station began in the late fall of 1958. Completed in 1966, it would relay warning of a missile attack to NORAD in Colorado. It was a massive undertaking, involving the construction of dormitories; mess halls; a warehouse; petroleum, oil, and lubricants storage and access roads; utilities; the relocation of forty-thousand-foot length of the Alaska Railroad; a transmitter and a computer building; a heat dissipation system and a radar transmitter building; wells and a pumphouse; a fire station and utilities; and assembly of a power-train generator with a five-thousand-kilowatt capacity, made necessary before the completion of a coal-fired generating plant with a capacity of 22,5000 kilowatts. Radio Corporation of America (RCA) installed the football-field-sized antennae and other equipment related to the missile warning system. The total cost of the BMEWS facilities exceeded $300 million.[35]

Defending Alaska, and by implication the North American continent, from incoming Soviet strikes did not depend entirely on radar detection. In 1955 Alaskan newspapers informed their readers that the military intended to develop a guided missile program in Alaska that would replace the 120-mm anti-artillery batteries that had protected the military installations near Fairbanks and Anchorage. From 1958 to 1959, initial construction of eight Nike Hercules missile sites began, at a cost of $33.3 million. By the late 1970s advancing technology had made all of them obsolete, and the military had deactivated them.[36]

The development of a modern communications network was essential for an effective early warning defense system. The Alaska Integrated Communications Enterprise, known as White Alice, used the propagation tropospheric scatter system, described above, to beam radio signals from a transmitting antenna and then bounce them off the troposphere back down to a receiving antenna. This new development was important for Alaska because of its strategic importance, vast distances, and often difficult and mountainous terrain in need of linkage.[37]

The first construction phase started in 1955, and by 1958 contractors had completed thirty-one sites at a cost of about $140 million. Eventually there were sixty sites, including big tropospheric scatter transmitters and smaller microwave stations. The technicians, mechanics, and housekeepers who staffed these self-contained outposts twenty-four hours a day were housed in dormitories, and airstrips permitted planes to land and deliver supplies.[38]

White Alice successfully linked DEW Line sites and Aircraft Control and Warning stations into an integrated network by relaying communications to Elmendorf and Eielson Air Force bases. Additionally, two routes had to be developed to send information from these stations and from the Clear Air Force Station BMEWS facility to NORAD. Called Rearward Communications, this phase added thirty-two stations to the complicated chain. One route roughly paralleled the Alaska Highway, while the other ran south along the Gulf of Alaska to Annette Island. From there it relayed data via submarine cable to Seattle. This added approximately $18 million to the total cost for the system. By 1961, work on the White Alice installations had been completed.[39]

Alas, technology changes, and by the early 1960s satellite developments had made the White Alice system obsolete. In 1967 Congress passed the Alaska Communications Disposal Act, which directed that all federally owned long-haul communications facilities in the state be transferred to private industry. In 1969, RCA created RCA Alaska Communications, Inc., soon Alascom, and successfully bid to acquire the network. One year later, the Alaska Public Utilities Commission granted authority to Alascom to begin the takeover, a complicated affair because of all the real estate, right-of-way, and easements issues, among other factors, involved in the acquisition. The Alaska District of the U.S. Army Corps of Engineers required thirteen years to complete the transfer.[40]

In 1975 the Alaska state legislature appropriated $5 million for the construction of small satellite earth stations in 125 villages with a population of twenty-five residents or more, and by 1985 Alascom had more than 160 earth stations scattered across Alaska. It was the construction of satellite earth stations that retired the last White Alice site at Boswell Bay on Hinchinbrook Island in Prince William Sound. Boswell Bay had formed a middle link in a communications path anchored at either end by White Alice sites at Neklasson Lake near Palmer and Middleton Island in the Gulf of Alaska. On January 15, 1985, Tim Pettis, an Alascom employee, threw the switch that caused the dials on the Boswell Bay transmitter to drop dead for the first time since late 1959.[41]

Nuclear Submarines and ACLMs

The Arctic Ocean is a forbidding and barren place, covering the top of the globe. It is covered by a permanent crust of ice that shifts perpetually, crumbles, and throws up ranges of jagged ridges. Fierce winds whip the surface, and underwater currents move the ice. Sudden rifts in the ice open apertures, called polynias or leads, uncovering an underwater domain that, close to the North Pole, plunges to almost five thousand meters in depth. The Lomonosov Ridge slices the Arctic Ocean in half, stretching from eastern Greenland to Russia. This towering underwater mountain ridge is a vestige of an old continental shelf, flanked on either side by two other mountain ranges. Despite the great height of the bordering ranges, water depth measures one thousand meters, more than enough room for a submarine to pass.[42]

The USS *Nautilus*, a nuclear submarine, became the first vessel to confirm the navigability of this underwater throughway in 1958, when it made the submerged passage from Point Barrow, Alaska, to the Svalbard Islands. Since then, many other submarines have traversed this expanse. And although sea ice covers the ocean virtually year round, there are always leads through which a submarine can surface, if only temporarily. The deep sea bed also makes detection virtually impossible.[43] The ambient noise of the pack ice drastically reduces the effectiveness of acoustical monitoring equipment, such as sonar systems, and the opaqueness of the Arctic Basin's ice cover renders visual monitoring methods practically useless.[44]

During the 1980s the increasing capabilities of ballistic missile nuclear submarines made them particularly suitable for arctic deployment. For example, both the Soviet Delta-class and American Trident submarines, operating in arctic waters, could pinpoint virtually all enemy targets from fixed patrol stations close to their respective homelands. Soviet Delta-class submarines equipped with SS-N-18 missiles could deliver nuclear warheads to military targets both in North America and Europe from arctic patrol stations. Similarly, American Trident submarines equipped with C-4 missiles could strike military targets throughout the Soviet Union from arctic waters.[45]

The latest generation of Soviet Typhoon-class and the American Ohio-class submarines were even more effective. The large, ice-reinforced Typhoon was especially designed to operate in arctic waters. These submarines were also equipped with Soviet SS-N-20 missiles, carrying six to nine warheads, or the even newer SS-NX-23 missiles. Likewise, the American Trident II, also called the D-5, carried eight to ten warheads. With a range of more than 4,800 miles, they are almost as accurate as land-based missiles. These submarines could also operate with relative safety in arctic waters because of the difficulties of locating, much less tracking, them under arctic conditions. The Arctic offers both ease of operations and comparative safety for these seaborne nuclear delivery systems.[46]

Air-launched cruise missiles (ALCMs) became another weapon of choice. They fly at relatively slow speeds and low altitudes in order to evade conventional air defense systems, and they can be guided and controlled all along their flight paths. Long-range cruise missiles in the early 1990s could travel up to 1,800 miles from their launch site. Prior to its collapse in 1991, the Soviet Union had mounted its ALCMs on the Blackjack-A bombers, which have a combat radius of 4,380 miles.[47]

Undoubtedly, the deployment of these ALCMs on the latest generation of long-range manned bombers reemphasized the role of the Arctic as a theater for military operations. The great circle route over

Alaska's Defense Role in the 1970s

In 1972, the newly created United States Pacific Command, headquartered on Oahu, Hawaii, assumed the responsibilities of the Alaska Air Command in the Aleutians and parts of the Arctic Ocean. This was the largest of the five U.S. unified commands, encompassing a 100-million-square-mile theater of operations in the Pacific area. The three components of the Alaska-based forces, namely the Alaska Air Command, the U.S. Army, and the Alaska and United States Sea Frontier, had until then maintained semiautonomous defense responsibilities in a regional unified command structure under the senior military officer in the state, the commander of the Alaska Air Command. This military reorganization elicited much criticism from state politicians and Alaska's congressional delegation, who wanted all military elements in Alaska to remain responsible to a single commander located in Alaska.

The Vietnam War decreased the state's military establishment except for the Military Airlift Command, which flew out of Cold Bay on the Alaska Peninsula to Cam Ranh Bay and Da Nang in South Vietnam. Elmendorf Air Force Base became a major refueling point for the C-5A Galaxy, C-141, and Lockheed C-131DC cargo planes, which resupplied ground forces in South Vietnam. A $10 million pipeline built between Whittier and Anchorage met the vastly increased demand for jet fuel.

Army units stationed in Alaska during this period at Forts Richardson, Wainwright, and Greely consisted of over five thousand troops of the 172nd Infantry, the Fourth Battalion Ninth Infantry, and support elements of the First Air Cavalry. The 21st Tactical Fighter Wing and support units, the 43rd Tactical Fighter Squadron, and the 5021st Tactical Operations Squadron were based at Elmendorf Air Force Base. Eielson Air Force Base south of Fairbanks was home to the Sixth Strategic Wing of the Strategic Air Command, consisting of RC-135 tankers and modified surveillance aircraft; the 18th Tactical Fighter Squadron and the 25th Tactical Air Support Squadron; and the 343rd Composite Wing. Other elements of the Alaska Air Command were based at Shemya Island in the Aleutians, namely the 5073rd Air Base Group; the 5071st Air Base Squadron at King Salmon on the Alaska Peninsula; and the 5072nd Air Base Squadron at Galena on the Yukon River. The navy maintained a token presence on Kodiak and Adak islands. It deactivated its Kodiak base in 1970 and moved its operations base to Adak Island. The Seventh Fleet (called the Pacific Fleet), headquartered in Hawaii, had primary responsibility for Alaska's seaborne defense. The navy also maintained an antisubmarine warfare program with nuclear antisubmarine depth charges kept at Adak. P-3 Orion aircraft could drop such charges into the ocean, and they were programmed to explode at preset depths.

Source: Jonathan M. Nielson, *Armed Forces on a Northern Frontier: The Military in Alaska's History, 1867–1987* (Westport, Conn.: Greenwood Press, 1988), 200–201.

the pole remains the shortest air route between North America and Eurasia. ALCMs launched from bombers operating in the airspace over the Arctic Basin were capable of reaching most military targets in North America, Western Europe, and the Soviet Union. Also, ionospheric irregularities in the Arctic interfere with the long-range over-the-horizon-backscatter radar systems for defense against these high-endurance bombers, especially those equipped with protective devices, like the B1-B.[48]

There are no effective ways of monitoring submarine activities; the only methods of tracking these crafts is to use nuclear attack submarines. Over half of the Soviet fleet of these submarines, many equipped with SS-N-15 or SS-N-16 nuclear antisubmarine missiles, were stationed with the Northern Fleet. It is probable that American Los Angeles–class nuclear submarines (SSNC) equipped with Harpoon antisubmarine missiles are still operating in the Arctic Basin.[49]

Alaska during the Reagan Years

Military spending in Alaska increased throughout the 1980s, reflecting President Ronald Reagan's commitment to expand America's ability in response to a Soviet military buildup and the Soviets' demonstration that they were willing to use military force as an instrument of policy. Alaska reaped huge benefits from the Cold War as a result of its strategic geographical location.

In November 1983, President Reagan spoke briefly at Elmendorf Air Force Base en route to Japan and Korea. Like other chief executives before him, the president emphasized Alaska's crucial role in national security policy consideration, concluding that the state was America's "first line of defense" and underscoring the postwar continuity of continental defense.[50]

Alaska's senior U.S. senator at the time, Theodore F. Stevens, vigorously supported President Reagan's defense policies, including prioritizing Alaska's military development. In 1983, Stevens, with the support of Lieutenant General Lynnwood Clark, chief of the Alaska Air Command, succeeded in his lobbying efforts when the air force increased the number of F-15 combat fighters from eighteen

to twenty-four, based at Elmendorf Air Force Base, and provided a similar increase in A-10 Skyhawks based at Eielson Air Force Base. Despite Stevens's best efforts, however, the navy did not increase its strength at its installation on Adak Island.

In April 1984, the army announced plans to create several light-infantry divisions as one component of a Rapid Deployment Force. The light infantry concept grew from the necessity to develop a more flexible conventional-force capability and the ability to respond quickly to situations described as "low-intensity conflicts" around the world. Alaska's congressional delegation, state politicians, and community leaders clamored to have one of the proposed new divisions based at either Fort Wainwright or Fort Richardson. Public hearings were conducted, and the army's Corps of Engineers prepared an environmental impact statement. Many individuals, particularly in Fairbanks, expressed concern about the impact such a division would have on the quality of life and community services and predicted disruptions in the local economy. On September 11, 1984, Secretary of the Army John J. Marsch, Jr., and Senator Stevens jointly announced that one of the two new light infantry divisions would be stationed in Alaska; the other was to find a home at Fort Drum, New York. After further deliberations the army decided to station the new unit at Fort Wainwright.[51]

The decision to station the new light infantry division at Fort Wainwright came just in time to rescue the area from the economic doldrums. Fairbanks had suffered major revenue declines, and local tax protest groups had successfully blocked increased property and sales taxes. City officials had despaired of funding necessary services, but the so-called 801 Housing Project at Fort Wainwright, designed to accommodate the new troops and their families, alone accounted for $18.9 million of the $19 million in total residential construction in 1987. It was $17 million above the 1986 spending levels.[52]

The new deployment was the first divisional strength unit to be stationed in Alaska since World War II. Troop strength increased from 8,300 to 12,000. The Sixth Division, trained for combat activities in subarctic environments, had the mission to defend Alaska, with a lower priority for service

The 171st Brigade at Fort Wainwright, whose history dates back to General George Custer and beyond, on field maneuvers.

(Courtesy of *Fairbanks Daily News-Miner*.)

elsewhere in the world where a crisis would require the airlift of a highly mobile combat force. As of the summer of 1986, Alaska had defensive as well as offensive conventional ground forces, complemented by an upgraded Alaska Air Command.[53]

In 1989, Congress appropriated $145 million for the initial construction of a Backscatter Air Defense Radar System in Alaska, with another $209 million planned to complete it. This system operates by bouncing signals off the ionosphere around the curvature of the earth. These over-the-horizon signals can detect airplanes or missiles at all altitudes at a range of 1,800 miles, vastly exceeding the 200-mile range capability of the DEW Line radars. The contractors, however, had not taken Alaska's unique

conditions into account, such as permafrost and the aurora borealis. As a result, the construction of the system was prolonged and resulted in cost overruns of at least $150 million. In the early 1990s work on the system stopped, partly due to the collapse of the Soviet Union.[54]

The Cold War's End and Its Consequences

On March 11, 1985, Mikhail Sergeyevich Gorbachev was elected general secretary, the leader of the Communist Party of the Soviet Union. In less than seven years, Gorbachev transformed the world and turned his own country upside down. He dissolved the Soviet empire in Eastern Europe and ended the Cold

Shemya Station: Small Island, Big Cold War Player

Shemya, a small, flat, isolated island, is located just east of Attu Island in the Aleutians. In 1943 it became the location of a heavy bomber runway, facilities for thousands of officers and men, and a 450-bed hospital. Together with the airfield on Attu Island it was an advance base for offensive strikes against the Japanese on the Kuril Islands.

During the 1950s and 1960s, Shemya Island served as yet another eye on the Soviet Union. By 1957, Air Force planners had decided to convert the island into an experimental radar station. Reconnaissance aircraft, based at Shemya, probed Siberian air space. Throughout the 1960s improvements continued at the base. All in all, the military had spent approximately $113 million there between 1943 and 1971.

After 1960, installations on Shemya monitored Soviet missile tests. During the 1970s new radar technology, such as Cobra Dane, brought the impact points of Soviet test missiles fired from Soviet bases within Shemya's surveillance capability. In 1984, Congress approved the construction of a rocket-launching base at the island, a response to increased Soviet military movements in and around eastern Russia. In addition, the United States needed to verify arms control agreements. Sounding rockets launched from the site carried instruments as far as the edge of the earth's atmosphere in order to monitor Soviet nuclear warhead tests. Construction on various other projects continued until 1995, including the completion of the remodeling of a three-story building for housing personnel, at a cost of $23,200,000. This city-under-a-roof included recreation and day rooms, atria, base exchange, snack bars, administrative offices, security police center with armory, barber and tailor shops, and laundry facilities on each floor.

In 1993 Shemya Station was renamed Eareckson Station. Then in 1995 the air force closed the station and turned it over to a civilian contractor, who maintained the facility in caretaker status with fifteen maintenance workers. B52 bombers can land on the runway, but air traffic is restricted to military aircraft or emergency landings.

Sources: Jonathan M. Nielson, *Armed Forces on a Northern Frontier: The Military in Alaska's History, 1867–1987* (Westport, Conn.: Greenwood Press, 1988), 204; Lisa Mighetto and Carla Homstad, *Engineering in the Far North: A History of the U.S. Army Engineer District in Alaska* (Anchorage: U.S. Army Engineer District, Alaska, 1997), 132–33, 271–72, 352–53; Alaska Department of Community and Regional Affairs, Alaska Community Database, Community Information Summary: "Shemya Station," available at www.state.ak.us/dca/commdb/cis.sfm, accessed May 20, 2009.

War that had dominated world politics and consumed the wealth of nations for nearly half a century. Finally, he disbanded the Soviet Communist Party, a vast institution that had made his political career possible. He then watched helplessly as the revolution he had started escaped his control, and the collection of peoples and cultures he considered one country fell apart. He had to step aside, and others were left to attempt to build something new out of the wreckage of the Soviet Union.[55] When Gorbachev resigned as president of the USSR on December 25, 1991, the Soviet Union already had effectively disappeared.

Today, the political rationale that drove military activities in the Arctic and elsewhere has virtually disappeared. In the early 1990s, the Pentagon made a number of proposals to cut costs, including a reduction of military personnel by three hundred thousand over the next four years and closing several bases throughout the United States. These base closures did not spare Alaska. Naval Air Facility Adak, which played an important role in the Cold War and was occupied by over five thousand navy personnel and their families, was officially reclassified and downsized as a limited air facility in 1994. Placed on a list of military base closures that Congress approved in 1995, it was to be shut down not later than January 1998. (It was officially closed in March 1997.) In late 1996, the navy selected Space Mark, Inc., a subsidiary of the Aleut Corporation, to be the contracted caretaker of the Adak facilities during the completion of environmental cleanup work on the base. Adak Reuse Corporation (ARC) is to make Adak, a complete town for five thousand, into a viable economic center of commercial activities. ARC, through one of its participating members, The Aleut Corporation (TAC), has historical and legal entitlements allowing it to play a key role in reuse planning. Furthermore, the Alaska Native Claims Settlement Act of 1971 provides a legal basis for the TAC to acquire Adak through federal land conveyance.[56]

TAC is the lead coordinator and principal partner with the ARC, U.S. Navy, Office of Economic Adjustment, U.S. Fish and Wildlife Service, and officials of the state of Alaska to ensure a smooth transition from caretaker status to the development of a viable economic center. In 1997, the Department of Defense spent $54 million on environmental cleanup activities. Plans are to concentrate on the fishing industry, trans-shipment-refueling support to airlines and ships, and trade with Asia. Tourism, industry support services, aggregate sales, sports hunting and fishing, and waste storage are other possible developments utilizing the former Naval Air Facility Adak.[57]

Fort Greely, located off the Richardson Highway about five miles south of Delta Junction and ninety miles south of Fairbanks, nearly became another casualty of the end of the Cold War. Initially a staging field for Air Transport Command operations, it was closed in 1945 but resuscitated in 1948 as Big Delta Army Air Field, housing the new Army Arctic In-

doctrination School. In 1955, the army built a larger facility and named it Fort Greely in honor of Arctic explorer Major General Adolphus W. Greely.[58]

In 1995, Fort Greely was selected for realignment, not closure, to save money. Only the Cold Regions Test Center (CRTC) and Public Works functions were to remain. Most of the post was to be closed and turned over to the city of Delta Junction for possible use as a prison. Those plans fell through. In 2001, headquarters for the Northern Warfare Training Center and CRTC were moved to Fort Wainwright, outside of Fairbanks. Though its command moved, CRTC continued operating from Fort Greely. The Northern Warfare Training Center also continued operations at its Black Rapids Training Facility.

After the United States announced its withdrawal from the Anti-Ballistic Missile Treaty, the army selected Fort Greely as a site for the Ground-Based Midcourse Defense system. Work started in 2002, with the plan to deploy twenty-five to thirty anti-ballistic missiles in underground silos by 2010. The Missile Defense Command took control of Fort Greely, and Delta Junction, which had been in a deep recession, boomed.[59]

As we have seen, World War II and the Cold War revolutionized Alaska. Once a territorial backwater, it now became America's strategic military outpost. The federal government spent many billions of dollars to build the defenses of the North. There was a brief period of apprehension at the end of World War II, when the United States rapidly demobilized its armed forces. By 1947, the Cold War rescued Alaska from economic doldrums with renewed spending on defensive installations.

The Cold War ensured continuing recognition of Alaska's strategic location and training environment. In fact, rising global tensions at the height of the Cold War made an adequate defense of the region of crucial importance because of its proximity to the Soviet Union. The relatively short polar routes made for a quick and efficient deployment of American armed forces, and this added to its military importance. Thus, from approximately 1947 throughout the Cold War, the Department of Defense kept a strong military presence in the state at Eielson and Elmendorf Air Force Bases; at Forts Richardson,

Wainwright, and Greely; as well as at several smaller air bases and a host of ever more sophisticated radar stations located throughout Alaska.

In the 1980s, President Ronald Reagan decided to significantly increase military spending to better enable the United States to deter Soviet military buildup and aggression. Alaska benefited through increased spending on upgrading the radar system and the improvement of many other military facilities. In addition, the number of conventional forces stationed at Alaskan military forts increased.

The collapse of the Soviet Union and the end of the Cold War have not diminished Alaska's strategic importance. Although defense spending decreased, the armed forces stationed in the North not only can defend America's military frontier but can be quickly transported to various trouble spots around the globe.

The twenty-first century brings a new agenda, including the removal of the environmental legacies the Cold War left behind. Although much of the arctic pollution is attributable to industrial and commercial activities, the U.S. military clearly has contributed to the problem. In its efforts to maintain superpower status, the former Soviet Union also wreaked ecological catastrophe both within its borders and beyond. This was particularly true in the Arctic. If these problems are not rectified, there is growing concern that past military activities may produce even greater destruction in the future. It will take many years to clean up the deadly environmental legacy of the Cold War.

PART IV

The State of Alaska

"End of the Trail."

(Courtesy of Alaska and Polar Regions Department,
Elmer E. Rasmuson Library, University of Alaska Fairbanks.)

Chapter 15

Alaska's Rocky Road to Statehood

While on a world tour at the end of his services in the administration of President Andrew Johnson, William Seward visited Sitka. There the former secretary of state and architect of the purchase of Russian America predicted that "the political society to be constituted here, first as a Territory, and ultimately as a State or many States, will prove a worthy constituency of the Republic."[1] No one on that August day in 1869 realized that it would take eighty-nine years for Alaska to achieve statehood.

The steps along the road to statehood included the First Organic Act of 1884, which provided Alaska with the rudiments of civil government; the grant of a voteless delegate to Congress in 1906; and the Second Organic Act, passed in 1912, which provided for an elected legislature. But the territory was left unable to regulate Alaska's fish, game, and fur resources or assume bonded indebtedness without congressional consent. These and other legislative restrictions soon led to demands for additional powers. As early as 1915 territorial legislators asked for changes in the Organic Act and even for statehood. Congress did not respond.[2]

The First Statehood Bill and President Harding's Visit

While the territorial legislature debated the merits of full territorial government and statehood, Alaska's delegate to Congress, James Wickersham (a Repub-

lican), introduced a bill to enlarge the powers of the territorial legislature. The most important feature of this measure would transfer management of Alaska's fish and wildlife resources to the territory. But the opposition of the commissioner of the United States Bureau of Fisheries killed the bill.[3]

Wickersham had given some thought to statehood as early as 1910, when he wrote an article for *Collier's* with the suggestive title "The Forty-ninth Star." In it he argued that Alaska was destined to become a state and had, as a matter of fact, "the constitutional right to Statehood." Wickersham also made known his intentions to introduce a statehood bill for Alaska late in 1910.[4] The promised statehood bill never appeared, and one can assume that he may have used the possibility of such a measure as a device to get the Second Organic Act through Congress.

In 1916 Wickersham sent up his first trial balloon by introducing an enabling act for the proposed state, patterning his bill after the 1906 measure that had gained admission for Oklahoma. That particular bill, he reasoned, was recent, contained many new ideas, and was liberal in its grants of money and land to the new state. He introduced the measure on March 30, 1916, the date of the forty-ninth anniversary of the signing of the treaty of cession of Russian America. He had carefully chosen the date to emphasize Alaska's long apprenticeship as a possession of the United States.[5]

The 1916 statehood bill, the first in a long line of such measures, was simple and skeletal. It contained the standard provision in enabling acts that the proposed new state would be admitted on an equal basis with the other states. The rights of Alaska's Indians, Eskimos, and Aleuts to lands claimed by them were protected in that the future state disclaimed all rights and title to any unappropriated public areas that were claimed by the various indigenous groups until Congress extinguished those rights.[6]

Congress, however, did not act on the Wickersham measure. In 1916, Alaskans reelected Wickersham on his own ambiguous platform, in which he favored extended powers for the territorial legislature and statehood "as soon as it can be organized in the interest and to the advantage of the people."[7] The issue of statehood was dead for the present, but it would soon reappear.

The year 1920 turned out to be a Republican year, with the election of Warren G. Harding of Ohio to the presidency. In the race for the delegateship in Alaska, Dan Sutherland, a Republican, prevailed over his Democratic opponent, George Grigsby. The new president appointed Scott Bone, former editor of the *Seattle Post-Intelligencer* and director of publicity for the Republican National Committee, to the governorship of Alaska.[8]

In 1923, President Harding decided to visit Alaska. This was the first time a chief executive had visited the territory during his term in office. The visit was of utmost importance to Alaskans, and they looked on it as an opportunity to present to the president their views on a variety of matters. Harding was interested in finding a solution to the administrative tangle in Alaska. At that time five cabinet officers and twenty-eight bureaus exercised authority over the territory. Many of the agencies were in bitter conflict over how best to develop and use the vast resources of the area. Secretary of the Interior Albert B. Fall, for example, consistently promoted a plan to concentrate the administration of Alaska into one department (presumably Interior), thus allowing private enterprise to exploit the natural resources as speedily as possible. Secretary of Agriculture Henry C. Wallace, in whose department was the conservation-minded Forest Service,

objected to Fall's plan. President Harding was torn between the conflicting opinions and wanted to investigate on the spot before making any decisions. The completion of the federal government's Alaska Railroad gave the president the opportunity not only to drive the official golden spike but also to learn more about the nation's neglected territory.

During his visit, Harding evidently concluded that few important changes of policy or administration were necessary or desirable. In his last major speech, given on July 27, 1923, a week before his death in San Francisco, he indicated that he opposed radical changes in Alaska's administration. He rejected Secretary Fall's idea of a sudden exploitation of Alaska's resources, endorsing instead the conservative policies of his predecessors. The president said that he favored a slow, planned evolution that would protect the territory's natural resources and yet permit their gradual use. Equally important to Alaskans, Harding declared that the territory was destined for ultimate statehood. "Few similar areas in the world present such natural invitations to make a state of widely varied industries and permanent character," he said. "As a matter of fact, in a very few years we can set off the Panhandle and a large block of the connecting southeastern part as a State." Alaskans' reaction to the president's speech was overwhelmingly favorable.[9]

The Secession Movement in Southeastern Alaska

At the conclusion of his Seattle speech, President Harding had suggested that it might be possible in a few years to set off the Panhandle and "a large block of the connecting southeastern part" of the territory as a state. A few weeks later, on August 22, the Ketchikan Commercial Club asked the mayor and town council to call a convention of those Alaskans who lived in the area defined by the president.[10]

The Ketchikan town council complied and issued the call. Arrangements were made for a referendum to be held on November 6 at all of the large southeastern towns, except Sitka, which was not notified in time. 1,344 voters approved of a new territory that day, and 89 voted against. The turnout, however, had been light. Only in Wrangell was the voting heavy; elsewhere only about half of the usual number of ballots were cast.[11]

Thereupon the common councils of Douglas, Haines, Juneau, Ketchikan, Petersburg, Skagway, and Wrangell selected delegates for a divisional convention, eleven delegates in all, and the governor appointed an additional two to represent the Panhandle's unincorporated parts. On November 15, the convention formally convened in Juneau and selected its officers and committees. One was to draft a memorial to Congress, another was to gather statistics to support it, and the third was to prepare an organic act for the new territory.[12]

What boundary was to be sought was the first question. Thereupon the convention invited the communities of Prince William Sound and the Copper River region to join the new territory. The business owners of Cordova responded that they were happy to join their areas with southeastern Alaska in forming a separate territory. What should it be named? Nobody wanted to abandon "Alaska," so the delegates tried out "Old Alaska," "South Alaska," "East Alaska," and "Southeast Alaska," settling on the last.[13]

On November 20 the convention approved of the work of its committees. The memorial, addressed to the president and Congress, asked for partition because the Southeast had a large enough population and expected economic growth, and its interests differed from those of the other divisions. The memorial also pointed out that while the Second and Fourth divisions together raised only as much tax revenue as the First Division, they received from both territorial and federal sources two and one-half times more money than the latter for roads, school, and special authorizations.[14]

After the preparation of the memorial, the convention recessed. Ralph Robertson, an attorney who had been the convention president, presented the memorial, supporting data, and proposed organic act to the House Committee on Territories. For three days, March 27–29, 1924, the committee held hearings on a measure its chairman, James Curry of California, had introduced to reapportion Alaska's legislature. The Department of the Interior had drafted the measure at the behest of Alaska's Governor Bone. Shortly after the hearings opened, chair-

man Curry, apparently with the agreement of his committee colleagues, stated that Alaskans "are not going to have two Territories and they are not going to have a State." Once Alaska's wealth was developed and it had a sufficiently large population, "they can have a state." The United States was not paying for two territorial governments in Alaska, which had a total population of only about fifty-six thousand. The government at present, Curry stated, spent over $7 million each year in Alaska, "and we get out of there about $400,000 in taxes."[15] That ended the matter of partition, and the reapportionment measure died as well.

New Leadership: Anthony J. Dimond and Ernest Gruening

In James Wickersham's 1930 candidacy for the seat of congressional delegate, his platform included, among other items, support for a more perfect form of territorial government and territorial control over Alaska's fish and game resources. Wickersham won the nomination and defeated his Democratic opponent, George Grigsby, in the fall elections. At seventy-four years of age, the veteran again assumed a seat in Congress.

The Great Depression spelled disaster for many Republican officeholders, among them Wickersham. Unopposed in the primary for a second term in 1932, he faced Democrat Anthony J. Dimond in the November election.[16] Dimond had moved to Alaska from Palatine Bridge, New York, early in the century. He worked as a high school teacher and miner and read some law. After a shooting accident forced him to abandon gold mining, he was admitted to the territorial bar and began the practice of law. He served as commissioner of the Chisana recording district in 1913 and 1914,[17] as mayor of Valdez for ten years, and as territorial senator for two terms. After a vigorous campaign, Dimond won the election by a substantial margin, and Alaska Democrats gained large majorities in both houses of the territorial legislature. The American public also voted for a national political change, and Dimond began his Washington career in an era of political ferment.[18] He served as delegate to Congress from 1933 to 1944, during which

Ernest Gruening, Alaska's territorial governor, 1939–53, and Alaska's junior U.S. Senator, 1958–68, in Barrow.

(Courtesy of the Rev. and Mrs. Klerekoper Collection, Alaska and Polar Regions Department, Elmer E. Rasmuson Library, University of Alaska Fairbanks.)

time he initiated the modern drive for statehood.

Despite Dimond's attempts, as delegate he accomplished no more for home rule than Wickersham had. However, changes in the governance of Alaska were made that affected the federal executive. Until 1934 federal relations with the territories had been conducted from the office of the chief clerk of the Department of the Interior. In that year the function shifted to the newly created Division of Territories and Island Possessions within the department.[19] Ernest Gruening became the first director.

Born in New York City in 1887, Gruening graduated from Harvard College and Harvard Medical School in 1912. Instead of practicing medicine, he pursued a career in journalism and became known for his editorship of a succession of Boston and New York newspapers as well as the liberal journal the Nation. In 1936 the energetic director visited Alaska for the first time, and within two weeks he had traveled approximately four thousand miles to familiarize himself with the North.[20]

As we saw in chapter 12, World War II led to the rediscovery of Alaska and its rapid development, a circumstance neither foreseen nor planned by the federal government. A day after the outbreak of war in Europe on September 2, 1939, President Roosevelt announced that John Troy had resigned from the governorship of Alaska because of ill health and that Ernest Gruening would take his place. In his inaugural address on December 5, 1939, Roosevelt predicted that Congress would be slow in granting statehood to the first noncontiguous territory and that hurrying the process would be desirable.[21]

The Beginning of the Modern Statehood Movement

In the 1941 progress edition of the *Daily Alaska Empire*, Dimond attempted to persuade Alaskans about the advantages of statehood. He pointed out that Alaska's population had increased substantially and that the federal government had initiated, if belatedly, a defense construction program. Dimond explained that statehood would enable Alaskans to manage their fish, fur, and game resources; have their own judicial system and police force, and gain federal matching funds for highway construction. Above all, it would bring voting representation in Congress.[22]

The war postponed any action on the matter, but early in 1943, Senator William Langer, a maverick Republican from North Dakota, drafted an enabling bill for Alaskan statehood that he introduced with conservative Democratic Senator Pat McCarran of Nevada on April 2, 1943. A short measure, eleven pages long, it dealt with drafting a constitution, establishing a federal district court in the state, and disposing of public land.[23] Several organizations and newspapers in Alaska considered the measure. Some reacted favorably, while others objected to the cost of statehood, fearing it would be excessive.[24]

On December 2, 1943, Delegate Dimond, who had talked so much about statehood, introduced his own measure. Very similar to Langer's bill, it also provided that the federal government convey to the state practically all public lands. Secretary of the Interior Harold Ickes conceded that ultimate statehood was desirable. But he objected to the general land transfer because he feared that special interests would resist adequate taxation, thereby tempting state lawmakers to allow wasteful exploitation of the lands to obtain needed revenues. None of the various executive departments most closely concerned with Alaska opposed the principle of statehood.[25]

Meanwhile, Delegate Dimond decided to retire from Congress in early 1944, and shortly thereafter President Roosevelt appointed him federal district judge for the Third Judicial Division, an office he had wanted to occupy. His protégé E. L. "Bob" Bartlett successfully overcame primary opposition and won the delegateship in the general election in September, 1944. He had made the issue of statehood one of his campaign planks.[26]

The territorial legislature met in early 1945 for its biennial session. On the fourth day of the session, Governor Gruening delivered his annual message, reminding his listeners that the platforms of both territorial political parties as well as the two opposing candidates for delegate had endorsed statehood in 1944. Furthermore, he said, few if any Alaskans rejected statehood in principle; they differed only on the timing of admission. The governor thought that a referendum on the question should be held but that first the voters had to have information on the issue. This information should be assembled impartially, published, and distributed widely.[27]

Members of Congress Visit Alaska

Several groups of lawmakers toured Alaska in the fall of 1945. One group was composed of the House Subcommittee on Appropriations for the Department of the Interior. Its members reported that although the majority of Alaskans favored statehood, they seriously doubted the territory's ability to assume the burdens of statehood. The reasons mentioned were absence of an adequate tax system and inadequate social legislation.

Representative John Rooney of New York amplified these views in a newspaper interview. People, he remarked, who allowed a major industry like fishing to take out about $60 million annually and retained only $1 million in taxes obviously were not ready for the responsibilities of statehood. Rooney observed that absentee fishing and mining interests controlled the legislature, but he blamed Alaskan citizens as much as the legislators for this state of affairs.

Source: U.S. Congress, House, Subcommittee of the Committee on Appropriations, *Official Trip of Examination of Federal Activities in Alaska and the Pacific Coast States,* 79th Cong., 1st sess., 11; *Washington Post,* August 14, 1945; *Ketchikan Alaska Chronicle,* August 25, 1945.

Debate on the Statehood Proposal

By mid-1945 the executive departments most concerned with the administration of Alaska had to take an official stand. Finally, on August 10, 1945, Secretary Ickes issued a statement on behalf of the Department of the Interior stating that statehood was now a part of the department's policy for Alaska. Ickes remarked that statehood would link Alaska more closely with the rest of the nation and encourage new settlers and the development of its resources. It would result in greater capital investment and bestow equality on territorial residents by giving them voting representation in Congress. The secretary dismissed as of no consequence the arguments used against admission, namely, the small population, lack of agricultural markets, seasonal unemployment, inadequate health services, underdeveloped economy, and higher costs of state over territorial government. He warned, however, that admission would not necessarily transfer the entire public domain to state control.[28]

Obviously an endorsement of statehood from this department was very important, since it had jurisdiction over mining, fish and wildlife, Native affairs, national parks and monuments, the Pribilof Islands' seal harvest, the Alaska Railroad, road construction and maintenance, the care and treatment of Alaska's insane, and the development, disposal, and surveying of the public lands. Its Division of Territories and Island Possessions generally supervised territorial affairs, and the president-appointed governor addressed his annual reports to the Interior secretary.

Governor Gruening was elated by the announcement and thought that if Alaskans voted affirmatively in the referendum, admission to the Union would not be too far behind.[29] The legislature had authorized a referendum, but no provisions had been made to inform the citizenry on the subject. Private citizens formed an Alaska Statehood Association and commissioned George Sundborg, a newspaperman and planner, to undertake a statehood study.[30]

In the meantime, Congress reassembled in 1946, and in his January State of the Union address President Harry S. Truman urged members to admit Ha-

waii and Alaska as states as soon as their residents had expressed their wishes. A short while later, on February 13, Secretary Ickes resigned, and the president appointed Julius A. Krug as secretary of the Interior.[31]

In August 1946, the new secretary went on a ten-day tour of Alaska to listen and learn, but he nevertheless did much of the talking. Many Alaskans were impressed by Krug, a large, jovial man, because he seemed sincere and interested. Krug cautioned residents that statehood was not the answer to all territorial problems but was a step in the right direction. Upon returning to Seattle, he told news reporters that Alaska "should comprise at least one state and perhaps two or three." He also remarked that Congress always moved slowly on major decisions unless it was "against the gun. This is not an issue on which it is against the gun."[32]

A few weeks after Krug left the territory, Alaskans received the statehood report George Sundborg had prepared. Printed both as a pamphlet and as a newspaper supplement titled "Statehood for Alaska: The Issues Involved and the Facts about the Issues," it was widely distributed throughout the territory. For many years this study was the authoritative reference work for the statehood forces. As might be expected, it clearly showed the sympathies of its author and the sponsoring group: of fifty-six pages only five were devoted to arguments against statehood.[33]

The Results of the Referendum

The Sundborg report stimulated public interest, as did the debates, speeches, meetings, and radio broadcasts that followed. About a month after the distribution of the report, Alaskans went to the polls to vote on statehood. In the referendum 9,630 residents voted affirmatively and 6,822 negatively.[34] The 3-to-2 vote was decisive, but not a landslide as proponents had hoped. Only 16,452 ballots had determined the issue, less than 23 percent of the 1939 population, but low voting participation was characteristic of Alaska.

Foremost among the businessmen opposing statehood was Austin "Cap" Lathrop, a entrepreneur whose interests in 1946 included apartment buildings, radio stations, motion-picture theaters, the Healy River Coal Company, and the *Fairbanks Daily News-Miner*. Alaska's wealthiest man, he was esteemed by many because he reinvested his profits in Alaska rather than outside. On the day before the referendum, his eighty-first birthday, he explained that he objected to statehood because of the "terrific financial burden" it would impose on a very small group of taxpayers. Business investment was needed, but capital would have to come from outside. High taxes would discourage investments. Once Alaska had more people, statehood would come easily.[35]

Although business owners generally shared Lathrop's views, many supported statehood nonetheless. Many of those living in incorporated towns firmly believed that statehood would be good for business because it would increase population and investment from outside the territory. A mass market would benefit everyone and also bring down the high cost of living. It was this perception that probably accounted for the widespread endorsement of statehood by chambers of commerce.[36]

Most Alaska politicians supported statehood, often because they believed in it and because it would expand the number of executive offices and judgeships and would also make available two U.S. Senate seats and one House seat. The prospect of reapportionment, however, did not appeal to the sparsely populated Second Judicial Division, where various politicians opposed statehood because their division stood to lose political clout.[37]

While Sundborg had conjured visions of population growth and economic development, these were precisely the features that many Alaskans, particularly old-timers, did not want. They were content with Alaska's unhurried pace, its leisure, independence, and outdoor life—untrammeled, for the most part, by regulations. If they preferred the amenities of city life, they said, they would live in Seattle.

Another point of resistance to statehood was Alaska's persistent regionalism, intensified by a massive population shift. From 1939 to 1950 the population of the Juneau area increased by only 2 percent and that of Ketchikan by 16 percent, while the Fairbanks and Anchorage areas increased by 241 percent and 658 percent, respectively. Massive federal spending for military bases caused these population increases, and in time many Juneau residents worried that Alaskans from those areas, not Congress, would decide the location of the capital.[38] In the last analysis, however, Alaskans were reluctant to close the door to statehood and also were dissatisfied enough with federal rule to cast a majority vote endorsing statehood.

The National Attitude toward Statehood for Alaska

Alaskans had indicated that they wanted statehood, and an even larger proportion of the American people were ready to accept Alaska as a state. On September 21, 1946, George Gallup, director of the American Institute of Public Opinion, announced that 64 percent of Americans favored admission, 12 percent opposed it, and 24 percent were undecided. Most of those who favored admission felt that Alaska was "vital to the defense of the nation" and that "it deserves equal representation in the body of states." In addition, dozens of national fraternal, business, labor, civic, patriotic, and other organizations supported statehood for Alaska. Foremost among supporting organizations was the General Federation of Women's Clubs. As early as 1944 the federation had adopted a resolution favoring statehood for Alaska.[39]

If Congress had reflected popular sentiment, it would speedily have admitted both Alaska and Hawaii. But many of the ninety-six members of the U.S. Senate did not favor the idea of diluting their power. If Alaska were admitted, Hawaii would not be far behind, making a total of four more senators. This consideration was not as important in the House, where the number of representatives was fixed at 435. Additionally, six or seven new members would be added to the electoral college, which chose the president.[40]

Partisan considerations were important as well. During most of the 1950s the Democratic and Republican parties were almost evenly balanced in the Senate. The admission of only one more state might shift that balance in favor of one or the other party. Hawaii had been Republican since the presidency of William McKinley, but Alaska had

Hawaii and Alaska statehood: "A case of paddling their own canoes."

(Courtesy of Alaska and Polar Regions Department, Elmer E. Rasmuson Library, University of Alaska Fairbanks.)

reflected the nation at large and had gone Democratic in the 1932 election.

Sectional considerations were also important. The West consistently and vigorously supported Alaska statehood, sharing with the territory many interests, such as extensive public lands, national forests, and extractive industries. In fact, in 1946 the Western Governors' Conference endorsed the admission of Alaska and Hawaii, and the National Governors' Conference followed suit in 1947.[41]

Congressional Hearings and Debate on Statehood

The House Subcommittee on Territorial and Insular Possessions, of the Public Lands Committee, held hearings on Alaska statehood in April 1947. Acting Secretary of the Interior Warner W. Gardner recom-

mended the enactment of the statehood measure but objected to the provisions that, with few exceptions, would have transferred to the new state title to practically all public lands. This, he stated, was contrary to the traditional practice followed throughout the American West, where public lands had always been retained by the federal government. Gardner proposed to grant Alaska about 21 million acres for schools, approximately 438,000 acres for the university, and another 500,000 acres for various internal improvements. He also objected that Native rights were not protected in the measure, and he proposed that the state and its people forever disclaim both the right and the title to all land retained by or ceded to the federal government by the statehood bill and to all land owned or held by Natives or Native "tribes, the right or title to which shall have been acquired through or from the United States or any prior sovereignty." Joining the Department of the Interior in seeking such a guarantee was James Curry, a Washington attorney for the National Congress of American Indians and the Alaska Native Brotherhood.[42]

Numerous Alaskans flew to Washington, D.C., to testify at the hearings, and most of them spoke in favor of the statehood bill. While generally sympathetic, the legislators worried about Alaska's willingness and ability to finance statehood. Eight days after the hearings ended, the members of the subcommittee voted 8 to 5 to defer reporting the measure until they had been able to visit Alaska personally.[43]

Between July 26, 1947, when the nation's lawmakers recessed, and November 17, when they reconvened, various groups of lawmakers visited Alaska and conducted statehood hearings. Five members of the subcommittee heard testimony from ninety-two people in various Alaska towns. Most of the testimony favored statehood, although some witnesses expressed fears about the added expenses.[44]

Another group touring Alaska consisted of Senator Hugh Butler of Nebraska and three other members of the Senate Public Lands Committee. They did not hold formal hearings. Butler had made it clear in 1946 that he opposed statehood for offshore areas and that, although Alaska was not offshore but a part of the North American land mass, he had decided "to remain a member of the jury" until the enabling bill came before his committee. Their trip was a fairly leisurely one; they did listen to Alaskans but made no record of their observations.[45]

When Congress reconvened in January 1948, Representative Fred Crawford of Michigan had become a crusader for Alaskan statehood. His trip to Alaska the previous year as a member of the House Subcommittee on Territorial and Insular Possessions had convinced him that statehood would correct much that was wrong in the North. Together with the three colleagues who had toured the territory with him, Crawford decided to recommend statehood favorably to the full subcommittee. When the subcommittee met to draft the measure, the Department of the Interior repeated its earlier recommendation that the state receive 21,930,000 acres of public lands to be selected from any lands in the public domain rather than being restricted to certain sections in each township.[46]

Chairman Richard Welch then instructed Delegate Bartlett to negotiate the size of the land grant with officials of the departments of the Interior and Agriculture. Eventually all agreed that Alaska was to receive four sections in each township. Under the provisions of a revised measure, which the subcommittee reported unanimously to the parent committee on March 4, the future state was to receive about 39 million acres of land. After some further debate about Native rights that left the bill unaltered, the Public Lands Committee finally reported the bill favorably.[47]

In the meantime, on February 6, 1948, Senator Butler had reported his findings to his full committee. It was more important to develop Alaska than to push for statehood, he concluded, but he thought that the Panhandle might be split from the rest, since it would be ready for statehood within the foreseeable future.[48]

After this flurry of activity, Speaker of the House Joseph Martin, Jr., refused to bring up the Alaska statehood bill because, as he stated, he did not believe that the Senate would act on it. Since all measures not acted upon at the end of the two-year Congress died, the whole process of introduction and committee review would have to be started again in 1949.[49]

The November elections returned control of both houses of Congress to Democrats and also retained President Truman in the White House. Many Alaskans were cheered when the Democrats pledged themselves to immediate statehood for Alaska and Hawaii, while the Republicans had promised only eventual admission. Alaskan voters had also rejected the "anti-governor, anti-statehood, anti-progress" legislators, who from 1941 through 1947 had blocked the enactment of a basic tax system for Alaska.[50]

Tax Reform and a Revived Statehood Movement

Alaska's basic tax system emerged from a special session of the Alaska legislature convened on January 6, 1949, followed by the regular session on January

24.[51] The most important part of this new structure was a net income tax, which required individuals and corporations to pay the territory 10 percent of their federal income tax obligation, calculated before the deduction of territorial taxes. The tax reform was important because it sent a signal to Congress that Alaskans were willing to tax the special interests and themselves to meet the responsibilities of modern government.

The 1949 session also created the Alaska Statehood Committee. An abortive effort in this direction had been made in 1947, but this time the legislature responded and appropriated eighty thousand dollars for the committee's operation. The legislature assigned several tasks to the committee, among them research, preparation for a constitutional convention, planning for the transition from territorial to state government, and aiding the delegate to Congress in lobbying for the enactment of enabling legislation.[52]

House Approval, Senate Obstruction

Meanwhile, the U.S. House considered Delegate Bartlett's new statehood measure, identical to the one approved in 1948 by the House Committee on Public Lands. In 1948 the House Subcommittee on Territories and Insular Possessions had consisted of twenty members, but in 1949 it had only ten, plus the delegates from Alaska and Hawaii and the resident commissioner of Puerto Rico. All the Republicans were subcommittee veterans, while all the Democrats, including Monroe Redden of North Carolina, the chairman, were new.[53]

Redden asked the committee members to study the published materials from the past two years; he planned to hold hearings in March. On March 3 his subcommittee unanimously approved statehood for Hawaii, and on the next day it held brief hearings on the Alaska measure, made minor amendments, and voted for it unanimously. On March 10 the two bills were reported to the House. The Rules Committee, however, bottled up the measures for the remainder of 1949. Early in 1950 the House Public Lands Committee voted to bypass the Rules Committee and instructed its chairman, J. Hardin Peterson, to take the necessary steps. Speaker Sam Rayburn of

Texas granted Peterson's request, and both statehood bills came to the floor of the House. On March 3, 1950, the Alaska measure passed by a vote of 186 to 146.[54]

The House had passed the Alaska statehood bill. Now the struggle shifted to the Senate, which until 1950 had seemed oblivious of the matter. One reason was that Bartlett was not a member of the upper house, and another was that Senator Hugh Butler had consistently obstructed action in his committee on the Alaska bills in 1947 and 1948.

On March 27, 1950, after approval by the House, Senator Joseph O'Mahoney's Committee on Interior and Insular Affairs scheduled hearings on the enabling bill for Alaska. To present an effective case to the Senate, the Anchorage Chamber of Commerce chartered a plane and flew interested Alaskans to Washington. They met with Bartlett and were told that it was essential to urge senators to approve the bill.[55]

On April 24, 1950, Alaska statehood hearings opened in the Senate. They were to be the most important and productive hearings held so far. Since Senator O'Mahoney was ill, Clinton P. Anderson of New Mexico presided. He had been a general insurance agent and President Truman's secretary of agriculture before his election to the Senate. The various executive department heads testified, among them Oscar L. Chapman, the new secretary of the interior. Various Alaskans told Anderson that they desired the committee not to alter the bill substantially lest it be lost in the final rush for adjournment. Finally Anderson told Edward Davis, an attorney representing the Anchorage Chamber of Commerce, that he did not intend to rubber-stamp the version passed by the House.[56]

On the fourth day of the hearings, Judge Winton C. Arnold, representing the Alaska Salmon Industry, Inc., a trade organization, appeared before the committee in opposition to the measure. All that day and part of the next, supported by an elaborate exhibit of charts and graphs, maps, and tables, he presented a brilliant analysis of the measure. The core of his testimony dealt with the natural resources provisions of the bill. Alaskans should oppose the measure because it "would doom the new State to perpetual pauperism and bureaucratic control." One reason was that the state could select only from vacant, unappropriated, unreserved public lands. This excluded about 27 percent of Alaska's land, because about that much had been withdrawn. Arnold also reminded the senators of his earlier warnings about the massive confusion the aboriginal land claims would cause.[57]

Arnold's testimony alerted senators to the inadequacy of the statehood bill under discussion and made clear that the western model of the public land state, with its township-section selections, was inapplicable to Alaska. In any event, Arnold's testimony provided the basis for a unique and generous land selection formula that, even though enlarged in subsequent years, did not change in concept.[58]

The Senate hearings ended on April 29, and on June 29 the Senate Interior and Insular Affairs Committee completed its revision of the Alaska statehood bill and reported it favorably. Although the statehood measure died in that particular Congress, the Senate report marked a turning point in the land-grant formula. As Delegate Bartlett related to his listeners in territory-wide broadcasts in July 1950, the Senate committee had "struck out in a novel and bold precedent shattering way in determining how land should be transferred to the new state." Instead of awarding to the new state sections 2, 16, 32, and 36 in each township, the Senate had granted the right to take from the public domain 20 million acres of vacant, unappropriated, and unreserved lands best suited to its particular needs.[59] Additionally, the measure granted about two hundred thousand acres from the national forests, the same amount adjacent to established or prospective communities, and another 1 million acres for internal improvements. Title to subsoil mineral rights, except where it conflicted with prior established ownership, was to pass to the new state as well.[60]

Once the historical precedent for the traditional land-grant formula, with its small land grants and specific township-section requirements, had been broken, the way opened for increasingly generous land-grant provisions in succeeding statehood bills. For the rest of 1950, however, the Southern Democratic–conservative Republican coalition prevented both the Alaska and Hawaii bills from coming to the floor of the Senate. This meant, of course, that the whole tedious process of getting a new bill through the House and then through the Senate had to be repeated.[61]

The Statehood Struggle Continues

On January 8, 1951, Senator O'Mahoney submitted an Alaska statehood measure for himself and eighteen of his colleagues of both parties. With the introduction of three companion bills in the House, the statehood struggle was joined again. Late in January 1951, the Senate Interior and Insular Affairs Committee began anew its study of the Alaska measure, but since extensive hearings had been held the preceding year and there was little that could be added, committee consideration of the bill was cursory. In May the committee reported the measure favorably by the narrow margin of 7 to 6. But with the outbreak of the Korean War in June 1950, national priorities had shifted, and Alaska statehood took very much a back seat. The years 1951 and 1952 were lean ones for the statehood forces, and even the Alaska Statehood Committee became somewhat moribund.[62]

With the end of the war in sight early in 1953, half a dozen new statehood bills were submitted, most of them identical to the 1951 bill. Delegate Bartlett doubled the land grant to 40 million acres in the measure he introduced on February 6, 1953, also including four hundred thousand acres from the national forests, a like amount for community and recreational purposes, and 2.5 million acres for internal improvements, a total of over 43 million acres. Representative John Saylor of Pennsylvania seconded Bartlett's bill with an identical measure of his own. The House Subcommittee on Territories and Insular Possessions of the renamed House Committee on Interior and Insular Affairs held hearings on a number of these measures and finally reported the Saylor bill favorably in June 1953, along with a number of amendments. The most important of these increased the proposed land grant from 40 million to 100 million acres. After this favorable treatment, the Alaska measure promptly disappeared into the House Rules Committee.[63]

Despite lack of legislative progress, by 1954 both House and Senate measures proposed to bestow some 100 million acres of land on the new state. This constituted a substantial land grant; more important, it followed the new formula that allowed Alaska to select its acreage in large blocks rather than take what luck gave it in the traditional township-section pattern.

In his 1955 State of the Union message, President Dwight D. Eisenhower, as he had the year before, strongly recommended the admission of Hawaii. For the first time in such an address, he mentioned the possibility of Alaska statehood, but only dubiously. He was reluctant to support Alaska statehood because he believed it would limit the president's ability to withdraw lands in Alaska for defense purposes. Frustrated, various individuals began considering the possibility of holding a constitutional convention before the territory's uncertain admission into the Union. But most Alaskans rejected the various alternatives to statehood that were suggested from time to time.[64]

One of the alternatives to statehood was the repeated proposal that Alaska and Hawaii become commonwealths. Commonwealth status, as its backers envisioned it, would grant Alaska exemption from the internal revenue laws of the United States but not much else. A report from the Library of Congress indicated that no incorporated territory had ever been exempted from federal taxes. Nevertheless, various small groups in Alaska supported the concept, still lured by the faint possibility of tax exemption. Delegate Bartlett remarked that commonwealth was mentioned only when there was a chance that Congress might approve Alaska statehood. Once legislation failed, talk of commonwealth also subsided.[65]

At the national level, the statehood movement did not fare well in 1955, though four statehood bills were introduced—one in the Senate and three in the House. The new Democratic-controlled House and Senate Interior and Insular Affairs committees prepared joint Alaska-Hawaii statehood bills, aware that it was important to satisfy President Eisenhower on this issue. The House again held hearings, primarily for the benefit of its new members. How to satisfy the president on statehood was a problem committee members faced. Secretary of the Interior Douglas McKay testified, favoring Alaska statehood

with a "proper bill." The secretary desired to exclude northern and western Alaska from the proposed state. Asked whether a military reservation should be inside or outside the state, McKay stated that it made little difference. Congressman Arthur Miller subsequently had prepared an amendment meeting McKay's requirements.[66]

Bartlett disliked the amendment, pointing out that neither the Department of Defense nor the president had indicated that it met their objections. Above all, the delegate had been given no opportunity to analyze the provisions of the amendment. He urged its omission, and the committee went along with him and voted it down. Soon thereafter, the Defense Department reported on the twin statehood measures. It raised no objection to Hawaii's admission but cautioned that no change be made in Alaska's status at that time. After more debate Bartlett compromised, and an amendment acceptable to all was worked out. Thereupon the committee approved the twin bill by a vote of 19 to 6.[67]

In the upper chamber Senator James Murray and twenty-five of his colleagues had reintroduced essentially the same bill that body had passed nine months earlier. Senator Henry M. "Scoop" Jackson's Subcommittee on Territories and Insular Affairs dealt with two markedly different executive reports. The Defense Department informed Jackson, as it had the House, that no changes should be made in the political status of Alaska, while the State Department asserted that admission of both territories would comply with the United Nations charter.[68]

After hearing testimony from various officials of executive departments, Senator Jackson and Congressman Miller wrote to the president asking him what sort of statehood legislation he would accept for Alaska. Eisenhower's answer was ambiguous. "I am in doubt," he wrote, "that any form of legislation can wholly remove my apprehension about granting statehood immediately. However, a proposal seeking to accommodate the many complex considerations entering into the statehood question has been made by Secretary of the Interior McKay, and should legislation of this type be approved by Congress, I assure your subcommittee that I shall give it earnest consideration." The president at last had indicated that he would at least consider Alaska statehood.[69]

Constitutional convention leadership. *Seated from left:* Frank Peratrovich, William A. Egan, and Ralph Rivers. *Standing from left:* Mildred Herman, Doris Arana Bartlett, Thomas B. Stewart, and Katherine Alexander.

(Courtesy of *Fairbanks Daily News-Miner.*)

The House sent its version of the twin bills to the Rules Committee, where Congressman Howard Smith of Virginia, the new chairman, was implacably opposed to statehood for either territory. After lengthy hearings, the committee granted a "closed rule" under which no modifications would be permitted except for the fifty-six amendments reported by the House Committee on Interior and Insular Affairs. On May 10, 1955, after two days of debate, the House recommitted the tandem bill by a vote of 218 to 170. The Senate, waiting for the outcome in the House, did not act at all.[70]

Alaska's Constitutional Convention and Success, at Last

In the meantime, the sentiment for holding a constitutional convention to boost Alaska's sagging fortunes found expression in measures introduced in the 1955 territorial legislature. Such a convention was finally convened, and after seventy-five days of labor, the fifty-five delegates produced a document that experts considered a model constitution.[71]

During their deliberations the delegates attached the so-called Alaska-Tennessee Plan ordinance to the constitution. The idea had originated with George H. Lehleitner, a public-spirited businessman from New Orleans who had become an advocate of Hawaii statehood. Finding that Hawaii would make no progress, Lehleitner then made statehood for Alaska a personal crusade. During his research into American history, Lehleitner had discovered that a number of territories had departed from the conventional procedures for seeking admission to the Union as states. Instead, these territories drafted state constitutions, elected two U.S. senators, and sent them to the nation's capital and asked for admission. Tennessee and six other territories had employed similar procedures.[72]

When the voters went to the polls in the general election on October 9, 1956, they elected three Democratic candidates for the positions described by the Alaska-Tennessee Plan: for U.S. senators, Ernest Gruening and William A. Egan; and for U.S. congressman, Ralph J. Rivers. Delegate Bartlett had agreed to the scheme even though he would lose

William A. Egan, president of the Alaska Constitutional Convention, signs the document in the University of Alaska gymnasium, February 5, 1956.

(Courtesy of Alaska and Polar Regions Department, Elmer E. Rasmuson Library, University of Alaska Fairbanks.)

his job if it was successful. The three men went to Washington, D.C., and although they were not seated, they lobbied hard for the cause.[73]

Meanwhile, the outlook for statehood had brightened in Washington. In March 1956 Secretary of the Interior McKay had resigned, and the president had appointed Fred Seaton to replace him. Seaton, a former publisher and broadcasting executive from Hastings, Nebraska, had been a supporter of Alaska statehood during his brief stint in the Senate, having been persuaded to support Alaska's cause by Ernest Gruening. In 1953 Eisenhower appointed him assistant secretary of defense for legislative and public affairs, and in 1955 he became a presidential assistant.

During his confirmation hearings, Seaton mentioned that he favored statehood for Alaska. He also pledged to allow the administration-requested defense withdrawals so that Alaska could join the Union. When asked how he stood on the immediate admission of Alaska to statehood, he replied, "Personally, I am for it. Furthermore . . . I should certainly be glad to do everything I can to work out [the withdrawal of lands necessary for defense] so that Alaska can become a state."[74] True to his word, Seaton staunchly supported Alaska statehood.

On the territorial level, when B. Frank Heintzleman resigned as territorial governor three months before the expiration of his term, he was replaced by Fairbanks attorney Mike Stepovich. The new governor told Alaskans in his inaugural address that the time had come to close ranks on the statehood issue and work toward the admission of the territory, since that was what the majority wanted.[75]

In 1957, at the request of Delegate Bartlett and Delegate John Burns of Hawaii, Senator James Murray introduced separate statehood bills for the territories, and each delegate introduced companion measures in the House. The new Alaska statehood measures differed somewhat from previous ones in that they considered the Alaska Constitution an accepted fact and thus became admission bills rather than enabling bills. In March the House Subcommittee on Territories and Insular Affairs held ten days of hearings on the subject. The Senate counterpart, presided over by Senator Jackson, devoted two days to it. In general, the two hearings were perfunctory, because many members of the House and Senate committees felt that little new could be added to the record.[76]

As finally reported to the House, the Alaska measure provided the state with 182 million acres of vacant, unappropriated, and unreserved land to be selected within a period of twenty-five years after admission. Native land claims were protected and left to be dealt with by future legislative or judicial action. In August the Senate committee reported its Alaska bill favorably, granting the state the right to select 103,350,000 acres from the vacant, unappropriated, and unreserved public domain within twenty-five years after admission to the Union.[77] In July 1957, Speaker of the House Sam Rayburn, hitherto a foe of Alaska statehood, finally changed his mind at Bartlett's urging and promised to give the territory "its day in court," but he advised Bartlett not to bring the bill to the House until 1958.[78]

In January 1958, President Eisenhower for the first time fully supported Alaska statehood and again urged Hawaii's immediate admission. Soon after delivering his address, however, Eisenhower again dimmed the hopes of Alaska statehood proponents when he advocated that the Hawaii bill be brought up simultaneously with the Alaska measure. At this critical point, Delegate Burns of Hawaii helped the Alaska cause when he asserted that "nothing should interfere with success in the consideration of [the] Alaska" statehood bill. He promised to remove the Hawaii measure from the Senate debate if that was necessary to ensure the success of the Alaska bill. The two bills were not combined.[79]

Toward the end of January 1958, Bartlett again received Rayburn's assurance that the Alaska statehood bill would come to a vote in the House. Not long after his talk with Rayburn, Bartlett "had a long, long talk with [Senate Majority Leader] Lyndon Johnson. Lyndon told me then that he was ready. He was ready to permit Alaska statehood to come to the floor of the Senate for action there."[80] At about the same time, Rayburn told Congressman Howard Smith, chairman of the House Rules Committee, that he wanted a ruling on the statehood bill. Bartlett was elated.[81]

In the House, Congressman Smith had not changed his opposition to statehood. Representative Clair Engle of California, chairman of the House Interior and Insular Affairs Committee, warned Smith that unless the Alaska bill was given the green light by the middle of March he intended to bypass the House Rules Committee by employing a little-used device under which statehood and a few other kinds of legislature were deemed privileged.[82]

In the meantime there were demonstrations for statehood in Anchorage and Fairbanks, and early in March the American television public saw an Alaska and Hawaii statehood debate on the CBS program *See It Now* with host Edward R. Murrow. Bartlett, Governor Stepovich, and Robert Atwood spoke in favor of Alaska statehood, while Winton C. Arnold; John Manders, an Anchorage attorney and member of a group called Commonwealth for Alaska; and Senator George Malone of Nevada spoke against it.[83]

In the House, Bartlett's friend Congressman Leo O'Brien announced that he would support four amendments to his bill. One would retain federal jurisdiction over Alaska's fish and game resources in the broad national interest. The others provided for a statehood referendum; a reduction of the land grant from 182 million to 102.55 million acres, with an additional four hundred thousand acres each of public lands and national forest lands, for a total of 103.35 million acres; and permission for the Federal Maritime Board to retain control of Alaska's seaborne trade with other states. Bartlett agreed to the other concessions but was unhappy with the federal retention of fish and game management.[84]

After the House Rules Committee stalled, the leadership decided to employ the bypass procedure. Representative Wayne Aspinall brought up the Alaska statehood measure as a privileged matter on May 21, 1958. Speaker Rayburn overruled various objections, and after lengthy debate and the adoption of four amendments, the House passed the Alaska statehood bill on May 26 by a vote of 210 to 166.[85]

Except for the likelihood of amendments being added to the bill, prospects looked bright in the Senate. However, if the Senate bill differed in important particulars from the House version, Bartlett worried, the statehood forces would "be catapulted into a morass." Bartlett and others therefore set up a meeting with Senator Jackson, floor manager of the bill, who agreed to abandon the Senate bill and take the House measure instead. The Senate debated Alaska statehood in the latter half of May and throughout June. On June 30 the Senate passed the Alaska statehood bill, 64 votes to 20. The long struggle had finally ended in victory.[86] President Eisenhower signed the Alaska statehood measure into law on July 7, 1958, and on January 3, 1959, he signed the proclamation officially admitting Alaska as the forty-ninth state of the Union.

Alaska's Huge Land Grant

The struggle had been an extended one, involving many people in Alaska, in Washington, and throughout the rest of the nation. Bartlett, summing up the long fight, stated that "it took fifteen years for fruition, and I think that given the nature of the opposition, the size of the project, the fact that no state had been admitted since 1912, that actually it was a pretty successful campaign."[87] Bartlett might well have decided that it was fortunate that statehood had not been attained earlier, under the meager bills then under discussion.

Together with vast changes in its political structure, Alaska received a total of 103,350,000 acres, to be selected from the vacant, unappropriated, and unreserved public lands within twenty-five years after admission. The magnitude of the federal land grant to the new state can best be understood in a comparison with the acreage turned over to the forty-eight contiguous states. Land grants to all of the contiguous states combined totaled approximately 225 million acres, with great variation in acreage granted to the individual states. The midwestern and southern states have received a larger percentage of their total area than have the eleven western states. Florida ranks first, with a grant of 24,119,000 acres of a total state area of 37,478,000 acres—an astounding 64.3 percent. Nevada ranks last, with a land grant of 2,723,647 acres of a total state area of 70,745,000 acres—3.8 percent. In the overall list of states, Alaska ranks seventh, with 27.9 percent of area granted, but it received by far the largest total acreage of any of the other public-land states.[88] Congress had been generous indeed.

Chapter 16

Managing Alaska's Oil Resources

Ever since the late 1890s gold rushes to Alaska, Alaska's fortunes have been tied to the vicissitudes of a resource-extraction economy. Successive mineral rushes and the exploitation of the region's rich salmon runs brought waves of settlers and periods of prosperity. The last of these petered out by the 1920s. Then World War II rediscovered Alaska, and the territory's strategic location became an important resource. The end of the war threatened to once again plunge Alaska into the economic doldrums when the Cold War rescued the territory and it became one of the cornerstones of Western defense against an aggressive Soviet Union.

A new boom began with the Richfield Oil Corporation's July 23, 1957, discovery of a commercial field at its Swanson River Unit No. 1. In 1950, the total number of oil and gas leases had covered a little over nineteen thousand acres, but by the end of December 1957, 12 million acres were under lease or had been filed on.[1] Many oil companies had come north, many major players as well as small wildcatters, and in the summer of 1958 twenty-three helicopter parties from various companies had conducted field research. In short, Alaska had entered the oil age. The difficult process of establishing the administrative and legislative foundation for managing this new resource was almost as arduous as the process of attaining statehood.

The Constitutional Convention and Alaska's Resources

The inadequacy of Alaska's tax system is an excellent historical marker to chart Alaska's struggle to gain increased political power, from a mere territory in the nineteenth century to one of fifty sovereign states in the mid-twentieth century. In territorial days, much of Alaskan resource development did not benefit its residents; the federal government and distant, large corporations and investors dominated Alaska's economic life. A central theme of the statehood struggle was to ensure that Alaska's residents would become the primary beneficiaries of Alaskan resource development. Taxes were one method that allowed northern residents, through their government, to prevent a greater share of Alaska's wealth from going south. As Alaskans struggled to increase local political authority, they also increased local taxation. Thus tax increases and statehood were linked as a means of constructing a permanent foundation for a stable society that would endure long after all the nonrenewable resources were gone.

In 1955, at the height of the statehood movement, Alaskans called a constitutional convention (see chapter 15). Anticipating that if and when Alaska achieved statehood, the new state's land endowment would be the cornerstone of its economic viability, the framers faced the challenge of drafting a resources article that would maximize potential benefits to Alaska residents. In order to aid them, the Alaska Statehood Committee hired the Public Administration Service of Chicago to prepare a series of background papers for the delegates on a wide variety of subjects to be included in the constitution, including Alaska's natural resources.[2]

The paper, authored by E. R. Bartley, professor of political science at the University of Florida at Gainesville, briefly discussed Alaska's resource potential and summarized the history of mining and the search for petroleum. It concluded that the "wise utilization of the state's potential mineral wealth will result not only in fullest development but in an orderly development calculated to return the greatest possible benefit to the people of the new state who are the real proprietors of these assets."[3]

It was clear that few topics facing the convention delegates were of greater long-range importance than a sound resource article. Practically all of the other territories that joined the federal Union as states had agriculture as an economic base. Alaska's future wealth and economic well-being, by contrast, would be largely based on its subsurface mineral resources and the wealth of its waters.

The Constitutional Convention invited Delegate E. L. "Bob" Bartlett to give the keynote address. He had read and was impressed by Bartley's staff paper, and he asked Bartley for help in drafting his speech, focused on resource policy. After a few preliminaries, Bartlett reminded the delegates that the statehood bills in recent years had called for a large land grant, approximately 100 million acres, or the size of California. This land mass, which would include "a tremendous acreage of submerged lands," represented "a veritable empire, a wealth of land and resources never before conferred on any state" except Texas, which had been allowed to retain all its public lands upon admission. These grants would provide the new state with a sound economic base for its future operations and activities.[4]

Bartlett reminded the delegates that too often in the past, entrepreneurs had exploited Alaska's natural resources while contributing very little "for necessary governmental services" or "for the permanent development of a sound economy for the people." Alaska's boom-and-bust economy, Bartlett charged, was "due in no small measure to the hard cold fact that mineral development was solely for the purpose of exploitation with no concern for permanent and legitimate growth." Corporate interests likewise had ruthlessly plundered the once-great fisheries "without regard to the welfare of the mass of average citizens."[5]

The delegate warned his listeners of two future dangers. Firstly, that corporate interests might exploit Alaska's resources as in the past without paying reasonable taxes for the support of state services and for the benefit of all Alaska's citizens. Secondly, that "outside interests, determined to stifle any development in Alaska which might compete with their activities elsewhere, will attempt to acquire great areas of Alaska's public lands in order *not* to develop them until such time as, in their omnipotence and the pursuance of their own interests," they see fit to do so. Alaskans demanded effective safeguards "against the exploitation of the heritage by persons and corporations whose only aim is to skim the gravy and get out, leaving nothing that is permanent to the new state except a few scars in the earth which can never be healed."[6]

Paradoxically, steps taken to avoid these dangers might lead to others, namely that upon statehood, Alaskans might desire to get resources developed quickly "at any and all costs." Although understandable because of the long years of territorial restrictions, such a course would eventually lead "to financial insolvency." If the Convention established long-range resource policies, the reward would be "true future development—not exploitation or non-use."[7]

In keeping with the tone set by Bartlett, the convention delegates established a framework of general guidelines that put the interests of Alaska's citizens ahead of private commercial ones. Article VIII, Section 1, of the Alaska Constitution states that it will be the "policy of the state to encourage . . . the development of its resources by making them available for maximum use consistent with the public interest." It adds in Section 2 that "the legislature shall provide for the . . . development . . . of all natural resources . . . for the maximum benefit of its people." State legislatures then were constitutionally required to enact resources development and leasing law consistent with the "maximum benefit to the people" standard.

Subsequently, territorial legislators showed decisiveness and ingenuity in drafting legislation anticipating an Alaskan oil boom. This happened at a time when the federal government owned more than 99 percent of Alaska's lands, and the territory held title to little more than one hundred thousand acres. The large land grants were still in the future, coming with the Alaska Mental Health Act of 1956 and the Statehood Act in 1958. Nobody then knew when Congress would pass these measures.

Early Natural Resources Legislation

The territorial legislature had already grappled with the land and resource management question a couple of years earlier. In February 1953, it had passed a Lands Act, Alaska's first effort to control its natural resources. This legislation established a Department of Public Lands and created the position of land commissioner, who was to administer any lands reserved for the support of public schools and also function in the territory's interest when the United States disposed of materials from lands withdrawn to support Alaska. The commissioner also was to prepare legislation to facilitate the administration, appraisal, leasing, and sale of all current and future territorial lands.[8]

In 1955 the territorial legislature expanded its efforts to create a meaningful authority over Alaska's natural resources by passing the Oil and Gas Conservation Act. Territorial commissioner of mines Phillip R. Holdsworth played a vital part in the development of this act. Armed with a degree in mining engineering and geology from the University of Washington, he had come to Alaska with his father, who built and operated a lode mill at the Skein-Lickner property on the Kenai Peninsula. Holdsworth worked as a mucker, a miner, an assayer, a timberman, and a gold miner as well as a government administrator. From 1931 to 1936 he was the mill superintendent for the Nabesna Mining Corporations at Chitina on the Copper River. He then took a job as mill superintendent for the Mindanao Mother Lode mines in the Philippines. Taken prisoner by the Japanese, he spent the war

years in a POW camp. He returned to Alaska in 1946, and Governor Gruening appointed him territorial commissioner of mines in 1952.[9]

Holdsworth's experience convinced him that the territory had to enact conservation measures before permitting additional petroleum exploration.[10] Designed primarily to conserve oil and gas reserves, the Oil and Gas Conservation Act broadly defined waste, which included the careless storage of oil, maintenance of an inefficient gas-oil ratio, and an excess gas escape. It also afforded the property owner the opportunity to produce his "just and equitable share" of any underlying pool.[11] The act also created the Alaska Oil and Gas Commission and gave it the authority to enforce the act. It consisted of the governor, the commissioner of mines, and the territorial highway engineer.[12]

The territorial legislature followed with other legislation. House Bill 216 dealt with oil and gas leasing in Alaska's public tide and shore lands. The land commissioner, with the approval of the commissioner of mines and the attorney general, was given authority to lease all such lands for oil and gas development. Borrowing from federal models, the bill established standards that were to govern the territory's oil leasing program. It required competitive bidding, with awards to the highest cash bonus offer. Successful bidders had to pay a royalty of at least 5 percent for the first ten years of new production, which rose to 12.5 percent thereafter. Exploration was to be completed within five years, at which time the initial lease expired. Under special circumstances the bill allowed a lease's renewal for an additional five years. Contiguous leases were restricted to 2,560 acres. No one was allowed to hold more than 100,000 acres unless the acreage was committed to an approved unitization plan.[13]

Lessees had to pay an annual rental of twenty-five cents an acre in advance. No rent was due for the second or third years unless the lessees discovered oil. In that case, the annual rent increased to one dollar per acre on rentals that produced oil, called "producing structures," or the required royalty payment, whichever was higher. The bill also allowed lease renewal as long as the structure produced. If there was no discovery, lessees renewed, paying the twenty-five cent annual rent during the fourth and fifth years. Thereafter, the rent increased to one dollar per acre.[14] Together, all of these terms created a starting point from which later legislation could be negotiated.

Shortly thereafter, territorial representatives Irene E. Ryan and Warren A. Taylor introduced legislation to amend the 1953 Lands Act. The new bill left most of the statute intact, but it expanded the section dealing with "duties and powers" of the land commissioner and wrote specific rules to govern the leasing of territorial lands for uses other than mineral extraction. It created a Board of Public Lands, composed of the land and agriculture commissioners and the attorney general, to handle several of the Department of Public Land's regulatory authorities. The board had no authority to lease petroleum lands. Land was to be leased competitively, and it could not be obtained for less than its appraised rental value. Payment had to be rendered in advance.[15]

During the legislature's first extraordinary session that year, Representative Ryan submitted another piece of petroleum legislation: the Oil Production Tax Act was to remove the speculative element that complicated assessing the value of oil or mineral rights in real property. House Bill 7 provided for a tax of 1 percent of "the gross value at the well of all oil and gas produced within" Alaska, including the royalty interest. Among other provisions, the statute specified that taxes were to be paid in full "in lieu of all ad valorem taxes now or hereafter imposed" by other government units on any property rights attached to producing leases, or on any "machinery, appliances and equipment used in and around any well producing oil or gas and actually used in the operation of such well."[16]

The unclear language of Ryan's bill later caused much confusion. Oil companies claimed that the law protected all of their facilities from local taxation, while local governments, such as the Kenai Peninsula Borough, disagreed, arguing that the "machinery" mentioned in the bill did not include more permanent production-related facilities such as refineries and pipelines. Years later, the state courts sided with the borough, although disputes over this issue continued for years, causing exten-sive debates and much animosity among the several parties involved.[17]

In 1957, the territorial legislature repealed the 1953 and 1955 land acts and passed a new measure, which established a Department of Lands, a Land Board, and the Office of the Land Director. Among its many other provisions, the act stated that oil and gas leases that Alaska issued were to "be in substantial conformity with the provisions of the Mineral Leasing Act of 1920, as amended." Only two provisions in the new land bill had leasing terms different from federal requirements. Article IX, Section 2(a) provided, in part, that if the land to be leased were on a known or producing geologic structure, or one reasonably believed to contain such a structure, it was to be offered only on a competitive bid basis. The territorial legislature added the qualification to the federal provision, allowing Alaska to offer leases on a competitive bid basis even though the land might not qualify as containing a proven structure by U.S. Geological Survey standards. Section 2(b) provided that in case the land to be offered was considered noncompetitive, a royalty of not less than 12.5 percent would be required. The wording change also applied to the 5 percent royalty provision for the first producer for the first ten years. Furthermore, Article IX, Section 3 of the Alaska Land Act provided that "leases issued shall be in substantial conformity with the provisions of the Mineral Leasing Act of 1920s, as amended," so that Alaska lands, adjacent to public lands, could be operated as a unit.[18]

The Discovery of Oil and the Development of Leasing Rules

In July 1957, the Alaska Land Board appointed Evert L. Brown director of the Alaska Department of Lands. Brown's job was to set up the new department, develop a records-and-appraisal system, and establish a fair market value for the paltry 106,000 acres of school lands to which the territory held title. He also was to prepare lease forms and regulations that were to govern oil and gas exploration and production, although he was unaware that Alaska had any potential oil and gas producing lands. In addition, his department was responsible for administering the developed tide lands that Congress by then had turned over to the territory.[19]

Although still in the organizational stage, the Alaska Department of Lands was functioning by early 1958. On January 11, 1958, Representative Ryan wrote Phil Holdsworth, then chairman of the Territorial Land Board, about newspaper articles that had quoted Director Brown expressing the view that generally the territory was better off "now to receive 90% of the income from oil and gas lease rentals [from federal land] than we would to receive 100% and to have the problem of administration." Ryan agreed that this probably was true for much of the public domain the territory might be able to select, but she argued that the 1957 discovery of the Swanson River oil field on the Kenai Peninsula had changed the situation. Oil companies had paid high cash bonuses and overriding royalties to the lease-holding speculators or middlemen in areas of oil potential. These financial benefits, she thought, should "rightly go to the benefit of the Territory as a whole." Ryan believed that the territorial "policy of selection and administration as a whole should now be reviewed." As knowledge of Alaska's oil provinces accumulated, she asserted, the territory should claim such blocks of land and offer them for competitive oil and gas lease sales."[20]

In 1956, Congress had passed the Alaska Mental Health Act, which transferred responsibilities for the care of the mentally ill to the territory. In order to help Alaska pay for these new responsibilities, the measure allowed the territory to select 1 million acres from the vacant, unappropriated, and unreserved public domain. By 1958, the selection process was under way, and territorial officials hoped that once title had been acquired, suitable acreage (with subsurface rights) would be available for oil and gas leasing. Congress had recently passed legislation giving the territory title to tidelands adjacent to or within incorporated municipalities, but the actual grant of these lands was held up pending U.S. Army Engineers surveys to determine the pierhead lines of these lands.[21]

By the early summer of 1958, the Alaska Department of Lands had drafted fifty-six proposed leasing rules and regulations. It then circulated the eighteen-page document for comments to the members of the Alaska Land Board. Brown also asked members of the Western Oil and Gas Association (WOGA) for aid in drafting regulations for state land leasing. Brown had written that "the oil industry is best equipped to aid him" in the task and that he would "appreciate any suggestions the industry might make in establishing a worthwhile set of oil and gas leasing regulations." The Public Lands Committee of the WOGA thereupon decided to arrange conferences between interested member companies and Brown.[22]

The Alaska Statehood Act, which President Eisenhower signed into law on July 7, 1958, set in motion massive changes in Alaska's government structure and its economy. The *Fairbanks Daily News-Miner* reported on August 19 that "Admission Will Open Way to Petroleum Development." The paper quoted the July 7 issue of the *Oil and Gas Journal,* which reported that Alaska's admission "will pave the way for what may the century's greatest drives to develop new oil reserves." The journal continued that the oil industry expected that the regulations governing oil and gas leasing and production to be adopted for state lands would "be more friendly [to the industry] than those of the federal government under which they now must operate."[23]

What this would mean specifically was made clear in the responses of the larger oil companies to Director Brown's call for suggestions for writing oil and gas regulations. For example, Humble Oil & Refining Company told Brown that Alaska should employ a competitive bidding system for all leases through sealed bids without acreage limitations on holdings. Such a policy, the company stated, would promote the development of the oil and gas resources, permit all qualified individuals to participate, benefit Alaska "as a state and royalty owner," and result in the timely development of these resources for the consumers of the state and nation."[24]

The smaller companies, such as Halbouty Alaska Oil Company, expressed a contrary opinion. The effort of the board to classify areas as competitive on the basis of suspected but unproven geological merit would result in classifying nearly all areas as competitive, thereby virtually eliminating independent operators who were unable to compete with the major companies in competitive bidding on large tracts. The company claimed that independent operators actually discovered far greater reserves than the major companies. Furthermore, the major companies customarily assembled large acreages and developed them slowly, while independents with much smaller budgets spent much of their money in exploration in a relatively short time. Any action the board might take that would tend to eliminate the independents "would simply mean that less oil will be found," and it would take much longer "to discover that which is found."[25] Independents liked the federal leasing system, which recognized the extraordinary risks, hazards, and costs involved in exploration and development operations for oil and gas. They asserted that only a system that provided adequate incentives and rewards, as the federal system did, could be successful in the development of large wildcat areas.[26]

As Land Board Commissioner Holdsworth informed the El Paso Natural Gas Products Company in October, the oil and gas leasing regulation as called for by the Alaska Land Act had not yet been prepared. First the Alaska Land Board intended to announce a policy for the disposition of oil and gas lands, both tidelands and uplands. The board intended to classify the lands according to their location relative to the petroleum provinces and basins the U.S. Geological Survey had laid out in its report "Geology of Possible Petroleum Provinces in Alaska." All tidelands and uplands adjacent to these provinces or basins as selected by the state were to be offered by predesignated tracts on a competitive basis. Holdsworth believed that such a system avoided "cluttering up our Land office with a lot of early applications or offers which would be rejected anyhow." Preparing proper control maps before offering various tracts on a competitive bid basis allowed for a more orderly management of these lands. Holdsworth also informed the company that, at present, the board intended to impose no acreage limitations.[27]

To clarify what must have been a confusing state of affairs, the Alaska Land Board issued a news release on November 15, 1958, in which it summarized the Alaska land situation, namely, that PL 505 authorized the Department of the Interior to lease the oil and gas deposits in lands beneath nontidal navigable waters in the territory until Alaska received title to these lands under statehood, and that PL 508, the Alaska Statehood Act, provided for a land grant in excess of 100 million acres (including subsurface rights) and also applied the Submerged Lands Act of 1953 to the state of Alaska. In addition, the Alaska Department of Lands was selecting a portion of the 1-million acre land grant under the provisions of PL 830, the 1956 Alaska Mental Health Act. The board had decided that in order to ensure that the lands be selected and managed in an orderly fashion "and to assure maximum benefit to the State and its people," it was necessary to establish and publicly announce a policy of land classification, selection, and management prior to Alaska's admission into the Union. The board promulgated these policies under the authority granted by Chapter 184, SLA 1957, the Alaska Land Act. It recognized that the new state legislature and governor might wish to amend the existing Land Act, but if Alaska hoped to manage its lands in an orderly fashion, "a policy must be established now" and carried out until the existing statute was amended.

Obviously, oil and gas leasing was the most important phase of land management, and the board announced as policy what Commissioner Holdsworth earlier had relayed to the El Paso Gas Products Company. Lands were to be classified into competitive and noncompetitive tracts. The lands available only on a competitive basis needed to "be identified, mapped and evaluated before they can be offered in such a manner as to bring maximum long range income to the State." The board also tentatively scheduled public hearings for December in Anchorage.[28]

The Public Hearings in Anchorage

At the end of November, the board had issued thirty suggested leasing rules and regulations to be discussed at the scheduled December public hearing in Anchorage. Commissioner Holdsworth expected wide interest in the December hearings and a big turnout. "The top brass of this phase of the oil industry will be there, each with their different pitch," he predicted.[29]

The December hearing in Anchorage was packed. Testimony began with Fred W. Bush of Union Oil Company, who spoke on behalf of fourteen operators interested in Alaskan oil and gas exploration and development. Bush stated that competitive bidding should govern all submerged salt water bottoms, conform to the existing federal policy, and be limited to producing structures; in all other cases, the state should grant noncompetitive leases, except that any particular parcel of land could be reclassified and shifted to competitive bidding. Further, sixty-day simultaneous filing periods should be made available to noncompetitive land leases when these acreages were selected or were made available for filing, but after the expiration of this period noncompetitive leases should be issued on a first-come, first-served basis. Bush declared that the companies favored five-hundred-thousand-acre limitations for noncompetitive, upland competitive, and saltwater bottom competitive leases, but that acreage limitations, called chargeability, be removed in all three categories as to producing or unitized leases or in leases subject to development contracts approved by the state or the Department of the Interior.[30]

Bush continued that Union Oil had served Alaska for forty-seven years. When Union Oil decided to take the financial risk involved in entering Alaska, the economic terms for land acquisition were an incentive and much different than those prevailing now. For example, low rental and a 5 percent royalty for ten years on discovery leases, including participating areas in a discovery unit, prevailed.

Bush assured the board that Union Oil was still willing to invest in Alaska but had to make certain that its investments be competitive with those in other areas of interest. He referred to Alaska's remoteness, harsh climate, and high cost of conducting business. Materials, supplies, labor, and transportation costs were all excessive. Somehow Alaskan oil had to be competitive with that from sources in Europe, Asia, South America, and the contiguous United States. He warned that any action adding to rather than subtracting from cost differentials that, at present, were unfavorable for Alaska "will delay, if not completely stall, that day in which Alaska can compete in the market place."

In short, Union had entered the territory when the basic ground rules had been attractive, but that had changed and profitable operations had become questionable. Bush urged that the board follow the Alaska Land Act, which indicated that it intended to conform to federal rules and regulations. The industry's future was at a crossroads in Alaska, Bush continued; for it to survive it needed fair tax laws, practical operating rules and regulations, and favorable public relations.[31]

Other companies expressed varying levels of agreement with Bush's presentation. The Western Oil and Gas Association, for example, made fifty-five suggestions concerning the proposed rules and regulations, while the Texaco-Alaska Company endorsed the presentation Bush had made, except that it opposed acreage limitations in any category. Humble Oil & Refining Company supported the WOGA statement but believed that the state was not married to the federal leasing system.[32]

After much testimony had been given, the lengthy Anchorage hearing adjourned early in the afternoon of December 12 and the board met in executive session. It discussed the results of the hearings and formulated the following policies for leasing state oil and gas lands:

1. Tidelands or salt water bottoms were all to be leased on a competitive basis.
2. Uplands were to be leased competitively if land was on a known or producing geologic structure or if additional information or public hearings determined that the lands were reasonably believed to contain such a structure.
3. If the lands were classified noncompetitive and there was a valid existing oil and gas lease offer or an application with the Bureau of Land Management that would be nullified by state selection, the board would honor that lease offer or application. If classified as competitive, an existing offer would not be given preference.
4. The board was governed by the acreage limitation provisions of Chapter 184, SLA 1957, the Alaska Land Act, which were identical with those of the federal Mineral Leasing Act (namely, 246,080 acres). The board, however, also had the right under the

terms of the act to enter into and approve operating and drilling contracts that one or more of the lessees had made under the same conditions applying to the secretary of the Interior at present.[33]

A few days after the Anchorage hearings, Bush wrote Holdsworth a letter. It stated that although many oil representatives had orally expressed their appreciation for Holdsworth's consideration and understanding of oil industry policy and problems in Alaska, he wanted to confirm it in writing. Holdsworth and the Land Board, he wrote, had "established a clear and concise policy that makes a lot of sense." It encouraged the continued investment of risk capital in Alaska and also allowed large and small businesses to participate. In short, the board's prompt action and business-like decisions were appreciated.[34]

The New Alaska State Legislature's First Steps

When the first state legislature met in Juneau in January 1959, it faced a formidable task—namely to help set up a new state government. Especially important was the matter of natural resources management. The final report of the Legislative Council of the twenty-third and last territorial legislature devoted a separate memorandum to the matter of oil and gas legislation. The memorandum described the interest in additional legislation to either regulate or help stimulate the development of the oil and gas industry in Alaska. There were those in Alaska, the authors pointed out, who strongly urged that the State of Alaska enact all measures necessary to fully protect its oil and gas resources and who believed that the maximum legislative encouragement possible be given to the oil and gas interests so that these resources could be developed in the shortest time feasible.[35]

The authors summarized existing federal and territorial (now state) laws affecting the oil and gas industry and concluded, in consultation with Commissioner Holdsworth, "that the existing laws, except for minor amendments, adequately safeguard the interests of the State of Alaska and its citizens." The December 1958 Anchorage hearings and correspondence the Alaska Legislative Council had received from industry leaders indicated that they were "well satisfied with the laws governing present and future exploration and development activities."[36]

By January of 1959, the Alaska Land Board had drafted a number of suggestions for amending the Alaska Land Act. Article IX needed to be amended, particularly to drop the statement about "substantial conformity with the provisions of the Mineral Leasing Act." Also, acreage limitations needed to be broadened.[37] So the Legislative Council held hearings in Juneau on possible amendments to the 1957 Alaska Land Act dealing with oil and gas land leases.

At these hearings, H. T. Sutherland, representing the Ohio Oil Company, stated that his company thought it unwise to give the Alaska Land Board the authority to classify as competitive any lands it may choose "purely on the basis of its belief that such lands are on a structure." He concluded, rather, that the legislature "was thinking of structure reasonably believed to contain oil and gas, and not just any structure." He also suggested that the state legislature increase the acreage limitation in leases and options from three to five hundred thousand acres. Further, the Ohio Oil Company was amenable to the proposals made in Juneau, but he objected "that Alaska lands be only leased under a system based entirely on competitive bonus bidding."[38] Representatives of other companies followed, and they all echoed the statements made at the December hearings in Anchorage.

Chapter 169

Finally, after extensive hearings and much work on the part of members of the Alaska Land Board and the lawmakers, the first state legislature drafted and passed Chapter 169, SLA 1959, titled "An Act Relating to Alaska Lands and Resources." It established a Division of Land within the Alaska Department of Natural Resources (ADNR) and the Office of the Land Director, prescribing duties and powers; it provided for the selection, acquisition, management, and disposal of Alaska lands and resources; and it repealed Ch. 189, SLA 1955, and Ch. 184, SLA 1957. Chapter 169 was approved on May 2, 1959.[39]

Article VIII, Section 3(7) of the act dealt with the leasing of oil and gas lands. It provided that all tide and submerged lands were to be leased by competitive bidding, "and whenever oil or gas is discovered in any well on Alaska land in commercial quantities," the commissioner was authorized to determine the additional lands in the same general area of the discovery well and lease those lands competitively.[40]

Competitive lands were to be leased to the highest responsible qualified bidder in units not exceeding 640 acres, except that tide and submerged lands were to be leased in units not exceeding 5,760 acres. The parcels were to be as nearly compact in form as possible, and the lessee was to pay a bonus as accepted by the commissioner. All other lands were to be leased noncompetitively to the first qualified individual applying, in units not exceeding 2,560 acres in any one lease. This increase in maximum acreage, from 640 to 2,560 acres, was a concession to the industry.

No concessions were made about royalty rates. Royalty was to be fixed in the lease, and in fact, the Alaska Land Act of 1959 went farther than the federal statute in that it stated royalties on competitive leases were to "be not less than 12½ percentum in amount or value of the production removed or sold from the lease."[41] The producer who discovered a new field was given the incentive of paying only a 5 percent royalty for ten years after the discovery. Thereafter, the royalty was to be no less than 12.5 percent.[42] In short, Article VIII was a flexible, well-crafted piece of legislation that accommodated the needs of the oil and gas industry in regard to acreage limitations but that protected the vital royalty interest of the state and its citizens.

Passage of the act, however, had been only the legislature's first step. On May 3, 1959, a joint legislature unanimously confirmed Phil R. Holdsworth as Alaska's first commissioner of the ADNR. Holdsworth's immediate goal was to establish rules and regulations that were attractive to the oil industry but that also protected the state's interest. With statehood, federal assistance had greatly diminished. The state needed an immediate cash flow, which oil and gas could provide. Holdsworth contacted the Western Oil and Gas Association and requested the temporary loan of a knowledgeable

attorney not representing any particular oil company. WOGA arranged for the temporary assignment of attorney James L. Wanvig from the law firm of Pillsbury, Madison, and Sutro of San Francisco. Wanvig arrived in Anchorage on May 12, 1959, and immediately set to work drafting an oil and gas leasing form.[43]

Wanvig completed the first draft of the regulations at the end of May, and in June he submitted his final draft. By September 14, 1959, the ADNR had completed its preliminary work and the state regulations took effect. On December 10 the state held its first offshore oil lease sale, producing bonus bids of $4,020,342 on thirty-two tracts along Cook Inlet and Wide Bay. Union Oil Company and the Ohio Oil Company provided the day's top bid of $1,001,123 for a 2,026 acre tract south of the Kenai River.

It had been a successful year for the new state. Unlike many older oil-producing states such as Texas, California, and Louisiana, it had drafted clear and simple laws attractive to the investment community while protecting its own interests. To the ADNR belonged much of the credit for that success. From a concept in the session laws, the department had established itself firmly within state government. It had recruited talented and committed professionals, enacted a workable land law, and created effective rules, regulations, and forms. ADNR's rational and competent land management boded well for Alaska's future.[44]

The Dispute over Wellhead Value

By the mid-1960s the ADNR had settled most basic disputes between the industry and the state except for one that plagued both parties for decades, namely, how to determine the wellhead value of Alaska's oil. It was a multifaceted problem. The Land Act required lessees to pay a 12.5 percent royalty in the "amount or value" of their production. Production quantities were to be determined at the "wellhead," where the oil was often dehydrated and cleaned. Both the lessee and the state aimed to maximize their potential gains and therefore resisted the other's attempts to establish a favorable wellhead price.[45]

In January 1959, Standard Oil Company of California claimed that its wellhead price was subject to adjustment. The company acknowledged that the oil's market price referred to its wellhead price, but it argued that transportation expenses might reasonably be deducted. The company shipped most of its oil to California and contended that its price should reflect the value of comparable California crude minus its transportation costs, which the U.S. Geological Survey estimated to be about nineteen cents per barrel. The state objected. It agreed to allow some transportation costs but questioned Standard Oil's deduction and maintained that locally refined oil was not subject to any amendment. For such oil, the Alaska Department of Law (ADL) allowed an adjustment to only cover transportation from an offshore platform to the Nikiski refinery on the nearby shore. Lessees, the ADL maintained, should pay royalty on a price about nineteen cents per barrel *above* the California price.[46]

The *Amerada Hess* Case

The differences between the producers and the state over the payment of royalties continued for years. The state received its oil and gas revenues, the bulk of its income, from six sources: the occasional lease sale bonuses, royalties, oil and gas production taxes, corporate income and property taxes, and a 90 percent share from oil and gas produced on onshore federal lands. It was of vital importance to the state to maximize its income from these nonrenewable resources. Over the years, state officials used two methods to maximize Alaska's royalty returns, namely, the legislature tried several statutory solutions, while the ADNR devised numerous administrative fixes. The ADNR thus alternated between negotiation and confrontation in its efforts to increase the wellhead price of the oil. These efforts were rarely immediately successful, but in the long run they helped the state to retain a greater percentage of its oil and gas wealth.

By 1968 the great Prudhoe Bay oil discovery on Alaska's North Slope added to the state's commercial oil and gas deposits, and on June 19, 1977, the first oil flowed into the Trans-Alaska Pipeline. On September 2 of that year the state filed a lawsuit, titled *State of Alaska v. Amerada Hess et al.*, that charged eighteen oil corporations (including Amerada Hess) with underpayment of royalty. All eighteen oil companies operated oil wells in the Prudhoe Bay oil field. At issue was the value of the state's royalty share for the oil pumped from that field.

By law, Alaska was to receive a royalty share equal to one-eighth, or 12.5 percent, of the total oil production. The state contended that the corporations had overreported their costs to lower their payments and also undervalued the final market value of the crude oil they sold in order to manipulate the royalties owed to Alaska. In short, the oil companies used bookkeeping tricks to create legal loopholes to increase their profits and shortchange the state. This was the beginning of fifteen years of litigations between the parties. The state spent about $108 million on outside legal counsel, and the state department of law expended about the same amount on the issue in-house. The oil companies spent huge sums of money on this legal battle as well.[47]

The monetary difference in the market value reported varied with each oil company, but it ranged from $1.00 to $1.25 in royalty per barrel. State officials estimated that the total value of the contested royalties came to a minimum of $80 million per year. Out of the eighteen defendants, Atlantic Richfield (ARCO, formerly Richfield Oil), British Petroleum (BP, formerly Sohio), and Exxon owned about 90 percent of the total revenues the state claimed.[48]

To claim that the companies undervalued the oil was one thing, but to prove it was another. State attorneys began with a simple argument that came to be known as the "upstream theory." It postulated that the value of crude oil for royalty purposes could be determined by first determining the market price of crude oil where it was sold, and then working upstream toward the source, on the way subtracting identified, approved costs. Eventually this procedure should yield the wellhead price.[49]

The oil companies did not dispute this basic idea. They disagreed with the state, however, over which costs applied and how much those expenses should be. The issue was further complicated because each oil company proposed a different market price and different means of arriving at that price. ARCO claimed that the West Coast oil glut made it difficult to earn a reasonable profit for its product. Therefore, it had to sell its oil to buyers in the Gulf of Mexico, which considerably increased transportation costs. It subtracted the expenses for moving the crude from the West Coast to the Gulf of Mexico, which, it claimed, resulted in the official price for its West Coast oil. State attorneys came to call this approach the "market theory" for determining the price on which royalty payments were based.[50]

BP either traded or exchanged oil it delivered to the West Coast for oil in the Midwest, where it had its own refineries. It was very difficult to verify these transactions because trading involved unequal amounts of different grades of oil from different locations. As with all trading deals, the economic advantage favored the participants but not the lessor to whom the royalties had to be paid.[51]

Exxon used whichever method worked best in a particular situation. It sometimes calculated value by subtracting transportation costs, and sometimes it traded oil, but often it did both. Exxon turned out to be the most aggressive of the three corporations in the lengthy litigation and was the last to settle.[52]

Two basic questions needed to be solved within the framework of the *Amerada Hess* case, namely, "where" and "how" should the value of the oil be determined? The state maintained that the oil's value should be determined at Pump Station Number One, located at the northern terminus of the Trans-Alaska Pipeline System (TAPS). The corporations argued that the "where" should be the wellhead. That meant that the companies would be allowed to deduct field costs before arriving at the value of the crude oil at the pump station. These consisted of two categories: expenses for delivering the crude oil to the pipeline and the treatment expenses, namely cleaning, dehydrating, and conditioning. The state disagreed. Royalty values were commonly based on the oil's value where it entered a pipeline. A major part of the argument was whether or not Alaska was unique. The state said no, the oil companies said yes. The litigation involving the "where" question was resolved by 1980. The question of how to determine the oil's royalty value took another twelve years.

Much happened during those years. One contentious question dealt with the interpretation of paragraphs fifteen and sixteen of the standard lease agreement that James Wanvig had drafted and that both the state and the companies had signed. Paragraph fifteen concerned the value; and sixteen, the price. Defining the difference between these two paragraphs and understanding their meaning took years. Determining allowable transportation costs, which involved establishing allowable deductions for pipeline and shipping expenses, was another hotly debated issue, partially resolved in a lawsuit the state of Alaska had filed against TAPS. In this litigation, the state sued the pipeline owners for deliberately overrepresenting the actual cost of moving the oil through the pipeline in order to reduce the tariff owed to the state.[53]

Still another problem to be resolved was how to determine the price oil companies received for their crude upon delivery. This was complicated by internal corporate manipulation of resources, lack of access to corporate records, and fraud charges the state filed. State lawyers also claimed that the oil companies waged a stalling campaign, thereby holding money and earning interest on funds that belonged to the state.[54]

The case dragged on, and the companies claimed that they could not receive a fair trial in Alaska because any settlement money would be deposited into the state's savings account and thus would benefit every Alaska citizen, including the personnel of the court system, in the form of their Permanent Fund dividend checks. The Alaska legislature solved this problem when it placed oil litigation funds into a budget reserve account instead of the general fund. That meant no money from the oil cases would go into the Permanent Fund, thus removing the potential conflict of interest.[55]

Amerada Hess Is Settled

In 1989, the state had estimated that the companies involved in the case owed back payments from 1977 totaling $902 million: BP owed $321.7 million; ARCO, $319.6 million; Exxon USA, $188.1 million; Phillips, $21.4 million; Getty-Texaco, $3.9 million; Union Oil, $2.7 million; Placid Oil, $855,661; Petro Lewis, $747,688; Marathon Oil, $585,616; Louisiana Land and Exploration, $545,832; Amerada Hess, $261,897; and Shell Oil, $157,195. Amerada Hess settled with the state on December 26, 1989, for $318,624. ARCO followed on September 12, 1990, for $285 million, or 86 percent of what the state claimed it owed. The ARCO settlement also established a royalty-computing formula, and the state dropped $100 million in fraud charges against the company.[56]

On November 6, 1990, Alaskans elected a new governor, Walter J. Hickel, who indicated that he would take a hard look at the Amerada Hess lawsuit. His attorney general, Charles Cole, stated that he wanted to study the case before making any comments.[57] In the meantime, Freeport McMoRan Energy Partners, Ltd. reached an agreement with the state in the fall of 1990 and paid $331,000, about 83 percent of the amount owed.[58]

By March 1991 Cole announced that the remaining claims had to be resolved. He had avoided the term "settlement" because it implied the state was giving up something in order to speed up the case. Cole wanted to resolve the issues but made it clear that he refused to give up even "five cents." By the end of March 1991 the state had resolved the issues with Marathon Oil Company, which paid $426,842, and Louisiana Land and Exploration Company, which paid $251,848. That left BP, Exxon, Phillips, Mobil, Chevron, and Texaco.[59] BP was particularly unwilling to settle with the state because it owed at least $335 million, and it fought hard to avoid paying that sum. Claims and counterclaims continued with BP, and Superior Court Judge Walter Carpeneti issued numerous opinions attempting to end the litigation.[60]

After many new motions and legal arguments, in early January 1992, BP settled and agreed to pay the state $185 million by the end of the month, settling all disputed claims through December 1991. The agreement also included a method for determining royalties on future oil and for establishing allowable deduction, as well as a dispute resolution method. The state received only 55 percent of the $335 million it had tried to collect from BP. It also had dropped the fraud charges against BP and the ability to recover punitive damages.[61]

BP apparently settled, at least in part, because of what it perceived as potential damage to its public image, but also because it wanted to avoid public disclosure of its business practices; it had the court seal some documents to protect its competitiveness and reputation. If the records had been opened, it is possible that the public might have suspected BP of dishonesty.[62]

By April 1992 all but one of the remaining defendants had settled. Mobil paid half of the $20 million Alaska claimed it owed, and Chevron received a similar deal. Texaco paid $3.2 million, 80 percent of the $4 million the state had claimed it owed. Phillips paid about $10 million. Now Exxon rented a downtown Anchorage building to house its lawyers, who were preparing to continue litigation and prepare for trial.[63]

Both Exxon and the state now engaged in a legal battle, which ended only when the formal trial began on April 13, 1992. After the court was recessed on the first day of trial, Attorney General Cole told Judge Carpeneti that the state and Exxon had settled the litigation and almost had reached a definitive agreement. Two days later Carpeneti was given the proposed agreement, which was similar to those BP and ARCO had negotiated. Exxon was to pay the state $128.5 million, 76 percent of the $170 million the state claimed it owed.[64]

The case, which had started fifteen years earlier, was finally over. Alaska received a little over $600 million of the $902 million it had claimed, settling for 67 cents on the dollar. The state had spent in excess of $100 million on outside legal counsel, and about the same amount on in-house legal counsel. Many Alaskans were disappointed. Alaska and the oil companies had established a method for computing oil royalties, but it provided the state with much less money than many thought it should receive.[65]

Ready for Statehood

During the struggle for statehood, many thoughtful northerners realized that as a state, Alaska would be dependent on natural resource extraction to build a viable future. For years, corporations headquartered outside of the territory had extracted fish and minerals from Alaska, leaving but a pittance in taxes. The framers of the state constitution wanted to avoid a continuation of this state of affairs, and so they drafted a resource article that provided for the development of all natural resources for the maximum benefit of Alaska's people.

Subsequently, territorial legislators drafted statutes in anticipation of an Alaska oil boom even though the federal government still owned more than 99 percent of Alaska's lands. The legislature had passed a Lands Act as early as 1953, a first effort to control Alaska's natural resources. In 1955 and 1957, it refined and augmented this legislation, and in 1957 the Alaska Land Board set about to develop oil land leasing rules in the wake of the Kenai oil discovery. By early 1958, the Alaska Department of Lands functioned and the oil rush was under way.

After Alaska entered the Union as the 49th state on January 3, 1959, the first state legislature built on the efforts of its predecessors and developed Alaska's leasing and royalty regulations. In 1968, the giant Prudhoe Bay discovery immensely increased the state's known commercial oil and gas deposits. On June 19, 1977, the first oil flowed into the Trans-Alaska Pipeline. Later that year the state filed a lawsuit, *State of Alaska v Amerada Hess et al.,* that involved the value of royalties in the past and the principles for determining their value in the future. Another issue brought up by the case was that the state did not have a good database for determining what was going on in the marketing of its oil. By the time the last involved oil company settled in the case, in 1989, the state stood to receive only a little over $600 million, much less than the $902 million it initially claimed. But now Alaska and the oil companies had finally established a method for computing royalties.

Raising the forty-nine-star U.S. Flag are, *from left,* Congressman Ralph J. Rivers, Secretary of the Interior Fred Seaton, U.S. Senators Ernest Gruening and E. L. "Bob" Bartlett, Mike Stepovich, and Waino Hendrickson. *Daily Anchorage Times* publisher Robert Atwood is holding the flag.

(Courtesy of Alaska and Polar Regions Department, Elmer E. Rasmuson Library, University of Alaska Fairbanks.)

Chapter 17

Transition to Statehood

Alaska entered the Union as the largest state, with an area of 378.3 million acres. Yet in 1958 the federal government owned 99.8 percent of Alaska's land mass, while only slightly more than 500,000 acres had passed into private ownership. Over the years various federal agencies had withdrawn and reserved for permanent public ownership more than 92 million acres, amounting to more than one-fourth of the total land area, while the remaining area, about 286 million acres, consisted of vacant, unappropriated, unreserved federal public domain lands under the stewardship of the U.S. Bureau of Land Management.[1]

The federal land-management policies had become the root of an increasingly bitter political controversy in Alaska. Most of the federal land-managing agencies seemed primarily interested in holding northern lands for some undetermined future use. Considering their role a custodial one, they had given little consideration to planning the future or coordinating the programs of the many federal agencies. Perhaps their attitude was conditioned by a lack of demand for the resources these lands could provide, but, still, many Alaskans had come to regard conservationists as a group of unscrupulous politicians retarding the settlement and development of the North through restrictive and unworkable land laws and the withdrawal and reservation of land.[2]

The Statehood Act was to change this land ownership pattern, because Congress authorized the new state to select 103,350,000 acres of vacant, unappropriated, unreserved federal land over the next twenty-five years. Although this land grant represented less than one-third of Alaska's total acreage, it was larger than California. Alaska's future, to a very large extent, would depend on the policies the state adopted for the selection, classification, and disposition of this vast, potentially resource-rich acreage covered with forests, containing minerals and water resources, inhabited by many species of wildlife, and blessed with magnificent scenery.

The Changing Alaska Economy

The large land grant promised future economic development, but the state of the economy in 1958 did not cheer anyone. Military spending had passed its peak in 1954 and had declined steadily since. Gold mining had never fully recovered from its virtual shutdown in the early 1940s, and salmon fishing faced a crisis brought about by years of federal mismanagement, overfishing, and recent high-seas salmon catches by the Japanese fishing fleets. Farm production was negligible, with only about twenty thousand acres under cultivation, and so was the income derived from furs.

The future for the timber industry looked brighter. In 1954 the first large pulp mill opened in Ketchikan, and thereafter the annual timber cut

A gold dredge at Coal Creek.

(Author's collection.)

increased considerably. In the years before 1954, the volume of timber cut in the Tongass National Forest had been modest, for it was primarily intended to meet local requirements for fish-trap pilings, packing cases, mine timbers, dock piles and timbers, and building lumber. But during the first four and a half years of the pulp mill's operation, the amount of timber cut amounted to 46.9 percent of the total cut for the entire previous forty-five years by all of Alaska's small sawmills. In 1959 the Alaska Lumber and Pulp Company, financed in large part by the Japanese Toshitsugu Matusi Company, began operating a pulp mill at Sitka.[3]

Another hopeful development occurred in 1957, when Richfield Oil Corporation discovered oil in commercial quantities at Swanson River, on the Kenai Peninsula; by 1959 three wells were producing. As exploration and development activities extended offshore to Cook Inlet, additional oil-and-gas fields eventually started production. Alaskans looking at historical patterns feared that the traditional boom-and-bust economic cycles would repeat themselves.

How had Alaska's economy developed over time? George W. Rogers, Alaska's most astute economist, conveniently summarized past development patterns in three broad phases, Native, Colonial, and

Military Alaska. The central theme of each phase, he maintained, can be summed up and compared in terms of the differing attitudes toward use of natural resources and the attitudes, interests, and aims that each phase has contributed to Alaska's alternating drift and drive toward an ill-defined and hazy future.[4]

In Native Alaska, land and marine resources were for subsistence—for the survival of the people. Differences in living standards and in the elaboration of Native cultures were directly related to the variety and availability of natural resources in each region. Shared by all, however, was the primary interest in simple survival, which is still dominant among Native peoples today. For despite the existence of welfare programs ensuring physical survival, individuals still struggle to preserve their cultures and identities while adapting to changing economic and social conditions.[5]

Native Alaska contributed the only stable and balanced element in the population, the only uniquely Alaskan art forms and culture, and the knowledge of how to survive and subsist in the more inhospitable areas of the land. Along with these assets came the problems arising from cultural differences and the economic, health, and welfare problems experienced by Native people in the throes of change.[6]

Colonial Alaska developed natural resources beyond the needs of subsistence. This phase was based primarily on the specialized and intensive exploitation of furs, salmon, and gold. Almost all the exploiters were non-Natives. Renewable and nonrenewable resources were usually exploited to the point of exhaustion. The raw materials and products were destined for nonresident markets, and capital, as well as much of the required labor, was imported. Industrial technology, too, was brought to Alaska, and this in turn stimulated some limited permanent settlement and local capital formation. In Alaska the absentee owners maintained a highly successful lobby that hampered and almost stopped the evolution of local self-government and impeded the imposition of a tax system required to provide the capital for further development.[7]

At the core of Military Alaska was the defense of the nation. Remoteness from the "mother country" and vast spaces, liabilities in Colonial Alaska, became assets in this third phase of Alaskan history. Strategic location, not natural resources, was its reason for coming into being. The basic activities of government and construction were carried on without concern for resources. Military Alaska produced an explosive expansion of the population, extension and improvement of surface and air transportation, and investment of more than $2 billion of public funds in defense construction. It also created local markets for some Alaska products, local capital, and labor pools. Military Alaska attracted people, and it produced employment and living amenities substantially beyond those that could have been supported from Alaska's own resources.[8]

Rogers concluded that upon attainment of statehood, Alaska's dominant characteristic was the lack of self-sustaining basic economic activity. Consumption, not production, was characteristic of Alaska, and both public and private investment had been primarily concerned with the improvement of living conditions rather than the fostering of solid economic development.[9] That was the situation in Alaska after the U.S. Senate passed the Alaska statehood bill on June 30, 1958.

Statehood Ushers in the First Elections

Even though most residents welcomed Alaska's admission to the Union as the 49th State, many remained uneasy about the impending changes. They feared higher taxes, continuing problems with the fishing industry, the elimination of federal cost-of-living allowances, and the possible suspension of federal welfare payments. One of the diehards probably best summed up the sentiments of those who remained opposed to statehood by stating, "Wait till the honeymoon is over and the taxes arrive."[10] His forebodings proved to be prophetic. Similar apprehension was present in a number of Eskimo and Athapaskan villages, where it was rumored that statehood would bring reservations, restrictions of traditional hunting and trapping activities, the closing of Native hospitals, and the suspension of federal welfare payments. Secretary of the Interior Fred Seaton denounced these rumors and reassured the Natives.[11] And despite these trepidations, statehood was achieved.

When President Eisenhower signed the statehood measure into law on July 7, 1958, it was up to Alaskans to undertake the necessary steps to get the new state functioning. On July 16, Governor Mike Stepovich announced that candidates for political office had until July 28 to file. The primary election was to be held at the end of August. Candidates for the U.S. Senate were to run for either the A or the B term, with the length of neither term identified.

In the forty-one days that elapsed between the governor's proclamation and the primary elections, many Alaskans felt called, filed for candidacy, and campaigned. A seasoned observer characterized the period as one in which an epidemic had been "let loose in the land." George Sundborg, editor of the *Fairbanks Daily News-Miner*, was amazed and amused that so many were "willing to sacrifice personal gain and give their all for the people of the great state." "The same number," he caustically remarked, "feel they very likely deserve it—after all, didn't I write a letter to the editor about statehood back in 1953?"[12]

At the primary election, the voters were also to decide on three propositions that had been inserted in the statehood bill: (1) Shall Alaska immediately be admitted to the Union as a state? (2) Shall the boundaries of the new state be approved? and (3) Shall all boundaries of the Statehood Act, such as those reserving rights and powers to the United States, as well as those prescribing the terms and conditions of the land grants and other property, be consented to? These were important propositions, and the Alaska Statehood Committee, Operation Statehood, and most candidates for office urged Alaskans to vote affirmatively.[13]

With no preregistration, any Alaskan nineteen years of age or older simply had to appear at the nearest polling place to vote. Officials expected a record turnout of 35,000 people, but instead 48,462 voters streamed to the polling places and overwhelmingly approved the three propositions by votes of 40,452 to 8,010; 40,421 to 7,776; and 40,739 to 7,500, respectively. Many polling stations ran out of ballots and had fresh supplies flown in or used sample ballots.[14]

There was no primary contest for U.S. Senate because Democrats E. L. "Bob" Bartlett and Ernest

Gruening ran unopposed. For Alaska's single seat in the House of Representatives, Democrat Ralph Rivers, former territorial attorney general, defeated Raymond Plummer, Alaska's former member of the Democratic National Committee, by a margin of 630 votes in the primary. Henry Benson, the Republican territorial commissioner of labor, won the Republican nomination and would oppose Rivers in November.

The field of Democratic hopefuls for the governorship was more crowded. In the primary William Egan defeated the territorial attorney general, J. Gerald Williams, and the territorial senate president, Victor Rivers.[15] John Butrovich of Fairbanks, a territorial legislator of long experience, ran unopposed for the Republican gubernatorial nomination, together with his running mate, Brad Phillips, an Anchorage businessman.

Alaska's voters had spoken, and the candidates prepared for the November 25, 1958, general election. The two former territorial governors, Gruening and Stepovich, dominated the thirteen-week campaign for the U.S. Senate seat. Stepovich had enjoyed much public exposure in recent months and had received 5,721 more votes in the primary than had Gruening. Knowing that he would have to work extremely hard to win, Gruening launched a well-organized campaign that blanketed Alaska.[16] As befitting Alaska's new dignity as the 49th State, national political figures journeyed north to help. Republican Vice President Richard M. Nixon, Democratic senators John F. Kennedy of Massachusetts and Frank Church of Idaho, and Secretary of the Interior Fred Seaton ventured to Alaska to endorse their candidates. Republican Seaton, overeager to ensure Stepovich's election, became controversial when in time-honored fashion he coupled his campaign with announcements of projects his department promised to undertake in the new state. In fact, Seaton's approach vastly overshadowed that of his protégé.[17]

On election day, despite the boost Secretary Seaton had tried to give Stepovich, he polled 23,464 votes to Gruening's 26,045. For the other Senate seat, a record number of 50,343 of an eligible 65,000 Alaska voters went to the polls to elect E. L. Bartlett to the U.S. Senate by 40,939 votes over

President Dwight D. Eisenhower signs the Alaska statehood bill. Looking on, *from left back,* Ralph J. Rivers, Ernest Gruening, E. L. "Bob" Bartlett, and, *to the left of the president,* Vice President Richard M. Nixon.

(Courtesy of Alaska and Polar Regions Department, Elmer E. Rasmuson Library, University of Alaska Fairbanks.)

7,299 for Ralph Robertson. Ralph Rivers comfortably outpolled his rival, Henry Benson, by a margin of 27,948 to 20,699, to win the lone U.S. House seat. In the race for governor, Democrat William A. Egan easily defeated Republican John Butrovich by 29,189 votes to 19,299. As many Republicans at the national level had sourly predicted, the voters gave Alaska's four top offices to Democrats. Voters favored Democrats just as decisively in the state legislative races, where they won thirty-three of the forty house seats and seventeen of the twenty senate seats.[18] The election was a disaster for the Republicans, probably because their Democratic counterparts were more experienced and better known. However, Alaska Republicans had also been badly factionalized for the last two decades and had fought as much with each other as with the Democrats.

Transition to State Government

After the votes were counted, the transition to state government lay ahead, and planning for it had already begun. In the transition, the Alaska Statehood Committee had again made substantial contributions, for one of its responsibilities was to gather information on how to bridge the gap between territorial and state government. Once before, in 1955, the Statehood Committee had engaged the services of the Public Administration Service (PAS) of Chicago to help prepare for the constitutional convention. Now the committee hired the PAS again, and it

began its work in the spring of 1958. PAS delivered detailed reports, outlining the organization of the executive, the judiciary, local government, and personnel administration.[19]

While all was being prepared in Alaska, President Eisenhower formally admitted Alaska as the 49th State when he signed the prescribed proclamation on January 3, 1959, together with an executive order creating a new flag for the United States. Soon thereafter U.S. District Court Judge Raymond Kelly administered the oath of office to Governor-elect William A. Egan and Secretary of State-elect Hugh Wade in the governor's office in Juneau, Alaska.[20]

Statehood Expenses

Alaska had finally become a state, and with two U.S. senators and one representative, it had also acquired modest influence and voting power in Congress. Soon enough the Alaska delegation found occasion to flex its muscles in speeding the passage of the Omnibus Bill for the new state—an afterthought, as it were, to the statehood bill.

As early as July 1958, the U.S. Bureau of the Budget had suggested to the president that a study was needed of the fiscal and administrative effects of Alaska's admission on federal legislation and activities. Similar studies had led to measures that had become law after the admission of Oklahoma, New Mexico, and Arizona. Since federal-state relations had been much simpler at that time, the bills reflected that simplicity.[21]

In May 1959, the Bureau of the Budget presented the results of its studies to the House and Senate Interior and Insular Affairs committees. Basically the recommendations were designed to put Alaska on an equal footing with the other states. Among other things, the apportionment and matching formulas of various federal grant-in-aid programs had to be revised. Equality of treatment also required that the federal establishment cease developing policies for and conducting governmental functions in Alaska that were now to be exercised by state and local governments.

The Alaska congressional delegation realized that equality would cost money; so did the Bureau of the Budget, which recommended assistance of $27.5 million in the form of transitional grants over a five-year period. Under this proposal the state was to receive $10.5 million for fiscal year 1960, $6 million each year for fiscal years 1961 and 1962; and $2.5 million each year for fiscal years 1963 and 1964. These monies were to be spent at the discretion of the new state government. The bureau believed that at the end of the five-year period enough revenue would be flowing into state coffers from oil and gas leases, the Pribilof fur-seal operations, and the sale of state lands that the state would be on its own.[22]

The state faced immediate expenses, such as the operation of the Anchorage and Fairbanks international airports and seventeen smaller airports.

Built by the federal government at a total cost of $41,460,200, the nineteen airports were expected to cost $1,438,000 a year to maintain, while earning $1,215,000, producing a deficit of $223,000 a year. The two international airports were expected to earn most of the revenues, but they were as yet unable to accommodate jet traffic. Major improvements were needed, and the estimated cost was about $9.8 million. By using $3.4 million of the transitional money, the state could obtain $6.4 million in matching funds, enough for the needed construction, under the Federal Aid Airport Act.[23]

Road construction and maintenance loomed as a large item in Alaska's state budget. The Bureau of the Budget proposed that Congress turn over to Alaska the highways, rights-of-way, and whatever real estate and equipment it owned to build and maintain roads. Excluded were roads in Mount McKinley National Park and in the national forests and equipment used for their construction and maintenance. To assist Alaska, the Bureau of the Budget therefore recommended $4 million for each of the fiscal years 1960 to 1962. Equality with the other states required that Alaska match 86.09 percent of federal monies with 13.91 percent of state monies. In other words, if the state could raise $5,940,877 a year for road-building purposes, it would receive $36,768,519 in federal matching funds. The state was not permitted to use any of the matching funds for maintenance expenses.

State officials foresaw the budgeting strain Alaska would surely experience after the expiration of the transitional grants, and Acting Governor Wade, representing the desperately ill Bill Egan, pleaded for permission to use matching funds for road maintenance. In return, the state was willing to compute only two-thirds of the eligible land area to arrive at the matching formula, knowing full well that this would reduce the maximum yearly grant by approximately $9.5 million.[24]

The Bureau of the Budget, however, insisted that no exception be made for Alaska, particularly since similar requests from other states had been denied because the basic purpose of the Federal Aid Highway Program was to speed road construction. In addition, because of the new state's vast land area, it would receive more funds than any other state and initially pay less in matching funds than any other state. The Bureau of the Budget was confident that the new state would be able to collect sufficient revenues within five years to pay for road maintenance. Another advantage Alaska had, Bureau of the Budget personnel pointed out, was freedom from bonded indebtedness. And Alaskans paid only 3.5 percent of their income in state taxes, as compared with a national average of 4.5 percent.[25]

About $7,190,000 for mental and general health care, already managed by Alaska, were included in the transitional grant of $27,500,000, and no more monies were to be paid under the old authorization. This was also the case with $200,000 that Congress had authorized the Department of the Interior to spend on the construction of recreational facilities in Alaska during fiscal year 1960–61.[26]

The Omnibus Bill

The Eisenhower administration was determined to shorten the transition period from federal to state control and therefore had requested no funds for civilian airports, roads, mental and general health programs, or recreational facilities for fiscal year 1960. Instead, it had asked that Alaska receive the first installment of the $27.5 million transitional grants. The Omnibus Bill also provided that the state could ask the president for continued federal operation of various functions until the state's staffing needs had been met and the functions could be transferred to state operation. Transitional monies were to be used for such operations. The state also had the option of contracting with the federal government on a reimbursable basis to provide needed services. In addition, the measure gave the president until July 1, 1964, to lend to the state or transfer outright federal property that had become surplus because of the termination or curtailment of federal activities in Alaska. The new state also was to receive $500,000 in unspent fines and fees collected by the federal district courts, monies that would help establish the Alaska court system.[27]

Some statutory inequalities were to remain, justified on the grounds that they did not affect federal-state relationships or general requirements of the Federal Aid Highway Act of 1921 that a state's feder-al-aid primary highway system not exceed 7 percent of its total highway mileage outside urban areas and federal reserves in 1921. This presented no problem in the contiguous United States, since the total mileage was nearly the same in 1959 as it had been in 1921. In Alaska, however, there had been less than two thousand miles of all kinds of road in 1921, and less than four thousand miles in 1959. Unless it was waived, the 7 percent requirement would keep Alaska's primary highway system very limited indeed. Precedent for making Alaska an exception existed, because the primary highway systems of Hawaii, Washington, D.C., and Puerto Rico were exempt.[28]

Still another exception concerned the National Housing Act. Because of the much higher construction costs in Alaska, Hawaii, and Guam, the federal housing commissioner was permitted to exceed the maximums on the principal obligations of federally insured mortgages by as much as 50 percent. Without this permission Alaskans would have been excluded from the program, unable to meet stiff federal standards of design and construction required for obtaining federal mortgage insurance.[29]

The Omnibus Bill also eliminated inappropriate statutory references to the territory of Alaska and included the state within the "continental United States." And while Congress considered the measure, members added several amendments, among them one by Ralph Rivers that increased the transitional funds from $27.5 million to $28.5 million.[30] Another Rivers amendment dealt with the provision of the admission act that temporarily retained federal jurisdiction over Alaska's fish and wildlife resources. Acting Governor Wade had already signed three pieces of legislation that met the state's responsibility. One of these created the Alaska Board of Fish and Game. Soon thereafter, Secretary of the Interior Seaton reported to Congress that Alaska had met the requirements of the admission act, thereby transferring effective control over its fish and wildlife resources to the state on January 1, 1960.[31]

The Omnibus Bill, with a minor change, passed the House of Representatives on a voice vote on June 1, 1959, after only one hour of debate, and a few days later it passed the Senate in a mere twelve minutes. Senator Bartlett remarked to a friend that during the afternoon before the Senate took up the bill, there had been a briefing session with staff members of the Bureau of the Budget. "And that night I studied the whole proposition for over two hours. That makes me madder than anything else." Bartlett jested "that he had wasted all that time without a single word of opposition or inquiry."[32]

When the president signed the measure on June 25, 1959, Alaska's transition to statehood had been accomplished.[33] The Alaska Statehood Act of 1958 and the clarifying Omnibus Act of 1959 had become a compact between the United States and its people and the State of Alaska and its people, transferring sovereign powers and responsibilities and agreeing on certain institutional rearrangements and conditions. Alaska was now creating its own political institutions.

The State Constitution

Statehood, contrary to the expectations of many, did not solve all of Alaska's problems. It did not appreciably diminish the federal role in Alaska, it did not result in instant economic growth, and it did cost money, most of which Alaskans now had to raise themselves. But Alaska's late entry into the Union had allowed its leaders to learn from the experience of other states and craft a constitution well-suited to the new state.

Recognizing that the territorial governor and the secretary of Alaska had been presidential appointees, that various other officials were popularly elected, and that many boards and commissions had been created over the years, the framers of the new state's constitution were determined to end "outside" control and executive fragmentation. The constitution provides for only one elected executive officer, the governor, while the secretary of state, today the lieutenant governor, is the governor's running mate. The framers limited the number of units within the executive branch to no more than twenty departments, each headed by a single person, appointed by and serving "at the pleasure of the Governor."[34] In case the legislature created a board or a commission to head any department, the governor not only would appoint members to such a group, subject to legislative confirmation, but also would have the power to reject their nominee.

The constitution, following ample precedent, provides for a bicameral legislature composed of a senate of twenty members elected for four-year terms from sixteen districts and a house of forty members elected for two-year terms from twenty-four districts. Subsequent reapportionments have changed the number of districts. The state legislature convenes annually on the second Monday in January and is now limited to a ninety-day session. A ten-member Legislative Council and a six-member Legislative Audit Committee are permanent interim committees. The governor has the responsibility for reapportionment and redistricting.

The Alaska court system constitutes the third branch of state government. Like Alaska's constitution as a whole, the judiciary article (article 4) is widely regarded as a good example of constitutional craftsmanship, embodying court reforms long sought in older states. The judicial system is efficient, independent, and accountable to the electorate. It is a unified system, which means that all the courts are part of a single state system. They are administered from one place, and all operate under the same rules. The state legislature finances the court system. The federal courts share this type of organization, but in most states the court system is fragmented. It may contain municipal courts and courts of special jurisdictions, county courts, and state appellate courts, each with its own peculiar jurisdiction, rules, and procedures, administration, and source of finance.

Article 13 provides for the formal amendment of the constitution. Delegates desired to make the amendment process difficult enough to prevent hasty and destructive changes but easy enough to allow the constitution to accommodate the legitimate needs of a changing society. They believed that since constitutional matters are of fundamental importance, all changes should be ratified by the voters, as is the custom elsewhere. They designed a two-step process allowing for deliberation, attention to detail, and reflection. Proposals for change must come from a deliberate body, either the legislature or a constitutional convention convened expressly for studying changes to the state's basic law. Only then can the proposed changes go to the electorate for ratification. The delegates sought to reduce the need for constitutional amendments by leaving to the legislature many matters that are usually included in the constitutions of other states, such as the powers of local government and the organization of the executive branch. They also created automatic mechanisms to deal with anticipated changes such as legislative reapportionment.

Article 15 provided a schedule of transitional measures. It established the legal continuity between the territory and the state and set in motion the new machinery of state government. This article fulfilled its function, and transitional measures became history. The courts have ruled that provisions of article 15 may be amended by statute, and it is therefore no longer a part of the constitution.

Local Government

Framers of the local-government article of the constitution were acutely aware of the inadequacies of the traditional pattern of local government—counties, cities, and towns—to accommodate the growing needs of an urbanizing country. They believed that Alaska would eventually develop substantial urban areas and that continued growth would create increasing sophistication in local affairs. But the delegates also realized that most of the urban settlements in the Alaska of the 1950s were very small, few in number, and widely separated. So they fashioned a local-government organization capable of serving both urban and rural areas, both as they existed then and as they might develop in the future. As a result the local-government article was designed to provide a simple, flexible system of local self-government with a minimum number of local-government units and to prevent duplication of tax-levying jurisdictions.[35]

The local-government article of the constitution mandated a new form of government called the "borough." There were two forms of boroughs, the "organized" and the "unorganized" (see "Types of Boroughs"). Standards for creating boroughs included population, geography, economy, transportation, and other factors. Each borough was to embrace, as much as possible, an area and population with common interests, making the borough

an area-wide unit stronger than the traditional form of the county.[36]

At the time of statehood, Alaska had about forty cities and twenty special districts. Fewer than half the cities had a population of one thousand or more. In 1960, Anchorage and Fairbanks had populations of forty-four thousand and thirteen thousand, respectively, accounting for more than one-fifth of Alaska's total population. Nearly another third of the residents lived in special districts and territory-serviced areas around the borders of these two large cities. There was practically no tax base except in the few populous areas. Federal and territorial agencies barely met the service, protection, and regulatory needs of settlements outside the larger cities.[37]

For the first few years after statehood, neither residents nor officials thought much about the constitutionally mandated creation of boroughs. In 1961, the legislature passed a measure authorizing borough incorporations and providing broad guidelines for local action. It required that all special-service districts be integrated with organized boroughs, or cities, in the case of certain public utilities, by July 1, 1963.[38]

Only one borough, the Bristol Bay Borough, was organized by initiative before the July 1963 deadline. Containing twelve hundred square miles and about one thousand inhabitants, this small borough is situated in southwestern rural Alaska. When the legislature met in January 1963, it seemed unlikely that any more boroughs would be formed before the deadline. So the legislature extended the life of the special districts for one year, and then it passed the Mandatory Borough Act, which required incorporation of boroughs in eight areas of the state containing public utility and independent school districts as of January 1, 1964.[39]

In 1963, under the threat of mandatory incorporation by the state, four local-option boroughs were established in Ketchikan, Sitka, Juneau, and the Kodiak Island region. Voters defeated incorporation proposals in the Fairbanks and Anchorage areas, whereupon those two areas and the Kenai Peninsula and Matanuska and Susitna valleys were mandatorily incorporated as boroughs on January 1, 1964. With the exception of Juneau's citizens, voters in the eight newly incorporated areas chose second-class

Ketchikan, 1962.

(Photo by Claus-M. Naske.)

rather than first-class status for their new boroughs, believing that, if boroughs had to exist, at least their powers should be limited. The majority of voters in all areas also preferred an elected chairperson, later renamed mayor, to the appointed manager as the form of borough executive. Thomas A. Morehouse, formerly a political scientist with the University of Alaska's Institute of Social and Economic Research in Anchorage and a specialist in local government, has stated that most Alaskans probably preferred the traditionally passive and weak mayor for their boroughs rather than the manager, which was popularly associated with more activist city governments.[40]

By 1972 there existed ten organized boroughs. The rest of the state, not part of an organized borough, was termed the "unorganized borough." There the state legislature exercised the powers and provided the services normally supplied by local government.[41]

Ownership and Use of Natural Resources

As we saw in chapter 16, another important consideration occupied the framers of the constitution: natural resources. In an effort to clear away the ambiguities of federal management policies, which sometimes favored exploitation by nonresidents,

Types of Boroughs

The delegates to the constitutional convention envisioned the borough as a mid-level governmental unit that would provide a framework within which city governments, school districts, and other local responsibilities could be administered. They did not have a clear vision of this unit, and that explains why the development of local institutions has been inconsistent throughout the state. Two separate local-government systems have emerged: one urban and the other rural. An integrated set of government institutions has developed in urban Alaska. Fewer than twenty-five local and regional governments serve the needs of the majority of the state's residents. Nine of these governments are boroughs—strong, county-like governments with broad powers and responsibilities—and about fifteen are cities. Three boroughs have become unified home-rule municipalities merged with the cities within them. Broad local-government powers are concentrated in these "organized boroughs," which have been well supported with revenues from state and local sources.

In rural Alaska, or the "unorganized borough," local and regional institutions have proliferated. Several hundred such units meet the needs of Native villagers and other rural Alaskans, who make up only a small part of Alaska's population. These units include traditional Native governments, state-authorized municipalities, Native regional and local corporations and nonprofit associations, boroughs, rural school districts, and other forms of special and quasi government. In 1993 there were more than five hundred such organizations in rural Alaska, most of them small "city" governments and village corporations established under the 1971 Alaska Native Claims Settlement Act. Most rural organizations are weak, poorly managed, and underfinanced.

The Borough Act of 1961 required that all special districts "integrate" with organized boroughs by July 1, 1963. Local groups were expected to petition for borough formation and to request the Local Boundary Commission's approval of the boundaries, structures, and functions they wanted for their borough government. Local voters could choose between an elected chair or an appointed manager for the executive, and could select first- or second-class borough status. First-class boroughs could acquire powers in areas outside cities by assembly ordinance, while in second-class boroughs a vote of the residents of those areas was required. Both classes of borough needed an areawide vote to take on additional areawide powers.

the state would "encourage the settlement of its land and the development of its resources by making them available for maximum use consistent with the public interest." The utilization, development, and conservation of all natural resources belonging to the state, including land and waters, were to be "for the maximum benefit of its people."

In 1956, when Alaskans went to the polls and ratified the constitution by a vote of 17,447 to 7,180, they also overwhelmingly accepted an ordinance providing for the abolition of fish traps for the taking of salmon for commercial purposes in the state's coastal waters. That vote was a lopsided 21,285 to 4,004.[42] But Alaska's salmon fisheries declined even after the abolition of fish traps and the transfer of management from the federal to the state government.

Consequently, a 1972 constitutional amendment allowed the state "to limit entry into any fishery for purposes of resource conservation, to prevent economic distress among fishermen and those dependent upon them for a livelihood and to promote the efficient development of aquaculture in the State."[43] Designed to limit fishing in Alaska waters by an elaborate system of permits, this limited-entry amendment soon became embroiled in heated controversy. In 1976, Kodiak Island fishers spearheaded an initiative drive to repeal limited entry. Voters, however, opted to keep the permit system.

The First State Government

As we have seen, Alaskans chose Democrats William Egan and Hugh Wade as their first governor and secretary of state. These two men faced the stupendous task of translating the provisions of the state constitution into working political institutions. Born in 1914 in the little Prince William Sound community of Valdez, Egan held a variety of jobs, including truck driver, bartender, gold miner, fisherman, and aviator. After wartime service in the Army Air Corps in 1943–46, he returned to Valdez, where he became proprietor of a general merchandise store. He was a member of the territorial House of Representatives between 1941 and 1945 and again from 1947 to 1953. Elected to the territorial Senate in 1953, he served one term. In 1955 fellow Constitutional Convention delegates chose Egan to preside over their deliberations. One observer later reported that "few deliberative assemblies have been so fortunate in their choice of chairmen" because he "presided with a combination of firmness, fairness, and humor" that helped to weld a group of comparative strangers, "inclined to be suspicious of one another, into a body of friends and co-workers united by their mutual respect and common purpose."[44]

The new administration got off to an inauspicious start when Egan became so ill that he required hospitalization and several operations in Seattle. Wade became acting governor, a difficult position for him to assume because Egan had not briefed his running mate. Wade recalled that Egan was essentially a "loner": "When I took over as Governor, on the first day, why, I hadn't talked with him for twenty minutes before or during the campaign." But Wade performed his duties as acting governor capably for more than three months, using the services of various territorial officials. Egan recuperated from his near-fatal illness, and in April 1959, during the closing days of the first session of the first legislature of the state of Alaska, he returned to Juneau, where he resumed his duties as chief executive.[45]

The first session of the first Alaska state legislature convened on January 26, 1959, amid an atmosphere of confidence as Alaska bravely stepped into a new era. Lawmakers were not greatly concerned with state finances and budgets, because Alaska started life as a state with a comfortably large surplus in its treasury acquired during the last prosperous years as a territory, with the certainty of five years of generous federal transitional grants, and with the prospects of a growing oil-and-gas boom. Relieved of money worries, the first session turned its attention to organizing the new state government.

In the State Organization Act of 1959, the new legislature created twelve departments: administration, law, revenue, health and welfare, labor, commerce, military affairs, natural resources, public safety, public works, education, and fish and game. Each department was to be headed by an executive appointed by the governor. The principal executive officers of the departments of education and fish and game were to be appointed by the governor from nominations made by boards affiliated with these departments. The legislature also drafted land laws and created a Division of Land within the Department of Natural Resources.

The division was to choose, manage, and dispose of the state's entitlement under the statehood act—more than 103 million acres. The state wished to select the resource-rich lands in order to stimulate economic development and create a year-round local economy, but the process was slow. No adequate inventories of Alaska's lands existed, and the U.S. Bureau of Land Management moved at a snail's pace in approving, surveying, and patenting state selections. Another inhibiting factor was awareness that landownership entailed expensive management responsibilities, such as classification, surveying, and fire control. The imposition of the land freeze in 1966 and the withdrawal of national-interest lands in the wake of the Alaska Native Claims Settlement

Act of 1971 further impeded state land selections (see chapter 19). As of March 31, 1971, the state had selected 68,818,500.34 acres and patented a mere 9,759,136.37 acres of state selections. Obviously, Alaskans optimistic expectations that statehood would free the new political entity from the constraints of the federal government were misguided.[46]

Alaskans quickly found that the federal government continued to play an important role in the state's government and economy. The U.S. Department of Defense, for example, continued to spend hundreds of millions of dollars a year on staffing, maintaining, and improving its defense installations in Alaska (see chapter 14). It also continued to operate the state's telephone and telegraph system until it was sold to private enterprise in 1971. The U.S. Department of the Interior loomed large in managing the extensive public domain and providing the range of social and other services found in the other states. The U.S. Department of Transportation operated the Alaska Railroad, and the Forest Service of the U.S. Department of Agriculture managed the state's two national forests. The list of federal agencies involved in Alaskan affairs seemed endless.

A few figures illustrate the pervasive federal influence. Of a total employed work force of 62,900 in 1959, 16,800 were federal employees. Although federal employment slowed in subsequent years, in 1971 federal workers still numbered 17,300 of a total employed work force of 110,600. By 1971 government employees made up more than one-third of the total employed work force; that growth was attributable to the expanding needs of local and state government. In 1959 local government employed a modest 3,000 workers, and state government employed 2,600. These figures had risen to 9,000 and 11,700, respectively, by 1971.[47]

Facing Up to the Economic Realities of Statehood

Alaskans had desired statehood in part because they believed that it would bring fairly rapid and diverse economic development. In fact, to survive as a political entity capable of fulfilling the role of a self-supporting state, Alaska desperately needed basic economic development. It possessed a few small lumber operations, two pulp mills, a mining industry consisting of one underground operation and several relatively minor placer operations, and an ailing and seasonal salmon-fishery and fish-processing industry. The only bright prospects were the potential expansion of tourism and the hope that oil and gas production would increase.

Patrick O'Donovan, a British newspaper correspondent, perhaps best summed up the dream and reality of Alaska shortly after the statehood bill passed Congress:

> They like to call this the last frontier. It is not. . . . A young man cannot come here with his hand and his courage and carve an estate out of the wilderness. You can get a 160-acre homestead from the Government for all but nothing. To develop it properly you are likely to need a capital of $25,000 or three generations of peasant labor. The banks will not be kind. You can work for a great corporation out in the wilderness, without women or drink, live like a Cistercian in a cell, have your cheeks scabbed by cold in winter, be fed each day like a prince hungry from the hunt and draw a salary of a bank manager. You can find temporary, chancy work in the city, but there is also unemployment. Alaska is a long-term, massive operation, conditioned by its inaccessibility, and its ferocious terrain. It is proper meat for the great corporations with capital the size of national debts and machines and helicopters and dedicated graduates from mining schools.[48]

Statehood proponents had been an optimistic lot, but soon after the attainment of their goal, many became convinced that they had attained a stage of political development before they had the economic base to support it fully. One tenacious opponent of statehood, Juneau lawyer Herbert L. Faulkner, strongly expressed the fears of many: "Well, I felt that Alaska was not ready for statehood, that it could not support it, that it would be much more expensive to have a state than to rely on the federal government for most appropriations to support what government we had." Faulkner also opposed new taxes to support the new state because "there's always got to be somebody opposing taxes or we'd be taxed out of existence."[49]

Statehood had been a means of accomplishing several goals: the achievement of full self-government accompanied by improved efficiency and a responsive local government, an increase of local control over natural resources, and the political means of severing the economic constraints of colonialism. But all of these goals would cost money, and Governor Egan called attention to this fact when he presented the first complete state budget in 1960. The governor explained:

> During the last half of the current fiscal year, we will have assumed full responsibility for the management of our fish and game resources, an excellent start will have been made on a State Land Management Program, the judicial and other purely state and local functions will have been fully assumed. How will we fare beyond June 30, 1961? Most immediately, we are faced with a progressive reduction of the transitional grants available under the Alaska Omnibus Act [a federal aid program], with those grants ending by June 30, 1964. At that time we will have to make up several millions of dollars if we are not to curtail services.[50]

By 1960 many Alaskans, as well as outside observers, began to share the doubts expressed for so long by Faulkner and others. Journalist Ray J. Schrick, reporting on "Alaska's Ordeal" in the *Wall Street Journal* in early 1960, observed that the "job of equipping the huge frozen back country with the political machinery for self-government is less than half-done."[51]

A financial crisis loomed ahead, and Alaska sectionalism had reasserted itself in bitter squabbling among numerous local factions over where highways should be located and how boroughs should be established. One group, centered in Anchorage, wanted to move the state capital from Juneau, while another wanted its region to secede from the new state entirely. Alaska's woes, Schrick continued, would affect all American taxpayers because the federal government might well be called upon to foot "as much as 74% of the bill for a proposed $323 million state construction program in the next six years."[52]

Meanwhile, basic services, like law enforcement, were proving difficult to finance. On February 20, 1960, the state officially took over state civil and criminal cases, which meant opening eight superior courts and replacing four former federal district courts, appointing ten district magistrates, and trying to settle over three thousand unfinished cases. The Nome Chamber of Commerce complained that the administration had assigned only one state trooper and no full-time prosecutor to its area, which is as large as the states of California and New York combined. "We were better off under the federal government," concluded many of Nome's citizens. One state official told Schrick that "economically you can't even justify Alaska's existence but it's here—just like Washington, D.C."[53]

Alaska's projected expenditures on highways alone for the next fiscal year amounted to $48 million, about $12 million more than the entire state general fund budget. Approximately $43 million of these monies would come from the federal government, but the state still had to raise $5 million as a match. The highway department had employed only twelve individuals in 1959; employment skyrocketed to nearly one thousand when the state took over the functions hitherto performed by the federal Bureau of Public Roads. Every mile of road built added between $800 and $1,500 a year in maintenance expenses.

Another problem lay in the downturn of one of the region's longstanding resources: salmon. The industry recorded a record low pack in 1959, and things were only made worse by continued fishing of Alaska-spawned salmon stocks by Japanese fleets in the Bering Sea and the mid-Aleutian area. Although the Japanese were fishing in international waters and west of a 170° west longitude demarcation line set up by international treaty, U.S. negotiators subsequently discovered that they had not placed the dividing line far enough toward Kamchatka; Bristol Bay salmon had been using this midocean area for a place to mature before returning to their home streams to spawn. Adding to these worries was the fact that for the first time, big Russian trawlers and factory ships were appearing in the Bering Sea, catching bottom fish species such as sole, haddock, flounder, rockfish, and cod. Americans, who generally did not use those species, were afraid that the Russians would soon be dragging the halibut grounds.[54]

Clearly, much had to be learned about fish-management techniques, and fishermen would eventually have to diversify and begin utilizing the great offshore resources of bottom fish. International conservation agreements also needed stronger enforcement. For years the coast guard had been handicapped in this enforcement because of lack of equipment, and Congress had been very slow in strengthening it.

Alaska's chief executive drew attention to some of these problems and also to the general causes for the increased financial costs of statehood in his 1960 budget message. Governor Egan also warned that available revenues would fail to meet those costs by several million dollars, but he hoped that monies would be forthcoming "from increased state land revenues, mineral lease receipts, stumpage payments, and other sources.[55]

Then he presented a balanced budget to the legislature that included proposed tax increases of two cents per gallon on highway motor fuel and one cent per gallon on marine motor fuel sales, plus the expenditure of approximately $15 million of federal transitional grants and withdrawals from the general fund surplus. Such a combination of monies would soon not be available, and it was the Alaska State Planning Commission that more fully explained just how far beyond its means the state would be living. At current rates of income and expenditures, the commission predicted, Alaska would be about $30 million in debt on operating programs by the end of the 1966 fiscal year and $70 million in debt if the financing of a minimum—and sorely needed—capital improvement program was included.[56]

The 1960 legislature, together with the Alaska State Planning Commission, gave the first accurate assessment of the new state government. Transfer of functions from the federal government to the state had almost been completed. The most dramatic revelation concerned the shift in monetary terms; from a high of $38 million per year during territorial days, the administration would be managing expenditures in excess of $104 million in 1961, and

state employment was to increase from 3,900 to approximately 4,600, including the employees of the University of Alaska and the Alaska State Housing Authority. Even the most optimistic, looking beyond the year immediately ahead, could not help but be disturbed by the financial crunch that had to be faced soon.

When the legislature met in 1961, it realistically considered Alaska's financial predicament and raised tax rates where they would do the least harm to future economic development. This legislature gave Alaskans the chance to do a fair job of managing the new state's financial affairs if spending restraints were used and the state encountered some luck along the way in the form of expansion in crude petroleum and gas production, income from competitive oil-and-gas lease sales, expansion in the fisheries through diversification, and expansion of the forest products industries.

And luck was with the new state. An increasing flow of new settlers, investors, and tourists had arrived in the new state in 1959. New motels, hotels, and resorts were in either the planning or construction phase, and more oil had been found. Alaska now possessed four modestly producing wells, and oil companies intended to undertake substantial exploratory work. This was reflected in the state's first competitive oil-and-gas lease sale in December 1959, when several companies paid approximately $4 million for a total of seventy-seven thousand acres. The Japanese investment groups that, together with American capital assistance, built the second pulp mill at Sitka had interested other Japanese companies in examining Alaska's coal, iron, and oil potential as a possible source of raw materials for Asia.[57]

These and other bright points allowed Alaska to get past this difficult transition period. A great deal would be accomplished by 1967, including growth in several key industries: A vigorous king crab fishery worth more than $10 million a year was created. The timber industry grew steadily; in 1960 it had an estimated annual payroll of $18.3 million and turned out wood products with an estimated end-product value of $47.3 million. By 1967 these figures had risen to $25 million and $77.7 million, respectively. And most significantly, the oil industry mushroomed: crude petroleum worth $1,230,000 was extracted in 1960; by 1967 the value would rise to $88,187,000. The value of gas production rose from $30,000 in 1960 to $7,268,000 in 1967. And Alaska's income from the oil industry grew accordingly. In 1960 the state treasury received a modest $3,372,000; by 1967 the figure had risen to a respectable $35,613,000.[58]

Party Politics of the 1960s

While many Alaskans worried about the state's economic future, the Alaska electorate trooped to the polls on November 8, 1960, to participate for the first time in a presidential election. Most observers except for a few die-hard Republicans believed that the state's three electoral votes were securely in the Democratic column. There was ample ground for Democratic optimism in the 49th State, since the Republicans had been successful only twice since World War II, once in 1946 and again in 1952.

Party labels, however, mean little in Alaska because issues important to the state do not fit traditional party molds. Voters from the left to the right on the political spectrum are freely distributed in both political parties, and notions of party loyalty are elusive at best. Within the state the Republican Party made an astounding comeback in 1960, reducing the number of Democrats in the statehouse from thirty-four to twenty-one. In the Senate the Republicans gained five seats. And although Alaska's congressional delegation was still Democratic and the state legislature boasted a Democratic majority, the 1960 election clearly ended the overwhelming Democratic predominance and, in effect, made Alaska a two-party state. Actually, statewide elections between 1958 and 1972 showed a substantial drift toward Republican voting, although the Democrats were dominant for most of the period.[59]

Perhaps reflecting the Republican drift, the Alaska electorate in 1966 voted out veteran Democrat William Egan, who was seeking a third term as governor, and narrowly elected colorful and ambitious Republican Walter J. Hickel, an Anchorage real estate developer and hotel owner. The new governor, perhaps best remembered for his decision to authorize a winter haul road from Livengood on the Yukon to Sagwon on the North Slope to improve transportation to the oil fields, quickly abandoned the executive mansion when President-elect Richard Nixon nominated him as secretary of the interior.

On the same day, December 11, 1968, the most powerful Alaskan in the history of the territory or the state, Senator E. L. Bartlett, died after undergoing arterial bypass surgery in a Cleveland hospital. Before Hickel's successor, Keith H. Miller, took over as governor, Hickel appointed Republican Ted Stevens to fill Bartlett's position in Congress. This was an ironic choice, because Stevens had recently lost his bid in the primary for the U.S. Senate when he was defeated by Elmer E. Rasmuson, president of the National Bank of Alaska and one of the state's wealthiest men.

Hickel made a wise choice in appointing Stevens, for he sent to Washington a man who had extensive contacts in the Department of the Interior and was well versed in Washington's folkways. Hickel needed Stevens's help, because before his Senate confirmation the rough-hewn and forthright Hickel had made reckless statements to the press that had aroused the ire of many. The secretary-designate had stated that he opposed placing federal lands "under lock and key" just for the sake of conservation and that it would be wrong to set water cleanliness standards so high that "we might even hinder industrial development." Senate foes held up Hickel's confirmation for weeks but eventually approved the new secretary.[60]

Governor Miller promptly named the winter haul road the Walter J. Hickel Highway. Unfortunately, the Hickel Highway turned into a canal in the spring of 1969 as the underlying permafrost began to melt and erode away. One observer called the highway, built to accommodate the trucking industry, "the biggest screw-up in the history of mankind in the arctic." And then, to add insult to injury, President Nixon fired his secretary of the interior in 1970.[61]

Responses to Natural Disasters

The first decade of Alaska statehood was an exciting and trying time for its citizens and its leaders alike. First, there was the continuing struggle to provide for an ever-growing array of badly needed state services in the face of strictly limited monetary resources. The state government had limped from one oil-and-gas lease sale to another.

Then, suddenly, on Friday, March 27, 1964, one of the greatest recorded earthquakes of all times, measuring 8.4 to 8.7 on the Richter scale, struck south-central Alaska and in a few minutes caused damage almost beyond description. Fortunately, the loss of life was relatively low, but property damage was estimated at $380 million to $500 million.[62]

Quickly technicians and mechanics arrived to restore essential service, and medical teams and rescue units "fanned out through the 900-mile coastal arc ripped by more than 10 million times the force of an atomic bomb to minister to the injured and prevent typhoid epidemics." Space was made available for the two thousand homeless in Anchorage alone, while Abe Romick, the state's commissioner of commerce, predicted that many Alaskans would never recover economically from the disaster. Kodiak's famous crab and salmon canneries were shattered, buildings from the towns had floated as far as two miles out to sea, and Seward's shoreline looked as though it had been bombed. In Valdez the waterfront looked "as though it was sawed off"; docks had been shattered, and homes had been "snapped from foundations and shredded into kindling." Most of the office buildings in the center of Anchorage had been destroyed or severely damaged, and one store had sunk so far into a fissure that only its roof showed on the buckled street level.[63]

The eyewitness report of twelve-year-old Freddie Christofferson, of Valdez, illustrates the enormity of the earthquake. Freddie had gone to the town dock to watch the unloading of the freighter *Chena,* which hailed from Seattle. The boy had just left the dock when "the earth started shaking." His companion hollered, "Earthquake!" and then took off running. "When I looked back," said Freddie, "I saw the ship up in the air. The water was up on the dock. The ship hit the dock. Then it blew the whistle and pushed off. The dock went up in the air after the ship left. It just exploded in a lot of planks. I never did see any of the people on it when it happened."[64]

Industry as well as government responded swiftly and generously. Commercial airlines and the mili-

Seward scene following a damaging tsunami in 1969.

(Courtesy of U.S. Army Corps of Engineers.)

tary dramatically displayed their capabilities by airlifting to the disaster areas hundreds of tons of emergency supplies, including drugs, food, water, electrical insulators, oxygen, blankets, flashlight batteries, heaters, and even sterile baby bottles. They also airlifted engineers and architects to inspect and restore damaged buildings and electricians and natural gas workers to restore utilities. Because of the swift response of the airlines and other industries, Alaska quickly returned to normal.[65]

At the urging of Senator Bartlett, President Lyndon B. Johnson established the Federal Reconstruction and Development Planning Commission for

Alaska, headed by Senator Clinton P. Anderson (D., N.Mex.). One month later a careful assessment showed that earthquake damage had amounted to $205,811,771 rather than the expected $400 million, and on August 14, 1964, President Johnson signed into law legislation that generously assisted Alaska with its reconstruction.[66]

South-central Alaska quickly recovered, but a few years later, in August 1967, the Chena River, which bisects the town of Fairbanks, overflowed its banks and put much of the city under about eight feet of water. Although the flooding was confined to that one city, property damage was heavy, and once again the federal government lent a helping hand. The Small Business Administration, as in the earthquake disaster, extended necessary long-term loans at favorable interest rates to put Fairbanks back on it feet.

The Euphoria of Oil and Planning for the Future

Early in 1968 the Atlantic Richfield Company (formerly Richfield Oil and known as ARCO) struck the 10-billion-barrel Prudhoe Bay oil field on Alaska's North Slope. In the subsequent oil-lease sale in 1969, the twenty-third since statehood, oil companies bid in excess of $900 million. Euphoria reigned, and there was hope that Alaska's perpetually rocky economy would now stabilize and diversify.

With over $900 million dollars in the state's coffers, many citizens believed that Alaska's financial problems had been solved. The question clearly was "What do we do with all the money?" The Legislative Council of the state of Alaska in association with the Brookings Institution scheduled a series of conferences in late 1969 with leading citizens to discuss directions for the future. In four successive meetings, a "representative" group of approximately 150 Alaskans examined and discussed the financial foundations of the future Alaska, the use of human resources, the quality of the natural environment, and alternative futures for the state.

Throughout the sessions, participants called for preserving the "unique" Alaska lifestyle, defining it as one that "affords the conveniences of technological innovation combined with the opportunity and values of living as close to nature as possible." Most agreed that compatibility between the oil industry and the Alaskan lifestyle could be achieved with "well enforced, proper regulation."[67] Members of the Brookings Institution team and outside experts in socioeconomic planning, however, tried to warn Alaskans that they probably could not eat their cake and have it too. The seminars certainly served to educate and inform the participants and the public, and the resulting recommendations were to serve as guidelines for legislators.

Not to be outdone by the Legislative Council, the Office of the Governor of Alaska contracted with the Stanford Research Institute to prepare planning guidelines for the state based on the state's identified or projected physical, economic, and social needs and the resources available to meet those needs over the next few years. The institute recommended substantial upgrading of urban services such as water, sewers, and solid waste disposal and improvements in education, personnel development, public welfare, and health. The consultants warned, however, that, far from transforming Alaska into an embarrassingly rich state, the North Slope oil discoveries at best would help place the state on a more comparable basis with its fellow states in terms of financial position and the availability of adequate public services. The high living costs and other disadvantages of a relatively remote and sparsely populated land would persist. In fact, the consultants warned, the oil boom might accentuate these factors unless the bonus money and other state revenues were used wisely and in the public interest.[68]

Chapter 18

Alaska's Oil Economy in the 1970s and 1980s

The discovery of the vast Prudhoe Bay oil field on state land in 1968 gave Alaskans a reprieve from the constant financial worries of previous years. Their new problem was enviable: what to do with the $900 million inflow of cash? Answering this question required some soul searching and careful listening, and Alaskans responded positively to the somewhat novel idea of creating a Permanent Fund that would directly benefit every Alaskan. Times were not flush for long, however, and the decade ended with the state again scrambling for cash.

The Question of Moving the Capital

Whether or not all of Alaska's public monies will be used wisely is still pretty much up in the air. One example will suffice to illustrate the ever-present urge to spend tax dollars foolishly. Soon after Alaska achieved statehood, Robert B. Atwood, the wealthy, powerful, and influential publisher of Alaska's largest newspaper, the *Anchorage Daily Times*, began campaigning to move the state capital from Juneau, in southeastern Alaska, considered fairly inaccessible, to somewhere closer to the state's population center. State voters decisively rejected initiatives for the move in 1960 and again in 1962 because of competing needs and scarcity of money.

In 1974, however, the move was approved, though it provided that the new capital could not be within a thirty-mile radius of either Anchorage or Fairbanks. This provision was included because politicians and business people in the two cities did not trust each other's intentions and had lobbied hard to make certain that the other city would not get the new capital.[1]

The new capital was to be established in an undeveloped area, but no specific sites had been listed on the referendum ballot, and no cost estimates were available. In short, citizens had voted for a concept without considering the ultimate costs or benefits. When asked why they desired to move the capital, Alaskans most often stated that they wanted to have the capital in a central and accessible location. Perhaps the post-Watergate distrust of government and the desire to have an open and visible government played a role in the vote as well.

Alaska's newly elected Republican governor, Jay S. Hammond, no friend of the move, acceded to the will of the voters and appointed a Capital Site Selection Committee headed by Willie Hensley, an Eskimo and former legislator from Kotzebue who had run unsuccessfully for Alaska's lone seat in the U.S. House of Representatives in 1974, when the capital move initiative was on the primary ballot. Hensley had spoken against it wherever he went, arguing that Alaska had many urgent needs to meet before the capital should be moved.

Now Hensley's committee was charged with proposing and evaluating possible capital sites. With a handsome budget and many consultants, and after much travel across the state, the committee came up with three possible sites: Willow, approximately thirty-five air miles north of Anchorage, with an estimated price tag of $2.46 billion; Larson Lake, about eighty miles north of Anchorage, at a cost of some $2.56 billion; and Mount Yenlo, approximately seventy air miles northwest of Anchorage, with a price tag of $2.7 billion. Consultants pointed out that in each case the state would have to assume only about one-fifth of the estimated costs. They expected private developers to supply the difference.[2]

Some state legislators attempted to give voters a fourth choice by adding to the ballot "none of the above," but their efforts failed. In 1976 voters chose Willow, the least expensive of the three proposed sites. The selected site was less than one mile east of the settlement of Willow and covered about one hundred square miles of state-owned land. Even before the Willow site was selected by the voters, private land in the Matanuska-Susitna valleys, particularly near Willow, rose enormously in paper value in anticipation of the move.[3]

Now the Hammond administration had to decide how the move was to be financed. There were two possibilities: to use revenues accruing to the state from the Prudhoe Bay oil field, which had begun flowing in June 1977, or to put the method of payment to the voters in the form of a bond proposition. Opponents of the move hoped for the latter course, assuming that a massive bond issue would force a rethinking of the issue. They therefore launched a petition drive in April 1977 to place on the 1978 ballot an initiative requiring Alaska voters to approve a bond issue before the capital could be moved. In the same year a group calling itself FRANK (Frustrated Responsible Alaskans Needing Knowledge) launched a petition drive seeking to put the true cost of the move on the ballot. The petition drive closed on December 15, 1977, both petitions succeeded, and Alaskans had a chance to do some rethinking in light of the costs involved.

Opponents of the move took heart in early 1977. Results of a survey conducted by the Anchorage-based Rowan Group, which was hired as part of the governor's Alaska Public Forum program, revealed that Alaskans still preferred Juneau, which has the most spectacular natural setting of any state capi-

tal, to any other site. Of a representative sample of urban and rural Alaskans, asked where the capital should be, 41 percent preferred Juneau; 15 percent, Anchorage; 13 percent, Willow; and 7 percent, Wasilla. The remainder were undecided or preferred other locations in the state.[4]

When Alaska voters trooped to the polls in the November 1978 general election, they decisively rejected a bond issue in excess of $900 million for moving the capital. Clearly, modern means of electronic communication can accomplish the goals of the proposed move—easy accessibility and communication—at a fraction of the cost. At the end of 1978, then, the voters had given conflicting directions to their legislators and the governor. Still on the books from 1974 was the approved capital move, yet in 1978 they had voted down the necessary funds to get the move under way. It is clear that more will be heard in the future about the pros and cons of relocating the capital.

The Upset Victory of Jay S. Hammond

The capital-move issue was only one of many major developments affecting the future of Alaska in the 1970s and 1980s. One of the most interesting of these developments was the election of Jay S. Hammond to the governorship in 1974. Born in Troy, New York, in 1922, the son of a Methodist minister, Hammond attended Pennsylvania State University and the University of Alaska, where he received a baccalaureate degree in biological sciences in 1948. Hammond was a U.S. Marine Corps fighter pilot in the South Pacific between 1942 and 1946. In 1952 he married Bella Gardiner, who was part Eskimo, in Palmer, Alaska. He was an apprentice guide, fisherman, hunter, and trapper in Rainy Pass in the Alaska Range between 1946 and 1949 and served with the U.S. Fish and Wildlife Service from 1949 to 1956 as a pilot-agent. Hammond established his own air-taxi service, became a registered guide, and built a sportsmen's lodge on Lake Clark and a fishing lodge among the Wood River Lakes.

First elected to the state house in 1959 as an independent, Hammond switched to the Republican Party two years later. He served for six years in the House, becoming minority and majority whip. He became mayor of the Bristol Bay Borough in 1965 and was elected in 1966 to the state Senate, where he served for the next six years, becoming majority party whip, majority leader, chair of the Rules and Resources Committee, and finally president of the Senate. Because his district was drastically reapportioned in 1972, Hammond chose not to run again, but once again he was elected mayor of the Bristol Bay Borough. He held that position until his election to the governorship in 1974.

Hammond's campaign for the governorship was a formidable undertaking because he had to defeat two former governors in the Republican primary—Walter Hickel and Keith Miller—and then incumbent Democratic Governor Egan in the general election. Hammond and his supporters started pounding the pavement, literally ringing thousands of doorbells. Hammond asked Lowell Thomas, Jr., son of the famous broadcaster and himself a member of the Alaska legislature, to run as his lieutenant governor. This was a smart move because Thomas had far greater name recognition than did Hammond at that point. A simple campaign brochure proclaimed: "It takes teamwork. . . . They will work together for Alaska. . . . We have only one special interest . . . the Alaskan people."[5]

Hickel, Nixon's former secretary of the interior, was heavily favored in the Republican primary because he was widely recognized and he had substantial financial backing from development interests. Hickel underestimated Hammond's candidacy, saving his money for his anticipated battle with Egan. To the chagrin of many Republicans, Hammond defeated both Hickel and Miller decisively in the primaries. (Miller, who was secretary of state under Hickel, had succeeded him as governor in 1968 when Hickel became secretary of the interior. In 1970 he was defeated in his bid for another term by Egan.) Then, after a hard-fought campaign, Hammond defeated Egan by a margin of 287 votes in the November general election.

Hammond readily admitted that he was an environmentalist, which is considered a political liability in Alaska because most important environmental lobbying efforts are identified with "outside" interests, particularly the California-based Sierra Club. These groups are accused by many Alaskans of de-

Governor Jay S. Hammond cruising on a new bike trail in Fairbanks, 1976.

(Courtesy of *Fairbanks Daily News-Miner.*)

siring to "lock up" the state forever from economic development. Hammond offered a middle course between those "who would develop for the sake of development" and those "who would conserve for the sake of conservation." He believed that each development project should be weighted individually by considering the question "Will the people of Alaska really profit from this?" Hammond proposed to formulate basic policy guidelines with the help of Alaska's voting public. These guidelines were to determine the "use of our resources, which will insure that our nonrenewable resources are developed when they can offer long-term benefits to all Alaskans, and that our renewable resources be maintained so there is a continual base for Alaska's economy."[6]

Although Hammond was intensely disliked by the development forces, particularly the *Anchorage Daily Times*, his rapport with the average voter seemed to be good. In a state that is unimpressed by formality, the governor fit in well. By and large, he did not isolate himself from the public with numerous aides and press spokespeople; he remained accessible, as were his top administrators. Bearded, casually dressed, and a colorful speaker, he projected an image of the typical Alaskan. Hammond insisted that development pay its own way. He was a fiscal conservative and emphasized that Alaskans should not rely on oil and gas revenues for operating the state government but rather should rely on income from renewable resources and general taxation. The governor repeatedly reminded Alaskans that of the $900 million in bonus monies the state received in the 1969 Prudhoe Bay lease sale, only $504 million was left by January 1975, and that was going fast.

The state had been spending more than it had taken in, using the bonus money to make up the deficit. This is not to say that the bonus money had been wasted; the monies had been used to increase spending for badly needed education, housing, welfare, and transportation programs. But the state's general fund budget had grown from $160 million in 1970 to about $725 million in 1975.[7]

Hammond emphasized that Alaska had to plan ahead and develop a sustaining economic structure based on something beyond the extraction of nonrenewable resources. It was no surprise, therefore, when he announced that he wished to run for a second term to complete his program.

In a crowded and confused 1978 election, Hammond reclaimed the governor's seat with 49,580 votes to Chancy Croft's 25,656 votes. Walter Hickel, who had launched a write-in campaign, received an astounding 33,555 votes.[8] The election highlighted the general difficulties of conducting elections in such a far-flung state. Hammond had alienated Republicans and unions alike in his first term by having refused to render special treatment to any one interest group. He was determined to deposit the monies from oil leases into an investment account, equitably disbursing benefits to all Alaskan shareholders in perpetuity, at the time an unpopular idea. As he later recalled, on election night 1978, he feared that he would not get reelected.[9]

Hammond and the Permanent Fund

In 1965, while Hammond was part-time manager of the Bristol Bay Borough, he had proposed the creation of an investment corporation financed by a proposed fish tax. Each local resident would be granted one share of stock for each year of Borough residency. Profits from "Bristol Bay, Inc.," Hammond proposed, would far exceed the fish tax payments. The voters rejected his idea. Hammond tried several other ideas to sell his Bristol Bay, Inc. to the Borough residents but failed.[10]

Now, as governor, Hammond believed that the best approach to divert some of the oil money cascading into state coffers was to create a dividend-dispensing investment account in which all Alaskans were stockholders. Initially the public reacted negatively, but Hammond introduced a measure to create "Alaska, Inc.," by amending the state constitution. Under the governor's proposal, Alaska, Inc. would receive 50 percent of all natural resource lease, bonus, royalty, and severance tax dollars. A statewide vote would be required before the principal could be spent. Fifty percent of the annual earnings were to be dispersed in cash dividends to all Alaskans in the form of one share of dividend-paying stock for each year of residency since statehood.[11]

The legislature was cool to the concept and, as Hammond wrote, referred it "to a multitude of committees for internment." A number of lawmakers did share Hammond's concern, however, and after much debate, they succeeded in persuading their colleagues to accept the concept. But the legislature created a statutory rather than a constitutional investment account, so lawmakers could tap into it any time. Also, only 25 percent of all resource lease, bonuses, and royalties were to be deposited, and there was no reference to severance taxes. The legislature had reduced Hammond's proposed contributions to the fund by almost 75 percent. Also, no mention was made of dividends or "Alaska, Inc."— instead the lawmakers called it the Alaska Permanent Fund.

In light of these major changes, the governor vetoed the measure and insisted that it be put to the electorate as a constitutional amendment. Alaskan voters approved the amendment in 1976. It required the state to deposit at least 25 percent of all mineral lease rentals, royalties, royalty sale proceeds, federal mineral revenue-sharing payments, and bonuses into the Permanent Fund. The amendment does not specify how the fund's investment income is to be used but merely provides that it be "deposited to the general fund unless otherwise provided by law."[12]

Despite the fund's constitutional status, Governor Hammond feared it would die unless assertive voters could fend off politicians "inclined to invade the trust on behalf of special interests." Thereupon Hammond introduced legislation to create a Permanent Fund Dividend program, which languished in legislative committee for some time. The governor let it be known that if lawmakers did not bring his bill to a vote, he would call them back into a special session the day after they adjourned. Additionally, he threatened to veto the special capital projects, in the budget bill, of those lawmakers who voted to keep his measure locked up in committee. Not only did the legislators bring Hammond's bill out onto the floor for a vote, but virtually all voted "Aye" on final passage. Now legislators rushed to claim coauthorship of the concept they had judged "dead on arrival" just a short time before.[13]

The governor's proposal was to grant each state resident one share of dividend-paying stock for each year of residency since statehood in 1959. The Alaska Permanent Fund Dividend became law, with the first dividend set at $50 per share. Thus, in 1980, those Alaskans living in the state since 1959 would receive twenty-one shares, or $1,050.[14]

It was on this retroactive feature that the program foundered. New residents Ron and Penny Zobel, both attorneys, believed the program was discriminatory and they sued the state. Eventually, after the case wound its way through the state courts, the U.S. Supreme Court sided with the Zobels and issued a restraining order on the distribution of dividends. The governor and legislature reworked the dividend program: Roughly one-half of the fund's annual earnings are distributed equally to all Alaskan residents, while a portion of the remaining earnings is used to "inflation proof" the fund. A five-year averaging method avoids wide annual dividend fluctuations. The first dividend check was arbitrarily set at one thousand dollars, about the accumulation during the three-year period of litigation.

Hammond signed the compromise legislation into law in June 1982. Although at first outraged at the Zobels' action, Hammond later realized that their suit had ensured that every Alaskan would receive the same annual dividend, thus strengthening the constituency that protects the Permanent Fund from raids by politicians.[15]

The Continuing Importance of the Permanent Fund

A special revenue fund derived from government-owned natural resources is not unusual; Alaska has the Mental Health and the University of Alaska trust funds, and there are examples in other states as well. Texas has a mineral trust fund for the support of the University of Texas; and the Canadian province of Alberta has the Alberta Heritage Fund. But the Alaska Permanent Fund differs from other state government mineral revenue trust funds primarily because of its immense size—approximately $34 billion in 2006 and $31 billion in June 2009.

Several factors account for this large size, namely, the high minimum contribution rate set by the constitution; the tremendous value of oil production from the Prudhoe Bay and Kuparuk oil fields; occasional special legislative appropriations to the fund; the fact that as much of the balance as necessary of the annual earnings, after about one-half has been distributed in the dividend program, shall be deposited to the principal to offset the effects of inflation; and the conservative management as an endowment trust following the "prudent investor" rule, adopted in 1980, which calls for an investment in a mix of high-quality bonds, stocks, and income-producing real estate partnerships, which generate a reasonable return without endangering the principal of the fund. All of these have allowed regular disbursements to every Alaskan.

The first one-thousand-dollar checks were issued

in 1982. Since that time, the annual dividend payments have been as follows:

1983	$ 386.15
1984	331.29
1985	404.00
1986	556.26
1987	708.19
1988	826.93
1989	873.16
1990	952.63
1991	931.34
1992	915.84
1993	949.46
1994	983.90
1995	990.30
1996	1,130.68
1997	1,296.54
1998	1,540.88
1999	1,769.84
2000	1,963.86
2001	1,850.28
2002	1,540.76
2003	1,107.56
2004	919.84
2005	845.76
2006	1,106.96
2007	1,654.00
2008	2,069.00
2009	1,305.00[16]

The state has expended in excess of $1 billion since the inception of the program in 1982, and the impact on individuals as well as the Alaska economy as a whole has been significant. The dividend program is particularly important in the bush, where unemployment rates and living expenses are high.[17] Dividends spent in the state create employment and generate more income from subsequent respending.

The federal and state governments regularly give money to citizens in the form of welfare checks, the food stamp program, loan subsidies, agricultural price supports, and other forms of direct or indirect payments to individuals, all supporting particular groups among the American citizenry. What is unique about the Permanent Fund Dividend (PFD) program is that all state residents receive the same payment. The wisdom of the program was hotly debated at the time it was a legislative proposal, but it has become extremely popular in the intervening years. In fact, most Alaskans have come to regard it as their birthright and will not tolerate any discussion about alternative ways to use the PFD, such as in support of state government programs. Clearly, the fund has created a powerful constituency that protects the principal of the fund and its conservative, income-producing investment management; it has also constrained the size and role of government in Alaska society.

Critics of the PFD argue that it is not good public policy, that the dividend money would be more productive if spent in the public domain to improve the quality of Alaska society and the public environment. Others point out that the unprecedented revenues flowing into state coffers will end when oil and gas reserves are gone, and that it would have been wiser for the legislature to create a fiscal plan of moderate spending and aggressive savings. That would have created a trust fund large enough to finance the state budget in perpetuity entirely from the earnings.[18]

Hammond left after his two terms in office ended in 1982. He wrote that "after eight years of tumult I had achieved the most important item on my agenda, and there was much to be thankful for."[19] During his administration the Trans-Alaska Pipeline had been completed; a budget surplus was achieved; and Alaska Native Claims Settlement Act corporations started to export timber, minerals, and seafood.

Hammond died in his sleep at his Lake Clark homestead on August 2, 2005, at the age of eighty-three. Alaska widely mourned the "man, myth, legend and, yes, politician." The *Anchorage Daily News* wrote that despite his "habitual plea 'I am not a politician,' [Jay S. Hammond] was a politician down to his very bones." Since leaving office, he had served Alaska as elder statesman and steadfast defender of the PFD program.[20]

The Post-Hammond Years

Governor Hammond was succeeded by a Democrat, William Jennings Sheffield, Jr. Sheffield grew up poor on a five-acre truck farm near Spokane, Washington. His life was made harder by a severe stutter, which remained with him well into adulthood. After a stint in the air force, he worked as a salesman in Alaska for Sears Roebuck. By the late 1950s, he was taking the first steps toward building Alaska's largest hotel chain.

Sheffield and his partner, Brad Phillips, leased the Anchorage Inn, a downtown apartment house, which they turned into a hotel to take advantage of the summer tourist trade. They then leased the Westward Inn, later called the Red Ram. When Phillips experienced financial difficulties, Sheffield bought out his partner, quit his Sears Roebuck job, and took over the enterprise alone. In 1964 Sheffield leased the Anchorage Travel Lodge, and in 1966 he built the Whitehorse Travel Lodge in the Yukon Territory. By the mid-1980s he had built the state's largest hotel chain.

In 1976 Sheffield decided to run for governor in the next election, but his wife, Lee Buhlert Sheffield, was diagnosed with lung cancer, so he quit politics and spent the time with her. She died in 1978. He launched his gubernatorial campaign in 1980, promising to bring to Juneau the same management principles that had made him successful. His opponent in the Democratic primary was Steve Cowper, a Fairbanks attorney and former two-term legislator who attracted little outside support and therefore had to rely heavily on personal savings to finance a shoestring campaign. Sheffield broke all records in the campaign, spending over $2 million, including six hundred thousand dollars of his own money. He defeated Cowper by a narrow margin of 280 votes, but he beat Republican Tom Fink decisively in the general election in 1982.

While campaigning, Sheffield had stated that he intended to place his company shares into a blind trust. Under such an arrangement, very common with individuals running for high elective office, it would have been a violation of state law for the trustee to provide information about the business to Sheffield. Sheffield never created such a trust, however, and after taking office, he twice acted on behalf of Westours, Inc., to which he was in the process of selling 33 percent of Sheffield Enterprises.

Later, Sheffield took offense when asked if he still involved himself in Sheffield Enterprises. "I'm sick and tired of the press and other people talking about the conflict of interest in my business. I don't have one. I don't recall ever saying I was going to put my stock into a blind trust. I didn't even know what a blind trust was." On his attorney's recommendation, he explained, he had placed his holdings "into a voting trust," which would not bar his involvement in company affairs. In any event, Sheffield stated, anybody who has worked hard has accumulated a certain amount of wealth. He did not run for the governorship "to get something." He ran for "office to do something for the people of Alaska. That's been my only motive . . . and I get a little upset when people question that."[21]

Sheffield had come to office with no political experience, and as a result, almost from the day he entered office the conflict of interest issue and pointed concerns about his conduct led to a number of investigations. From the start Governor Sheffield was in trouble with the press, the legislature, and the public over a series of scandals and political blunders. In 1983, he was investigated for possible infractions of the state's campaign finance law. In 1984, he was investigated for charges that his administration had pressured state workers to contribute money to the Democratic Party. 1985 brought investigations into additional questionable campaign contributions, and later that year, the governor fought against corruption charges in a case involving a top campaigner. The jury in this last case did not believe Sheffield, called him "unfit" for office, and suggested he had committed perjury. The special prosecutor recommended that the legislature consider impeaching him. After two weeks of hearings, the Senate Rules Committee found insufficient evidence to send articles of impeachment to the House.

Although many believed the prosecutor had made a case for impeachment, the Republican majority was unable and unwilling to muster the two-thirds majority for the impeachment resolution to set in motion the process in the House. There was speculation that some senators did not comprehend what was wrong in helping a campaign contributor. Others felt bound by the "unwritten political code that you don't stone anyone in power today 'lest you be stoned tomorrow.'" Others probably recognized that Sheffield had committed official misconduct but just did not have the courage to say so.[22]

In the end, the Senate not only rejected the special prosecutor's recommendation but destroyed the contents of a subsequent Rules Committee resolution that denounced Sheffield for questionable veracity and important irregularities. Instead it called for a study of state procurement procedures. It added a rebuke to the investigators in a resolution asking that the Alaska Judicial Council "study the use of the power of the grand jury to investigate and make recommendations . . . to prevent abuse and assure basic fairness." Five years later, after memories of the event had faded, the legislature even reimbursed the then ex-governor for his legal expenses of $302,653 in a measure ostensibly passed to fund the state's longevity bonuses. In 1992, after Bill Clinton became president of the United States, Sheffield became Clinton's patronage dispenser in Alaska.[23]

Sheffield had survived the biggest crisis of his political career, and he felt vindicated. But others continued to view his actions with suspicion. Part of the problem, according to some, was his view of the gubernatorial role. The state's chief prosecutor, Dan Hickey, who had worked under the last three governors, said the principal trait that distinguished Governors Bill Egan and Jay S. Hammond from Sheffield was that Sheffield felt he could do whatever he wanted to do as governor "in terms of furthering his own political interests or those of his friends." If not, what was "the point of being governor?" Sheffield had compared state government to a private corporation, with himself "as the chairman of the board." Unfortunately, Sheffield viewed the corporation not as a publicly owned one with many shareholders but rather as a business he owned, accountable to him rather than the citizenry. Symptomatic of his management style was that he insisted that his signature, rather than that of the commissioner of administration, "be on all payroll checks for state employees." He wanted to impress "on every state employee that they worked for Bill Sheffield."[24]

Despite his legal troubles, Governor Sheffield met the state's growing financial troubles head-on. Initially, he was not in favor of keeping the Permanent Fund sacrosanct. For example, soon after he took office, Sheffield proposed spending 25 percent of the Alaska Permanent Fund's earnings on large public works projects, such as the Susitna River hydroelectric project, which quickly died (see "The Susitna Hydroelectric Project"). He also backed repeal of the Permanent Fund Dividend program because if it survived much longer, it would be politically impossible to kill. The governor, however, changed his views, probably because of widespread public opposition, and stated that to put money directly into the hands of Alaskans benefited the state's economy. This quick change showed that Sheffield had no vision of what Alaska's future should be, and that he had no fixed compass to follow but instead was satisfied to formulate policy based on public opinion alone.[25]

During his first two years in office, Sheffield resisted considerable legislative opposition to deposit $700 million of general funds into the Permanent Fund. He also joined forces with fiscally conservative legislators to reduce the $2 billion plus operating budget, which had grown 15 to 20 percent a year under his predecessor. Sheffield used his veto to cut spending, although some legislators accused him of zeroing in on their pet projects for political rather than financial reasons.

The governor did have reasons to worry about the budget. In January 1980, Alaska's lawmakers had wondered what to do about a projected $3.6 billion surplus for fiscal year 1981. By 1985, the huge surpluses were gone, and the state had taken in only about $2.68 billion during fiscal year 1986 (July 1985 through June 1986). For that year, the legislature had appropriated about $2.58 billion from the state's general fund and spent another $1 billion from other sources. In the coming fiscal year, 1987, the Alaska Department of Revenue had forecast about $1.4 billion from taxes, fees, federal money-sharing programs, and resource leases and sales. Unused money, oil company back taxes, and other sources were expected to bring the money available to spend to about $1.78 billion—not enough to cover expected expenditures. The legislature had already appropriated $2.58 billion for fiscal year 1987. By mid-July, the governor had cut that to $2.17 billion and suggested cuts of another $90 million, expecting a $300 million deficit.[26]

On March 24, 1986, Sheffield had announced at

The Susitna Hydroelectric Project

As early as 1952, the U.S. Bureau of Reclamation had identified a large number of possible hydroelectric power sites throughout Alaska. Among all the potential possibilities, the Susitna River was the most strategically situated because of its proximity to Anchorage and Fairbanks and the connecting Railbelt region. The Bureau of Reclamation identified three possible dam sites on the Susitna River. Site 1 was near the upstream end of the seventy-five-mile canyon section; Site 2 was located thirty-six miles below Site 1, at a location where the bottom is less than three hundred feet wide and rock slopes rise far above the river at forty-five-degree angles. Site 3, Devil Canyon, was located thirty miles downstream from Site 2. Here the rock walls rise steeply, almost vertically in places, to heights of six hundred to one thousand feet above the stream. A dam high enough to raise the water 525 feet would have a crest length of 1,000 feet and create a backwater to Site 2. The active storage capacity would be 1 million acre-feet, and the annual firm energy production would amount to more than 2.6 billion kilowatt hours.

Over the years, the federal and state government conducted various studies and analyses of the Susitna hydroelectric project. Early in 1976, Alaska's U.S. Senator Mike Gravel assumed leadership of the project. Gravel announced that the U.S. Army Corps of Engineers estimated that a two-dam project would cost $1.5 billion, considerably more than the 1974 estimated cost of $682 million. Although the senator was confident that the project would gain federal authorization, he cautioned that Alaska was perceived as a rich oil state and that Congress would tell the state to use its own funds. Interest lagged thereafter until Governor Sheffield again promoted the Susitna Dam.

Source: Claus-M. Naske and William R. Hunt, *The Politics of Hydroelectric Power in Alaska: Rampart and Devil Canyon, A Case Study* (Fairbanks: Institute of Water Resources, University of Alaska Fairbanks, October 1978).

---

the Seventh Alaska Energy Conference in Anchorage that the state would not spend another cent on the multibillion-dollar Susitna River hydroelectric project. He had always favored the project, but not at any cost. He told the conferees that he would ask the Alaska Power Authority (APA) to reevaluate all possibilities for meeting the Railbelt's future power needs, including coal, natural gas, and smaller-scale hydroelectric projects. He added that he "would kill any special funding for any single Railbelt projects" until the reevaluation had been completed. The state had spent about $145 million since 1980 in project studies and federal license preparations. The next day, the Alaska Power Authority board of directors voted to kill the project. Two APA reports had concluded that bonds for Susitna could be sold only if guaranteed by income from the $7.2 billion Permanent Fund, which was politically unacceptable.[27]

In July 1986 Sheffield appealed to state workers to take a 10 percent pay cut—a politically unappealing move that the unions rejected. In essence, the governor was convinced that the Alaska oil boom had ended, and he blamed himself for having failed to convey the economic seriousness of the situation to the Alaskan public.

The 1986 Campaign

Governor Sheffield campaigned vigorously in the 1986 primary campaign, telling voters throughout

Alaska that he deserved another four years at the helm of state government. Once again, his opponent in the primary was Fairbanks attorney Steve Cowper, who had little of his own money to contribute yet was determined to make a race of it. Cowper knew that Sheffield was in deep political trouble, but he also knew that Democratic loyalists would be reluctant to desert their incumbent governor. But as the early 1986 polls showed a steady decline in Sheffield's numbers, Cowper's campaign picked up steam. The Republicans attacked Sheffield relentlessly. They sought their own party's nomination, but there was no clear leader. Cowper gained the benefit from the Republican disarray while remaining above the fray. His poll numbers began to climb, and many voters began to think of him as the alterative to Sheffield. Indeed, the idea that Sheffield ought to be replaced was catching the attention of voters.

At the beginning of August 1986, three weeks before the primary election, the first statewide poll showed Cowper in the lead. As the election approached, Sheffield contributed $235,000 of his own money to his campaign, but it was too late. In the final week, a Cowper TV spot featured an earnest-looking woman who told her audience that "the only way to beat Bill Sheffield is to vote for Steve Cowper." The voters responded, and on primary election night Cowper led Sheffield by nine thousand votes.

Sheffield did not suffer terribly from the loss. In 1987, he sold his hotels to Holland America. He sat on boards and ran an environmental company for a year while it was in bankruptcy. Then Governor Tony Knowles appointed Sheffield to the Alaska Railroad board of directors. He was elected chair, and two years later he became president, a position he held until 2001. In that year, George Wuerch, then the mayor of Anchorage, asked Sheffield to serve as the interim director of the Port of Anchorage. He still served as the director of the port in 2009.[28]

The 1986 Republican primary race for governor was described as "Snow White and the Seven Dwarfs"—with Arliss Sturgulewski playing the part of Snow White. Sturgulewski was a moderate champion of campaign finance reform, which appealed to many voters tired of government scandals and politicians trying to buy their way into public office. She won the Republican primary by a two-thousand-vote margin over runner-up Walter Hickel. Although she outpolled the two biggest spenders in the race, Hickel and Joe Hayes, her campaign was not cheap, approaching $800,000 in the primary and rising to more than $1.4 million by the November general election, including about $400,000 from her own pockets. Both Hickel and Hayes had also spent hundreds of thousands of dollars of their own money.

In the November election, Cowper and Sturgulewski faced each other. Both candidates were the most liberal in their respective parties, with reputations as political reformers. Conservatives felt they had nobody to vote for, while liberals felt they could not lose. Between the end of August and the beginning of November, Cowper received $640,000 in contributions, with another $200,000 after the election was over. Sturgulewski received $573,000 in the same period. The unknown in the election was Joe Vogler, a longtime Fairbanks miner and founder of the Alaska Independence Party. His gubernatorial campaign had attracted little attention until the final weeks, when he mounted a modest TV ad campaign, hoping to attract conservatives disenchanted with the two main candidates. Many were surprised when Vogler received ten thousand votes in the November election. If most of those had gone to Sturgulewski, she might have won.

Steve Camberling Cowper, born August 21, 1938, in Petersburg, Virginia, was sworn in as Alaska's seventh chief executive on Monday, December 1, 1986. Sheffield had left a brief message, clipped to a sheaf of papers on his desk in his office on the third floor of the Capitol Building, for his successor. It read: "Steve, Good luck. —Bill." Cowper would need it, because the precipitous fall in oil prices, beginning in December 1985 and continuing through the first six months of 1986, had deepened the recession that had began before the price drop. Republicans stated that they probably would not criticize Cowper for cutting the budget because it was useless "to be part of the problem."

Boom to Bust

In 1986, Alaska's recession began. It was quite a difference from January 1980, when Alaska's lawmakers, awash in oil money, had wondered what to do about a projected $3.6 billion surplus for fiscal year 1981. These excess funds were gone by 1985, and the state had taken in only about $2.68 billion during fiscal year 1986 (July 1985 through June 1986). Oil prices declined from about twenty-eight dollars per barrel in the peak years to eight dollars a barrel in 1986. The state's economy collapsed.

But while the boom lasted, a large wave of migrants entered Alaska between 1980 and 1985. In-migrants outnumbered out-migrants by about 90,666, almost one-third of Alaska's 1986 population. Housing construction boomed. Soon, blocks of elegant homes and condos sprang up, some alongside the jerry-built apartment houses, tarpaper shacks, and trailer courts that housed earlier arrivals. The Seattle-based Nordstrom chain of expensive apparel and other goods renovated the store it had bought in Anchorage in 1975 in anticipation of the customers working well-paying jobs in the oil industry. Elegant restaurants and boutiques shot up within weeks. Anchorage grew at a frantic pace. In 1983, the city issued permits for over $1 billion worth of construction. That exceeded the combined building permits of the thriving cities of Seattle, Portland, and Honolulu in that same year.[29]

Bankers from Alaska and the contiguous states flocked to Anchorage, willing to lend and fully taking advantage of state programs that guaranteed loans. Easy credit fueled the boom, and opportunities abounded for large-scale private profiteering. The story of entrepreneur Peter Zamarello was typical of the boom; he rose from rags to riches in Alaska in just a few years and saw his wealth disappear in just a few months. Born in Greece in 1927, he came to New York in 1953 and came to Alaska in the 1960s to seek his fortune as a carpenter. He saved enough money for a down payment on a loan to buy a parcel of land. He discovered that credit checks were weak in Alaska, so that when the money ran out from one bank loan he could get another from a bank down the street.[30]

With his first construction loan of $150,000 in 1969, Zamarello built a shopping center near the gates of Elmendorf Air Force Base in a section of Anchorage called Muldoon. Small store owners soon rented space in the complex after noticing the steady traffic. Next he bought a 568-unit trailer park. Then he bought cheap land around Anchorage, convinced that the imminent oil rush would make the city boom. In front of the development frenzy that transformed Anchorage and its environs, Zamarello borrowed, built, and borrowed some more, creating an empire, worth perhaps $1 billion, consisting of dozens of shopping centers, malls, office plazas, condos, and trailer parks. Alaska and Washington state banks sought his business. They rarely questioned his one-page, unaudited financial worth statements.

By 1985 Zamarello had become the largest, richest, and most flamboyant developer in the state, known as the "king of the strip malls." One-thousand workers toiled for him, and his personal fortune reportedly grew to $292 million. Doing his best to live up to the title of "wealthiest man in Alaska," he lived in a $1.2 million mansion in Anchorage, bought condos for himself and his wife in Tacoma, Washington, and owned an $850,000 residence in Honolulu, Hawaii. Zamarello invested millions in four financial institutions, and he boasted of an $11 million collection of art, furniture, and jewelry. He was particularly proud of his $80,000 gold-and-diamond watch. He also paid much of a $3 million bill for the cathedral that became the headquarters of the Alaska Diocese of the Russian Orthodox Church. Although an atheist himself, he did it, he said, to honor his parents. He also donated forty acres of lakefront property and cash valued at $480,000 to Alaska Pacific University because he wanted others to have the education he had missed. Additionally, he made a substantial contribution to build a mobile dental clinic for children in Greece.[31]

By late 1985, University of Alaska economists were warning of an Anchorage building glut. In 1986, Zamarello's lease income dropped from about $13.2 million to $7.2 million. The banks that had lent him money looked more carefully at his financial worth statements and soon found his business in distress. Real estate began a freefall. When a contractor sued Zamarello to collect a due payment of $4.3 million, his empire collapsed, and in August 1986, he filed for protection under Chapter 11 of the bankruptcy laws. During the proceedings it became clear that Zamarello owed about $150 million and that about 250 very unhappy creditors were pursuing him. His became the most complicated bankruptcy case in Alaskan history, as court-appointed examiners tried to unscramble his seven interlocking companies but found that Zamarello had no memory of what had happened to his fortune. He claimed that he had no job, no income, and no cash except for the eight or ten dollars in his pockets. He was colorful on the stand during the proceedings, at one point stating, "I'd rather be a pimp with a purple hat . . . than be associated with banks." Zamarello returned from bankruptcy in 1989 and rejoined the business world with but a fraction of his former holdings. He insisted that he would never build anything in Alaska again, "not even my tomb." Despite it all, he was one of the lucky ones, for he lost other people's money, not his own.[32]

The Banking Crisis

Zamarello's crash was one of the first in the severe recession that hit Alaska in 1986. Banks, suppliers, in fact, the entire real estate industry suffered. Home owners could no longer make payments on fifteen-year mortgages with variable interest rates, and landlords, unable to find renters, declared bankruptcy or simply walked away and left the lending institutions to deal with the problem.[33]

The Alaska Teamsters Federal Credit Union became the first major casualty when federal regulators took it over and later merged it with another credit union. The next casualty was Peninsula Savings and Loan, based out of Soldotna. Then the first bank failed when federal regulators shut down Security National Bank. Within five months all three varieties of Alaska's regulated financial institutions— credit unions, savings and loans, and banks—had been hit. By year's end the list had grown to five. It quickly became obvious that these were not isolated cases but marked the beginning of very hard times for financial institutions.[34]

By 1986 more than half of Alaska's banks and all of the savings and loans were losing income. Nonperforming loans climbed to $325 million. Other real estate owned (OREOs), or bank-owned properties, doubled to $87 million. The Federal Deposit Insurance Corporation (FDIC) moved into Alaska in full force, and credit union membership began to fall for the first time. 1987 proved to be a disaster for an increasing number of Alaska's financial institutions. Hundreds of banking jobs disappeared. Federal regulators either shut down or merged one more savings and loan and four more banks during 1987.[35]

The most spectacular of these involved Alaska Mutual, the state's second largest bank. Two days before year's end, federal regulators merged Alaska Mutual Bank with another troubled bank, United Bank of Alaska, to create the Alliance Bank. Combined, these banks lost $71 million in 1986 and another $231 million in 1987. They were merged instead of shut down because given the size of their assets, some people believed that their collapse would reverberate throughout Alaska's economy and cause irreparable harm. In the long run the FDIC thought it cheaper to bail them out than to let them fail. The FDIC shelled out $295 million and a private investment group put in another $65 million (90 percent guaranteed by the FDIC) to recapitalize the newly formed Alliance Bank. Early in 1988 the United Bank of Alaska Southeast was also merged into the Alliance Bank, temporarily creating the state's largest bank.

The failures continued, with two more in 1988. Since the Great Depression of 1929 no financial institutions had failed in Alaska, and in 1987 alone there were six. Poor management was certainly one reason. If these institutions had not been as eager to grow quickly and had been more careful screening loans and developing a strong deposit base, they might not have failed. All deposits up to one hundred thousand dollars had been insured, but many businesses and individuals with larger deposits in failed institutions lost part of their money. And the recession hastened the exodus of the state's residents. Between 1985 and 1990, civilian out-migrants, about 143,200, outnumbered in-migrants,

The Lure of the Big Project

In February 1987, Governor Cowper requested five hundred thousand dollars from the legislature to create a lobbying arm and pay for the public relations effort he hoped would convince Americans that the Arctic National Wildlife Refuge be opened to oil exploration. The request rushed through the legislature with supporting resolutions from all local governments and civic bodies. Here again, as in the past, politicians and many Alaskans supported great crusades and the expenditure of millions in public funds to convince their fellow citizens, or the American public at large, that salvation lay in some huge project. For example, the construction of the Susitna Dam, the largest dam project under the American flag, was supported by editorial pages and slick brochures by the Alaska Power Authority. Partisan groups tried to justify expending billions of oil dollars and bonding indebtedness payable by future generations to build those monumental concrete piles. Similarly, in the 1960s Senator Ernest Gruening and a powerful coalition of businessmen and politicians had dreamed up the multimegawatt Rampart Dam. Few of its supporters actually believed that the project would produce electrical power at 3.5 mills per kilowatt at tidewater. Even if it had, who would have bought that incredible output?

But then, as now, all eyes were on construction dollars and the immediate boost they would give the Alaskan economy, especially if the federal government would pay for it. And one should not forget the Alaska bid to become the breadbasket of the world. The Delta Project I and II and the Point Mackenzie agricultural venture siphoned off huge numbers of state dollars and the energies of hundreds of devoted participants. Everything had to be accomplished in a hurry because there was no time to lose—never mind that a rational clearing method could have utilized the wood from the forests that had to be removed before planting could begin. At Point Mackenzie, smoke from miles of burn piles containing millions of torched board feet of lumber blackened the sky. Later, of course, large-scale Alaska agriculture collapsed, and the federal government paid the Delta and Point Mackenzie farmers large sums to keep their acres out of production. And the hoped-for rescue? Once again, it was only a stop-gap measure.

about 83,000, by roughly 60,000. Out-migration was greater than in any other period.[36]

Eventually the FDIC assumed $1.5 billion in bad loans and defaulted property from Alaska's failed financial institutions. On a per capita basis, the federal bailout rivaled the national savings and loan scandals that followed. The FDIC sued thirty-three former bank officers and directors in 1991 for $55 million in an attempt to retrieve some of the losses. Most of the defendants, considered pillars of the Alaska establishment, were charged with gross mismanagement, breach of duty, and reckless real estate lending.[37]

The Problem of Taxation

To make up for part of the revenue lost when the collapse of oil prices cut Alaska's oil wealth in half, in early 1987 state legislators were whispering about imposing new state taxes. Alaska's budget stood at $2.2 billion, but revenue forecasters estimated that the state would collect only $1.3 billion in the next fiscal year. Any cash reserves had to be applied toward reducing an estimated $875 million deficit in the 1986–87 budget.

Revenue officials estimated that an income tax, which the legislature had abolished in 1980, would, at its former rate of 16 percent of the federal income tax rate, raise about $400 million annually, while a 1 percent sales tax would bring in an estimated $37.6 million per year. Governor Cowper made things clear when he stated, "[E]verybody understands that we ought to be getting revenue from someplace other than the oil industry." The next question was, who wanted to be taxed? And the answer was, nobody. As Cowper said, everybody understood "the pickle we're in but nobody wants to pay taxes. That's where we are right now."[38] Alaska was, and still is, a tax heaven when compared with other states. Individual Alaskans, then as now, paid virtually no state taxes. The oil industry, through severance, property, and income levies, paid better than 90 percent of general fund tax collections. Alaskans paid an eight-cent-per-gallon tax on fuel and levies on alcohol and tobacco. Most Alaskans paid sales or property taxes, or both, to local governments. However, neither Anchorage nor Fairbanks, home to well over half the state's population, had a sales tax.

Alaskans generally paid modest local taxes when compared with other states. Anchorage, with about half the state's population in 1985, ranked forty-fourth in property tax load among fifty-one cities surveyed in a District of Columbia tax-rate study. The study showed that an Anchorage property owner paid $940 a year on $100,000 in property. Boston and Chicago, median among the study cities, paid property taxes of $1,640 for every $100,000 in assessments. What held local taxes down in Alaska was state aid in the form of revenue sharing, municipal grants, and education funding.[39]

Governor Sheffield's transition team had left a report on possible new state revenue sources, including increases in existing taxes and creation of new levies. It included a variety of oil taxes and other business taxes and licensing fees, sin taxes, individual taxes, and a state lottery (see table 1). In 1986, the state's oil taxes had included the severance tax, levied on oil as it came out of the ground. The tax rate ranged from 15 percent on Prudhoe Bay production to zero on most Cook Inlet fields. The Economic Limit Factor (ELF) was a provision of state tax law that provided lower severance taxes on low-production oil and gas fields. The state also taxed oil and gas production and transportation facilities or

equipment, and there was a tax on oil and gas corporate income. For years legislators have debated whether or not the oil industry should be taxed only on its Alaska income. Revenue officials have pointed out that this method, called separate accounting, meant more revenue when the Alaska oil industry was very profitable. It could bring in less, however, when Alaska profits were low. That was because when Alaska profits were low, worldwide industry revenues, taxable under the prevailing system of modified apportionment, were often higher and acted as a buffer. Whatever the accounting method, an increase in the income tax rates for both oil and non-oil businesses, with a higher rate applied to bigger profits, could raise an additional $280 million a year.

Other business taxes and license fees included the corporate income tax, which applied to nonpetroleum businesses; a fuel tax, which applied to highway, marine, and aviation fuels; a tax on business gross receipts paid by most businesses; and taxes on canned salmon and floating and shore-based fish processors. In fiscal year 1987 the state expected about three hundred thousand dollars in revenue from the mining license tax, the only tax applied exclusively to mining.

So-called sin taxes were levied on tobacco and alcohol. Liquor was taxed at a higher rate than wine and beer. Possible individual taxes included the personal income tax, and it might also be possible to add a state sales tax or to reinstate the school head tax. The state levied no sales tax, although seven boroughs and fifty-nine municipalities collect sales taxes at rates ranging from 1 to 5 percent. Forty-five out of fifty states also levied such a tax, exempting certain goods and services such as food, clothing, and utilities. In earlier years the state had also assessed each citizen a ten-dollar tax to help pay for school needs, but the legislature had repealed the school head tax along with the personal income tax in 1980. Alaskan politicians were not seriously considering other individual taxes, like a real property tax, personal property tax, or land speculation tax. One more source of income that was increasingly common in the contiguous states was the lottery. In the 1986 legislative session a lottery was proposed for Alaska, estimated to raise about $12 million per year.[40]

TABLE 1

Real and Possible Revenue from Taxes in Alaska, FY 1987, 1988

TAX	ESTIMATED REVENUE ($) 1987 (OR 1988)	ESTIMATED REVENUE ($) WITH INCREASE
Severance tax	470.6 million	540–620 million[a]
Property tax on oil and gas production facilities	89 million	105 million
Oil and gas production income tax	130 million	410 million[b]
Non-oil corporate income tax	17 million	110 million
Fuel tax	33.3 million	66.6 million
Business income tax	(38.4–62.3 million)	NA
Fish taxes	22 million	NA
Mining license tax	300,000	NA
Tobacco tax	7 million	8.5 million
Alcohol tax	123.8 million	128.5 million
Income tax	—	400 million
Sales tax	—	29.2–37.6 million
School head tax	—	5 million
Lottery	—	12 million
Total	**931.4–955.3 million**	**~1.8 billion**

Source: *Anchorage Daily News,* January 16, 1987.

[a]By eliminating or modifying the ELF, FY1988.
[b]Oil and nonoil businesses.

There was, however, little enthusiasm for, or even adamant opposition to, any taxes. State Senator Rick Halford stated that he thought that "the public feels the first step is to reduce government spending." State Representative Ben Grussendorf thought that "the general public is going to have to be educated [about the fiscal crisis]. And this is not going to occur for many months." Dick Randolph, a former Libertarian Party leader and unsuccessful Republican candidate for governor, an-nounced that he would "make a lot of noise" if the governor and the legislature imposed new taxes. Randolph had led initiative petition drives to accomplish other political goals. He acknowledged that article 11, section 7, of the Alaska State Constitution barred the use of citizen initiatives to kill taxes, but he stated that "you can be sure we'd look at advisory petitions, anything to get across that thousands of Alaskans oppose new taxes."[41]

In March 1987, Senator Don Bennett, a Fairbanks

area legislator, sponsored a day-long session where revenue-raising ideas were discussed. Fred Pratt, a columnist for the local newspaper, wrote that most of them did "not hold much water" when examined closely. "None will make nearly enough money to do what their champions claim." The Alaska Department of Revenue, Pratt pointed out, had warned the legislature that it would "be practically impossible to replace petroleum revenues with taxes on individuals or other industrial sectors given the present structure of the Alaskan economy."[42]

The 1987 legislative session did not deal with the fiscal gap, nor did subsequent ones. Governor Cowper asked the legislature in 1987, 1988, and 1989 for permission to spend as much as $500 million in Permanent Fund earnings on state government, but the lawmakers turned him down. In 1989, he barnstormed Alaska with his plan to create an Education Endowment. His plan would have diverted Permanent Fund earnings into this special account that eventually would produce about $700 million annually to support public schools, although not the University of Alaska. It would, if approved, have cut the growth of the Permanent Fund and with it, the dividends paid to Alaskans each year. That meant that the Permanent Fund itself would no longer have kept pace with inflation.[43] Cowper's idea did not resonate with either the legislature or the public.

Deeply disappointed with his inability to translate any of his ideas into effective policies and legislation, Cowper decided not to seek a second gubernatorial term. He traveled to Fairbanks and met with reporters at the *Fairbanks Daily News-Miner* on the morning of March 25, 1989. There he announced his decision. His intention was to give his party time to recruit a suitable successor. During his meeting with reporters, he was handed a note from the Governor's Office, telling him that the tanker *Exxon Valdez* had run aground on Bligh Reef near Valdez in Prince William Sound on the previous night, spilling more than 11 million gallons of North Slope crude oil. Governor Cowper, now a lame duck, had his hands full dealing with that massive disaster. It was, to date, the worst oil spill in U.S. history. Things were looking grim as Alaska entered the 1990s.

Chapter 19
Native Land Claims

There can be no doubt that the descendants of Alaska's aboriginal inhabitants historically have participated but little in Alaska's economic development and its attendant social benefits. As a consequence they have suffered loss of lands and resources essential to their traditional ways of life.[1] Organized protest had been weak, sporadic, and divided along ethnic and geographical lines.

The First Organic Act of 1884 and the Second Organic Act of 1912 contained disclaimers for lands used and occupied by Natives. The Statehood Act of 1958 renewed this pledge, specifically stating that the new state and its people disclaimed all rights or title to lands "the right or title to which may be held by Eskimos, Indians, or Aleuts" or held in trust for them. It did not, however, define the "right or title" that Natives might have, correctly leaving this for future action by Congress or the courts. More important, Congress granted the new state the right to select over 100 million acres from vacant, unappropriated, and unreserved public lands, and hundreds of thousands of acres from the national forests and other public lands. Congress intended that new state become "master in fact of most of the natural resources within its boundaries."[2] In the meantime, Alaska Natives, who made up about one-fifth of the state's population in 1960, continued to live mostly where they constituted a majority—in approximately two hundred villages and settlements widely scattered across rural Alaska. They confidently expected to continue using the land as their ancestors had used it for thousands of years.

Soon, however, threats to Native land rights emerged, to which Natives responded by forming local and regional organizations, eventually uniting statewide. The fear of losing their land aroused many Natives and radicalized them. An identity revolution occurred in villages across Alaska during the 1960s, and by 1968 the inhabitants of the most remote settlements understood what was at stake. A number of factors had contributed to that revolution: one was the establishment on October 1, 1962, of the *Tundra Times*, the first statewide Native newspaper, under the capable editorship of Point Hope Eskimo artist Howard Rock; another was the emergence of several energetic and able young Native leaders who were able to identify simultaneously as U.S. citizens and as Natives.

While the 1968 Prudhoe Bay oil discovery captured public attention, of perhaps greater long-range importance for Alaska was the Alaska Native Claims Settlement Act of 1971, known as ANCSA. The provisions of this legislation embraced two basically unrelated causes: the fight of Native Alaskans for a greater share and role in Alaska's development and a national concern that the course of this development would not endanger lands of special conservation value.

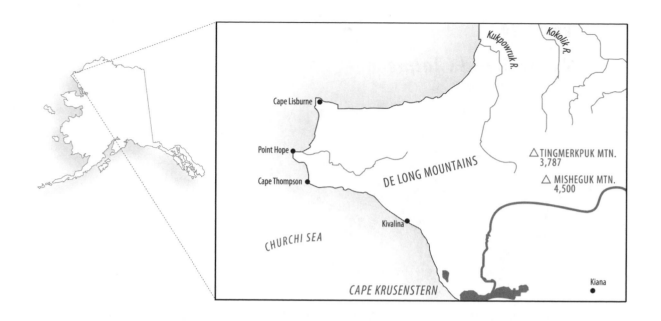

The Cape Thompson Area

Project Chariot and Iñupiat Paitot

The first government threat to Native lands oc-curred as early as 1957. On June 19 of that year the Atomic Energy Commission (AEC) established the Plowshare Program to develop the peaceful uses of atomic energy. In November scientists at the Ra-diation Laboratory at the University of California at Berkeley recommended to the AEC that large earth excavations promised the earliest success in the Plowshare Program. By the end of the year they had designed a massive explosion, equal to 2.4 million tons of TNT, known as Project Chariot.[3]

After considering a number of ideas, the physicists decided to blast an artificial harbor—or at least a hole that could be made to look like a harbor—at Cape Thompson, on Alaska's northwest coast. In 1958 the AEC asked the U.S. Geological Survey for a study of the geological and oceanographic factors relevant to excavating a harbor on the Alaska coast between Nome and Point Barrow. Later it requested a detailed report on the twenty-mile coastal strip south of Cape Thompson, and the Radiation Laboratory contracted with the E. J. Longyear Company to study the eco-nomic potential of minerals along the coast. No travel money was authorized for either study.[4]

Whale rib grave marker at Point Hope on the Arctic coast.

(Courtesy of John Trent, Alaska Department of Fish and Game.)

In April 1958, both reports came back. The Geological Survey found "the northwest coast of Alaska . . . relatively unknown geologically," while the Cape Thompson area was "largely unexplored" and ice-blocked nine months of the year. Longyear reported optimistically that within twenty-five years a port at Cape Thompson would handle the "substantial" amounts of oil and coal believed to be abundant near the cape. Both reports had been based on literature searches of relevant data rather than on investigations on the spot. On June 5, 1958, Lewis Strauss, a chairman of the AEC, requested a 1,600-square-mile withdrawal of land and water from the public domain in the Cape Thompson area. The explosion was scheduled for 1960.[5]

In July 1958, Edward Teller, the famous physicist and father of the hydrogen bomb, led a group of scientists and AEC officials to Alaska to sell Project Chariot. Teller assured his Alaska audiences that two-thirds of the projected $5 million targeted for the project would be spent in Alaska. The Alaska press wholeheartedly supported the blast because it would funnel needed federal funds into the new state and put Alaska on the map, but business leaders were skeptical of the alleged mineral deposits and the need for a harbor. A few members of the

science faculty of the University of Alaska, a handful of citizens, and a few key government officials questioned the alleged safety of the proposed blast.

Alaska dissenters demanded that the AEC establish a scientific basis for its assertion that Project Chariot would harm neither human life nor livelihood. Faced with this task, the AEC lost faith in the project and announced it would have to be dropped for lack of support in the state. Lawrence Laboratory physicists quickly recognized that a crisis existed. Two of them toured the state warning that Project Chariot's fate depended on endorsements by chambers of commerce and the state legislature. Soon some chambers of commerce were backing the project, and others were falling into line, while the legislature gave its official blessing. Preparations resumed, but then the AEC announced that the project would be only an excavation experiment because the harbor likely would not be commercially useful.[6]

The officials of the AEC apparently did not consider it important to consult the people of Point Hope, who utilized the resources of the coast, including those of the Cape Thompson area. Prehistoric Iñupiat hunters had discovered a spit of land jutting twenty miles into the Chukchi Sea, pointing like a finger back across the water to Asia, just

160 miles away. They called the place Tikiraq, the Iñupiaq word for "forefinger." The peninsula was an ideal place for intercepting migrating sea mammals, and from there the people of Tikiraq hunted walrus, seals, polar bears, and beluga and bowhead whales, and they collected the eggs of nesting seabirds from the inland cliffs near a little stream called Ogotoruk. Oral history accounts agree that the early inhabitants of the region around Tikiraq organized themselves into a social system similar to a modern nation. They occupied a precisely defined territory, defended it, and sometimes penetrated several hundred miles into neighboring dominions. In time, they became the largest and most powerful society in northern Alaska.[7]

In 1960 the village had a population of about eight hundred residents. In March of that year AEC officials visited Point Hope and a string of other Arctic villages. Their intention, obviously, was to warm the residents to the idea of excavating a harbor at Cape Thompson, because the Geological Survey report had shown that along the 1,600-mile coastline from Nome to Point Barrow there were only eleven locations as much as twenty miles away from any human habitation. The village council members of Point Hope listened politely and then voted unanimously to oppose Project Chariot. On March 3, 1961, the Point Hope village Health Council wrote President John F. Kennedy in opposition to the proposed chain explosion of five atomic bombs. The blast, they objected, would be "too close to our hunting and fishing areas. We read about the cumulative and retained isotope burden in man that must be considered. We also know about strontium 90, how it might harm people if too much of it gets into our body. We have seen the summary Reports of 1960, National Academy of Science, on 'The Biological Effects of Atomic Radiation.' We are deeply concerned about the health of our people now and for the future that is coming."[8]

The Point Hope residents had deep roots in the past and were unwilling to jeopardize the continued existence of their village. Archaeological records indicted a continued existence for at least five thousand years at that village on a spit of land projecting like a finger into the Chukchi Sea, and for that same period the inhabitants had depended on the fish, seals, and whales of the sea and the game animals, chiefly caribou, of the immediate hinterland. An atomic explosion, they feared, could end the existence of Point Hope.

Meanwhile, another controversy was brewing in Barrow, the state's northernmost settlement. State Representative John Nusunginya, an Iñupiat, was arrested for shooting ducks outside the hunting season established by an international migratory bird treaty. Barrow Eskimos had hunted ducks, geese, and other migratory waterfowl since time immemorial. The treaty had long made this practice unlawful, but federal agents in Alaska had overlooked the Barrow Eskimo hunting practices. Now Natives insisted that it was their right to hunt, and they intentionally and en masse broke the law. Two days after Nusunginya's arrest, 138 other men shot ducks and presented themselves to federal game wardens for arrest, but they were merely cited for their violations. The federal government dropped all charges against them in 1961, in essence recognizing that Native hunting practices had precedence over international treaties.[9]

Finally, in November 1961, representatives from all along the coast met at Point Barrow for a conference on Native rights sponsored by the Association on American Indian Affairs, a private charitable organization based in New York City. They discussed many of their mutual concerns. The Native representatives claimed that the proposed site for Project Chariot belonged to them and asked the Department of the Interior to revoke the research license the Bureau of Land Management (BLM) had granted to the AEC. The representatives opened their report by saying: "We the Inupiat have come together for the first time ever in all the years of our history. We had to come together in meeting from our far villages from Lower Kuskokwim to Point Barrow. We had to come from so far together for this reason. We always thought our Inupiat Paitot [the people's heritage] was safe to be passed down to our future generations as our fathers passed down to us. Our Inupiat Paitot is our land around the whole Arctic world where the Inupiat live."[10]

Eskimo resistance and public opposition eventually forced the government to abandon Project Chariot at Cape Thompson. Furthermore, the conference won the attention of high officials of the Department of the Interior and also led to the development of the first regional Native organization to be established since the founding of the Alaska Native Brotherhood nearly half a century earlier. The new organization adopted the name Iñupiat Paitot (the People's Heritage) and elected as president Guy Okakok of Barrow.

Protesting State Land Selections in the Minto Flats

Project Chariot had been aborted, but there were other dangers to Native land rights. The Alaska Statehood Act constituted the greatest threat, because while it recognized the right of Natives to lands that they used and occupied, it did not and could not provide any means of assuring such use and occupancy. State land selections thus endangered the continued use of lands by Natives.

It was in the Minto Lakes region of interior Alaska that state land selections first conflicted with Native hunting, fishing, and trapping activities. In 1961 the state wanted to establish a recreation area near the Athapaskan village of Minto and construct a road into the area to make it accessible to Fairbanks residents. State officials also had an eye on the future development of oil and other resources in the area.[11] In the fall of 1961, the Alaska Division of Lands filed land selection applications that requested the BLM to convey to the state legal title to 4.16 million acres of land near the Athapaskan villages of Minto, Northway, and Tanacross.

Learning of these state plans, the village of Minto asked the U.S Department of the Interior to protect their rights and reject the state's application for the land. In response, James Hawkins, the Alaska area director of the Bureau of Indian Affairs (BIA), instructed his acting area director to protest the approval of the state land selection. Late in 1961, the bureau began filing protests on behalf of the Natives of Minto, Northway, Tanacross, and Lake Alegnagik over land totaling approximately 5,860,000 acres and conflicting with some 1,750,000 acres of state selection.[12] Shortly after the protest, the bureau transferred Hawkins to its office in Minneapolis, Minnesota.

Attempts to block state land selections caused an uproar in Alaska and put great political pressure on the Department of the Interior. In January 1962, the Alaska Commissioner of Natural Resources, Phil Holdsworth, publicly expressed concern that the Native protest filings would hold up the whole program of state land selection. In February 1962, Dan Jones, the head of the BLM's Fairbanks office, dismissed Hawkins's protests and stated that the villages could technically appeal to the secretary of the interior.

As early as December 1961, the Department of the Interior reacted by ordering the state director of the BLM for Alaska to dismiss protests unless the claims clearly fell within the regulation that "lands occupied by Indians, Aleuts, and Eskimos in good faith are not subject to entry or appropriation by others." On February 20, 1962, the regional solicitor for the Department of the Interior issued an opinion in which he asserted that "Indian title" was involved in the protest and that therefore a determination of the facts had to be made.

Subsequently BLM managers were told not to accept protests of this kind. The solicitor suggested that the protests be dismissed on jurisdictional grounds because the only occupancy recognized in BLM regulations was that which led to the issuance of allotments under the Alaska Native Allotment Act. Following these instructions, BLM personnel in 1962 dismissed a number of Native protests, which the claimants then appealed to the director of the BLM. Early in 1963 the director advised Alaska BLM offices to make no more decisions at the local level and instead to forward case records to Washington for consideration.[13]

While Native leaders and the BIA undertook the complex procedures involved in the protest and appeal process and the BLM weighed what steps to take next, the Alaska Conservation Society met in Fairbanks in February 1963 to discuss the proposed Minto Lakes recreation area. Attending the meeting were about 150 local sportsmen and conservationists, as well as Richard Frank, chief of the Minto Flats people, who hunted and fished and found some seasonal employment with the river barge companies and as firefighters. The Minto Flats people used more than 1 million acres of land, including the lakes where the state planned its recreation area, in their search for food. Frank told his listeners that the lakes belonged to his people, that the area was their traditional hunting ground, and that without the use of the area his people would go hungry. Frank also told how the BIA had asked his people in 1937 whether they wanted to go to a reservation. The village had rejected the idea, but Frank's father, then the chief, had made a map showing the area where they hunted and fished. In 1951 the Minto Flats people had filed a land claim with the Fairbanks office of the BLM. The chief at that time had simply taken a map and indicated with a circle the approximate area his people used. Later, in the wake of oil and gas exploration around nearby Nenana in 1961, Frank had taken his father's map to the BLM office and indicated what lands his people claimed. Frank resented the fact that the state now planned to build a road across village-claimed lands without consultation.[14]

Meanwhile, the BIA appealed the dismissal of Hawkins's original protest to John Carver, the assistant secretary of the interior for public land management, who supervised both the BLM and the BIA. When the files reached his office, he decided not to act on them. So the three village land applications were consigned to a filing cabinet. Six months later, Senator E. L. "Bob" Bartlett inquired about their status. Carver told him that the appeals raised "extremely complex" issues that required "extensive study and research" to resolve.[15]

Roscoe Bell, head of the Alaska State Division of Lands, suggested that the state and the Minto people resolve their differences. He proposed that the state select and patent the land and then sell parcels of it back to the Indians. Frank flatly refused to go along with the scheme: "As long as I'm chief, we won't give up our land. We have the same idea the state has. The state wants to develop this land and that's our aim, too." Thereupon the Minto people hired attorney Ted Stevens, who had just spent a number of years in the solicitor's office at the Department of the Interior. Stevens offered his services for free.[16]

The *Tundra Times* spread Frank's fighting words to every Native community in the northern part of Alaska. Editor Howard Rock, commenting on what was happening in Minto, wrote: "We Natives should realize that we will not be able to compete fully with big business for a long time yet. Since we cannot do that now, we should try to hold on to our lands because that is the greatest insurance we can have. . . . Without land, we can become the poorest people in the world."[17]

The Rampart Canyon Dam Project

Between 1962 and 1966, threats to Native-claimed lands multiplied, and the story of Minto was repeated over and over again. The most spectacular involved the proposal for building a dam at the Rampart Canyon, on the Yukon River. At a cost of several billion dollars, the dam would generate 5 million kilowatts and would put the entire Yukon Flats—a vast network of sloughs, marshes, and potholes that is one of the largest wildfowl breeding grounds in North America—under several hundred feet of water. The proponents of the scheme, the U.S. Army Corps of Engineers, intended to create a lake with a surface greater than that of Lake Erie or the state of New Jersey; it would take approximately twenty years to fill.

An organization named Yukon Power for America, armed with an initial budget of one hundred thousand dollars, intended to lobby the Rampart project through Congress. Businessmen, newspaper publishers, chambers of commerce, and mayors of Alaska's principal cities belonged to the group. Yukon Power for America published a colorful brochure titled *The Rampart Story,* which extolled the benefits of cheap electrical power, namely, three mills per kilowatt-hour. This power would in turn attract industry, it was said, notably the aluminum industry. Alaska's junior U.S. senator, Ernest Gruening, wholeheartedly supported the project.[18]

The U.S. Fish and Wildlife Service, on the other hand, reported to the Army Corps of Engineers that "nowhere in the history of water development in North America have the fish and wildlife losses anticipated to result from a single project been so overwhelming." The authors of the report strongly opposed authorization of the Rampart Canyon Dam and Reservoir. Paul Brooks, a conservation writer, estimated that about 1,200 Natives would have to be relocated elsewhere; that the livelihood of 5,000 to 6,000 more in Alaska and approximately 3,500 in Canada's Yukon Territory would be affected by the reduction in the salmon run; and that the moose range, with an estimated eventual carrying capacity of twelve thousand animals, would disappear, together with wildfowl breeding grounds and the smaller furbearers.[19]

Rampart Dam eventually died a quiet death for a variety of reasons, including adverse ecological and economic reports backed by the opposition of Alaska's Natives and an increasingly well-informed public.

Alternatives for Settling Native Claims

During these controversies the state had continued to claim its allotted lands, and by 1968 it had selected 19.6 million acres, some 8.5 million acres of which had been tentatively approved and over 6 million acres of which had been patented. In the same year, Alaska Natives had legal ownership of fewer than five hundred acres and held in restricted title only fifteen thousand acres. Some nine hundred Native families lived on twenty-three reserves administered by the BIA. These reserves, which included 1.25 million acres of reindeer lands, totaled 4 million acres. An estimated 270 million acres of land remained in the public domain. About 37,000 rural Alaska Natives lived on that land and the twenty-three Native reserves, while another 15,600 of their kin lived in Alaska's urban areas. The only recourse open to Natives consisted of filing protests to the state land selections, and between 1961 and April 1, 1968, Native protest filings covered some 296 million acres; by the middle of 1968 the filings covered almost 337 million acres.[20]

Early in 1963 the Alaska Task Force on Native Affairs, established by the Department of the Interior, issued a report that stated that a resolution of Native land rights was long overdue. The report cited the failure of the First Organic Act to provide the means by which Natives might obtain title to land and noted that in the following seventy-eight years Congress had "largely sidestepped the issue of aboriginal claims." If Congress ever was going to define Native rights, the report concluded, it should do so promptly. The Alaska Task Force also included

An Eskimo woman cooking in camp along the shores of the Chukchi Sea.

(Photograph by Robert Belous; courtesy of the National Park Service.)

specific recommendations for solving the Native land problem. It called for the prompt granting of up to 160 acres to individuals for homes, fish camps, and hunting sites; withdrawal of "small acreages" for village growth; and designation of areas for Native use—but not ownership—in traditional food-gathering activities.[21]

With the help of the Association on American Indian Affairs and its executive director, William Byler, Alaska Natives successfully opposed the implementation of the task force recommendations. Part of the opposition was based on the fact that they included no provisions for cash payment for land lost or for mineral rights for lands Natives would receive. Alaska's congressional delegation offered differing approaches as well. Senator Gruening favored settlement through the U.S. Court of Claims, while Representative Rivers felt that would take too long. He favored congressional extinguishment of Native claims coupled with cash compensation. Senator Bartlett urged that state land selections be allowed to proceed before a land settlement was reached. One million acres for villages would be sufficient, he suggested, while cash payment should be made for other lands Natives claimed.[22]

At that point four basic courses of action seemed plausible: Natives might seek the establishment of reserves under existing laws, resolve their claims in the federal Court of Claims, obtain legislation at the state level to protect their land rights, or attempt a congressional settlement. Reserves would be held in trust for Natives by the federal government, and thus that option did not hold great appeal. The history of reservations outside Alaska showed Natives that they were no more than holding pens, which was no solution. Earlier experience with the long delays in the court system, with claims taking over twenty-five years to resolve, made the judicial alternative unattractive. (Congress had allowed the Tlingit-Haida to sue in 1935 [see chapter 11], but not until 1959 had the Court of Claims supported the case and decreed that their claims were compensable. Later the compensation was fixed at $7.5 million.) State action was rejected because most state legislators agreed that Native land rights could be resolved only by Congress.[23]

Native leaders briefly considered state legislation that might protect their rights. One proposal would have created twenty-square-mile reservations surrounding villages, a proposal rejected as inadequate. But most Native leaders also realized that congressional settlement was enormously uncertain; because Congress was sovereign, it could extinguish or recognize rights, grant little or no land, or decide to give compensation only for surrendered lands. While the various alternatives were being examined and discussed, none was pursued. That would have to await the formation of a statewide Native organization with sufficient financial resources to pursue a settlement.

The AFN and the Land Freeze

What made the organization of a statewide group difficult was the deeply rooted mistrust that many Natives harbored for people outside their own geographical regions. Yet throughout the 1960s various Native groups and organizations and numerous individual villages met in Anchorage to form the organization that was to become the Alaska Federation of Natives (AFN). In the preamble to its constitution, adopted the following year, the AFN made its purpose clear. It was to secure the rights and benefits to which Natives were entitled under the laws of the United States and Alaska, enlighten the general public about Natives, preserve cultural values and seek an equitable solution to Native claims, promote the common welfare of Alaskan Natives, and foster continued loyalty and allegiance to Alaska and the United States.[24]

Despite some disagreements with Eskimos and interior Athapaskans, the AFN began to function in 1967. Before it became a reality, however, Secretary of the Interior Stewart Udall acted on one of the AFN's recommendations and imposed a "land freeze," effectively stopping all transfers of federal lands until Congress had settled the land claims issue. Udall's action followed Native protests against state plans to sell gas-and-oil leases on the North Slope on lands tentatively approved for patent to the state.[25]

In the meantime, Governor Egan had lost to Republican Walter Hickel in the 1966 elections, while Republican Howard Pollock had defeated Representative Ralph Rivers, who had not favored a settlement. Before Hickel's election, the Egan administration and the Democratic congressional delegation had maintained that the land claims were a federal problem. During his campaign, Hickel had not stressed the claims issue but had concentrated on the theme of getting Alaska moving economically.[26]

After he became governor, Hickel promptly overrode a BLM decision not to allow the lease sale, which then proceeded as planned. In the meantime, Native leaders tried to enlist the governor's support for a settlement. After initial resistance, Hickel proposed the outlines of such a settlement, calling for granting Natives full title to some lands around their villages and surface rights to a larger acreage.[27]

In May 1967, the Department of the Interior finally drafted a settlement bill for congressional consideration. In essence the measure proposed a grant of fifty thousand acres to each Native village and the payment of a small amount of cash to each individual. The Department of the Interior, however, would maintain its paternalistic role and control both the land and the money.[28]

The AFN, learning of the proposal, met in Anchorage and voted to oppose it. It asked Senator Gruening to introduce legislation making possible a Court of Claims settlement instead. In the late fall the AFN met again, this time to listen to Hickel's attorney general, Edgar Paul Boyko, urge cooperation between Native communities and the state against the Department of the Interior, which he characterized as a common enemy. The state was eager to come to a settlement, afraid that lengthy litigation would cause the oil companies with lease holdings in the Arctic to leave. Boyko promised to compensate Natives for lands already taken on the basis of their value at the time of statehood in 1959 and to give full title to other lands as well. A few weeks later Hickel appointed thirty-seven members of a Land Claims Task Force, which was to write a mutually acceptable bill.[29]

The state was eager to find a solution; the land area affected by Udall's freeze had rapidly grown as Natives had filed additional claims, ranging from a 640-acre claim by Chilkoot village to the 58 million acres claimed by the Arctic Slope Native Association. Because many of the claims were overlapping, the total acreage amounted to 380 million acres, more than the state's land area.[30]

In January 1968, the Land Claims Task Force delivered its report, recommending that legal possession of 40 million acres be given to Native villages, that all lands currently used for hunting and fishing activities be available for such purposes for one hundred years, that the Native Allotment Act enabling Alaska Natives to obtain legal title to 160-acre homesteads (see chapter 10) remain in force, and that 10 percent of the income from the sale or lease of oil rights from certain lands be paid to Natives, up to a total of at least $65 million. The settlement was to be carried out by business corporations,

one of which would be statewide, the rest organized by villages and regions. The task force also recommended that the state legislature pass companion legislation providing $50 million to Natives from mineral revenues from certain lands, but only if the freeze was lifted before the end of 1968.[31]

In 1968, Senator Gruening introduced a bill based on the recommendations of the Land Claims Task Force. The Senate Interior and Insular Affairs Committee promptly held a three-day hearing in Anchorage, which opened on February 8, 1968. A large crowd, including many Eskimos, Indians, and Aleuts from across the state, attended the hearing. Committee members listened to Native leaders explain the proposed settlement and urge prompt action on the measure.

The principal opposition came from the Alaska Sportsmen's Council, which objected to the granting of public lands but approved of cash payments. On the other hand, the Alaska Miners' Association, represented by George Moerlein, of its Land Use Committee, claimed that the U.S. government was "neither legally nor morally obligated to grant any of the claims put forth by the various Native groups or by the Native Land Claims Task Force."[32]

Committee members also listened to older village people describe why a settlement was needed. Peter John, of Minto, described how plentiful game used to be around his home but how increasing hunting pressure from non-Natives had caused a steep decline. He said that there had once been an abundance of furbearing animals, such as muskrats, mink, fox, beaver, and otter. Mining activities, however, had filled many of the lakes and creeks with silt, driven away the furbearing animals, and killed most of the fish. Walter Charley, of the Copper River Indians, said: "Game, up to a few years ago, was always plentiful. Some of my people still hunt moose as well as caribou. They have to live. We also fish. Two years ago the state put very strict limits on the number of fish that each family could take. We were only allowed twenty sockeye salmon and five king salmon." (After much protest, this limit had been increased to two hundred fish.) There were few jobs; out of a total of five hundred people in the Copper River area, only twelve held full-time jobs. "The rest of

Eskimo hunters at Cape Krusenstern National Monument, Alaska.

(Courtesy of the National Park Service.)

our people live from hand to mouth and the living they can make from a little bit of trapping, fishing, and firefighting." George King, an Eskimo from Nunivak Island, complained that the federal government had reserved the island as a national wildlife refuge in the 1930s: "The island has apparently been set aside for ducks, musk ox, and reindeer. We have not even been able to get a townsite, and, according to the Executive Order establishing the reservation, we are not even there. It is hard for us to understand why the government reserves all of Nunivak Island for the animals and left none of it for the people." The government, contrary to previous pledges, had deprived the Nunivak Islanders of all their land.[33]

The Hickel administration generally supported the proposed settlement but urged speedy lifting of the land freeze because it prevented oil leasing on federal lands. Since the state received 90 percent of the federal revenues from such leases, it was losing money. After the election of Republican Richard Nixon to the presidency in 1968, Native leaders worried about the continuation of the land freeze, which, in Udall's words, had "held everyone's feet to the fire." Just before giving up his office, Udall signed an executive order changing the informal freeze into law.[34]

President-elect Nixon chose Governor Hickel to replace Udall. Hickel, who had a reputation as a developer, needed all the support he could obtain, including that of the AFN, because powerful conservationist groups objected to his Senate confirmation. In return for AFN support, Hickel promised to extend the land freeze until 1971 or until the claims were settled. He was confirmed by the Senate as Nixon's new secretary of the interior.[35]

In 1968, Senator Henry Jackson, chairman of the Senate Interior and Insular Affairs Committee, asked the Federal Field Committee for Development Planning in Alaska to carry out a comprehensive study dealing with the social and economic status of the state's Native peoples. Headed by Joseph H. Fitzgerald, this small federal agency had been established following the 1964 Good Friday earthquake to coordinate planning among federal and state agencies. Early in 1969 the committee completed its 565-page study of the Native land problem. The committee recommended a land grant of between 4 and 7 million acres, granting Natives the right to use public lands for subsistence, a $100 million compensation for lands taken in the past, and a 10 percent royalty on mineral revenues from public lands in Alaska for ten years.[36]

Congressional hearings on proposed claims legislation were held in 1969, but no bill emerged from the committees. The Native cause was strengthened through the continuation of the land freeze, support from the Association on American Indian Affairs, and various national newspapers. Furthermore, former Supreme Court Justice Arthur Goldberg represented the AFN, enhancing its national image. Soon Ramsey Clark, former U.S. attorney general, joined Goldberg.[37]

Still More Proposals

In the meantime, the Department of the Interior proposed a settlement differing considerably from that endorsed by Hickel's task force. The department proposed to give Natives about 12.5 million acres of land instead of 40 million, and $500 million instead of $20 million, but no royalty or any sort of revenue sharing. Soon the Natives presented their own proposal, which included full title to 40 million acres of land, allocated among the villages according to their size; $500 million and a 2 percent royalty in perpetuity on all revenues from all other public and state lands in Alaska; and the creation of a statewide Native development corporation and up to twelve regional corporations, coinciding with areas inhabited by various Native groups, who were to manage the land and money received in the settlement.[38] It was a far-reaching proposal, designed to avoid problems that had arisen elsewhere with Indian claims settlements. It avoided a per capita distribution of cash—which could be quickly squandered—and also retained the Native concept of communally held land but adapted it to changing times.

The various interest groups responded quickly. The Department of the Interior recommended that all federal reservations, including Naval Petroleum Reserve No. 4, which Alaskans and the oil industry had long been trying to open for development (see chapter 11), be used in settling the claims. The Forest Service objected to including any portions of the Chugach and Tongass national forests in the settlement. Conservationists wanted Native communities to receive as little federal refuge land as possible and also wanted guarantees that none of the land would pass out of Native hands. The Natives strenuously ob-

Eskimo drying caribou meat, Brooks Range, Alaska.

(Courtesy of the Alaska Department of Fish and Game.)

jected to any Department of the Interior trusteeship.

The oil and gas industry worried because the Federal Field Committee had suggested that competitive leasing should be required throughout the state, not just in areas known to contain oil. The various independent companies knew that this would mean bonus leasing, requiring large outlays of cash at the time leases were sold, and feared that they would be unable to compete with the major oil companies. Ten Canadian independent oil companies had a special problem because they had filed for noncompetitive federal oil and gas leases in Alaska between March 1967 and November 1968. The lease applications covered approximately 20 million acres and had cost $3 million altogether. But because of

State of Alaska oil lease at Sydney Laurence auditorium, 1969. At the microphone is Governor Keith Miller.

(Courtesy of Ward Wells Collection, Anchorage Museum of History and Art.)

the Native protests and the land freeze, the BLM had not processed these applications. The Canadian companies wanted language in the bill protecting their priority rights.[39]

The Western Oil and Gas Association wanted to be sure that existing federal and state mineral leases were not changed, while other oil companies and the state wanted to make sure that tentative approval for patent, as well as actual patenting, would be considered an "existing right." The state had al-

ready leased some 2.4 million acres, mostly on the North Slope, which were only tentatively approved for patent by the BLM at the time of the land freeze. Furthermore, the state planned to offer more leases on tentatively approved land at its September 10, 1969, lease sale.

While the settlements proposed by the Department of the Interior recognized tentative approval as a valid right, the Natives argued that their claims took precedence over the Statehood Act and that they should be allowed to take tentatively selected state lands. This cast a shadow on the validity of the state oil and gas leases on these lands. The state also worried about Native claims to tentatively approved lands, and Governor Keith Miller's administration argued that mineral rights to any land given to Natives remain under state control since the Statehood Act had given the state control over all leasable minerals. Giving these rights to individuals or corporations constituted a violation of that compact.[40]

Senate Interior and Insular Affairs Committee Chairman Henry Jackson, angry over the bickering within his committee and leaks to the press, announced that his committee planned to disregard all previous settlement proposals and start from scratch. The committee was back where it had been the previous summer.[41] In the meantime, the state held its twenty-third competitive oil lease sale in Anchorage on September 10, 1969, bringing in over $900 million in bonus bids. The sale was the psychological high point for Alaskans since the discovery of the Prudhoe Bay field in 1968.

Soon the Trans-Alaska Pipeline System (TAPS), the incorporated joint venture of Atlantic Richfield, British Petroleum, and Humble Oil, applied to the Department of the Interior to construct a hot-oil pipeline from Prudhoe Bay, in the Arctic, to Valdez, on Prince William Sound, a distance of 798 miles. Interior Secretary Hickel was under pressure from opposing interest groups: the oil companies and most Alaskans wanted the $900 million project to get under way, while conservationists wanted it delayed because of the innumerable environmental, technical, and economic questions that the project posed.[42]

After much negotiating—and when Secretary Hickel was just about to issue the permit for the construction of the North Slope haul road—on March 9, 1970, five Native villages asked the federal district court in Washington to stop Secretary Hickel from issuing the permit. The villages said they were claiming the ground over which the pipeline and the road would pass. Avoiding the Native claims issue, Federal Judge George L. Hart, Jr., enjoined the Interior Department from issuing a construction permit across 19.8 miles of the route over the land claimed by sixty-six residents of Stevens Village. A few days later three conservation groups sued the Department of the Interior, asking for a halt in the TAPS project because it violated stipulations of the 1920 Mineral Leasing Act and the new National Environmental Policy Act. On April 13, 1970, Judge Hart issued a temporary injunction against the TAPS project.[43] By now the oil companies realized that there would be no pipeline unless the Native land claims were settled first. British Petroleum soon agreed to help lobby for a Native claims bill and agreed to persuade its partners to do likewise.

Alaska Natives Finally Compensated

In mid-April 1970, Senator Jackson outlined the provisions of a bill on which his committee had tentatively agreed. It awarded $1 billion to Alaska Natives but authorized revenue sharing for only a limited number of years. Natives would receive only a little more than 40 million acres of land, and instead of the twelve regional corporations that the AFN sought, the measure authorized one corporation for the Arctic Slope and two statewide corporations, one for social services and another for investments. Within five years of enactment the educational and social programs of the BIA would be terminated. Despite Native protests, the full Senate adopted the Jackson measure. The AFN now had to look to the House for a more favorable bill.[44]

The organization sought help from groups in Alaska and beyond. Strapped for cash, it had received a $100,000 loan from the Athapaskan village of Tyonek, on Cook Inlet. Tyonek had earlier reached a cash settlement with the federal government over land disputes and therefore had been able to help bankroll the struggle. Still, there was not enough cash, and the AFN appealed for voluntary contributions. At that point the Yakima Indian Nation of the State of Washington extended a $250,000 loan to the hard-pressed AFN, enabling it to continue its congressional lobbying efforts. The lobbying apparently bore fruit: soon thereafter the House Subcommittee on Indian Affairs informally agreed that Natives should be granted 40 million acres.[45]

There were other good omens. The National Congress of American Indians decided to give unqualified support to the AFN's struggle to obtain a congressional claims settlement. This action gave the AFN a significant source of national support. In Alaska, Keith Miller was defeated in the gubernatorial election by former Governor William Egan, who had expressed a willingness to work with the AFN. Nick Begich, a state senator who had stated that 10 million acres was an inadequate settlement, was elected to Alaska's lone seat in the House of Representatives. Furthermore, the Arctic Slope Native Association, which had earlier withdrawn from the AFN over a disagreement, rejoined by the end of the year. With the AFN unified once again, its settlement proposal kept the twelve regions and the $500 million initial compensation, plus the 2 percent share in future revenues from public lands. It raised the land provision to 60 million acres and accepted the Arctic Slope argument that the regions with the largest land area should also receive the most land and money.[46]

Soon after Congress convened in 1971, senators Fred Harris (D-OK) and Ted Kennedy (D-MA) introduced the measure in the Senate, while Congressman Lloyd Meeds (D-WA) submitted the companion measure in the House. Key features of these measures were full title to 60 million acres of land, $500 million, perpetual sharing in mineral royalties from lands given up, and the establishment of regional corporations. Another Senate bill introduced was that of Senator Henry Jackson, which had passed that body in 1970. Wayne Aspinall (D-CO), chairman of the House Committee on Interior and Insular Affairs, introduced a measure that provided only about one hundred thousand acres of land, making additional lands for subsistence use available on a permit basis.[47]

The final drive now started. Efforts centered on the progress of the Meeds bill in the House because attempts to have the Jackson measure amended in the Senate had failed during the previous year. Lobbyists descended on Congress, but perhaps the most important factor in moving the White House and Congress toward a settlement was the continuing delay in construction of the Trans-Alaska Pipeline. Oil companies and contractors had made enormous investments and impatiently waited to recover them.

On September 28, 1971, by voice vote, the House Interior and Insular Committee reported HR10367, providing $925 million and 40 million acres of land for Alaska Natives to settle their land claims. They would receive $425 million from the U.S. Treasury over a ten-year period, and $500 million from mineral revenues that would otherwise have gone mainly to the state. Twelve regional corporations and a network of village corporations were to administer Native assets. The House approved the bill on October 20 in essentially the same form after clearing a strong challenge from twelve conservation groups.[48]

The Senate also acted swiftly and reported a measure that would provide $500 million from the federal treasury and a like amount from mineral revenue sharing. It would provide 50 million acres of land, but 20 million would be for subsistence use, not ownership, and it established only seven regional corporations. Senator Mike Gravel of Alaska had proposed a land-use planning commission, which was also included. In November the Senate passed the measure with but little opposition.[49] The conference committee reported its measure in early December, having compromised on several dozen items.

The Alaska Native Claims Settlement Act

The terms of ANCSA are many and complex. First, Alaska Natives would receive both surface and subsurface rights to 40 million acres, divided among some 220 villages and twelve regional corporations. Villages would receive the surface estate only in about 18.5 million acres in the twenty-five townships surrounding each village, divided among the villages according to population. In addition, the villages were to receive an additional 3.5 million acres of surface estate for a total of 22 million acres. The regional corporations were to divide this additional acreage among the villages on equitable principles. The regional corporations were to receive the subsurface estate in the 22 million acres patented to the villages, and full title to 16 million acres selected within the twenty-five township areas surrounding the villages, to be divided among the twelve regional corporations on the basis of the total area in each region.[50]

An additional 2 million acres, which completed

the total of 40 million acres, were to be conveyed, with existing cemetery sites going to the regional corporations; the surface estate on not more than 23,040 acres, or one township, was to go to each of the Native groups too small to qualify as a Native village. The regional corporations were to receive the subsurface estate. Each Native who had a principal residence outside a Native village was to receive not more than 160 acres of surface estate, while the regional corporations gained the title to the subsurface estate. Natives in four towns that originally were Native villages but that now contained predominantly non-Native inhabitants were to receive the surface estate not to exceed 23,040 acres. These conveyances were to be near the towns but far enough away as not to inhibit the expansion of these towns. The regional corporations were to receive the subsurface estate. If there was any balance left of the 2 million acres, it was to be conveyed to the regional corporations. In case the entire 40 million acres could not be selected from the twenty-five township areas surrounding the villages because of topography or restrictions on the acreage that could be selected within the Wildlife Refuge System, the secretary of the interior was to withdraw in lieu selection areas as close to the twenty-five township areas as possible.[51]

The monetary settlement consisted of $962.5 million. $462.5 million was to come from the federal treasury and be paid to the twelve regional corporations, which were to be organized under the act over an eleven-year period. The remaining $500 million was to be paid from a 2 percent royalty on production and 2 percent royalty on bonuses and rentals from lands in Alaska thereafter conveyed to the state under the Statehood Act of 1958 and from the remaining federal lands in Alaska, excluding, however, Naval Petroleum Reserve no. 4.

Resident Natives in each of the villages were to be organized as a profit or nonprofit corporation that was to assume title to the surface estate in the land conveyed to the village, administer the land, and receive and administer a part of the monetary settlement. The twelve regional corporations were to take title to the subsurface estate in the land conveyed to the villages and full title to the additional land divided among the regional corporations, which

would also receive the full monetary grant, divided among them by Native population. Each regional corporation had to divide among all twelve regional corporations 70 percent of the mineral revenues received.[52]

Each regional corporation also had to distribute among the village corporations in the region no less than 50 percent of its share of the $962.5 million, as well as 50 percent of all revenues received from the subsurface estate. This provision, however, did not apply to revenues received from their investments in business ventures. For the first five years after the act became law, 10 percent of the revenues from the first two sources mentioned above were to be distributed among the individual Native stockholders of the corporations. Those Alaska Natives no longer residents of the state were permitted to create a thirteenth regional corporation if a majority so elected. (Those Natives did create The 13th Regional Corporation, headquartered in Seattle. It received only a portion of ANCSA's cash settlement, but no ANCSA lands or other benefits.)[53]

ANCSA stock was issued, without charge, in blocks of one hundred shares to all U.S. citizens with one-fourth or more Alaska Indian, Eskimo, or Aleut blood who were living when the settlement became law, except members of the Annette Island community of Metlakatla. About eighty thousand individuals received the block of one hundred shares each. Natives born after that date were not entitled to receive ANCSA stock except through inheritance or child custody disputes. Many Natives feared that individual stockholders would sell their shares after December 1991 and control of Native corporations and their lands would pass out of Native hands.[54]

Native village residents enrolled as shareholders in one of the twelve regional corporations, as well as being shareholders in the nonprofit corporation of the village in which they lived. Thousands of Natives who were urban residents did not receive village stock but were enrolled and received stock as at-large shareholders in one of the twelve regional corporations.[55]

Population size largely determined village and region land allocations; that is, the larger the population, the more land the village or region received. Six regions with small populations had relatively

Tour of Sealaska's Southeast Timber operations, June 1985. *From left:* Joe Wilson (former chair, Sealaska Board), Toshiaki Sasaki, general manager of the Seattle Branch of the Bank of Tokyo, and Byron Mallott.

(Courtesy of Ross V. Soboleff, Sealaska Corporation.)

large land claims. They gave up or lost more land in the settlement than regions with large populations. Section 12(c) of ANCSA was to correct this inequity by allowing these regions to select an additional 16 million acres. Unlike the village selections, Ahtna, Arctic Slope, Chugach, Cook Inlet, Doyon, and NANA regional corporations received title to both the subsurface and surface estate of these 16 million acres. The remaining 2 million acres were allocated among the four "urban" Native corporations, nine or ten Native groups, cemeteries and historical sites, Native primary places of residence, and some Native allotments. After all these distributions had been made, any remaining land was to be allocated among all but The 13th Regional Corporation on a population basis. The twelve regional corporations all obtained some surface lands. In the case of the more populous regions, this amounted to several hundred thousand acres. Sealaska, the southeast Alaska regional corporation, discovered this to be a very important source of old-growth timber.[56]

Southeast Alaska's Natives had become beneficiaries of the long, drawn-out Tlingit and Haida land claims case, which in 1968 had resulted in a mon-etary award of $7.2 million. As a result, ANCSA limited the ten southeast Alaska villages to one township (23,040 acres) each. Most of these lands were located in the Tongass National Forest, which enabled some of the regional, village, and urban corporations to obtain considerable wealth from timber sales.[57]

ANCSA originally had planned a total settlement of 40 million acres, but the eventual settlement came to about 45.5 million acres. This increase came about because section 19 of ANCSA extinguished all the existing administratively created Indian reservations in Alaska with the exception of Annette Islands Reserve. It allowed the village corporations on those former reservations to select the surface and subsurface estate of those lands but forgo all other ANCSA benefits, including the cash payments, in settlement of their land claims. Four of the large reservations took advantage of this provision, with combined total claims of about 4 million acres, in addition to the stipulated 40 million acres. The four large reservations and their associated villages were Saint Lawrence Island Reserve and the villages of Gambell and Savoonga; Elim Reserve

Japanese customers visit Sealaska Timber Corporation's log "sort yard" on Prince of Wales Island near the community of Klawock. The log sort yard at Klawock is the only dry land storage and loading dock in southeast Alaska. The dry storage yields a superior grade log to those stored in water.

(Courtesy of Ross V. Soboleff, Sealaska Corporation.)

and the village of Elim; Chandalar Reserve and the villages of Venetie and Arctic Village; and Tetlin Reserve and the village of Tetlin. Klukwan Reserve and Chilkat Indian Village was the fifth and much smaller reserve, with only eight hundred acres. In 1976 Congress amended ANCSA to allow the village corporation, Klukwan, Inc., to select a township under ANCSA if it conveyed the lands of the former reserve in fee to the Chilkat Indian Village tribal government. Klukwan, Inc. conveyed the eight hundred acres, then ran out of land selection in the Haines area, and chose Long Island in the Tongass National Forest in 1977.[58] The in-lieu subsurface selection of five regional corporations added another 1.6 million acres.

ANCSA contained numerous other major provisions. It established, for example, a Joint Federal-State Land Use Planning Commission, with important advisory functions; it authorized the secretary of the interior to withdraw from selection by the state and regional corporations, but not village corporations, and from the operation of the public land laws up to but not to exceed 80 million acres of unreserved lands for possible inclusion in the National Parks, National Forests, Wildlife Refuges, and Wild and Scenic River systems; it authorized the secretary of the interior to withdraw public lands and classify or reclassify such land, and to open to entry, location, and leasing in such a manner that would protect the public interest and avoid a "land rush" and massive filings on public lands in Alaska after the expiration of the land freeze. The act also provided for appropriate public access and recreational site easements on lands granted to Native corporations to protect the public interest. It limited attorney and consultant fees to $2 million, and it protected all valid existing rights, including inchoate rights of entrymen and mineral locators. It limited the acreage that could be granted to Native villages located in national forests. The conference committee believed that the secretary of the interior, through his or her withdrawal authority, could protect all Native interests in subsistence needs by closing necessary lands to entry by nonresidents when subsistence resources of these lands were in short supply or threatened. Congress expected both the secretary of the interior and the State of Alaska to collaborate in protecting the subsistence lifestyle.[59]

A Mixed Blessing

Congress passed ANCSA with stunning speed. The settlement of these land claims for decades had seemed remote. It was the discovery of Prudhoe Bay, North America's largest oilfield in 1968, which promised to alleviate the nation's dependency on foreign imports, that pushed Congress to finally settle the longstanding land claims. Prudhoe Bay oil could be delivered to market only through the construction of a pipeline. The oil companies, the state, and the business community at large realized that Alaska Natives would have to be satisfied before there was any chance for the pipeline.

The urgency played into the hands of the AFN, which had won the support of influential groups and individuals. After intense lobbying on the part of the many interested groups, Congress forged the ANCSA legislation in December 1971. It was a compromise among four often competing interests, namely, Alaska's Natives, the state of Alaska, the federal government, which held about 217 million acres of Alaska lands, and finally, the environmental interests, which had become concerned about the effect of these land settlements on wildlife and other ecological values. ANCSA seemingly resolved the conflict between the state's land selections and aboriginal claims. Section 17(d)(2) in ANCSA called for a later withdrawal of federal lands for various environmental purposes. This section was known simply as "d-2" in the Alaska National Interest Land Conservation Act of 1980, which added 104.3 million acres to conservation systems in Alaska.

ANCSA was a complex piece of legislation, drawn up in haste. It contained many ambiguities, and it is no wonder that every Congress since 1971 has amended the act. As a result of ANCSA, both Native communities and Alaska underwent massive changes. There is doubt that the Native subsistence culture, which is the way Alaska Natives and their ancestors had lived from time immemorial, will survive. Numerous conferences have been held around the state since the passage of ANCSA in which participants assure each other that they will be able to maintain the traditional ways and also fully participate in modern American life. The talk is illusory, however. Natives must learn to think and act like those in the majority culture to succeed with their corporations. At best, ANCSA has eased Native transition into the modern world. Natives face very tough choices; as Chris Wright, a mental health counselor for the Copper River Native Association, pointed out in 1991, "If you leave the village, you desert your family. If you stay in the village, you desert your future."[60]

Chapter 20

The Native Regional Corporations

By the early summer of 1972 the twelve Native regional corporations had organized, renting office space and hiring a cadre of professionals, including land planners, economists, and accountants, to begin their corporate existence. By midsummer they received the first U.S. Treasury checks for five hundred thousand dollars each. Most of this money was to be passed to the villages, which incorporated as soon as the enrollment of individual Natives had been completed.[1]

By the spring of 1977 only 3.5 million acres of land of the 45.5 million acres due to the Native corporations had been conveyed; the cumbersome federal bureaucracy was working very slowly indeed. But there was no doubt that Native investments had already made a substantial impact on Alaska's economy. Money from the settlement had been flowing steadily into corporate treasuries. By December 1975, the regional corporations had received $170,306,168 of the monetary settlement.[2]

The 1976 Omnibus Act

It was to be expected that a complex piece of legislation like the Alaska Native Claims Settlement Act (ANCSA) would be ambiguous in parts and that Congress would soon be asked to define its intent more clearly and rectify some of the apparent injustices. In 1975, Congress passed such an omnibus act, which became law in 1976. A major part of the new law concerned the Cook Inlet Region, Inc. (CIRI), where not enough lands were available for regional and village corporation selections. The law authorized a complicated exchange of lands among the United Sates, the Cook Inlet Region, Inc., and the state of Alaska as a means of satisfying the region's entitlement under the ANCSA.

To accomplish this land exchange with state lands required state legislation. To meet a congressionally mandated deadline, the state legislature quickly enacted the necessary legislation authorizing the exchange, to become effective March 12, 1977. The lawmakers recognized that more comprehensive legislation was needed for future land exchanges. After much deliberation and helpful guidance from the Joint Federal-State Land Use Planning Commission, the legislature enacted the necessary regulations that clearly spelled out the requirements to be met before land exchanges could be made by the executive branch.[3]

The Omnibus Act clarified many more sections of the ANCSA. For example, it extended Native enrollment for one more year and provided that monies received under ANCSA were not to be used in lieu of various federal programs but only for extinguishing land claims.[4]

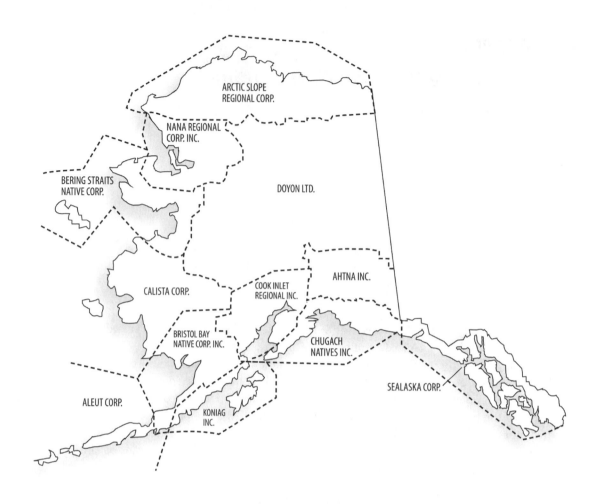

Boundaries of the Twelve Native Regional Corporations

Problems of the Native Regional Corporations

One of the most troublesome issues affecting the regional corporations was the dispute over the distribution of revenues derived from their land entitlements. There was bitter fighting and much ill will as the corporations tried to determine how the revenues from oil, minerals, and forests could be distributed equitably to all Alaska Natives. The "7i dispute," as it became known after the paragraph and subchapter in ANCSA, was finally settled in 1982. According to the agreement, each regional corporation retained 30 percent of its revenues from

natural resources, while it paid the remaining 70 percent into a resource pool of income from all of the regional corporations. These pool funds were then redistributed according to the number of shareholders each regional corporation had. The regional corporation then redistributed half of the funds to the village corporations in its region and to at-large shareholders, while the remainder was income for that regional corporation and its shareholders.[5]

There was much dissatisfaction with this among many Alaska Natives. Jeanie Leask, the 1984 president of the Alaska Federation of Natives (AFN), which had originally taken the lead in lobbying for the passage of the act, charged that ANCSA was surrounded by myths and misconceptions. For example, there was the belief that the settlement act was to address and solve all the problems Alaska Natives faced, running the gamut from alcoholism to the inadequacies of village life. Leask stated that she often heard the remark that the "Natives were given all that land and money—why do they want more?" In reality, she continued, ANCSA was only a limited economic tool, a land settlement that did not affect the special relationship Natives enjoyed with the federal government. Nor did it affect Native rights to self-government under the Indian Reorganization Act of 1934 (IRA) and the Alaska Reorganization Act of 1936. But it certainly did not further extend any self-government rights, as the legislation and subsequent court decisions proved. As Native leaders and shareholders came to realize the limitations of the corporate structure, they began to study the possibility of vesting control of the 45 million acres in tribal governments, represented by traditional councils or Indian Reorganization Act Councils, and to consider membership organizations in which participation would not depend on stock ownership. Consideration of these alternatives, she concluded, was urgent because of the looming deadline of 1991, when shareholders would be able to sell their stock and other protections in ANCSA would expire as well.[6]

The whole question of tribal government charters, or the Native sovereignty issue, perplexed many Alaskans. Apparently it caught even the governor unprepared. In April 1984, Alaska's Governor Bill Sheffield asked the Department of the Interior to delay issuing a tribal government charter, under the provisions of the IRA and its 1936 extension to Alaska, to the Native village of Eagle on the Yukon River. Don Wright, a Fairbanks resident, the former president of the AFN, and a longtime champion of Native self-government, immediately claimed that the governor's action broke a campaign promise he had made in 1982 to respect tribal sovereignty. Horace Biederman, Jr., the president of the Eagle village corporation, reminded Sheffield that he had promised the village that he would not oppose IRA governments. Obviously, Biederman concluded, Sheffield "speaks with a forked tongue." What was clear was that Sheffield, on the campaign trail, apparently

was not acquainted with the Indian Reorganization Act of 1934, or the 1936 Alaska Reorganization Act. Furthermore, it is easy to make promises on the campaign trail, but once one was elected, issues became much more complex. This seemed to be the case in this matter.

John Shively, Sheffield's chief of staff and a former Native corporation executive, issued a statement clarifying the governor's intent. Sheffield had only asked for time to study the Eagle constitution because it differed in important respects from the approximately seventy existing IRA constitutions, mostly issued in the 1940s. While those documents were general in nature, the Eagle constitution specifically identified some powers, such as taxing authority and the right to issue business charters. In short, Shively explained, Governor Sheffield continued to support the issuance of IRA constitutions but desired that they continue to be general in nature.[7]

Congress, at the time of ANCSA's enactment, had expressed the hope that the act's approach of settling Native land claims "should be accomplished rapidly, with certainty, and in conformity with the real economic and social needs of Natives, without litigation, with maximum participation by Natives in decisions affecting their rights and property" and without creating racially defined "institutions, privileges, or obligations." There were to be no reservations, no lengthy ward or trusteeship, no adding to the categories of property and institutions that enjoyed special tax advantages.[9]

But the U.S. House Committee on Interior and Insular Affairs concluded in 1987 that few of these goals had been accomplished. While a few of the regional corporations could be considered financially secure, most were only marginally successful and a few were on the verge of total bankruptcy. The village corporations were in worse conditions. Implementing ANCSA had been extremely difficult and costly. Native leaders had to establish more than two hundred corporate entities, select 44 million acres of land, and seek business opportunities where often none existed. In addition, the federal government had delayed land conveyances, and there had been almost continuous litigation because of ANCSA's inherent ambiguities. It had been an onerous and costly burden.

The Alaska Native Review Commission

Among many Alaska Natives, uneasiness about ANCSA and its implementation spread in the 1970s and early 1980s, particularly in view of the financial misadventures of most of the regional corporations and the seemingly unending litigation between village, group, and urban corporations as to what, among other topics, Congress meant when it described the lands conveyed to these entities as "surface estate," and those conveyed to the regions as "subsurface estate." As a result, the Inuit Circumpolar Conference in 1983 created the Alaska Native Review Commission to examine the intent of ANCSA and its consequences for Alaska Natives. It hired Thomas Berger, a former chief justice of British Columbia, Canada, who had gained international recognition for his pursuit of Native rights issues in his country, to chair the commission. Berger's charge was to hold extensive hearings in urban and rural Alaska and listen to people discussing their expectations of and experiences with ANCSA. Berger's mandate was to examine the social and economic status of Alaska Natives, the policies the United States historically followed in settling Native American claims, including ANCSA, the functions of the Native corporations ANCSA had created, and the significance of ANCSA to indigenous peoples throughout the world.[8]

After attending many hearings in urban and rural Alaska, Berger issued his report and recommendations in 1985. His first recommendation was that lands should be severed from the regional corporations and transferred to tribal governments. Congress had complied with Native wishes and specifically created the corporate format to induce Natives to join the capitalist world. But if corporations kept the land, Berger warned, it would not remain in Native hands. Alaska Natives wanted and deserved their own tribal governments and had to assume responsibilities as sovereign peoples. Congress and the state government had to fully acknowledge that Native governments were legitimate political institutions and had a right to retain their ancestral lands in perpetuity. Native governments also had to be given jurisdiction over fish and wildlife management in order to defend and continue their subsistence lifestyle.

Berger recognized that the implementation of these recommendations might involve complications in sorting out many ANCSA issues, such as shares, dissenter's rights, the land bank, and children born after 1971, among many others. But he pointed out that the main concerns were land, self-government, and subsistence. These issues were linked, and together they were the means by which Native people could regain control over their land, their communities, and their lives.

Berger's report was published in 1985, but his recommendations were not adopted.

Source: Thomas R. Berger, *Village Journey: The Report of the Alaska Native Review Commission* (New York: Hill and Wang, 1985), 155–66.

AFN president Leask described the situation in a 1984 report to the President's Commission on Indian Reservation Economics. Native people and their institutions had experienced an overwhelming legal and administrative burden during the last thirteen years, and implementing ANCSA had become an end in itself. The effort had consumed tens of millions of dollars that should have been put into business investments, personnel training and technical assistance for village corporation employees, and communications between stockholders and corporation leaders. Regions had paid dearly for implementation costs, she continued, and it had been worse for villages, especially smaller ones, because they had but little cash from the Alaska Native Fund to start with. Many villages were practically broke because of implementation costs. They did not make any money, nor had they undertaken much economic development. Now they probably would have to sell some of their land to keep going. The AFN leadership also realized that the protections given by the stock restrictions and tax exemptions for underdeveloped ANCSA lands were fast ending, and corporation lands were vulnerable to creditors' claims in case of bankruptcy.[10]

Steve Colt, a University of Alaska Anchorage economist with the Institute of Social and Economic Research, analyzed the performance of the Alaska Native regional corporations between 1973 and 1993 and found that they had lost more than $380 million in direct business operations. He estimated that village corporations had lost approximately the same amount as the regional corporations over the same time span, which meant that about $760 million of the $962.5 million Alaska Natives had received for the extinguishment of their aboriginal claims in 1971 had disappeared.[11]

The Sale of NOLs and Other Solutions

The immediate need was to stop the financial bleeding and refinance the cash-strapped Native corporations. In 1986 Senator Ted Stevens had Congress insert into the Internal Revenue Code a provision that allowed ANCSA corporations to sell their accumulated financial losses. These net operating losses, or "NOLs," could be sold to profitable corporations

for the value of the tax write-off given to the buyers. For example, in 1986 Doyon, Ltd. lost $238 million by selling a Canadian company the right to develop an asbestos deposit located on land it had selected. In 1988, it sold that $238 million loss to the Marriott Corporation and the Campbell Soup Company for a cash payment of $77.5 million.[12] In short, the NOLs enabled Congress to refinance the Native corporations.

Other regional corporations were convinced by lawyers that NOLs did not necessarily have to be losses in cash but could also be land devalued when oil or gas exploration was unproductive or when falling timber and oil prices made land less valuable than at the time Congress had conveyed the property. These were also losses to the corporations. Thereupon CIRI, the most profitable and one of the best managed of the thirteen regional corporations, sold $102 million from losses created from devalued oil and gas reserves.[13] Consequently, within a few years of the NOL tax break, many of the Native corporations had generated more than $1 billion in new capital, in essence refinancing ANCSA. For several corporations, it meant the difference between bankruptcy and survival.[14] Congress closed the NOL tax loophole in 1988, but by that time the American taxpayer had been billed to recoup the money the regional and village corporations had lost.

Senator Stevens further aided Alaska's Natives when he wrote a provision to the procurement preference law that sparked a boom for the regional and village corporations through a Small Business Administration program, the Department of Defense, and other channels. The provision exempted the companies from a $5 million cap on no-bid contracts imposed on other small or disadvantaged firms, and Alaska Natives also did not have to run the firms. Unlike individually owned companies, the Alaska Native regional and village corporations can have more than one company in the program at a time. From 2000 to 2004, the number of contracts awarded to the firms quadrupled and were worth $1.1 billion; of these, 77 percent were awarded without competitive bids.[15]

The Native regional and village corporations had become firmly established in Alaska's economy, and they contributed somewhat to diversifying the state's economy. Many problems, remained, however. The settlement provided a twenty-year tax moratorium on Native lands, which put much pressure on corporate leadership to put lands into production, and it soon became apparent to many that regional corporate profit goals were often incompatible with village subsistence. In 1988 Congress passed an extensive set of ANCSA amendments that virtually restructured the act. The amendments continued the restrictions on the sale of ANCSA stock and provided indefinite tax exemptions and protection from creditors for ANCSA lands as long as they remained undeveloped. The amendments also made it possible for ANCSA corporation shareholders to decide if they wanted to admit as new shareholders children born after December 18, 1971. ANCSA shareholders were also given the authority to eliminate the stock restrictions or adopt various options for limited stock sales.[16]

Between 1988 and 1998, three regional ANCSA corporation and three village corporation shareholders voted to issue shares to the children of the original shareholders. Issuing new stock, however, would dilute the voting rights and property interest of the original shareholders. Using 1990 census figures for Alaska Native fertility and various demographic studies, economist Steve Colt showed that issuing stock to all of the children of the original shareholders then alive would about double the number of shareholders in each of the corporations, reducing the voting power and dividend rights of the original shareholders by about 50 percent. It followed that the more children born, the greater the dilution would become over time.[17]

Congress continued amending ANCSA practically every other year and slowly relieved the ANCSA Native corporations of some of the obligations normally accompanying corporate activities. No doubt, ANCSA will continue to evolve. Appendix G gives a picture of Alaska Native Regional Corporations as of September 2006.

Amendments to Securities Law Exemptions

ANCSA mandated Alaska Native corporations, but they were organized under state law and have always been unique. The 1976 ANCSA amendments made clear the corporations' uniqueness. They exempted the ANCSA corporation from the federal securities laws through December 31, 1991, and the 1987 amendments extended these securities law exemptions indefinitely for each Alaska Native corporation as long as the corporation did not issue unrestricted stock, ended the restrictions on its stock, or filed a registration statement with the Securities and Exchange Commission.

The state of Alaska responded to the 1976 federal securities law exemption with the so-called "Alaska mini-securities statutes," which apply only to the larger Alaska Native corporations. Under these statutes, Native corporations with both five hundred or more shareholders and $1 million in assets have to follow unique state securities regulations. Generally, they require full disclosure of information pertaining to the performance of the board of directors and the company's financial performance at each annual shareholder's meeting. Those soliciting proxies or those who want to put propositions before the shareholders also have to make full disclosures. The 1976 amendments allowed the merger of village and urban corporations within regions and with regions. Available under state law, the amendments prohibited the exercise of dissenter's rights in Native Corporations mergers.[18]

The 1987 amendments extended the authority to merge corporations as long as the "Settlement of Common Stock" of the merging corporations was subject to "alienability restrictions." Very few villages merged, with the notable exception of the merger of six villages on the Upper Kuskokwim River to form the Kuskokwim Corporation. NANA and Ahtna villages have also merged with their regional corporations, with the exception of one village corporation. This merging led, by 1998, to a reduction of the original 204 village corporations to 173.[19]

Under corporate law, dividends must be distributed to all owners of each particular class of stock, but Native corporation shareholders often pressured the corporate boards to make payouts to benefit particular members of the community, such as elders or those facing family emergencies. That clearly contradicted the equal distribution rule, but the 1987 ANCSA amendments specifically allowed corporations to create "settlement trusts" to provide such benefits if they promoted "the health, education, and welfare" of the trust beneficiaries or preserved Native heritage and culture. Some Natives challenged the unequal benefits to shareholders, and the Alaska Supreme Court agreed, but Congress, in a 1998 ANCSA amendment, specifically allowed Native corporations to provide such disproportionate health, education, or welfare benefits directly to Native shareholders and their immediate family members.[20]

Dividends

Economist Colt analyzed the ANCSA corporations as to their ability to pay dividends. He divided them into three groups: The highest dividend paying group included CIRI, the Barrow-based Arctic Slope Regional Corporation (ASRC), and in third place, further back but still a member of the top group, Sealaska Corporation. The second group included Ahtna, Inc., Bristol Bay Native Corporation, Doyon Ltd., and NANA Regional Corporation, which all paid smaller dividends than the top three corporations. The third group consisted of Aleut Corporation, Bering Straits Native Corporation, Calista Corporation, Chugach Alaska Corporation, Koniag Inc., and The 13th Regional Corporation. These six all have paid small or no dividends over the years.[21]

CIRI has consistently paid quarterly dividends. They are among the highest of any of the Native regional corporations. CIRI shareholders have received regular quarterly dividends since it started payments in 1980, with a special dividend paid right before Christmas. In 2001, the first and second quarter dividends were $8.38 per share. In 2000 the corporation set the dividend at $6.28 per share, per quarter, for the year. Since 1980, CIRI has distributed $115,000 to the average shareholder.[22] In December 2000, CIRI made headlines in Alaska and beyond when it paid a special distribution dividend of $500 per share. The average CIRI shareholder owns about one hundred shares and therefore received a check for $50,000. In total, the approximately seven thousand CIRI shareholders received a $314 million payout of corporate wealth. Then in May 2001, CIRI distributed another $94.3 million, or $150.29 per share. Both distributions were related to CIRI's sale

of VoiceStream Wireless Corp. stock that the corporation exchanged for past partnership interests.

ASRC ran a good second in dividend payments. It sold drilling rights to oil and developed several successful oil-field service companies. In 2000, it paid its shareholders an annual dividend of $9.66 per share, down only slightly from $10.07 in 1999. ASRC continues to enroll new members as they are born. Most ANCSA corporations limited their membership to those born before the 1971 passage of the act. Younger shareholders in most other corporations receive shares either as gifts or in estates.[23]

ASRC, CIRI, and virtually all the other regional corporations contribute substantially to social and economic development programs that enhance shareholder well-being, and they also may pay significant cash awards. For example, ASRC pays approximately $120 per month to shareholders who are over sixty-five years of age. It also runs a generous scholarship program, as well as supporting a variety of non-economic activities. These include donations to the AFN, the Inuit Circumpolar Conference, and various dance groups.[24]

Long-Term Consequences

Perhaps most importantly, most of the Native corporations have realized that they are business corporations first and foremost, and Native corporations second. This has contributed to the split between the village Natives and the so-called Brooks Brothers Natives—individuals who have seen and experienced a much larger segment of the world than their village relatives and have assumed leadership in the corporations and in political life. It can be safely assumed that the corporate structure, just like the historic white incursions, will materially contribute to the disappearance of traditional Native lifestyles. Before the settlement, Alaskan Natives roamed over much of Alaska in search of subsistence; since the settlement they have become landowners, their domain defined by one stake in each of four corners. Now Natives worry about trespassing and rights-of-way just as their non-Native neighbors do.

Donald Craig Mitchell, an Anchorage attorney long involved with the AFN and Alaska Native legal matters, wrote a two-volume definitive history of how Congress enacted ANCSA. His concluding personal observations are worth summarizing. The majority of Alaska's Natives, he wrote, were not involved in the implementation of ANCSA beyond their status as shareholders of regional and village corporations. Most importantly, the 44 million acres of land ownership rights and $962.5 million paid to regional and village corporations, as well as to individual Alaska Natives, did little to alleviate the economic and social problems widespread in Native villages.[25]

When Natives realized this, a new political movement began in Alaska Native communities. The "tribalization movement" stems from the idea that each resident of Alaska's more than two hundred Native villages is a member of a separate "federally recognized tribe," whose governing body possesses "inherent" sovereign powers of self-government to govern the "Indian country" surrounding each village. It began as a fringe movement in 1983, but today tribalization is seen by more people as the solution to all village problems. In fact, Mitchell writes, "no Native leader who wishes to remain one any longer publicly questions that judgment."[26]

Many Natives have come to believe that tribalization, that is, turning ANCSA lands over to the individual tribes, would solve the multitude of problems confronting Native villages. Mitchell dismissed such talk as romanticized stereotyping and instead focused on the need for honest discussions about three questions: What is the future of Native villages in the twenty-first century? If villages have a future, what must Congress and the Alaska state legislature, other federal and state policymakers, and all individual Native and non-Natives who care about these matters do to make such a future possible? And if many villages have no future, what has to be done?[27] Unfortunately, such honest discussions are not taking place.

Despite much talk about ANCSA's responsibility to protect Native lands and traditional cultures, most Natives have measured the success of regional and village corporations by the size and frequency of the dividend checks. Mitchell gave numerous examples. In 1990, Sealaska sold a subsidiary for $62 million. Almost half of Sealaska's 15,700 shareholders petitioned the board of directors to give each shareholder a four-thousand-dollar dividend, a payout that would have distributed more than $60 million. President Byron Mallot objected, pointing out that this would amount to a partial liquidation and be equal to "corporate suicide." Nevertheless, the board of directors responded to shareholder pressure and paid each shareholder a $2,000 dividend.[28]

In this and many other cases, shareholders come close to liquidating or severely impacting the corporations' continued existence. Mitchell pointed out that shareholders used the money to purchase goods and services they now consider necessities. In fact, Alaska Natives have sought as much access as possible to the ever-expanding array of goods and services modernity offers. It is no wonder that Alaska Natives measure the success of the regional and village corporations by the size and frequency of their dividend checks. In short, from southeast Alaska to the Beaufort Sea at Barrow, shareholders have pressured boards of directors of regional and village corporations "to write dividend checks that distribute money earned through the ownership of businesses or acquired by selling operating losses, natural resources located on or under a corporation's land, or the land itself."[29]

All that can be said with any kind of assurance is that ANCSA is an experiment that is still evolving, and will be for a long time into the future. In the meantime, the ANCSA corporations have become a most important part of Alaska's economy.

Chapter 21

Land Claims and Land Conservation

Many different factors made possible the Alaska Native Claims Settlement Act (ANCSA) of 1971. Among these must be counted the civil rights revolution of the 1950s, which led to the landmark Supreme Court decision in *Brown v. Board of Education of Topeka, Kansas* in 1954, and the Civil Rights Acts in 1957 and 1960. The court decision and federal legislation, together with the work of civil rights activists and women's rights advocates, sensitized Americans to the plight of minorities.[1] Although Alaska was remote from the civil rights struggles in the contiguous states, modern communications media—television, radio, newspapers, and magazines—carried the news of the civil rights struggle into every town and village in the North. Many Indians, Aleuts, and Eskimos watched, listened, and in time became politicized, a development hastened by their long-standing demands for compensation for the lands taken from them. The state government's selections of acreage under the statehood grant conflicted with Native claims and speeded political awareness.

Thus the climate had changed by the time the Atlantic Richfield Company discovered the huge Prudhoe Bay oil field in 1968, and when it became apparent that the pipeline necessary to transport the oil from the Arctic to tidewater at Valdez would have to cross lands claimed by Natives, the majority listened to minority concerns and demands. In addition, the need to get the oil to market resulted in a sustained and energetic effort to resolve the Native claims. As we saw in chapter 20, an unlikely coalition of interest groups, each with its own agenda and goals, worked together to solve the Native claims issue. Included in the effort to produce ANCSA were the oil companies, the state of Alaska, various environmental organizations, Native leaders, Congress, and the executive branch of the federal government. But perhaps the problems had just begun, because now the Native communities, the state, and the various executive agencies of the federal government scrambled to cut up Alaska.

Conservation Legislation and the d-2 Controversy

There can be no question that Congress passed the ANCSA at a time when the nation had moved into a new era in federal land planning and management, which emphasized protection of natural and other environmental values on the remainder of the public domain. Several major pieces of legislation passed by Congress in the 1960s and 1970s reflected this changing national mood and had important bearing on the evolving controversy over Alaska lands. The first of these was the Wilderness Act of 1964, which directed the major federal land-management agencies to conduct detailed reviews of roadless areas under their jurisdiction and to recommend which lands Congress should include in a national wilderness preservation system.[2]

Then, on January 1, 1970, President Nixon signed into law the National Environmental Policy Act as the first measure in what he called the "environmental decade of the 1970s." Many commentators and observers originally thought the measure to be only a vague statement of environmental consciousness. It quickly became clear, however, that it was a firm directive requiring federal agencies to prepare lengthy and detailed environmental-impact statements on all federal actions that might significantly affect the quality of the environment.[3] Whenever a federal land-management agency in Alaska proposed to add to its landholdings, it became subject to the act's provisions, necessitating the development of full environmental impact statements. Not only did these studies employ an army of consultants, but they also ensured that both economic and environmental values came under closer public scrutiny.

During the legislative battle for passage of ANCSA, Congress included section 17(d)(2) in the measure to gain the support of the conservation forces. It authorized the secretary of the interior to withdraw up to 80 million acres of vacant, unreserved, and unappropriated federal public lands in Alaska for study as possible additions to the national park, forest, wildlife refuge, and wild and scenic river systems. The secretary withdrew 78 million acres in 1972. Congress, however, had until December 1978 to decide precisely which lands were to be put into which categories. In the meantime, the conservationists, the state, and various extractive interests lobbied for their pet schemes. Section 17(d)(2) created an uproar in Alaska, and in Congress as well, pitting conservation groups against development-minded interests.

The Joint Federal-State Land Use Planning Commission, not without dissent among its members, made its first recommendation in August 1973. Established in 1972 by the state of Alaska and the federal government as part of ANCSA, it served during a time when major changes in landownership and land management took place. Its goal was to create a framework for the use and protection of Alaska lands and resources in the years to come.[4] Reflecting its largely Alaskan composition, it stressed the "multiple-use" concept for the 78 million acres withdrawn in 1972. The commission urged that more than 60 million acres be opened for limited mineral development.[5]

At the same time, conservation groups lobbied vigorously for the creation of parks, wilderness areas, and refuges, and an Alaska task force in the Department of the Interior formulated alternative proposals for the 78 million acres. The task force was subject to the varying pressures of industry interests, conservationists, and the state, all wanting the land for themselves. But it also had to deal with federal agencies: the Forest Service intended to create vast national forests, while the Bureau of Land Management desired to maintain its control. Then in December 1973, Secretary Rogers C. B. Morton asked Congress that out of 78 million acres withdrawn, 63.8 million be added to make parks and refuge systems.[6]

In the meantime, as a result of increasing demands for natural resources, such as timber, minerals, and energy from public lands, Congress passed several pieces of legislation designed to improve the land-planning and management functions of the Forest Service and the Bureau of Land Management. This legislation was also a response to the growing national concern for environmental quality, with an emphasis on protection, preservation, and recreational, nonexploitative uses of the land. In 1960 the Multiple Use–Sustained Yield Act had given the Forest Service its first statutory authority to manage the lands under its jurisdiction for a number of different uses simultaneously. It also gave the Forest Service the legal basis for fending off pressures from single-use advocates, such as wildlife and wilderness champions and timber interests. Two other pieces of legislation extended and reemphasized that policy. The Forest and Rangeland Renewable Resources Planning Act of 1974 and the National Forest Management Act of 1976 required that national forest lands be managed on the basis of detailed inventories of the resources, future-demand projections, careful consideration of alternative land uses and management schemes, extended public participation in the planning process, and consultation and coordination with local, state, and federal agencies.[7]

With the passage of the Federal Land Policy and Management Act of 1976, also known as the Bureau of Land Management Organic Act, Congress established similar policies for the BLM. The Organic Act changed the bureau from primarily a land-disposal agency to a land-management agency. Congress instructed the BLM to manage the remaining public domain lands for multiple uses. The BLM was now included within the authority of the Wilderness Act of 1964, which required it to conduct wilderness studies of all its roadless areas. In effect, the act marked the closing of the public domain by ending land disposals with but few exceptions.[8]

The Battle for Lands Brews

With passage of the Federal Land Policy and Management Act of 1976, a battle began for the control of the last of the nation's uncommitted lands in Alaska. Each of the federal land-management agencies now studied the d-2 lands and staked out large acreages. The Forest Service proposed that 44 million acres be added to its holdings in the form of fourteen new national forests. The National Park Service claimed some of the same lands and asked for 33 million acres to establish several large new national parks and to expand the boundaries of existing parks. The Fish and Wildlife Service wanted 30 million acres for new wildlife refuges to protect waterfowl nesting and breeding grounds, as well as other habitats. About half of this acreage conflicted with either National Park Service or Forest Service proposals. The BLM had not officially become a land-management agency until passage of the act of 1976. Therefore, it was in a weak position to claim lands for permanent management and watched, practically helpless, as other federal land-management agencies prepared proposals that would have left the bureau with scattered parcels of marginal lands that neither the state of Alaska, the Natives, nor the other federal agencies wanted.

As the d-2 battle proceeded, each federal agency sought political support for its particular proposals. Various interest groups began to fall in line behind one or the other agency in preparation for the upcoming congressional battle. Environmental groups in Alaska and the contiguous states desired that maximum acreage be placed under the management of the National Park Service and the Fish and Wildlife Service, where it would be managed almost exclusively to safeguard natural values and wildlife habitat or recreational uses that would not impair the wild character of the land. Development interests cried foul and described this kind of management as a "lock-up" of America's last remaining storehouse of resource wealth. They demanded that the Forest Service and the BLM, the two multiple-use agencies, obtain jurisdiction over the maximum acreage. The Native community was divided in this battle. Many rural villagers favored the conservationists, hoping to be provided greater protection for their subsistence style of living, while regional corporation leaders, intent on maximizing income, more often joined those supporting the multiple use of federal lands.

When legislative proposals to resolve the d-2 land issue were introduced in Congress in 1977, officials of President Jimmy Carter's administration, members of Congress, Alaskans, conservationists, developers, and national lobbyists for varied interests joined in emphasizing the importance of the legislation.[9] The questions to be addressed were, How much and which federal public lands in Alaska should be permanently reserved to protect their natural values, and under what management systems should this be done? Much of the most bitter fighting in Congress centered on these issues. But several other questions also had to be dealt with at the same time. What effect would wilderness preservation have on Alaska's and the nation's economies? Should the state of Alaska play only an advisory role in the management of federal lands, or should it be given considerable powers to affect federal land-management policy? What actions were necessary to protect the subsistence lifestyles of Alaska Natives and other rural residents, and to what extent, if any, should sport hunting be allowed in the new units of the national park system? What impact would the fractured landownership patterns have on Alaska's wildlife, particularly species, like the caribou, that migrate over large areas? How would the new federal units affect state and Native land selection and management, and what could be done to ensure that the state of Alaska, the Natives, and other landowners would have access across new federal conservation units? Finally, how could the state's need for transportation corridors across Alaska's vastness be satisfied without adversely affecting natural values in the areas crossed?

In the congressional hearings, politicians received widely differing recommendations on how to approach these questions. Obviously the variance stemmed from the very dissimilar perceptions various interest groups had about what constituted the "national interest" in Alaska's lands and resources. Many Alaskans and those associated with resource-extractive industries viewed the lands as representing important economic opportunities that could benefit the whole nation—but only if a large percentage of the lands remained open to multiple use. These groups argued that not enough was known about the resources of the lands to make a wise decision about their potential. It was premature to "lock up" the lands in restrictive management units, because only further resource exploration could reveal their full potential.

Environmentalists had a totally different point of view. They argued that Alaska's national-interest lands represented the last opportunity to save intact a significant portion of the nation's wilderness. The state and the Natives had already selected the lands with the highest potential for development of oil, gas, mineral, and other resources, they claimed. Any resources found on national-interest lands should be left in place for eventual future use.

Congress at an Impasse

These widely divergent views were evident in a host of bills introduced in Congress in 1977. Congressman Morris Udall (D-AZ) sponsored H.R. 39, which quickly became known as "the conservationist measure." Udall proposed to create a total of 116 million acres of new conservation-system units in the state. All the units were to be made a part of the national wilderness preservation system, effectively precluding any resource development. In June of the same year, Senator Ted Stevens (R-AK) introduced S. 1787, representing the views of the Alaska state government and strongly supported by development interests. At the opposite end of the spectrum from the Udall bill, it proposed to put 25 million acres in new conservation units without the protective wilderness designation. An additional 57 million acres were to be placed in a new category called Federal Cooperative Lands, to be managed on a multiple-use basis under joint commission oversight, somewhat along the lines proposed by the Joint Federal-State Land Use Planning Commission for Alaska. Secretary of the Interior Cecil Andrus presented the Carter administration plan, which fell within the two extremes, proposing to set aside 92 million acres in new conservation units. Of these, 43 million acres were to be protected with the wilderness designation.

Obviously, a significant departure from section 17(d)(2) of the ANCSA had taken place. That law had directed that 80 million acres be set aside for study, and there had been no intention of designating some or all of the new conservation units as wilderness. The wilderness issue, however, became centrally important in the congressional d-2 land debate. Resource development interests and Alaska state government officials rejected the proposed creation of these "instant wilderness" areas, maintaining that they bypassed the formal procedures required in the Wilderness Act, which mandated agency review, public hearings, and presidential recommendations to Congress. Supporters of the concept argued that the d-2 lands had already been studied extensively in the eight years that had passed since the passage of ANCSA, and that this amounted to a de facto compliance with the Wilderness Act.

To mollify state and development interests, the House Interior Subcommittee revised H.R. 39 to include less acreage and wilderness. The compromise measure, which passed the House of Representatives on May 19, 1978, by a vote of 277 to 31, included about 100 million acres in new conservation units with only 66 million acres designated as wilderness. Conservationists were jubilant—but they had not reckoned with the Senate.

Alaska's two senators, Ted Stevens and Mike Gravel, rejected the House measure and worked closely with the Senate's Energy and Natural Resources Committee and its chairman, Senator

Henry Jackson of Washington, to change it. In early October 1978, the Senate committee reported out a measure that protected about one-third less in conservation units and designated just about half as much wilderness as H.R. 39 did. In the final hours before adjournment, House and Senate leaders tried to reach a compromise. Agreement on a measure that would have put 96 million acres in conservation units and designated 50 million acres of this total as wilderness emerged, but at the last moment Senator Gravel balked and threatened to filibuster the bill if it reached the Senate floor. Thereupon negotiations fell apart, and the measure died. Unable to reach a compromise, congressional leaders introduced legislation to extend the d-2 land withdrawals for another year, but Senator Gravel threatened to filibuster that as well, and Congress adjourned without action on Alaska lands legislation.

Congress had given itself until December 18, 1978, to pass Alaska lands legislation. It had failed to do so. Shortly before the deadline, the Carter administration acted. Using the emergency withdrawal authority provided by section 204-e of the Federal Land Policy and Development Act of 1976, Secretary Andrus withdrew 110 million acres of Alaska lands on November 16. This withdrawal renewed the protection for the original 80 million acres of d-2 lands, together with an additional 30 million acres of new lands. On December 1, 1978, President Carter used his authority under the 1906 Antiquities Act to designate 56 million acres of Alaska lands as permanent, new national monuments and also directed Secretary Andrus to administratively designate 40 million acres as permanent wildlife refuges. At the request of the president, Robert Bergland, the secretary of agriculture, closed to mining another 11 million acres of lands in the Tongass and Chugach national forests. Altogether, about 120 million acres were included in the different withdrawals, and only Congress could reverse these executive actions.

When the Ninety-sixth Congress convened in 1979, conservationist and development interests faced each other again in the battle over Alaska's lands. On one side were the state and national environmental organizations—the so-called Alaska Coalition—which eventually included fifty-two nationwide environmental organizations. Although representing differing philosophical views, these groups were able to come together on the Alaska lands issue and form a formidable power base in the capital. They were supported by a national constituency of several hundred thousand members who on short notice were able to put grass-roots pressure on their senators and congresspeople. Reinforcing the coalition's efforts was Americans for Alaska, a small but vocal organization whose membership included prestigious individuals such as photographer Ansel Adams, scientist Jacques Cousteau, singer John Denver, and Lady Bird Johnson, to name but a few.

On the other side were the Citizens for Management of Alaska's Lands (CMAL), representing the state of Alaska and many of its citizens and business interests, as well as many of the nation's most important oil, timber, and mining corporations. The U.S. Chamber of Commerce, the National Association of Manufacturers, and the National Rifle Association supported CMAL, and the Alaska Legislature had appropriated $5.7 million for lobbying, possible litigation, and a national media campaign to publicize CMAL's views.

The Planning Commission Reports

On May 30, 1979, the Joint Federal-State Land Use Planning Commission for Alaska issued its final report. Commission members were convinced that the issues to be decided were comparable in scope to those facing the American West in the last century. But the federal government's approach to Alaska had differed markedly from the often imprudent expansion into the western states, because in the meantime a new land ethic had evolved. No longer would resources be exploited without attention to conservation and environmental protection. Wilderness had been recognized as a scarce national resource meriting protection and preservation. Most lands remaining in the public domain would be retained in public ownership. Federal policies toward the Natives sought to foster self-determination and avoid paternalism. The commission members stated that the public interest demanded that planning precede and regulations govern significant resource development and land use.[10]

The years of labor by commission members cul-minated in its final report. Commission members had looked at the state as a whole and considered the myriad public goals and interests as integrally related to the protection and use of Alaska's land and resources. Its recommendations reflected this viewpoint:

1. New national parks and national wildlife refuge systems should be added to those already existing and also join complimentary areas adjacent to established national parks, wildlife refuges, and forests to these existing units.
2. Certain lands with high natural values as well as resource potential should be managed in a flexible manner compatible with the land's natural values and largely primitive character.
3. Boundaries of new national interest units and additions to existing ones should follow hydrologic, physiographic, or other natural features and exclude privately owned areas.
4. A statewide system of wild, scenic, and recreational rivers should be created on both federal and state lands.
5. The state legislature, by statute, should recognize the public value of recreation and direct agencies to provide public recreational opportunities.
6. The state should manage fish and wildlife. Hunting, fishing, and trapping should be allowed on all national interest units. Subsistence use of fish and wildlife, where scarce, should be given preference over sport and commercial use.
7. Boundaries of proposed national parks and wildlife refuges should avoid including Alaska's major natural transportation corridor routes where possible.
8. All federal lands remaining after selections by the state of Alaska and Native corporations should be retained in public ownership.[11]

The commission then made specific recommen-dations providing a policy framework for future land-use decisions affecting the Arctic. Together with the general recommendations, these were meant to apply to other regions as well. There was also a host of other recommendations, but those summarized above give a flavor of the commission's thinking. It is doubtful, however, that Congress made use of much of the commission's work.

Congress Acts

In early 1979, Congressman Udall reintroduced H.R. 39 and the House passed it, 360 to 65. Udall's bill included 127 million acres of conservation units, with 65 million acres carrying the wilderness designation. As in the previous year, the Senate En-ergy and Natural Resources Committee approved a measure with much smaller acreages. At that point conservationists persuaded Senate leaders to negoti-ate anew.

Out of these deliberations emerged a substitute bill representing a compromise between the Udall measure and the pro-development Senate measure. Not until a year later, on August 19, 1980, after several days of debate and frantic lobbying efforts, did the Senate vote on the Alaska Lands Bill, and it finally passed the substitute bill by a vote of 78 to 14. The measure put 104 million acres in new conserva-tion units; of these, 57 million acres were designated as wilderness.

There were significant differences between the House and Senate versions that would have required a conference committee for resolution. Senate lead-ers informed the House, however, that if the House made any important changes in the Senate version, Alaska's two senators would filibuster the measure, thereby killing any chances of enacting an Alaska lands bill in that Congress.

In November 1980, American voters rejected Carter and swept Republican Ronald Reagan into the presidency. Conservationists feared that Reagan, a conservative and a westerner, would open the pub-lic domain to unbridled exploitation. Furthermore, the Senate gained a Republican majority, and the House, although still Democratic, was more conser-vative. Udall, House leaders, and the conservation lobby quickly realized that the Senate bill was better than nothing. They realized that if they put off the decision for the next Congress, they would probably

A tranquilized polar bear sow with two cubs, 1971.

(Photograph by Larry B. Jennings; courtesy of Alaska Department of Fish & Game.)

lose all the gains they had made in the four-year congressional battle. Thereupon the House quickly passed the Senate version on November 12, and President Carter signed the Alaska National Interest Lands Conservation Act into law on December 2, 1980.[12]

The Alaska National Interest Lands Conservation Act

The 156-page Alaska National Interest Lands Conservation Act of 1980 (ANILCA) is a complex measure. ANILCA not only established the boundaries for federal, state, Native, and private lands but also created a framework for dealing with future conflicts in land use. Those supporting economic development and those favoring environmental protection had fought bitterly over practically every provision in the act, and although it resolved many important issues, it hardly touched that basic conflict. The battleground now shifted from Congress to the land itself. This is an ongoing process with no end in sight, and undoubtedly further legislative efforts will be made to modify ANILCA.

Specifically, ANILCA added 104.3 million acres to conservation systems in Alaska. Of these, 43.6 million are in national parks and preserves; 53.8 million are in wildlife refuges; 3.4 million are in national monuments within the Tongass National Forest; 2.2 million are in national conservation and recreation areas; and an additional 1.2 million are included in twenty-two wild and scenic rivers. Thirty-six conservation units are scattered throughout the state and are interspersed with large and scattered state and Native lands.[13] Taken together, the conservation units established in Alaska before 1980 and those added by ANILCA embrace 150.8 million acres, or about 41 percent of the total area of the state. Adding the BLM lands outside the conservation system brings federal holdings to 60 percent of the lands in Alaska.

Obviously, the federal government has significant landholdings in Alaska. In fact, when state and Native land selections were finally completed in 1993, federal holdings in Alaska amounted to 30 percent of all federal lands nationwide. Designating almost 57 million acres of new wilderness within various units of the conservation system was a highly controversial aspect of ANILCA. With this legislation, the size of the national wilderness preservation system throughout the United States was more than tripled, increasing from 24 million to 80 million acres. Alaska now contains about 71 percent of all federal lands classified as wilderness in the United States. When all land transfers have taken place (which could take decades[14]), the state will own about 104 million acres, or approximately 28 percent of Alaska's land area; private lands will amount to about 2 million acres, or 1 percent; the federal government will own approximately 228 million acres, or 60 percent of Alaska's land area; and the Native Regional Corporations will own about 44 million acres, approximately 12 percent of Alaska's land area.

All lands in the park and refuge systems not designated wilderness were to be studied for possible later inclusion in the national wilderness preservation system, and Congress was to receive recommendations within seven years from the date of the passage of the lands act. ANILCA, however, provides for only one study area of roughly 1.5 million acres in the Chugach National Forest. Environmentalists were particularly bitter about the exclusion of about 150,000 acres from the Misty Fjords Wilderness Area, in the Tongass National Forest near Ketchikan, to accommodate a large molybdenum exploration undertaking. In addition, to pacify the lumber interests and avoid a possible reduction in timber production because of prohibitions on logging in national forest wilderness areas, ANILCA provided for maintaining a production of 4.5 billion board feet per decade, considered to be close to the maximum. To attain that goal, the act authorized an intensive forest management program to be funded by Congress at $40 million a year.[15]

Conservationists were also unhappy that Congress excluded roughly 1 million acres in the Arctic National Wildlife Refuge to allow seismic exploration for oil and gas. Opponents continue to argue that the Porcupine caribou herd, which calves on the coastal plain, the polar bears denning there, and other wildlife, as well as natural values, could be irreparably harmed by resource extraction activities. Since major oil deposits are suspected to lie under the coastal plain, it is clear that this area will remain one of contention.[16]

It is also clear that the land and resource issue will continue in Alaska well into the twenty-first century. The question remains, How will the new landownership patterns affect the state's economic development? The percentage of the federal lands in Alaska open to a variety of commercial uses is fairly high. About 50 percent of all federal lands are open to new mining claims; about 12 percent to homesteading, settlement, and other land disposals; and 75 percent to all other uses, including oil and gas development. In fact, Congress excluded from the conservation units lands with known commercial value and allowed sport and trophy hunting in national preserves. This allows hunting on about 40 percent of the Alaska national park system classified as preserves. Only about 10 percent of all lands in Alaska are excluded from all commercial uses, namely, the national parks and parts of national preserves designated as wilderness.

There are other provisions favorable to development. For example, Title 15 of ANILCA gives the president the authority to recommend to Congress that mineral exploration and development be permitted on all Alaska federal lands except the national parks and Arctic National Wildlife Refuge if he determines that national needs dictate such a course of action. If Congress were then to enact a joint resolution supporting the presidential recommendation, it would take effect.

Other sections of ANILCA directed the secretary of the interior to study all federal lands on the North Slope for oil and gas potential, wilderness and wildlife values, and transportation requirements. Within eight years after the act was made law, the secretary was to submit a final report to Congress on how national interests can best be served in the area. Other provisions of the act established procedures allowing pipelines, highways, power lines, and other transportation systems to cross conservation units even where existing law prohibits such uses.

ANILCA also guaranteed subsistence and other traditional users access into and through conservation units, including parks, and also authorized occupancy permits for cabins in national parks, salmon aquacultural activities in national forest wilderness and wilderness study areas, and public-use cabins and shelters in wilderness areas. Finally, Senator Stevens inserted a clause declaring that no more executive land withdrawals exceeding five thousand acres may be made in Alaska without congressional consent.[17]

The Subsistence Question and the Alaska Land Use Planning Council

Congress realized that the ANCSA of 1971 did not transfer enough land to maintain subsistence activities among Alaska's rural peoples. It therefore included complex provisions in ANILCA to ensure the continuation of the subsistence lifestyle. Federal land managers were to give highest priority to subsistence use of resources by rural Alaskan residents (of any ethnicity), and the state was to continue to manage fish and wildlife on federal lands as long as it adhered to that basic priority. If the state failed to do so, the federal government would take over fish and wildlife management on federal lands for subsistence purposes.

To comply with these provisions, many local and regional subsistence councils and commissions were established throughout Alaska to ensure that rural residents had a voice in the decision-making process. Not all was smooth sailing, however. During the congressional debate over ANILCA, sport-hunting groups opposed the subsistence provisions, asserting that Natives relinquished subsistence rights with the passage of ANCSA. In 1982, Alaska sportsmen's groups undertook a statewide campaign to repeal the state subsistence law passed in 1978 to accommodate the ANILCA subsistence provisions. The voters rejected the initiative, which, if passed, would have resulted in the federal assumption of fish and wildlife management. But Alaska sportsmen (mostly urban dwelling) continued to challenge state and federal laws that supported rural residents' priority in taking fish and game when those resources were limited. Ultimately, sportsmen prevailed at the state level and brought on federal participation. To date the subsistence section

of ANILCA has withstood legal challenge, and federal and state overseers continue to practice divided management of hunting and fishing on federal lands in Alaska.

In 1996, Congress also established an Alaska land bank, designed to protect undeveloped lands and promote cooperative land management among the various landowners. This was a voluntary effort in which a Native corporation or anyone else could cooperate with other landowners to shield unimproved and undeveloped land from taxation. It will be recalled that, under the provisions of the ANCSA, lands conveyed to Native corporations were not to be taxed for twenty years as long as they remained undeveloped. The land-bank program protected village corporation lands that were selected primarily to protect subsistence activities. Lands placed in the land bank could not be sold or developed except as provided in the agreement. Furthermore, management of those lands had to be compatible with that of adjacent state or federal lands. Lands could be withdrawn again, but if they were then developed, they would become taxable. The land bank concept, an untried one, was not used as far as we can determine.[18]

Looking toward the Future

The division of Alaska's land has resulted in an often confusing patchwork of ownership. Unfortunately, it has too often proved impossible to draw rational boundary lines. Various natural resources have been divided by mixed ownership—and wildlife, which requires extensive habitats, pays no attention to landownership. The Joint Federal-State Land Use Planning Commission anticipated many of these problems early in the 1970s and analyzed a variety of institutional mechanisms suitable for cooperative planning and management after passage of ANILCA. What is clear is that it will take time, much litigation, and also considerable goodwill among all of Alaska's landowners to implement the intent of the Alaska National Interest Lands Conservation Act of 1980.

Chapter 22

The Oil Boom

No single event in Alaska's history has had an impact on the region comparable to that of Atlantic Richfield's discovery of the gigantic Prudhoe Bay oil field in 1968. But it involved luck, and as we shall see, it followed years of wrangling over how to manage Alaska's gas and oil resources. The road to Prudhoe was paved with power struggles, political infighting, and conflicting interests. It also resulted from the hard work of a group of committed and dedicated state employees.

Marshall's Folly

Roscoe Bell, the state's first director of the division of lands within the Department of Natural Resources, recruited geologist Tom Marshall in the fall of 1960 as an assistant land selector, and shortly thereafter he was promoted to land selection officer. Bell asked Marshall to stay at his job at least one year; it turned out that he stayed eighteen years. Marshall had earned a degree in geology from the University of Colorado and had worked for various oil companies in Wyoming before becoming an independent consultant, assembling lease plays. He moved to Alaska in 1958, hoping to homestead and confident that he could make a living in the recent oil boom.[1]

In his state job, Marshall familiarized himself with the applicable federal and state statutes. Under the 1958 Statehood Act, Congress had given the new state the right to select in excess of 103 million acres from the vacant, unreserved, and unappropriated public domain. Marshall recalled that the Bureau of Land Management (BLM) and the state had agreed that the latter would select 4 million acres a year in square or rectangular parcels for more efficient land management. The state complied with the BLM's request for a number of years, selecting marginal and higher value lands to comply with the bureau's compactness standard.[2]

In 1961 Marshall proposed that the state select 1,507,630 acres of Arctic North Slope land, basing his selection on information about the area he had obtained from a U.S. Geological Survey publication. Marshall stated that he used "regional geology . . . in my selection criteria. . . . I transferred my Rocky Mountain oil and gas exploration experience." The same publication was available to the BLM and the oil companies, "but they had their own ideas." Marshall gave his "selection the highest priority for its geologic promise," but it did not meet BLM's "square and compact" criteria.[3]

After Marshall had prioritized the land selections in 1962, he became the state's only petroleum geologist in the division of mines and minerals. John Fryburg, his former subordinate, now was in charge of land selections. Marshall, however, still attended Division of Land Monday staff meetings. He learned from Fryburg that the BLM had abandoned its compactness standard, which meant there was hope for Marshall's "misshapen North Slope coastal selection." The BLM apparently had realized that it would be a protracted nightmare to determine who owned the navigable waters. The state claimed ownership out to the three-mile limit. BLM surveyors had stated that there was a small tidal range on the North Slope. The land was so flat that it would take years to figure out the tidal effect, so state ownership of the narrow coastal strip made sense to BLM. Another issue emerging was Native land claims. A number of Native groups had begun to file conflicts with the BLM land selection, and the agency realized that Alaska could "not be divided into tidy manageable segments."[4]

Many in the Department of Natural Resources disagreed with Marshall's priority. The goal of the selection process was to enhance revenue, but the bureau and the oil companies both seemed less than enthusiastic about Marshall's selection. Indeed, Marshall's was the first selection the state ever made that had no known surface uses. But on January 1964, the state officially selected Marshall's priority. After that Marshall received much communication from politicians and citizens alike. Politicians wanted to know the basis for his "Arctic wasteland selection." Others, oil companies among them, called his selection "Marshall's icebox" and "Marshall's folly." Fellow homesteaders referred to it as "worthless tundra." In short, Marshall did not win any popularity contests.[5]

By October 1964 the BLM had granted the state tentative approval on its North Slope selection. On December 9, 1964, the state received $5.6 million in bonus monies from lease sales covering the Kuparuk-Ugnu areas of the North Slope—not spectacular compared with future income, but sufficient to cover the filing fees and have some left over.[6]

North Slope Lease Sales

Before the Atlantic Richfield (ARCO) discovery, however, politicians had to smooth the way to encourage interested oil companies to bid on state lease sales. Oil companies had asked Alaska's Governor William Egan to include North Slope acreage in a lease sale scheduled for November 22, 1966. Yet no such acreage was included, so state lands direc-

tor Bell asked the governor on October 7, 1966, to allow him to offer nearly thirty-eight thousand acres offshore in Prudhoe Bay. The land lay atop the promising Prudhoe Bay structure. Governor Egan refused permission. His reason for not allowing the lease sale of this acreage was because on October 4, 1966, the Arctic Slope Native Association had filed a lawsuit seeking to enjoin the state from selecting or leasing North Slope land because the Iñupiats claimed aboriginal title to the land, which they had used and occupied from time immemorial, and no law, treaty, or sale had ever terminated that title (see chapter 19).[7]

In essence, Egan denied the requests of ARCO and Exxon to include the offshore acres, and this decision "cut the heart out of the scheduled November state lease sale." Only a single well was tentatively planned for the entire North Slope. Egan had withdrawn those tracts that ARCO and other oil companies needed before they could commit to drilling at Prudhoe Bay. In November of that year, however, Alaskans went to the polls and elected Republican Walter Hickel as their governor. Hickel's selection was to benefit ARCO, Exxon, and British Petroleum (BP).[8]

Hickel's victory was in no small way aided by the support of Alaska's Native leaders who had tired of what they perceived to be Egan's weak support for their land claims. Hickel now had to deal with the North Slope oil and gas leasing, which had become a contentious issue between the Natives and the oil companies. Eskimos now claimed all of the North Slope, while the oil companies wanted to lease more of it.[9]

Egan and Hickel were very different in temperament. Egan consulted everybody even remotely connected with a policy issue, and then waited to the last moment before making a decision. He played his cards close to his vest and did not tell even his wife before making his decision public. Hickel, on the other hand, was instinctive and spontaneous. Thus with the election, the state's oil leasing climate changed overnight, from caution to action. Hickel reversed Egan's withdrawal order, and less than two months after his inauguration the state offered the Prudhoe parcels at a special oil and gas lease sale.[10]

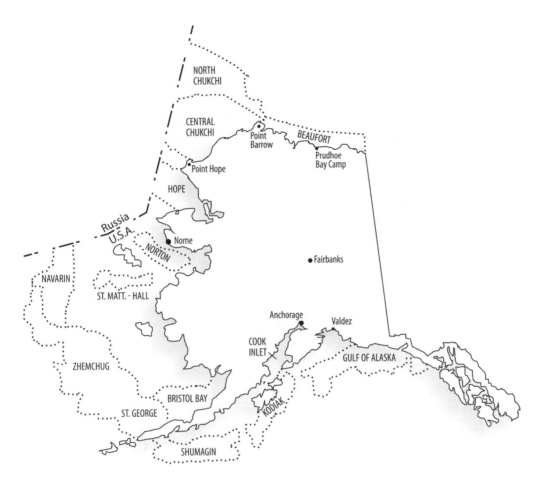

Alaska's Sedimentary Basins with Possible Oil and Gas Deposits

Native leaders opposed the sale, but Hickel believed that besides helping the oil companies, the sale might speed the federal courts or the Congress to settle Native land claims. A few days before the sale, Hickel met Native leaders and persuaded them not to file protests against it. In exchange, he pledged that the state would join them in their claims against the federal government. Oil lease money, Hickel promised, would not be locked in escrow, and many Natives believed that circulating cash would help the local economy.[11]

The ARCO Strike

The January 24, 1967, Prudhoe Bay oil lease sale offered forty-seven thousand acres. ARCO, Exxon, and BP bid on the parcels offered. ARCO now wanted to start drilling, and it moved its Susie drill to Prudhoe Bay and began drilling onshore in April 1967. Work at Prudhoe Bay State No. 1 was suspended after less than two weeks at a depth of about two thousand feet because of the state's drilling ban after spring breakup. It did not start again until late November.[12]

A month after resuming drilling, ARCO found gas and oil. Company geologists soon realized that they had made a spectacular find, but to be certain they needed to drill a second well for confirmation. Geologist Gill Mull, who represented Exxon, recalled "that we probably had a gas well." On December 27, gas blew to the surface under tremendous pressure, was ignited, and "blew strongly for hours,"

Kuparuk and Sadlerochit Oil
Fields, Prudhoe Bay.

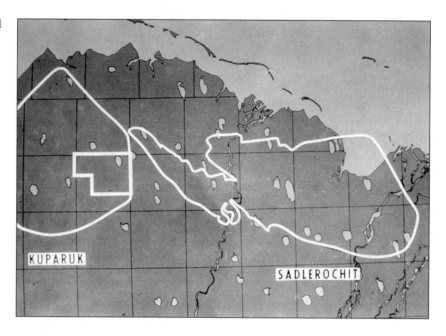

KUPARUK

SADLEROCHIT

sounding "like the roar of a nearby jetplane." The flare, visible for miles around, still burned on the morning of December 28. It burned for twenty-four hours, and although ARCO wanted to keep the find a secret, rumors soon circulated. In mid-January 1968, the company went public, announcing that it had discovered gas, not oil. By February there were increasing signs of oil. A press release announced that the well had "sealed off a 470-foot sand section of which the top 400 feet is gas producing and the lower 70 feet is oil saturated."[13]

In March, ARCO announced that the well produced 1,152 barrels of oil per day. ARCO was cautious, however, and stated that although the test had been encouraging, additional information was needed to determine if the well was commercially feasible. The company wanted to maintain tight security on the well, because ARCO chairman Robert O. Anderson did not want the company accused of manipulating its stock price with leaked information. ARCO executive Harry Jamison described the period after the January announcement as the "goldfish bowl atmosphere." One of the company's geologists "briefed planeloads of executives, politicians, United Nations representatives, reporters, and others as they toured Prudhoe Bay."[14]

Soon ARCO drilled its second, confirmatory well—Sag River No. 1—at the mouth of the Sagavanirktok River. Security was extremely tight. In late June 1968 ARCO announced that the Sag River well could produce 3,567 barrels of oil per day. Soon it became apparent that the two wells, seven miles apart, would produce 20,000 to 30,000 barrels of oil per day, equivalent to Middle East volumes. The Sag River well confirmed the discovery of a world-class giant oil field on Alaska's North Slope.[15]

In late July 1968, the international geological consulting firm DeGolyer & McNaughton described the Prudhoe Bay discovery as "one of the largest petroleum accumulations known to the world today." Specifically, the consultants wrote that the Prudhoe Bay field contained 21 billion barrels of oil in place and almost 38 trillion cubic feet of natural gas. The Sadlerochit reservoir sandstone, at a depth of about 8,800 feet, was expected to contain 9.6 billion barrels of recoverable oil, in excess of 21 trillion cubic feet of recoverable gas, and another 16 trillion cubic feet in solution with the oil. The Prudhoe Bay oil was of medium gravity, with less than 1 percent by weight sulfur content. The Prudhoe Bay field covered an area of about forty-five miles by eighteen miles. That made it North America's largest oil field.

In July 1968 there had only been four drill rigs on the North Slope. By the end of 1968 there were more than a dozen, and at least a dozen oil companies had seismic crews working on the North Slope, including Amerada Hess, Marathon Oil, Getty, Louisiana Land and Exploration, and H. L. Hunt.[16]

Naval Petroleum Reserve No. 4

The Prudhoe Bay discovery was not the first oil find in the North. As far back as 1923, President Warren G. Harding had created Naval Petroleum Reserve No. 4 (NPR-4), a reserved area on the North Slope of approximately thirty-seven thousand square miles. At the request of the U.S. Navy, the U.S. Geological Survey conducted a topographic and geological reconnaissance of NPR-4 to map the petroleum reserves. There was no follow-up work, however, and it was not until the summer of 1943 that the U.S. Bureau of Mines conducted field examinations on the Arctic Slope and recommended further and more definitive surveys.[17]

In March 1944, Secretary of the Navy Frank Knox informed President Franklin D. Roosevelt that his department had formulated a definite and comprehensive program for the exploration of NPR-4. The president approved the proposal, and Congress appropriated $1 million to the navy to start exploration work. The navy intended to drill six wells, and in testimony on the naval appropriation bill, Secretary Knox told the congressmen that he "proposed to use Seabees [naval construction battalions], ideal men for that type of work," for the drilling operations. Before the navy dispatched the Seabees, however, it sent a reconnaissance team to survey conditions on the Arctic Coast of Alaska. The team made a surface examination of the geological structure along the Colville River about one hundred miles from its mouth and found promising indications of oil. In the meantime, the navy had obtained a light drilling outfit and shipped it by cargo vessel to Barrow, from where it had to be hauled overland to the proposed testing site.[18]

By April 1944, the reconnaissance party had found a good oil structure at Umiat Mountain, on the Colville River, and geological mapping of the area "revealed a closed anticlinal structure with live gas and oil seeps." Secretary of the Navy James Forrestal decided to start drilling at Umiat in the winter of 1945, while directing further geophysical exploration and core drilling at Cape Simpson to determine the oil-bearing structure. Additionally, Seabees were surveying a prospective pipeline route and conducting reconnaissance work in the southeastern part of the reserve in the spring of 1945. Above all, the secretary was determined to have the navy undertake a long-range exploratory program with a minimum expenditure of power, time, and effort "to determine the presence and quantity of oil in Naval Petroleum Reserve No. 4." The Naval Appropriations Bill for 1946 contained $1,620,000 to cover the work for the coming year.[19] At the end of 1945, Secretary Forrestal informed the president that by the time the work in NPR-4 was finished "there will have been expended approximately $8,000,000 and if oil is found in justifiable volume, a development program for readiness involving an expenditure in the order of $150,000,000 may be indicated."[20]

By early 1946, much had changed. The end of the war and the demobilization of naval personnel had made necessary a reevaluation of the navy's future course in exploring the reserve. The Seabees, in NPR-4 since the spring of 1944, had been "mustered out of the service and no other qualified personnel [were] available." Therefore, contractors from the petroleum industry had to be found to continue the work. Exploration so far had been limited to the eastern third of the reserve. The navy and the U.S. Geological Survey had collaborated on the work, and now these two and the photographic section of the army were correlating the collected data and preparing maps for the use of surface geological parties in the summer of 1946. Some work had also been accomplished in the southern section of the reserve and at Cape Simpson. A test well at Umiat, approximately 1,900 feet deep, had already encountered five separate oil-bearing sands, but so far none had been of commercial value. The preliminary pipeline survey had been completed, and a study had shown a recoverable reserve of between 400 and 500 million barrels of oil, with a potential production of one hundred thousand barrels a day, which was required to economically support such a venture.[21]

In support of the exploratory work, the navy had established a base camp at Barrow with secondary camps at Umiat and Cape Simpson. During the summers of 1944 and 1945, approximately twenty-six thousand tons of equipment and supplies had been landed at Barrow, and during the coldest winter months when the ground was sufficiently frozen to bear the weight of sled trains it was taken to the secondary camps. The navy had built landing fields at Barrow, Umiat, and Cape Simpson and emergency strips midway between Fairbanks and Barrow and Barrow and Umiat. In 1947, Congress appropriated $9.6 million to continue the work until 1950, making continued funds available until 1953. Contractors and field parties of the U.S. Geological Survey ranged over the reserve from 1946 until 1953 and also explored a similarly large area of public land contiguous to the reserve. Seabees had drilled the first wildcat well in 1945. Although it showed light gravity oil, it could not be completed as a producer because there was not enough oil. The same was true of a second well.[22]

In 1946, Arctic Contractors, a joint venture of three specially qualified firms, continued to carry out all the phases of exploratory work except for geological research, which was performed by members of the U.S. Geological Survey. The contractors drilled eleven wells in the Umiat area, outlining a field that contained an estimated 100 million barrels of recoverable oil.[23]

Between 1944 and 1953, when the navy suspended its exploration of the reserve, thirty-six wildcat wells had been drilled and forty-four core holes had been sunk, varying in depth from 2,000 to 11,872 feet. Arctic Contractors found two minor oil and three natural-gas fields but made no commercially significant discoveries. The navy's findings suggested that the area north of the Brooks Range might contain extensive oil and gas reserves. But while the navy could claim some success, the area was not as rich as many had hoped.[24] By the end of 1952 some 153 wells and core tests had been drilled in Alaska since 1901, but no commercial quantities of oil or gas had been found.

Alaska Propane and NPR-4

When the Eisenhower administration terminated the NPR-4 exploration program in 1953, it was not the end of federal involvement in NPR-4. The Department of the Interior now had to decide what to do with the geological data accumulated over the years. What plans did the BLM have for vacating Public Land Order 82, thereby opening the land to development, and how would it deal with the special leasing problems once that had happened?[25] How were territorial Governor B. Frank Heintzleman and other Interior officials to deal with pressures various parties interested in developing northern Alaska's energy resources exerted on them? Interior key personnel met on May 17, 1954, in Washington, D.C. to arrive at a consensus on what to do next.[26]

The navy had surplused the considerable amount of drilling equipment and other materials remaining and decided to sell it to the public once various federal agencies with an interest had made their selections. Governor Heintzleman mentioned that a Fairbanks group had opposed any such sales until it had obtained leases on the withdrawn lands that were to be opened. The BLM indicated that it was ready to revoke Public Land Order 82 as early as June 1954. There was to be no oil and gas leasing, however, until a ninety-day waiting period giving interested parties an opportunity to study the technical data and until a land survey net had been projected on paper over the area opened for leasing. One conference participant pointed out that if NPR-4 had established the commercial viability of gas in the Gubik field, then the area would have to be opened to competitive rather than noncompetitive bidding. After some discussion, the participants agreed that such commercial viability had been established.[27]

Other members of the group raised the question as to whether or not private interests might wish to acquire not only the surplus equipment but also the whole Barrow base camp, including its buildings. Or perhaps the territorial government might be interested in purchasing the navy's materials, equipment and facilities. Governor Heintzleman expressed an interest in federal legislation that would transfer all of this to the territory "without exchange of funds." Conferees discussed special problems that might arise through mining claims or surface entries by private interests thus obtaining rights in NPR-4 in airfields and building sites, among others. All agreed that the questions the conferees had raised had to be answered speedily.[28]

In June 1954, Alaska Propane Gas and Oil Company, Inc. of Fairbanks, which James W. Dalton and others had founded, informed the director of the BLM that it wanted to have "that portion of Public Law 82, which comprises the Gubec [*sic*] structures north of the Brooks Range, removed from withdrawal." The company operated gas distribution lines in and near Fairbanks and had a franchise to furnish gas to the residents of the city. It also intended to supply the two military bases, as well as the Golden Valley Electric Association and the Municipal Utilities System of Fairbanks, with cheap power "for their electrical and steam users."[29]

The Alaska Propane Gas and Oil Company wrote the BLM that fuel costs in Fairbanks varied widely. Coal was the cheapest, at about thirteen dollars per ton, or seventy-six cents per million BTUs. The estimated 300 billion cubic feet of gas in the Gubik structure at seventy-six cents per million BTUs would be worth 228 million dollars. This gas volume allowed considerable leeway in setting a price required for amortization of the gas line and development and would bring cheaper fuel to the Fairbanks area.[30]

The company proposed to build a pipeline to Fairbanks from the Gubik structure, located approximately 465 miles north of Fairbanks and the Brooks Range and east of Umiat. The estimated cost of building a twelve-inch pipeline, including survey, clearing, grading, and river crossings; drilling twelve gas wells; and installing distribution lines at the pipeline terminal was $35,925,342, or $65,065 per mile. A sixteen-inch pipeline would cost $42,864,507, or $79,988 per mile. The company had arranged to secure $6 million in equity capital either in the Alaska Propane Gas and Oil Company or a new corporation set up for this purpose. The Metropolitan Life Insurance Company had agreed to lend $30 million for the pipeline construction "if the test wells established a minimum of 300 billion cubic feet of recoverable gas."[31]

On October 1, 1954, nationally syndicated columnist Drew Pearson reported that plans to lease "rich Alaskan oil lands" to private interests were about to be announced despite "heavy navy and congressional opposition." Further, Pearson suggested that a conflict of interest existed for some of the principle parties, including Vice President Nixon. The rumor spread that the secretary planned to release large tracts of publicly owned Artic land, much more than those that Public Land Order 82 had withdrawn.[32]

In the face of this criticism, the lands were not released, despite all the investment of time and money and Alaskans' real need for a natural gas source. The executive of the Alaska Propane Company contacted Secretary of the Interior Douglas McKay on October 5 and thanked him for his personal interest and assistance. But the company could do nothing if the lands were not released. The Gubik gas field was not developed, and no pipeline was constructed to bring gas to Fairbanks.[33]

Interest in the Kenai National Moose Range

Still, oil industry leaders dreamed of sudden riches to be wrested from Alaska's several promising oil structures. In the fall of 1954 Texas oilman F. Kirk Johnson, along with a group of wealthy businessmen, including movie actor Jimmy Stewart, filed on more than two hundred thousand acres of oil leases in the Kateel River country west of Fairbanks. Oil prospectors had become excited about this property because geologists believed that the oil basin the navy had discovered at Point Barrow and Umiat extended south of the Brooks Range and that oil could be found in the Norton Sound area, a much more accessible, and therefore less expensive, region to develop.[34]

Many geologists believed that a great inland sea laid down the Point Barrow oil reserve eons ago. After the basin was created, these geologists reasoned, the Brooks Range uplifted and cut the big oil basin in half. Therefore, half of the oil lands lay north of the range, and the rest to the south. Geologists found rock formations in the Brooks Range that matched formations found underground in the Barrow and Umiat region. Oil shale formations on the south of the Brooks Range indicated that these mountains uplifted through oil deposits. Hopes ran high that wells drilled on these leases "will tap the same rich oil beds the navy found north of the mountains." Although most interested parties realized that large oil companies had to perform considerable prospecting to locate the oil basins underlying Alaska, expert geologists were convinced that Alaska had "great oil reserves, and someday these reserves will be [its] biggest sources of income.[35]

In the 1950s the U.S. Congress increased the oil and gas acreage an individual or company could hold to one hundred thousand acres under lease and two hundred thousand acres under option. Obviously, Congress wanted to encourage oil and gas leasing in the North. Soon oil companies began to pay attention to the Kenai Peninsula and Cook Inlet and began filing lease applications.[36]

The Kenai National Moose Range had originally been closed to oil and gas leasing in 1953, but the Department of the Interior allowed Richfield Oil Corporation and two minor oil company partners into the range in that same year. Secretary of the Interior Fred Seaton had stated that it was a test to see if oil could be produced without destroying the wildlife. He said that more leasing would be allowed after stricter regulations had been adopted and Fish and Wildlife officials had decided how much of the range to open to oil development.[37]

While the oil companies focused their attention on the Kenai, the early 1950s witnessed the formation of a leaseholder's clique that utilized its position at the center of the Anchorage business world to advance the future of Alaska oil. Locke Jacobs, a clerk at the Anchorage Army-Navy Surplus store, had come to Alaska in 1947 and worked at a variety of jobs throughout the territory before he arrived in Anchorage in 1952. There he started his education in the oil and gas leasing business, which soon made him one of the great sources of oil-lease knowledge in Alaska. Locke did not have the financial means or the business connections of some other members of the group that formed around him, but he did all the legwork, filing applications, making maps, and copying records. Without his work the clique would not have functioned. Therefore, Glenn Miller and John McManamin, the owners of the Army-Navy

Surplus store, insisted that their enterprising clerk fully share in any of the group's profits from oil and gas leasing.[38]

The Spit and Argue Club, as the members called their group, had fourteen members. These included hotelman Wilbur Wester and Willard Nagley, whose parents owned the land on which Wester's Westward Hotel was built; Fred Axford, a versatile entrepreneur who was a jeweler and an ice cream and office supply store owner; George Jones, an accountant whose clients included the *Anchorage Daily Times*, the Westward Hotel, and the Army-Navy Surplus store; Phil and Ray Raykovich, the owners of the bar next to the surplus store; contractor C. R. "Kelly" Foss; and National Bank of Alaska vice president Rod Johnston. Elmer Rasmuson, the president of the National Bank of Alaska, Robert B. Atwood, the editor and publisher of the *Anchorage Daily Times* and Rasmuson's brother-in-law, were also members, as was Howard Carver.[39]

The members of the Spit and Argue Club were at the center of Alaska's oil fever. The landmen (geologists who scouted out land with oil deposits) and other employees of the major oil companies stayed at Wester's Westward Hotel when they came to town. They bought clothing and outdoor gear at the Army-Navy Surplus store, and publisher Atwood interviewed them. Some opened accounts at Rasmuson's National Bank of Alaska. Axford and Jones served on the Anchorage City Council. Most of the members met each week for lunch at the Elks Club the day after City Council meetings, and much of the discussion dealt with local politics.[40]

In 1955, the club applied for more than one hundred thousand acres of leases in the Kenai National Moose Range, then closed to leasing. Richfield Oil Corporation had asked the club to lease the land on its behalf because it had already filed leases on one hundred thousand acres, which was the limit. The Spit and Argue Club also signed an agreement to transfer the leases to Richfield if they were ever issued.[41]

Swanson River

Fast forward to 1957, a year that long will be remembered by the industry. Humble Oil & Refining

Alaska Gulf & Oil Company drilling rig at Knik, 1955.

(Author's collection.)

Company drilled the most promising dry hole ever in Alaska, the Bear Creek wildcat. Though it went to 14,900 feet and showed signs of both oil and gas, it was not a commercial find. It was, however, a very expensive well, at a cost of about $6 million.[42]

On July 23, 1957, Richfield Oil Corporation cored into the oil sands of what became the Swanson River field, establishing Alaska's first truly commercial oil production. It was Richfield's first wildcat in the territory, and the company had been lucky indeed, because its drilling rig, situated on the Swanson River oil structure, nearly missed the reservoir. Richfield completed its Swanson River Unit 1 on September 29, 1957, after drilling to a depth of 12,384 feet. Oil flowed from the discovery well at a rate of 900 barrels a day, and it also produced 112,000 cubic feet of gas a day. A second well was started in the same year and completed in 1958. Eventually, eleven dry wells were drilled in the task of outlining the boundaries of the Swanson River field.[43]

On a December day in that same year, Alaska's delegate to Congress, E. L "Bob" Bartlett, sat alone in his Washington office, dictating a memo. He recounted how he had been "an observer," the day before, "at one of the most adroit performances I have ever witnessed." He and a few top officials of the

Eisenhower administration "had seen the curtain raising on the final act of a three-year drama played mostly behind the scenes, to bring the oil industry to Alaska." Spit and Argue member Wilbur Wester was the star of the day. He wanted to make sure that the Department of the Interior would lease the Kenai National Moose Range acreage. More specifically, the issue was whether leases would be made noncompetitively, namely, on a first-come, first-served basis. If that happened, he and his partners in the Spit and Argue Club would get leases on tens of thousands of acres Richfield had promised to buy from them.[44]

There was also another group, opposed to the Spit and Argue Club, led by Dan Cuddy, president of the First National Bank of Anchorage, and developer and contractor Walter J. Hickel, who favored competitive leases because they would bring more money into the territorial treasury and give everyone a chance to compete for the leases. Amidst accusations and counter-accusations between the two groups and intense lobbying of officials at the Interior Department, someone discovered that Interior had issued the Richfield lease while a prohibition on all leasing in wildlife refuges was in effect. That was true, and Richfield, two minor oil company partners, and the Spit and Argue Club held the only leases in the moose range—all issued while a leasing suspension was in effect.[45]

On January 8, 1958, Secretary of the Interior Fred Seaton announced new wildlife range leasing regulations. They prohibited oil and gas leasing on wildlife refuge lands except in Alaska. Because of the extreme interest in Alaskan oil development, Seaton had placed the Kenai National Moose Range into a separate category. The U.S. Fish and Wildlife Service was to determine which areas of the range should be opened to oil development. Feeling pressured by the industry and its boosters, the service rushed through its survey of the moose range and proposed to open half of it to development. Seaton wanted the service to take more time to study the issue, but it had been four years since his Anchorage friends in the Spit and Argue Club had first applied for leases in the moose range, and only limited exploration had been allowed. Richfield's discovery

made it difficult to wait while Seaton "fretted over what to do."[46]

Meanwhile, in early February, Congress asked that all oil and gas leasing in Alaska be suspended again while it considered increasing rents and royalties. This congressional delay was the same fight Hickel had waged the year before—namely, why should oil companies get leases in Alaska for half of what they paid in the contiguous states? In the territory, leases were twenty-five cents an acre, but they were double that everywhere else in the country. Lease applicants had to pay a one-year advance rent payment. That meant shelling out five hundred dollars, on average. Oil company lobbyists and territorial officials argued that the lower rate was needed as an incentive to explore in Alaska. But since oil had been discovered, was an incentive still needed?[47]

In an April hearing before the Senate Committee on Interior and Insular Affairs, Senator Clinton P. Anderson (D-NM) wanted an investigation to determine why Interior was giving away twenty-five-cent-an-acre leases without competitive bidding in a proven area. Anderson was particularly troubled that territorial officials and Delegate Bartlett supported these giveaways. The delegate, realizing that the rents would soon be doubled, lobbied and made certain that the new law provided a one-year rental break of twenty-five-cents an acre for leases "on which application had been filed before May 3, 1958"—safeguarding Richfield and the Spit and Argue Club.[48] Seaton ordered half of the moose range opened, and August 14, 1958, was the day land would become available for leasing on a first-come, first-served basis at the BLM office in Anchorage. First in line that day were Kenai homesteader Ruby Coyle, Dr. Michael Beirne, and lawyer James Tallman.

Three weeks after Seaton had opened the moose range to leasing in August 1958, the Spit and Argue Club received leases to about seventy thousand acres. Under the 1955 agreement, the club transferred the leases to Richfield and its new partner, Standard Oil Company of California, now Chevron U.S.A. Work proceeded slowly in the new field, but on March 21, 1960, a rig on a Spit and Argue Club lease struck oil, at 3,400 barrels a day the biggest find since the original Richfield discovery. All the oil discovered in the second area, the Soldotna Creek side, came from club leases. The two fields merged into one called the Swanson River field.[49]

Even though Coyle, Beirne, and Tallman had been the first that day to apply for the land they wanted, BLM decided in October 1959 that those leases should go to the Spit and Argue Club, whose members had applied four years earlier when the range had been closed to leasing. The law allowed noncompetitive leases in areas with no proven oil deposits. In the Kenai there had been a major strike, and therefore federal regulations called for competitive bidding. Interior Department officials led Congress to believe that this would happen to most of the leases pending on the moose range. Ultimately, however, it was up to the secretary to decide which method to use. Seaton did not require competitive bidding.[50]

For Coyle, Beirne, and Tallman it meant the beginning of a six-year, ultimately unsuccessful court fight to claim the leases to which they felt entitled. Tallman contacted Beirne, Coyle, and nine others whose applications had been rejected. He filed a formal complaint with the BLM, arguing that since the moose range had been closed to leasing since August 1953, the BLM should not have accepted any lease applications at that time.[51]

The director of the BLM and the secretary of the interior, however, both affirmed the decision granting the leases to the Spit and Argue Club. Then the Court of Appeals for the District of Columbia reversed BLM and the secretary, holding that Executive Order 8974, creating the Kenai National Moose Range in 1941, had withdrawn the contested lands from leasing under the Mineral Leasing Act of 1920. The lands, therefore, should have remained closed to leasing until reopened by a revised departmental regulation on August 14, 1958. The lease applications the Spit and Argue Club had filed while the lands were closed were therefore ineffective.

The case next went to the U.S. Supreme Court, which upheld the leases. It argued that ever since the promulgation of Executive Order 8979 and Public Land Order No. 487, regulating disposition of public lands located in the Kenai National Moose Range, the secretary of the interior had consistently construed both orders not to bar the issuance of oil and gas leases. Section 17 of the Mineral Leasing Act of 1920 stated that a person first making application for a lease was entitled to such a lease without competitive bidding. The BLM had issued the leases effective September 1, 1958. The Tallman applications reached the BLM for processing in October 1959 and were rejected because the land had already been leased to the prior applicant.[52]

The Spit and Argue Club members and their heirs fared well. The *Anchorage Daily News* compiled an estimate of what each of the fourteen members earned between 1962 and 1988, determined through state and federal records. The twenty-seven-year average per year for each member was $107,157, or a total of $2.9 million per club member. These payments have continued since 1988 and will continue until the Swanson River field runs dry. Tallman, Beirne, and Coyle, like most Alaskans, found themselves excluded from Alaska's new oil wealth.[53]

Oil Development after Statehood

After Richfield Oil Corporation completed its second well on the Swanson River, it made an agreement with Standard Oil Company of California, naming it as operator of its Cook Inlet basin holdings. Tanker trucks took the first oil from the Swanson River field to Seward for shipment to refineries in the contiguous states. Then Richfield and Standard built the first modern crude oil pipeline to move oil from the wells to the Nikiski Beach terminal, which Standard had built. The first shipment of Alaska crude a tanker transported from Nikiski Beach to the contiguous states occurred on November 12, 1960.[54] In 1962, Standard began construction at Nikiski Beach of Alaska's first petroleum refinery, which produced jet and diesel fuel and asphalt.[55]

In 1959, Union Oil of California (Unocal) discovered Alaska's first commercial gas at the Kenai and Cannery Loop fields southwest of the Swanson River field. Unocal partnered with the Ohio Oil Company (later Marathon Oil Company) as operators of a co-venture to develop the gas field. A pipeline was built to Anchorage and furnished the city with

Concern for Oil Conservation

In the mid-1950s it had been territorial legislator Irene Ryan who had advised territorial governor Ernest Gruening on oil and gas matters. Ryan had a degree in mining and petroleum geology from the New Mexico School of Mines. She designed small airports in Alaska for the Civil Aeronautics Administration and then opened an Anchorage engineering and land surveying office. She was knowledgeable about the oil industry and knew many of its players. She informed Governor Gruening that Alaska had great oil and gas reserves that would someday be found, and convinced him that the territory needed a conservation law like the one in Texas. Without such a law, reckless oil drilling practices would waste valuable natural reservoir pressures in oil fields and permit the escape of huge amounts of hydrocarbons. The law would compel lessees competing for oil in a field to coordinate drilling. It would control well spacing and also prevent drainage of oil from future state lands lying next to federal lands.

Territorial Commissioner of Mines Phil Holdsworth attended meetings of the thirty-three-member Interstate Oil Compact Commission and returned with valuable materials on the subject. During the 1955 legislative session, Ryan and Holdsworth drafted the Alaska Oil Conservation Act, which the legislature passed and the governor signed into law. The 1955 legislature also passed a 1 percent gross oil and gas production tax in lieu of local petroleum taxes. It also passed an eight-cent-per-barrel "conservation tax" not to exceed seven hundred thousand dollars in any one year, to be levied on any oil or gas to be found in the territory. The money was to pay for the administration of a newly created Alaska Oil and Gas Conservation Commission.

During the last territorial legislature before statehood, in 1957, lawmakers passed the Alaska Land Act patterned on the U.S. Mineral Leasing Act of 1920. To be offered only by competitive bid were the 1 million acre Mental Health Lands that Congress had granted the territory in 1956, all University of Alaska lands, and all lands lying three nautical miles seaward of mean high tide, the so-called tide and submerged lands. The Territorial Land Board had authority to classify oil and gas uplands as either competitive, cash bidding or noncompetitive, or first-come, first-served. Alaska became an oil state sooner than expected. The territorial government was surprised when, by the end of 1957, major oil companies, independents, lease brokers, and individuals had filed for leases on more than 10 million acres in Alaska.

Source: Jack Roderick, *Crude Dreams: A Personal History of Oil and Politics in Alaska* (Fairbanks/Seattle: Epicenter Press, 1997), 95, 99–101.

its first natural gas. In the 1960s and throughout the 1970s operators discovered several more gas fields on the inlet's northwest side, but none began production until the 1980s.[56]

In 1960 the state opened Cook Inlet to oil and gas leasing. In 1962 Pan American Petroleum discovered the Middle Ground Shoal oil field. Shell Western Exploration and Production, Inc. and Unocal, with Richfield as a partner, operated Alaska's first offshore oil field. Shell's engineers successfully designed the first offshore platform in Cook Inlet—a very difficult environment, with among the world's highest tides rising and falling more than thirty feet, twice a day. The inlet's waters have strong currents, and in the winter, ice threatens to crush the platform. Platform A came to the inlet in 1964, and in 1964–65 it withstood the most brutal conditions of the worst winter in one hundred years. It began production in 1967, an engineering success for Shell's designers.[57]

In 1965 Unocal and Marathon discovered the Trading Bay and McArthur fields. In 1966 the companies put two offshore platforms in place: the 7,200-ton Grayling platform over the McArthur field and the Monopod platform over the Trading Bay field. The latter was another first for Alaska and the world's oil industry, the first single-legged offshore platform ever erected. By the early 1990s fifteen offshore platforms operated in Cook Inlet, extracting oil from four fields. Thirteen of these were put into place prior to 1969. In 1990–91 Unocal acquired 100 percent operational control of the Middle Ground Shoal and Granite Point fields through sales and purchase agreements with Amoco, Chevron, and Texaco. Unocal then concluded an exchange agreement with ARCO in which Unocal acquired three of ARCO's producing properties in Cook Inlet in exchange for certain Unocal exploration acreage on the North Slope and in Cook Inlet. In the agreement Unocal got the Swanson River field.[58]

In the late 1990s Unocal operated ten platforms in Cook Inlet and produced an average of 31,370 barrels of oil per day, and it also operated six natural gas fields that produced close to 320 million cubic feet per day. Marathon produced about 27 percent of Cook Inlet oil and owned or had an interest in

Offshore exploratory drilling rig.

(Author's collection.)

seven of the offshore platforms. Other producers of Cook Inlet oil and gas were Phillips, Mobil, Chevron, Shell, Stewart Petroleum, and Forcenergy. Although production in the region has been in decline for many years in the older fields, new technologies as well as discoveries once thought uneconomical continue to keep the fields alive.[59]

Because of the limited in-state market for natural gas, Phillips and Marathon submitted separate proposals to a group of Japanese utilities to export liquefied natural gas (LNG). The companies agreed to work jointly on a project, and in 1967 construction began on platforms, pipelines, and plant and loading facilities. The Japanese built and installed the

Tyonek production platform in the North Cook Inlet gas field, where it began production. At the same time crews installed two underwater pipelines extending more than thirteen miles from shore. Marathon installed eighteen miles of onshore pipelines. The liquification plant and loading facilities were built at Nikiski, north of Kenai. They have operated continuously since the company made its first LNG on June 8, 1969. That fall the nation's first large-scale commercial LNG export came from Alaska's shores. Phillips owns 70 percent of the plant and two LNG tankers, and Marathon owns the remaining 30 percent.[60]

Tesoro Corporation built a refinery at Nikiski and sold the first made-in-Alaska gasoline to the state's residents in 1975. In 1977, after it had made extensive upgrades to its refinery to process the Prudhoe Bay oil, it was the first to sell in-state gasoline refined from that feedstock. Tesoro supplied Alaskan markets by pipeline, rail, truck, air, and marine vessels. Finally, in 1968 Unocal dedicated one of the world's largest chemical complexes, in Kenai. In 1978 it expanded the plant at a cost of $250 million. The complex produced over 1 million tons of ammonia per year, half of which was used to produce over 1 million tons of urea for the Alaskan and the West Coast markets. Both are key ingredients of fertilizers used to boost crop production. Furthermore, some of the urea was used to make de-icer and fertilizer in Alaska.[61] In 2007 Unocal closed the plant because of a natural gas shortage.

Attempts to Increase Oil Taxes

In the meantime, the new state of Alaska fought to get a share of the oil wealth. Since the federal government owned the land, the companies had to pay a 12.5% royalty. Under the provisions of the statehood compact, Alaska received 90 percent of all the royalties derived from federal onshore lands. Swanson River generated $2.4 million in royalty income for the state. But the only state tax in place for the first decade of Swanson River production was a 1 percent severance tax the territorial legislature had passed as part of a more comprehensive measure.[62]

Oil industry advocates had pushed for this tax, and the industry used it to avoid other levies. (Companies paid the tax instead of local property taxes on oil production facilities.) The result was that as the Kenai Peninsula struggled to deal with the effects of the oil boom, it was unable to tax the industry that created the burdens. State Senator Bob Blodgett (D-Teller), who supported oil development (and in fact supported all development), had stated that the 1 percent tax "was a sweetheart deal for the oil companies." Blodgett was one of the few lawmakers who, after statehood, tried time and again to increase oil taxes. But every measure to that effect that he introduced quickly died. Proposals to study oil tax problems did not get through the legislature, either. One such plan died in 1963, and a 1965 request for a tax study and a 2 percent tax increase also died quickly. In 1966, legislators introduced seven oil tax measures, all of which were immediately killed. Legislators from those days remembered no oil company lobbyists in Juneau to fight these tax proposals, but everyone knew who they were, namely, Atwood and Rasmuson, both members of the Spit and Argue Club who made more than $91,000 in 1966 from their share of the leases.[63]

Finally, in 1967, the legislature increased the severance tax from 1 to 2 percent in response to the disastrous Fairbanks flood of that year. By then, Swanson River oil production was close to its peak, and soon it was to begin an uneven but gradual decline. Between 1962 and 1974, the state had received a total of $16,580,000 in severance taxes from the combined Swanson River and Soldotna Creek fields. In the subsequent years, the effective severance tax rate dropped to 0 percent due to the Economic Limit Factor as Swanson River became a marginal field.[64]

Environmental Effects of Oil Development

Interior Secretary Seaton had delayed opening the Kenai National Moose Range in part until regulations protecting the wildlife had been developed. How did the oil industry affect the moose range? Ray Arnett, the Richfield geologist who first explored the area, told a reporter in 1990 that opposition to drilling came from individuals who did not understand the oil business and who "were afraid we would crack the moose eggs." He maintained that there was not a reason in the world the refuges and oil wells were incompatible. Refuges were not sacrosanct, he argued; in fact, the only reason to save wildlife was for "man's enjoyment and mankind has to be taken care of." Arnett related that his company worked in the moose range with wildlife conservation in mind. "Even with the road and well site in there you couldn't see anything," he said. He described overflights of the area during which he would tell people that the plane was coming upon the well site. He asked the visitors to point it out, but there was such a maze of spruce trees that they would watch out of the right side of the plane "and they would fly right over the damn thing. They couldn't find the damn thing."[65]

Others had a different point of view. David Spencer, a longtime moose range manager who later became the head of all the wildlife refuges in Alaska, related that he and his staff objected right away to "this straight bulldozed line right across the countryside for miles and miles, a road running east and west across the range." J. C. Saylor II, director of refuges for the U.S. Fish and Wildlife Service, wrote in 1962 that an aerial view of the oil development looked like "a site of a major military conflict, with Caterpillar tractor trails running everywhere, frequent large gravel pits, untreated spoil banks, and sludge pits. Every eighty-acre parcel had a road and most often was surrounded by roads on all four sides. Pipelines and power lines radiated to all points of the compass, kids, school buses, cats and dogs abounded." Plus it seemed that all the new oil workers had become moose hunters; the moose population dropped from a high of 4,736 in 1959 to 2,719 in 1961. Saylor's summation: "It is a hell of a mess." In the late 1960s, the oil companies began a cleanup, "at least in that part of the development that could be easily seen." But over the decades that followed great parts of the moose range became polluted.[66]

A major disaster occurred in January 1972 at a gas-injection facility, where a major explosion tore open pipes filled with a fluid containing deadly PCBs, polychlorinated biphenyls, and spread them onto ice and snow. PCBs were not yet recognized as deadly carcinogens, although Congress finally banned their manufacture in 1976. In the meantime, the company collected the contaminated soil and stored it at waste oil facilities. In 1983 and 1984, the toxic soil, mixed with the waste oil, was spread throughout the range to control dust on roads. The contamination was discovered in 1985, and one of the largest environmental cleanup projects on any U.S. wildlife refuge got under way, a several-year-long effort to pick up approximately eighty thousand tons of soil. A 1982 General Accounting Office study documented oil pollution in moose range streams. David Spencer reflected that oil had brought many benefits, but none had "accrued to the moose, or the wildlife refuge."[67]

The Beginning of the Boom

One might say that the 1957 Swanson River Richfield oil discovery triggered an oil rush and a leasing boom in the territory, which officially joined the Union as the 49th State in 1959. By September 28, 1965, Alaska held its fifteenth competitive lease sale since the first one on December 10, 1959. The state offered a total of 3,728,456 acres for lease during those six years, of which 66.9 percent, or 2,494,714 acres, was snapped up by the oil companies. The state had taken in a total of $66,134,155 in its fifteen lease sales, averaging $26.51 for every acre leased.[68]

By 1965 the oil industry had become an important part of Alaska's economy; five oil and eleven gas fields had been developed. Between 1958 and January 1, 1966, the state received a total of $122,223,000 in direct cash payments from the oil industry—approximately $480 per person in Alaska—compared to $756,805 the territorial government had received between 1947 and 1957. Most of the money came from bonuses on competitive leases, which provided more than $66 million. In addition, the state received 90 percent of the rentals paid to the federal government for leases on onshore federal lands. It also collected 90 percent of the royalty paid to the federal government for production from the Swanson River field.[69]

By 1966, in the short span of nine years since the first truly commercial discovery in 1957, the oil industry had become an integral part of Alaska's economy. Natural gas heated homes in Anchorage, and Chevron's Nikiski refinery produced jet, diesel, and heating fuels and asphalt products. The oil industry and many Alaskans were optimistic about future prospects. Experts believed that the upper Cook Inlet area had not been fully explored and still held much promise; the lower Cook Inlet was virtually untouched, and Geophysical Service, Inc. had sent seismic crews into the Bristol Bay area and the Gulf of Alaska to perform exploratory work for some twenty oil companies. Although industry leaders seemed almost certain that Alaska's North Slope contained sizable reserves, the region's inaccessibility and climatic rigors put them off. The industry estimated that it needed to discover between 200 million and 500 millions of recoverable oil before it could establish an economically viable field on the North Slope. In 1966 industry spokesmen estimated that producing and moving oil to markets, even after the discovery of such a big field, would "test the ingenuity of the American petroleum industry," adding, "there's nothing to be done with the gas."[70]

While geologists and seismic crews roamed Alaska's wide spaces, annual crude oil production rose from 187,000 barrels in 1959 to 74 million barrels in 1969; and natural gas, from 310 million cubic feet to 149 billion cubic feet. Wellhead value of this production, on which the state levied its taxes, had risen from $1.5 million in 1960 to $219 million in 1969—at which point the oil industry had become Alaska's foremost natural resource extractive industry.[71]

Chapter 23

The Oil Industry Matures

After the discovery of the Prudhoe Bay oil field on the Alaska North Slope (ANS), the state was changed forever. Industrial activity grew from a single operational oil field at Prudhoe Bay to a complex web of working oil fields and their interconnecting roads, pipelines, and power lines that extend from the Colville River in the west to near the border of the Arctic National Wildlife Refuge in the east. Wealth poured into (and out of) the state, the population boomed, and the economy was tied, once again, to the fluctuating price of a nonrenewable resource. Along with great wealth, the oil industry brought with it complex issues that further complicated state politics. The tragedy of the *Exxon Valdez* and other spills also brought the values of environmental conservation and economic development into more immediate conflict.

The Prudhoe Bay Oil Field

Prudhoe Bay is the world's twelfth-largest oil field and the largest discovered in North America, with recoverable reserves of approximately 13.7 billion barrels of crude oil and condensate and 26 trillion cubic feet of natural gas. In comparison, only two other fields discovered in the United States—the East Texas and the Wilmington—initially contained recoverable reserves in excess of 2 billion barrels of oil. Except for these two, more oil had been re-

moved from the Prudhoe Bay field during it first 4.5 years of production than from any other North American field. At the end of 1985 more than 4 billion barrels of oil had been pumped from the Alaska North Slope (ANS). By early 1986 approximately six thousand tankers had berthed at the pipeline terminal at Valdez. For the week ending January 9, 1986, vessel cargo sizes ranged from 279,000 to 1,795,000 barrels a load.[1]

Initial industry sources estimated the total oil in place in the vicinity of the Prudhoe Bay field at about 60 billion barrels. This total included 23 billion barrels of oil in place at Prudhoe Bay, 5.5 billion in the Kuparuk River field, and 3 billion in the Lisburne formation underlying the Prudhoe Bay field. In addition, estimates of oil in place in the West Sak Sands and Ugnu heavy oil zones overlaying the Kuparuk River field ranged between 21 and 36 billion barrels. Known oil resources on the ANS outside the immediate vicinity of Prudhoe Bay could bring the total oil in place in the region to 80 billion barrels.

Industry in the 1970s could economically recover only a fraction of the oil in place, referred to as "recoverable reserves." Still, given the prevailing economic conditions during the 1970s, the expected profitability of the Prudhoe Bay field was sufficient to finance the investment in the Alyeska Pipeline Service Company and the basic infrastructure on the ANS without considering

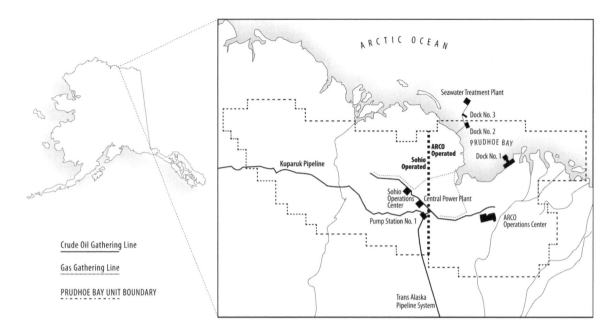

ARCTIC OCEAN

Seawater Treatment Plant

Dock No. 3

Dock No. 2

PRUDHOE BAY

ARCO Operated

Sohio Operated

Dock No. 1

Kuparuk Pipeline

Sohio Operations Center

Central Power Plant

Pump Station No. 1

ARCO Operations Center

Trans Alaska Pipeline System

Crude Oil Gathering Line

Gas Gathering Line

PRUDHOE BAY UNIT BOUNDARY

Prudhoe Bay Oil Field

Valdez Terminal with the tanker ARCO *Juneau.*

(Author's collection.)

ARCO JUNEAU

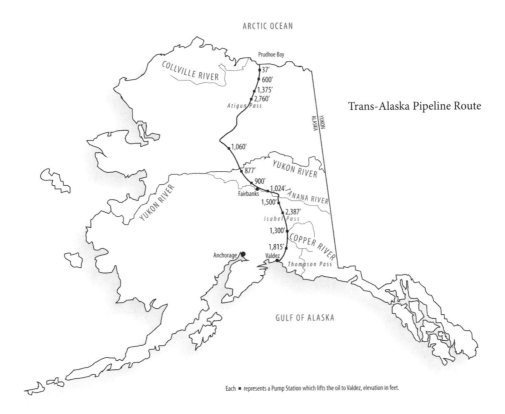

ARCTIC OCEAN

Trans-Alaska Pipeline Route

Each ■ represents a Pump Station which lifts the oil to Valdez, elevation in feet.

any potential production outside the Sadlerochit reservoir at Prudhoe, the main oil pool.[2]

By 2006, total ANS production had reached 15.1 billion barrels. Prudhoe Bay's main reservoir ultimate oil recovery is estimated at 13.7 billion barrels, with about 2.4 billion barrels remaining to be produced from that reservoir. There are seven separate oil fields on the ANS and a total of twenty-nine separate oil pools. The total estimated remaining recoverable oil on the ANS was about 7 billion barrels in 2006.[3] In the meantime, about nineteen thousand tankers had berthed at Valdez by April 2006. Each tanker has an average deadweight of 134,724 tons, and most of the fleet is now double-hulled. Also, the terminal has eighteen crude tanks, each holding 510,000 barrels for a total of 9.18 million barrels.[4]

Techniques for Recovering More Oil

Prudhoe Bay began producing oil in 1977. By the summer of 1984, about six hundred wells were flowing, and the field yielded an average of 1.5 million barrels a day, the maximum efficient rate (MER) that the Alaska Oil and Gas Conservation Commission had established. Standard Oil of Ohio (Sohio) was of the opinion that the MER could be sustained until 1987, but it also estimated that the field's MER could drop by more than 50 percent by 1992 under conventional recovery methods. Producers could employ a variety of alternative methods to prolong the field's productive life into the 1990s and beyond, extracting an additional 2 billion barrels of oil.

Technological problems with extracting the oil are particularly challenging in the West Sak Sands, at a depth of 3,500 to 4,000 feet, and in the Ugnu formation above West Sak Sands, at about 2,500 to 3,000 feet. Over much of the ANS permafrost extends to depths of as much as 2,000 feet. Oil just below that depth is much cooler than reserves at greater depth. For example, oil from the Prudhoe Bay field flows at about 190 degrees Fahrenheit,

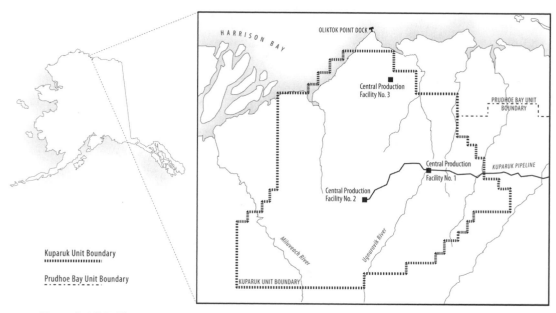

HARRISON BAY

OLIKTOK POINT DOCK

Central Production
Facility No. 3

PRUDHOE BAY UNIT
BOUNDARY

Central Production
Facility No. 1

KUPARUK PIPELINE

Central Production
Facility No. 2

Miluveach River

Ugnuravik River

KUPARUK UNIT BOUNDARY

Kuparuk Unit Boundary
....

Prudhoe Bay Unit Boundary
- - - - - - - - - - - - - - -

Kuparuk Oil Field

while the oil in West Sak Sands is about seventy degrees and Ugnu oil is between forty and fifty degrees. In fact, if one had Ugnu oil in a jar, it would not pour without first being warmed.

Flow rates illustrate the importance of the oil's temperature to maximum recovery. Oil from Prudhoe Bay's Sadlerochit formation flows between 10,000 and 20,000 barrels a well day. Each Kuparuk well yields between 2,000 and 3,000 barrels a day. But the cooler West Sak Sands oil, without specialized recovery methods, would flow at a maximum rate of only 200 barrels a day. That is the crux of the problem—how to add heat to the oil to decrease its viscosity. This calls for sophisticated tertiary recovery methods, such as steam flooding or in situ combustion.[5]

In the 1980s there existed no system to export

Prudhoe Bay's estimated 26 trillion cubic feet of gas—it had no market because it was too expensive—and the producers reinjected it back into the reservoir rock to maintain sufficient pressure to push out more oil. The rest was used as fuel for field facilities and Alyeska's pipeline facilities. In 1984 operators began using secondary recovery techniques, including injection wells to force water or gas (in processes called water flooding and gas injection, respectively) into the reservoir to push out more oil through the reservoir rock to production wells. Operators invested $2 billion in a water-flood project in which Beaufort Sea water is processed in a treatment plant and pumped into the oil formation through injection wells. Water extracted simultaneously with oil from production wells is also used for injection. A seawater treatment plant with

Exposed permafrost along the route of the Trans-Alaska Pipeline is examined by a geologist employed by the line's builders. Permafrost is defined as "unconsolidated deposits or bedrock that continuously has had a temperature below zero degrees Centigrade for two years or more." In areas where the permafrost is "ice-rich" the pipeline is elevated to avoid thawing the ground and thus losing support for the pipe.

(Courtesy of Alyeska Pipeline Service Company.)

Heat pipes with finned radiators are installed in vertical support members for the Trans-Alaska Pipeline. More than 62,000 heat pipes are required on above-ground portions of the 800-mile long pipeline.

(Courtesy of Alyeska Pipeline Service Company.)

daily capacity in excess of 2 million barrels removes seawater impurities. Over the life of the field, water flooding is expected to account for production of about 1 billion barrels of oil.[6]

A tertiary recovery program called the Prudhoe Bay Miscible Gas Project was designed to further maximize oil production. "Miscibility" is the ability of two substances to mix perfectly; in this project the operators combined water-flooding with the injection of miscible mixtures of hydrocarbon gases into the reservoir. The project calls for some of the natural gas produced from the field to be enriched with propane and butane. This enriched mixture is then injected into the reservoir, where it mixes with the oil, creating a solvent effect that helps the oil flow more easily through the reservoir to production wells. In addition, the gas-processing plant also produces a natural-gas liquid stream in excess of 30,000 barrels daily, which is blended with the crude oil entering the Trans-Alaska Pipeline System (TAPS). The Miscible Gas Project was expected to yield an additional 400 million barrels of oil and natural-gas liquids from the Prudhoe Bay reservoir.[7]

A section of forty-eight-inch mainline pipe is lowered into a ditch by side boom tractors in the Brooks Mountain Range, about 175 miles south of Prudhoe Bay. Almost half of the 800-mile-long pipeline is buried.

(Courtesy of Alyeska Pipeline Service Company.)

The Rise of BP Amoco

In the meantime, BP and the American oil giant Amoco announced on August 11, 1998, that they planned to merge, creating Great Britain's largest company. The new entity was to be called BP Amoco, headquartered in London, and it would be one of the world's top three international oil producers. The new group confirmed that it would cut six thousand jobs worldwide, and BP share prices soared 15 percent after the merger announcement. Amoco's share prices also rose, from forty to forty-six dollars per share. Sixty percent of the merged company stock was to be held by BP shareholders; and 40 percent, by Amoco shareholders. BP chief executive Sir John Browne hoped that the merger would increase pretax profits of the two partners by at least $2 billion by the end of 2000.[8]

Hungry for other properties, the new entity announced plans to merge with ARCO. Consumer groups and the Federal Trade Commission (FTC) challenged the proposed merger, stating that it would raise prices for crude oil used to produce gasoline and other petroleum products. The FTC charged that BP Amoco controlled crude oil prices on the West Coast by exporting to Asia at lower prices, and that the merged entity could manipulate trading of crude oil futures. The deal also would violate antitrust laws, lessening competition in the exploration and production of ANS crude oil and its sale to West Coast refineries, and in the market for pipeline and storage facilities.[9]

BP Amoco addressed all objections and negotiated with the states of Alaska, Washington, Oregon, and California. The FTC had particularly objected that the proposed merger would give the new corporation about a 75 percent share of exploration, production, and transportation of ANS crude oil, substantially lessening competition. BP Amoco and ARCO accepted the FTC order to sell all of ARCO's Alaska assets to Phillips Petroleum Company. The result of this divestiture gave Phillips about a 30 percent share of ANS crude oil exploration, production, and transportation; in fact, Phillips would have even more crude oil to sell on the open market than ARCO. BP Amoco acquired two West Coast oil refineries that had been a part of ARCO. Under the agreement, BP Amoco continued to produce about 45 percent of ANS crude, Phillips about 30 percent, and Exxon Mobil Corporation about 22 percent.

TABLE 2

Largest Alaska North Slope Oil Spills since 1985

DATE	OIL FIELD	QUANTITY (GALLONS)	CAUSE
March 5, 2006	Prudhoe Bay	267,000	Pipeline leak
July 28, 1989	Milne Point	38,850	Other
February 19, 2001	Prudhoe Bay	38,000	Pipeline failure
August 21, 2000	Prudhoe Bay	30,030	Truck overflow
August 25, 1989	Kuparuk	25,200	Leak
December 10, 1990	Lisburne	25,200	Explosion

Source: *Anchorage Daily News,* March 7, 2006.

Each of the producers owns an interest in TAPS and the oil tanker fleet that is roughly proportionate to its share of ANS crude oil production.[10]

On April 13, 2000, BP Amoco and ARCO announced that the FTC had approved the merger of their companies, initially agreed upon a year earlier. It created a combined group with a market capitalization of some $200 billion. The transaction was finalized in London on April 18, 2000.[11]

Spills and Other Environmental Hazards

Generally, Alaskans have welcomed the oil industry, for it provides jobs and feeds the state treasury. But some individuals have been consistently critical of the oil industry and the danger oil spills pose to the environment. The biggest spill occurred on March 24, 1989, when the *Exxon Valdez* ran up on Bligh Reef in Prince William Sound and punctured eight of its oil tanks, spilling more than 11 million gallons of crude oil into the sound. More-minor oil spills occur fairly frequently. Table 2 provides a list of the biggest ANS oil spills since 1985.

Pipeline leaks are another problem. On March 5, 2006—very early on a bitterly cold day—a BP worker driving along an empty access road at Prudhoe Bay suddenly smelled oil. On the side of the road, covered by snow, a massive oil slick of crude oil had spread over almost two acres of tundra. An aging pipeline, installed in the 1970s, had corroded from

the inside and oozed oil out of a quarter-inch hole, about the size of a pencil eraser. The BP leak had gone undetected for at least five days, having failed to trip any of the pipeline's leak detection alarms. In all, about 267,000 gallons of crude escaped, making it the biggest spill ever on the ANS.[12]

This accident once again raised questions about the operations of the oil industry in Alaska. The easily extractable oil reserves were drying up inexorably. The U.S. Senate had passed a largely symbolic budget amendment in support of opening the Arctic National Wildlife Refuge (ANWR) to development; in the meantime, the thirty-year-old pipelines that stretch like a giant cobweb over the North Slope's oil fields needed more and costlier maintenance, as did the eight-hundred-mile-long pipeline that carries the crude to Valdez. The 2006 spill once again focused attention on the question of whether or not the oil companies, focused on their bottom line, can be trusted to protect Alaska's fragile environment.

One opinion came from Dr. Richard Fineberg, who has closely observed Alaska's oil development for three decades as a prize-winning reporter, advisor to the governor of Alaska on oil and gas policy, and an independent consultant to investors, government agencies, and nonprofit organizations. Over the years, Fineberg has called attention to the serious operational and management problems on the Trans-Alaska Pipeline System into which the feeder lines from the various oil fields on the ANS deliver the oil. He maintains that these problems pose a serious environmental risk and threaten the West Coast's crude oil supply.

Fineberg wrote that in early April 2006 an Alyeska financial analyst was asked to leave the company after he refused requests to provide inflated reports of how much Alyeska spends on anticorrosion measures. A few days later another report revealed that an Alyeska worker at the pipeline's Marine Terminal had falsified environmental compliance documents between 2001 and 2003.[13] Fineberg charged, in essence, that Alyeska, in order to save money, was automating the TAPS, laying off employees, and scrimping on pipeline repairs and maintenance.

Another critical report came in 2003 from the National Academy's National Research Council, which had studied the environmental effect of more than three decades of oil and gas exploration on the ANS. The report found that the roads, rigs, and pipelines necessary to produce and transport the oil have been affecting the ANS environment since the Prudhoe Bay discovery in 1968. The consequences have been mounting over time, despite enormous strides the oil industry and regulatory agencies have made in reducing environmental effects. (For example, advances in locating and targeting oil have reduced the number of exploration wells, and the use of remote sensing to find oil have reduced off-road travel. Oil drilling platforms are smaller, thus leaving smaller physical imprints on the tundra. Some roads and drilling sites are now being built with ice instead of gravel.)

The report found several accumulating effects on animal populations; for example, bowhead whales have traveled a different route in their fall migration to avoid the noise of seismic exploration, although the exact extent of their detour is not known. Increased human population on the ANS has resulted in more refuse for scavenging bears, foxes, ravens, and gulls, which has boosted their numbers. These animals prey on the eggs and nestings of many bird species, some of which are listed as endangered or threatened. In some years and in some places, reproductive success among birds is too low to allow populations to persist without additional birds joining them from elsewhere.[14] The cumulative effects of oil development, so far, have not resulted in large declines in the overall size of the Central Arctic caribou herd on the ANS, but they have at times affected their geographical distribution and reproductive successes.

Extensive off-road travel has also altered the tundra. Networks of trails used for seismic exploration have harmed vegetation and caused erosion. The trails degrade the visual experience of local residents and visitors alike. New technology has lessened but not totally eliminated the impact of seismic exploration on the Alaskan landscape. Roads have made access to the ANS easier and have had significant environmental effects.[15]

The oil revenue stream has led to profound social and economic changes on the ANS. Many of the residents view this in a positive light. Schools, health care, housing, and other community services have improved. At the same time, however, balancing the economic benefits of oil activities against the accompanying loss of traditional culture and other societal problems that occur is a dilemma for ANS residents. For example, rates of alcoholism and diabetes have increased. The council reminded planners to try to head off potential problems that may occur in ANS villages when oil production declines.[16]

The council also reported that Alaska Native subsistence harvesting has been affected. The Iñupiats have had to travel farther out to sea for the fall whale hunt because these mammals are avoiding the noise of oil-exploration machinery. This means that hunters face a greater risk of running into bad weather, endangering their lives. Agreements in the late 1990s between the whalers and the industry do limit exploration activities during the whale's fall migration. The council also interviewed Gwich'in Indian representatives, who reported that they perceive any oil development threatening the Porcupine caribou herd calving grounds as a deadly threat to their culture.[17]

The council wrote that decisions about the timing, placement, and environmental protections needed for oil activities on the ANS have been made on a case-by-case basis by agencies that have not communicated well with each other. It recommended the development of a comprehensive framework and plan so that regulatory decisions are consistent with overall goals. The plan should consider long-range environmental consequences and should cover all phases of oil and gas development, including the dismantling and removal of equipment as well as environmental restoration. The council recommended further research into environmental effects that are continuing to accumulate. The council also urged scientists to take advantage of the rich and detailed knowledge of local residents. Attention needs to be paid to air pollution and water and food source contamination caused by oil exploration and production. Particular attention has to be paid to how climate changes are affecting the relationship between oil development and the environment. If the current warming trend continues, as expected, it could affect the usefulness of present oil-development technologies as well as the number of plants and animals on the ANS and their geographical distribution.[18]

The Dangers of Oil in Prince William Sound

In 1974 Friends of the Earth, Inc., with sister organizations of the same name in other countries working for the preservation, restoration, and more rational use of the earth, published a volume titled *Cry Crisis! Rehearsal in Alaska.* The authors reviewed three centuries of American energy: 1776 to 2006 and a half century of Alaska oil, 1923 to 1973, focusing on the innumerable grievous faults of building TAPS and operating a supertanker shuttle system. The book also offered alternatives to the Prudhoe Bay-Valdez pipeline.

Valdez, on an arm of Prince William Sound, was among the most beautiful of harbors, quiet and mountain-ringed. The Prince William Sound fishermen then did a $20 million annual wholesale business. The authors predicted that oil would change all this. Once in operation, two million barrels of oil would move out of Valdez on a daily basis across fifty miles of restricted sound waters before reaching the sea. On the way out they would pass empty tankers going the other way. "The potential for a major collision is obvious."[19]

Tankers did not collide, as the authors feared, but despite the Alyeska promise that a fleet of double-hulled tankers would come into Port Valdez, virtually all the ships that called there were single-hulled until very late into the twentieth century. Each month, eighty ships, or between two or three a day, were loaded at the terminal before traveling across Prince William Sound toward the Gulf of Alaska, the roughest water any U.S. tanker has to travel. From there the tankers sailed to ports on the lower West Coast. There were numerous near misses over the years, including one as early as 1979, when the supertanker *Prince William Sound* lost power and steering in high winds. The tanker was within half an hour of running aground on the rocks when the wind luckily shifted and moved it back into deeper waters and it regained power. Small oil spills occurred with regularity within the Port of Valdez.[20]

There were also questions about the reliability of the tanker fleet. During the 1970s tankers were replaced regularly as they aged, but during the 1980s, because of declining oil prices, the companies sharply reduced the purchase of new vessels. On average, the age of the ships in the Alaska fleet was fifteen years greater that that of the U.S. fleet at large. Because of their size and the weight they carry, tankers are designed to flex in rough waters so as not to break apart. Because the hulls twist and heave so much as they navigate the Gulf of Alaska, metal fatigue and cracking is a great danger.[21]

In 1988 the U.S. Coast Guard released its *Ma-rine Structural Casualty Study,* which revealed that structural failures in the Alaskan fleet were unusually high. Although Alaskan ships represented only about one-eighth of the large ships surveyed, they experienced more than half the cracks and other structural failures. For example, in January 1989 the tanker *Thompson Pass* leaked 72,000 gallons of oil into Port Valdez, the largest spill up to that time in Prince William Sound. The tanker had been observed to be leaking in San Francisco, but BP officials decided to send it north for one more trip before undertaking repairs. In Valdez a boom placed around the tanker was left unwatched. It was not long before the leaking oil rode the water and spilled over the boom. Alyeska cleanup crews required fifteen days to recover the crude. Two weeks after that spill, the tanker *Cove Leader* spilled 2,500 gallons into Port Valdez.[22]

Resistance from the CDFU and the Town of Valdez

Prince William Sound fishermen are represented by the Cordova District Fishermen United (CDFU), not a union but something more like a lobby willing to legally represent its members. Based in Cordova, a small fishing community some seventy miles east of Valdez, the CDFU, with six hundred members, represents more than half of the fishing permit holders in Area E fishery, namely, Prince William Sound. CDFU had opposed the pipeline's construction from the beginning and then fought for a landline down Canada to the contiguous states. At the start of pipeline construction, the fishermen were starting the salmon hatchery system in Prince William Sound, and they were afraid that oil spills would ruin their livelihoods. They filed suit against the secretary of the interior's approval of the pipeline and terminal construction. In 1973, that suit, consolidated with several others, received a favorable Federal District Court ruling, which the U.S. Supreme Court subsequently upheld. Pipeline proponents, however, enlisted Congress, and in late 1973 legislation to circumvent court rulings on environmental grounds was introduced. In the U.S. Senate, Vice President Spiro Agnew broke the tie vote, and the bill soon became law.[23]

In 1985 CDFU, together with oil broker Charles Hamel, filed notice of intent to sue over the mismanagement of the water ballast treatment plant at the terminal and the discharge of toxic pollutants into the Port of Valdez. The Environmental Protection Agency (EPA) and the Alaska Department of Environmental Conservation followed with compliance orders requesting Alyeska to build a system to monitor, remove, and dispose of sludge. Alyeska's response was spotty over the years that followed.[24]

John Devens, the mayor of Valdez, learned of the January 1989 *Thompson Pass* leak and decided to form a committee to investigate Alyeska's safety problems. What he discovered about Alyeska water and air pollution alarmed him. A town meeting was called for Thursday evening, March 23, 1989. Alyeska declined to send a representative. Devens instead invited Cordova fisherwoman and scientist Dr. Riki Ott to give a presentation on the Alyeska terminal and marine transport of oil. A member of the CDFU board of directors at the time, Ott holds a doctorate in sediment toxicology as well as an Area E drift gillnet permit. During her presentation, via teleconference, Ott talked about oil revenues and Alaskan politics, about unauthorized design changes in the Alyeska terminal, and about its overtaxed pollution control system. She talked about Alyeska's failure to live up to its promises, pointed out that only one part-time DEC employee monitored the entire terminal, and described the poor condition of the tanker fleet. Like many, she believed that it was not a question of whether a major oil spill would occur, but rather when. She told her audience that Alyeska was increasingly incapable of containing and cleaning up a major spill. She felt that Alaska fishermen were playing a game of Russian roulette. At the conclusion of her talk, she was pleased with the questions her audience had asked. She bicycled home and went to bed.[25]

Early on the morning of March 24, 1989, Ott woke up to wild banging on her door. She opened the door to find Jack Lamb, acting president of the CDFU. Lamb asked her to get dressed quickly because "we've had the Big One. There is a tanker aground on Bligh Reef. It's lost ten million gallons, but there's four times that still on board." Dr. Ott recounted that the two stared "into each other's eyes for a moment, then I gazed past him up Orca Inlet and across Hawkins Island to the northwest." For an instant her mind went blank, and then "a tidal wave of emotion flooded back in—denial, a hot white flame of anger, a surge of adrenaline, a cascade of ideas." Within ten minutes the two were headed to the CDFU office. "It would be a week—and a lifetime—before I returned."[26]

The Spill

The Exxon *Valdez* had docked at the Alyeska Terminal at 10:48 P.M. on March 22. Chief Mate James Kunkel and Captain Joseph Hazelwood were on the ship's bridge. The captain, at age thirty-two, ten years after graduating from the New York Maritime College, had become the youngest captain in Exxon's fleet. He quickly gained an excellent reputation in the industry for his seamanship, his feel for the vessel, and his skill at extricating ships from dangerous situations. He was an intelligent and skillful man who wanted to be at sea but had but little patience for the reams of paperwork his job entailed.[27]

The crew spent the night on the tanker, which measured 166 feet at the beam and 987 feet from bow to stern, or longer than three football fields. The tanker loaded 1,286,738 barrels of crude, slightly under its capacity of 1,484,829 barrels, or 211,000 deadweight tons. Early the next morning the crew began discharging the ballast water and filling the twelve cargo tanks with crude. By 7:24 P.M. on March 23, the tanker was loaded. The officers and crew had worked long hours and were tired, and if the congressionally mandated requirement that officers have six hours off-duty time within the twelve-hour period prior to departure had been obeyed, the Exxon *Valdez* would not have departed that night.[28]

Tanker crews generally were tired after loading and unloading. Exxon, in a cost-cutting measure with little regard to its negative impact, had reduced crew size, citing the increasing automation of the ships as a justification. At the same time, the company insisted on the speedy delivery of crude. This made it impossible for the crews to both perform the work and follow crewing regulations. In fact, prior to the spill, Exxon Shipping had planned to reduce crew levels further, from twenty to sixteen by 1990.[29]

Hazelwood had spent part of Thursday, March 23, running errands in town, and he apparently drank two or three vodkas at the Pipeline Club and later something unidentified at the Pizza Palace. The tanker got under way at 8:30 P.M., and when the captain appeared on the bridge, William Murphy, who would pilot the tanker out of Valdez, smelled alcohol on his breath. Hazelwood went below deck to finish some paperwork, and then he returned to the bridge.

From that point onward, throughout the journey and after grounding, no one on the ship thought the captain to be deficient in any way. Reports of Hazelwood's drinking were later spread widely, but there is no clear evidence that the captain was drunk at the time of the spill. His crew members insisted he was not, and the Coast Guard found that the measures he took after the grounding were exemplary.[30]

The tanker left the dock without incident, passed Entrance Island, near the mouth of the Port of Valdez, at 10:20 P.M. and started to turn into the Valdez Narrows, where passage was restricted to one-way only. The sea was calm and there was a light wind. There were warnings of ice ahead in Valdez Arm. Eventually the tanker cleared the narrows and entered Valdez Arm, where there were two lanes for inbound and outbound traffic. Hazelwood returned to the bridge and called the Valdez Traffic Center (VTC) to get permission to change from the outbound to the inbound lane in order to avoid ice from the Columbia Glacier. Gordon Taylor, on duty at the VTC, testified later that tankers commonly changed lanes to avoid the ice flow and that sometimes they left the shipping channel altogether. Taylor's relief, Bruce Blandford, stated that their radar monitored the narrows but that it often did not reach Bligh Reef. Many of the officers navigating the tankers had not been informed of this. In the early 1980s the Coast Guard had downgraded the radar system to save funds even though its operations manual still required that Valdez Arm, which extended to Bligh Reef, be continually monitored.[31]

Blandford assumed his duties just before midnight, when Taylor told him that the Exxon Valdez radar image was "getting hard to hold onto." Blandford did not attempt to see or contact the tanker. He described this as routine practice. The Coast Guard administered the VTC, and the VTC staff who administered the radar permitted the tankers to leave and enter the Port of Valdez in a sloppy fashion. Blood tests taken from Taylor and Blandford afterward showed marijuana traces and alcohol use, respectively. In Blandford's case, the alcohol could not be clearly linked to consumption before or during his watch. In any case, this carelessness eventually resulted in the investigation of the Exxon Valdez grounding being taken away from the Coast Guard and assumed by the National Transportation Safety Board.[32]

The heavy ice was visible by radar and by sight, stretching across the lanes from Point Freemantle to within one mile of Bligh Reef. By 11:24 P.M. the ship traveled close to eleven knots, the speed at which it maneuvered most effectively. Hazelwood told Third Mate Gregory Cousins that they would go around the ice and ordered a course change to 180° (due south), which would take them to a point just off Busby Island. The captain ordered helmsman Harry Claar to put the ship on autopilot, but he did not inform Cousins. Moments later Robert Kagan relieved Claar, who told him that he was steering "one-eight-zero" and that he was on autopilot. Cousins stood next to Claar and took the tanker off autopilot. The captain told Cousins he wanted to "bring it down abeam of Busby, and then cut back to the lanes." Cousins plotted the course, and when asked if he felt comfortable with the maneuver he replied in the affirmative. Hazelwood asked Cousins if he felt good enough about the maneuver to allow him to go below deck to finish some paperwork, Cousins again replied in the affirmative. The captain then ordered the engines to be placed under a computer program, increasing engine speed from 55 rpm to sea speed full ahead at 78.7 rpm or a little over fourteen knots. The tanker would not attain sea speed until forty-five minute later, and thus it would retain peak maneuverability as long as it was in the Bligh Reef area.[33]

At 11:54 P.M. Hazelwood went below to his quarters. About eleven or twelve minutes past midnight, the Exxon Valdez ran hard aground. Hazelwood, who had been gone for fifteen minutes, returned to the bridge. At 12:20 A.M. the captain ordered the engines shut down, and at 12:26 he called the VTC in Valdez to report the grounding. At 12:40 the captain had the engines restarted and attempted to move the tanker off the reef, but in later testimony it appeared that he had instead tried to drive it deeper onto the reef in order to stabilize it.[34]

The Damage

An environmental nightmare had begun that would despoil Prince William Sound for decades to come. Several investigations got under way to determine the spill volume. The Alaska Department of Environmental Conservation and Exxon jointly contracted Caleb Brett, a company that gauges tanker loads for the oil industry, to estimate the spill volume. The company, however, refused to make public its finding, citing its employer-client relationship. After review of the several investigations, Dr. Ott concluded that the State of Alaska's conservative estimate of 30 million gallons rather than Exxon's reported 11 million gallons should be used.

After two days of calm weather, a horrific storm spread the oil through the sound and out into the Gulf of Alaska. Ultimately, over 3,200 miles of Alaska's shorelines were oiled—from the sound, past the Kenai Peninsula and Kodiak Island, to parts of the Alaska Peninsula, some 1,200 miles distant from Bligh Reef. For comparison, a similar-sized spill would have oiled the shores from New York to Cape Canaveral, Florida.

Walter Meganack, the traditional village chief of Port Graham, a Native village on the Kenai Peninsula, stated one year later that "the excitement of the season had just begun, and then [we] heard the news: oil in the water, lots [of] oil killing lots of water. It is too shocking to understand. Never in the millennium of our tradition have we thought it possible for the water to die, but it is true."[35]

The runaway slick left devastation in its wake. It killed more wildlife than any other oil spill ever in the world. Among those killed were thousands of marine mammals, such as sea otters, seals, and orcas, and hundreds of thousands of birds, like murres, marbled murrelets, harlequin ducks, scoters, bufflehead, goldeneyes, cormorants, and many

others. Millions of salmon and herring were killed by an invisible cloud of dissolved and dispersed oil that spread underwater, shadowing the path of the surface slick and hanging offshore from the oiled beaches in the sound. The killing, however, did not stop with the oil, because Exxon shoreline cleanup continued to kill plant and animal life that had survived the initial oiling. The pressurized hot water wash uncovered huge beach areas normally covered with rich sea plants and animal communities. Dr. Ott estimated that by the end of 1989, the cleanup had killed by weight as much plant and animal life as the initial oiling.[36]

In the meantime, confusion raged, and the questions of who was in charge and what was the proper relationship among the four institutional entities, namely, Exxon, the Coast Guard, the state of Alaska, and various federal agencies, were never resolved. Officials had to address two priorities: to contain the spill and to pump the remaining oil out of the tanker. Exxon was clearly in charge of the pumping operation. There were many problems, such as obtaining fendering (fencelike) material to put between the stricken tanker and the lightering tanker, the *Baton Rouge*, which was trying to pump the remaining oil out of the *Exxon Valdez*. The main problem was determining the sequence for taking oil off the Valdez and reballasting the ship so that it did not collapse or capsize. It was a dangerous and delicate operation, and after several setbacks, including pumps that did not work, spillage from hoses, and a storm that spun the rafted ships—two tankers and four tugs—twelve degrees, the operation was eventually completed successfully.[37]

The initial cleanup of the spill took three years, employed thousands, and cost over $2.1 billion. Unlike most spills worldwide, the effects of the *Exxon Valdez* spill and cleanup were both well studied by both public-trust and Exxon-funded scientists. During 1990 and 1991 Exxon's was virtually the only voice in the news; the public-trust scientists were under a secrecy order because of pending litigation over the loss of wildlife and its habitat. Exxon waged a media campaign during that time, inundating the public with messages that Prince William Sound had recovered rapidly and everything had returned to normal after the spill. In essence, the company papered over the spill's effects, and it perpetuates this charade to this day.

Gradually the popular understanding of the spill, cleanup, and biological effects of this tragedy became Exxon's story. By the time the public-trust story of the spill emerged in 1993, Exxon's version had been widely accepted. The residents of the sound watched what was happening there, and reality departed further and further from Exxon's spill story. Dr. Ott followed the happenings in the sound and learned about the persistence of sick wildlife and the long-term and pervasive health problems cleanup workers suffered.[38]

Legal Consequences

Both the federal government and the state filed criminal charges against Exxon and civil claims for damages to and recovery of wildlife and public lands the spill had harmed. On October 9, 1991, the U.S. District Court approved a settlement among the federal and state governments and Exxon. Under the criminal plea agreement, Exxon was fined $150 million and forgiven $125 million because of its cooperation in the cleanup. The North American Wetlands Conservation Fund received $12 million, and the national Victims of Crime Fund received $13 million. Exxon paid $100 million for criminal restitution, evenly divided between state and federal governments. Under the civil settlement, Exxon agreed to pay $900 million in annual payments over a ten-year period, three times lower than the minimum estimate for damages calculated from public surveys. It amounted to about $500 million after deducting tax breaks and accounting for inflation and the ten-year payment schedule.[39]

The 1991 civil settlement created a council of state and federal trustees, named the Exxon Valdez Oil Spill Trustee Council, to oversee the restoration of damaged wildlife and habitat and use the $900 million for that purpose. Section 17 of the 1991 civil settlement contained a "Reopener for Unknown Injury," which requires Exxon to ante up another $100 million to restore wildlife or habitat for harm that "could not reasonably have been known nor . . . anticipated" based on the scientific understanding of oil effects at the time.[40] In May 2006 the state and federal governments served notice on Exxon, demanding another $100 million under the reopener clause.

On September 16, 1994, a jury in the Anchorage Federal District Court returned a $5.5 billion punitive damages verdict against Exxon to thirty-four thousand fishermen and other Alaskans whose property and jobs were either harmed or totally ruined in 1989. The company appealed, and continued to appeal. On August 4, 1998, the *Anchorage Daily News* reported that these appeals paid handsomely, earning Exxon $90,000 an hour, $2 million a day, or nearly $800 million a year on the $5.5 billion as long as the case drags on and the money stays in its coffers.[41]

On January 27, 2006, Exxon attorneys asked a panel of three judges of the Ninth U.S. Circuit Court of Appeals to erase the $5 billion in damages a federal district court had ordered the company to pay in 1994. Attorney Walter Dellinger told the judges that Exxon should be liable for no more than $25 million in punitive damages, which were meant to deter and punish misconduct. Exxon had reported third-quarter earnings of $10 billion. Dellinger told the judges that Exxon had spent more than $3 billion on cleanup work and to settle other federal and state lawsuits from the spill. Dellinger said that deterrence had been accomplished by that amount. He added that because of the money Exxon had already paid out over the last sixteen years, "the harm has been largely avoided." That comment provoked chuckles from a packed courtroom, which included fishermen whose livelihoods had been damaged by the spill. Max McCarty, a former Prince William Sound fisherman, stated that their lives "were trashed." He now worked as a substitute teacher in Arizona and sold fish at a local market. Attorneys have estimated that hundreds of Seattle fishermen could receive millions of dollars if the award stood.[42]

Exxon had another appeal pending, and the endless legal wrangling went on. With the award money tied up in court, some fishermen and affected Alaskan communities have settled independently. After oral arguments in January 2006, the case eventually wound up in the U.S. Supreme Court.[43] At the end of June 2008, the U.S. Supreme Court voided Exxon's punitive damages in the worst oil spill in

U.S. history, cutting the damages from $2.5 billion to $500 million. Under the new arithmetic, each of the thirty-three thousand victims would receive an average of fifteen thousand dollars, a reduction of 80 percent. The business community praised and environmentalists and Alaskans decried the court's decision.[44]

The five-to-three ruling came almost two decades after the *Exxon Valdez* supertanker ran onto Bligh Reef in the Prince William Sound and ruined the fisheries, the wildlife, and the Native subsistence economy. Justice David Souter wrote for the court that punitive damages may not exceed what the company already paid to compensate victims for economic losses. Overall, Exxon had paid about $3.4 billion in fines, penalties, cleanup costs, and other expenses resulting from the spill. Looked at another way, however, the $507.5 million represented slightly more than four days of profits for Exxon Mobil during the last quarter of 2007. The commercial fishermen, Native Alaskans, landowners, businesses, and local governments involved in the lawsuit each received about fifteen thousand dollars for "having their lives and livelihoods destroyed," according to Jeffrey Fisher, their attorney before the Supreme Court, but they had not "received a dime for emotional distress damages."[45]

Exxon was to release $383 million for distribution to the thirty-three thousand plaintiffs. Lawyers for the plaintiffs and Exxon continued to battle over another $70 million, as well as potential interest of $488 million, accrued on the penalty during the lengthy litigation, which Exxon said it did not owe. In June 2009, the Ninth U.S. Circuit Court of Appeals ordered Exxon to pay the interest, set at 5.9 percent a year. Exxon stated that it would not appeal the ruling, agreeing to pay the $470 million in interest on the $507.5 million in punitive damages. That seems to have ended the long legal battle.[46]

In the meantime, Captain Hazelwood lost his job with Exxon and stood trial in a state court in Anchorage in 1990, accused of a felony, second degree mischief, and two misdemeanors, operating a watercraft under the influence of alcohol and reckless endangerment. The Anchorage jury returned a verdict on only one of the four charges against him, namely, the negligent discharge of oil. The judge fined the captain fifty thousand dollars and sentenced him to one thousand hours of community service, cleaning Alaska beaches. After eight years of unsuccessfully appealing the sentence, he began his cleaning job in 1999. Nobody hired him again as a captain after the spill, so he became a technical expert for a maritime insurance agency.[47] Finally, the company renamed the ill-fated *Exxon Valdez*, after repairs, the *Sea River Mediterranean*. Later renamed *Dong Fang Ocean*, it was refitted in 2008, and continues to sail as an ore carrier. Alaska barred her from ever entering state waters again. Exxon applied to have the court ruling reversed, but the appeal was rejected.[48]

One has to be creative when looking for any positive results from the spill. As a direct result of the disaster, governments imposed tighter environmental regulations on many industries. Unfortunately, the Republican administration that came into office in 2000 assiduously worked to administratively weaken these regulations. Perhaps the most important regulation to protect against a repeat of the spill is the modern tanker standard, which requires double hulls on new ships. If the outer skin is punctured, no oil will leak. After years of complaints about air pollution at the tanker terminal, in 1997 Alyeska installed a vapor recovery system at berths four and five, used to recover tanker vapors during the loading process. It resulted in a substantial reduction of air emissions at the Valdez Main Terminal. Another benefit is that substantial tracts of land have been added to the Kenai Fjords National Park with funds from the Exxon fines.

The Oil Economy

Despite tragedies like the *Exxon Valdez* spill, many in the North still support oil development, which has brought substantial economic well-being to the majority of Alaskans. But Alaska, like many lesser developed regions, suffers from the negative results of resource development. Like other oil exporters, the state has had difficulties translating its oil wealth into a stable, diversified economy. A good example is the decades-long debate over how best to cushion the state government's budget and its economy against declining ANS production and oil price fluctuations. Many proposals have been made to balance the state budget by using some of the earnings of the Alaska Permanent Fund (APF), a petroleum savings account that has grown to about $33 billion in three decades. Some view the APF as a model for handling petroleum revenue wisely, while others think it strange that the state's citizens think they have a revenue shortfall with such a massive nest egg.

As explained in chapter 18, the Alaska state legislature funds an annual Permanent Fund Dividend (PFD) payout to all eligible Alaskans. This program, which began in 1982, is part of a remarkable social experiment, testing whether a part of public resources revenues might benefit Alaska more in the hands of individual citizens than in the hands of their state government.[49] Some Alaskans maintain that the PFD program is fundamentally flawed and fosters a pro-extraction and anti-conservation bias. It buys citizen support for more extraction, tending to pervert public policy processes favoring more sustainable development scenarios.

But most Alaskans have come to think of the PFD as a birthright, an entitlement, and any politician hoping to be reelected had better be a staunch defender of the program. Criticism of the PFD program is seldom heard in Alaska, and indeed, many citizens want to enshrine the PFD program in the state constitution. This would guarantee an automatic and direct payout of a certain percentage of Alaska's oil wealth to its citizens without annual legislative approval. Indeed, when state fiscal issues are debated, a multitude of Alaskans shout, "Do not touch my dividend!" This essentially ends any meaningful discussion of whether to use some portion of the APF to balance the state budget.

For example, in 2004 Governor Frank Murkowski made solving the state's chronic budget crisis his top priority. He convened a three-day statewide gathering of civic leaders to make recommendations to the legislature on four revenue management issues. One would have enshrined the PFD in the state constitution. Absent from the governor's instructions was any mention of generating new revenues to balance the budget. For example, the meeting might have considered reinstating the personal income tax, abolished in 1980 in the grip of oil wealth euphoria. Consequently, the statewide gathering accomplished nothing, and Alaskans have become almost totally dependent on the oil industry to pay state government expenses. This has severed the citizen's stake in government spending and indeed has made all of Alaskans recipients of state welfare funded by oil royalties and taxes on the oil companies.

In the meantime, while Alaska has not fared very well, the three major operators on the ANS have made very decent profits. Dr. Fineberg reported in 2005 that despite reduced production during the last two decades, ANS oil operations and TAPS continue to be profitable to investors and competitive internationally. The international consulting firm of Wood Mackenzie reviewed the operations of about sixty international petroleum provinces. It found that despite relatively high costs, including pipeline operations, Alaska ranked in the top quartile in value per barrel to the industry. Government incentives generally rank in the top half from a company perspective, so it is profitable to operate in Alaska. Conoco Phillips, the only ANS producer that publishes Alaska-specific data, confirmed that it anticipated a better return on past Alaska exploration and development investment than it will earn on similar investments elsewhere in the world.[50]

Fineberg analyzed the net revenue from ANS production and associated pipeline operations—that is, the difference between the price received for a barrel of oil and the costs to produce and deliver it to the refinery. His findings confirmed the profitability of these operations. The results were as follows: When ANS oil averaged $38.84 per barrel in 2004, the industry net revenue take on ANS production and associated pipeline operations was about $15 million per day in dollars not adjusted for inflation, or 53.8 percent of the total net revenue. The state received $7.7 million or 27.6 percent; and the federal government, $5.2 million or 18.6 percent.[51]

When oil prices averaged $12.55 per barrel in adjusted dollars in 1998, the industry profits on ANS production and pipeline operations were $2.3 million per day, and $2.6 million per day at $14.33 per barrel in 2005 dollars. Thus ANS production remains profitable even at low prices, which separates the industry from national profit leaders such as IBM, General Motors, and Ford, to name but a few, who lose money in bad years.[52]

Effects on the State Budget

Unfortunately, the state of Alaska has become largely dependent on oil revenues for its operating and capital budgets. In 1978, Texas, Louisiana, and Oklahoma received 19.6, 29.2, and 15 percent, respectively, of their state revenues from the oil industry. In 1982, the state of Alaska received 86.5 percent of its revenues from oil resources. Petroleum income fueled state spending, and for about a decade Alaska's labor force, population, and personal income increased faster than those of any other state. Very little of this growth would have occurred without the five-fold price increase for Middle Eastern crude oil in 1973–74 and the resulting three-fold increase in the market value of U.S. domestic crude oil, which made it economically possible to develop the Prudhoe Bay field and construct the Trans-Alaska Pipeline.[53] World oil prices increased again in 1979–80, and at their peak in 1981, oil revenues flowed into the state treasury at an annual per capita rate of more than ten thousand dollars. State spending for government operations, transfer payments, loan programs, and public works kept pace with state revenues. In 1980 the state legislature abolished personal income taxes.

By the second quarter of 1981, crude oil prices began to decline, but most private and government planning had assumed that oil prices would keep rising. This implied that Prudhoe Bay would generate more and more revenues for the state, which in turn, promised more public-and private-sector jobs and also sustained high levels of exploration activity on state and federal lands and on the federal outer continental shelf. This would undoubtedly bring about major new discoveries, and a few were made. Rising oil prices also convinced sponsors of the Alaska gas pipeline that they all but could ignore the difficulty of marketing ANS gas as a constraint on the project's feasibility.

Ever-increasing oil prices also seemed to assure Alaska a petrochemicals boom based on the growing cost advantage that ANS natural gas-liquids would have over oil-based petrochemical feedstocks used elsewhere. It also seemed to guarantee development of Alaska's coal for export. Increasing oil prices also meant that natural gas and coal would soon be too valuable to use for generating electric power, and

planners and lawmakers used this argument as a rationale for planning various hydroelectric generating plants, including a multibillion-dollar plant on the Susitna River in south central Alaska.[54]

It was estimated that state revenues from oil production on state lands, primarily Prudhoe Bay, would peak in 1987 and then decline rapidly. In November 1982, the Governor's Council on Economic Policy focused a day of discussions and presentations on the question "Is there life for the State of Alaska after Prudhoe Bay?" A diverse group of economists, oil-industry experts, and state officials concerned about the ominous Prudhoe Bay production curve met to share their views. How could state government be funded at present levels when the revenue flow from Alaska's oil industry began its steep decline in the 1990s? Three points of view were identified in the roundtable briefing paper: (1) Projections of state oil revenues are unduly pessimistic; therefore state expenditures will continue to be important in bolstering Alaska's economy. (2) State oil revenue may decline, but other sources of revenue will be developed to make up the difference. (3) Oil revenues may decline, and no other significant sources of tax revenues may be found. But by the time revenues drop sharply, the unsubsidized private sector will have grown enough to offset the adverse economic impact of reduced state spending.

There was also a more pessimistic view that maintained that the revenue projections were valid, that other significant sources of tax revenue either did not exist or could not be developed without damaging the private sector or precluding new investments, and that the private sector would not grow sufficiently to offset the decline in state spending. In fact, one economist predicted that Alaska's oil boom was short-lived and would be followed by the most severe depression experienced since statehood in 1959.[55]

By the spring of 1986 the economic bust had begun. Lower oil prices meant smaller Alaska petroleum revenues. In 1988 dollars, the state took in $2.4 billion in 1970, $4.4 billion in 1982, $1.4 billion in 1987, $1.9 billion in 1988, and $1.7 billion in 1990. Cutting budgets was called for, but what many citizens regarded as spending for fat, others considered spending for essential services or entitlements. Whatever was cut would hurt some Alaskans. But even before Alaska became oil rich, the state government spent two to three times the average of other states, largely because of higher costs in the North. The oil-fueled state spending in the late 1970s and 1980s started from a base that was already substantially above that of other states.[56]

Alaska's population doubled between 1967 and 1987, and inflation nearly tripled prices. Therefore, state spending would have to be six times larger in 1989 just to keep pace with population and prices. In 1987, however, state spending was sixteen times greater than in 1967. What happened is that the state expanded existing programs, delivered more expensive services, added new spending, and increased public employee wages. To balance the state budget became very complicated because state spending created economic and political forces that in fact resisted such moves—in essence, most individuals, municipalities, school districts, and the entire Alaska economy. Many interest groups resisted budget cutting, and Alaskans were not about to give up the PFD program and other special benefits. Most importantly, Alaska's citizens were unwilling to pay more taxes.[57]

Between 1981 and 1988, $34 billion (or about $36 billion in 1988 dollars) passed through the state general fund, an average of about $4 billion per year. That included not only operating and capital spending, but also some savings and investments. State agencies spent about one-third of the money on operating and capital expenses. Alaska's urban and rural school districts received about 14 percent, or almost $5 billion. The legislature deposited more than $4 billion, or 12 percent, into the Permanent Fund in addition to the $2.8 billion that went into the Permanent Fund as the constitution required. Alaska's local governments received about $3.4 billion in state operating and capital aid, about 10 percent of the total. The state's public corporations, quasi-state agencies that do everything from subsidizing home mortgage rates to building dams, received $2 billion, or 6 percent of the total. Individual Alaskans collected almost $2 billion, or 6 percent, in cash or services through programs other than the PFD, such as the state's welfare programs and the

Longevity Bonus Program, to name but a few.[58]

Alaskans received $1.7 billion between 1983 and 1988 in Permanent Fund dividends, about 5 percent of the total $34 billion. The University of Alaska statewide system received $1.4 billion in operating and capital funds for 1981 through 1988, or about 4 percent. Funds that loan money to students, farmers, fishermen, and others received $1.3 billion, or 4 percent, between 1981 and 1988. Debt service on state general obligation bonds, excluding the large bonded debt the state's public corporations owe, cost about 3 percent in the 1980s. One-time special expenses cost about 3 percent of the total. The biggest was a $295 million payment the state owed the Alaska Native Corporations, and the $160 million individual Alaskans received in refunds with the repeal of the individual income tax. Nonprofit corporations and others that provided various kinds of services received about $600 million, or 2 percent of total spending from 1981 to 1988.[59]

Petroleum has driven Alaska's economic growth since 1970, and oil revenues have paid most of the government's general expenses and supported thousands of public and private sector jobs since the late 1970s. The most volatile influence on the state's economy has been the price of crude oil. Alaska's growth has mostly been due to fortunate good timing. The peak flow of oil from Prudhoe Bay field coincided almost exactly with peak world oil prices. Since ANS production began in 1977, the state has watched prices rise to all-time highs and then fall precipitously.[60]

In 1981, oil prices were triple what they had been in 1970 and ten times higher than in 1968. The high prices increased exploration and led to the discovery of numerous new and promising deposits. Oil prices, however, crashed in 1986 as consumers and industry conserved energy and move to lower-priced fuels. After the crash, oil prices hovered between fifteen and twenty dollars per barrel until the middle of 1997, when a severe recession started in East Asia, which had driven oil consumption in the previous decade. As demand fell, oil from other sources came on the market. Oil prices fell throughout 1998, averaging about eleven dollars a barrel for the year. After 2000 international markets shifted, and in 2004 prices averaged almost thirty-

TABLE 3

Total Alaska Oil Profits, 1969–1987

REVENUES	Production revenues	97.6 billion
	TAPS revenues	33.7 billion
	Total revenues	131.3 billion
EXPENSES	Depreciation	12.1 billion
	Operating expenses	9.1 billion
	Exploration expenses	4.1 billion
	Overhead	0.8 billion
	Interest	7.5 billion
	Royalty	11.8 billion
	Severance tax	10.4 billion
	Property tax	3.5 billion
	State Income tax	3.6 billion
	Windfall profits tax	6.4 billion
	Federal income tax	19.4 billion
	Total expenses	88.7 billion
PROFITS		42.6 billion

Source: *Fairbanks Daily News-Miner*, March 26, 1989.

nine dollars per barrel. The next year they rose to seventy dollars and were still hovering around this price by mid-2006.[61]

Addressing the Fiscal Gap

In the meantime, at the urging of Governor Steve Cowper, in 1989 the legislature passed a measure to modify the Economic Limit Factor (ELF), a little known provision of state law that was supposed to be a tax break to encourage development of Alaska's poorer oil fields. The legislature had rewritten it in 1981, at the same time it had abandoned the separate accounting method of oil industry income taxes. The severance tax was raised slightly to make up for the income Alaska would lose without a full tax on oil industry profits. The ELF was rewritten at that time because the state needed to keep the sever-

ance tax from being a burden on smaller fields and yet keep Kuparuk, the second largest field, paying its share of taxes. By 1987, the ELF was losing the state millions of dollars in revenue. Governor Cowper instructed the Office of Management and Budget and the Department of Revenue to study the problem. By 1988 the ELF had become a major issue in the legislature, and when the legislature passed the ELF modification in 1989, it raised approximately $141 million in extra revenue from the oil industry.[62]

On March 16, 1989, the state had also released a report that consultant Dr. Edward B. Deakin, an internationally recognized authority on oil industry accounting, had prepared for the Alaska Department of Revenue. Dr. Deakin's report presented a picture of the Alaska oil industry's profits entirely different from the one Alaskans had been getting "from the industry's advertisements and speeches."

Editorial writer Fred Pratt of the *Fairbanks Daily News-Miner* wrote that "since oil company spokesmen have lately been questioning the 'credentials' of us benighted Alaskans who dare to comment on their statistics," it was appropriate to cite Deakin's numbers, summarized in table 3.[63]

Several factors probably helped persuade the legislature to amend the ELF formula in 1989 to raise taxes on the oil industry, among them the Deakin's report, the grounding of the *Exxon Valdez* and subsequent massive oil spill in Prince William Sound, and the growing fiscal gap.

In 1989, economist Oliver Scott Goldsmith of the Institute of Social and Economic Research of the University of Alaska Anchorage initiated a research project that also dealt with Alaska's fiscal gap. It resulted, during the next decade, in a series of Fiscal Policy Papers in which Goldsmith and his colleagues addressed the problem and suggested solutions. The problem was easy to explain: state government spent more than it collected in taxes. He predicted that if state government spending stayed at the current level of $2.25 billion (in 1989 dollars), the difference between current spending and projected revenues would soon grow to $1 billion annually. The fiscal crisis loomed because oil production, which supplied 85 percent of the state's general fund revenues, was expected to drop soon, as Prudhoe Bay declined. Goldsmith speculated that likely new petroleum production, higher oil prices, and other economic activity in the coming decade would not generate nearly enough tax and royalty income to make up for the Prudhoe Bay decline.[64]

Goldsmith wrote that if future revenues were larger than anticipated, the fiscal gap could be reduced for a short time but the overall picture would remain the same. Such a gap could not persist. The legislature would have to balance the budget by cutting spending, raising taxes, using the state's savings, or some combination of the three. These changes would affect not only everyone who enjoyed state services, worked for state government, or paid taxes, but also everyone who benefited from local government services like schools and street maintenance. It would also affect recipients of government transfer payments, including PFD payment recipients and businesses that depended on the purchasing power

of a large public sector. In short, balancing the budget would affect all Alaskans because the state's economy was dangerously dependent on oil revenue that financed state government spending. Even in 1989, after several years of recession and a precipitous drop in revenues, state government spending still accounted directly and indirectly for more than one in four Alaska jobs.[65]

Goldsmith outlined four possible scenarios to deal with the fiscal gap between 1989 and 2010. The first was to "stumble from year to year." This assumed that the state would attempt to maintain current spending for as long as possible by using all available reserves except the principal of the Permanent Fund, and then cut spending to match reduced revenues. The second was to "deplete the Permanent Fund," which would maintain the current budget level by spending the principal of the Permanent Fund. The third was to "freeze the budget"—in effect cutting the budget by the annual inflation rate. The fourth was to "cut spending and raise taxes." This would reduce state spending, reimpose the personal income tax, and eliminate the PFD. Goldsmith recognized that there were other possible combinations, but these four encompassed the main options. He recognized the enormous political difficulties inherent in exercising any of these options. Some would require changes in law or even amendments to the Alaska Constitution. All were certain to generate intense public debate, and most would face extremely strong opposition from specific groups or from Alaskans in general.[66]

Goldsmith proposed a "soft landing" approach to deal with the fiscal gap: cut state spending year by year, implement an income tax, institute user taxes, and cap dividend payments. Whatever decisions were taken, however, would have significant economic consequences. Goldsmith and his colleagues continued to produce information about the implications of different choices for policy makers and the general public in subsequent years.

The 1990 legislature was concerned about the fiscal gap. Among other measures it considered, it put a constitutional amendment on that year's November ballot creating a state budget reserve fund. Voters approved the amendment. The new budget reserve account was to be funded by settlements the state would receive from tax disputes with the oil industry and from proceeds from the resolution of disagreements with the federal government over Alaska's share of offshore oil and gas revenues. The legislature expected more than $5 billion from these sources over the next several years. The amendment stated that funds could be spent only through a majority vote of the legislature if monies available for appropriation in any year were less than the amount appropriated the previous year. Withdrawals, however, could not be used to exceed the pervious year's budget total. A three-fourths vote could commit the fund for a public purpose, but any money withdrawn would have to be repaid as soon as possible from excess cash available at the end of the following budget years.[67]

The legislature and the governor also conducted a series of workshops between March 11 and March 25, 1990, in Valdez, Anchorage, Juneau, Kodiak, Mat-Su, and Nome, concluding with a television program on March 28 that was carried by all public television stations. They also developed a four-page brochure, sent to most Alaskans, that showed the facts of the state budget and asked citizens to answer a series of questions with a yes or no answer: Would you favor reductions in the following areas? (1) state government operations or (2) assistance to individuals and local governments. Would you favor increasing revenues in the following ways? (1) taxes, (2) user fees, (3) reallocate cash and reserves. Before the legislature and the governor distributed the questionnaire, they had conducted workshops in Fairbanks, Homer, Barrow, Kenai, Soldotna, Eagle River, Seward, Kotzebue, Unalaska, and Dillingham.[68] No fiscal plan emerged, however, from these workshops.

By June 1990, the state faced an estimated deficit for fiscal year 1991 of somewhere between $500 million and $900 million, depending on the oil price used for the calculations. The price of oil had been heading for the ten-to-twenty dollars per barrel price range because of the world oil glut and cheating on the production rate OPEC had imposed on its member states. The price per barrel of oil in calculating Alaska revenue projections is important because each dollar change in oil prices equals about $150 million in the projected state budget. Based on

these revenue forecasts, Governor Cowper vetoed $350 million from the state's operating budget, and the legislature went along with his action.[69]

The veto caused distress in municipalities and school districts because they had to reduce already approved fiscal year 1991 budgets after mill rates had been set for the next fiscal year. Then, when the Gulf War began on August 6, 1990, oil prices jumped to almost thirty dollars per barrel. This revised revenue projections again, and now the state expected a $700 million surplus for fiscal year 1991.[70]

The Future

The oil, gas, and pipeline story is far from over, for oil revenues still provide Alaska with much of its unrestricted revenue and experts believe that fully one-third of the nation's undiscovered recoverable oil and gas may still lie under Alaska and its continental shelf. Over the years, the Department of the Interior has sold substantial lease acreage in the Gulf of Alaska and the Beaufort and Bering seas. In 1983, for example, eighty-four leases for tracts in three offshore Alaska areas, the Navarin, Saint George, and Norton basins, netted the federal government about $1.4 billion in revenues. The oil industry, together with consultants and academic communities, has embarked on an ambitious research and exploration program to enable it to eventually extract oil and gas from these offshore areas.[71] In short, the federal government looks to Alaska and its outer continental shelf for the single largest increment in new oil-and-gas supplies to meet national energy needs in the twenty-first century and beyond.

However, all talk about bridging the fiscal gap in the face of declining oil prices has stopped. Alaska's state budget increased from $4.1 billion in 1990 to $11.2 billion in 2008. Economist Goldsmith, who has dealt with the projected budget gap for years, and his associates asked, Who paid for the budget growth? The state's oil revenues dropped by half in the 1990s, which tore big holes into the budget. Additionally, Alaska has no personal income tax or other broad-based taxes. Although oil has accounted for the biggest revenue stream for the last twenty years, fees, interest income, and non-oil taxes pay

A moose passes beneath a section of above-ground pipe for the Trans-Alaska Pipeline. There are about eight hundred natural and man-made animal crossings along the right-of-way where the pipline is above ground.

(Courtesy of Alyeska Pipeline Service Company.)

for some spending, as does the federal government. The state kept deficits from growing ever larger by cutting or at least holding steady general fund revenues for programs ranging from resource management to municipal revenue sharing. So who paid for the $7.1 billion budget growth from 1990 to 2008?

The answer is that more than half was in federal money, which pays for designated expenses. Some of the growth was financed by other state sources, especially fees from people and businesses. Spending from fees and from earnings of public corporations multiplied. People and businesses pay fees for enterprises like ferries, the university, and airports,

and for everything from licenses to leases. Management fees for state retirement systems and for trust funds (mainly the Permanent Fund) also increased, as did earnings of public corporations like the Alaska Housing Finance Corporation. These earnings mainly pay for corporation operating costs, but the state has also recently used earnings of the Alaska Housing Finance Corporation, the Alaska Industrial Development and Export Authority, and the Science and Technology Foundation to pay general expenses.[72]

Unrestricted general fund spending for major population-driven programs grew 60 percent between 1990 and 2002. Alaska's overall population grew about 17 percent, but numbers of Alaskans in some population-driven programs grew much more. The number of school children grew 22 percent, the number of persons receiving Medicaid climbed nearly 150 percent (and medical costs soared), the numbers of prisoners grew 90 percent, and the Adult Public Assistance caseload (low-income older and disabled Alaskans) grew 117 percent. The state's general fund spending for these programs grew apace, from $678 million in 1990 to $1.1 billion in 2002. (No comparative studies have been made since 2002.) Meanwhile, annual federal funding in Alaska leaped from $574 million to $2.3 billion. The biggest increases were for building transportation projects (which grew from $164 million in 1990 to $667 million in 2002) and funding Medicaid (from $84 million in 1990 to $527 million in 2002), but programs throughout the budget saw more federal money.[73]

With a sizable surplus, the 2006 legislature submitted a 2006 fiscal year budget of $8,666.7 billion. Of this, $4,469.8 billion, or 51.57 percent, came from the general fund, $2,829.5 billion from federal expenditures, and $1,367.4 from other funds.[74] The good times seemed to be here again, but then a recession began in late 2007. Although Alaska was not hit as hard as the rest of the country, severe belt-tightening looms in the near future.

Alaskans continue to argue among themselves about whether or not energy development has been a worthwhile trade-off for the increased economic activity and prosperity. There are those who maintain that the oil boom has irreparably harmed the delicately balanced ecology of the Arctic and has wrought havoc with the independent lifestyle of the state's residents. Those favoring economic growth point to the long-term economic benefits the state is reaping, including a vastly improved infrastructure made possible by abundant oil revenues. In any event, Alaskans themselves have had very little say in the decisions to develop the state's energy resources. The energy crisis of 1973–74, the subsequent explosion in crude oil prices, and the national drive toward an illusionary energy "self-sufficiency" have been the factors that combined to, and continue to spur, Alaska's development.

What is certain is that a larger population has put greater pressures on the state's land, water, fish, and wildlife resources. Above all, oil development has generated a momentum of its own, and it is largely unaffected by what the state may or may not do. Thomas Morehouse, a seasoned observer of Alaska, has concluded that if the state government is to have any control over the speed of development, it will have to "rely primarily on policies other than the direct control of petroleum resources—on environmental regulations, tax policies, expenditure programs, and other policy actions that can both mitigate undesirable effects of petroleum development and distribute its benefits more equitably." But perhaps it was an old sourdough who best summed up the momentous changes in Alaska when he said: "They sure have gotta lotta things they never had before, ain't they?"[75]

PART V

Modern Alaska

Chapter 24

The Unconventional Walter "Wally" J. Hickel

Wally Hickel had left the governorship in 1968 to become President Nixon's Secretary of the Interior. He lasted two years in that job before Nixon fired him, and he left with a decent reputation as a guardian of America's natural and scenic resources. He came back to Alaska and quickly involved himself in state politics again. It took him twenty-two years, however, to regain the governorship he had left in 1968.

The 1990 Election

In the Republican Party primary in August 1990, state Senator Arliss Sturgulewski won, together with her running mate, State Senator Jack Coghill. Jane Arliss Sturgulewski grew up in northwestern Washington state during the Great Depression in a poor family. In 1945, after having saved enough money, she enrolled at the University of Washington to study accounting, one of three women in the degree program. After receiving her degree, she remained in Seattle for a few years and worked as an accountant. In 1952 she drove the Alcan Highway north to take advantage of "lots more possibilities in Alaska, more men and more jobs."[1]

She quickly found a job as a bookkeeper and also met Bernard Sturgulewski, an engineer. The two married in 1953. In December 1968, Bernard was killed in a plane accident. Through the years, the couple and their young son had lived on Bernard's earnings and invested her pay, so she was financially independent upon her husband's death. She now devoted her time to politics. After several positions in municipal government in Anchorage, voters elected her to the state senate in 1978.[2]

Former two-term Anchorage mayor Tony Knowles won the Democratic primary. His views differed only slightly from Sturgulewski's moderate positions. Joe Vogler, the president of the Alaska Independence Party (AIP), had won 10 percent of the vote in the 1986 election, and so his party was guaranteed a place on the 1990 ballot. Vogler's party called for secession of Alaska from the United States. The 1990 party convention selected former University of Alaska Anchorage chancellor and rural newspaper publisher John Lindauer as its standard bearer, and Jerry Ward as the number two man on the ticket.[3]

On the evening of September 18, 1990, Anchorage bank executive David Cuddy hosted a meeting at his home to ask Sturgulewski some questions. Those attending the meeting included around thirty of the Republican Party's social conservatives, as well as Lindauer, the Independence Party's candidate. Sturgulewski listened and told the attendees what she could and could not do. She could not, for example, commit to reducing the state budget during the next four years, nor would she alter her pro-choice stand on abortion. Clearly, Cuddy's hope that she adopt a conservative platform would not be fulfilled.[4]

Sturgulewski's refusal to compromise helped convince Coghill to jump ship. Edgar Boyko, a former Alaska attorney general and conservative Republican, had tried for weeks to get Coghill to dump Sturgulewski and form a ticket with Walter J. Hickel. Coghill had refused. But at midnight on September 18 he called Hickel and suggested that the two form an AIP ticket. Boyko subsequently made the necessary arrangements. Lindauer and Ward dropped out of the race; Joe Vogler gave his blessings and appointed Hickel and Coghill as the AIP candidates. On the afternoon of September 19, Boyko listened in on a series of phone calls between Hickel and numerous interested parties. John Sununu, President George H. W. Bush's chief of staff, urged Hickel not to join the race. Boyko surmised that Alaska's junior U.S. Senator Frank Murkowski was the main force behind the call. Boyko called it "the Polish connection," referring to a relationship by marriage between the Sturgulewski and Murkowski families. "To neutralize it," Boyko stated, "we're going to get an endorsement from Lech Walesa" (Poland's premier).[5]

Hickel probably was reminded of a call to service he had received at the end of December 1989 from a number of Anchorage citizens, dissatisfied with Governor Steve Cowper's leadership and worried about Alaska's future. As Hickel jumped into the gubernatorial race, he probably recalled the full page appeal in the *Anchorage Daily News*. Among the individuals sponsoring the ad were Steve McCutcheon, James M. Rockwell, and Ken Mears. Their appeal was headlined "Governor Hickel, the State of Alaska Needs You." The undersigned considered the next five years crucial. "We are terrified. No announced candidate for governor has the experience, foresight, or guts to lead Alaska out of fiscal disaster. Worse yet, no candidate . . . has the backbone to make the tough decisions that will have to be made over the next four years. . . . However, we know we won't survive another four years of timid leadership." The group asked Hickel to run for governor, win, and execute an action plan that included, above all else, making decisions instead of merely talking about the problems. Anyone could run for governor, that ad pointed out, all it took was fifty dollars and a ballpoint pen. Alaska needed a chief executive

who would lead, "not a warm body that dodges the tough issues facing us." The seventeen individuals concluded their appeal to Hickel: "You file for governor, we'll get you elected. You have to call us and let's get cracking." At the time, Hickel did not heed the call to service.

Now things were different. A few days later Hickel told the media that Sununu had suggested that Hickel's proposed gas pipeline would be endangered if he made a third-party bid for governor. That threat, Coghill commented, "simply helped firm Hickel's resolve to enter the race." Now both Hickel and Coghill campaigned under the AIP banner, although Coghill stated, "they both still consider themselves Republicans at heart."[6]

Hickel's sudden entry into the race six weeks before the election threw the race into chaos. Upon Coghill's departure, Republican candidate Sturgulewski recruited her closest challenger in the August 28 Republican primary, Jim Campbell, as her new running mate. Sturgulewski remarked that she was dismayed and sad at the turn of events, "but it's a new day and we're going forward with great hope for the future of Alaska." Mike States, an Anchorage Republican conservative and anti-abortion activist, said, "When [Democratic candidate] Tony Knowles woke up yesterday morning, it appeared he would be elected governor. When John Lindauer dropped out, . . . it appeared Sturgulewski would be governor. When Hickel entered the race at 4 P.M., it became certain she'll never be governor. It's a two-way race now between Hickel and Knowles."[7] On the other side, Senate President Tim Kelly, whom Coghill had defeated in the Republican primary for lieutenant governor, dismissed the chances of the Republican turncoats. "You've got two old dogs who want one more bay at the moon, but Alaskans are not going to turn the clock back 30 years and elect Jack Coghill and Wally Hickel."[8]

Hickel and Coghill ran an aggressive media campaign and emphasized the need to cut state operating expenses by at least 5 percent and to promote economic growth. Both men stressed their difference from both Sturgulewski and Knowles, and voters elected the Hickel-Coghill team with 39 percent in the three-way vote.[9] Hickel was sworn into office on December 3, 1990. On December 6 he visited

Fairbanks to thank the town's citizens who had rallied around his third-party ticket and given him 50 percent of the local vote. He told the crowd jammed into the local Elks Lodge, "When the last governor took office, he had said 'All bets are off.' I want to tell you—'all bets are on.'"[10] What Hickel did not tell the crowd was that Cowper had realized when he took office that even assuring Alaskans that normal state services would continue was impossible because of the low oil prices. And it was revenues from the oil industry that fed 90 percent of the general fund.

In his inaugural address Hickel promised a new era in state politics, stating, "It is time for Alaska to recapture its glory. It is time we establish for all the world to see that Alaska is 'one country one people.'" He asked legislators to help him lead Alaska into "a new era of optimism and unity" by approving an ambitious public works program. He asked for a 5 percent cut in the state operating budget, proposed limiting legislative sessions to seventy-five days, and legislative terms to eight years. He rejected demands for Native sovereignty, and he promoted a voucher system to make private schools more affordable. Most legislators, however, were not impressed by the governor's speech, which "was long on big proposals and his 'owner-state' rhetoric, but short on the how-to-do it details they wanted to hear."[11]

Governor Hickel

Hickel was back in the spotlight: thinking big, being unconventional, and making the political establishment uncomfortable. In just eight weeks in office, Hickel had enthusiastically immersed himself in controversy as he tried to recast Alaska in his own predevelopment image. He appointed a former oil company president as commissioner of the Department of Natural Resources, which rankled environmentalists. He proposed significant cuts in the state operating budget, even though Alaska expected a $1 billion windfall because of the higher oil prices caused by the Gulf War. The governor proposed to put the windfall into an investment fund to finance costly, Alaska-sized projects designed to help diversify the state's economy. These projects included a huge port near Anchorage, extension of the state's railroad, and an $11 billion pipeline to bring natural

President Richard M. Nixon and his Secretary of the Interior, Walter J. Hickel, 1971.

(Courtesy of *Fairbanks Daily News-Miner*.)

gas to Asian markets. These were all part of his vision of Alaska as a unique "owner state," where government owned most of the land, subsurface, and natural resources and had an obligation to develop and manage them for maximum public benefit. The governor maintained that such a role was foreign to government in the United States because it had been structured "to be a regulator." Hickel wanted to build a modern transportation and energy system, allowing private industry to develop the state's vast resources and create jobs.[12]

Alaska's political establishment reacted to Hickel with a mixture of anxiety and humor. Juneau, Alaska's capital, quickly became known as "Wally World" after the goofy theme park in the movie *National Lampoon's Vacation*. An Anchorage newspaper maintained a "Wallywatch" to track the average age of the "old white men" who comprised Hickel's cabinet. Juneau's Democrats billed their inauguration party as the "Back to the Future Ball."[13]

Bill Ray, former state legislator turned lobbyist and a longtime Hickel friend, described the governor as "a progressive, conservative liberal. He's for progress, yet he is a conservative, but he's liberal in getting it done." Since Hickel had financed his own independent campaign, he owed special interests and the Republican Party nothing. Ray remarked that the governor was "a mustang. He's running wild and he has no reins on him. He drinks from any puddle he wants." In short, Hickel did not respond to political pressure like other politicians. "But for all the bluster, Wally Hickel is a pretty sophisticated guy. He is no tobacco chewin' hick."[14]

The 1991 legislative session pitted Hickel, who promised budget cuts and favored big development projects, against a Democratic-led House coalition that supported modest growth in the operating budget and a Republican-led coalition in the Senate that responded to interest group pressures and public sector forces to continue unchanged the operation of popular programs. The legislative budget came to almost $3 billion, about $200 million over the governor's recommended total. The governor cut 2 percent of the operating budget and 2.5 percent of capital funding. The legislature did not call itself into a special session to try overriding the budget reductions. The operating budget cuts were transferred to the municipalities, which depended on state funding for between 20 to 30 percent of their revenue, through the municipal assistance and revenue sharing pass-through programs. The House and Senate passed the education budget almost one month before the end of the session so that if it were vetoed, the legislature would still be in session to override the vetoes. The governor let it pass without his signature.[15]

The State Senate voted on April 17, 1991, to increase the interest the state charged on the oil industry's nearly $4 billion in disputed state tax bills. In 1990 the Cowper administration had proposed just such an increase, spearheaded by Hugh Malone, the commissioner of revenue. The oil industry viewed Malone as something of a sinister figure, and the Senate, which oil industry friends dominated, gutted Malone's proposal and then passed a final bill so late that it died. But now the Senate passed Hickel's version of the bill. That was not the first time the governor had stiff-armed the oil firms in a big financial fight. Right after he took office, Hickel could have lifted outgoing Commissioner Malone's new rule forcing oil companies to pay more of their sev-

erance taxes up front instead of stalling payments through years of litigation. Malone's rule ended up in court, and Hickel vigorously defended it. The state prevailed.[16]

The Recall Movement, Ethics Issues, and Conflict with Jack Coghill

Hickel was a controversial governor, and as early as April 1991, a grassroots movement had been gathering signatures to put a Hickel-Coghill recall petition on the ballot. In early October 1991, the petitioners put on a "Recall Ball" in Fairbanks, which attracted more than 250 area residents. Lou Brown, one of the organizers, hoped the party would help them raise one thousand dollars, to be used to buy large advertisements in the Anchorage newspapers, including petitions that readers could cut out and send to the organizers. The event featured an auction, and the most popular item was a Hickel administration poster, hyping the governor's plan to build a gigantic water pipeline to bring arctic waters to thirsty Californians. The recall committee, with most of its supporters based in Fairbanks, had gathered 12,000 signatures out of a total of 19,754 needed to put it on the ballot. But the initiative never made it to the ballot.[17]

In early December 1991, Chip Thoma, a Juneau political activist, filed ethics complaints against the governor for owning 12 percent of the shares of the Anchorage-based Yukon Pacific Corporation, which Hickel had founded nearly a decade earlier to build a proposed trans-Alaska natural gas pipeline and market the state's gas to Pacific Rim nations. The stock was potentially worth millions of dollars. A special prosecutor thereupon charged the governor with violating the state ethics laws because his stock ownership posed "a clear conflict of interest" in that the governor's actions could affect the stock's value. Hickel was angry about the charges, and his administration was worried that they could add fuel to the recall campaign.[18] The whole matter was settled quickly, however, when Hickel signed an agreement establishing a charitable foundation to which he donated his shares. It stated that the governor and his family could never profit from the stock, but it allowed him to deduct the donation from his 1991 federal income taxes. Thereupon, the state Personnel Board dismissed the ethics charges against Hickel, and he formally approved the settlement.[19]

In the meantime, differences had developed between Hickel and his lieutenant governor, Jack Coghill. Hickel had promised his running mate in 1990 that Coghill would review and change, if necessary, all proposed state regulations. However, this promise extended far beyond Coghill's constitutional task of administratively acknowledging the regulations. The constitution only gives the lieutenant governor the jobs of running elections and keeping the state seal. Coghill, as a member of the constitutional convention in 1955–56, which drafted the document, should have known better, but sometimes a politician's greatest achievements come back to haunt him in later life. The constitution gives all the power in the executive branch to the chief executive. If someone wrote bad regulations, it was the job of the commissioner of that department to correct them. If the commissioner failed, it was the governor's and the attorney general's job to correct him.[20] Hickel could not change this by executive order.

Coghill's reaction was to declare a political divorce in December 1991, and he accused the governor of breaking campaign promises, declaring that Hickel's action "effectively dissolves the Hickel-Coghill team." One week later, however, after having met with the governor, Coghill was contrite and stated that "our differences, which have now been resolved, were made public hastily." He stated that he respected Hickel and what the governor had tried to accomplish and was confident that "our team is solid."[21]

Hickel and State Budget Shortfalls

Despite a recession in the oil industry in the late 1990s, the economies of Alaska and the United States were fairly stable throughout the decade. A number of factors promoted stable prices in the face of increased worldwide demand. Among these was Saudi Arabia's willingness to accommodate American needs. Whenever short supplies threatened to drive up prices, it simply pumped more oil. Saddam Hussein apparently had targeted the al-Saud family in his drive to control the world's oil supply, and his defeat in Desert Storm had greatly relieved the kingdom's fears.

But Hickel was restrained in his budgets because the price of oil hovered at around twenty dollars a barrel throughout Operation Desert Storm, severely pinching Alaska's general fund. Oil was also cheap from 1992 to 2001, and as a producer, Alaska suffered. Certainly tourism was a bright spot in the state's economy; in fact, over 1 million visitors had come to Alaska for the first time in 1994. But oil production continued to diminish, and experts predicted no end to the decline. Diminishing oil revenues inevitably resulted in projections of state budget shortfalls.

By April 1992, after sixteen months in office, the governor acknowledged that he had a tough time fulfilling campaign promises to reduce state spending. In his campaign he had promised to cut the budget by 5 percent. But he managed to rationalize a victory: after cutting 5 percent below the 1992 budget, absorbing the cost of living increases, he had actually cut more than 10 percent. "So to even hold it even is pretty much of a victory."[22]

In his 1992 State of the Budget address, the governor urged the citizens "to think rich again," but he offered few clues to how he would deal with projected revenue shortfalls in 1993. The governor recommitted his administration to an activist, pro-development agenda that would "overwhelm the forces of no growth." Alaskans had been spoiled by Prudhoe Bay's riches; their courage and creativity had been sapped by living too lavishly for too long. He maintained that affluence too often stunts creativity. "We're not poor—we're thinking poor." Hickel did acknowledge the state's increasingly dismal fiscal picture. Oil prices had declined in recent weeks and revenue had fallen off, and it could get worse. Many legislators were not impressed with the governor's address, and one characterized it as "a lot of fluff—a lot of show and no tell."[23]

Hickel presented an operating budget of $2.43 billion for fiscal year 1993. He proposed to pay for it with oil prices at $18.90 a barrel. Alaska's legislature always spends the first half of the annual session waiting for the March oil revenue estimates,

Suing the U.S. Government

In his State of the State address in January 1992, Governor Hickel announced that he planned to sue the federal government for violating terms of Alaska's statehood compact and "treating the nation's largest state like a colony." He declared, "Today we must draw a line. Alaska has had enough." He cited, among other examples, the refusal of Congress to open the Arctic National Wildlife Refuge to oil drilling and the increasing restrictions on logging the vast Tongass National Forest. Hickel maintained that the statehood compact had guaranteed Alaska the chance to build an economy so its citizens "can afford to govern ourselves and so all our people can have a decent standard of living."

In July 1993, the state filed its lawsuit. The governor asked for $29 billion, "a conservative estimate of the amount the guaranteed mineral revenue Alaska was denied in the past 34 years as Congress withdrew federal lands from resource development." The governor stated that $29 billion was only the minimum, and that the lawsuit could be worth up to $70 billion. Congress had withdrawn more than 100 million acres of federal lands, "forever preventing it from producing any income to the state, and often preventing access for development of state lands." The twelve-page lawsuit claimed that Congress "induced" Alaskans to ratify the Statehood Act in 1958 by promising the state broad opportunities to develop federal lands. A spokesman for the Secretary of the Interior suggested that the lawsuit would not be taken very seriously in Washington. "There may be a political basis for the suit, but there clearly is no legal basis. We are unaware of any legal reasons why we'd be obligated to fork out $29 billion."

Indeed, after winding its way through the U.S. Court of Federal Claims, the suit received a hearing and the judge found in favor of the United States. That was the end of Hickel's suit. This was the fourth, and by far the biggest, lawsuit Hickel had filed against the federal government. The others had sought to assert the state's claim to its navigable waterways, to assert its right to manage its fish and game on federal lands, and to overturn the federal ban on foreign export of North Slope oil.

Sources: *Fairbanks Daily News-Miner,* January 15, 1992, July 3, 1993; *Charles E. Cole, Attorney General, State of Alaska, Plaintiff, v. United States of America, Defendant,* Compliant for Just Compensation, July 22, 1993; Harold M. Brown and Stephen V. Bonse, "Memorandum in Support of State of Alaska's Motion for Partial Summary Judgment," November 29, 1994, 17 (in author Naske's files).

the last reliable data the legislature receives before it adjourns. The March estimates, after winter oil usage, are the year's highest, permitting the lawmakers to spend the maximum amount. But in 1992 there were only unpleasant surprises. Oil prices had dropped, and the national recession and a warm winter had further reduced demand. The Department of Revenue's forecast estimated the next fiscal year's oil prices at $15.86 a barrel. The estimates projected a shortfall of $235 million for the current fiscal year. Fiscal year 1993 revenue projections fell $435 million below those projected in the fall of 1991. Such a deficit would have sent shudders through legislative bodies in other states. In Alaska it merely added to the usual tensions during the annual budget debates. It was not even deemed worthy of front page coverage in the state's major newspapers.[24]

The explanation for this probably was the state's ability to finance deficits more easily than other states. Included in the state's financial cushion are the Alaska Housing Finance Corporation and other state corporations, whose assets would produce over $1 billion in revenues annually. The Alaska Permanent Fund was valued at $13.4 billion in early 1992. Paying the annual Permanent Fund Dividend, a hugely popular program, cost $430 million in fiscal year 1992. The fund annually generates almost $500 million, which is allocated to inflation proofing in an earnings reserve account. The legislature could appropriate this money by a simple majority vote of both houses of the legislature. Then there was the $1 billion settlement between the state of Alaska, the U.S. Justice Department, and Exxon resulting from the *Exxon Valdez* oil spill, part of which the legislature could tap. Finally, in 1992, ARCO Alaska, Inc., BP Exploration (Alaska), Inc., and Exxon Co. USA agreed to pay the state $633 million to settle the long-running dispute over royalty payments to the state (see chapter 16). In short, Alaska's public resources were more than adequate to meet public needs. Additionally, Alaska's tax base was largely underutilized. There were no state income or sales taxes and only very moderate property taxes.[25]

The Budget Reserve Issue

Governor Hickel again proposed a status quo budget of $2.34 billion for fiscal year 1994, some $10 billion less than the fiscal year 1993 amount. The governor initially proposed a $328 million capital budget that, including federal matching funds, would total $714 million. He proposed spending $150 million annually over four years on school construction and university maintenance, funded from earnings of the Permanent Fund. Many legislators rejected this idea. After the BP tax settlement, the governor suggested that the state use the entire $633 million to create a school construction and maintenance fund.

Most policy makers agreed that funds were needed for school construction and improved maintenance, but they disagreed with Hickel's proposal to use the settlement monies for this purpose. Republican leaders in both houses of the legislature asserted that the windfall should be saved in the constitutional budget reserve. Attorney General Charles Cole advised that because the BP settlement had been reached informally, the proceeds could immediately be deposited in the state's unrestricted general fund. If the funds were deposited in the budget reserve, both houses of the legislature would have to deliver a three-fourths vote to remove the funds. That would be difficult to achieve, even for a popular measure like school construction.[26]

The two houses compromised with a plan to use the BP settlement for public school construction and renovation. The legislature made direct grants for school construction in the state's largest urban areas and proposed a 70 percent debt reimbursement for school bonds in urban areas. The total urban school package reached $500 million. The governor approved the total capital budget of $735.6 million, but late in the fiscal year Senate Republicans asserted the use of the money was unconstitutional and promised to sue in state court. After making some slight reductions in the operating budget, such as capping welfare benefits and phasing out the Longevity Bonus Program, which gave Alaska senior citizens $250 a month to continue living in the state, the legislature agreed on a $2.42 billion operating budget. The governor signed it into law in late June 1993. In short, Alaska's fiscal year 1994 budget was $3.23 billion, about $500 million above the previous year's budget. Including federal funds, it totaled more than $5.1 billion.[27]

The majority of Republican legislators had approved the capital budget, but they nevertheless sued to determine the legality of their actions. Former Governor Cowper also sued the state, asserting that the actions of the legislature and governor were unconstitutional. Superior Court Judge John Reese ruled in November that the $924 million tax settlement funds had been illegally diverted from the state's constitutional budget reserve and ordered the legislature and governor to replace it. The Alaska Supreme Court upheld Judge Reese's preliminary ruling in late January 1994.[28]

The Republicans then codified their intent in legislation to make it easier for the legislature to spend reserve funds by simple majority vote and to narrowly define the source of revenue for the budget reserve. Opponents sued, and Judge Reese declared the legislation unconstitutional as well. In April, the Alaska Supreme Court declared that "administrative proceedings" between the state and the oil companies began at the moment the state declared that the companies had underpaid their taxes. Judge Reese ended legislative attempts to get around the three-fourths vote requirement by declaring the new law "unconstitutional in its entirety."[29]

Less than a month before the end of the session, the House and Senate compromised on the budget reserve issue and voted unanimously and without debate to place $1 billion into the budget reserve, returning the oil-tax settlement proceeds that they had spent improperly. Most of the $1 billion was then transferred immediately into the general fund to balance the fiscal year 1994 budget, which was short about $670 million because of low oil prices. Minority Democrats, in return for making the three-fourths vote possible, received full school funding to the tune of $635 million in the fiscal year 1995 budget, as well as full funding of the state's share of school construction debt. The governor signed the measures into law within hours after it had passed both houses unanimously.[30]

Once again, the legislature and the governor had avoided dealing with the big issues, namely, how to wean the state off its dependence on oil taxes and royalties. They had once again failed to tax Alaska's citizens for the government services they enjoy; they had not capped the PFD or dedicated the Permanent Fund earnings for the support of state government.

A Maverick Governor?
Or, the Art of the Possible?

1994 was an election year, and after more than three years in office, Governor Hickel drew both praise and criticism. The newly elected governor had gone to Juneau in 1991 to cut the budget, assert state rights, and make Alaska a friendlier place for developers and business owners. Many praised him for having made some inroads on the latter two of his promises, but many conservative supporters felt betrayed when reviewing the governor's record. Fritz Pettyjohn, an Anchorage Republican analyst, voiced their sentiments when he stated that many had be-

lieved that Hickel "would go down there and shake up the system and make some serious big-time changes." Instead he had become "sort of a status quo governor." Most critically, Hickel had failed to reduce state spending.[31]

Hickel responded to his critics by stating that "cutting the budget has not been as easy as [he] once thought. Politics is the art of the possible." Furthermore, nobody could "say this is exactly what's going to happen." Lieutenant Governor Coghill was probably one of Hickel's severest critics. He stated that the state "could have saved $250 million to $300 million over the last three years if middle managers and duplicative services had been eliminated from the bureaucracy. The administration has allowed all of the money to pour through like . . . water through a sieve, and without any restraints."[32]

There was much speculation over whether or not Hickel would run again. In mid-April he partially answered that question when he abandoned the AIP and changed his voter registration back to Republican. Hickel explained that if he "did run, which is just a doubtful thing, at least there is an organization there. I just don't know if I'm going to run."[33] On April 16, 1994, Coghill announced that he was seeking the AIP nomination for governor. "The Hickel administration's highest ranking malcontent," as some observers had come to characterize him, accused Hickel of not reorganizing government, not increasing services to residents, not simplifying state regulations, and not opening more natural resources to Alaskans. Coghill apologized for the breach of the administration's 1990 campaign promises and said that he had "really tried. I guess, if you really want to get the job done sometimes you have got to just do it yourself." On August 16, Hickel announced that he would not seek reelection, thereby ending months of speculation. His announcement came just one week before the primary, and some of the thirteen candidates vying to replace him complained that potential contributors had been waiting for Hickel's plans before giving money.[34]

In 1990, Alaska's Republican Party had changed the rules of Alaska's blanket primary system. Voters previously had been able to cast ballots for any party's candidates, no matter what their registration status. Now the Republicans closed their primary to Democrats and other party registrants in order to avoid raiding and crossover voting. Nondeclared and nonpartisan voters, comprising 54 percent of Alaska's registered voters, were allowed to vote, and it was possible to change party affiliation at the polls. Republican party leaders had hoped that these primary changes would improve the prospects of fiscal and moral conservative candidates. This "classic open" primary system was first used in 1992, and it confused voters. In the 1994 primary, fewer than four of every ten voters opted for the Republican primary. Jim Campbell, lieutenant governor candidate for the party in 1990 and former CEO of Spenard Building Supply, the state's largest hardware chain, as well as the Alaska Railroad, won the primary with under 52 percent of the vote.[35]

On the Democratic side, three candidates vied for the nomination: Tony Knowles, the party's 1990 gubernatorial candidate, two-term Anchorage mayor, assemblyman, and restaurateur; Steve MacAlpine, former Valdez mayor and two-term lieutenant governor; and Sam Cotten, former House speaker from Eagle River. Knowles won the primary with more than ten thousand votes. Coghill won the AIP primary with practically no opposition.

Knowles and Campbell shared similar positions on job development, balancing the state budget, and dealing with state-federal conflicts, particularly subsistence. Coghill advertised himself as "Conservative, Constitutionalist, and Christian," hoping to capture the religious right from the Republican Party and to enlarge his support from miners, pioneers, small business owners, and protest voters, who had kept the AIP alive for nearly twenty years. Republican leaders urged Coghill to drop out of the race. Tom Fink, however, endorsed him over Campbell.[36]

Knowles won the election with barely 40 percent of the vote, with a lead of 339 votes over Campbell. The final count and recount gave Knowles a lead of 562 votes, the second closest race in state history. Although Knowles had been expected to win,

nobody had predicted such a close contest. Coghill, who had won 13 percent of the gubernatorial vote, had been a major factor in Knowles's victory. Coghill had spoiled Campbell's race.[37]

Republican Congressman Don Young easily defeated Tony Smith, his Democratic challenger and former commissioner of the State Commerce Department. With Republican control of the U.S. House and Senate, Young became chair of the House Resources Committee. Senator Frank Murkowski assumed the chair of the Committee on Energy and Natural Resources, while Senator Ted Stevens became chair of the Senate Rules Committee. To have Alaska's representatives in the House and Senate chair these committees gave the state much clout over decisions affecting federal lands in the state.[38]

When Hickel's term ended in December 1994, both Republicans and Democrats praised him, particularly since his last two budgets had continued the status quo. Cuts in state government had occurred through attrition. Hickel had negotiated a number of tax settlements with oil companies. On November 17, 1994, he announced a $1.4 billion out-of-court tax settlement with BP, the largest in state history. The three-year payout corresponded approximately to the anticipated budget deficits in fiscal years 1995 through 1997, cushioning the blow. On November 18, Hickel announced a settlement with ARCO in the amount of $269 million, eliminating oil and gas production tax disputes going back to 1990. Hickel left Alaskan electoral politics as a leader who promoted Alaska's interests as a "corporate state," where its citizens owned the natural resources and had a duty to utilize and manage them wisely.[39] Walter J. "Wally" Hickel died on May 7, 2010, at age ninety of natural causes at an Anchorage assisted-living facility. At his wish, he was buried upright in his teak coffin so that he could come out swinging when he reached heaven.

Chapter 25

The Knowles Years, 1994–2002

The 1990s were a time of both continuity and change in Alaska. Oil continued to dominate the state economy, and the problem of budget short-falls dominated political discussion as oil prices remained low. A Republican majority in the state legislature hampered the efforts of Democratic governor Tony Knowles and his administration, but they succeeded in changing attitudes toward education and children's health and safety.

A New Governor Faces the Fiscal Gap

Tony Knowles was sworn in as Alaska's ninth governor on December 5, 1994. The new governor, born Anthony Carroll "Tony" Knowles in Tulsa, Oklahoma, served in Vietnam and earned a degree in economics from Yale University, where he was a Delta Kappa Epsilon fraternity brother of George W. Bush. After graduation he moved to Alaska and worked on oil drilling rigs on the North Slope and in Cook Inlet. In 1969, he started the first of his four restaurants, including the Anchorage Downtown Deli & Café. Knowles served three terms on the Anchorage Assembly and served two terms as mayor of Anchorage, from 1981 to 1987.[1]

The new governor appealed for harmony and reiterated his campaign themes of job creation, support of schools and families, and the need to be aware of the needs of Alaska's citizens. Knowles completed his cabinet appointments in March 1995

and continued the appointment of Bruce Botello, Hickel's attorney general. Within six weeks of his inauguration, however, Knowles suspended Alaska's controversial wolf control program and blamed the Department of Fish and Game for poor management. The governor also directed the Department of Law to drop the suit against the federal government over Native subsistence issues. That displeased Republican legislators who had relished confrontations with the federal government over land and resources issues. They first tried to reinstitute the suit, and failing in that, they criticized the attorney general, who had defended the suit in the Hickel administration. Observers criticized the governor for not having been actively involved in the legislative process, but blamed his inexperience. Knowles, however, used his veto power and showed the Republican legislature that it would have to acknowledge his priorities and agenda in the future. An opinion poll taken at the end of June 1995 found that Knowles was more popular than any of his predecessors except Alaska's first chief executive, Bill Egan.[2]

The Prudhoe Bay oilfield continued its decline. Fewer barrels pumped and lower oil prices translated into lower state revenues. The legislature for years had refused to tax Alaska's citizens for the many state services they enjoyed, instead relying on oil revenues to fund approximately 80 percent of the general fund. In March 1995, Governor Knowles gained support from the legislature's Republican leadership to form a joint executive-legislative fiscal planning commission to make recommendations to close the growing fiscal gap.

The Fiscal Planning Commission

The Fiscal Planning Commission consisted of fifteen members, including two Democratic and two Republican legislators, the director of the Office of Management and Budget, two former Democratic legislators, a former commissioner of revenue, the chancellor of the University of Alaska Anchorage, and several local business leaders.[3]

The commission issued its report in October 1995. Its preface stated that Alaska was spending $524 million more than it would take in during fiscal year 1996 (by June 30 of that year that amount had dropped to $330 million). The report estimated that the gap would grow to $1.3 billion annually by the year 2005. To balance the budget in three years, the commission recommended a combination of spending cuts, revenue increases, and changes in the Permanent Fund. The report recommended spending cuts of $40, $30, and $30 million in 1996, 1997, and 1998, respectively. With compounding, that would total $300 million in 1996 dollars. It also proposed reducing state general fund spending, including federal contributions, from $4.020 to $3.692 billion, or $3.255 billion in 1996 dollars by 2000.[4]

The commission also proposed revenue increases, including taxes of one dollar per pack of cigarettes, producing an estimated $43 million, and ten cents per alcoholic drink, producing $20 million. Gas taxes were to be raised from their 1961 level of eight cents to twenty-two cents per gallon, producing $44 million. An increase in user fees would bring in $3 million per year. Doubling motor vehicle license fees and eliminating license fee exemptions would produce $32 million. A new tourist tax would raise $20 million. Increased taxes on fisheries and other resources would raise another $30 million.[5]

The most unpopular recommendations involved the state's Permanent Fund and dividend program. The commission proposed to establish the Permanent Fund as an endowment to partially replace declining oil revenues. The endowment would pay up to 4 percent of the Permanent Fund's five-year average market value to the general fund for dividends and state services dedicated to K–12 education. The principal would be constitutionally protected by including long-term inflation proofing into the endowment plan. To increase the fund's earning power, the commission recommended five changes: building the fund's principal, which contained $18.5 billion in June 1996, through additional special deposits, including increasing minimum annual deposits and retaining additional earnings; depositing $600 million from the Constitutional Budget Reserve (CBR) into the Permanent Fund in 1996; ending the Permanent Fund earnings reserve once the endowment was established by depositing its 1.2 billion into the fund; increasing to 50 percent the maximum contribution to the fund from oil, gas, and mineral lease revenues; and retaining earnings in excess of 4 percent annual payout in the fund.

The commission's most controversial recommendation was to cap the Permanent Fund dividend pool. It would reduce the total amount spent for the dividend program from $565 million in 1996 by $50 million per year for three years. This would decrease individual dividends from about $970 in 1995 to $900 in 1996, $800 in 1997, and $700 in 1998. The commission recommended the maintenance of the CBR at $1.5 billion as a cushion against oil revenue volatility. The commission did not recommend an immediate reinstitution of the state income tax, which the legislature had abolished in 1980. It suggested, however, that the issue be revisited in late 1998 or early 1999 to adjust the overall plan as needed for the succeeding five to ten years. By that time the budget would be balanced and state leaders would know more about ANWR, the gasline, and federal budget changes, and then additional spending cuts, tax increases, and/or further dividend reductions might be considered.[6]

Alaskans had already discussed many of these ideas to fix the fiscal gap in the preceding years, so there were few new ideas. The commission's plan would reduce the size of government only minimally. It would increase taxes where opposition would be the least. But commission members did not achieve unanimity among themselves. Some members objected to making the Permanent Fund an endowment for future government spending, fearing that it would increase future budget deficits. One member called for the immediate reimposition of the income tax, which would force nonresidents, as much as 25 percent of the workforce, to contribute to the general fund.[7]

The responses to the commission's recommendations were less than enthusiastic. Republicans thought that there had been too few budgets cuts. Jay Hammond, one of the originators of the fund and perhaps the strongest defender of the dividend program, opposed the proposal to cap dividends and instead urged the reimposition of the income tax. Governor Knowles also disagreed with the proposal to cap dividends. He preferred an income tax or other tax increases to any change in the dividend program.[8]

Fairbanks columnist Fred Pratt, a frequent critic of state government, stated that "capping dividends diverts money to the operating budget and takes away the public's direct interest in guarding the Permanent Fund."[9] Legislators continued to discuss the commission report for the first part of the session, but their discussion did not help in the development of a consensus about how to close the fiscal gap.[10]

A Republican Majority in the State Legislature

1996 was an election year, with all forty state House seats and half (ten) of the Senate seats up for election. Republicans enlarged their majorities in both houses of the legislature, gaining two seats in the House for a total of twenty-four, and one in the Senate for a total of thirteen. After the election, two Democrats changed parties in the Senate, giving Republicans control over three-fourths of the seats. Together with those who changed parties in the House and rural, conservative, or perhaps opportunistic Democrats who voted with Republicans, the Republicans had a majority of twenty-eight out of forty seats in the House for the biggest Republican majority in state history, with forty-three out of sixty seats in both houses. Now the leadership could overturn gubernatorial vetoes on most bills and came close to the three-fourths majority needed to tap the CBR.[11]

The state and federal government had frequently butted heads over numerous issues. By mid-March 1997, legislators had passed five resolutions against the federal government. Senate Joint Resolution 16 urged Congress to amend the Endangered Species Act so that it would not hinder resource development. Senate Joint Resolution 20 encouraged similar amendments to federal wetlands preservation law in the Clean Water Act of 1972. Senate Joint Resolution 13 questioned the Clinton administration's "illegal and arbitrary re-interpretation" of RS 2477, right-of-way legislation, which prevented the state from claiming myriad trails across the public domain. House Joint Resolution 24, which was highly critical of President Clinton's timber "preservation" policies, opposed the use of an Alaskan tree from the Tongass National Forest in the capital for Christmas festivities: "The Alaska State Legislature recognizes harvesting Alaska's trees to provide pleasure for those far removed is symbolic of a failed national policy which has cost Southeast Alaska communities thousand of year-round, family-supporting jobs and caused untold personal suffering." House Joint Resolution 14 supported Congressman Don Young's attempts to bar agreements with the United Nations for "biosphere reserves" and "world heritage sites," which Young had called a method of creating new parks by bypassing Congress.[12]

A federal court decision in late 1996 brought up the issue of Native rights to self-government. Arctic Village and Venetie, two small Athapaskan villages in the interior, petitioned the federal courts for powers of "Indian Country," which would allow them to tax village residents, regulate land use, establish tribal courts, and otherwise exercise power equivalent to those of the state government. The U.S. Court of Appeals for the Ninth Circuit supported this claim. The governor and the legislature objected strenuously, fearing that it would create sovereign Native jurisdictions in more than 225 Native villages. It would decrease the state's ability to generate revenue without necessarily reducing its expenditures in rural areas. By general consensus, early in the 1997 legislative session there was agreement to spend $1 million to support the state's position before the U.S. Supreme Court.[13] The Supreme Court rendered its decision on February 25, 1998; a unanimous court reversed the lower court's decision and held that with the exception of Metlakatla,

"Indian Country" did not exist in Alaska.[14] Private attorney John Roberts argued on behalf of the state before the U.S. Supreme Court. In 2005 he was nominated and confirmed to be chief justice of the nation's highest court.

Subsistence is another issue that has not lent itself to any easy solution. In 1978 the state legislature had passed a subsistence measure to reduce conflicts between Native and non-Native Alaskans in their use of fish and game resources. This measure had gone around the state's constitutional prohibition of discrimination in the allocation of fish and game by establishing zones distant from urban areas for the preferential allocation of fish and game. Provisions of the Alaska National Interest Lands Conservation Act (ANILCA) in 1980 granted preferential use of fish and game to rural users (both Native and non-Native) in times of insufficient resources. In 1989, the Alaska Supreme Court overturned the state's subsistence law in the McDowell decision because it conflicted with the state constitution. Thereupon, state fish and game authorities allocated these resources on a nondiscriminatory basis, which violated the ANILCA provisions. Negotiations with federal authorities did not settle the issue. In the early 1990s the Department of the Interior took over the subsistence management of game species on federal lands. The state's influential congressional delegation was unable to persuade Congress to amend ANILCA to bring it into conformance with the state constitution. ANILCA delayed assumption of federal management control over fisheries until December 1, 1998.[15] On October 1, 1999, the federal government took over subsistence management of fisheries in federal public waters as well.

Governor Knowles attempted to solve the subsistence issue. Late in 1997, the governor persuaded the Republican legislative leadership to join him in endorsing a constitutional amendment authorizing the rural subsistence preference. The majority caucus buried the proposal in committee, but eventually lengthy debates resulted in the passage of a new state subsistence law. Advised that the measure still violated the terms of ANILCA, Knowles vetoed it. The governor called a special session to consider a proposal that dealt with most of the governor's and the Native leaders' concerns. It fell short by two votes of the two-thirds majority necessary to put a constitutional amendment on the general election ballot in November.[16] The issue has not been settled to this day.

Alaska's Republicans and Democrats saw pretty much eye to eye on access to land and the sanctity of the Permanent Fund. Social and economic conservatives, however, had controlled Alaska's Republican Party since 1990. Few of the forty-three-member Republican majority supported abortion rights, for example. Republicans' control of the legislature enabled them in 1997 to implement part of their agenda, and the legislature enacted two restrictive abortion bills. One banned partial-birth abortions, which had never been performed in Alaska. The other required underage women to gain parental consent or the authorization of a district court judge before undergoing an abortion. Governor Knowles vetoed both bills, but lawmakers overrode his vetoes. The Republican majority also passed legislation that would publicly name juveniles arrested for serious offenses. "No frills" legislation for Alaska's correctional system made it austere, and an automated telephone system was to notify crime victims whenever the individual who assaulted them was released from custody. Another law also expanded rights for individuals holding concealed weapons permits.[17]

The Republican majority, over the governor's veto, limited his budgetary powers by requiring chief executives to release their entire spending package by December 15 and preventing any changes before its introduction to the legislature in January. Another measure allowed political parties to gain a spot on the ballot only if their membership totaled at least 3 percent of the vote in the previous gubernatorial race. The Republicans reasoned that since small parties would no longer be able to run candidates for governor, it would be more likely that the two major party nominees would no longer face spoilers. In the last four gubernatorial contests, the Alaska Libertarian or Independence Parties had figured prominently, playing spoiler roles in 1982 and in 1994, the latter election resulting in the victory of Democrat Tony Knowles. The Republican majority also weakened Alaska's environmental laws, over the governor's veto. In short, the 1997 legislative session was the most partisan and conservative in state history.[18]

The 1998 Elections

In 1998, Alaskans again elected a governor and lieutenant governor, forty out of sixty state legislators, and two of the state's three-member congressional delegation. U.S. Congressman Don Young (R) retained his seat, for a fourteenth term, and the state's junior U.S. senator, Frank Murkowski (R), had only token opposition and retained his seat with two-thirds of the vote.[19]

The August 1998 primary involved a three-way race for the Republican gubernatorial nomination: state senator Robin Taylor from Wrangell; Wayne Ross, an Anchorage attorney; and John Lindauer, briefly chancellor of the University of Alaska Anchorage and economics professor, one-term legislator, and the owner of several rural newspapers and radio stations. Neither Taylor nor Ross was able to raise sufficient funds to conduct a viable statewide campaign. At the start of the primary, Lindauer had $880,000 in the bank, and he spent it lavishly on TV spots and full-page newspaper ads in which he accused the Knowles administration of planning to end the Permanent Fund Dividend (PFD) program, selling out state's rights on subsistence, failing to develop Alaska's economy, defending a choice in abortion, and favoring privacy rights. Lindauer claimed that the governor's stands were out of touch with the views of conservative Alaskans. He received 23 percent of the gubernatorial vote, and Taylor and Ross took 17 percent each in the primary, which saw voter turnout of only 31 percent.[20]

Lindauer created much drama in the general election. The media noticed that his proposals changed with each city and region he visited. Lindauer also claimed that Bill Allen, the CEO of Veco Corporation, Alaska's largest oil field services company, and also the publisher of the conservative newspaper *Voice of the Times*, had sold out to Governor Knowles. Allen thereupon sued Lindauer for slander.[21]

A short time after the primary, questions about Lindauer's finances arose and quickly destroyed what remained of his credibility. Initially, Lindauer had asserted that his campaign funds came from a family trust established before his first wife died. When pushed by Republican leaders, he claimed he had earned six hundred thousand dollars in

consulting and other fees.[22] A couple of weeks later, Lindauer's campaign manager resigned, complaining that he could not believe his candidate any longer. In early October the Republican steering committee proposed to withdraw Lindauer from the ticket. He appeared before the full forty-eight-member Republican Central Committee, where his explanations apparently kept him on the ticket. Yet within a week of his meeting with the committee, news reports about Lindauer's finances revealed a web of lies. His trust account had little income, as his newspaper and radio station assets had no value. On top of that, the IRS had put liens on his property for failure to pay back taxes. His money actually came from Dorothy Doremus, his second wife, who was a wealthy Chicago attorney and cement business heiress. The money had been a gift and a loan guarantee. Two weeks before the November election, the Republican leadership abandoned Lindauer and endorsed a Robin Taylor write-in campaign. The courts turned down the Republican Party's attempt to postpone the general election. Knowles received 51.2 percent of the votes; and Taylor, 21 percent, all write-in votes. Lindauer received 17 percent. He had spent $1.7 million of his wife's money and the Alaska Public Offices Commission had fined him.[23]

1998 Ballot Measures

Several measures on the 1998 ballot evoked considerable controversy. Ballot measure no. 2 proposed amending the constitution to define marriage as "between one man and one woman." Republican legislators had placed it on the ballot because an Anchorage superior court judge had ruled that Alaska's marriage law, which two gay men had contested when denied a marriage license, might be unconstitutional because of an apparent violation of the constitutional right to privacy in Alaska. The ballot measure passed overwhelmingly with a $500,000 contribution from the Church of Jesus Christ of Latter-day Saints.[24]

Ballot measure no. 6, part of the national English-only movement, sought to require the state to use English in all government functions and actions. The Native community opposed it but was unable to defeat it. It passed handily. Ballot measure no. 9 would have prohibited the use of snares for trapping wolves and would also prohibit possession, purchase, or sale of wolf hides known to have been obtained with snares. It arrayed animal rights activists nationally against Alaska trappers and hunting groups. The measure failed to pass by a large margin.[25]

Republicans won twenty-six of the state House seats and fifteen of the Senate seats, for an overall majority of forty-one out of sixty legislative seats, greater than the two-thirds majority required to override gubernatorial vetoes. The addition of rural Democrats to the House and Senate majorities gave the Republicans large majorities in each House, but they fell short of the forty-five Republican votes, the three-fourths majority, required to withdraw money from the state's CBR or to deny the governor's requested amount.[26]

More Economic Woes

It was Governor Knowles's misfortune to be chief executive at a time when oil prices hit bottom, as well as having to work with a legislature with a large Republican majority. By the late 1990s, however, the state's economy had attained some stability. Unemployment had dropped to below 6 percent, and the population increased at a steady rate of 1.5 percent. In fact, in 1999 Alaska had 675,000 residents. That ranked it forty-eighth among the fifty states, slightly ahead of Wyoming and Vermont.[27]

In 1998–99, the oil industry was in a recession. At the beginning of 1998, oil sold for $15 per barrel. By June, the price had dropped to $9.56 per barrel, bottoming out at $8.63 per barrel of North Slope crude on December 21. If adjusted for inflation, this would have been equivalent to $3.26 per barrel in 1977, a figure 75 percent lower than the actual oil price that year. Adjusted for inflation, oil was cheaper in December 1998 than it had been any time since the systematic tracking of oil prices began in 1949.[28]

In December 1998, the Department of Revenue predicted a $3 billion revenue shortfall for the next three years. The fiscal year 2000 deficit was estimated at $1.1 billion. ARCO and BP, Alaska's primary oil producers, announced layoffs of 10 and 30 percent of their employees, respectively, at an estimated loss of three thousand jobs. But the oil companies had no intention of leaving Alaska. In fact, they planned to continue exploration activities, and BP and ARCO applied for eighteen new drilling permits in 1998, hoping to find replacements for the declining Prudhoe Bay and Kuparuk reservoirs. The companies also bid for leases in the National Petroleum Reserve-Alaska, which the Department of the Interior had opened for exploration early in the year.[29]

In late March 1999, OPEC ministers voted to cut production by 2.1 million barrels daily. That decreased global supply by 2.6 percent. By early May, North Slope crude sold for over $17 per barrel for the first time in sixteen months. The Department of Revenue forecast that oil prices would average $13.57 per barrel through fiscal year 2000, higher by $1.32 than the fiscal year 1999 average, but experts predicted oil prices would not top $20 per barrel in the foreseeable future.[30]

Additionally, the salmon industry suffered from reduced runs, a lower demand from the traditional Japanese market, and stiff competition from lower-cost farm-raised salmon. In fact, the dire situation in western Alaskan villages dependent on the fishery led Governor Knowles to urge legislators to provide timely financial relief.[31]

Finally, the markets for food exports declined sharply, and the Japanese-owned Alaska Lumber and Pulp Company, Inc. shut down its Sitka pulp mill in 1993 and closed its Wrangell sawmill in 1994. At full capacity, the Sitka mill had employed 450, producing wood fiber used in the production of rayon fabrics and paper. The Ketchikan Pulp Company shut its doors in March 1997. The region's pulp mills represented a foundation for industrial infrastructure as well as a substantial source of revenue for their host communities. Pulp manufacturers utilized by-product chips from independent sawmills, laid the foundation for small operators to acquire timber supplies, provided an outlet for wood that could not be processed by others, and cushioned the cyclical trends in the wood products markets. The pulp and sawmill closures hit southeastern Alaska hard.[32]

There were some economic bright spots, such as tourism, which brought almost $1.5 million visitors to Alaska in 1998. It was the state's second largest industry, after oil, and the largest private employer in Alaska. Mining expanded in the late 1990s, with the development of two new gold mines in the Fairbanks area and the development of Green's Creek Mine near Juneau. Low gold prices discouraged exploration plans but did not lead the mining multinationals to abandon Alaska.[33]

Federal, state, and local government employment was the foundation of Alaska's economy in the late 1990s. Alaska's military bases, federal land and resource management offices, and Native affairs and social welfare program administration accounted for thousands of jobs. Senator Stevens, in his position as chair of the Senate Appropriations Committee, used earmarks to funnel many millions of dollars into the Alaska economy. Also, the state did not lose a major military installation during the first and second rounds of base closings, in large part due to Senator Stevens's clout.[34]

In short, although the state lost high-paying jobs in the oil industry, fisheries, timber, and state and local governments in the late 1990s, it also added jobs. But most of those occurred in the low-paying sectors of tourism, retail sales, and other service areas. This lowered Alaska's per capita income, which in 1998 grew only 2.8 percent, the fifth lowest rate in the nation. Average earnings were $25,675, below the national average by $750, putting Alaska in twentieth place nationally in per capita personal income.[35]

Status of the Permanent Fund

Economist Scott Goldsmith, who for years has written extensively about Alaska's looming fiscal gap, reported in 1998 that a couple of recent changes made Alaska's fiscal condition better than many thought. One was that the Permanent Fund had grown faster than expected, having nearly doubled since 1991 and reached more than $23 billion. Fund earnings constituted the largest source of state revenues. General fund spending had dropped to $2.3 billion, $1 billion less than it would have been if it had grown with population and inflation since 1991. This meant that the state could indefinitely sustain the current spending level. In 1998, state spending totaled $2.3 billion from the General Fund and $850 million for Permanent Fund dividends. Even with a general fund deficit of $420 million in 1998, Goldsmith based his estimate of sustainable spending on the revenue-generating capacity of Alaska's oil reserves, the Permanent Fund, and the CBR—all three available for broad government purposes. Goldsmith estimated that prudent management of those assets, together with non-oil general fund revenues, could yield about $3.2 billion in annual revenues.[36]

The managers of the Alaska Permanent Fund announced that a stock market correction in late August 1998 had cost the fund $1.7 billion in unrealized profits. By year's end, most of that had been regained. In September, the Permanent Fund Corporation revealed that each eligible Alaskan would receive a dividend check of $1,540.88. The October distribution of the checks boosted the state's economy by a multiplier of 1.6 as check recipients purchased snowmobiles, airline packages, or other large-ticket items, paid off debts, or saved.[37]

In January 1999 the Permanent Fund's market value had climbed to $25.1 billion—including $18.6 billion in the fund principal, which could only be used for income-producing investments. Some $3.9 billion were unrealized gains representing appreciation (paper profits) in the value of stocks and other equities in the Permanent Fund. Another $2.5 billion was in the Permanent Fund earnings reserve, used to "inflation proof" the fund. These monies were re-deposited into the fund's principal, were used to pay dividends, or were made available for other legislative action.[38]

Attempts at Long-Range Planning

In mid-December 1998 Governor Knowles proposed a flat general fund budget of $2.2 billion. Including federal and other funds, it would reach $4.2 billion. He also proposed an expansion of his Smart Start program for early childhood education, child protection, and health care. The $32 million this program needed was to come partly from federal funds and partly from settlement money paid by the tobacco industry to the states to resolve Medicaid-related lawsuits. In January 1999, in his State of the State address, Knowles proposed an increase in the gasoline tax to generate matching dollars to make Alaska elegible for the plentiful federal transportation grants to states. To balance Alaska's budget deficit, he suggested that the state cash in the $4 billion in Permanent Fund earnings and deposit them in the CBR, and also that the state income tax, which the legislature had abolished in 1980, be reimposed. Knowles argued that the income tax was necessary to capture some of the earnings of nonresidents. About 20 percent of Alaska's workforce consisted of nonresidents, who earned about $1 billion tax-free dollars annually. The governor suggested that the tax apply only to families, both residents and nonresidents, with two full-time incomes totaling over sixty thousand dollars. Knowles estimated this would yield about $350 million annually for the general fund. He said that both the income tax and Permanent Fund diversion should be voted on by the electorate in a special election.[39]

The 1999 legislature did not seriously consider raising taxes and instead focused on spending cuts. The final fiscal year 2000 total operating budget came to about 4.8 billion. The legislative session ended on May 19, 1999. The governor then called the legislature into special session with only one agenda item, namely a long-range fiscal plan. The compromise plan they came up with, in which Knowles played an important role, would consolidate the CBR and the Permanent Fund's earning reserve account into the new "Alaska Income Account," which would be housed within the corpus of the Permanent Fund. Some 5.88 percent of the market value of both the Income Account and the Permanent Fund would be deposited into the Alaska Income Account. Half of the deposit would be used to stabilize the general fund, and the other half, averaged over five years, would be paid out in dividends. The PFD would be guaranteed at $1,700 for two years, declining to $1,340 by 2001. Any remaining earnings would be used to inflation proof the Permanent Fund.[40]

The resulting ballot proposition asked voters if "after paying annual dividends to residents and inflation-proofing the permanent fund, should a portion of the permanent fund investment earnings be used to help balance the state budget?" Most Chambers of Commerce, development interests, and leaders in the public sector and the oil industry supported the proposition. Former governors Hickel, Cowper, and Sheffield endorsed the plan, as did Governor Knowles and most elected officials, including the Republican legislative leadership.[41]

Opposed were former Governor Hammond, who believed a state income tax should be reimposed before funds earnings were used to help close the fiscal gap; the *Anchorage Daily News,* which argued that the proposal was regressive; and environmental groups and taxpayer associations, who all objected to the proposed "theft" of individual dividends, which most Alaskans had come to regard as a God-given right. Eighty-four percent voted against the proposition. It failed in every precinct of the state. Only 30 percent of Alaska's residents turned out to vote and the vote was not binding on the legislature, yet it nevertheless killed the plan, demonstrating a lack of political leadership and courage.[42]

The 2000 state elections and subsequent legislative organization did not materially alter the relationship between the executive and legislature. In the previous six years, the legislature had refused to fund most of the governor's initiatives and vetoed several of his board and commission appointments. It had reduced the number of state departments through combination and reorganization. It had filed suit against executive actions on subsistence, fish and game management, and state lands issues. This all happened because Governor Knowles had the weakest partisan support in the legislature of any of his predecessors.[43]

A Natural Gas Pipeline?

In September 2000 Alaska's major oil producers announced plans for a 17 percent production increase in the next five years. Part of that was to come from the new wells to be drilled at Prudhoe Bay or in satellite localities. Throughout 2000 and into 2001 oil prices fluctuated, but to the state's advantage they were on the high side. A number of factors were responsible for these price movements. Strong economic growth in 1999 and early 2000 had increased demand, which pushed North Slope crude prices to $35.62 in September 2000, its highest level since the early 1980s. Then the U.S. economic slowdown pushed North Slope crude prices down to $21 per barrel by late December 2000. A recurrence of violence in the Middle East in late 2000 scared oil markets and held prices high. And finally, Saudi Arabia, which led the eleven-member OPEC cartel, increased production limits three times in early and mid-2000 in order to lower prices. Then, in order to reverse falling oil prices, the cartel cut production by 5 percent in January 2001, and another 4 percent in mid-March. This put crude prices at $26.70 per barrel in May. The state's department of revenue projected an average crude price of $27.92 for the 2001 fiscal year.[44]

The Alaska Permanent Fund produces more revenue than do oil and gas. The principal cannot be touched, and the earnings are dedicated to issuing PFD checks to Alaskans and to inflation-proof the fund. In 2000 each eligible Alaskan received $1,964, the largest amount in the program's history. In early October 2000, the state distributed $1.2 billion to 585,000 eligible recipients. Alaskans enrolled in the program since its inception in 1982 had received a total of $18,511. But future distributions of dividends, the department of revenue warned, would probably not match the increase in recent years because of the stock market's vagaries.[45]

Diversification of Alaska's economy was an ongoing concern. In 2001 there was much talk about bringing to market the 35 trillion cubic feet of proven natural gas reserves, about 20 percent of known U.S. reserves. Natural gas prices had doubled in the domestic American market in previous years, and BP, Phillips, and Exxon, the owners of Alaska's gas reserves, were eager to get it to markets. But natural gas production would not solve the state's fiscal problems since royalties, taxes, and other charges would probably produce only between $200 million and $400 million in annual revenues and gas line construction was estimated to cost between $6 and $10 billion. It would, however, generate employment. In late August 2000, Governor Knowles stated that his administration was committed to the construction of a gas line within two years.[46]

Several questions remained about how to transport the gas. Should it be liquefied and shipped, or transported solely in pipelines to markets in the contiguous states? Yukon Pacific Corporation advocated shipping Alaska liquified natural gas to Asian markets. These countries, however, had closer gas resources, within their region. Alaskans were keenly interested in pipeline routing. Three alternatives were proposed: (1) a North Slope to Valdez route, paralleling the Trans-Alaska Pipeline System; in Valdez it would be liquified and shipped in tankers, (2) a line from the North Slope to Canada, crossing the Alaska Highway and connecting to existing pipelines near Calgary, and finally, (3) an offshore route from Prudhoe Bay to Canada along the Beaufort Sea, the shortest but environmentally most challenging route.[47] However, since then there has been much talk but little movement on the proposed gasoline or other schemes to bring the gas to market.

Drilling in ANWR and Other Issues

In 2000 and 2001 many Alaskan citizens debated a couple of issues that concentrated their attention on the federal government. The first of these involved the possible opening of the Arctic National Wildlife Refuge (ANWR) to oil exploration and production. The refuge encloses the eastern end of the five-hundred-mile-long North Slope between the Brooks Range and the Beaufort Sea. The election of George W. Bush to the presidency in 2000 had given developers and many Alaskans hope because the new president supported the opening of ANWR. The National Research Council, at the request of Congress, had conducted an eighteen-month study of the cumulative effects that oil development has had on the environment, landscape, and residents of Prudhoe Bay. It concluded that oil development had materially and negatively altered the ecology and environment of the North Slope. For their part, industry experts argued that new technologies had radically reduced pollution and other environmental problems, while scientists from conservation groups held that oilfield expansion would irrevocably ruin the country's wildest and most fragile landscape. Native leaders decried the negative impact on their culture from oil development despite the jobs and other benefits it had brought.[48]

The first few months of the Bush administration seemed auspicious for opening ANWR, which required congressional authorization. Representative Young and Senator Murkowski introduced legislation in early 2001 to open ANWR. Arctic Power, a prodevelopment consortium that received almost $2 million from the Alaska legislature to lobby Congress on ANWR and was not required to account for how it spent the money, aided the effort. President Bush made drilling ANWR the focus of his campaign to boost domestic energy production. Federal geologists estimated that ANWR could produce 1 million barrels of crude a day.[49]

Most of the Democratic members of Congress opposed opening ANWR, and so did many Republicans. In early 2001, the House Budget Committee refused to include ANWR lease income in its budget resolution because it was too large a fight to handle in the budget process. The Senate Budget Committee chair also said that no ANWR language would be in his measure either, because at least one Republican would not support it.[50]

In March and April, environmental groups opposed to drilling, including the Natural Resources Council, the Sierra Club, the Alaska Wilderness League, and the National Audubon Society, waged a media blitz, costing nearly $1 million, which focused national attention on the issue. The president's support wavered in the face of concerted opposition, although his energy plan included opening a portion of ANWR to drilling. In any event, the Bush effort to open ANWR failed.[51]

Another issue of concern to Native Alaskans was debated throughout the year. Delegates from about one-quarter of Alaska's 229 federally recognized tribes signed an agreement in April 2001 formalizing relations between state government and tribal leaders. The agreement established a temporary committee of four state officials and four tribal leaders to develop recommendations on tribal-state relations that were expected to lead to improved delivery of services such as health care and education and more control over subsistence hunting and fishing. Governor Knowles applauded the agreement, while some tribal leaders criticized it because it recognized state sovereignty.

Subsistence fishing was another issue; it presented a conflict between federal laws, granting rural residents priority for hunting and fishing on federal lands and waters, and the Alaska State Con-stitution, which states that all Alaskans have equal access to the state's fish and game. In 1990 the state denied Native requests to put up subsistence fish camps. In 1991, Katie John, an Athapaskan elder, sued the Department of the Interior, asking it to force the state to let her place subsistence salmon nets at her Copper River fish camp. U.S. District Court Judge H. Russell Holland agreed with John. In 1995, on appeal, the Ninth U.S. Circuit Court of Appeals ruled that the federal government possessed jurisdiction in Alaska's navigable waters and in "federal reserve waters." This led to the 1999 federal takeover of Alaska's fisheries in federal waters. In early May 2001, the Ninth U.S. Circuit Court of Appeals upheld Judge Holland's ruling in an 8–3 decision. Quickly, sport hunters' groups, whom Republican legislators supported, demanded that the state pursue the issue in the U.S. Supreme Court. One Republican legislator went so far to demand that Governor Knowles should be impeached if he did not appeal the circuit court's decision.[52] The Knowles administration chose not to appeal the decision.

In the meantime, the executive and the legislature sparred over the size of the 2002 fiscal year operating and capital budgets. The legislature had allocated $112 million from the general fund for the $1.4 billion capital budget, the difference coming from federal funds. The operating budget drew $2.290 billion from the general fund, an increase of $120 million from the previous year. The total, including federal funds, came to $4.668 billion, excluding the $1.4 billion capital budget monies, as well as $693 million Permanent Fund inflation proofing and $1.136 billion in fund dividends. The total authorization, including all funds, came to $7.32 billion, the highest spending of any American state on a per capita basis. Knowles was satisfied that the legislature had increased spending on his priorities, namely, public safety, health, education, and providing services business needed for economic development.[53]

The 2002 Election

In the 2002 election, voters returned Senator Stevens and Congressman Young to Washington, each gaining about three-quarters of the vote. The gubernatorial contest pitted Republican Frank Murkowski against Democrat Fran Ulmer. Murkowski, a twenty-two-year veteran of the U.S. Senate, had attended public schools in Ketchikan and studied at the University of Santa Clara and Seattle University. After serving in the U.S. Coast Guard, he had become a banker and served as Alaska's commissioner of economic development from 1966 to 1970. In 1970 he ran unsuccessfully for Alaska's lone seat in the U.S. House. In 1980 he ran again and won the U.S. Senate seat with 53.7 percent of the vote.[54] Alaskans reelected him in 1980 and 1992, and in 1998 for the term ending January 3, 2005. Murkowski was the favorite to win the governorship, and at the start of his campaign in early 2002 polls showed him leading Ulmer by a fifteen-point margin. By the end of the campaign, that margin had practically closed.

Born in Madison, Wisconsin, Ulmer had earned a degree in political science and economics and a law degree from the University of Wisconsin. She clerked for a federal judge and worked as a legal counsel to the Alaska Legislature. She was a legislative assistant to Governor Hammond and then headed his Division of Policy Development and Planning. At the end of Hammond's second term, Ulmer launched her own political career. She ran for mayor of Juneau in a five-way race and won in a landslide, outpolling all four opponents and taking 56 percent of the vote. Three years later she ran for the State House in Juneau's District 4, defeated two fellow Democrats in the primary, and then swamped her Republican opponent by a two-to-one margin in the general election. Three elections later, in 1994, Ulmer ran for lieutenant governor, securing the nomination as Tony Knowles's running mate and joining him, after a recount, in a more traditional Alaska landslide; that is, they edged out Republicans Jim Campbell and Mike Miller by fewer than six hundred votes. After eight years as lieutenant governor, Ulmer was now the Democratic Party's candidate for governor. She had been deeply involved in all the major Alaska issues of the late twentieth century, from the Alaska Native Claims Settlement Act to the Alaska National Interests Lands Conservation Act. Associates admired

her skill in summarizing and clarifying positions and presenting rational reasons for the positions she advocated.[55]

Both candidates ran vigorous campaigns. Murkowski wanted to get Alaska "moving" again and to end what he claimed were the economic stagnation and gridlock of the past eight years. He opposed the reimposition of the income tax and promised to fight any efforts to spend Alaskans' PFD. He promised to control state spending and submit responsible budgets to the legislature, as well as use his line item veto authority. He planned to conduct a top-down audit of every state agency to review the effectiveness of state services. He claimed that he could create "good paying jobs for Alaskans" by revitalizing the resource industries. Above all, he hoped to get in place the regulatory and financial incentives to have the engineering, if not actual construction, of a gas pipeline under way.

Murkowski had a long list of measures to revitalize mining and other resource-extractive industries and to improve education, both K–12 and the university. Predator control would restock Alaska's wildlife, infrastructure construction of water and sewer systems would modernize the villages, and road construction would open Alaska to resource development. In short, he was not concerned about the fiscal gap because resource development would solve it, and in fact, it would allow him to establish a special fund for education. That prompted economist David Reaume to write that either Murkowski had inside information yet to be made public, he was unaware of certain hard facts, or he knew better but was unwilling to tell the truth about the state's true fiscal position. For even if new resource development should materialize, it could not make a serious budgetary difference in less than five to ten years.[56]

For her part, Ulmer wanted to base a new prosperity for the state on creating good jobs for Alaskans, providing excellent schools, and closing the fiscal gap in a way that ensured essential services and protected the PFD program. She thought that by 2006 Alaska's economy would include more value-added jobs in the resource industries and that technology would drive the economy. The Alaska natural gas pipeline should be under construction by 2006. She hoped for a constitutional spending cap that would least harm the economy and a fiscal plan that preserved the PFD program, and she predicted that Alaskans would find a common path to bridge the gap between urban and rural Alaska.[57]

The fiscal gap was the key issue in the campaign. In nine out of the past eleven years, the legislature had allocated more money than revenues had generated. That had necessitated filling the gap with money from the CBR to the tune of $4.8 billion. Some $2.15 billion remained in the reserve. Ulmer proposed to deal with the fiscal gap with a cap on state spending, with increases only for inflation and population growth; a promise to veto any budget that spent Permanent Fund earnings; and finally, a "parachute plan" whereby tax measures, to be determined with legislators, would kick in if the CBR fell below $1 billion.[58]

When Alaskans went to the polls on November 5, 2002, they elected Frank Murkowski the state's new governor by 56.1 to 40.5 percent. Murkowski called his victory a message that voters supported his platform of controlling the budget and aggressively pushing economic development.[59]

A Republican Majority

Murkowski's victory and those of Republican legislators from across the state gave the GOP control of both the executive and legislative branches for the first time since the Hickel administration. Since statehood, Alaska's legislature had rarely been ruled by the chief executive's party. Divided government had been the rule more often than not. Most of Alaska's governors had been able to blame people in the other party for impeding their agenda. This new majority meant that neither Governor Murkowski nor the legislature could complain about all the things they could be doing if only the other party were not obstinately blocking their agenda. The governor stated that the stars were "in alignment, with unity in Juneau and Washington."[60] The next four years looked bright.

Murkowski was only the fourth U.S. senator in U.S. history to leave that office and win the governorship. Upon his inauguration, Murkowski resigned his Senate seat. The previous legislature had anticipated Murkowski's election and set back the dates for filling the Senate vacancy. For months Murkowski and his aides had released long lists of people he was said to be considering for his replacement. He staged a set of interviews with some of them, trying to make the process as interesting as possible. This show for public consumption was part of Republican Party politics; Murkowski was reaching out to conservatives and moderates and all those in between. There were seven on the list who had never held an elective office in Alaska, including a plastic surgeon, an archbishop, an active general, and a retired general. Those who closely followed Murkowski's career knew that he would not appoint any of these individuals. On December 12, 2002, he appointed his daughter, Lisa, becoming the first U.S. senator to bestow his seat upon his daughter.[61]

Tony Knowles had served eight years as Alaska's governor. He had faced a Republican legislature throughout his time in office, and the relationship between the executive and legislative branches was often hostile. Despite that, Knowles was proud of the economic opportunities and job growth that had occurred. Three-fourths of the state's jobs were in the private sector, and unemployment was low. He was disappointed that the legislature had not brought the subsistence issue to a public vote. Knowles had battled every year over the legislature's draconian budget cut proposals, which severely endangered the state's ability to manage public safety and transportation and meet the state's stewardship responsibilities for managing its fish and game resources. His administration held the line on those issues and managed to obtain increased education funding. Knowles was disappointed that despite several efforts to solve the fiscal gap, these had failed; he concluded that the citizenry was not yet ready to embrace taxes to balance the state budget. He was proud that his administration had built a new attitude and approach to child protection and children's health and had initiated programs to enable them to get a safer, healthier start in life so that they could become productive adults. In short, despite divided government, Knowles felt that during his eight years "there was growth and progress on the issues that define us as a just and civilized society."[62]

Chapter 26

Into the Twenty-first Century

As the twentieth century came to a close, Alaska's problems and opportunities carried over into the new century. Despite endless discussions, the threat of a fiscal gap continued. Alaska remained dependent on its natural resources to feed the general fund.

The Rising Price of Oil

Oil has dominated Alaska's economy since the 1968 Prudhoe Bay discovery and the subsequent construction of the Trans-Alaska Pipeline System (TAPS) in the early 1970s. At the peak of production in 1988, some 2.3 million barrels of crude oil per day moved through the pipeline from Prudhoe Bay to Valdez. Enhanced recovery methods and the discovery and development of satellite oilfields have reduced the rate of decline. As a result, in 2003 some 1 million barrels of crude oil daily were still shipped through the pipeline.[1]

The good news for Alaska and its new governor, Frank Murkowski, was that oil prices increased to their highest level ever in 2002–2003, reaching nearly thirty-eight dollars per barrel in late February 2003. Several factors accounted for this, including a modest economic recovery in the United States, which increased demand, and unusually cold spells during the winter. International events, however, had the largest impact on prices. Interruptions in global supply, such as the temporary withdrawal of Venezuela from the oil market, raised global prices, as did the instability in Nigeria in 2002 that reduced oil production. As the United States edged closer toward a military conflict with Iraq, apprehension about the situation in the Middle East increased oil prices. After the U.S. occupation of Iraq, that country, which had produced 2.1 million barrels daily under Saddam Hussein, was slow to resume production and put out only 1 million barrels daily by June 2003. OPEC did not noticeably expand or reduce production throughout the year. In any event, oil prices were around thirty-two dollars per barrel in early June 2003, while the average price during the period was about twenty-nine dollars per barrel. That was higher than the state Department of Revenue had estimated, and it reduced the annual withdrawal from the Constitutional Budget Reserve to balance the budget.

By 2005, only 916,000 barrels of crude oil passed through TAPS daily, and the estimate for 2006 was 854,000 barrels daily. Oil production from the peak in 1988 to 2004 had been declining at an average annual rate of 4.5 percent. Fortunately, oil prices in 2005 began at fifty dollars per barrel, rose to fifty-three dollars per barrel in June, up to over sixty dollars in early August, and after Hurricane Katrina struck the Gulf Coast at the end of August 2005, they rose to sixty-eight dollars per barrel. Prices continued to rise to over seventy-five dollars per barrel by late April 2006 and stayed in this range into the new fiscal year.

The U.S. Department of Energy forecast that oil prices would stay above fifty dollars per barrel for years. The state's Department of Revenue noted that oil revenues would fund some 85 percent of Alaska's general fund budget until at least 2008 and predicted that oil prices would average $57 per barrel for the next fiscal year. In March 2006 it raised its estimate to $58.72 per barrel for 2006.[2]

The Career of Ted Stevens

Another boost to the state's economy came from Alaska's Republican delegation to Congress. Foremost was the work of Ted Stevens, Alaska senior U.S. senator. Perhaps the November 2005 cover of *Alaska*, a monthly magazine, best expressed the role Stevens played in Alaska's economy, reading "Uncle Ted: Can Alaska Survive Without This One-man Economic Force?" In 2007, Stevens had represented the state for thirty-nine years, and as the magazine put it, "Alaska Has Enjoyed the Benefits of Having a Powerhouse in the U.S. Senate. Economic Juggernaut Ted Stevens Is Famous to Some—to Some Notorious—For Bringing a Lot of Federal Dollars Home to Alaska."[3]

Theodore Fulton "Ted" Stevens was born in 1923 in Indianapolis, Indiana. During World War II, he flew for the Fourteenth Army Air Corps Transport Section, which supported the Flying Tigers throughout the China theater. After leaving the Army Air Corps at the end of the war, Stevens received a degree in political science at UCLA. He then received his law degree from Harvard.[4]

Stevens was then recruited by Mike "Northcut" Ely, who headed a Washington, D.C., law firm that specialized in natural resource issues. Ely later recalled that Stevens "was a vigorous chap, highly effective. He was very personable, with a good sense of humor." Ely assigned Stevens to handle the legal affairs of Emil Usibelli, an Alaska client who was trying to sell coal to the military. Interested in natural resources law, Stevens wanted to pursue it in government and not in private practice. After volunteering for Dwight D. Eisenhower's presidential campaign, he took a job with Charles Clasby, Usibelli's lawyer in Fairbanks.[5]

Stevens and his wife, Ann, moved to Fairbanks in the winter of 1952 and quickly got acquainted with the small town's Republican establishment. Stevens became friends with C. W. Snedden, the owner of the town's newspaper, and became the paper's attorney. In 1956, after a stint as district attorney, Stevens returned to Washington to take a job as acting legislative counsel for the Department of the Interior. During the push for statehood, Snedden recommended Stevens to Secretary of the Interior Fred Seaton, who thereupon appointed Stevens as legislative counsel, and about a year later, as assistant to the secretary. On his next trip to the nation's capital, Snedden found a hand-lettered cardboard sign on Stevens's office door reading "Alaskan Headquarters." Stevens quickly became known as "Mr. Alaska" in the department.[6]

Stevens effectively organized the statehood drive from the executive branch. He later recalled, "[W]e were violating the law; . . . we were lobbying from the executive branch, and there's been a statute against that for a long time." The statehood campaign ended successfully, and Alaska became the 49th State on January 3, 1959.[7]

Stevens and his wife and five children left Washington, D.C., in 1961 and headed for Anchorage. He opened a law practice and, among other clients, represented oil companies seeking to drill on state leases. He also did legal work for the *Anchorage Daily Times* and the *Anchorage Daily News*, the state's two largest newspapers. Then, in 1962, he ran against U.S. Senator Ernest Gruening. After making personal attacks on the senator based on his age (Gruening was seventy-five years of age at that time), Stevens lost by a 3–2 margin.[8]

In 1964 Stevens ran for the state House of Representatives and won, and he won again in 1966, the same year Walter Hickel was elected to his first term as Alaska's governor. Stevens served as House majority leader in 1967 and 1968. He was not re-elected in 1968.[9] Instead, that year he ran for the Republican nomination for the U.S. Senate. He faced Elmer E. Rasmuson, the CEO of Anchorage-based National Bank of Alaska. Stevens lost against Rasmuson, whose political experience had been limited to the chairship of the University of Alaska Board of Regents and a brief term as mayor of Anchorage. Stevens's political career seemed over.[10] That same

Stevens v. Gravel

But much happened between 1968 and 2007. There was the long feud between Stevens and Senator Mike Gravel, a Democrat from Alaska elected in 1968 who served for twelve years. The two fought over just about every Alaska issue that Congress dealt with. They fought most bitterly over the Alaska National Interest Lands Conservation Act (ANILCA). In 1978, Stevens blamed Gravel for derailing a compromise measure. The latter accused Stevens of selling out Alaska's interests and contributed twenty-four thousand dollars of his own campaign money into the coffers of Stevens's Democratic challenger, Anchorage electrical contractor Don Hobbs. The money financed advertisements that told Alaskans that a vote for Stevens "was a vote for compromise," while a vote for Hobbs "was a vote to fight."

The derailment meant that Citizens for Management of Alaska's Lands, Alaska's leading organization for lobbying Congress and battling environmentalists, needed more money. The group scheduled a fund-raiser for December 4, 1978, in Anchorage. Stevens attended Governor Hammond's second inauguration in Juneau that day. To make it to the fund-raiser, Stevens, his wife Ann, and five others flew in a private Learjet to Anchorage. The plane was hit by gusty crosswinds on the approach to the Anchorage International Airport and flipped. Stevens and Tony Motley, the head of the citizen group, were the only survivors. His wife's death devastated Stevens. In House testimony in early 1979, Stevens stated that the fateful flight would not have been necessary had Gravel kept his word and supported the ANILCA compromise. The statement was widely interpreted as accusing Gravel of causing his wife's death. In any event, Congress passed the ANILCA in 1980.

Source: *Anchorage Daily News*, August 12, 1994.

---

year Alaska's senior senator, E. L. "Bob" Bartlett, died of complications following heart surgery. Governor Hickel chose Stevens to fill the vacancy. After serving out the two-year remainder of Bartlett's term, Stevens was elected in his own right in 1970 and thereafter he was reelected in 1972, 1978, 1984, 1990, 1996, and 2002. On April 13, 2007, Stevens became the longest-serving Republican in U.S. Senate history. With thirty-nine years in office, Stevens had been a Republican senator for more than a quarter of the time the party had been in existence, since its founding in 1854.[11]

Senator Stevens and Federal Appropriations

Smart and hard working, Senator Stevens became a superb politician. His seniority gained him considerable clout in the Senate, which he used to benefit his home state. In 1997, he left the chairmanship of the Senate Governmental Affairs Committee and took over the chairmanship of the Senate Appropriations Committee, replacing retiring Mark Hatfield (R-OR). His power translated into big money for Alaska over the years.

Contrary to cherished Alaskan myths, federal spending has played a major role in Alaska's economy since the United States bought it from Russia in 1867. Alaskans are not, by and large, rugged individualists who survive by their own wits. In 1999, for example, Alaska ranked second in per capita federal spending, at $7,763. Stevens provided the state with approximately $1.4 billion annually in federal funds for projects ranging from supercomputers to logging-town subsidies. Federal spending in Alaska increased 46 percent between 1990 and 1998, from over $3 billion to slightly under $5 billion in 1998.

In 1990, 18,700 nonmilitary federal workers in the state received combined salaries of slightly over $400 million. In 1998, some 17,200 nonmilitary federal workers received combined wages of about $550 million.

In the mid-1990s the Boys and Girls Clubs of Greater Anchorage opened a branch in Tyonek, a Cook Inlet village. Until then, youths in the village committed suicide at an alarming rate, but after the opening of the club there were no more suicides. Tyonek thanked Stevens, who had increased funding for community-centered social programs from $20 to $50 million between 1996 and 1999. In Alaska, the funds resulted in a 200 percent increase in the number of Boys and Girls Clubs. That has given an additional eight thousand youths a safe and enriching place to spend their spare time.

In fact, Stevens was the catalyst behind hundreds of millions of dollars of federally financed construction each year, which has built hospitals, military barracks, and airport runways. His Denali Commission funneled millions of dollars to get quick action on rural sewage and sanitation problems and leaking underground fuel tanks. The University of Alaska Fairbanks (UAF) research establishment also benefited from the support Stevens rendered. In 1998–99 the senator directed at least $50 million to the university; $10 million went to the International Arctic Research Center as the federal share, $8 million to aurora research, $5 million to the new university museum; $4 million to advanced weather forecasting software, and $18 million to supercomputer operating funds.[12]

Stevens fended off critics for two years while insisting that the Cray research supercomputer should be funded through the Department of Defense budget and placed at the UAF to study how "to harness the power of the aurora borealis." Scientists and politicians rejected the idea. Many thought the idea of gaining electricity from the northern lights was crazy. Academics in institutions in the contiguous states charged that earmarking the $25 million supercomputer for UAF violated all tenets of competitive grants and peer review.

Stevens held firm and stated in 1992 that he was ready "to take my lumps for looking over the horizon. . . . [T]his supercomputer will help cement UAF's reputation as a premier institution in arctic research." Since 1999, tapping electricity from the northern lights has remained a pipe dream, but the supercomputer has anchored UAF in arctic research. In the meantime, the original Cray has been replaced with faster, bigger, better computers, and the funding Stevens initiated has persisted. By 1999, UAF received $10 million a year through the Department of Defense as one of fourteen centers for processing military data. University President Mark Hamilton stated that "Stevens' legacy will transcend Alaska and speak to the health, economic and scientific needs of the circumpolar regions. There are few people who share this vision."[13]

Between 1990 and 1999 Congress directed approximately $1.5 billion in cost-of-living adjustments for federal workers to Alaska; another $1 billion for bypass mail, which allows bush air carriers to deliver bulk items to villages at very reasonable postal rates; more than $800 million for military construction and another $400 million for water and sewer improvements in rural Alaska; some $400 million in logging subsidies to southeastern Alaska; $265 million for Native hospital construction; $160 million for a new Elmendorf Air Force Base hospital (located near Anchorage); some $120 million for the construction of state ferries that connect communities in southeastern Alaska; and $46 million for the Denali Commission, which Stevens created in 1998 to improve rural infrastructure.[14]

There is much more. New visitor centers were built in Alaska's national parks, and the Alaska Railroad tracks have been rebuilt and reach new destinations. Some money arrived with a flourish, like $300 million a year in road money, or $38 million for the Alaska Peninsula village of King Cove for a new health clinic and airport and a road to neighboring Cold Bay. Stevens never added up the funds he funneled to Alaska, but his aides stated that he probably directed as much as $1.4 billion to Alaska annually. In any event, he was probably the second-largest engine, after oil, driving the Alaska economy. The U.S. Senate Appropriations Committee writes thirteen funding bills each year, and Alaska was prominent in most of them.[15]

But critics were unhappy with the senator's earmarking activities. In September 1999 the *Wall*

Street Journal ran a scathing editorial titled "The Spenders," illustrated with a picture of Stevens with the caption "Republicans like pork, too." Some of his colleagues, like Senator John McCain (R-AZ), characterized him as among the biggest "pork barrel" spenders. Others worried about what would happen to the Alaska economy when Stevens left office. John Katz, who was Alaska's chief lobbyist and had served seven governors by 2007, told an interviewer in 1999 that he was very conscious of what happened when Oregon's long-serving U.S. senator, Mark Hatfield, Washington's U.S. senators Warren G. Magnuson and Henry M. "Scoop" Jackson, and House Speaker Tom Foley left office: their states dropped to the bottom of the pile. Katz also remarked in the interview that "as far as Stevens not being in the Senate, that's a prospect I don't even want to contemplate." Mike Doogan, newspaper reporter, author, and legislator, wrote that Alaskans were afraid that if something happened to Stevens, "our economy will do one of its famous crash dives." How afraid were Alaskans? Doogan asked. He answered his own question: "I tell people that the day I hear Stevens has a head cold, I'm putting my house on the market. And I'm not entirely kidding."[16]

Representative Don Young and Pork Barrel Spending

Congressman Donald Edwin Young was born and raised in California, graduating with a degree in education from Chico State College in 1958. After a stint in the U.S. Army, he moved to Alaska, where he tried commercial fishing, trapped, did some gold mining, and then taught school in Fort Yukon in a Bureau of Indian Affairs Day School for ten years. He captained his own tug and barge operation and delivered supplies to villages along the river. In Fort Yukon he met and married a young bookkeeper, Lula Fredson, daughter of Athapaskan leader John Fredson. Young had two daughters with "Lu."[17]

Young started his public service career in 1964, when he was elected mayor of Fort Yukon. Two years later he won election to the statehouse, where he served until 1970. Elected to the state Senate, he served there from 1970 to 1973. Alaska's at-large congressman, Democrat Nick Begich, disappeared

in a plane crash on October 16, 1972. He was reelected to the House that November but declared dead on December 29. Young, who had been the Republican candidate against Begich in November, ran in the special election in March 1973 and won, just barely defeating Democrat Emil Notti.[18]

Congressman Young was reelected in 1974 and has won every election since then. In 2006 Alaskans reelected him to his eighteenth term, and he became the third ranking Republican member and the seventh ranking overall member of the U.S. House of Representatives. He served as chairman of the House Resources Committee from 1994 to 2000 and chairman of the House Transportation and Infrastructure Committee from 2000 to 2006. After the Democrats retook the House in the 2006 elections, Young returned to the Resources Committee as the ranking minority member. In 2008 Alaskans elected Young to his nineteenth term.[19]

Young has used his muscle as a senior member of the House and as chairman of major committees to steer money to Alaska, some of it questionable. For example, he wanted to build a bridge connecting the city of Ketchikan, population 14,500, to Gravina Island (population 50 on a good day), where the Ketchikan Airport is located. The island is twenty miles long, with two mountain ranges and a big valley of forest and muskeg. The island has no stores, restaurants, or paved roads. Its airport hosts fewer than ten commercial flights a day. The planned bridge would be nearly as long as the Golden Gate Bridge and eighty feet taller than the Brooklyn Bridge. In 2005, Young secured $941 million for Alaska and earmarked $223 million for that bridge and another $231 million for another bridge, to connect Anchorage with Point Mackenzie, north of Knik. If it were built, the bridge would be named "Don Young's Way." It would not save commuters into Anchorage any time. Walt Parker, a former commissioner of the Alaska Department of Transportation and Public Facilities, remarked that neither bridge "makes much sense, but a lot of people are going to make a lot of money building the bridge . . . and it will have to be maintained."[20]

The Gravina Island bridge was one of a record 6,371 "earmarks" in the 2007 Transportation Equity Act, a six-year, $286 billion measure that paid particular attention to the pork barrel. Alaska, the third least populated state, was the fourth-biggest recipient of transportation funds. The measure spent $86 per person on a national average, but an estimated $1,500 on every Alaskan.[21]

Erich Zimmermann, a senior policy analyst for Taxpayers for Common Sense, a Washington group opposed to corruption and government waste, wrote that Young "let his power go to his head." The two Alaskan legislators, especially Young, had been loud and proud about their ability to harness big transportation bucks. They "repeatedly bragged that new roads and bridges will spur development and industry in Alaska." While addressing a Ketchikan crowd, Young referred to Stevens's ability to round "up pork" and stated that he would like "to be a little oinker myself." Young was so proud of the House version of the transportation bill that he named it "TEA-LU, after his wife, Lu." He said that he stuffed the bill "like a turkey."[22]

But perhaps bragging about pork was not politically wise. Keith Ashdown, the spokesman and chief sloganeer for Taxpayers for Common Sense, had been stewing about how to describe Alaska's Gravina Island bridge in a news release. He wanted a catchy phrase that clearly spelled out the enormous cost and dubious need for the mile-long span. As he stood beneath a Miller Lite sign at a bar, he had a brainstorm: "Bridge to Nowhere!" Four years later the phrase did what few political slogans can do. It shaped public opinion, influenced an election, and pressured Congress to change its rules. Repeated countless times in newspapers and on radio and television, it became shorthand for political pork and a Congress that was out of touch. Language columnist William Safire called it "the phrase that launched a thousand editorials." Columnist George Will wrote after the November 2006 elections that "Republicans now know where the bridge to nowhere leads: to the political wilderness."[23]

"The Bridge to Nowhere" Haunts Alaskan Politics

On June 12, 2003, Ashdown issued a press release announcing that the Golden Fleece Award, presented annually to a public official for wasting public

money, was going to Young for his sponsorship of the Gravina Island bridge earmark. In the spring of 2004, Timothy Egan of the *New York Times* wrote a story about the Gravina and Knik Arm bridges. Titled "Built with Steel, Perhaps, but Greased with Pork," it portrayed the "gold-plated bridge to nowhere" as part of a money grab by Alaska's congressional delegation. The next day, on *Meet the Press*, when Senator John McCain was asked about boosting military spending without increasing the deficit, he complained about "bridges to nowhere in Alaska."[24]

In the summer of 2005, when Congress began considering a highway bill, journalists repeated the phrase in stories that criticized the pork-laden bill. As criticism mounted, Young told the Associated Press that "these people keep saying it's nowhere, they're just smoking pot." Congress passed Young's highway bill with the bridges tucked inside, and President Bush signed it into law on August 10, 2005.[25]

Perhaps the story might have ended there. But Rep. Duke Cunningham (R-CA) again drew attention to congressional pork because he earmarked money for a defense contractor in return for bribes. When hurricane Katrina devastated New Orleans and the coastal region, cost estimates for reconstruction soared. Members of Congress began looking for expensive federal projects that could be cut or delayed. Ashdown's phrase exploded in the media. Editorials, op-ed columns, and television news shows cited the bridges as an example of federal priorities gone awry. Rep. Young rejected the idea that the money be eliminated and sneered that the critics "can kiss my ear." Senator Tom Coburn (R-OK) proposed cutting federal money from the Gravina and Knik Arm bridges and channeling much of it to repair a span that the hurricane had damaged in Louisiana. Senator Stevens, in a fist-pounding speech, accused Coburn of attacking not the bridges but Alaska itself. He said that if the Senate discriminated against Alaska and took "money only from our state, I will resign from this body." The Coburn amendment went down to defeat 82–15.

A few weeks later *Parade* magazine, with a circulation of 34 million, ran a cover story titled "A Visit to The Bridge to Nowhere." The phrase had reached critical mass. Rep. Jeff Flake (R-AZ) wrote House Speaker Dennis Hastert warning that the phrase was damaging their party. Flake wrote that if one asked what the "bridges to nowhere" were, the answer would be that "they are a serious example of a Republican Congress bringing home some of the most expensive bacon in history on the taxpayer's dime." There were many other criticisms across the country, and congressional leaders eventually removed the earmarks for the bridges but did not cut Alaska's transportation money by the same amount. The state was still free to use federal dollars for the structures.[26]

The bridges again became an issue in the 2006 elections. Brian Riedl, an analyst with the Heritage Foundation, a conservative think tank, said that the phrase was as evocative as the four-hundred-dollar hammer that had symbolized Pentagon waste in the 1980s. Although the Iraq war and disapproval of President Bush were the major reasons that the Democrats regained the House and Senate that year, the bridges did play a role. When the Democrats took control in January 2007, they changed the House rules to require more disclosure of individual projects. Yet when the new leadership had to pass a spending bill in April 2007, it was still stuffed with pork.[27]

Alaska's congressional delegation, which had funneled $705 million in special projects to Alaska in 2005, was now faced with much less to work with under new White House targets for cutting pork barrel spending by half. The economic repercussions threatened all of Alaska, from rural villages to Anchorage. In 2005 the veteran earmarkers, Senator Stevens and Representative Young, directed as much money to Alaska as did the state's PFD checks. Like the dividend, the federal money has become part of the state's identity. Senators Stevens and Murkowski and Representative Young all warned Alaskans in April 2007 about the new Washington environment. All three lawmakers suggested that the state start using the Permanent Fund's interest to meet the state's future infrastructure and development needs that had so far been met through earmarks.[28]

University of Alaska Anchorage economist Scott Goldsmith wrote in 2007 that one in three jobs in Alaska can be traced to federal spending, either through earmarks, matching funds, or other spending. That included military spending, which at $183 million constituted the largest part of the 2005 earmarks. The Alaska congressional delegation maintained that earmarks are not pork. Many bush villages still had honey buckets and lack sanitary water supplies. Solving those problems was not pork but rather meeting basic needs. Some powerful Democrats supported Alaska's delegation. Rep. Jim Oberstar (D-MN), who then chaired the House Transportation and Infrastructure Committee, remarked that earmarking was "particularly important for small and rural communities. . . . It is irresponsible for the Bush administration to threaten these alternative funding sources." In any event, leaner times were ahead for Alaskans.[29]

Stevens's Troubles

In August 2007, Michael Carey, the former editorial page editor of the *Anchorage Daily News* and now a freelance writer, penned a piece titled "The Ways 'Stevens Money' Changed Lawmaker, Alaska." On July 3, 2007, federal agents had searched Stevens's home in Girdwood, Alaska, seeking records related to his relationship with the oil services contractor Veco, Corp. Carey wrote that he could not "believe that he [Stevens] has engaged in old-fashioned favors-for-votes bribery." But he thought it possible that Stevens "became careless or indifferent to his legislative and personal affairs. So it's not difficult to believe that after years of having his way with the federal Treasury, he eventually became the subject of a government investigation."[30]

The senator's troubles had started earlier when the *Los Angeles Times* published lengthy articles examining Stevens's record. The authors wrote that the senator wielded extraordinary power in Washington, D.C., and eventually held "sway over nearly $800 billion a year in federal spending." Outside the U.S. Senate, often called "the Millionaires' Club," Senator Stevens struggled financially. In 1997, he got serious about making money "and in almost no time, he too was a millionaire—thanks to investments with businessmen who received government contracts or other benefits with his help." Stevens's new partnerships and investments illustrated how it was possi-

The Corrupt Bastards Club

According to Lori Backes, the executive director of the Alaska Alliance, the name "The Corrupt Bastards Club" was coined in the spring of 2006 as a barroom joke among Alaska legislators linked to large campaign contributions from Veco. In a guest column for the *Anchorage Daily News,* Backes named twelve lawmakers who had received money from Veco, including Ben Stevens, the son of Senator Stevens. Those named made a joke about it and even made hats with "CBC" on them. The FBI was not laughing when agents served a warrant at Veco headquarters and raided the offices of six legislators, looking for financial ties between the company and the lawmakers. They looked for documents dealing with Governor Murkowski's proposed gas pipeline contract and a related rewrite of the Alaska oil production tax laws. Included in the search were the offices of four legislators associated with the Corrupt Bastards Club, namely Ben Stevens, Pete Kott, John Cowdery, and Vic Kohring. Also searched were the offices of Donald Olson and Bruce Weyhrauch. At the end of 2007, the federal probe had produced four indictments, three convictions, and three guilty pleas. In 2008 a fourth conviction was added when former lawmaker Kohring received a sentence of three and a half years in prison.

Alaska's U.S. Representative Don Young has been under federal investigation over his ties to Veco, the use of earmarks, and his close connection to disgraced lobbyist Jack Abramoff. He also came under scrutiny for adding earmarks to transportation legislation that would benefit a Wisconsin trucking company and a Florida real estate mogul, both of whom contributed generously to his campaign. Young reputedly has spent in excess of $1 million in legal fees to defend himself. Undoubtedly, these investigations have weakened the influence of Alaska's congressional delegation. And in July 2008, a grand jury indicted Senator John Cowdery on bribery and conspiracy counts in the federal investigation of corruption that already sent three former lawmakers to prison.

Sources: *Anchorage Daily News,* September 5, 2006; *Fairbanks Daily News-Miner,* June 2, 2008; *Anchorage Daily News,* August 5, 2007.

---

ble to build a personal fortune if one was "one of the United States' most influential senators." They also showed how lax ethics rules allowed members of Congress and their families to profit from personal business dealings with special interests.[31]

The authors then gave examples of how Stevens became wealthy. Armed with the power his committee posts gave him over the Pentagon, Stevens helped save a $450 million military housing contract for an Anchorage businessman, who in turn made the senator a partner in a series of real estate investments that turned his $50,000 stake into at least $750,000 in six years. A Native company that

Stevens helped to create also received millions of dollars in defense contracts through preferences he wrote into the law. By 2003, the company paid $6 million annual rentals for an office building the senator and his business partners owned, and the senator continued to further legislation benefiting the company.[32]

An Alaska communications company benefitted from Stevens's activities on the Commerce Committee. His wife, Catherine Stevens, earned tens of thousands of dollars from an inside deal involving the company's stock. Responding to questions from the *Los Angeles Times,* Stevens wrote that in all these cases his official actions were motivated by a desire to help Alaska. He played no role in the day-to-day management of the ventures into which he invested.[33]

When the FBI and the IRS searched Stevens's home in July 2007, they were seeking records of a 2000 renovation project that more than doubled the size of his home. Bill Allen, the CEO of Veco Corp. who oversaw the renovation project, had pled guilty to bribing Alaska state legislators. Allen had founded Veco, an Alaska-based oil field services and engineering firm that received tens of millions of dollars in federal contracts.[34] He resigned from Veco and awaits sentencing, as does Rick Smith, a Veco vice president who pled guilty to similar charges.

The FBI retrieved a note Stevens had written to former U.S. Attorney Wev Shea in which he wrote that he and his wife had paid "over $130,000" for the Veco-supervised home renovation. Stevens had told reporters that he had paid every bill he had received. That left open the possibility that Veco had not billed him for all the work performed. Critics contended that all the work done could not have been accomplished within that budget.[35]

On February 21, 2008, Stevens filed for reelection for his eighth term in the U.S. Senate. On July 29, 2008, he was indicted on seven federal criminal counts. His corruption trial began on September 22 of that year, and in October a jury found him guilty on all seven charges. Stevens was to be sentenced in April 2009, but on April 1, U.S. Attorney General Eric Holder moved to drop all charges against the former senator, who had lost his reelection bid to Mark Begich, formerly the Democratic mayor of Anchorage. Justice Department lawyers told a federal court that they had discovered a new instance of prosecutorial misconduct on top of earlier disclosures that had raised questions about the way the case was handled, and they asked that the convictions be voided.[36]

One day later, Governor Sarah Palin echoed a call from the Alaska Republican Party for Senator Begich to resign in light of the Justice Department's actions and stated that "a special election should be held to fill the seat." Alaska Republican Party Chairman Randy Ruedrich stated that Alaskans should get a chance to choose between Begich and Stevens without the "improper influence of the corrupt Department of Justice." The Republicans pointed out that Begich beat Stevens by a mere 3,953 votes.[37]

What the Republicans failed to mention is that Begich filed for the Senate seat before Stevens's troubles began. Furthermore, a victory by 3,953 votes can be considered a landslide in Alaska, where many contests are decided by only hundreds of votes. Nothing will come of the Republican bluster, and Begich will serve his six years. All Alaskans are relieved that Stevens does not have to go to jail, and all wish him a happy retirement. He deserves it after serving his state faithfully for forty years.

Governor Murkowski's Administration

Newly elected Governor Murkowski had announced that the stars were aligned after his victory. He had promised during his campaign to "hit the ground running." But after his election it took him some time to select a new slate of state administrators. Governor Knowles had permitted several commissioners to live and work out of Anchorage, but Murkowski demanded that all commissioners keep offices and residences in Juneau. Commissioner's salaries, most starting at less than the governor's eighty-five thousand dollars, also limited Murkowski's choices and required sacrifices on the part of the appointees. By late January 2003 Murkowski had filled most of the top positions in state government with old white men, with a few women and Natives.[38]

The governor's administrative style displeased many Alaskans. Shortly after the election he went pheasant hunting in Scotland without informing the media. Several weeks later he went on a hunting trip to the contiguous states. After reporters queried his commissioners and deputies about administration policies, Murkowski asked the media to channel all inquiries through his chief of staff and press secretary. The news media, used to the informal access to former governors, revolted. Clearly, the governor was used to the U.S. Senate style of doing business. He rescinded his order, but not until he had made all his cabinet appointments. Then there was the seventy-year-old governor's health. Shortly after his election he underwent an angioplasty procedure in

Anchorage. A month later he underwent a similar procedure in Seattle.[39]

During his campaign Murkowski had stated that he wanted to base predator control on solid science and not politics. He had opposed the reluctance of the Knowles administration to limit the state's wolf population, especially in areas of special interest to moose hunters. Murkowski had replaced most of the members of the state Board of Game with individuals sympathetic to sport hunters. The new Game Board, thereupon, approved a predator control plan for the McGrath area and adjoining interior regions of the state. The board authorized the use of helicopters for wolf control in mid-March 2003. Animal rights groups responded immediately, and some threatened to boycott Alaska tourism. The new administration, in the face of the opposition, prohibited the use of low-flying aircraft and state personnel in controlling wolves. A final legislative compromise allowed land-and-shoot predator control by authorized civilians. That effectively overturned previous citizens' initiatives that had banned such methods.[40]

Budget Cuts and Tax Increases

In mid-February 2003, Murkowski presented a fiscal year 2004 operating budget request of $2.167 billion, compared to the previous year's budget of $2.223 billion. Murkowski estimated that his proposal would necessitate a withdrawal of $393 million from the Constitutional Budget Reserve, as compared to $1.1 billion at the introduction of the previous administration's fiscal year 2003 budget. What programs to cut and how to raise revenues were the next questions. The Longevity Bonus Program, began in 1972 to reward those who had arrived before statehood in 1959 and had thereby contributed to the state's development, was first on the cutting block. Constitutional challenges had required the opening of the program in the mid-1980s to all Alaskans over sixty-five years of age. The legislature closed the rolls in 1996, but the program still cost the state $47 million annually. Murkowski also proposed cuts to the State Department of Education and Early Development for learning grants and bus transportation expenses, termination of the Alaska Science and Technology

Foundation endowment, intended to stimulate Alaska businesses, and the state's central correspondence school, duplicated in several urban and rural school districts.[41]

The governor proposed five revenue enhancements, namely, an increase in the motor fuel tax from eight cents to twenty cents a gallon; a ten-dollar fee for studded tires; a wildlife conservation pass similar to a hunting and fishing license, to be required of nonconsumptive users of wildlife, at forty-five dollars per pass; an increase in the state business license fee from twenty-five to two hundred dollars annually; and a 5 percent tax on gross receipts of pull tab operators. He also asked the legislature to decide which one of two broad-based taxes to adopt, a seasonal sales tax or reimposition of the school tax, which had been collected annually from each employee's first paycheck. Legislators told the governor to choose among the two. Murkowski estimated that the revenue enhancements would contribute about $100 million annually to the general fund. The governor opposed an income tax or an increase in corporate income taxes.[42]

Unlike the proposals Knowles had made, each of Governor Murkowski's proposals was scheduled for a hearing. The strongest opposition developed to the elimination of the $250 monthly longevity bonus, but various groups also opposed the other suggested enhancements. Eventually, the legislature increased the state business tax to $100 annually, enacted a small increase in vehicle registration and license taxes, and also imposed a tax on all new and studded tire sales.[43]

The governor used his line item veto authority to reduce legislative appropriations by $138 million. He cut local government assistance by $37 million and eliminated the Longevity Bonus Program. The legislature had approved Murkowski's request to give a severance tax credit of 20 percent to companies drilling new exploration wells more than three miles from current activity, and 40 percent to those drilling more than twenty-five miles from production facilities. That cost the state an estimated $50 to $100 million annually. In the end, the fiscal year 2004 budget was much like the budget of the previous year. It came to $7.6 billion, including $479.2 million drawn from the CBR.[44]

Lisa Murkoswki's Reelection

There were four ballot propositions in the 2004 general election. The most important, ballot measure no. 4, cancelled the governor's power to make temporary appointments to vacant U.S. Senate seats. This was in reaction to Murkowski's appointment of his daughter, Lisa, to the U.S. Senate seat he had vacated. It passed with 55 percent of the vote.

Former Governor Knowles ran against Lisa Murkowski in the 2004 general election. It was the most expensive campaign in state history. Knowles raised $5.8 million, with major support from lawyers, investment firms, and realtors and some 80 percent from individual donations. Murkowski raised $5.7 million, with main support from the oil and gas industry, lawyers, and medical professionals. She received twice as much from political action committees as did Knowles, but 20 percent less in individual donations.

The two candidates had few differences on major issues. Both promised to open ANWR to oil and gas development and assist in building a gas pipeline. They both pledged to increase jobs in Alaska and improve welfare. Murkowski was vulnerable on the nepotism issue, which made most voters unhappy. It was, perhaps, best expressed in the bumper stickers that read "Yo, Lisa! Who's yer daddy?" Senator Stevens and Representative Young helped her in a campaign blitz in the last days of the campaign, and Murkowski won the race, with 49 percent to Knowles's 45 percent of the vote.[45]

In good health at age eighty-six, Stevens probably would have enjoyed several years of satisfying retirement. On August 9, however, a 1957 DeHavilland DHC-3T owned by GCI Communications, on the way from its fishing lodge to a fish camp, crashed on a mountainside about seventeen miles north of Dillingham in southwestern Alaska, taking the life of Ted Stevens and four other passengers. Four additional passengers survived. Alaska and his many friends mourned the death of "Uncle Ted," Senator Ted Stevens.

Efforts to Change the Retirement System

The major issue that occupied the time and energy of legislators was reform of the state Personnel Retirement System (PERS) and the Teacher Retirement System (TRS). Over the years, the legislature had addressed the retirement issue on several occasions. During the pipeline years, as public employees were deserting their positions to make big money in pipeline construction, the legislature had sweetened the retirement package by adding health insurance. The legislature later canceled the health insurance and other benefits, leaving those who had entered the system when it was in place in the "first tier" of the system and creating other tiers.

The Murkowski administration early on had planned to align Alaska's retirement system with President Bush's goal to transform Social Security into largely private savings accounts. Also, more American businesses were abandoning defined-benefit retirements and replacing them with defined-contribution retirement systems, or 401(k) plans, which are personal savings accounts with modest employer contributions. They pay out only what has accumulated in the account, plus earnings, regardless of the individual's life span.

Therefore, in 2003, Murkowski's commissioner of administration replaced a capable and nationally respected director of retirement and benefits with an individual charged with the task of dismantling the existing retirement system. The commissioner requested the retirement boards made up of teachers, state employees, and the commissioner of administration to establish a committee to formulate a new retirement tier. Retirement funds were used to finance a study of the retirement system that the legislature was to use in its deliberations. Despite the fact that each board had three members appointed by the new administration, no committee member recommended a pure defined-contribution plan. The administration, in turn, insisted that a pure defined-contribution plan be recommended. Thereupon, the new director worked hard with supporters of any bill in the legislature that supported the defined-contribution plan.[46]

Several lawmakers sounded the alarm early in 2005. The state was bleeding money. In 2004 rising health care costs for first-tier state employees constituted 34 percent of total benefits paid in that year. The systems had an unfunded liability of $5 billion. In late March 2005, members of the PERS and TRS boards urged lawmakers to focus on controlling the cost of the current system instead of abolishing it. Mercer, a human resource consulting firm, had concluded that in twenty-five years the two retirement systems would be short the $5.6 billion needed to pay expected benefits. Kerry Jarrell, a new Murkowski appointee to the TRS board, told the Senate Finance Committee that this forecasted shortage was "no reason to gut the retirement system." Small changes, such as less than projected health care cost increases, could significantly change the estimate.

These comments irked Bert Stedman, an influential member of the Senate Finance Committee who had done much of the work on the new defined-contribution retirement legislation. The state could not afford inaction on the matter. It spent more money every year for increased retirement needs when the money could be used for other pressing needs. The Senate legislation called for combining the governing boards that oversaw PERS and TRS with the Alaska State Pension Investment Board to "correct a fractured governing structure." There were other proposals as well, all designed to remove beneficiaries of the system from the boards.[47]

In April the state Senate, on a straight party-line vote of 12–8, approved the Retirement Security Act. It provided for a 401(k) savings account for new employees and combined the three boards. Democrats and some Republicans complained throughout the remainder of the session that the Senate measure did not solve the $5.4 billion deficit. The House rejected the Senate plan, which included a one-year sunset clause, on a 17–23 vote.[48] The House then passed its own version, and the Senate rejected it, which put the issue into conference committee where it remained until adjournment.

In retaliation, Governor Murkowski threatened to veto hundreds of millions of dollars in public work projects around the state unless the legislature

eliminated the traditional pension system. In the meantime, national labor leaders and the White House pressured House members in opposite directions.[49] The stalemate persisted and the legislature adjourned. Governor Murkowski then called a special session of the state legislature (the governor sets the agenda for such a session). Murkowski's priorities were reform of the state's workman's compensation law to make it more business-friendly; reform of the retirement system, and four other measures, namely, a provision to allow soft money in campaigns, a proposal to grant the University of Alaska 250,000 acres of state land, a revision of the state insurance laws, and construction of a virology lab in Fairbanks.[50]

In the special session, after intense negotiations over the capital budget, the House and Senate solved the deadlock over the retirement reforms. Senate leaders agreed to directly fund the entire state Department of Education and Early Development list of deferred school maintenance projects in the unorganized borough (rural Alaska), and they also agreed to moderately increase employer contributions to the new defined-contribution (401k) retirement account. These concessions bought enough rural votes to bring about House passage of the new State Employment Security Act. The House also agreed to reform worker's compensation by freezing physician rates. It established an appeals board of gubernatorial appointees that would decide how injuries would be covered. Agreement was also reached on transferring 250,000 acres of state land to the University of Alaska, required as a state match for an equal amount of federal lands. The agreement required negotiators to remove several tracts of land to which environmentalists had objected. At the conclusion of the two-week special session, the legislature adopted the operating and capital budgets of $2.214 and $1.656 billion, respectively.[51]

The legislature left for the future issues such as how to deal with the unfunded retirement liabilities; how to attract and retain employees for public sector employment because the pension reform broadened the gap in salaries and benefits of public and private sector jobs; and finally, how to pay for government services without a sound fiscal plan.

The Oil Tax and the Natural Gas Pipeline

In 2006, a proposal to increase taxes on oil companies and the contract for an Alaska natural gas pipeline dominated state politics. Both turned out to be very controversial. The governor proposed to revise the state's system of taxing the oil companies, essentially unchanged since 1977 when oil first entered the TAPS. Under this system, the state collected royalties from the oil companies, assessed property taxes, which are shared with local governments, and charged an income tax, as does the federal government. The state also charged a severance tax on the oil as it leaves the ground. Together, oil taxes and royalties produced between 65 to 85 percent of the state's general fund budget.

For years, critics questioned whether or not the state, as owner of the resources, received a fair share of the bounty. Two factors increased these concerns, the first pertained to the very high profits reported by the multinational companies doing business in Alaska, and second was the impact the Economic Limit Factor (ELF) would have on company taxes as Alaska's oil is drawn down. As previously discussed, the state devised and implemented the ELF to encourage oil companies to develop smaller fields. These would be taxed at lower rates or not at all. Economist used taxes on the second largest oil field, Kuparuk, as an example. In 2000, the field produced 212,000 barrels of oil a day and had an ELF rate of 0.6, or an effective 9 percent production tax. With declining production, this tax rate would be lowered to 3.75 percent by the year 2006, and by 2007 it would generate no taxes at all, even though it was still producing 125,000 barrels of oil per day.[52]

The governor had been negotiating with the three major oil producers for a gas line project. The companies also discussed the existing state's oil taxation. In late January 2006, as the negotiations neared completion, the governor announced that he had combined changes in the oil tax system with the gas line. On February 21, Murkowski announced that the negotiations had been concluded. He had combined agreement on a natural gas pipeline with legislative acceptance of a new oil production tax. Parts of the proposal included a 20 percent tax

on company net profits, a 20 percent deduction to companies for capital and operating expenses, a 20 percent tax credit on investment in Alaska, and a standard deduction of $73 million annually for each company in the Alaska oil business. The change was expected to increase the state's take by 6 percent and produce $1 billion more in tax revenue for the state when oil prices were high. At twenty-five dollars per barrel or less, however, the state would earn less.[53]

Murkowski stated that the oil companies had offered to pay 12.5 percent of net profits. He thought that 20 percent was more balanced and would still attract exploration and investment. An Exxon spokesperson commented that "the oil contract terms consistent with the governor's proposed oil tax bill would provide the predictability . . . necessary to advance the gas project to the next phase."[54] However, Conoco Phillips and BP ran an intensive ad campaign on Alaska's television stations and radio stations and in newspapers, claiming that tax increases would stifle oil industry investments in Alaska and damage the state's economy. Several Anchorage lawmakers responded that the state Department of Revenue had released a report on the oil industry that showed that it would earn some $7 billion in profits in 2006 from existing fields at prices of sixty dollars a barrel—a 43 percent profit margin—which would drop to $3.9 billion if the price of oil dropped to forty dollars a barrel.[55]

In the meantime, lawmakers had been discussing the governor's changes to the state's tax regime for better than a month. They had increased the governor's proposed rate of 20 percent to as high as 25 percent and reduced some of his tax credits. The oil industry had urged the lawmakers to pass the governor's changes in the oil tax system. They claimed they reluctantly supported these because they made a gas line possible. Lawmakers commented that they understood that the oil companies acted in the best interest of their shareholders, but they had the responsibility to act in the best interest of the state and its citizens.[56]

Many Alaskans participated in the tax debate by speaking at public forums, e-mailing their legislators, and writing letters-to-the-editor as well as public opinion pieces for the major newspapers.

Alan Boraas, a professor of anthropology at the Kenai Peninsula College, weighed in with a piece titled "Norway Sets Standard for Oil Taxation." He pointed out that Norway taxed net oil profits at 50 percent and then added a 28 percent corporate tax, for a total that amounted to a 78 percent tax. The multinationals objected, but as a Norwegian economist pointed out, they still made a profit of 15 to 18 percent when oil was below sixty dollars per barrel. With oil at over sixty dollars per barrel, oil companies took in after-tax profits of 30–35 percent. Norway exported about three times the oil Alaska did but generated six times the value of the $34 billion Alaska Permanent Fund.[57]

A few days later the Senate approved switching the state's production tax to the governor's petroleum profits tax (PPT), setting a base tax rate of 22.5 percent while allowing a 25 percent credit on capital investments. The tax rate increased by 0.2 percentage points for every one dollar prices climb above fifty dollars a barrel, based on North Slope crude prices. Murkowski criticized the Senate version. He continued to defend the deal he had worked out with Exxon Mobil, BP, and Conoco Phillips as a part of the $25 billion gas pipeline. Under the terms of the deal, the tax rate would be locked in for thirty years to provide the producers fiscal certainty on their future tax liability.[58]

When the legislature adjourned on May 9, it had failed to adopt the PPT or any version of it. Murkowski, therefore, called a special session to evaluate the complex gas line draft agreement that he had finally released. Most criticized the 352-page contract as "full of lucrative incentives for the producers" and great risk to the state. Above all, it offered no guarantee that the pipeline would ever be built.[59]

During part of the first and throughout the second special session, both houses of the legislature held hearings and meetings on the proposed contract. The senate created a special committee on the gas pipeline, and during the forty-five-day public comment period the administration received more than two thousand individual comments. Although most everyone wanted to see a gas pipeline built, opinions differed on routing, state ownership and its implications, antitrust problems, guarantees,

tax rates, viability of a gas pipeline, and the speed of construction. At the conclusion of the second special session, the legislature had failed to take any action on the gas pipeline contract or associated matters.

But the legislature did reach agreement on oil taxation changes. The new production tax established a 22.5 percent tax rate on oil company net profits and included a 20 percent credit of investment, close to the governor's original proposal. The PPT had an escalator provision, which became effective when oil prices would rise above fifty-five dollars per barrel. The measure also included a provision preventing the state from subsidizing repairs necessitated for oil field shutdowns caused by poor maintenance of the infrastructure.[60]

Reviewing the Murkowski Years

It had been a rough four years for Murkowski. His tenure seemingly had been mired in controversy almost from the moment he first took office in 2002. One after another of his appointees had come under investigation: One of the governor's appointees to the Alaska Oil and Gas Conservation Commission (AOGCC), Republican Party chairman Randy Ruedrich, was forced to resign his state job after Sarah Palin, chair of the AOGCC, accused him of unethical conduct. Palin resigned after exposing Ruedrich. The governor's commissioner of the Department of Commerce, Community, and Economic Development was forced to resign because of an ethics scandal. The governor's former commissioner of the Department of Health and Social Services was under investigation for alleged ethics violations. His attorney general, Gregg Renkes, resigned over conflict of interest charges. Murkowski appointed Dave Marquez as his replacement even though he also had significant conflicts of interest. The governor appointed former political aide Mike Menges as commissioner of the Department of Natural Resources to replace Tom Irwin, who had been dismissed after he sent a memorandum to Attorney General Marquez, raising several legal questions about the Stranded Gas Development Act negotiations held between the state and the three major North Slope producers. Six deputy commissioners, directors, and a project assistant all quit in support of Commissioner Irwin.[61]

Murkowski had refused to release the gas line deal he had negotiated behind closed doors with the major producers and instead kept it secret. He then linked the rather difficult gas deal to a very complicated oil tax revision plan. This placed the legislature in the position of trying to make a major decision with only half of the necessary information.[62]

Murkowski attempted to use $2 million in federal homeland security funds to purchase a jet for his use as governor. The federal government rejected his request, so the governor next lobbied the legislature to have $1.4 million inserted into the state budget in January 2005. He was refused. He later suggested selling one of several planes the Department of Public Safety owned to provide capital to lease a jet. The legislature also rejected his request, but the governor did get his jet. The department sold a C-12 turbo-prop aircraft and used the proceeds for the down payment on a Westwind II jet aircraft. The total price for the jet was $2,692,600 in November 2005. The public was not amused.

The Alaskan electorate had given Murkowski ten consecutive statewide election victories. As a U.S. Senator, Murkowski endlessly repeated the platitudes about resource development most Alaskans love to hear. He was a steadfast warrior in the state's continuous battle with the federal government over a multitude of issues, ranging from rights-of-way across federal lands to the management of fish and game resources on the public domain. Murkowski did not deviate from the prevailing political orthodoxy. His record in the U.S. Senate was modest, no major legislation bears his name, and senior Senator Stevens overshadowed him throughout his twenty-two years in office. Being governor, however, required a different skill set, which he never acquired. His Senate colleagues accepted his gruff demeanor, aggressive business style, and imperial and arrogant manner. Alaskans did not.

The 2006 Election

Dave Dittman, a former Murkowski consultant, released a poll shortly before the GOP primary in August 2006. The poll of 514 likely Republican primary voters showed the governor running a distant third behind former Wasilla Mayor Sarah Palin, who received 40 percent of the vote from the respondents, and former state Senator John Binkley, who got 29 percent. Murkowski wound up with just 17 percent. Undecided voters comprised 14 percent of those surveyed. The poll had a 4.3 percent margin of error.[63]

Murkowski's reelection slogan was "Courage, Leadership, Experience." Voters, however, looked at it differently. They saw stubbornness, arrogance, and too many years in the nation's capital. At first Binkley appeared to be the Republican favorite. Fifty-three years of age, he and his prominent Fairbanks family ran the remarkably successful Riverboat Discovery tourism enterprise. He was telegenic, well respected in Republic Party circles, and very likeable. He also had amassed a substantial campaign chest of $1 million. One television ad showed him checking the dipstick on his small bush plane, a reminder to voters that he flew his own small aircraft, in contrast to Murkowski, who traveled in comfort in a jet at state expense. Binkley seemed to promise the voters a continuation of the governor's conservative business and social policies but without Murkowski's personality defects.

On August 23, 2006, however, voters told Binkley that they did not want a new, improved Murkowski. A little better than half voted for Sarah Palin, an unknown until 2002 when she lost her bid for lieutenant governor. She had become widely known when she blew the whistle on Republican Party chairman Randy Ruedrich, forcing him to resign.

Forty-two-year-old Sarah Palin displayed a formidable ability to connect with and inspire voters. A former beauty queen and high school basketball star, she was a natural on television, with her good looks and easy manner. During the campaign she cast herself as the future and the governor as the past. She promised to bring transparency and high ethical conduct to state government. Besides that, she repeated the usual Alaskan political sentiments about stimulating oil and gas development, protecting the Permanent Fund, keeping taxes low, and demanding responsible state budgets.[64]

She did not talk about her stand on abortion, which she opposed for any reason, except to save the life of a mother. She opposed teenagers' access to information on contraception, prevention of unplanned pregnancy, and safe-sex practices. She supported abstinence-only sex education. As a fundamentalist Christian, she favored adding "intelligent design" Christian creationism to the science curriculum in public schools. (Palin is also skeptical of the science connecting human actions to global warming.)[65] The churches Palin attended all teach a literal interpretation of the Bible. She believes in the power of prayer: as governor she addressed a gathering of the Assembly of God Church in Wasilla. Among other things, she talked about the intersection of faith and public life. She encouraged her listeners to pray that "God's will" be done in bringing about the construction of the gas pipeline. She suggested that her work as governor would be hampered "if the people of Alaska's heart isn't right with God." In short, she is convinced that she is God's servant.[66] None of these beliefs were aired during the campaign.

Murkowski lost the Republican primary, receiving 12 percent of the vote. It was only the fourth time in the state's history that Alaskan voters in a primary election booted out a statewide office holder. In the November general elections, Sarah Palin, the Wasilla "hockey mom," defeated Democrat Tony Knowles in his comeback attempt.

What were Murkowski's achievements as governor? He worked hard in attempting to resolve a commercial dispute over the mothballed Healy Clean Coal Project, a fifty-megawatt new-technology power plant that should have been supplying power to the regional electric grid but was not—a problem he inherited from previous governors. His greatest achievement, no doubt, was to overhaul the state's seriously defective oil and gas production tax laws. The new Petroleum Profits Tax was a real achievement, for he faced opposition from the industry and his fellow Republicans in the legislature.

In the meantime, Alaskans welcomed their first female governor, the first chief executive to be born after statehood.

ACES and New Oil Tax Reform

One of the first major issues Governor Palin faced was corruption. In May 2007, Bill J. Allen, chief executive officer of Anchorage-based Veco Corporation, an oil field services company, and Rick Smith, a Veco vice president, pleaded guilty to bribing state legislators with cash and the promise of jobs and favors in exchange for backing bills the company supported (see "Stevens's Troubles" above). The two pleaded guilty to extortion, bribery, and conspiracy to impede the Internal Revenue Service. The pleas came after the indictments of one current and two former Republican members of the Alaska House of Representatives on federal bribery and extortion charges related to the 2006 negotiations for a new oil and gas tax and a proposed natural gas pipeline.[67] By December 2007, two former House members had been sentenced to five- and six-year jail terms, respectively, and a third one received a prison sentence of three and a half years in 2008.[68]

In light of all of these events, Governor Palin developed and introduced Alaska's Clear and Equitable Share plan (ACES), a hybrid valuation plan that incorporated gross and net features to ensure that the state would receive appropriate value when oil prices were high, share risks during downturns, and credit companies for new private sector investments.[69]

Palin asked the legislature to approve a sensible rewrite of the PTT. Instead, in a special session, the legislature passed a measure boosting oil revenues almost four times more than she had proposed with her ACES plan. Why did an appropriate oil tax bill finally pass? The political climate was far more favorable for a tax increase than the governor, the producers, and most politicians had guessed. Most legislators became convinced that corruption had played a role in the shaping of the 2006 PTT legislation. The three major producers denied they had anything to do with it, but they were among the chief beneficiaries of the corruption. Furthermore, as global oil prices rose, jurisdictions around the world were boosting their share of the oil profits. Also, the oil industry's image in Alaska had suffered. With North Slope oil spills, BP's big fine for price fixing and environmental crimes, and Exxon's umpteenth oil spill penalty appeal, all occurring as producers posted record profits—all of this had exhausted the public's patience, particularly with ever-rising prices for gasoline, diesel, and heating oil.[70]

In March 2007, the governor introduced the Alaska Gasline Inducement Act as a new vehicle for building a natural gas pipeline from the North Slope to the contiguous states. Both Republicans and Democrats supported the act, which the governor signed into law in June 2007. During the 2008 legislative session, and in response to high oil and gas prices and the resulting state budget surplus, the governor proposed giving Alaskans a one-hundred-dollar-a-month energy debit card to be used for home heating fuel, electric, or gas, and grants to electrical utilities so that they would cut customer rates. She later dropped these ideas and instead proposed to give every resident a $1,200 grant and suspend the state fuel tax for a few months. The legislature went along.[71]

Governor Sarah Palin and her family, 2007.

(Courtesy of the Alaska Governor's Office.)

First Dude

With a woman in the governor's office for the first time, Alaskans became especially interested in her husband, Todd Palin. Sarah Heath met Todd Palin at a high school basketball game. They eloped in 1988, six years after graduation. British Petroleum trained Todd Palin as a production operator in a facility that separates oil from gas and water. In December 2006, when Sarah ran for governor, he took a leave of absence to avoid a potential conflict of interest and to have more time with their four children.[72]

In mid-February 2007, the "first dude" rode his snowmachine across two thousand miles of wintry tundra, tracing the entire Iditarod trail from Anchorage to Nome plus an additional leg to Fairbanks, to win his fourth Iron Dog championship since 1993. Governor Palin flew to Fairbanks "to wave her exhausted husband across the finish line."[73]

Like other first spouses, Mr. Palin has been asked to champion an array of causes or institutions since his wife took office in December 2006. After spending years in manual labor in the fishing and oil industries, both physically very demanding, he has decided to steer young Alaskans toward stable jobs in the oil and gas industry.[74]

Palin on the National Ticket

On August 24, 2008, Senator John McCain, the Republican nominee for president, called Sarah Palin with the news that he was considering her as his running mate. It was a short call. Palin, attending the Alaska State Fair in Palmer, had difficulties hearing McCain over the crowd. McCain was intrigued and asked that his staff fly her down to Arizona. She arrived in Flagstaff on Wednesday, August 27. Mark Salter, coauthor of McCain's books and a close adviser, and Steve Schmidt, a McCain aide, met her and talked with her late into the night, looking for gaps between her views and McCain's. While Salter was cautious, Schmidt favored Palin from the beginning, seeing in her the "potential as a conservative populist, the kind of throw-'em-red-meat, bash-the-elites politician who thrilled the Republican base."[75]

The next morning the two men drove Palin to McCain's cabin in Sedona, Arizona. There they met with McCain for about an hour. After a brief reflection, McCain asked Palin to join his ticket, and she instantly accepted. On August 29, the candidate introduced his running mate to the world in a high school gym in Dayton, Ohio. Palin was an instant hit. McCain's crowds suddenly swelled to Obama-size numbers—five to ten to fifteen thousand—most there to see and hear Palin.[76]

Palin's speeches were rousing at rallies of true believers. Early one morning in Clearwater, Florida, with an enormous American flag suspended over her head, she began her speech with "God bless America—you guys get it!" The crowd of several thousand, virtually all white, screamed "Drill, baby, drill." Then she started in on Barack Obama: "I am just so fearful that this is not a man who sees America the way you and I see America." She brought up William Ayers, a former Weather Underground bomber who was casually acquainted with Obama through Chicago politics. "I'm afraid that this is someone who sees America as imperfect enough to work with a former domestic terrorist who targeted his own people."[77]

The polls showed that Palin succeeded in rallying the Republican base but also caused countless independent voters to turn to Obama. Her Republican handlers scripted her appearances and restricted news media access to her because they suspected she was not qualified to be a heartbeat away from the presidency. In interviews with ABC's Charlie Gibson and CBS's Katie Couric, she was unable to define the Bush Doctrine, identify Supreme Court rulings with which she disagreed, or name a newspaper that she read. Columnist Maureen Dowd wrote after the election that Palin seemed "disturbingly unconcerned about how much she did not know." Dowd quoted Palin when she defended herself against the contention that she got confused about Africa: "My concern has been the atrocities there in Darfur and the relevance to me with that issue as we spoke about Africa and some of the countries there that were kind of the people succumbing to the dictators and the corruption of some collapsed governments on the continent, the relevance was Alaska's investment in Darfur with some of our Permanent Fund dollars. Never, ever did I talk about, well, gee, is it a country or a continent, I just don't know about this issue."[78]

Columnist Leonard Pitts, Jr., of the *Miami Herald* commented that every politician wants to be seen as Everyman or Everywoman, and that is why every primary season brings the curious sight of millionaires in plaid shirts "wandering through county fairs eating fried things on sticks." In that sense, Palin was nothing new. "The 'g' dropping, moose shootin', eye-winkin', hockey mom" had plenty of antecedents. The difference was that "those antecedents were smart, wonkish people pretending to be one of us. Sarah Palin 'is' one of us." By that Pitts meant "the lowest common denominator us, the us of myth and narrative, the us of simple mind, the reactionary, ill-informed, impatient with complexity, utterly shallow us."[79]

The McCain-Palin ticket lost as the American electorate chose Barack Obama as the forty-fourth president of the United States on November 4, 2008. Sarah Palin returned to Alaska to resume her job as governor. Shortly after the election, Palin told Greta Van Sustern of Fox News, "my faith will guide [me] on a 2012 run. I'm like, Ok, God, if there is an open door for me somewhere—this is what I always pray—don't let me miss the open door. . . . Show me where the open door is, even if it's cracked open a little bit, maybe I'll plow right on through that and maybe prematurely plow through it." Dowd wrote that Palin now thought she was "even bigger than her vast state" and threw open the door to the national press "letting them hang in her Wasilla kitchen as she makes moose chili and cake and baby formula and hefty servings of spin."[80]

Palin's remarks prompted a Fairbanks resident to write to the town's daily newspaper, "God doesn't care whether Sarah Palin runs for president in 2012 or even for the U.S. Senate next year. Omnipotent and omnipresent though He may be, He has more important things to think about than the governor's political future, and it's more than a little vainglorious for her to think otherwise."[81]

Now the governor had to mend broken political fences. Many Alaska Democrats—her allies in passing key legislation—were outraged by her partisan attacks on Obama and by the McCain-Palin campaign tactics. Oil prices, which provide the bulk of state revenue, were more than one hundred dollars per barrel when she left in late August to campaign. At the years' end they were south of sixty dollars a barrel, below the level needed to balance the state budget. Increased scrutiny of Palin's time as governor painted an often unflattering portrait of her administration and showed her to be consumed with personal matters and vindictiveness, particularly in the firing of her public safety commissioner in what became known as "Troopergate." In any event, she had her work cut out for herself.

Then on July 3, 2009, after just two and a half years in office, Governor Palin stunned political observers by announcing that she would resign her office and turn it over to Lieutenant Governor Sean Parnell on July 26. Many northern residents had the impression that Palin's heart was not in her job since she returned from the presidential campaign trail in the fall of 2008. Lawmakers complained that she failed to take an interest in the state's politics, and she limited her access to Alaska's media. After her State of the State Address in January 2009, one legislator observed that the only eye contact she made in the legislative chamber was with the television camera.[82]

Palin held a short news conference outside her lakeside home in Wasilla, where she made her announcement in an often "rambling address." She had decided not to seek reelection at the expiration of her first term and therefore did not think it fair to her constituents to continue in office. At times in the course of her remarks, "delivered in a voice often seemed rushed and jittery, she sounded at times like a candidate with continued national aspirations" as, for example, when she suggested she "could fight for all our children's future from outside the governor's office." Later in the afternoon, as Republicans wondered exactly what she intended to do, she posted a notice on her Twitter site: "We'll soon attach info on decision not to seek re-election. . . . This is in Alaska's best interest, my family's happy. . . . It is good, stay tuned."[83]

Economist Gregg Erickson, publisher of a newsletter and long-time political observer, stated that with all the thorny issues enveloping her in Alaska, like the various ethics complaints, she probably just wanted to cut her losses. "The drum-beat of adverse news coverage from Alaska would likely have continued and intensified had she remained governor," Erickson stated. "It would have become an increasing liability to her national campaign." Palin, he added, had received adulation from social conservatives in the contiguous states, but in Alaska "she's become a lightning rod for criticism and controversy."[84]

Perhaps it is all simpler than that. She was following the money. She had a multimillion dollar book deal and invitations to be active on the conservative radio and television circuit. She could become a rich woman, but as a sitting governor she could not take advantage of these opportunities while in office.

Fifty Years of Statehood

The first fifty years of statehood, most Alaskan residents would agree, have brought monumental changes to the 49th State, some for the better, others for the worse. Alaska is an urban state. Most of its 698,473 inhabitants live in urban centers that offer most of the conveniences found elsewhere in urban America, from box stores to traffic jams. Then there are the Native Alaskans who, if they have not moved to the urban centers, live in more than 200 villages scattered across the state, the majority not connected to the road system, who lack most of these modern conveniences.

Alaskans like to imagine that their state still offers untrammeled freedoms and limitless horizons. This myth lies behind the resistance to all designations of land designed to protect natural landscapes and wildlife habitat, or to prevent environmental degradation. Such attitudes, however, foreclose the freedoms they supposedly defend. There is no escaping into the past of the 1860s before boundary lines and private property, before "No Trespassing" signs, before cities and urban areas had changed the landscapes through which explorers and prospectors traveled laboriously on foot, horseback, dog team, and boat. We are still attracted to the romance of that past, but that world has disappeared. When local activities threaten national parks, national wildlife refuges, and national forests, among others, we each lose. Not only our generation but also those of our children and grandchildren will suffer that loss.

As citizens of this state we must ask, before we allow ourselves to be deluded by those who claim to represent our interests, which schemes will have unfortunate, unpredictable, and long-term consequences: who will benefit from these multiplying mining sites, highways, and bridges to everywhere? Who loses and what are the losses? It is important to keep Alaska a good place to live, maintaining a sense of spaciousness and our individual ties to wild lands so close to our homes. That is a real part of why we live here. It will require vision, wisdom, and experience to manage the inevitable changes the next fifty years will bring. The first fifty years of statehood have been, at times, tumultuous. Hopefully, we can steer the inevitable changes the next fifty years will bring into avenues that benefit all Alaska residents and preserve those lifestyles we cherish.

Appendix A

COMMANDERS IN ALASKA AND EFFECTIVE DATES OF COMMAND; COMPOSITION AND TOURS OF DUTY OF THE ALASKA GARRISONS

Commanders in Alaska and Effective Dates of Command

Military District and Department of Alaska

Brevet Major General Jefferson C. Davis, Colonel, Twenty-third Infantry
(September 6, 1867–July 9, 1870)

Military District of Kenay

Brevet Brigadier General John C. Tidball, Major, Second Artillery
(September 17, 1868–September 17, 1869)
Brevet Colonel Edward B. Williston, Captain, Second Artillery
(September 17, 1869–May 27, 1870)
Brevet Brigadier General John C. Tidball, Major, Second Artillery
(May 27, 1870–September 18, 1870)

Post of Sitka

Brevet Major General Jefferson C. Davis, Colonel, Twenty-third Infantry
(October 29, 1867–December 1, 1868)
Brevet Lieutenant Colonel William Neil Dennison, Captain, Second Artillery
(December 1, 1868–July 7, 1869)
Brevet Lieutenant Colonel George K. Brady, Captain, Twenty-third Infantry
(July 7, 1869–September 23, 1870)
Major John C. Tidball, unused rank of Brevet Brigadier General, Second Artillery
(September 23, 1870–September 20, 1871)
Major Harvey S. Allen, Second Artillery
(September 20, 1871–January 4, 1873)
Major Joseph Stewart, Fourth Artillery
(January 4, 1873–April 20, 1874)
Captain George B. Rodney, Fourth Artillery
(April 21, 1874–August 7, 1874)
Captain Joseph B. Campbell, Fourth Artillery (August 17, 1874–March 24, 1875)

Captain Edward Field, Fourth Artillery
(February 24, 1875–March 24, 1875)
Captain Joseph B. Campbell, Fourth Artillery (March 24, 1875–June 15, 1876)
Captain John Mendenhall, unused rank of Brevet Lieutenant Colonel, Fourth Artillery
(June 15, 1876–March 5, 1877)
Captain Arthur Morris, Fourth Artillery
(March 5, 1877–June 14, 1877)

Fort Wrangell

Brevet Captain John H. Smith, First Lieutenant, Second Artillery (May 5, 1868–October 8, 1869)
Brevet Lieutenant Colonel Thomas Grey, Captain, Second Artillery
(October 8, 1868–March 7, 1869)
First Lieutenant William Borrowe, Second Artillery
(March 7, 1869–May 11, 1870)
First Lieutenant M. R. Loucks, Second Artillery (May 11, 1870–July 14, 1870)
First Lieutenant William Borrowe, Second Artillery
(July 14, 1870–September 22, 1870)
From September 1870 to September 1874 Fort Wrangell was closed.
Second Lieutenant Alexander B. Dyer, Fourth Artillery (September 18, 1874–January 19, 1875)
First Lieutenant John A. Lundeen, Fourth Artillery
(January 19, 1875–August 19, 1875)
Captain Stephen P. Jocelyn, Twenty-first Infantry
(August 19, 1875–November 9, 1876)
Captain Eugene A. Bancroft, Fourth Artillery
(November 9, 1876–June 12, 1877)

Fort Tongass

Captain Charles H. Peirce, Second Artillery
(April 21, 1868–November 7, 1869)
First Lieutenant Franklin M. Ring, Second Artillery
(November 7, 1869–March 5, 1870)
Captain Charles H. Peirce, Second Artillery
(March 5, 1870–May 10, 1870)

First Lieutenant John M. Smith, Second Artillery (May
    10, 1870–July 15, 1870)
Captain Charles H. Peirce, Second Artillery
    (July 15, 1870–October 7, 1870)

Fort Kodiak

First Lieutenant Eli L. Huggins, Second Artillery (June
    6, 1868–September 21, 1868)
Brevet Brigadier General John C. Tidball, Major,
    Second Artillery
    (September 21, 1868–September 17, 1869)
Brevet Colonel Edward B. Williston, Captain, Second
    Artillery
    (September 17, 1869–November 19, 1869)
First Lieutenant Eli L. Huggins, Second Artillery
    (November 19, 1869–December 4, 1869)
Brevet Colonel Edward R. Williston, Captain, Second
    Artillery
    (December 4, 1869–May 27, 1870)
Second Lieutenant Edwin G. Curtis, Second Artillery
    (May 27, 1870–June 3, 1870)
Brevet Lieutenant Colonel Carl A. Woodruff, Captain,
    Second Artillery
    (June 3, 1870–September 18, 1870)

Saint Paul's and Saint George's Islands

First Lieutenant James L. Mast, Second Artillery (May
    22, 1869–June 13, 1870)
First Lieutenant Eli L. Huggins, Second Artillery (June
    13, 1870–September 7, 1870)

Fort Kenay

Brevet Captain John McGilvray, First Lieutenant,
    Second Artillery (April 17, 1869–March 16, 1870)
Second Lieutenant Medorem Crawford, Second
    Artillery (March 16, 1870–September 15, 1870)

Composition and Tours of Duty of the Alaska Garrisons

Sitka

Company F, Ninth Infantry:
    September 1867–July 1869
Company H, Second Artillery:
    September 1867–September 1870,
Company E, Twenty-third Infantry:
    July 1869–June 1871
Company I, Second Artillery:
    September 1870–June 1872
Company C, Second Artillery:
    June 1871–January 1873
Company H, Second Artillery:
    June 1872–January 1873
Company C, Fourth Artillery:
    December 1872–August 1874
Company D, Fourth Artillery:
    December 1872–August 1874
Company F, Fourth Artillery:
    August 1874–June 1876
Company L, Fourth Artillery:
    August 1874–June 1877
Company M, Fourth Artillery:
    January 1875–June 1877
Company N, Fourth Artillery:
    June 1876–November 1876
Company G, Fourth Artillery:
    June 1876–June 1877

Fort Wrangell

Detachment, Company E, Second Artillery:
May 1868–October 1868

Company I, Second Artillery:
    October 1868–September 1870
Detachment, Companies F and L, Fourth Artillery:
    September 1874–January 1875
Detachment, Company M, Fourth Artillery:
    January 1875–August 1875
Company B, Twenty-first Infantry:
    August 1875–November 1876
Company A, Fourth Artillery:
    September 1876–June 1877

Fort Tongass

Company E, Second Artillery:
    April 1868–October 1870
Company H, Second Artillery:
    March 1869–June 1869
Company F, Ninth Artillery:
    March 1869–June 1869

Fort Kodiak

Company G, Second Artillery:
    June 1868–September 1870
Company F, Second Artillery:
    August 1868–April 1869

Saint Paul's and Saint George's Islands

Detachment, Company G, Second Artillery:
    May 1869–September 1870

Fort Kenay

Company F, Second Artillery:
    April 1869–September 1870

———————

Source: Stanley Ray Remsberg, "United States Administration of Alaska: The Army Phase, 1867–1877: A Study in Federal Governance of an Overseas Possession" (PhD diss., University of Wisconsin, 1975), 460–65.

Appendix B

IMPORTANT PLACER GOLD DISCOVERIES

First Alaska gold discovery by the Russians on the
    Russian River on the Kenai Peninsula, 1848
Stikine River near Telegraph Creek, British Columbia,
    1861
Sumdum Bay, 1870
Indian River on the outskirts of Sitka, 1871
Cassiar district in Canada, in the Stikine River
    headwaters country, 1872
Silver Bay near Sitka, 1874
Juneau, 1880
Fortymile, 1886
Yakutat, 1887
Lituya, 1887
Resurrection, 1888
Rampart, 1893
Circle City (Birch Creek), 1893
Seventymile, 1895
Klondike, 1896
Sunrise, 1896
Chistochina, 1898

Shungnak, 1898
Manley Hot Springs, 1898
Nome, 1898
Fairbanks, 1902
Valdez Creek, 1903
Bonnifield, 1903
Kantishna, 1905
Richardson, 1906
Chandalar, 1906
Innoko, 1906
Ruby (Poorman), 1907
Aniak, 1907
Melozitna, 1907
Iditarod, 1909
Kiana, 1909
Hughes (Indian River), 1910
Nelchina, 1912
Chisana (Shushana), 1912
Marshall, 1913
Livengood (Tolovana), 1914

Source: Donald J. Orth, *Dictionary of Alaska Place Names*,
Geological Survey Professional Paper 567 (Washington,
D.C.: U.S. Government Printing Office, 1967).

Appendix C

FEDERAL DISTRICT COURT JUDGES BEFORE STATEHOOD

District of Alaska, headquartered in Sitka

Ward McAllister, 1884–85
Edward J. Dawne, August–December 1885
Lafayette Dawson, 1885–88
John H. Reatley, 1888–89
John S. Bugbee, 1889–92
Warren D. Truitt, 1892–97
Arthur K. Delaney, 1895–97
Charles D. Johnson, 1897–1900
On June 6, 1900, President Theodore Roosevelt signed a measure creating three judicial districts in Alaska. An additional district was added in 1909.

First District: Juneau

Melville C. Brown, 1900–1904
Royal Arch Gunnison, 1904–1909
Thomas R. Lyons, 1909–13
Robert W. Jennings, 1913–21
Thomas Milburne Reed, 1921–28
Justin W. Harding, 1929–34
George Forest Alexander, 1934–47
George W. Folta, 1947–55
Raymond John Kelly, 1955–60

Second District: Nome

Arthur H. Noyes, 1900–1902
Alfred S. Moore, 1902–10
Cornelius D. Murane, 1910–13
John Randolph Tucker, Jr., 1913–17
William A. Holzheimer, 1917–21
Gudbrand J. Lomen, 1921–32
Lester O. Gore, 1932–34
J. H. S. Morison, 1935–44
Joseph W. Kehoe, 1944–51
J. Earl Cooper, 1952–53
Walter H. Hodge, 1954–60

Third District: Eagle, Fairbanks, Valdez, Anchorage

James Wickersham, 1900–1907
Silas H. Reid, 1908–1909
Edward E. Cushman, 1909–12
Peter D. Overfield, 1912–13
Frederick M. Brown, 1913–21
Elmer E. Ritchie, 1921–27
E. Coke Hill, 1927–32
Cecil H. Clegg, 1932–34
Simon Hellenthal, 1935–45
Anthony J. Dimond, 1945–53
J. L. McCarrey, 1953–60

Fourth District: Fairbanks

Peter D. Overfield, 1909–12
Frederick E. Fuller, 1912–14
Charles E. Bunnell, 1915–21
Cecil H. Clegg, 1921–32 (moved to Third District in 1932)
E. Coke Hill, 1932–35
Harry Emerson Pratt, 1935–54
Vernon D. Forbes, 1954–60

Claus-M. Naske and Herman E. Slotnick, *Alaska: A History of the 49th State,* 2nd ed. (Norman: University of Oklahoma Press, 1987), 294.

Appendix D

DELEGATES TO CONGRESS

In 1906, Congress authorized Alaska to send a voteless delegate to the House of Representatives. The following individuals served in that capacity:

Frank H. Waskey, 1906–1907.

Thomas Cale, 1907–1909.

James Wickersham, 1909–17.

Charles A. Sulzer, 1917. Contested election.

James Wickersham, 1918. Seated as delegate.

Charles A. Sulzer, 1919. Elected, died before taking office.

George Grigsby, 1919–21. Appointed.

James Wickersham, 1921. Seated as delegate, having contested the 1919 election and resulting appointment.

Dan A. Sutherland, 1921–31.

James Wickersham, 1931–33.

Anthony J. Dimond, 1933–44.

Edward Lewis (Bob) Bartlett, 1944–58.

In 1956, members of the Alaskan Constitutional Convention signed the constitution they had drafted for the future state. When Alaskans went to the polls in April 1956, they overwhelmingly approved their constitution, together with the so-called Alaska Tennessee Plan. In the general election on October 9, 1956, they elected three Democratic candidates for the positions described by the Alaska-Tennessee Plan: as senators, Ernest Gruening and William A. Egan, and as representative, Ralph J. Rivers, all of whom served from 1956 to 1958. Statehood was proclaimed on January 3, 1959.

Alaska's First Congressional Delegation

U.S. Senators

Edward Lewis (Bob) Bartlett, 1959–68. Died in office, December 11, 1968.

Ernest Gruening, 1959–68.

Mike Gravel, 1968–80.

Theodore F. Stevens, December 11, 1968–2008. Appointed to E. L. "Bob" Bartlett's vacant seat; elected in 1972 in his own right. Reelected in 1978, 1984, 1990, 1996, and 2002. Democrat Mark Begich defeated Stevens in 2008.

Francis Hughes "Frank" Murkowski, 1980–2002. Reelected to consecutive terms, resigned his seat in 2002 upon election as governor of Alaska. Appointed his daughter, Lisa Murkowski, to his seat. She won election to a six-year term in her own right in 2004.

Lisa Murkowski, 2004–present.

U.S. Representatives

Ralph J. Rivers, 1959–66.

Howard Pollock, 1966–70.

Nicholas Begich, 1970–72. On October 16, 1972, Begich boarded a small plane to continue his campaign for reelection. Bound for Juneau, the plane took off from Anchorage and disappeared. Thirty-nine days of intensive air, land, and sea search revealed no trace of the aircraft, its passengers, or it pilot.

Donald Edwin "Don" Young, 1973–present. Young was elected to Congress in a special election in March 1973 after Congressman Begich was declared dead on December 29, 1972. Young was elected to a two-year term and has been reelected ever since, the last time in 2008.

Appendix E

ALASKA'S POPULATION, 1880–2003

TABLE 4

Alaska's Population by Region, 1880–1980

YEAR	TOTAL	SOUTHEAST	CENTRAL	SOUTH	SOUTHWEST	INTERIOR
1880	33,426	7,748	4,352	13,914	2,568	4,844
1890	32,052	8,038	6,112	12,071	2,333	3,498
1900	63,592	14,450	10,000	13,000	5,600	20,642
1910	64,356	15,216	12,900	12,049	13,064	11,127
1920	55,036	17,402	11,173	11,541	7,964	6,956
1930	59,278	19,304	11,880	12,118	8,246	7,730
1940	72,524	25,241	14,881	12,846	10,345	9,211
1950	128,643	28,203	50,093	17,715	23,008	9,624
1960	226,167	35,403	108,851	21,001	49,128	11,784
1970	300,382	42,565	162,001	26,491	56,479	12,846
1974	351,159	50,232	194,569	28,165	63,151	15,042
1975	404,634	50,438	229,492	28,428	78,614	17,662
1976	413,289	51,172	244,056	28,488	68,572	21,041
1977	411.211	53,162	252,836	26,512	58,208	20,493
1980	400,331	53,613	235,465	28,659	67,154	15,440

Source: George W. Rogers and Richard A. Cooley, Alaska's Population and Economy: Regional Growth, Development and Future Outlook, vol. 1 (Fairbanks: Institute of Business, Economic, and Government Research, 1963).

TABLE 5

Alaska's Population by Region, 1990–2003

YEAR	ANCHORAGE/ GULF COAST	INTERIOR	NORTHERN	SOUTHEAST	SOUTHWEST	MATSU
1990	266,021	64,063	92,111	20,380	68,989	38,479
2000	319,605	73,799	97,417	23,789	73,082	39,239
2002*	334,311	75,399	99,003	23,851	71,972	39,310
2003	341,476	75,261	96,397	23,905	71,841	39,938

Source: Alaska Department of Labor and Workforce Development, Alaska Population Overview: 2001–2005 Estimates and Census 2000 (Juneau: ADLWD, February 2006).

*Provisional figures.

In 1985–86 Alaska had a total population of 550,700, an increase of 6,800 from the period 1984–85, an annual rate of growth of 1.24 percent. As the figures in tables 4 and 5 show, population statistics for the territory and state of Alaska have historically been characterized by periods of expansion and contraction, dictated by the economic climate of the time. The net result has been an overall increase. Before the gold rushes in the 1880s, Alaska's population was quite small. Early territorial censuses were incomplete. The gold rushes doubled the territory's population between 1890 and 1990. After the turn of the twentieth century, Alaska's population remained stable for the next forty years. The 1900 population stood at 63,592, but by 1939 only 59,278 persons remained. The territory's gold production had declined precipitously and thrown many out of work.

World War II saw the construction of bases and facilities throughout the territory, as well as the building of the Alaska Highway. As a result, the population grew dramatically, from 72,524 in 1940 to 128,643 in 1950. The war and military construction throughout the territory played a key role in the development of both Anchorage and Fairbanks. Although Alaska's military population as a share of the total has declined since World War II, the military continues to play a substantial role. In 1990, about 10 percent of the population was made up of military personnel and dependents; by 2002, they accounted for only 7 percent.

Alaska's population grew quickly from the end of World War II to 1952, with an average annual increase of 9.5 percent. The population grew at a slower, smoother pace from 1952 to 1965, with an average annual rate of change of 2.7 percent. Alaska had about 224,000 residents at statehood in 1959. From 1965 to 1973, the population growth rate gradually increased to 3 percent per year.

The construction of the eight-hundred-mile Trans-Alaska Pipeline dramatically affected population growth in the 1970s. Construction began in 1973 and peaked in 1975, with a migration gain of over 30,000 persons. The average annual rate of population change during this period came to 6.6 percent per year. A bust followed the pipeline boom, lasting from 1977 to 1980. Alaska lost about 6,400 residents between 1977 and 1978. The annual

average rate over the four-year period (1977–80), however, averaged a positive 0.6 percent per year.

Between mid-1980 and mid-1985 Alaska experienced its largest economic boom. Rapid growth came from construction and infrastructure development driven by a combination of state spending based on oil revenues, major federal expenditures, and private development. As a result, Alaska's population grew by 25 percent in five years, making it the fastest growing state in the nation. The most growth occurred in the 1981–83 period, during which the annual rate of growth averaged 6.8 percent per year. The growth pace began to slow during 1983–84, with a rate of change of 4.8 percent, declining further in 1984–85 to 3.6 percent.

In 1985–89 recession again gripped Alaska, as falling oil prices combined with declining crude oil production. In 1986–87, the population declined at a rate of 1.8 percent. The cumulative loss of residents to net outmigration in 1985–86 was about 45,900 persons, as compared to a net outmigration of 20,400 during the post-pipeline period. This population loss equaled about 8.3 percent of the state's peak 1986 population. Proportionately, this loss would be the equivalent of Washington state losing Spokane; or California, the San Diego metropolitan statistical area. By 1989, net outmigration slowed enough to allow the natural increase of births over deaths to produce the first increase in population since 1986. From July 1, 1980, to July 1, 1990, the average annual rate of population increase in Alaska was 2.8 percent. For the United States during the period the change averaged 0.9 percent per year.

Between 1990 and 2000, the state's population continued to increase. Population growth averaged 1.3 percent annually, ranging from a low of 0.2 percent in 1994–95 to a high of 3 percent in 1991–92. Since 1993, it has been natural population increase, more births than deaths, that has constituted the major growth element. Alaska still has one of the nation's highest rates of natural increase. (In the nation as a whole, birth rates are currently falling.) The number of military personnel and dependents declined substantially because of base closures and reorganizations during the mid-1990s. Alaska, therefore, experienced a protracted period of net military outmigration, offsetting any civilian inmigration during this period. During the late 1990s, excellent economic opportunities in the contiguous states, which traditionally provide most of Alaska's migrants, combined with the state's lack of growth in income and the continued high living costs dampened inmigration to Alaska to levels seen in the 1980s and 1990s. With the onset of the 1999 economic decline nationally, most movement nationwide declined. As opportunities in Alaska's feeder states declined, in-migration became positive for the first time in 2001–2002, which resulted in modest growth equaling about 50 percent of the state's rate of natural increase in that year.

Government spending and policy decisions also affect economic and population growth in the state. For example government remains Alaska's largest primary employer. In 2002 the military, federal, state, and local governments employed almost one-third of Alaska's total labor force. Reductions in federal agency spending, state operating revenues, and loss of revenue sharing to local communities have slowed Alaska's economy and population growth in the past. Since 1990 the service sector has been the largest positive factor in employment. Alaska no longer offers attractive salaries in almost every segment of the economy, relative to those in Washington, Oregon, and California. In short, Alaska, like most western states, will probably continue its boom-bust economic cycles for years to come.

Births and deaths are a significant component of population change, and Alaska's fertility rate has always been well above the national average. In 1990, Alaska had one of the higher levels of fertility among the states, with 2.6 children per family. Following a brief increase in the birth rate around 1990, birth rates have declined somewhat in Alaska and nationwide. In 2002, Alaska's fertility was about 2.2 children per family.

Most of the growth in Alaska's Native population has been due to natural increase. Birth rates among Native Americans, traditionally very high, have been declining. In 2001–02, the crude birth rate for Native Americans in Alaska was 21.4 per 1,000, and the crude death rate was 6 percent per 1,000, for a natural increase of 1.5 percent per year. In 1970, the average number of children for Native American families was 4.6, but that declined to a low of 2.7

in 1976. After that, it has risen again slowly. The average number of children in 1990 returned to a peak of 3.9 children per family. In 2002, the average Native American household in Alaska had again declined to about 2.9 children per family, a number approaching the 1976 low.

The number of white Alaskan families has been relatively stable since the mid-1970s. The crude white birth rate in 2001–2002 was 13.4 per 1,000, and the crude death rate was 4.4 per 1,000, for a natural increase of 0.9 percent. The size of the average white family has declined only slightly, to about 2.7 children per family by 2002. The low white fertility rate came during the economic recession of the late 1980s when white families averaged close to 2.0 children per family. It is once again approaching that low.

Alaska has one of the highest levels of migration to and from the state, and the highest level of gross migration of any state in the Union. Migration to and from Alaska depends partly on federal military and program policies. These result from unique historical events rather than easily predictable trends. The general economic conditions prevailing in the Pacific and Mountain regions relative to those in Alaska strongly influence migration to and from the state. When employment is relatively weak in Washington, Oregon, and California, then many look north for opportunities, and vice versa.

The vast majority of residents living in Alaska at the time of the 2000 Census were migrants to the state. Only 38.1 percent of residents were born in Alaska. Regionally, these proportions varied from a low of 25 percent born in the Aleutians West Census Area, which the highly transient city of Unalaska dominates, to a high of 94.1 percent for the Wade Hampton Census Area. Generally, over 75 percent of Alaska's rural residents were born in the state, compared to 32.1 percent for Anchorage, 29.5 percent for Fairbanks, and from 33 to 38 percent for the Matanuska-Susitna, Kenai, and Juneau areas. Among persons not born in Alaska, 23.2 percent were born in the West, 13.5 percent in the Midwest, 11.2 percent in the South, and 6.5 percent in the Northeast. Another 1.3 percent were born abroad to American parents, and 5.9 percent of Alaskans were foreign born. The proportion of foreign-born in 1990 was 4.5 percent. This increase reflects but is lower than the general U.S. trend. In 2000, some 11 percent of all persons in the U.S. were foreign born. Similarly, 2.7 percent of all Alaskans were not U.S. citizens, compared to 6.6 percent of residents in the U.S. as a whole.

In the late 1990s, the Federal Office of Management and Budget redefined the way citizens could identify themselves as multirace. In recent decades one could choose only one of four races, namely, white, black or African American, American Indian or Alaska Native, or Asian and Pacific Islander. In the 2000 Census, people could choose all of the races they thought defined them. As a result, race as reported in 2000 is no longer compatible with the earlier data, and statistics on race are far more complex. For this reason, determining the real number of Alaska Natives in 2000 has become difficult. But

in 2002 some 102,523 individuals, or 15.9 percent of Alaska's population, identified themselves as American Indian or Alaska Native alone.

Alaska's population is younger than the national average, but because of a recent slowdown in migration, the gap is narrowing. In 2001, the median age in the contiguous states was 35.6, while in Alaska it was 32.7 years. The percentage of Alaskans 65 years of age and older was 6 percent in 2002, a substantial increase over the 4 percent figure in 1990 and significantly higher than the 2.9 percent proportion in 1980. Still, Alaska has the smallest percentage of persons over 65, but it is following the national trend toward an increasingly larger share of older persons.

In 1999, Alaska had twenty cities large enough to be considered urban, with a population greater than or equal to 2,500 (see table 6).

TABLE 6

Alaskan Cities with More than 2,500 Residents, 1990, 1999, 2000–2002

	JULY 1, 2002 (Estimate)	JULY 1, 2001 (Estimate)	APRIL 1, 2000 (Census)	APRIL 1, 1990 (Estimate*)	CITY RANK, 2002	CITY RANK, 2000	CITY RANK, 1999
Anchorage, Municipality of	269,070	263,940	260,283	226,338	1	1	1
Juneau City and Borough	30,981	30,675	30,711	26,751	2	2	3
Fairbanks City	29,670	29,558	30,224	30,902	3	3	2
Sitka, City and Borough	8,894	8,836	8,835	8,588	4	4	4
Ketchikan City	7,845	7,565	7,951	8,263	5	5	5
Kenai City	7,166	6,925	6,942	6,340	6	6	6
Kodiak City	6,544	6,396	6,334	6,365	7	7	7
Wasilla City	6,343	5,614	5,469	4,049	8	9	10
Bethel Census Area	5,736	5,488	5,471	4,674	9	8	8
Valdez City	4,171	3,981	4,036	4,068	13	13	9

Source: Alaska Department of Labor and Workforce Development, Research and Analysis Section, *Alaska Population Overview: 2001–2002 Estimates and Census 2000* (Juneau: ADLWD, February 2004).

*1990 population estimate for population in 2000 boundaries.

Alaska is the largest state in the union and has the lowest population density. Larger than Texas, California, and Montana combined, it has an average population density of only 1.1 persons per square mile. (The average U.S. population density was 79.6 persons per square mile in 2000.) This portrait of population settlement in the state, however, is misleading. According to the Alaska Department of Natural Resources, the federal government owns 60 percent of Alaska's land, the state another 28 percent, and Native corporations 11 percent. Only about 1 percent of the state is in private ownership. Most of the federal and state lands are in parks and refuges or have development prohibitions or restrictions. Although Native-owned lands are potentially available for development, generally they are not for sale. Of the land potentially available for development, much is very rugged, inaccessible, or otherwise unsuitable. Taking this into account, a fairer picture of settlement densities on available, usable land in the state is likely to be closer to 100 persons per square mile. Contrary to widely held perceptions, Alaska's population is chiefly found in relatively dense settlements set in or near large tracts of unsettled land. In 2002, 74.5 percent of the state's population lived in places with populations of at least 2,500, only slightly below the national average.

The Municipality of Anchorage is the state's largest city and home to 41.8 percent of the overall population. Anchorage has 65.4 percent of the population living in places of 2,500 or more residents. The remaining 34.6 percent of this population live in localities ranging in size from 2,794 to 30,981 residents. Alaska's population in places of fewer than 2,500 made up 25.5 percent of the state's population. These individuals lived in some 291 small villages (18.2 percent) or outside any community (7.3 percent).

Slightly under three-fifths of Alaska's land area lies outside of any incorporated city or borough. In these places, called the Unorganized Borough, the state performs all governmental functions. The 2002 estimate was that 20,481 people, or 3.2 percent of the state's population, lived in the Unorganized Borough.

The demographic profile of Alaska reflects economic trends. As the state shifts away from a frontier economy, it will see more women in the population, more families forming, more middle-aged individuals (35–55) staying, and a general shift to the demographic profile of an older state.

Source: Alaska Department of Labor and Workforce Development, Research and Analysis Section, *Alaska Population Overview: 2001–2002 Estimates and Census 2000* (Juneau: ADLWD, February 2004).

TABLE 7

Alaska, Narrative Profile: 2005–2007 American Community Survey Three-Year Estimates, Data Profile Highlights

SOCIAL CHARACTERISTICS	ESTIMATE	PERCENT	U.S.
Average household size	2.80	(X)	2.60
Average family size	3.34	(X)	3.19
Population 25 years and over	418,136		
High school graduate or higher	(X)	90.2	84.0%
Bachelor's degree or higher	(X)	26.2	27.0%
Civilian veterans (civilian population 18 years and over)	74,267	15.5	10.4%
Disability status (population 5 years and over)	90,855	15.0	15.1%
Foreign born	45,498	6.7	12.5%
Male, Now married, except separated (population 15 years and over)	134,405	48.9	52.6%
Female, Now married, except separated (population 15 years and over)	131,653	52.0	48.5%
Speak a language other than English at home (population 5 years and over)	95,858	15.3	19.5%
Household population	654,219		

ECONOMIC CHARACTERISTICS	ESTIMATE	PERCENT	U.S.
In labor force (population 16 years and over)	368,891	71.4	64.7%
Mean travel time to work in minutes (workers 16 years and over)	18.0	(X)	25.1
Median household income (in 2007 inflation-adjusted dollars)	61,766	(X)	50,007
Median family income (in 2007 inflation-adjusted dollars)	72,008	(X)	60,374
Per capita income (in 2007 inflation-adjusted dollars)	27,988	(X)	26,178
Families below poverty level	(X)	7.6	9.8%
Individuals below poverty level	(X)	10.4	13.3%

HOUSING CHARACTERISTICS	ESTIMATE	PERCENT	U.S.
Total housing units	279,293		
Occupied housing units	233,861	83.7	88.4%
Owner-occupied housing units	149,008	63.7	67.3%
Renter-occupied housing units	84,853	36.3	32.7%
Vacant housing units	45,432	16.3	11.6%
Owner-occupied homes	149,008		
Median value (dollars)	213,400	(X)	181,800
Median of selected monthly owner costs			
With a mortgage (dollars)	1,654	(X)	1,427
Not mortgaged (dollars)	474	(X)	402

ACS DEMOGRAPHIC ESTIMATES	ESTIMATE	PERCENT	U.S.
Total population	676,778		
Male	351,442	51.9	49.2%
Female	325,336	48.1	50.8%
Median age (years)	33.4	(X)	36.4
Under 5 years	49,670	7.3	6.9%
18 years and over	493,869	73.0	75.3%
65 years and over	45,075	6.7	12.5%
One race	627,739	92.8	97.9%
White	463,815	68.5	74.1%
Black or African American	25,429	3.8	12.4%
American Indian and Alaska Native	90,702	13.4	0.8%
Asian	31,165	4.6	4.3%
Native Hawaiian and Other Pacific Islander	3,646	0.5	0.1%
Some other race	12,982	1.9	6.2%
Two or more races	49,039	7.2	2.1%
Hispanic or Latino (of any race)	37,280	5.5	14.7%

Source: Reprinted from U.S. Census Bureau, 2005–2007 American Community Survey, available at www.census.gov/acs/www/Products/ (accessed June 30, 2009).

Note: Although the American Community Survey (ACS) produces population, demographic and housing unit estimates, it is the Census Bureau's Population Estimates Program that produces and disseminates the official estimates of the population for the nation, states, counties, cities and towns and estimates of housing units for states and counties.

Appendix F

The Governors of Alaska

Governance of the Department of Alaska

Between 1868 and 1877, Alaska was under the jurisdiction of the War Department and administered by U.S. Army officers. The army withdrew in 1877, and the Treasury Department took over control of the territory. The highest ranking federal official in the territory from 1877 to 1879 was the collector of customs under the Treasury Department. The U.S. Navy was given jurisdiction over the Department of Alaska in 1879.

Table 8 includes the names of the individuals in charge during this time, their dates in office, and the branch of service in which they were serving.

TABLE 8

Governance of Alaska, 1867–1884

NAME	DATES IN OFFICE	BRANCH OF SERVICE
Brevet Major General Jefferson C. Davis	October 18, 1867 to August 31, 1870	Army
Brevet Lieutenant Colonel George K. Brady	September 1 to September 22, 1870	Army
Major John C. Tidball	September 23, 1870 to September 19, 1871	Army
Major Harvey A. Allen	September 20, 1871 to January 3, 1873	Army
Major Joseph Steward	January 4, 1873 to April 20, 1874	Army
Captain George B. Rodney	April 21 to August 16, 1874	Army
Captain Joseph B. Campbell	August 17, 1874 to June 14, 1876	Army
Captain John Mendenhall	June 15, 1876 to March 4, 1877	
Army Captain Arthur Morris	March 5 to June 14, 1877	Army
Montgomery P. Berry	June 14 to August 13, 1877	Customs
H. C. DeAhna	August 14, 1877 to March 26, 1878	Customs
Mottrom D. Ball	March 27, 1878 to June 13, 1879	Customs
Captain Lester A. Beardslee	June 14, 1879 to September 12, 1880	Navy
Lieutenant Commander Henry Glass	September 13, 1880 to August 9, 1881	Navy
Commander Edward P. Lull	August 10 to October 18, 1881	Navy
Commander Henry Glass	October 19, 1881 to March 12, 1882	Navy
Commander Frederick Pearson	March 13 to October 3, 1882	Navy
Commander Edgar C. Merriman	October 4, 1882 to September 13, 1883	Navy
Commander Joseph B. Coghlan	September 15, 1883 to September 13, 1884	Navy
Commander Albert G. Caldwell	September 14 to September 15, 1884	Navy
Commander Henry E. Nichols	September 14 to September 15, 1884	Navy

Governors of the District of Alaska

In 1884 the Department of Alaska was redesignated as the District of Alaska, an incorporated but unorganized territory with a civil government. The governors were appointed by the U.S. president:

John Henry Kinkead: July 4, 1884 to May 7, 1885
Alfred P. Swineford: May 7, 1885 to April 20, 1889
Lyman Enos Knapp: April 20, 1889 to June 18, 1893
James Sheakley: June 18, 1893 to June 23, 1897
John Green Brady: June 23, 1897 to March 2, 1906
Wilford Bacon Hoggatt: March 2, 1906 to
    May 20, 1909
Walter Eli Clark: May 20, 1909 to Aug. 24, 1912

Governors of the Territory of Alaska

The District Alaska was organized into Alaska Territory in 1912.

Walter Eli Clark: August 24, 1912 to April 18, 1913
John Franklin Alexander Strong: April 18, 1913 to
    April 12, 1918
Thomas Christmas Riggs, Jr.: April 12, 1918 to
    June 16, 1921
Scott Cordelle Bone: June 16, 1921 to
    August 16, 1925
George Alexander Parks: August 16, 1925 to
    April 19, 1933
John Weir Troy: April 19, 1933 to December 6, 1939
Ernest Gruening: December 6, 1939 to
    April 10, 1953
Benjamin Franklin Heintzleman: April 10, 1953 to
    January 3, 1957
Waino Edward Hendrickson: 1957 (acting
    governor)
Michael Anthony Stepovich: April 8, 1957 to
    August 9, 1957
Waino Edward Hendrickson: 1958–1959
    (acting governor)

Governors of Alaska

The Statehood Act was signed into law on July 7, 1958, and on January 2, 1959, Alaska officially entered the Union as its forty-ninth state. These are its governors:

William A. Egan: January 3, 1959 to
    December 5, 1966
Walter J. Hickel: December 5, 1966 to
    January 29, 1969
Keith Miller: January 29, 1969 to
    December 7, 1970
William A. Egan: December 7, 1970 to
    December 2, 1974
Jay S. Hammond: December 2, 1974 to
    December 6, 1982
Bill Sheffield: December 6, 1982 to
    December 1, 1986
Steve Cowper: December 1, 1986 to
    December 3, 1990
Walter J. Hickel: December 3, 1990 to
    December 5, 1994
Tony Knowles: December 5, 1994 to
    December 2, 2002
Frank Murkowski: December 2, 2002 to
    December 4, 2006
Sarah Palin: December 4, 2006 until her resignation,
    which took effect on July 26, 2009.
Sean Parnell: July 26, 2009, to present.

Appendix G

Native Regional Corporations, 2006

CORPORATION NAME/LOCATION	SHAREHOLDERS AND REVENUE	BUSINESS ACTIVITIES AND SUBSIDIARIES	2005 REVENUE SOURCES
Ahtna Inc. Glennallen, Alaska	Shareholders: 1,200 Land conveyed: 1,556,670 acres 2004 revenue: $83,809,270 2005 revenue: $95,313,783	**Service, construction, and 8(a)[a]** Ahtna Construction & Primary Products Corp.; Ahtna Enterprises Corp. **Service contracts:** Ahtna Development Corp.; Ahtna Government Services Corp. **Service contracts and 8(a)[a]:** Ahtna Technical Services, Inc.	Service contracts: $67,309,000 Trust and agency fees: $2,627,000 Rental properties: $3,321,000 Fuel sale: $20,913,000 Section 7(i): $1,211,000 Permanent Fund earnings: $137,000 Investment income: $117,000 Gravel sales: $185,000 Water utility: 38,000 Other: $188,000 Total: 95,313,783
The Aleut Corp. Anchorage, Alaska	Shareholders: 3,249 Land conveyed: 1,638,000 acres 2004 revenue: $64,173,000 2005 revenue: $96,046,000	**Base operations-defense contractor:** Aleut Management Services LLC; Fuel Operations at Adak and Cold Bay, Port Operations, Airport Services and Commercial Fisheries: Aleut Enterprise Corp. LLC, Anchorage **Water utility:** Midtown Estates Water Utility LLC **Property rental:** Aleut Real Estate LLC **Interest entities:** Alaska Trust	Operations and maintenance contracts: $67,309,000 Trust and agency fees: 2,627,000 Rental properties: 3,321,000 Fuel sale: 20,913,000 Section 7(i): 1,211,000 Permanent Fund earnings: 137,000 Investment income: 117,000 Gravel sales: 185,000 Water utility: 35,000 Other: 188,000 Total: 96,046,000

CORPORATION NAME/LOCATION	SHAREHOLDERS AND REVENUE	BUSINESS ACTIVITIES AND SUBSIDIARIES	2005 REVENUE SOURCES
Arctic Slope Regional Corp.	Shareholders: 9,000 Land conveyed: 5,000,000 acres 2004 revenue: $1,329,9000,000 2005 revenue: $1,587,222,000	**Government contract holding company:** ASRC Federal Holding. LLC **Technical Services:** ASRC Aerospace Corp.; ASRC Communications Ltd.; ASRC Airfield and Range Services, Inc.; ASRC Management Services, Inc.; Field Support Services, Inc.; Arctic Slope World Services, Inc. **Petroleum, refining and marketing:** Petro Star, Inc. **Energy services:** ASRC Energy Services, Inc. (AES) **Energy services operations and maintenance:** AES-Operations and Maintenance, Inc. **Construction:** AES-Pipeline, Power and Communications. Inc.; Omega Natchiq, Inc.; ASRC Constructors, Inc.; Arctic Slope Compliance Technologies, Inc.; ASRC Construction Holding Co.; ASRC Civil Construction LLC, (ACCL) **Petroleum engineering:** Tri Ocean Engineering, Inc. **Retail services:** Eskimos, Inc. **Accommodation services:** Tundra Tours, Inc. **Permitting:** AES-LYNX, Inc. **Management services:** ASRC Service Center, Inc. **Finance:** Alaska Growth Capital (BIDCO) **Other:** ASRC Wireless Services, Inc.	Contracting – Sales and Service: 1,566,487,000 Natural resource revenue: $20,735,000 Total: $1,587,222,000

CORPORATION NAME/LOCATION	SHAREHOLDERS AND REVENUE	BUSINESS ACTIVITIES AND SUBSIDIARIES	2005 REVENUE SOURCES
Bering Straits Native Corp. Nome, Alaska	Shareholders: 6,334 Land conveyed: 2,300,000 acres 2004 revenue: $16,491,000 2005 revenue: $21,692,769	**Real estate development:** Bering Straits Development Co. **Auto and equipment rentals:** Stampede Ventures, Inc. **Quarry service:** Cape Nome Products JV **Construction and environmental services:** Inuit Services, Inc. **Electrical contracting:** Eagle Electric LLC; Eagle Eye Electric LLC-Nevada **8(a) facilities support services**[a]**:** Bering Straits AKI LLC; Bering Straits Aerospace LLC **Mining and services:** Golden Glacier, Inc. **IT support:** Bering Straits Information Technology LLC	Investment income: 225,519 Gain on investment securities: 202,645 Resource revenue/ other corporations: $2,360,052 Natural resources: $1,064,554 Rentals: 3,699,527 Contract revenue: 14,038,837 Other: 101,635 Total: 21,692,769
Bristol Bay Native Corp. Anchorage, Alaska	Shareholders: 7,900 Land conveyed: 3,052,000 acres 2004 revenue: $259,842,000 2005 revenue: $321,065,000	**Design services:** BBKP; Village Corporation Gifting and Estate Services; Bristol Bay Corporate Services **Environmental remediation design services:** Bristol Environmental and Engineering Services Corp. **Oilfield services and construction management:** CCI, Inc. **Corrosion inspection services:** Kakivik Asset Management **Card-lock fueling system:** PetroCard Systems **Environmental services, engineering and technical services:** SpecPro, Inc. **IT and engineering support services:** Vista International Operations	Petroleum sales operations: 223,389,000 Investment earnings: 9,888,000 Contract services: 83,486,000 Natural resources: 2,593,000 Other: 1,709,000 Total: 321,065,000

CORPORATION NAME/LOCATION	SHAREHOLDERS AND REVENUE	BUSINESS ACTIVITIES AND SUBSIDIARIES	2005 REVENUE SOURCES
Calista Corp. Anchorage, Alaska	Shareholders: 13,000 Land conveyed: 6,500,000 acres 2004 revenue: $48,514,073 2005 revenue: $56,865,445	**Printing and title companies:** Holding company for Calista's partial ownership in Alaska: Alaska Newspapers, Inc., Camai Printing (f. 1998) is a full-service print shop offering Web press and full-sheet press services. Solstice Advertising is a full-service advertising agency (est. 1997 and acquired by ANI in 2005) specializing in corporate identity development/logo and media design. Via Llikista, Calista owns 40 percent of Pacific Northwest Title Co. of Alaska; Fairbanks Title Agency; Title Agency of Juneau; and Southcentral Title Agency of Kenai/Soldotna. JV with Nordic Well Servicing-Work Over, Completion and Coil-Tubing Services on North Slope, Prudhoe and Kuparuk; OOkichista Drilling Services **8(a) company-wide range of professional and technical services to government agencies:** Yulista Management Services, Inc. **Camp leasing/management/services/cooking/housekeeping/janitorial/expediting:** Mayflower Catering **8(a) company non-ANSCA commercial property management and construction**[a]**:** Tunista, Inc.	Contracting and professional services: 35,319,658 Construction services: $43,836 Rental and property management: 1,964,274 Printing and newspapers: 4,473,589 Camp services and catering: 4,689,695 Regional resources: 1,335,917 Other region resources: $5,287,502 Equity in earning of ventures: 2,479,886 Investment security portfolio: 1,251,090 Total: $56,865,445

CORPORATION NAME/LOCATION	SHAREHOLDERS AND REVENUE	BUSINESS ACTIVITIES AND SUBSIDIARIES	2005 REVENUE SOURCES
Chugach Alaska Corporation Anchorage, Alaska	Shareholders: 1,991 Land conveyed: 797,983 acres 2004 revenue: $700,040,030 2005 revenue: $785,450,665	**Facilities maintenance, temporary employment services, oil spill response service:** Chugach Development Corp. **Facilities maintenance and general construction:** Chugach Industries, Inc. **General construction, education services and environmental services:** Chugach McKinley, Inc. **Base operating services/ civil engineering:** Chugach Management Services, Inc. **Base operating services and construction management:** Chugach Support Services **Telecommunications:** Chugach Telecommunications and Computers, Inc. **Information technology:** Chugach Systems Integration	Contract revenues: 783,824,835 Resources sales: 90,381 Section (7i) income: 1,534,118 Tourism revenue: 1,331 Total: 785,450,665
Cook Inlet Region, Inc. Anchorage, Alaska	Shareholders: 7,292 Land conveyed: 605,399 acres of surfaces estate; 1,344,427 acres of subsurface estate 2004 revenue: $77,868,000 2005 revenue: $97,500,000	**Construction services:** Peak Oilfield Service Co.; Alaska Interstate Construction LLC **Investments:** Hyatt Regency at Lake Las Vegas Resort, NV; Ritz-Carlton Resort at Lake Las Vegas, NV; The Westin Kierland Resort, AZ **Telecommunications:** Cook Inlet VoiceStream PCS **Tourism:** CIRI Alaska Tourism; Anchorage RV Park; Kenai Fjords Tours; Prince William Sound Cruises and Tours; Seward Windsong Lodge; Talkeetna Alaskan Lodge	Real estate: 12,693,000 Construction services: 6,762,000 Telecommunications: 7,402,000 Tourism: 36,833,000 Natural resources: 6,349,000 Other managed funds: 27,461,000 Total: 97,500,000

CORPORATION NAME/LOCATION	SHAREHOLDERS AND REVENUE	BUSINESS ACTIVITIES AND SUBSIDIARIES	2005 REVENUE SOURCES
Doyon Limited Fairbanks, Alaska	Shareholders: 14,000 Land conveyed: 9,831,818 acres 2004 revenue: $161,400,000 2005 revenue: $172,034,962	**Government contracting:** Doyon Development Corp.; dba Doyon Government Services **Oil and gas drilling:** Doyon Drilling, Inc. **Tourism:** Doyon Tourism, Inc.; The River Cabins Inc.; dba Denali River Cabins; Kantisha Roadhouse, Inc. Doyon Aramark; Denali National Park Concession JV **Real estate:** Doyon Properties, Inc. **Telecommunications:** Doyon Communications. Inc. **Catering and security services:** Doyon Universal Services LLC **Security services:** Doyon Security Services Corp. LLC **Logistics, base operations and maintenance:** Doyon Logistics LLC **Construction and project management:** Doyon Project Services LLC **Engineering services:** Doyon Environmental and Engineering LLC **Aerospace parts manufacturer:** Angeles Composite Technologies, Inc.	Oil and gas drilling: 59,164,636 Natural resources: 539,841 Real estate: 2,811,110 Tourism: 20,607,315 Investment income: 13,156,211 Revenue from other regions: 3,376,662 Catering and security: 54,707,580 Construction and other govt. contracting: 17,671,607 Total: $172,034,962

CORPORATION NAME/LOCATION	SHAREHOLDERS AND REVENUE	BUSINESS ACTIVITIES AND SUBSIDIARIES	2005 REVENUE SOURCES
Koniag, Inc. Anchorage, Alaska	Shareholders: 3,555 Land conveyed: 935,351 acres 2004 revenue: $147,553,587 2005 revenue: $147,897,000	**Aircraft composite parts:** Angeles Composite Technologies, Inc. **Fluid reprocessing and environmental services/ government contracting:** Clarus Technologies LLC **Telecom and Security, Government Contracting:** Frontier Systems Integrators LLC **Diesel engine/fuel research, IT, aerospace services, infrastructure support and development:** Integrated Concepts and Research Corp. **Land and natural resource management and sport hunting and fishing:** Karluk Wilderness Adventures **Holding company:** Koniag Development Corp. **Information sciences, government contracting:** Professional Computing Resources, Inc. **Government contracting, consulting:** Washington Management Group/FSI **Logistical services:** XMCO, Inc. **Commercial real estate:** Nunat Holding LLC	No information on record except for total revenue. Total: 147,897,000

CORPORATION NAME/LOCATION	SHAREHOLDERS AND REVENUE	BUSINESS ACTIVITIES AND SUBSIDIARIES	2005 REVENUE SOURCES
NANA Regional Corporation, Inc. Kotzebue, Alaska	Shareholders: 11,100 Land conveyed: 3,085,532 acres 2004 revenue: $331,000,000 2005 revenue: $526,900,000	**Professional and management services:** NANA Management Services LLC; NANA Colt Engineering LLC; DOWL Engineers LLC; Worksafe; Inc.; ASCG, Inc. **Contracted government services:** Akima Management Services, Inc. (Akima); TKC Management Services LLC (TKC); Ki LLC (Ki); NANA Services LLC; NANA Pacific LLC **Oilfield and mining support:** NANA Oilfield Service, Inc. (NOSI); NANA Lynden Logistics LLC; NANA Major Drilling LLC **Hospitality and tourism:** Courtyard by Marriott; Springhill Suites by Marriott-Anchorage; Springhill Suites by Marriott-Fairbanks; Residence Inn by Marriott; Nullagvik Hotel; Arctic Caribou, Inn	Business operations: 514,654,000 Investment income: 2,892,000 Natural resources: 9,354,000 Total: $526,900,000

CORPORATION NAME/LOCATION	SHAREHOLDERS AND REVENUE	BUSINESS ACTIVITIES AND SUBSIDIARIES	2005 REVENUE SOURCES
Sealaska Corporation Juneau, Alaska	Shareholders: 17,300 Land conveyed: 289,800 acres of surface estate; 600,000 acres of subsurface estate 2004 revenue: $151,799,000 2005 revenue: $144,300,000	**Timber development and marketing:** Sealaska Timber Corp. **Forest management and silviculture:** Natural Resources Department **Managed investment portfolio:** Finance Department **Minority/diversity/8(a) initiatives[a]:** Office of Diversity Solutions **Rock, sand, and gravel:** Alaska Coastal Aggregates **Injection molding, plastic and manufacturing:** Nypro Kánaak GDL; Nypro Kánaak Iowa **Life sciences/plasma products:** International BioResources **Prototyping/new product development/manufacturing:** Synergy Systems, Inc. **Injection molding, plastics and manufacturing:** Nypro Kánaak Alabama **Environmental consulting and remediation:** Sealaska Environmental Services **Cultural programs/scholarship management:** Sealaska Heritage Institute	Natural resources: 64,483 Manufacturing: 49,891 Investments: 24,342 Corporate and other income: 5,605 Total: $144,300,000

CORPORATION NAME/LOCATION	SHAREHOLDERS AND REVENUE	BUSINESS ACTIVITIES AND SUBSIDIARIES	2005 REVENUE SOURCES
The 13th Regional Corporation Tukwila, Washington	Shareholders: 6,188 Land conveyed: 0[b] 2004 revenue: $30,809,762 2005 revenue: $9,125,800	**Government contracting:** NW Business Service Group LLC **Land development:** Cold Bay Land Development, Inc. **Construction/government contracts:** M. Kennedy Co., Inc.; North Star Industrial Contractors LLC **Government contracting-electrical:** Alindeska Electrical Contractors LLC **Scholarships:** The 13th Regional Heritage Foundation (Nonprofit)	Construction: 3,500,199 Electrical: 5,468,369 Net investment: 157,232 Total: $9,125,800

Source: *Alaska Business Monthly*, September 2006, 72–79.

a. The Small Business Act contains the 8(a) program, created to help small / disadvantaged business compete in the marketplace and to assist them in gaining access to federal and private procurement markets. To be admitted to the program, a company must meet the eligibility criteria set out in 13 CFR part 124, including (1) the size criteria to be a small business as established in SBA regulations and (2) the requirement of majority ownership by economically and socially disadvantaged individuals.

b. Congress never granted any land to the 13th Regional Corporation. It did get about $54 million out of the total $962.5 million distributed to Native corporations after the 1971 passage of ANCSA. By 2009, the 13th Corporation had all but closed down. See "Native 13th Regional Corp. Future Murky at Best," November 1, 2008, Anchorage Daily News Web site, available at www.adn.com/money/industries/native_corporations/story/575677.html (accessed June 30, 2009).

Notes

Introduction

1. Tom Kippel, *Lost World: Rewriting Prehistory—How Science Is Tracing Ice Age Mariners* (New York: Atria Books, 2003), 39–40; *National Post*, October 28, 2000.

2. *Fairbanks Daily News-Miner,* March 20, 2009.

3. Curtis J. Freeman, "'Humdinger' of a Year: 2006 Great Year for Mining Industry," *Alaska Business Monthly*, November 2006, 75.

4. Ben Grenn, comp., "2007 Forecast for Alaska's Key Industries," *Alaska Business Monthly*, January 2007, 25–26.

5. Ibid., 26.

6. The total comes to 101 percent because of rounding.

7. *Alaska Visitor Statistics Program V, Interim Visitor Volume Report,* Summer 2008 (Juneau: McDowell Group, 2008), 1, available at www.dced.state.ak.us/oed/toubus/research.htm (accessed May 1, 2009).

8. Quoted in Walter R. Borneman, *Alaska: Saga of a Bold Land* (New York: Harper Collins, 2003), 471.

9. Committee on Cumulative Environmental Effects of Oil and Gas Activities on Alaska's North Slope, Board on Environmental Studies and Toxicology, Polar Research Board, Division on Earth and Life Studies, National Research Council of the National Academies, Cumulative Environmental Effects of Oil and Gas Activities on Alaska's North Slope (Washington, D.C.: The National Academies Press, 2001).

Chapter 1. Alaska's Prehistory: The Land and the First Americans Debate

1. Alfred H. Brooks, *The Geography and Geology of Alaska,* U.S. Geological Survey Professional Paper no. 45 (Washington, D.C.: Government Printing Office, 1906), 11.

2. Based on information supplied by David Stone of the Geophysical Institute of the University of Alaska; and on Clyde Wahrhaftig, *Physiographic Divisions of U.S. Geological Survey* Professional Paper no. 482 (Washington, D.C.: Government Printing Office, 1965).

3. J. E. Ransom, "Derivation of the Word Alaska," *American Anthropologist*, July 1940, 550–51.

4. Map no. 55, by Ivan Lvov (about 1710), in A.V. Yefinov, ed., *Atlas of Geographical Discoveries in Siberia and North-Western America,* IVII–XVIII (Moscow: Nauka, 1964).

5. Vladimir Jochelson, "People of the Foggy Seas," *Natural History 4* (1928): 413.

6. Ibid.

7. A. L. Seeman, "Regions and Resources of Alaska," *Economic Geography,* October 1937, 334; "The Aleutians," *Alaska Geographic 7,* no. 3 (1980): 30.

8. The discussion of Alaska's geography and climate is based on U.S. Department of the Interior Bureau of Reclamation, *Alaska: Reconnaissance Report on the Potential Development of Water Resources in the Territory of Alaska,* H. Doc 197, 82nd Cong., 1st sess. (Washington, D.C.: Government Printing Office, 1950); and National Resources Committee, *Alaska: Its Resources and Development* (Washington, D.C.: Government Printing Office, 1938). For those interested in further reading, the following publications are very helpful: Resource Planning Team, Joint Federal-State Land Use Planning Commission for Alaska, *Resources of Alaska Regional Summary,* rev. ed. (Anchorage: Joint Federal-State Land Use Planning Commission for Alaska, 1975); and Lidia L. Selkregg, *Alaska Regional Profiles,* sponsored by State of Alaska, Office of the Governor, in cooperation with Joint Federal-State Land Use Planning Commission for Alaska, 6 vols. (Fairbanks: Arctic Environmental Information and Date Center, University of Alaska, 1974–ca 1980). The volumes deal exhaustively with Alaska's six geographical regions.

9. Elaine Dewar, *Bones: Discovering the First Americans* (Toronto: Random House Canada, 2001), 50.

10. Ibid., 152–84.

11. Tom Kippel, *Lost World: Rewriting Prehistory—How Science Is Tracing America's Ice Age Mariners* (New York: Atria Books, 2003), 39–40.

12. *National Post,* October 28, 2000.

13. Dewar, Bones; E. James Dixon, Bones, Boats, and Bison: Archeology and the First Colonization of Western North America (Albuquerque: University of New Mexico Press, 1999); James C. Chatters, Ancient Encounters: Kennewick Man and the First Americans (New York: Simon & Schuster, 2001).

Chapter 2. Alaska's Ancestral Native Peoples

1. Vladimir Jochelson, "People of the Foggy Seas," *Natural History 4* (1928), 413.
2. In Greenland and Canada, the term "Eskimo" has been supplanted by "Inuit," and many assume that the same is true in Alaska. However, "Eskimo" continues to be used in the 49th State because it includes both Yupik and Iñupiat, whereas "Inuit" does not. See the website of the Alaska Native Language Center at the University of Alaska Fairbanks, at www.uaf.edu/anlc (accessed April 20, 2009).
3. Philip Drucker, *Indians of the Northwest Coast* (Garden City, N.Y.: Natural History Press, 1963), 1–176.
4. Wendell H. Oswalt, *This Land Was Theirs: A Study of the North American Indian* (New York: John Wiley and Sons, 1967), 312–13.
5. James VanStone, *Athapaskan Adaptations: Hunters and Fishermen of the Subarctic Forests* (Chicago: Aldine Publishing Co., 1974), 1–89; Professor Jean Aigner, University of Alaska Fairbanks, personal communication; Marie-Francoise Guedon, *People of Tetlin, Why Are You Singing?* (Ottawa: National Museum of Man, National Museum of Canada, 1974), 204–208.
6. VanStone, *Athapaskan Adaptations,* 1–89.
7. Guedon, *People of Tetlin,* 205–217.
8. Ibid.
9. VanStone, *Athapaskan Adaptations,* 54–58.
10. Ibid., 56–64.
11. Ibid., 67–69.
12. Margaret Lantis, "The Aleut Social System, 1750–1810, from Early Historical Sources," in *Ethnohistory in Southwestern Alaska and the Southern Yukon: Method and Content, ed. Margaret Lantis* (Lexington: University of Kentucky Press, 1970), 179.
13. Svetlana G. Fedorova, *The Russian Population in Alaska and California: Late 18th Century–1867* (Kingston, Ontario: Limestone Press, 1973), 160–65, 2-3–204, 165–66.

14. Raisa V. Makarova, *Russians on the Pacific, 1743–1799,* trans. and ed. Richard A. Pierce and Alton S. Donnelly (Kingston, Ontario: Limestone Press, 1975), 78–82.
15. Ibid.
16. Jane Aigner, University of Alaska Fairbanks, personal communication.
17. Lantis, "The Aleut Social System," 292–95; see also Don E. Dumond, *The Eskimos and Aleuts* (London: Thames and Hudson, 1977), 55–56.
18. Lucien M. Turner, *An Aleutian Ethnography,* ed. Raymond L. Hudson (Fairbanks: University of Alaska Press, 2008), 103–160.
19. Ibid.
20. Lantis, "The Aleut Social System," 292–95.
21. Hans-Georg Bandi, *Eskimo Prehistory,* trans. Ann E. Keep (College: University of Alaska Press, 1969), 7–8.
22. Michael E. Krauss, professor of linguistics and director, Alaska Native Language Center, University of Alaska Fairbanks, personal communication; and Jane Aigner, University of Alaska Fairbanks, personal communication.
23. Bandi, *Eskimo Prehistory,* 8.
24. Ibid., 9–11.
25. Michael E. Krauss, personal communication. Steve J. Langdon, *The Native People of Alaska* (Anchorage, Alaska: Greatland Graphics, 1993), 26–53.
26. William C. Sturtevant, gen. ed., *Handbook of North American Indians,* vol. 5, *Arctic,* ed. David Damas (Washington, D.C.: Smithsonian Institution, 1984), 14–16.
27. Wendell H. Oswalt, *Bashful No Longer* (Norman: University of Oklahoma Press, 1990), 12–39.
28. Wendell H. Oswalt, *Eskimos and Explorers* (Novato, Calif.: Chandler and Sharp, 1979), 213–16.
29. Langdon, *The Native People of Alaska,* 26–53.
30. Jane Aigner, University of Alaska Fairbanks, personal communication.

Chapter 3. Russian Expansion into Siberia and Exploration of North America

1. Richard A. Pierce, *Russian America: A Biographical Dictionary* (Kingston, Ontario: The Lime-Stone Press, 1990), 120–21.
2. Robert K. Massie, *Peter the Great: His Life and World* (New York: Alfred A. Knopf, 1980).
3. Pierce, *Russian America*, 31–32.
4. Ibid., 32.
5. Ibid., 34.

6. See Raymond H. Fisher, *Bering's Voyages: Whither and Why* (Seattle: University of Washington Press, 1977); Orcutt Frost, *Bering: The Russian Discovery of America* (New Haven: Yale University Press, 2003), 340. For example, historian Orcutt Frost, author of a recent biography of Bering, writes that Bering's mission was to map the way from Tobolsk to Kamchatka and from there to the Bering Sea. Sighting islands or the American continent was incidental to the mission. In short, Bering was to use some existing map in order to create a new and better one. See Frost, *Bering,* 40.

7. Frost, *Bering,* 34–35.

8. Ibid., 40–41.

9. Ibid., 43–45.

10. Ibid., 46–47.

11. Ibid., 49–50.

12. Ibid., 52.

13. Ibid., 53–54.

14. Ibid., 55–57.

15. Ibid., 58.

16. Ibid., 59–61.

17. Ibid., 62–63.

Chapter 4. The Second Kamchatka Expedition

1. There still is no agreement on a commonly recognized name for this expedition, as it did not have an official name. The name most commonly found in documents is the Kamchatka Expedition or the Second Kamchatka Expedition. The name "Kamchatka," however, excluded hinterland Siberia and the Arctic Ocean, where the expedition's several voyages and activities occurred, thus giving rise to other names. Thus the expedition is sometimes called the Siberian and Kamchatka Expedition. Alexander P. Sokolov, who wrote the first detailed narrative of the expedition, called it the Northern Expedition. It was also called the Siberian–Pacific Ocean Expedition and even the Great Northern, Second Kamchatka Expedition of Bering or the American Expedition. The most commonly used term is the Second Kamchatka Expedition. See Raymond H. Fisher, *Bering's Voyages: Whither and Why* (Seattle: University of Washington Press, 1977), 108–109.

2. Ibid., 109–10.

3. Orcutt Frost, *Bering: The Russian Discovery of America* (New Haven: Yale University Press, 2003), 65.

4. Fisher, *Bering's Voyages* 110–11.

5. Frost, *Bering,* 63.

6. Ibid., 65–70.

7. Bering left his two older sons, aged ten and twelve years of age, in the care of a gymnasium professor and his wife in Revala, Estonia, where he had been stationed for a short time during the Great Northern War.

8. Frost, *Bering,* 74.

9. Ibid., 85–86.

10. Ibid., 87.

11. Ibid., 87–89.

12. Ibid., 90.

13. Ibid., 91.

14. Georg Wilhem Steller, *Journal of a Voyage with Bering, 1741–1742,* ed. O. W. Frost, trans. Margritt A. Engel and O. W. Frost (Stanford, Calif.: Stanford University Press, 1988), 48–49.

15. Richard A. Pierce, *Russian America: A Biographical Dictionary* (Kingston, Ontario: The Lime-Stone Press, 1990), 117.

16. Steller, *Journal of a Voyage,* 54–61.

17. Frost, *Bering,* 134.

18. Ibid., 138–40.

19. Ibid., 140–43.

20. Ibid., 144.

21. Ibid., 202–204.

22. Donald J. Orth, *Dictionary of Alaska Place Names,* Geological Survey Professional Paper 567 (Washington, D.C.: U.S. Government Printing Office, 1967), 825.

23. Steller, *Journal of a Voyage,* 61.

24. Ibid., 64.

25. Ibid., 65.

26. Frost, *Bering,* 160.

27. Ibid., 166–71.

28. Ibid., 171–81.

29. Ibid., 182–87.

30. Ibid., 187–88.

31. Ibid., 189–96.

32. Steller, *Journal of a Voyage,* 109.

33. Ibid., 111–13.

34. Ibid., 119, 122.

35. Ibid., 132.

36. Frost, *Bering,* 233–36.

37. Ibid., 236, 219.

38. Steller, *Journal of a Voyage,* 138, 141; Frost, *Bering,* 238.

39. Frost, *Bering,* 241.

40. Steller, *Journal of a Voyage,* 142–43.

41. Ibid., 144–45.

42. Ibid., 154, 165–67.
43. Ibid., 169.
44. Frost, *Bering,* 268.
45. Ibid., 273–74.
46. Ibid., 275–79.

Chapter 5. The Early Russian Fur Trade

1. Orcutt Frost, *Bering: The Russian Discovery of America* (New Haven: Yale University Press, 2003), 65.
2. Lydia T. Black, *Russians in America, 1732–1867* (Fairbanks: University of Alaska Press, 2004), 59.
3. Black, *Russians in Alaska,* 59–61; Vasilii Nikolaevich Berkh, *A Chronological History of the Discovery of the Aleutian Islands, or the Exploits of Russian Merchants,* trans. Dmitri Krenov, ed. Richard A. Pierce (Kingston, Ontario: Limestone Press, 1974), 1–2.
4. Raisa V. Makarova, *Russians on the Pacific, 1743–1799,* trans. and ed. Richard A. Pierce and Alton S. Donnelly (Kingston, Ontario: Limestone Press, 1975), 98–101.
5. Ibid., 102–104.
6. Ibid., 98.
7. Ibid., 105.
8. Ibid., 107.
9. Ibid.
10. Ibid., 107–108.
11. Ibid., 108–10.
12. Ibid., 110–17.
13. Ibid., 111–12.
14. Ibid., 113–14.
15. Ibid., 115.
16. Richard A. Pierce, *Russian America: A Biographical Dictionary* (Kingston, Ontario: The Lime-Stone Press, 1990), 412–13.
17. Ibid., 172–73.
18. Ibid., 454–55.
19. Ibid., 456.
20. Ibid., 456–57.
21. Makarova, *Russians on the Pacific, 1743–1799,* 125–26.
22. Ibid., 126–28.
23. Svetlana G. Fedorova, *The Russian Population in Alaska and California: Late 18th Century–1867* (Kingston, Ontario: Limestone Press, 1973), 115–16.
24. Walter A. McDougall, *Let the Sea Make a Noise. . .: A History of the North Pacific from Magellan to MacArthur* (New York: Basic Books, 1993), 83.
25. Ibid., 83–84.
26. Ibid., 83–84.
27. J. Arthur Lower, *Ocean of Destiny: A Concise History of the North Pacific, 1500–1978* (Vancouver: University of British Columbia Press, 1978), 26, 28–29.
28. Fedorova, *The Russian Population in Alaska,* 116–18.
29. Makarova, *Russians on the Pacific, 1743–1799,* 129–31.
30. Ibid., 131–32, quote on 131.
31. Black, *Russians in Alaska,* 109–10.
32. Ibid., 111, 114.

Chapter 6. The Age of Alexander A. Baranov, 1790–1818

1. Lydia T. Black, *Russians in America, 1732–1867* (Fairbanks: University of Alaska Press, 2004), 121.
2. Ibid., 121–22.
3. Ibid., 123–25.
4. Richard A. Pierce, *Russian America: A Biographical Dictionary* (Kingston, Ontario: The Lime-Stone Press, 1990), 21.
5. Ibid.
6. Ibid.
7. Ibid., 127.
8. Black, *Russians in Alaska,* 126.
9. Ibid.
10. Ibid., 128.
11. Ibid., 129.
12. Pierce, *Russian-America: A Biographical Dictionary,* 22.
13. Ibid., 419.
14. Ibid., 458–60.
15. Andrei Val'Terovich Grinev, *The Tlingit Indians in Russian America, 1741–1867* (Lincoln: University of Nebraska Press, 2005), 107.
16. Ibid., 108–109.
17. Ibid., 109.
18. Ibid., 109–10.
19. Ibid., 110.
20. Grinev, *The Tlingit Indians in Russian America,* 111.
21. Svetlana G. Fedorova, *The Russian Population in Alaska and California: Late 18th Century–1867* (Kingston, Ontario: Limestone Press, 1973), 133–34.
22. K. T. Khlebnikov, *Baranov: Chief Manager of the Russian Colonies in America* (Kingston, Ontario: Limestone Press, 1973), 40–41.
23. Pierce, *Russian America: A Biographical Dictionary,* 393–419.

24. Black, *Russians in Alaska,* 161.

25. Fedorova, *The Russian Population in Alaska,* 134.

26. Pierce, *Russian America: A Biographical Dictionary,* 418–19; A. I. Alekseev, *The Destiny of Russian America, 1741–1867* (Kingston, Ontario: Limestone Press, 1990), 128–29.

27. Pierce, *Russian America: A Biographical Dictionary,* 419.

28. P. A. Tikhmenev, *A History of the Russian-American Company,* trans. and ed. Richard A. Pierce and Alton S. Donnelly (Seattle: University of Washington Press, 1978), 91–93.

29. Ibid., 92–94.

30. Ibid., 94.

31. Ibid., 98–99.

32. Richard A. Pierce, ed., *The Romance of Nikolai Rezanov and Concepcion Argüello: A Literary Legend and Its Effect on California History,* by Eve Iverson, and *The Concha Argüello Story: Memory Visits with Old Vinnie,* by Father Maurice M. O'Moore, O.P. (Kingston, Ontario: Limestone Press, 1998), 3.

33. Ibid., 3–4.

34. Ibid., 4.

35. E. O. Essig, Adele Ogdenand, and Clarence John DuFour, *Fort Ross: California Outpost of Russian Alaska 1812–1841* (Kingston, Ontario: Limestone Press, 1991), 1.

36. Ibid., 63–64, 67–68.

37. Pierce, *Russian America: A Biographical Dictionary,* 475; Alekseev, *The Destiny of Russian America,* 137–137, quote from S. N. Markov, *Lotopis' Alisaski,* 1948, 77.

38. Alekseev, *The Destiny of Russian America,* 137.

39. S. B. Okun, *The Russian-American Company,* ed. and with introduction by B. D. Grekov, trans. Carl Ginsburg (New York: Octagon Books, 1979), 189.

40. Ibid., 188.

41. Pierce, *Russian America: A Biographical Dictionary,* 48, 376–77.

42. Ibid., 377.

43. *Colonial Russian America: Kyrill T. Khlebnikov's Reports, 1817–1832,* trans. with introduction and notes by Basil Dmytryshyn and E. A. P. Crownhart-Vaughan (Portland: Oregon Historical Society, 1976), 4–5, 101–102; Tikhmenev, *A History of the Russian-American Company,* 99.

44. Howard I. Kushner, *Conflict on the Northwest Coast: American-Russian Rivalry in the Pacific Northwest, 1790–1867* (Westport, Conn.: Greenwood Press, 1975) 11–17; James R. Gibson, *Imperial Russia in Frontier America: The Changing Geography of Supply of Russian America, 1784–1867* (New York: Oxford University Press, 1976), 158–59.

45. Gibson, *Imperial Russia in Frontier America,* 158–61.

46. Ibid.

47. Glynn Barratt, *Russia in Pacific Waters, 1715–1825* (Vancouver: University of British Columbia Press, 1981), 172–74.

48. Ibid., 174–75.

49. Ibid.

50. Ibid., 445–46; Alekseev, *The Destiny of Russian America,* 149.

51. Alekseev, *The Destiny of Russian America,* 150.

52. Ibid., 150–51.

53. K. T. Khlebnikov, *Baranov: Chief Manager of the Russian Colonies in America* (trans. Colin Bearne, ed. Richard A. Pierce (Kingston, Ontario: Limestone Press, 1973), 92–100, Golovnin quote on 98.

55. Black, Russians in Alaska, 183–84.

Chapter 7. Russian Naval Rule, 1818–67

1. S. B. Okun, *The Russian-American Company,* ed. and with introduction by B. D. Grekov, trans. Carl Ginsburg (New York: Octagon Books, 1979), 95–99.

2. Ibid., 101.

3. Ibid., 95–101.

4. Walter A. McDougall, *Let the Sea Make a Noise . . .* (New York: Basic Books, 1992), 147; Howard I. Kushner, *Conflict on the Northwest Coast: American-Russian Rivalry in the Pacific Northwest, 1790–1867* (Westport, CT: Greenwood Press, 1975), 26–30.

5. McDougall, *Let the Sea Make a Noise,* 31–32.

6. Kushner, *Conflict on the Northwest Coast,* 31–32.

7. W. Bruce Lincoln, *The Romanovs: Autocrats of All the Russias* (New York: The Dial Press, 1981), 402–407.

8. Kushner, *Conflict on the Northwest Coast,* 31–32.

9. Ibid., 32.

10. Glynn Barratt, *Russia in Pacific Waters, 1715–1825* (Vancouver: University of British Columbia Press, 1981), 217–19.

11. James R. Gibson, *Imperial Russia in Frontier America: The Changing Geography of Supply of Russian America, 1784–1867* (New York: Oxford University Press, 1976), 162–65.

12. Mykhaylo Huculak, *When Russia Was in America: The Alaska Boundary Treaty Negotiations, 1824–25, and the Role of Pierre de Poletica* (Vancouver, BC: Mitchell Press Limited, 1971), 51–78.

13. Ibid., 174.

14. A. I. Alekseev, *The Destiny of Russian America: 1741–1867* (Kingston, Ontario: Limestone Press, 1990), 175.

15. John S. Galbraith, *The Hudson's Bay Company as an Imperial Factor* (Berkeley and Los Angeles: University of California Press, 1957), 139–40.

16. Richard A. Pierce, *Builders of Alaska: The Russian Governors, 1818–1867* (Kingston, Ontario: Limestone Press, 1986), 12–13.

17. Peter C. Newman, *Caesars of the Wilderness: Company of Adventurers,* vol. 2 (Markham, Ontario: Penguin Books Canada, 1987), 254.

18. Ibid., 255.

19. Gilbraith, *The Hudson's Bay Company as an Imperial Factor,* 154.

20. Ibid., 161–62.

21. Ibid., 156.

22. Gibson, *Imperial Russia in Frontier America,* 205.

23. Ibid., 206.

24. Galbraith, *The Hudson's Bay Company as an Imperial Factor,* 161; Gibson, *Imperial Russia in Frontier America,* 207–208.

25. Galbraith, *The Hudson's Bay Company as an Imperial Factor,* 169–71.

26. Glynn Barratt, *Russia in Pacific Waters, 1715–1825* (Vancouver: University of British Columbia Press, 1981), 211; Pierce, *Builders of Alaska,* 7.

27. Pierce, *Builders of Alaska,* 7.

28. Ibid., 8–9.

29. Ibid., 9.

30. Lydia T. Black, *Russians in Alaska, 1732–1867* (Fairbanks: University of Alaska Press, 2004), 199.

31. Ibid., 200; Pierce, *Builders of Alaska,* 13.

32. James VanStone, introduction to *Lieutenant Zagoskin's Travels in Russian America, 1842–1844,* ed. Henry N. Michael (Toronto: University of Toronto Press for the Arctic Institute of North America, 1967), xii.

33. Ibid., 14.

34. Ibid.; Richard A. Pierce, *Russian America: A Biographical Dictionary* (Kingston, Ontario: The Lime-Stone Press, 1990), 380.

35. Pierce, *Builders of Alaska,* 13, 16–17.

36. Black, *Russians in Alaska, 1732–1867,* 209–13.

37. Ibid., 209.

38. Svetlana G. Fedorova, *The Russian Population in Alaska and California: Late 18th Century–1867* (Kingston, Ontario: Limestone Press, 1973), 148–49; Okun, *The Russian American Company,* 172–73.

39. Captain P. N. Golovin, *The End of Russian America: Captain P. N. Golovin's Last Report, 1862,* trans. Basil Dmytryshyn and E. A. P. Cownhart-Vaughan (Portland: Oregon Historical Society, 1979), 13–14.

40. Ibid., 257–58.

41. Fedorova, *The Russian Population in Alaska,* 156.

42. Golovin, *The End of Russian America.* 14–16; Fedorova, *The Russian Population in Alaska,* 154–58.

43. P. A. Tikhmenev, *A History of the Russian-American Company,* trans. and ed. Richard A. Pierce and Alton S. Donnelly (Seattle: University of Washington Press, 1978), 470n21.

44. Golovin, *The End of Russian America,* 21–22; William S. Laughlin, "The Aleutians," *Alaska Geographic* 7, no. 2 (1980): 100.

45. Golovin, *The End of Russian America,* 21–22; Okun, *The Russian-American Company,* 198.

46. Golovin, *The End of Russian America,* 23.

47. Quoted in Okun, *The Russian-American Company,* 200.

48. Pierce, *Russian America: A Biographical Dictionary,* 521.

49. Ibid., 521–22.

50. Ibid., 522.

51. Ibid.

52. Golovin, *The End of Russian America,* 54–55.

53. Ibid., 53.

54. Ibid., 54–56.

55. Ibid., 56–57.

56. Ibid., 54.

57. Sir George Simpson, *Narrative of a Journey Round the World During the Years 1841 and 1842* (London: Henry Colborn, 1847), vol. 2, 190.

58. Okun, *The Russian American Company,* 226–27.

59. Ibid., 220.

60. Gibson, Imperial Russia in Frontier America, 42.

Chapter 8. The Sale of Russian America

1. Raisa V. Makarova, "Toward a History of the Liquidation of the Russian American Company," in *Russia's American Colony,* ed. S. Frederick Starr (Durham, N.C.: Duke University Press, 1987), 64.

2. N. N. Bolhovitinov, *Russian-American Relations and the Sale of Alaska, 1843–1867* (Kingston, Ontario: Limestone Press, 1996), 84–85.

3. Ibid., 85.

4. Ibid., 86–88.

5. Richard A. Pierce, *Russian America: A Biographical Dictionary* (Kingston, Ontario: The Lime-Stone Press, 1990), 486.

6. Bolkhovitinov, *Russian-American Relations,* 81–82.

7. Basil Dmytryshyn and E. A. P. Crownhart-Vaughan, introduction to *The End of Russian America: Captain P.N. Golovin's Last Report, 1862* (Portland: Oregon Historical Society, 1979), xi–xii.

8. Bolkhovitinov, *Russian-American Relations,* 97–98.

9. Baron Ferdinand Petrovich von Wrangel, quoted in Bolkhovitinov, *Russian-American Relations,* 99–100.

10. Bolkhovitinov, *Russian-American Relations,* 101–102.

11. Ibid., 103–106.

12. Ibid., 106–107.

13. Ibid., 108–109.

14. Ibid., 109–12.

15. Ibid., 112–13.

16. Ibid., 116–17.

17. Ibid., 64–65.

18. Pierce, *Russian America: A Biographical Dictionary,* 257.

19. Dmytryshyn and Crownhart-Vaughan, introduction to *The End of Russian America,* xiii.

20. Ibid., xiv, xiii.

21. Ibid., xv.

22. Bolkhovitinov, *Russian-American Relations,* 127–33.

23. Ibid., 134–38.

24. Ibid., 170–74.

25. Ibid., 178–82.

26. Ibid., 185–88.

27. Ibid., 189–204.

28. Ibid., 207–208.

29. Bolkhovitinov, *Russian-American Relations,* 43.

30. Ibid., 208.

31. Ibid., 209–11.

32. Ibid., 212–17.

33. Frederick Seward, cited in Bolkhovitinov, *Russian-American Relations,* 217–18.

34. Ibid., 223.

35. Ronald J. Jensen, *The Alaska Purchase and Russian-American Relations* (Seattle: University of Washington Press, 1975), 79.

36. Ibid., 83–92.

37. Ibid., 93–97.

38. Ibid., 101; Pierce, *Russian-America: A Biographical Dictionary,* 255.

39. Lydia T. Black, *Russians in Alaska, 1732–1867* (Fairbanks: University of Alaska Press, 2004), 286, 285. The name Alaska had apparently been gradually established by local use. Derived from a Native term referring to the southwestern end of the Alaska Peninsula, it gradually included the whole subcontinent. Secretary of State Seward; Charles Sumner, U.S. senator and chairman of the Committee on Foreign Relations; and Major General Halleck, commander of the Military Division of the Pacific, proposed to name Russian America "Alaska" in 1867. Who had the idea first is not known. See Donald J. Orth, *Dictionary of Alaska Place Names,* Geological Survey Professional Paper 567 (Washington, D.C.: Government Printing Office, 1967), 60.

40. Jensen, *The Alaska Purchase and Russian-American Relations,* 101; Bolkhovitinov, *Russian-American Relations,* 278–80.

41. Ibid., 280.

Chapter 9. American Settlement of Alaska: The Army, Treasury Department, and Navy Phase, 1867–84

1. Ted C. Hinckley, *The Americanization of Alaska, 1867–1897* (Palo Alto, Calif.: Pacific Books, Publishers, 1972), Johnson quote on p. 37.

2. Richard A. Pierce, *Builders of Alaska: The Russian Governors, 1818–1867* (Palo Alto, Calif.: Pacific Books, Publishers, 1972), 48.

3. Hinckley, *The Americanization of Alaska,* 30–31.

4. Ibid., 31.

5. Pierce, *Builders of Alaska,* 47.

6. Ibid.

7. Ibid., 47–48.

8. Hinckley, *The Americanization of Alaska,* 24, 32.

9. *Alta California,* November 23, 1867, cited in Hinckley, *The Americanization of Alaska,* 34–35.

10. Hinckley, *The Americanization of Alaska,* 34–35.

11. U.S. Army, Alaska, *The Army's Role in the Building of Alaska,* Pamphlet 360-5, April 1, 1959 (Headquarters, U.S. Army, Alaska, 1969), hereafter cited as USARAL Pamphlet 360-5, pp. 9–16.

12. Ted C. Hinckley, "Alaska as an American Botany Bay," *Pacific Historical Review* 42, no. 1 (1973): 1–11.

13. Hinckley, *The Americanization of Alaska,* 40–57.

14. Ibid., 49–52.

15. Jeannette P. Nichols, *Alaska: A History of Its Administration, Exploitation, and Industrial Development during Its First Half Century under the Rule of the United States* (Cleveland, Ohio: Arthur H. Clark, 1924), 44.

16. Bobby Dave Lain, "North of Fifty-Three: Army, Treasury Department, and Navy Administration of Alaska, 1867–1884" (PhD diss., University of Texas at Austin, 1974), 109–119.

17. Stanley Ray Remsberg, "United States Administration of Alaska: The Army Phase, 1867–1877: A Study in Federal Governance of an Overseas Possession" (PhD diss., University of Wisconsin-Madison, 1975), 170.

18. Ibid, 171.

19. Ibid., 220–21.

20. Ibid., 220–23.

21. Ibid., 226–27.

22. Morgan B. Sherwood, *Exploration of Alaska, 1865–1900* (Fairbanks: University of Alaska Press, 1992), 87.

23. Ibid., 93–118.

24. Ibid., 115.

25. USARAL Pamphlet 360-5, 34.

26. Ibid., 34–44.

27. Hinckley, *The Americanization of Alaska,* 99.

28. Lain, "North of Fifty-Three," 230–31.

29. Ibid., 231–32.

30. Ibid., 232–33.

31. Ibid., 232–35

32. Ibid., 234.

33. Sheldon Jackson College closed its doors for good in June 2007, unable to overcome its financial difficulties.

34. Lain, "North of Fifty-Three," 232–35.

35. William R. Hunt, *Arctic Passage* (New York: Charles Scribner's Sons, 1975), 117, 132–33, 122.

36. George W. Rogers, *The Future of Alaska: Economic Consequences of Statehood* (Baltimore: Johns Hopkins Press, 1962), 89.

37. House Committee on the Territories, *Civil Government for Alaska: Report to Accompany S. 153*, 48th Cong., 1st sess., 1884, H.R. 476, 2.

38. Remsberg, "United States Administration of Alaska," 261–62.

39. Ibid., 231.

40. Ibid., 236–37.

41. Ibid., 237–39.

42. Ibid., 242–43.

43. Ibid., 246.

44. Ibid., 248.

45. Ibid., 419–20.

46. Ibid., 421–22.

47. Ibid., 422, 424–25.

48. Ibid., 425–27, 432.

49. Ibid., 433–34.

50. Ibid., 435–37.

51. Lain, "North of Fifty-Three," 221–23.

52. Ibid., 224.

53. Ibid., 225–26.

54. Ibid., 235–36.

55. Ibid., 237–39.

56. Ibid., 240–42.

57. Ibid., 242–44.

58. Ibid., 228.

59. Ibid., 228–29; Richard A. Cooley, *Politics and Conservation* (New York: Harper & Row, 1963), 25–26.

60. Morgan B. Sherwood, *Exploration of Alaska* (New Haven: Yale University Press, 1965), 45–46.

61. Ibid.

62. Ernest Gruening, *The State of Alaska*, 2nd ed. (New York: Random House, 1968), 67–70; Hinckley, *The Americanization of Alaska*, 92; Alfred H. Brooks, *Blazing Alaska's Trails*, 2nd ed. (Fairbanks: University of Alaska Press, 1973), 270–71; Nichols, *Alaska*, 47–49.

63. Sherwood, *Exploration of Alaska*, 44.

64. Lawrence W. Rakestraw, *A History of the United States Forest Service in Alaska* (Anchorage: Alaska Historical Commission, Department of Education, State of Alaska and Alaska Region. U.S. Forest Service, Department of Agriculture, with the assistance of the Alaska Historical Society, 1981), 7.

65. Brooks, *Blazing Alaska's Trails*, 300–301.

66. Robert N. De Armond, *The Founding of Juneau* (Juneau: Gastineau Channel Centennial Association, 1967), 74.

67. Ibid., 89.

68. Brooks, *Blazing Alaska's Trails*, 303–306.

69. De Armond, *The Founding of Juneau*, 110.

70. Ted C. Hinckley, "Prospectors, Profits, and Prejudice," *American West* 2 (Spring 1965): 59–63.

71. Brooks, *Blazing Alaska's Trails*, 327–28.

72. Ibid., 332–34.

73. Ibid., 334.

74. Lain, *North of Fifty-Three*, 246–47.

75. Ibid., 248–51.

76. Secretary Thompson, as reported by Beardslee and quoted in Lain, *North of Fifty-Three*, 258–59.

77. Beardslee, quoted in Lain, *North of Fifty-Three*, 260–61.

78. Lain, *North of Fifty-Three*, 262–64.

79. Sitka preamble, cited in Lain, *North of Fifty-Three*, 264–65.

80. Lain, *North of Fifty-Three*, 266–67.

81. Ibid., 269–70.

82. Nichols, *Alaska*, 67–68.

83. Gruening, *The State of Alaska*, 565–66.

84. Hinckley, *The Americanization of Alaska*, 153–56.

85. Claus-M. Naske, "The Shaky Beginnings of Alaska's Judicial System," *Western Legal History* 1, no. 2 (Summer/Fall 1988): 164–65.)

86. Ibid., 165–66.

87. Ibid.

88. Benjamin Harrison, quoted in Naske, "The Shaky Beginnings," 166.

89. *Annual Report of the Secretary of the Interior,* in *The Executive Documents of the House of Representatives for the First Session of the Fiftieth Congress, 1877–1888,* vol. 1 (Washington, D.C.: Government Printing Office, 1889), 64–65; Nichols, *Alaska,* 72.

90. *Annual Report of the Secretary of the Interior,* 160–66.

91. Ted C. Hinckley, "Sheldon Jackson and Benjamin Harrison," in *Alaska and Its History,* ed. Morgan Sherwood (Seattle: University of Washington Press, 1967), 306–307.

92. Hinckley, *The Americanization of Alaska,* 167.

93. Ibid., 81–82.

94. Ibid., 115–16.

95. Ibid., 98–99; Brooks, Blazing Alaska's Trails, 488–92.

Chapter 10. The Great Gold Rush and Its Aftermath

1. Robert N. DeAmond and Terrence Cole, "George Holt: First White Man across the Chilkoot Pass," *Alaska History,* 21, no. 1 (Spring 2006), 39–44.

2. William R. Hunt, *North of 53<dg>: The Wild Days of the Alaska-Yukon Mining Frontier, 1870–1914* (New York: Macmillan Publishers, 1974), 1–4.

3. Pierre Berton, *The Klondike Fever* (New York: Alfred A. Knopf, 1958), 12–13.

4. Ibid., 13–15.

5. Ibid., 15.

6. Ibid.

7. Ibid., 15–17.

8. Remittance men were young gentlemen who came to the American West and Alaska either willingly or under parental pressure. For the most part, they lived on money sent from home.

9. Berton, *The Klondike Fever,* 18, 23, 27.

10. Mayo was farther down the river at Minook Creek. Harper and his partner, Joseph Ladue, had settled in Canadian territory along the river.

11. Berton, *The Klondike Fever,* 28–29, 32–33.

12. Ibid., 34–35, 37–39.

13. Ibid., 39–41.

14. A derogatory term for Natives.

15. Berton, *The Klondike Fever,* 43–51.

16. Ibid., 51, 73, 96–100.

17. Alfred H. Brooks, *Blazing Alaska's Trails,* 2nd ed. (Fairbanks: University of Alaska Press, 1973), 335.

18. Ibid., 376.

19. Ibid.

20. Ibid., 390–91.

21. Hunt, *North of 53<dg>,* 113; Brooks, *Blazing Alaska's Trails,* 397–98; Terrence Cole, "Nome," *Alaska Geographic* 11, no. 1 (1984); 73–79.

22. Edward S. Harrison, *Nome and Seward Peninsula,* (Seattle: n.p., 1905), 54.

23. Act of June 6, 1900, *An Act Making Further Provision for a Civil Government for Alaska, and for Other Purposes,* ch. 786, 32 Stat. 321 (1900).

24. Evangeline Atwood, *Frontier Politics: Alaska's James Wickersham* (Portland, Oreg.: Binford & Mort, 1979), 59.

25. *Laws Other than Criminal Relating to Alaska,* H.R. Doc. No. 99, 55th Cong., 3rd sess. (1898); for an excellent discussion of the origin of the Alaska and Oregon codes, see Frederick E. Brown, "The Sources of the Alaska and Oregon Codes: Part I, New York and Oregon," *UCLA-Alaska Law Review* 2 (1972): 15–22; and Brown, "The Sources of the Alaska and Oregon Codes: Part II, The Codes of Alaska, 1867–1901," *UCLA-Alaska Law Review* 3 (1973): 87–112.

26. Harrison, *Nome and Seward Peninsula,* 197–201.

27. Terrence Michael Cole, "A History of the Nome Gold Rush: The Poor Man's Paradise," (PhD diss., University of Washington, 1983), 164–166.

28. Ibid., 166.

29. Ibid., 166–69.

30. Ibid., 169–71.

31. 33 Cong. Rec. 56th Cong., 1st sess. (1900), 4418.

32. Ibid.

33. Ibid., p. 3739.

34. Ibid., p. 4310.

35. Cole, "A History of the Nome Gold Rush," 177; 33 Cong. Rec., 56th Cong., 1st sess. (1900), 3928, 3934, 4471; Petition to President William McKinley, n.d. (1900), RG 60, National Archives, Washington, D.C. (hereafter NA); D. E. Morgan to President of the United States, March 21, 1900, Appointments, Alaska, RG 60, NA; List of Endorsements for Arthur H. Noyes, n.d., RG 60, NA; D. F. Morgan to President McKinley, April 19, 1900, Appointments, Alaska, RG 60, NA..

36. United States Ninth Circuit Court of Appeals, "In the Matter of Arthur H. Noyes, et al.," "Transcript of Proceedings and Testimony," section titled "Statement of W. T. Hume," 2: 394, 391, Records of the Department of Justice, RG 60, NA.

37. Ibid., at 400–04; *In re Noyes,* 121 F. 209 (9th Cir. 1902).

38. Cole, "A History of the Nome Gold Rush," 198–201.

39. *In re Noyes*, 121 F. 209 (9th Cir. 1902); Cole, "A History of the Nome Gold Rush," 203.

40. C. S. A. Frost to Attorney General John W. Griggs, August 16, 1900, Records of the Department of Justice, file 10000/1900, box 1215, RG 60, NA.

41. William W. Morrow, "The Spoilers," *California Law Review* 4 (1916), 108; *In re Alexander McKenzie*, 180 U.S. 536–51 (1901); William H. Metson to Attorney General, October 8, 1900, Records of the Department of Justice, file 10000/1900, box 1215, RG 60, NA.

42. Cole, "A History of the Nome Gold Rush," 204–05.

43. Ibid., 206–208.

44. Cole, "A History of the Nome Gold Rush," 161–62.

45. *In re Noyes*, 121 F. 209 (9th Cir. 1902).

46. Ibid.

47. James Wickersham, *Old Yukon: Tales-Trails-and Trials* (Washington, DC: Washington Law Book Co., 1938), 371.

48. Terrence Cole, *Crooked Past: The History of a Frontier Mining Camp, Fairbanks, Alaska* (Fairbanks: University of Alaska Press, 1991), 22–26.

49. Cole, *Crooked Past*, 27–60.

50. A reorganization of the Alaska Commercial Company in 1901 resulted in the creation of the Northern Commercial Company. For more, see L. D. Kitchener, *Flag over the North* (Seattle: Superior Publishers, 1954).

51. David B. Wharton, *The Alaska Gold Rush* (Bloomington: Indiana University Press, 1972), 264–66.

52. Ibid., 131–34.

53. For a full account of this misadventure, ass Keith A. Murray, *Reindeer and Gold,* occasional paper no. 24 (Bellingham, Wash.: Center for Pacific Northwest Studies, Western Washington University, 1988).

54. U.S. Army, Alaska, *The Army's Role in the Building of Alaska,* Pamphlet 360-5, April 1, 1959 (Headquarters, U.S. Army, Alaska, 1969), 3–7 (hereafter cited as USARAL Pamphlet 360-5).

55. Ibid., 45–47.

56. Jeannette P. Nichols, *Alaska: A History of Its Administration, Exploitation, and Industrial Development during Its First Half Century under the Rule of the United States* (Cleveland, Ohio: Arthur H. Clark, 1924), 159–62.

57. Ernest Gruening, *The State of Alaska*, 2nd ed. (New York: Random House, 1968), 113.

58. USARAL, Pamphlet 360–5, pp. 26–28.

59. Thomas A. Bailey, *A Diplomatic History of the American People* (New York: Appleton-Century-Crofts, 1950), 507–10.

60. George W. Rogers and Richard A. Cooley, *Alaska's Population and Economy: Regional Growth, Development and Future Outlook*, vol. 2, *Statistical Handbook* (College, Alaska: Institute of Social, Economic, and Government Research, 1963), 7.

61. Robert D. Arnold et al., *Alaska Native Land Claims* (Anchorage: Alaska Native Foundation, 1976), 83.

62. Ibid.

63. Gruening, *The State of Alaska*, 355–81; Senate Committee on Interior and Insular Affairs, *Alaska Native Claims Settlement Act of 1971: Report Together with Additional and Supplemental Views to Accompany S. 35*, 92nd Cong., 1st sess. (October 21, 1971), 91.

64. Fitzgerald et al, *Alaska Natives and the Land* (Washington, D.C.: Federal Field Committee for Development Planning in Alaska, 1968), 434–35.

65. Stanton H. Patty, "A Conference with the Tanana Chiefs," *Alaska Journal*, Spring 1971, 2–10.

66. Ibid., 11, 18.

67. *Alaska Native Claims Settlement Act of 1971*, P.L. 92-203, p. 91.

68. Orlando W. Miller, *The Frontier in Alaska and the Matanuska Colony* (New Haven: Yale University Press, 1975), 17.

69. Ibid., 17–18.

70. William H. Wilson, *Railroad in the Clouds: The Alaska Railroad in the Age of Steam* (Boulder, Colo.: Pruett Publishing Co., 1977), 4–15. For a good source on railroad development, consult Frank W. Burch, "Alaska's Railroad Frontier: Railroads and Federal Development Policy, 1898–1915" (PhD diss., Catholic University of America, 1965).

71. Petroleum News-Alaska, "Katalla to Prudhoe Bay: An Entertaining Look at the First 100 Years of the Oil and Gas Industry in Alaska," Commercial Printing/*Anchorage Daily News,* no date [1998?], 8.

72. *Anchorage Daily Times*, November 9, 1981.

73. Ibid.

74. Ted A. Armstrong, "Alaskan Oil," *Oil and Gas Journal*, August 22, 1966, 95–96.

75. Gruening, *The State of Alaska,* 144; Nichols, *Alaska,* 251.

76. Nichols, *Alaska,* 330–32.

77. Herman E. Slotnick, "The Ballinger-Pinchot Affair in Alaska," *Journal of the West* 10, no. 2 (1971): 337–47.

78. Nichols, *Alaska,* 283–84, 308–309; Gruening, *The State of Alaska,* 142–45.

79. Nichols, *Alaska,* 385–89.

80. Gruening, *The State of Alaska,* 151–52.

81. Ibid., 159–63, 173–74.

82. Ibid., 177; Edward Fitch, *The Alaska Railroad* (New York: Frederick A. Praeger, 1967), 43.

83. *Alaska v. Troy,* 258 U.S. 101 (February 27, 1922).

Chapter 11. Normalcy, the Depression, and the New Deal

1. Ernest Gruening, *The State of Alaska,* 2nd ed. (New York: Random House, 1968), 270, 272.

2. Richard A. Cooley, *Politics and Conservation* (New York: Harper & Row, 1963), 26.

3. Ibid., 73.

4. Ibid., 75–76, 78–82; H.R. 13543, 59th Cong., 1st sess. (1906).

5. Cooley, *Politics and Conservation,* 97–98.

6. Ibid., 95–96.

7. Ibid., 96.

8. Ibid., 87–89, 104–105. For the definitive study of the hatchery program, see Patricia Roppel, *Alaska's Salmon Hatcheries, 1891–1959,* Studies in History, no. 20 (Anchorage: Alaska Historical Commission, 1982).

9. Ibid., 106–108.

10. Ibid., 118.

11. Ibid., 125–27, 129.

12. George W. Rogers, *The Future of Alaska: Economic Consequences of Statehood* (Baltimore: Johns Hopkins Press, 1962), 91.

13. William H. Wilson, *Railroad in the Clouds: The Alaska Railroad in the Age of Steam, 1914–1945* (Boulder, Colo.: Pruett Publishing, 1977), 155, 195–238, 254–261.

14. U.S. Department of the Interior, Bureau of Reclamation, *Alaska: Reconnaissance Report on the Potential Development of Water Resources in the Territory of Alaska,* H. Doc 197, 82nd Cong., 1st sess. (Washington, D.C.: Government Printing Office, 1950), 65–66.

15. Gruening, *The State of Alaska,* 271.

16. Rogers, *The Future of Alaska,* 62.

17. Lawrence W. Rakestraw, *A History of the United States Forest Service in Alaska* (Anchorage: Alaska Historical Commission, Department of Education, State of Alaska and Alaska Region. U.S. Forest Service, Department of Agriculture, with the assistance of the Alaska Historical Society, 1981), 108–109.

18. *Anchorage Daily Times,* November 9, 1981; Ted A. Armstrong, "Alaskan Oil," *Oil and Gas Journal,* August 22, 1966, 95-96.

19. In addition to the four naval petroleum reserves established by Executive Order between 1912 and 1923, three oil share reserves were similarly established: Shale Reserve No. 1, Colorado, December 6, 1916; Shale Reserve No. 2, Utah, November 17, 1924; and Shale Reserve No. 3, Colorado, September 27, 1924. See "Summary of the History of the Naval Petroleum Reserves," in folder of the same name, February 7, 1951, box 98, Papers of Oscar L. Chapman, Harry S. Truman Library, Independence, Missouri.

20. Mary C. Mangusso, "Anthony J. Dimond: A Political Biography" (PhD diss., Texas Tech University, 1978), 166–68, 183.

21. Rakestraw, *A History of the United States Forest Service,* 95–100.

22. Cooley, *Politics and Conservation,* 136–39.

23. Ibid., 147–49.

24. Ibid.,151.

25. Ibid., 151, 156.

26. Orlando W. Miller, *The Frontier in Alaska and the Matanuska Colony* (New Haven: Yale University Press, 1975), 38–45.

27. Ibid., 62, 69–71.

28. Ibid., 83–87, 98–99.

29. Ibid., 88–89.

30. Ibid., 102–104.

31. Mangusso, "Anthony J. Dimond, 188–95; Miller, *The Frontier in Alaska,* 166–75.

32. Stat. 984; 49 Stat. 1250, sec. 2; Gruening, *State of Alaska,* 364–65.

33. Gruening, *State of Alaska,* 367; Robert D. Arnold et al., *Alaska Native Land Claims* (Anchorage: Alaska Native Foundation, 1976), 88.

34. Later on, a court held that the Hydaburg Reservation had not been established legally. Native villages, however, continued to submit petitions to the secretary of the interior requesting reservations. By 1950 eight villages had submitted such petitions embracing approximately 100 million acres. The Department of the Interior, however, did not act on any of them, probably because by then public opinion seemed opposed to the reservation system because it represented racial segregation and discrimination. Arnold, *Alaska Native Land Claims,* 88.

35. Compare Rogers, *The Future of Alaska,* 248–50, and Gruening, *The State of Alaska,* 255–59, 364–68.

36. Arnold, *Alaska Native Land Claims,* 85, 88–89, 91.

37. National Resources Committee, *Alaska,* 19; Harold Ickes, *The Secret Diary of Harold Ickes* (New York: Simon and Schuster, 1954), 2:449–50.

38. Ernest Gruening, Many Battles: The Autobiography of Ernest Gruening (New York: Liveright, 1973), 283.

Chapter 12. Alaska's Strategic Role in World War II

1. U.S. Army, Alaska, *The Army's Role in the Building of Alaska,* Pamphlet 360-5, April 1, 1959 (Headquarters, U.S. Army, Alaska, 1969), hereafter cited as USARAL Pamphlet 360-5, 74,

2. Ibid., 70.

3. Ibid., 71.

4. Ibid.

5. Claus-M. Naske, *An Interpretative History of Alaskan Statehood* (Anchorage: Alaska Northwest Publishing Co., 1973), 56.

6. USARAL, Pamphlet 360-5.

7. Ibid., 74.

8. Naske, *An Interpretative History,* 56–57; USARAL, Pamphlet 360-5.

9. Samuel Eliot Morison, *History of United States Naval Operations in World War II,* vol. 4, *Coral Sea, Midway and Submarine Actions* (Boston: Little, Brown, 1962), 163–65.

10. Brian Garfield, *The Thousand-Mile War: World War II in Alaska and the Aleutians* (Garden City, N.Y.: Doubleday, 1969), 12.

11. Morison, *The Coral Sea,* 75.

12. Ibid., 3–7.

13. Ibid., 17–28.

14. Ibid., 7, 25.

15. Ibid., 180–81. For the story of the Joneses and Etta Jones's students, see Mary Breu, *Last Letters from Attu* (Portland, Ore.: Alaska Northwest Books, 2009).

16. Ibid., 169, 181.

17. Ibid., 183.

18. Ibid., 5.

19. Ibid., 4.

20. Ibid., 12–13.

21. Ibid., 12–13.

22. Garfield, *The Thousand-Mile War,* 146–47, 149–50.

23. Deane R. Brandon, "War Planes to Russia," *Alaska Magazine,* May 1979, 14–17.

24. Garfield, *The Thousand-Mile War,* 153–55.

25. Morison, *Naval Operations,* vol. 7, *The Aleutians, Gilberts, and Marshalls,* 17.

26. Ibid., 22; Garfield, *The Thousand-Mile War,* 178–79.

27. Ibid., 251–52.

28. Ibid., 256.

29. Ibid.

30. Morison, *The Coral Sea,* 54, 57–59.

31. Ibid., 59–60.

32. Ibid., 63–64.

33. UASRAL, Pamphlet 360-5, 96.

34. George W. Rogers, *The Future of Alaska: Economic Consequences of Statehood* (Baltimore: Johns Hopkins Press, 1962), 95.

35. Lyman L. Woodman, "An Alaskan Military History," *Alaska Sportsman,* March 1969, 26.

Chapter 13. Ramifications of War: Evacuations and Censorship

1. Dean Kohlhoff, *When the Wind Was a River: Aleut Evacuation in World War II* (Seattle: University of Washington Press; Anchorage: Aleutian/Pribilof Islands Association, 1995), 18–21.

2. Executive Order 9066, *Federal Register,* vol. 7 (1942), 1407; Roger Daniels, *Concentration Camps America: Japanese in the United States and Canada During World War II* (Malabar, Fla.: Robert E. Krieger, 1981), xvi.

3. Kohlhoff, *When the Wind Was a River,* 52.

4. Ibid., 33–34.

5. Ibid., 44–46.

6. Ibid., 70–71.

7. Ibid., 71–72.

8. Ibid., 72–77, quote on 72.

9. Ibid., 87–137.

10. Ibid., 136–43.

11. Ibid., 85–87, 180. See also Galen Roger Perras, *Stepping Stones to Nowhere: The Aleutian Islands, Alaska, and American Military Strategy, 1867–1945* (Vancouver: University of British Columbia Press, 2003), 82.

12. Claus-M. Naske, "The Evacuation of Alaska's Japanese," *Pacific Northwest Quarterly* 74, no. 3 (July 1983), 124.

13. Ibid.

14. Ibid.

15. Ibid., 124–25.

16. Ibid., 125, originally quoted in the *Daily Alaska Empire* (Juneau), December 8, 1941.

17. Ibid., 125.

18. Ibid.

19. Ibid.

20. Ibid., 125–26.

21. As Gruening was often absent during his governorship, Bartlett, the secretary of Alaska, served as acting governor. Ibid., quote on 128.

22. Ibid.

23. Ibid.

24. Ibid., 129.

25. Ibid., 130.

26. Ibid., 131.

27. Ibid.

28. Ibid., 132.

29. Ibid.

30. Kohlhoff, *When the Wind Was a River*, 183.

31. Ibid., 183; PL 100-383, August 10, 1988 (102 Stat. 903). No monetary compensation, however, could repair the hardships and deprivations the relocation program had inflicted upon the evacuees.

32. Kohlhoff, *When the Wind Was a River*, 180–81.

33. Ernest Gruening memorandum for Secretary Harold L. Ickes, November 10, 1942, folder 9-1-96, World War, General, RG 126, National Archives, Washington, D.C. (hereafter NA).

34. Ibid.

35. E. L. Bartlett to Governor Gruening, February 11, 1942, folder 9-1-96, World War, General, RG 126, NA.

36. Lewis to Commanding General, Alaska Defense Command, Fort Richardson, Alaska, January 11, 1942, folder 9-1-96, World War, General, RG 126, NA.

37. Lyle C. Wilson to Brigadier General A. D. Surles, February 2, 1942, folder 9-1-96, World War, General, RG 126, NA.

38. Governor Gruening to Byron Price, February 17, and Price to Gruening, February 18, 1942, folder 9-1-96, World War, General, RG 126, NA.

39. Ernest Gruening Diaries, January 20, 1947, Ernest Gruening Papers, University of Alaska Fairbanks Archives, Fairbanks, Alaska.

40. Confidential memorandum for Secretary Ickes from Ruth Gruber, October 5, 1942, folder 9-1-6, part 3, National Defense, RG 48, NA.

41. Norman Littell to Harold Ickes, November 10, and Governor Gruening to Ickes, November 17, 1942, folder 9-1-96, World War, RG 126, NA.

42. Gruening Diaries, January 20, 1947, Ernest Gruening Papers, University of Alaska Fairbanks, Fairbanks, Alaska.

43. Byron Price to Governor Gruening, November 23, 1942, folder 9-1-96, RG 126, NA.

44. Gruening Diaries, January 20, 1947, Ernest Gruening Papers, University of Alaska Fairbanks Archives, Fairbanks, Alaska; Byron Price to Stephen Early, December 10, 1942, OF 400, folder Appointments, Alaska, 1942, box 2, Franklin D. Roosevelt Library, Hyde Park, New York.

45. Ernest Gruening, Many Battles (New York: Liveright, 1973), 313–14; Byron Price to Stephen Early, December 10, 1942, OF 400, folder Appointments, Alaska, 1942, box 2, Franklin D. Roosevelt Papers, Hyde Park, New York; Gruening Diaries, January 20, 1947, Ernest Gruening Papers, University of Alaska Fairbanks Archives, Fairbanks, Alaska; Byron Price to President Roosevelt, November 11, and President Roosevelt to Byron Price, November 15, 1944, OF 400, folder Appointments, Alaska, 1944–1945, box 3, Franklin D. Roosevelt Papers, Hyde Park, New York.

Chapter 14. The Cold War

1. "Alaska: Airman's Theater," *Time*, November 6, 1950, 28.

2. U.S. House of Representatives Committee on Territories, *Official Trip to Conduct a Study and Investigation of the Various Questions and Problems Relating to the Territory of Alaska*, February 15, 1946, House Report 1583, 79 Cong., 2nd sess. (Washington, D.C.: Government Printing Office, 1949), serial 11022, 1, 6, 18.

3. "Remarks by Brigadier General Elmer J. Rogers, Jr., United States Air Force, Director of Plans and Operations, Headquarters Alaskan Command," Appendix A, *Report of the Alaskan Task Force, Seventh Report of the Preparedness Subcommittee of the Committee on Armed Services*, U.S. Senate, March 1, 1951, Senate Document 10, 82 Cong., 1st sess. (Washington, D.C.: Government Printing Office, 1951), serial 11503, 46; Lyman L. Woodman, *The Army Corps of Engineers in Alaska Starting in 1896* and *History of Its Alaska District During 1946–1974* (Anchorage: Alaska District, 1976), 27.

4. Captain John J. Teal, Jr., "Alaska, Fulcrum of Power," *Foreign Affairs,* October 1948, 86, 90.

5. Ibid., 92–93, 95.

6. "Another Pearl Harbor? An Interview with Ernest Gruening, Governor of Alaska," *U.S. News & World Report*, November 18, 1949, 32–36.

7. *New York Times*, March 13, 16, 1949.

8. "Alaska: Airman's Theater," *Time*, November 6, 1950, 28.

9. *New York Times*, March 13, 16, 1949.

10. Ibid., March 19, 1949.

11. Ibid.

12. Ibid.

13. Ibid., March 21, 1949.

14. Ibid., March 26, 1949; January 3, 1949.

15. Ibid., March 26, 1949, 7; January 3, 1949, 9.

16. Brent R. Bowen, "Defense Spending in Alaska," *Alaska Review of Business and Economic Conditions* (Fairbanks: Institute of Social, Economic and Government Research, July, 1971), 4.

17. *New York Times*, June 25, 1950.

18. Ibid., June 27, 1950.

19. Ibid., November 2, 1952.

20. Ibid., January 6, 1954; July 27, 1954.

21. Claus-M. Naske, "Alaska and the Federal-Aid Highway Acts," *Pacific Northwest Quarterly*, 80, no. 4 (October, 1989): 133–38.

22. Lyman Woodmen, "An Alaska Military History, 1940–1968," *Alaska Sportsman*, March 1969, 26; Truman Strobridge, *Strength in the North: The Alaska Command 1947–1967* (Elmendorf Air Force Base, Anchorage, Alaska, 1966), 37.

23. Jonathan M. Nielson, *Armed Forces on a Northern Frontier: The Military in Alaska's History, 1867–1987* (Westport, Conn.: Greenwood Press, 1988), 187.

24. Ibid.

25. John Dyson, *The Hot Arctic* (Boston: Little, Brown and Company, 1979), 177; Lisa Mighetto and Carla Homstad, *Engineering in the Far North: A History of the U.S. Army Engineer District in Alaska* (Anchorage: U.S. Army Engineer District, Alaska, 1997), 265.

26. Ibid., 266–67.

27. Howard La Fay, "DEW Line: Sentry of the Far North," *National Geographic,* July 1958, 133; T Sgt. Pat McKenna, "The Border Guards, NORAD: The Eyes and Ears of North America," *Airman* 40, no. 1 (January 1, 1996): 2, 3, 87.

28. La Fay, "DEW Line," 131.

29. Ibid.

30. Ibid.

31. Ibid., 129, 144.

32. Ibid., 136.

33. Oran R. Young, *Arctic Politics: Conflict and Cooperation in the Circumpolar North* (Hanover, N.H.: University Press of New England, 1992), 193–96;

Fairbanks Daily News-Miner, March 29, 1999.

34. Dyson, *Hot Arctic*, 178.

35. Mighetto and Homstad, *Engineering in the Far North*, 269–70.

36. Ibid., 270–71.

37. "The End of White Alice, the End of an Era," *Alascom Spectrum* 6, no. 1 (March 1985): 18–21.

38. Mighetto and Homstad, *Engineering in the Far North*, 273.

39. Ibid.; "The End of White Alice, the End of an Era."

40. Mighetto and Homstad, *Engineering in the Far North*, 273–74.

41. Ibid., 274.

42. Nielson, *Armed Forces,* 200–201.

43. John Honderich, *Arctic Imperative: Is Canada Losing the North?* (Toronto: University of Toronto Press, 1987), 87–88.

44. Oran R. Young, *Arctic Politics: Conflict and Cooperation in the Circumpolar North* (Hanover, N.H.: University Press of New England, 1992), 191–92. In the twenty-first century, the circumpolar pack ice has decreased steadily, and many scientists predict an ice-free Arctic Ocean by midcentury.

45. Ibid., 88.

46. Young, *Arctic Politics,* 191–92.

47. Ibid., 192–93.

48. Ibid., 193–94.

49. Ibid., 194.

50. Ibid., 195.

51. Nielson, *Armed Forces*, 202.

52. Ibid., 203–204.

53. Ibid., 204.

54. AbsoluteAstronomy.com Web site, "Over-the-Horizon Radar," 2009 (accessed May 20, 2009).

55. Robert G. Kaiser, *Why Gorbachev Happened* (New York: Simon & Schuster, 1992) 85, 491.

56. In September 2000 TAC signed an agreement with the U.S. Navy and the Department of the Interior. It allowed the United States, acting through the navy and the Department of the Interior, to enter into a land exchange agreement with TAC that took place in March 2004. The exchange transferred 47,271 acres of the northern portion of Adak, including the downtown area, housing units, and industrial facilities, to TAC. The latter exchanged surface and subsurface property from its ANCSA entitlement lands, mostly in the Shumagin Islands. Under the terms of the agreement, the Adak airfield was transferred to the Alaska Department of Transportation and Public Facilities for operation and

maintenance. Population on the island ranges from fifty to three hundred, depending on the season.

57. Kaiser, *Why Gorbachev Happened,* 11.

58. See "Challenge," www.adakisland.com/challenge/. The facility provided selected officers and enlisted men instruction in summer and winter military operations, including survival in far northern environments, mountaineering, and tactical, technical, and logistical support. The Arctic Training Company within the school served as a tactical and administrative school and also assisted the Test and Development Section with its equipment and clothing. The Test and Development Section, later renamed the Arctic Test Board and later still the Arctic Test Center, was responsible for conducting summer and winter tests of various types of equipment, armament, rations, clothing, and techniques to be used in far northern operations. See U.S. Army, Alaska, *The Army's Role in the Building of Alaska,* Pamphlet 360-5, April 1, 1959 (Headquarters, U.S. Army, Alaska, 1969), 96, 100.

59. Fort Greely Public Affairs Office, "Ft. Greely Fact Sheet," January 9, 2006, City of Delta Junction, Alaska Web site, www.ci.delta-junction.ak.us/ft_greely/index.htm (accessed May 20, 2009).

Chapter 15. Alaska's Rocky Road to Statehood

1. *Speech of William H. Seward, at Sitka, August 12, 1869* (Washington, D.C.: Philip & Solomons, 1869), 15–16.

2. Territorial Senate, *Senate Journal,* 1915, 4–5, 95, 98, 100, 137, 150, 192–93; *Alaska Daily Empire,* March 31, 1915, April 9, 13, 1915.

3. U.S. Congress, House, HR 6887, 64th Cong., 1st sess. (January 4, 1916); 64th Cong., 1st sess., *Congressional Record,* 1916, 53, pt. 15: A1520.

4. James Wickersham, "The Forty Ninth Star," *Collier's,* August 6, 1910, 17.

5. Claus-M. Naske, *49 at Last: The Battle for Alaska Statehood* (Kenmore, Wash.: Epicenter Press, 2009), 49–50; H.R. 13978, 64th Cong., 1st sess. (March 1916).

6. Naske, *49 at Last,* 51.

7. *Daily Alaska Dispatch,* September 1, 1916.

8. *Alaska Daily Empire,* July 13, 1921.

9. Claus-M. Naske, *49 at Last:* 61.

10. Warren G. Harding, *Speeches and Addresses of Warren G. Harding, President of the United States, Delivered during the Course of His Tour from Washington, D.C., to Alaska and Return to San Francisco, June 20 to August 2, 1923,* reported and comp. by James W. Murphy (Washington, D.C.: 1923), 347–49, 360–61; *Ketchikan Alaska Chronicle,* August 22, 1923.

11. *Alaska Daily Empire (Juneau),* November 7 and 9, 1923.

12. U.S. Congress, House, Committee on the Territories, *Reapportionment of the Alaska Legislature: Hearings on H.R. 8114,* 68th Cong., 1st sess (March 27–29, 1924), 14–16.

13. *Alaska Daily Empire (Juneau),* November 15–17, and 19, 1923.

14. House Committee on the Territories, *Reapportionment of the Alaska Legislature: Hearings on H.R. 8114,* 68th Cong., 1st sess. (March 27–29, 1924), 17–20.

15. Ibid., pp. 1, 3.

16. Naske, *49 at Last,* 73.

17. The commissioner was the lowest-ranking federal judge. Miners within an area recorded their claims in the appropriate recording district, where the commissioner served as recorder of claims.

18. Author Claus-M. Naske's interview with Sister Marie Therese, Dimond's eldest daughter, Trinity College, Washington, D.C., April 20, 1975.

19. Ernest Gruening, *The State of Alaska,* 2nd ed. (New York: Random House, 1968), 316.

20. Ernest Gruening, *Many Battles: The Autobiography of Ernest Gruening* (New York: Liveright, 1973), 3–87, 210–28. For a biography of Gruening, see Claus-M. Naske, *Ernest Gruening: Alaska's Greatest Governor* (Fairbanks: University of Alaska Press, 2004).

21. *Alaska Daily Times,* September 2, 1939; *Daily Alaska Empire,* December 6, 1939.

22. *Daily Alaska Empire,* Progress Edition, March 23, 1941.

23. *Anchorage Daily Times,* June 25, 1942; *Daily Alaska Empire,* April 24 and June 23, April 24, 1943; S. 951, 78th Cong., 1st sess. (April 2, 1943).

24. *Daily Alaska Empire,* July 9, 15, and 29 and September 2, 1943; Juneau Chamber of Commerce, Legislative Committee, *Report of Legislative Committee, Juneau Chamber of Commerce, on Senate Bill No. 951, Entitled "A Bill to Provide Admission of Alaska into the Union"* (Juneau: Juneau Chamber of Commerce, 1943).

25. H.R. 3768, 78th Cong., 1st sess. (December 2, 1943); Dean Sherman, "The Statehood Question," *Alaska Life*, June 1944, 15–18.

26. *Daily Alaska Empire*, January 18 and 24, 1944; State of Alaska, Territorial Canvassing Board, "Alaska General Election, September 12, 1944."

27. Alaska Legislature, House, *Journal* (1945), 46–47, Elmer E. Rasmuson Library, University of Alaska, Fairbanks (hereafter EERL).

28. *Daily Alaska Empire*, August 13, 1945.

29. Ibid.

30. *Anchorage Daily Times*, November 2, 1945; E. Atwood to Gruening, December 26, 1945, E. L. Bartlett Papers, Statehood file, folder Correspondence, General, 1944–45, box 6, University of Alaska Fairbanks Archives, Fairbanks, Alaska (hereafter UAFA); *Daily Alaska Empire*, March 12, 1946.

31. U.S. President, *Public Papers of the Presidents of the United States, Harry S Truman, 1946* (Washington, D.C.: Office of the Federal Register, National Archives and Records Service, 1962–66), 66; *Anchorage Daily Times*, February 13, 1946; *Daily Alaska Empire*, February 26, 1946.

32. *Daily Alaska Empire*, August 20 and 22, 1946; *Ketchikan Alaska Chronicle*, August 21, 1946.

33. George Sundborg, *Statehood for Alaska: The Issues Involved and the Facts about the Issues* (Anchorage: Alaska Statehood Association, August, 1946).

34. Territory of Alaska, Territorial Canvassing Board, "Official Returns, General Election, October 8, 1946," author Claus-M. Naske's files.

35. *Fairbanks Daily News-Miner*, July 22, 1952.

36. *Anchorage Daily Times*, October 5, 1946.

37. *Jessen's Weekly*, December 28, 1945.

38. U.S. Bureau of the Census, *Census of Population, 1950*, vol. 2, pt. 56, pp. 5–6; U.S. Congress, House, Subcommittee on Territorial and Insular Possessions of the Committee on Public Lands, *Alaska: Hearings Pursuant to H. Res. 93*, 80th Cong., 1st sess. (August 30–September 12, 1947), 356–60.

39. *Anchorage Daily Times*, September 26, 1946; U.S. Congress, House, Subcommittee on Territories and Insular Possessions of the Committee on Interior and Insular Affairs, *Statehood for Alaska: Hearings on H.R. 20, H.R. 207, H.R. 1746, H.R. 2684, H.R. 2982, and H.R. 1916*, 83rd Cong., 1st sess. (April 14–17, 1953), 138; *Daily Alaska Empire*, April 28, 1944.

40. Edward Latham, ed., *Statehood for Hawaii and Alaska*, Reference Shelf, vol. 25, no. 5 (New York: H. W. Wilson, 1953), 68; *Congressional Record*, 81st Cong., 2nd sess., 2748.

41. Ernest Gruening, *The Battle for Alaska Statehood* (College: University of Alaska Press, 1967), 5–6.

42. U.S. Congress, House, Subcommittee on Territories and Insular Possessions of the Committee on *Public Lands, Statehood for Alaska: Hearings on H.R. 206 and H.R. 1808*, 80th Cong., 1st sess. (April 16–24, 1957), 428.

43. Ernest Gruening, *Message to the People of Alaska: A Report on the Eighteenth Territorial Legislature from Governor Ernest Gruening* (Juneau, 1947), 4, EERL; *Daily Alaska Empire*, April 9 and 21 and May 2, 1947; *Jessen's Weekly*, May 9, 1947.

44. U.S. Congress, House, Subcommittee on Territorial and Insular Possessions of the Committee on Public Lands, *Alaska: Hearings Pursuant to H. Res. 93*, 80th Cong., 1st sess. (August 30–September 12, 1947), 115, 120, 155–56, 159, 166, 160, 169, 374–75; *Anchorage Daily Times*, August 30 and September 13, 1947; *Ketchikan Alaska Chronicle*, September 13, 1947.

45. *Daily Alaska Empire*, December 10, 1946, September 12, 1947; *Anchorage Daily Times*, July 1 and September 5, 1947; *Ketchikan Alaska Chronicle*, August 1 and September 3 and 15, 1947; U.S. Congress, House, Subcommittee on Territorial and Insular Possessions of the Committee on Public Lands, *Alaska: Hearings Pursuant to H. Res. 93*, 80th Cong., 1st sess. (August 30–September 12, 1947), 374; *Jessen's Weekly*, September 12, 1947.

46. *Daily Alaska Empire*, February 21, 1948.

47. E. L. Bartlett to Burke Riley, March 1, 1948, E. L. Bartlett Papers, Statehood file, box 7, folder Correspondence, General, 1948, UAFA; *Daily Alaska Empire*, March 3, 1948; *Ketchikan Alaska Chronicle*, March 3, 1948; U.S. Cong., House, *Providing for the Admission of Alaska into the Union*, H. Rept. 1731 to accompany H.R. 5666, 80th Cong., 2nd sess. (February 27, 1948), 3–6; E. L. Bartlett to Burke Riley, March 1, 1948, E. L. Bartlett Papers, UAFA; *Daily Alaska Empire*, March 5 and 26, 1948; *Ketchikan Alaska Chronicle*, April 17, 1948; E. L. Bartlett to Friend, April 8, 1948, D'Ewart to Felix S. Cohen, March 29, 1948, Frances Lopinski to Friend, April 26, 1948, all in E. L. Bartlett Papers, Statehood file, box 16, folder Legislative History, 1948, UAFA; U.S. Congress, *Congressional Record*, 85th Cong., 2nd sess., 13734–35.

48. *Ketchikan Alaska Chronicle*, February 6, 1948.

49. *Alaska Federationist* (Juneau), June 1948; *Daily Alaska Empire,* May 8, 1948.

50. Kirk H. Porter and Donald Bruce Johnson, *National Party Platforms, 1840–1960* (Urbana: University of Illinois Press, 1961), 435, 453; *Ketchikan Alaska Chronicle,* November 6 and 8, 1948.

51. Alaska Legislature, House, *Journal,* 1949, 49, EERL; *Daily Alaska Empire,* June 24, 1949; *Anchorage Daily Times,* December 18, 1948.

52. *Daily Alaska Empire,* January 23 and February 14 and 20, 1947; *Ketchikan Alaska Chronicle,* February 22, 1947; Alaska Legislature, House, *Journal,* 1947, 320, EERL; Senate, *Journal,* 1949, 432, 541, 614–16, EERL; House, *Journal,* 1949, 1022–23, EERL; Territory of Alaska, *Session Laws,* 1949, 270–71, EERL.

53. U.S. Cong., House, Subcommittee on Territorial and Insular Possessions of the Committee on Public Lands, *Statehood for Alaska: Hearings on H.R. 331 and Related Bills,* 81st Cong., 1st sess. (January 3, 1949); U.S. Cong., House, Subcommittee on Territorial and Insular Possessions of the Committee on Public Lands, *Statehood for Alaska: Hearings on H.R. 206 and H.R. 1808,* 81st Cong., 1st sess. (April 16–24, 1947), 393–394.

54. *Daily Alaska Empire,* March 4, 1949; House Subcommittee on Territorial and Insular Possessions of the Committee on Public Lands, *Statehood for Alaska: Hearings on H.R. 331 and Related Bills,* 81st Cong., 1st sess. (March 4 and 8, 1949), 31, 34–35; House Subcommittee on Territories and Insular Possessions, *Providing for the Admission of Alaska into the Union,* H. Rept. 225 to accompany H.R. 331, 81st Cong., 1st sess., 36–52; George B. Galloway, *The Legislative Process in Congress* (New York: Thomas Y. Crowell Co., 1955), 343–45; *Congressional Record,* 81st Cong., 2d sess., 2780–81.

55. *Ketchikan Alaska Chronicle,* January 24, 1949, March 27, 1950, and April 24 and 27, 1950; Claus-M. Naske, *49 at Last,* 142–43.

56. U.S. Senate, Committee on Interior and Insular Affairs, *Alaska Statehood: Hearings on H.R. 331 and S. 2036,* 81st Cong., 1st sess. (April 24–29, 1950), 1, 26, 49, 79, 160, 164.

57. Ibid., 317–18.

58. Author Claus-M. Naske's interview with Mary Lee Council, Washington, D.C., July 20, 1969.

59. Under the traditional system, sections would be determined under the requirements of the Public Land Survey System, which began in the surveying of public lands performed after the Revolutionary War. The system imposed a grid system across much of the country. This provided a fair, economical way to divide and describe land into uniform parcels. Public Land Survey Townships were subdivided into thirty-six sections, each section approximately one mile by one mile in dimension. Sections were numbered from 1 to 36 and labeled in a switch-back pattern.

60. Senate Committee on Interior and Insular Affairs, *Providing for the Admission of Alaska into the Union,* 81st Cong., 2d sess., S. Rep. 1929, 11; transcript of E. L. Bartlett radio address, recorded for station KINY, Juneau, July 5, 1950, E. L. Bartlett Papers, Statehood file, Legislative History, June–July 1950, box 16, UAFA; E. L. Bartlett Memorandum, "Public Land Provisions in Modern Alaska Statehood Legislation," June 27, 1957, E. L. Bartlett Papers, Statehood file, Legislative History, June–July 1950, box 16, UAFA.

61. *Congressional Record,* 81st Cong., 2nd sess., 15919–16035.

62. Naske, *49 at Last,* 165, 167.

63. Ibid., 184–86.

64. *Anchorage Daily Times,* May 17, 1954.

65. Naske, *49 at Last,* 205–214.

66. Ibid., 224–226.

67. Ibid., 226–27.

68. Ibid., 227–28.

69. Ibid., 228–29.

70. Ibid., 229.

71. For the story of the convention, see Victor Fischer, *Alaska's Constitutional Convention* (Fairbanks: University of Alaska Press, 1975).

72. Ibid., 52–53; Gruening, *The Battle for Statehood,* 383.

73. Territory of Alaska, "Official Canvass of Results, Alaska General Election, Tuesday, October 9, 1956," author Claus M. Naske's files.

74. Naske, *An Interpretative History,* 106; Senate Committee on Interior and Insular Affairs, *Nomination of Frederick A. Seaton to Be Secretary of the Interior,* 84th Cong., 2nd sess. (June 5, 1956), 2–30, quote on 30.

75. *Congressional Record,* 85th Cong., 1st sess. (1957), A4651.

76. Naske, *49 at Last,* 257–58.

77. Naske, *An Interpretative History,* 159.

78. Ibid., 159–60.

79. Ibid., 160–61.

80. E. L. Bartlett interview with Val Trimble and Scott Hart, Washington, D.C., August 1, 1965, Vide Bartlett private papers.

81. Naske, *An Interpretive History,* 98–99.

82. Ibid., 162.

83. Naske, *49 at Last,* 273.

84. Ibid., 275.

85. Ibid., 277.

86. Naske, *An Interpretive History,* 164–66.

87. Bartlett interview with Val Trimble and Scott Hart, August 1, 1965, E. L. Bartlett Papers, UAFA.

88. Claus-M. Naske, "103,350,000 Acres . . . the Land Grant Provisions of Alaska Statehood Bills from 1916 Onward," *Alaska Journal,* Autumn 1972, 11–12.

Chapter 16. Managing Alaska's Oil Resources

1. Alaska Legislative Council, "Memorandum on Oil and Gas Legislation," 1958, author Claus-M. Naske's files. (Naske worked as a counsel for the State of Alaska and for several Alaska law firms. The attorney-general's office collected many historical materials and distributed them to the attorneys, including Naske. They are still in his personal files.)

2. Public Administration Service, "The Alaska Constitution and the State Patrimony: The Constitution and Natural Resource," November 1955.

3. Ibid., 14, 17.

4. E. L. Bartlett, "Meeting the Challenge," November 8, 1955, College, Alaska, pp. 2–4, E. L. Bartlett Papers, Statehood file, 1955, University of Alaska Fairbanks Archives, Fairbanks, Alaska.

5. Ibid., 5.

6. Ibid.

7. Ibid.

8. Alaska Territorial Legislature, *House Journal,* 1953, 200; *Session Laws of Alaska,* 1953, ch. 126, Sec. 9, 11, Elmer E. Rasmuson Library, University of Alaska, Fairbanks (hereafter EERL).

9. Claus-M. Naske, John S. Whitehead, and William Schneider, *Alaska Statehood: The Memory of the Battle and the Evaluation of the Present by Those Who Lived It* (Fairbanks: Alaska Statehood Commission, n.d.), 82.

10. Ibid.; *Session Laws of Alaska,* 1955, ch. 40, EERL.

11. *Session Laws of Alaska,* 1955, Sec. 2, pp. 11, 12, EERL.

12. Ibid., Sec. 1, 3.

13. *Session Laws of Alaska,* 1955, ch. 189, Sec. 2, and Sec. 3–5, EERL.

14. Ibid., Sec. 4.

15. *Session Laws of Alaska,* 1955, ch. 183, Sec. 9(a)(2), EERL.

16. Ibid., ch. 7, Sec. 2, EERL. Taxes determined by and object's worth are deemed "ad valorem," meaning "according to value."

17. Geoffrey T. Bleakley, "A Policy History of Alaska Oil Lands Administration, 1953–1974" (PhD diss., Washington State University, May 1996), 37–38.

18. J. Gerald Williams, Attorney General, to Empire Printing Company, July 9, 1957, author Naske's files.

19. Videotape Deposition of Evert L. Brown, State of Alaska, Office of the Attorney General, Royalty Litigation Collection, *State of Alaska v. Amerada Hess,* May 21, 1987, Anchorage, Alaska, vol. 1, Juneau.

20. Irene E. Ryan to Phil R. Holdsworth, January 11, 1958, author Naske's files.

21. Claus-M. Naske, "Bob Bartlett and the Alaska Mental Health Act," *Pacific Northwest Quarterly,* 71, no. 1 (January 1980): 31–39; Evert L. Brown to Robert E. Stevens, the Superior Oil Company, May 12, 1958, author Naske's files.

22. Alaska Department of Lands, "Rules and Regulations Relating to Lease of Alaska Lands" (May 1956); Gwen D. Phillips to Phil R. Holdsworth, June 2, 1958; Minutes of the Meeting, Public Lands Committee, Western Oil and Gas Association, August 15, 1958—all in author Naske's files.

23. *Fairbanks Daily News-Miner,* August 19, 1958.

24. Humble Oil & Gas Refining Company to Evert L. Brown, September 14, 1958, author Naske's files.

25. Halbouty Alaska Oil Company to Alaska Land Board, December 5, 1958, author Naske's files.

26. Reserve Oil and Gas Company to Alaska Land Board, December 8, 1958; Exploration Services to Phil R. Holdsworth, December 10, 1958—both in author Naske's files.

27. Phil R. Holdsworth to El Paso Natural Gas Products Company, October 30, 1958, author Naske's files.

28. "Alaska Land Board Schedules Oil and Gas Hearings," November 15, 1958, author Naske's files.

29. Phil R. Holdsworth to Evert L. Brown, November 21–6, 1958, author Naske's files.

30. "Statement of Fred W. Bush," Alaska Land Board Hearing, December 11 and 12, 1958, author Naske's files.

31. Ibid.

32. Transcript, "Alaska Land Board Hearing," December 11 and 12, 1958, Anchorage, Alaska, author Naske's files.

33. Ibid.

34. Fred W. Bush to Phil Holdsworth, December 17, 1958, author Naske's files.

35. Alaska Legislative Council, "Final Report of the Legislative Council of the 23rd Legislature, Territory of Alaska," Publication No. 23–10, Juneau, Alaska, 1959; Alaska Legislative Council, "Memorandum on Oil and Gas Legislation," 1959.

36. Ibid.

37. Phil R. Holdsworth to J. Gerald Williams, January 13, 1959, author Naske's files.

38. Statement of H. T. Sutherland, the Ohio Oil Company, January 15, 1959, author Naske's files.

39. State of Alaska, *Session Laws, Resolution and Memorials,* 1959 (Juneau, Alaska, 1959), 229–247, EERL.

40. Ibid.

41. Ibid.

42. Ibid.

43. Bleakley, "A Policy History", 83–85.

44. Ibid., 88, 91, 94–99.

45. Ibid., 121–122.

46. Ibid., 123.

47. William R. Johnson, Jr., "Alaska v Amerada Hess: Alaska Litigates for Oil Royalties, 1977–1992" (PhD diss., Washington State University, 2005), 2.

48. Ibid., 3.

49. Ibid., 2–3.

50. Ibid., 4.

51. Ibid.

52. Ibid., 4–5.

53. Ibid., 5–6, 3.

54. Ibid., 6–7.

55. Ibid., 108–33.

56. *Anchorage Daily News*, October 19, 1989.

57. Johnson, "Alaska v Amerada Hess," 194.

58. *Anchorage Daily News*, October 6, 1990.

59. Ibid., March 20, 30, 1991.

60. William R. Johnson, Jr., "Alaska v Amerada Hess," 119–94.

61. Ibid., 210–12.

62. Ibid., 212–13.

63. Ibid., 215.

64. Ibid., 215–38.

65. Ibid., 215–41.

Chapter 17. Transition to Statehood

1. Richard A. Cooley, *Alaska: A Challenge in Conservation* (Madison: University of Wisconsin Press, 1967), 21–23.

2. Ibid., 24.

3. George W. Rogers, *Alaska in Transition: The Southeast Region (Baltimore: Johns Hopkins Press, 1960),* 74–75; Lawrence W. Rakestraw, *A History of the United States Forest Service in Alaska* (Anchorage: Alaska Historical Commission, Department of Education, State of Alaska and Alaska Region, U.S. Forest Service, Department of Agriculture, with the assistance of the Alaska Historical Society, 1981), 128.

4. George W. Rogers, *The Future of Alaska: Economic Consequences of Statehood* (Baltimore: Johns Hopkins Press, 1962), 266.

5. Ibid.

6. Ibid.

7. Ibid., 266–67.

8. Ibid., 267–68.

9. Ibid., 269.

10. "The 49th State," *Time,* July 14, 1958, 16.

11. *Fairbanks Daily News-Miner,* August 9, 14, and 25, 1958; Robert B. Atwood, "Alaska's Struggle for Statehood," *State Government,* Autumn 1958: 208.

12. *Fairbanks Daily News-Miner,* July 16 and 19, 1958; George Sundborg to E. L. Bartlett, July 4, 1958, Vide Bartlett, private papers.

13. *Anchorage Daily Times,* July 15 and 24, August 20, 1958; Donald R. Moberg, "The 1958 Election in Alaska," *Western Political Quarterly* 12 (1950): 259–60.

14. *Fairbanks Daily News-Miner,* August 19 and 25, 1958; *Daily Alaska Empire,* July 13 and August 16, 1958.

15. Ralph and Victor Rivers were brothers. "Statehood Primary Election Results," August 26, 1958, Alaska Historical Library, Juneau.

16. Ibid.

17. *Fairbanks Daily News-Miner,* August 2, 1958, November 4 and 28, 1958; "Fred and the 49th," *Time,* November 24, 1958; Moberg, "The 1958 Election in Alaska," 260–62; *Daily Alaska Empire,* December 1, 1958.

18. "Alaska Official Returns of the Special Statehood Referendum Election, August 26, 1958, and the General Election, November 25, 1958," Office of

the Secretary of Alaska, Juneau Alaska, copy in author Naske's files.

19. Thomas B. Stewart to E. L. Bartlett, May 25, 1957, E. L. Bartlett Papers, Statehood file, box 12, folder Correspondence, General, May 1957, University of Alaska Fairbanks Archives, Fairbanks, Alaska (hereafter UAFA); "Minutes of the Meeting of the Alaska Statehood Committee," March 7–8, 1958, UAFA; "Minutes of Meeting, Executive Committee of the Alaska Statehood Committee," July 12–13, 1958, and "Contract Amendment," E. L. Bartlett Papers, box 2, folder Alaska Statehood Committee, 1958–59, UAFA; *Session Laws of Alaska,* 1957, 471, Elmer E. Rasmuson Library, University of Alaska, Fairbanks (hereafter EERL); *Session Laws of Alaska* Public Administration Service, *Proposed Organization of the Executive Branch, State of Alaska: A Summary Report* (Chicago: Public Administration Service, 1958); Public Administration Service, *Proposed Organization of the Judicial Branch, State of Alaska* (Chicago: Public Administration Service, 1959); Public Administration Service, *Local Government under the Alaska Constitution: A Survey Report* (Chicago: Public Administration Service, 1959); Public Administration Service, *Functional and Staffing Charts for the Proposed Organization of the Executive Branch, State of Alaska* (Chicago: Public Administration Service, 1959).

20. *Fairbanks Daily News-Miner,* January 3 and 12, 1959.

21. 86th Cong., 1st sess., *Congressional Record, S. 1541, March 25, 1959, p.* 8737; *H.R. 6091, March 26, 1959; Cong. Rec. 86, p. 9472.*

22. House Subcommittee on Territorial and Insular Affairs, *Alaska Omnibus Bill: Hearings on H.R. 6091 and H.R. 6112,* 86th Cong., 1st sess. (1959), 25–36, 55–56; Senate Committee on Interior and Insular Affairs, *Alaska Omnibus Bill: Hearings on S. 1541,* 86th Cong., 1st sess. (1959).

23. House Subcommittee, *Hearings on H.R. 6091,* 86th Cong., 1st sess. (1959), 67–73; Omnibus Bill, *Congressional Record,* 86th Cong., 1st sess., 9473; Senate Committee, *Hearings on S. 1541,* 86th Cong., 1st sess. (1959), 11.

24. House Subcommittee, *Hearings on H.R. 6091,* 45, 59–63; Senate Committee, *Hearings on S. 1541,* 10–11; Paul F. Royster to Ralph Rivers, September 25, 1959, Ralph J. Rivers Papers, Legislative file, 1959–66, box 18, folder Omnibus Bill, UAFA.

25. House Subcommittee, *Hearings on H.R. 6091,* 61–78.

26. Senate Committee, *Hearings on S. 1541,* 11; House Subcommittee, *Hearings on H.R. 6091,* 26–35.

27. House Subcommittee, *Hearings on H.R. 6091,* 27–39; *Anchorage Daily Times,* March 25, 1959.

28. House Subcommittee, *Hearings on H.R. 6091,* 56–58; P.L. 86-70, 85th Cong., H.R. 7120, June 25, 1959 (73 Stat. 141), Alaska Omnibus Act, Sect. 21, Highways.

29. Senate Committee, *Hearings on S. 1541,* 5–8, 74.

30. *Anchorage Daily Times,* May 11, 1959; House Subcommittee, *Hearings on H.R. 6091,* 79–80.

31. *Session Laws of Alaska,* 1959, 89–104; *Anchorage Daily Times,* April 21 and 28, May 11, 1959.

32. *Omnibus Bill,* HR 7120, 86th Cong., 1st sess. (1959); *Congressional Record* (May 14, 1959), 9470, 9480, 9482–84; *Anchorage Daily Times,* May 28, June 15, 1959; E. L. Bartlett to Hugh Wade, June 4, 1959, Bartlett Papers, Alaska Statehood File, folder 1959–62, UAFA.

33. *Omnibus Act,* 86th Cong., 1st sess., *Congressional Record 34, (*May–June 1959), 9470, 10568, 9678–79, 10594.

34. Constitution of the State of Alaska., art. 3, sec. 25.

35. Ibid., art. 10.

36. Ibid.; Thomas A. Morehouse, Gerald A. McBeath, and Linda Leask, *Alaska's Urban and Rural Governments* (Lanham, MD.: University Press of America, 1984), 26.

37. Morehouse, McBeath, and Leask, *Alaska's Urban and Rural Governments,* 39.

38. Ibid., 42.

39. Ibid., 43–44.

40. Ibid., 45.

41. Constitution of the State of Alaska, art. 10, sec. 1.

42. Ibid., art. 8; Elaine Mitchell, ed., *Alaska Blue Book,* 1st ed. (Juneau: State of Alaska, Department of Education, Division of State Libraries, 1973), 148.

43. Constitution of the State of Alaska, art. 8, sec. 15.

44. Claus-M. Naske, *An Interpretative History of Alaskan Statehood* (Anchorage: Alaska Northwest Publishing Co., 1973), 142.

45. Author Naske's interview with Hugh J. Wade, Anchorage, Alaska, December 30, 1976.

46. Mitchell, *Alaska Blue Book, 1975,* 2nd ed. (Juneau: Alaska Department of Education, 1975), 196–97.

47. State of Alaska, Department of Economic Enterprise, *Alaska Statistical Review, 1972* (Juneau: Division of Budget and Management, Office of the Governor, 1972):15–16.

48. Patrick O'Donovan, "The Forty-Ninth Star on the U.S. Flag," *London Observer,* July 13, 1958.

49. Author Claus-M. Naske's interview with Herbert L. Faulkner, Juneau, Alaska, August 11, 1969.

50. "Message of Governor William A. Egan to the Second Session, First Alaska State Legislature, Recommending Appropriations for Fiscal Year 1961," in *State of Alaska Budget Document, 1960–61* (Juneau), January 27, 1960, 1–4, EERL.

51. Ray J. Schrick, "Alaska's Ordeal," *Wall Street Journal,* March 16, 1960.

52. Ibid.

53. Ibid.

54. "Main Trails and Bypaths," *Alaska Sportsman,* January 1960, 7.

55. "Message of Governor William A. Egan to the Second Session," 1–4.

56. Ibid., 7, 20; Alaska State Planning Commission, *State of Alaska Capital Improvement Program,* 1960–1966, January 29, 1960, C-4–C-7, EERL.

57. "Main Trails and Bypaths," 7; Schrick, "Alaska's Ordeal."

58. State of Alaska, Department of Economic Development, Industrial Development Division, *Alaska Statistical Review, 1968* (Juneau: Office of the Governor, 1969), 3, 23, 28, 56; "Bob" Bartlett, "Big Gains in Fish, Timber," *Fairbanks Daily News-Miner,* March 17, 1966.

59. Herman E. Slotnick, "The 1960 Election in Alaska," *Western Political Quarterly,* March 1961: 300; Thomas A. Morehouse and Gordon A. Harrison, *An Electoral Profile of Alaska* (Fairbanks: Institute of Social, Economic, and Government Research, 1973), 2–3.

60. *The Nomination of Governor Walter J. Hickel of Alaska to Be Secretary of the Interior: Hearings before the Committee on Interior and Insular Affairs,* U.S. Senate, 91st Cong., 1st sess. (January 15–18 and 20, 1969), parts 1 and 2, pp. 16, 17–91.

61. Jan Juran and Daniel Raff, "Theodore F. Stevens, Republican Senator from Alaska," in *Ralph Nader Congress Project: Citizens Look at Congress* (Washington, D.C.: Grossman Publishers, 1972), 8; Tom Brown, *Oil on Ice: Alaskan Wilderness at the Crossroads* (San Francisco: Sierra Club, 1971), 42–43.

62. State of Alaska, Office of the Governor, "Alaska Earthquake Disaster Damage Report" (preliminary), April 4, 1964, in author Naske's files.

63. *Washington Daily News,* March 30, 1964. The massive Good Friday earthquake was not confined to Alaska. Huge tidal waves called tsunamis battered the Pacific coast. Crescent City, California, experienced four such tsunamis, which severely damaged the town and killed ten (another fifteen were reported missing). And at Depoe Bay, Oregon, a tsunami killed four. See *Washington Post,* March 31, 1964.

64. *Washington Post,* March 31, 1964.

65. E. L. Bartlett Press Release, April 3, 1964, in author Naske's files.

66. E. L. Bartlett to Clinton B. Anderson, April 11, 1964, in author Naske's files; *Fairbanks Daily News-Miner,* May 20, 1964; *An Act to Amend the Alaska Omnibus Act...,* P.L. 88-451; 88th Cong., 2nd sess., (August 19, 1964), S. 2881.

67. Brookings Institution, Advanced Study Program, in Association with the Legislative Council of the State of Alaska, "Conference on the Future of Alaska," Fall 1969, EERL.

68. Planning Guidelines for the State of Alaska, prepared for the Office of the Governor, State of Alaska (Menlo Park, Calif.: Stanford Research Institute, 1969).

Chapter 18. Alaska's Oil Economy in the 1970s and 1980s

1. Capital Site Selection Committee, "Information for Participants," 1974, author Naske's files.

2. Capital Site Selection Committee, "The Birth of a City, segment 1 and 2: "Nobody Told Juneau," *Alaska Review* (monthly television program funded by the Alaska State Legislature and the Alaska Humanities Forum), 1977.

3. Ibid.

4. *Ketchikan Daily News,* January 15, 1977.

5. Hammond campaign brochure, in author Naske's files.

6. Ibid.

7. State of Alaska, Department of Revenue, *Alaska '75: Facing the Crunch* (Juneau, 1975), 16 pages.

8. *All Alaska Weekly,* December 22, 1978.

9. Jay S. Hammond, *Tales of Alaska's Bush Rat Governor* (Fairbanks/Seattle: Epicenter Press, 1974), 215, 225.

10. Ibid., 153.

11. Ibid., 248.

12. Ibid.; Constitution of the State of Alaska, art. 9, sec. 15.

13. Hammond, *Tales of Alaska's Bush Rat Governor,* 249.

14. Ibid., 251–52.

15. Ibid., 253.

16. "The Permanent Fund Dividend," Alaska Permanent Fund Corp. Web site, www.apfc.org/home/Content/alaska/dividentPrgrm.cfm (accessed May 26, 2009).

17. Gunnar Knapp, Scott Goldsmith, Jack Kruse, and Gregg Erickson, *Permanent Fund Dividend Program: Economic Effects and Attitudes* (Anchorage: Institute of Social and Economic Research, University of Alaska Anchorage, 1984). The authors based this study on a survey of 1982 and 1983 dividend recipients.

18. See Scott Goldsmith, "Sustainable State Spending Levels from Alaska State Revenues," *Alaska Review of Social and Economic Conditions*, 20, no. 1 (February 1983).

19. Hammond, *Tales of Alaska's Bush Rat Governor*, 274.

20. *Anchorage Daily News*, August 3, 2005.

21. *Anchorage Daily News*, August 3 and 5, 2005.

22. John Strohmeyer, *Extreme Conditions: Big Oil and the Transformation of Alaska* (New York: Simon & Shuster, 1993), 136.

23. Ibid., 136–37.

24. *Anchorage Daily News*, August 24, 1986.

25. Ibid.

26. Ibid.

27. Ibid.

28. Melissa Campbell, "Former Governor Keeps Going Strong," *Alaska Journal of Commerce*, March 13, 2006, www.AlaskaLegislature.com (accessed May 26, 2009).

29. "The Characteristics of Alaska Migrants: Boom and Bust Migration, 1960–2000," in Lance Howe, "Understanding Alaska," Institute of Social and Economic Research, available at www.iser.uaa.alaska.edu/isser/people/elhowe/research.html (page now discontinued); Strohmeyer, *Extreme Conditions*, 154.

30. Ibid., 154–55.

31. Ibid., 155–57.

32. Ibid., 158–59; Terrence Cole to author Claus-M. Naske, February 24, 2007, Fairbanks, Alaska; Strohmeyer, *Extreme Conditions*, 159–60; *The Wall Street Journal*, February 24, 1987.

33. Strohmeyer, *Extreme Conditions*, 160.

34. Alaska Department of Labor, *Alaska Economic Trends*, (Juneau: Department of Labor, 1988), 7.

35. Ibid., 7–8.

36. Ibid.; "The Characteristics of Alaska Migrants: Boom and Bust Migration, 1960–2000."

37. Strohmeyer, *Extreme Conditions*, 158–61.

38. *Anchorage Daily News*, January 16, 1987.

39. Ibid.

40. *Anchorage Daily News,* August 3 and 5, 2005.

41. Ibid.

42. *Fairbanks Daily News-Miner*, March 1, 1987.

43. Anchorage Daily News, October 28, 1989.

Chapter 19. Native Land Claims

1. Joseph H. Fitzgerald et al., *Alaska Natives and the Land* (Washington, D.C.: Federal Field Committee for Development Planning in Alaska, 1968), 19–22.

2. *Alaska Native Claims Settlement Act of 1971*, P.L. 92-203, 85 Stat. 688, , 92nd Cong., 1st sess. (December 18, 1971), 94.

3. Paul Brooks, *The Pursuit of Wilderness* (Boston: Houghton Mifflin, 1971), 64.

4. Ibid., 66.

5. Ibid.

6. Ibid., 67.

7. See Ernest S. Burch, Jr., *The Iñupiaq Eskimo Nations of Northwest Alaska* (Fairbanks: University of Alaska Press, 1998).

8. Brooks, *The Pursuit of Wilderness*, 62–63.

9. Pamela R. Stern, *Historical Dictionary of the Inuit* (Lanham, Md.: Scarecrow Press, 2004), 47.

10. Robert D. Arnold et al., *Alaska Native Lands Claims* (Anchorage: Alaska Native Foundation, 1976), 95–96; Brooks, *The Pursuit of Wilderness*, 72–73.

11. Arnold, *Alaska Native Land Claims*, 100.

12. *Alaska Native Claims Settlement Act of 1971*, 96.

13. Ibid.; Mary Clay Berry, *The Alaska Pipeline: The Politics of Oil and Native Land Claims* (Bloomington: Indiana University Press, 1975), 44.

14. Berry, *The Alaska Pipeline*, 34–35.

15. Donald Craig Mitchell, *Take My Land, Take My Life: The Story of Congress's Historic Settlement of Alaska Native Land Claims, 1960–1971* (Fairbanks: University of Alaska Press, 2001), 88–90.

16. Berry, *The Alaska Pipeline*, 37.

17. Ibid.

18. Brooks, *The Pursuit of Wilderness*, 78–90.

19. Ibid., 91–92.

20. *Alaska Native Claims Settlement Act of 1971*, 96; Berry, *The Alaska Pipeline*, 44.

21. Arnold, *Alaska Native Land Claims*, 103–105.

22. Ibid.

23. Ibid., 106–107.

24. Berry, *The Alaska Pipeline*, 47.

25. Ibid., 48, 49.

26. Ibid., 48–49.

27. Ibid., 50.

28. Ibid.

29. Ibid., 51.

30. Arnold, *Alaska Native Land Claims,* 119.

31. Ibid., 120.

32. Senate Committee on Interior and Insular Affairs, *Alaska Native Land Claims: Hearings on S. 2906, S. 1964, S. 2690, and S. 2020,* 90th Cong., 2nd sess. (1968), 441, 189, 237.

33. Ibid., 45–46, 289–90, 371–72.

34. Arnold, *Alaska Native Land Claims,* 123–25.

35. Berry, *The Alaska Pipeline,* 60–61.

36. Arnold, *Alaska Native Land Claims,* 126; Berry, *The Alaska Pipeline,* 62. See the full report, Federal Field Committee for Development Planning, *Alaska Natives and the Land, Anchorage, Alaska, October 1968* (Washington, D.C.: Government Printing Office, 1968).

37. Arnold, *Alaska Native Land Claims,* 132.

38. Berry, *The Alaska Pipeline,* 65.

39. Ibid., 67–68.

40. Ibid., 69.

41. Ibid., 69, 81.

42. Ibid., 102–103.

43. Ibid., 117–18, 121.

44. Arnold, *Alaska Native Land Claims,* 134.

45. Ibid.

46. Ibid., 135–36.

47. Ibid., 137.

48. Ibid., 141–42.

49. Ibid.

50. *Alaska Native Claims Settlement Act, Conference Report to Accompany H.R. 10367,* 92nd Cong., 1st sess. (December 14, 1971), S. Conf. Rep. 12-581, 35.

51. Ibid.

52. Ibid.

53. Ibid., 36.

54. David S. Case and David A. Voluck, *Alaska Natives and American Laws,* 2nd ed. (Fairbanks: University of Alaska Press, 2002), 160.

55. Ibid., 159–160.

56. Ibid., 160.

57. Ibid. 161–62.

58. Ibid., 162.

59. Ibid.; John Strohmeyer, *Extreme Conditions: Big Oil and the Transformation of Alaska* (New York: Simon & Schuster, 1993), 188.

60. Anchorage Daily News, May 18, 1991.

Chapter 20. The Native Regional Corporations

1. Mary Clay Berry, *The Alaska Pipeline: The Politics of Oil and Native Land Claims* (Bloomington: Indiana University Press, 1975), 148–49.

2. Rosemary Shinohara and Virginia McKinney, "Natives Taking Leadership in Business Community," *Alaska Industry,* January 1976, 37–38, 40–47, 53–54.

3. Chapter 19, State of Alaska, *Session Laws of Alaska,* 1976, ch. 19 and 240, Elmer E. Rasmuson Library, University of Alaska, Fairbanks.

4. *Omnibus Act,* P.P. 94-204, 99th Cong., 1st sess. (January 2, 1976).

5. "A Year of Change for Alaska's Regional Native Companies," *Alaska Business and Industry,* September, 1983, 24.

6. *Fairbanks Daily News-Miner,* April 25, 1984.

7. Ibid., April 20, 1984.

8. Alaska Native Review Commission, "Overview Hearings Agenda," *Alaska Native News,* March 1984, 26.

9. *Alaska Native Claims Settlement Act,* 92nd Cong., 1st sess. (December 14, 1971), Report No. 92-581, 33.

10. David Case and David A. Voluck, *Alaska Natives and American Laws,* 2nd ed. (Fairbanks: University of Alaska Press, 2002), 168–69.

11. Steve Colt, "Alaska Natives and the New Harpoon: Economic Performance of the ANCSA Regional Corporations," revised February 2, 2001 (Institute of Social and Economic Research, University of Alaska Anchorage, 2001), 3.

12. Donald Craig Mitchell, *Take My Land Take My Life* (Fairbanks: University of Alaska Press, 2001), 507–508.

13. CIRI had been able to pick up only about half of its allotments because much of the land in the Anchorage area was already claimed. CIRI, thereupon, persuaded Congress in 1981 to give it a $200 million credit in exchange for the unavailable land. It used these credits to bid at auctions of surplus federal property. Newspapers estimated that by 1991 CIRI had built a billion-dollar real estate empire that included more than thirty former federal properties in places ranging from Miami Beach, Florida, to Alexandria, Virginia, and also holdings in Hawaii and California. CIRI also used tax breaks given to broadcasting corporations that sell their business to minorities. Those opportunities gave CIRI major interest shares in television stations in New Haven, Connecticut,

and Nashville, Tennessee, as well as radio stations in Boston, Washington, D.C., Chicago, Seattle, and three other metropolitan areas. See John Strohmeyer, *Extreme Conditions: Big Oil and the Transformation of Alaska* (New York: Simon & Schuster, 1993), 185.

14. Mitchell, *Take My Land*, 507–508.

15. *Anchorage Daily News*, July 7, 2006.

16. Case and Voluck, *Alaska Natives and American Laws*, 170.

17. Ibid., 178–79.

18. Ibid., 183.

19. Ibid.

20. Ibid., 183–84.

21. Will Swagel, "Feast or Famine: Dividends for Native Shareholders," *Alaska Business Monthly*, September 2001.

22. Ibid., 31.

23. Ibid., 32.

24. Ibid.

25. Donald Craig Mitchell, *Take My Land, Take My Life*, 503–504.

26. Ibid., 504–505.

27. Ibid., 506.

28. Ibid., 507.

29. Ibid.

Chapter 21. Land Claims and Land Conservation

1. Congressional Quarterly Service, *Congress and the Nation, 1945–1964: A Review of Government and Politics in the Postwar Years* (Washington, DC: Congressional Quarterly Service, 1965), 1597, 1606, 1530.

2. *Multiple-Use Sustained-Yield Act of 1960*, P.L. 86-517, H.R. 10572, 86th Cong., 2nd sess. (June 12, 1960), 16 U.S.C. 530; *Wilderness Act*, P.L. 88-577, 88th Cong., 2nd sess. (September 3, 1964), codified at 16 U.S.C. 1131–1136. The major federal agencies to conduct these reviews were the Forest Service, the Fish and Wildlife Service, and the National Park Service. Congress included the Bureau of Land Management in 1976 when it passed the Federal Land Policy and Management Act (P.L. 94-579). During this period Congress also passed legislation establishing national wild and scenic river and national trail systems, an act protecting endangered animal and plant species, and several measures dealing with air and water quality.

3. *National Environmental Policy Act*, P.L. 91-190, codified at 42 U.S.C. 4321.

4. Joint Federal-State Land Use Planning Commission for Alaska, *The Final Report of the Joint Federal-State Land Use Planning Commission for Alaska: Some Guidelines for Deciding Alaska's Future* (Anchorage: Joint Federal-State Land Use Planning Commission for Alaska, May 30, 1979), 1.

5. Mary Clay Berry, *The Alaska Pipeline: The Politics of Oil and Native Land Claims* (Bloomington: Indiana University Press, 1975), 250.

6. Ibid., 251, 252–54.

7. *Multiple-Use Sustained-Yield Act of 1960*, P.L. 86-517, H.R. 10572, 86th Cong., 2nd sess. (June 12, 1980), codified at 16 U.S.C. 528-31; *Forest and Rangeland Renewable Resources Planning Act of 1974*, P.L. 93-378, 88 Stat. 475, as amended (August 17, 1974), codified at 16 U.S.C. 1600-14; *National Forest Management Act of 1976*, P.L. 94-588, 90 Stat. 2949, as amended (October 22, 1976), codified in various sections of 16 U.S.C.

8. *Federal Land Policy and Management Act*, Public Law 94-579, 90 Stat. 2743.

9. House *Subcommittee on General Oversight and Alaska Lands of the Committee on Interior and Insular Affairs, Inclusion of Alaska Lands in National Park, Forest, Wildlife Refuge, and Wild and Scenic River Systems: Hearings on H.R. 39, H.R. 1974, H.R. 2876, H.R. 5505, to Designate Certain Lands in the State of Alaska as Units of the National Park, National Wildlife Refuge, Wild and Scenic Rivers, and National Wilderness Preservation Systems, and for Other Purposes; H.R. 1454, to Establish the Lake Clark National Park in the State of Alaska, and for Other Purposes; H.R. 5605 and H.R. 8651, to Establish Admiralty Island National Preserve in the State of Alaska*, 95th Cong., 1st sess. (1977). Hearings were held on various dates, starting on April 21, 1977, and ending on September 21, 1977. The hearings comprise sixteen volumes. Testimony given in Alaska is contained in vols. 8–13, and that in Washington, D.C., in vols. 1–3 and 14–16; testimonies given in Chicago, Atlanta, Denver, and Seattle are found in vols. 4–7, respectively.

10. Joint Federal-State Land Use Planning Commission for Alaska, *The Final Report of the Joint Federal-State Land Use Planning Commission for Alaska*, 1.

11. Ibid., 13–15.

12. *Alaska National Interest Lands Conservation Act*

(ANILCA), P.L. 96-487, 94 Stat. 2371 (December 2, 1980).

13. Ibid.

14. As of 2008, 13 million acres remained to be transferred; 59 million were waiting on the patenting process; 7 million acres remained to be transferred via ANCSA, and almost three thousand Native Allotment parcels had yet to be transferred.

15. *ANILCA,* sec. 708, sec. 705.

16. Ibid., sec. 1002.

17. Ibid., Title 1, sec. 101(d).

18. Ibid., Title IX, sec. 907, a–g.

Chapter 22. The Oil Boom

1. Lisa Wolff, *Katalla to Prudhoe Bay: An Entertaining Look at the First 100 Years of the Oil and Gas Industry in Alaska* (Anchorage: Petroleum News Alaska, 1997), 42.

2. Ibid.

3. Ibid.

4. Ibid.

5. Ibid., 42–43.

6. Ibid., 43.

7. Jack Roderick, *Crude Dreams: A Personal History of Oil and Politics in Alaska* (Fairbanks/Seattle: Epicenter Press, 1997), 204.

8. Ibid., 205.

9. Ibid., 209.

10. Ibid., 210.

11. Ibid., 212–13.

12. Ibid., 213–14.

13. Ibid., 217–19.

14. Ibid., 219.

15. Ibid., 222–23.

16. Ibid., 222, 225.

17. William R. Hunt, "Notes on the History of North Slope Oil," *Alaska Magazine,* February 1970, 8–10; Ruth Hampton to Abe Fortas, Under Secretary of the Interior, January 21, 1944, Files of Under Secretary Abe Fortas, Territories, Alaska, RG 48, National Archives, Washington, D.C. (hereafter NA); Frank Know to President Franklin D. Roosevelt, March 4, 1944, and Van Valin to President Roosevelt, May 20, 1944, OF 400-Alaska, container 3, folder Appointments, Alaska, 1944–45, Franklin D. Roosevelt Papers, FDR Library, Hyde Park, New York.

18. William B. Heroy to R. K. Davies, Deputy Petroleum Administrator, September 22, 1944, Harold L. Ickes Papers, Library of Congress, Washington, D.C.

19. James Forrestal to the President, March 31, 1945, Official Files 400, Alaska, Oil-Naval Petroleum Reserve (1), Harry S. Truman Papers, Harry S. Truman Library, Independence, Missouri (hereafter Truman Papers).

20. James Forrestal to Harry S. Truman, December 10, 1945, and Secretary Ickes to Harold D. Smith, Director, Bureau of the Budget, January 17, 1946, Official Files 400, Alaska, Oil-Naval Petroleum Reserve (1), Truman Papers.

21. James Forrestal to President Truman, January 22, 1946, Official Files 400, Alaska, Oil-Naval Petroleum Reserve (1), Truman Papers.

22. Ibid.; James Forrestal to President Truman, March 10, 1947, General File, Alaska, box 112, Truman Papers; Memorandum from director, Naval Petroleum Reserves, November 26, 1952, Records of John C. Reed, Staff Geologist for the Division of Territories and Island Possessions, Correspondence with Navy, 6.3, RG 57, NA.

23. Ted A. Armstrong, "Alaskan Oil," *Oil and Gas Journal,* August 22, 1966, 96.

24. Gene Rutledge, Prudhoe Day…Discovery (Anchorage: Wolfe Business Services, 1987), IV. 3.

25. Public Land Order 82 was part of a larger land withdrawal made by Acting Secretary of the Interior Abe Fortas in 1943. This action withdrew 67,440,000 acres of public lands from all forms of appropriation under the public land laws, including the mining and mineral leasing laws. Secretary Seaton lifted Public Land Order 82 in 1960, making it possible for the state to pick the future Prudhoe Bay selection.

26. Conference on Northern Alaska, May 17, 1954, Records of the Office of Territories, Central Classified Files, Part 1, Alaska, Lands, Public Land Order #82, RG 126, NA.

27. Ibid.

28. Ibid.

29. Clinton Brown, President, Alaska Propane Company, Incorporated, to Director, Bureau of Land Management, June 11, 1954, Records of the Office of Territories, Central Classified Files, Part 1, Public Land Order #82, RG 126, NA.

30. Alaska Propane Co., Inc., "Summary of Proposed Development of the Gubik Structure and Construction of Pipeline," August 6, 1954, Records of

the Office of Territories, Central Classified Files, Part 1, Alaska, Lands, Public Land Order #82, RG 126, NA.

31. Ibid.

32. Drew Pearson, "The Washington Merry-Go-Round," October 1, 1954, typewritten copy in Records of the Office of Territories, Central Classified Files, Part 1, Alaska, Lands, Public Land Order #82, RG 126, NA.

33. Sczudlo to McKay, October 5, 1954, Records of the Office of Territories, Central Classified Files, Part 1, Alaska, Lands, Public Land Order #82, R.G. 126, NA.

34. *Fairbanks Daily News-Miner*, October 12, 1954.

35. Ibid., September 3, 1954. Those were prophetic words.

36. Roderick, *Crude Dreams*, 60–61.

37. *Anchorage Daily News*, February 11, 1990.

38. Roderick, *Crude Dreams*, 57–63.

39. Ibid., 62; *Anchorage Daily News*, February 11, 1990.

40. *Anchorage Daily News*, February 4, 1990.

41. Ibid.

42. Armstrong, "Alaskan Oil," 96.

43. Ibid.

44. *Anchorage Daily News*, February 9, 1990.

45. Ibid.

46. Ibid.

47. Ibid.

48. Ibid.

49. Ibid., February 11, 1990.

50. Ibid.

51. Ibid.

52. *Udall v. Tallman*, 380 U.S. 1 (1965).

53. *Anchorage Daily News*, February 11, 1990.

54. Wolff, *Katalla to Prudhoe Bay*, 24.

55. Thirty years later, Chevron (formerly Standard Oil) shut down its refinery and pulled its exploration and production operations from the state.

56. Wolff, *Katalla to Prudhoe Bay*, 24–25.

57. Ibid., 25.

58. Ibid., 26.

59. Ibid, 27.

60. Ibid., 38.

61. Ibid.

62. *Anchorage Daily News*, February 11, 1990.

63. Ibid.

64. Ibid.

65. Ibid.

66. Ibid.

67. Ibid.

68. Armstrong, "Alaskan Oil," 91.

69. Ibid.

70. Ibid., 86.

71. Ibid., 82–83.

Chapter 23. The Oil Industry Matures

1. Scott Goldsmith, "Sustainable Spending Levels from Alaska State Revenue," *Alaska Review of Social and Economic Conditions,* February, 1983, 3; *The Insider*, January 24, 1986; author Naske's interview with Kay Herring, Public Relations Department, Alyeska Pipeline Service Company, January 24, 1986, Anchorage, Alaska.

2. Matthew Berman, "Alaska North Slope Oil Production and Revenue Projections," *Alaska Review of Social and Economic Conditions,* February 1985, 1–2. The Alyeska Pipeline Service Company was formed in 1970 by seven oil companies as a separate entity to coordinate the construction, operations, and maintenance of the Trans-Alaska Pipeline System.

3. Bill Van Dyke, Alaska Department of Natural Resources, Division of Oil and Gas, to author Naske, March 29, 30, 2006.

4. Ruth E. Black, Valdez Communications Manager, Alyeska Pipeline Service Company, to author Naske, March 9, 2006.

5. Paul Laird, "North Slope's Shallow Crude Defies Technology, Economics," *Alaska Business Monthly,* March 1985, 16–17.

6. Richard Wheatly, "Getting the Most Out of Prudhoe Bay," *Sohio*, Summer 1984, 2–4.

7. Richard Wheatly, "One-Billion Barrel Increase Is Goal of North Slope Projects," *Sohio*, Winter 1985, 25.

8. BP International, "BP: The BP Logo Used from 1989 to 2001," BBC Online Network, August 11, 1998.

9. "FTC to Challenge BP Amoco/ARCO Merger Alleging that Deal Would Raise Prices for Crude Oil Used to Produce Gasoline and Other Petroleum Products," FTC announcement, Washington, D.C., February 2, 2000, available at www.ftc.gov/oka/2000/02/bpamocopr.shtm (accessed January 4, 2010).

10. Statement of FTC Commissioners Anthony, Swindle, and Leary in BP Amoco/ARCO, File No. 991-0192, Docket No. C-3938, available at www.ftc.gov/05/2000/04/bpstateask.htm.

11. DieselNet, What's New page, "BP Amoco-ARCO Merger Approved by U.S. Government," April 13, 2000, www.dieselnet.com/news/2000/04bp.php (accessed May 30, 2009).

12. *Fairbanks Daily News-Miner*, March 19, 2006.

13. FinebergResearch.com, "Documents Reveal Trans-Alaska Pipeline in Trouble: Monitors Punt," April 22, 2006, www.finebergresearch.com/archives.html (accessed May 30, 2009).

14. National Research Council of the National Academies, Committee on Cumulative Environmental Effects of Oil and Gas Activities on Alaska's North Slope, Board on Environmental Studies and Toxicology, Polar Research Board, Division on Earth and Life Studies, *Cumulative Environmental Effects of Oil and Gas Activities on Alaska's North Slope* (Washington D.C. : The National Academies Press, 2003), 1–225.

15. Ibid.

16. Ibid.

17. Ibid.

18. Ibid.

19. Harvey Manning, et al., *Cry Crisis! Rehearsal in Alaska,* ed. by Hugh Nash (San Francisco: Friends of the Earth, 1974), 155.

20. John Keeble, *Out of the Channel: The Exxon Valdez Oil Spill in Prince William Sound* (New York: Harper Collins Publishers, 1991), 18, 22.

21. Ibid., 22–23.

22. Ibid., 23

23. Ibid., 23–24.

24. Ibid., 24.

25. Ibid., 24–25.

26. Dr. Riki Ott, *Sound Truth and Corporate Myth$: The Legacy of the Exxon Valdez Oil Spill* (Cordova, Alaska: Dragonfly Sisters Press, 2005), 1.

27. Keeble, *Out of the Channel*, 31, 12.

28. Ibid., 32.

29. Ibid., 32–33.

30. Ibid., 33–34.

31. Ibid., 37–39.

32. Ibid., 39.

33. Ibid., 39–40.

34. Ibid., 42–45.

35. Walter Meganack, quoted in Keeble, *Out of the Channel,* 6.

36. Ibid.

37. Ibid., 51–53.

38. Ott, *Sound Truth and Corporate Myth$*, 8–9.

39. Ibid.

40. Ibid.

41. *Anchorage Daily News*, August 4, 1998.

42. *Seattle Post-Intelligencer*, January 28, 2006.

43. Ibid.

44. *Fairbanks Daily News-Miner,* June 26, 2008.

45. Ibid.

46. *Anchorage Daily News,* June 29, 2009; *Fairbanks Daily News-Miner,* June 16, 2009.

47. *Anchorage Daily News*, March 23, 1990; "Joseph Hazelwood," Wikipedia Web site, last modified May 25, 2009, available at http://en.wikipedia.org/wiki/Joseph_Hazelwood (accessed June 1, 2009). A massive scientific and popular literature has developed on the subject of the spill over the years. The most recent and most critical book on the subject is Dr. Riki Ott, *Sound Truth and Corporate Myth$,* 2005; excellent and informative are John Keeble, *Out of the Channel: The Exxon Valdez Oil Spill in Prince William Sound*, 1991; and Jeff Wheelwright, *Degrees of Disaster, Prince William Sound: How Nature Reels and Rebounds,* 1994.

48. "*Exxon Valdez*," Wikipedia Web site, last modified May 31, 2009, available at http://en.wikipedia.org/wiki/Exxon_Valdez (accessed June 1, 2009).

49. Clifford John Groh and Gregg Erickson, "The Permanent Fund Dividend Program: Alaska's Noble Experiment," *Alaska Journal* 13, no. 3 (Summer 1983): 141.

50. Richard A. Fineberg/Research Associates, "The Profitability and Economic Viability of Alaska North Slope and Associated Pipeline Operations," April 27, 2005, commissioned by Prince William Sound Regional Citizens' Advisory Council, www.pwsrcac.org/docs/d0014100.pdf (accessed June 1, 2009), 4.

51. Ibid., 4–5.

52. Ibid., 5.

53. Scott Goldsmith, "Sustainable Spending Levels from Alaska State Revenue," *Alaska Review of Social and Economic Conditions,* February 1983, 1.

54. Ibid.

55. Bob Dixon, "Experts View State's Fiscal Future When Oil Revenues Begin to Decline," *Alaska Business and Industry,* January 1983, 10–11.

56. "Facts and Fables of State Spending," Fiscal Policy Paper no. 2, Institute of Social and Economic Research, University of Alaska Anchorage, October 1989, 13.

57. Ibid., 2.

58. Ibid., 3–4.

59. Ibid., 4–5.

60. Arlon Tussing and Linda Leaska, "The Changing Oil Industry: Will It Affect Oil Prices?" Fiscal Policy Paper no. 11, Institute of Social and Economic Research, University of Alaska Anchorage, May 1999, 1.

61. Ibid., 2; Fineberg, "Profitability and Economic Viability," 5.
62. Personal communication to author Naske from Dr. Richard Fineberg, March 1, 2007.
63. *Fairbanks Daily News-Miner,* March 26, 1989.
64. Oliver Scott Goldsmith, "The Alaska Fiscal Gap," Fiscal Policy Paper no. 1 (August 1989), Institute of Social and Economic Research, University of Alaska Anchorage.
65. Ibid., 1–2.
66. Ibid., 12.
67. 1990 Alaska State Legislative Summary, Juneau, Alaska, July 1990, 11 pages, in author Naske's files, p. 9.
68. *Closing the Budget Gap* (brochure), Juneau, Alaska, 1990, in author Naske's files.
69. Gerald A. McBeath, "Alaska, 1991," in *Proceedings, Roundtable State Budgeting in the 13 Western States,* ed. Robert Huefner, F. Ted Hebert, and Carl Mott (Salt Lake City, UT: Center for Public Policy and Administration, University of Utah, 1991), 6.
70. Ibid., 7.
71. "Results of Recent Alaska Offshore Leasing by the U.S. Government," *Alaskan Update,* Spring 1984, 1.
72. Scott Goldsmith, Linda Leask, and Mary Killorin, "Alaska's Budget: Where the Money Came From and Went, 1990–2002," Fiscal Policy Paper no. 13 (May 2003), Institute of Social and Economic Research, University of Alaska Anchorage, 3, 1.
73. Ibid., 4.
74. Joan Brown, State Office of Management and Budget, personal communication with author Naske, June 27, 2006.
75. Thomas A. Morehouse, "Petroleum Development in Alaska," Alaska Review of Social and Economic Conditions, March 1977, 15; Fairbanks Daily News-Miner, July 18, 1977.

Chapter 24. *The Unconventional Walter "Wally" J. Hickel*

1. *Anchorage Daily News*, May 30, 1986.
2. Ibid.
3. Gerald A. McBeath, "Alaska," in *Proceedings, Roundtable State Budgeting in the 13 Western States,* ed. Robert Huefner, F. Ted Hebert, and Carl Mott (Salt Lake City, UT: Center for Public Policy and Administration, University of Utah, 1990), 7.
4. Ibid., September 20, 1990.
5. Ibid.
6. *Fairbanks Daily News-Miner*, September 21–22, 1990.
7. Ibid., September 20, 1990.
8. Ibid.
9. McBeath, "Alaska," 1990, 7.
10. *Fairbanks Daily News-Miner*, December 6, 1990.
11. Ibid., January 23, 1991.
12. Ibid., January 28, 1991.
13. Ibid.
14. Ibid.
15. McBeath, "Alaska," 1992, 7–8.
16. *Anchorage Daily News*, April 20, 1991.
17. *Fairbanks Daily News Miner*, November 11, 1991.
18. Ibid., December 12, 1991.
19. Ibid., December 13–14, 24, 1991.
20. Ibid., December 30, 1991.
21. Ibid., January 7, 1992.
22. Ibid., April 26, 1992.
23. *Fairbanks Daily News-Miner*, January 17–18, 1992.
24. *Anchorage Daily News*, March 17, 1992.
25. McBeath, "Alaska," 1992, 5–6.
26. Ibid., 1993, 9–10.
27. Ibid., 10–11.
28. *Anchorage Daily News*, February 28, 1994.
29. Ibid., March 17, 1994, April 13, 1994; *Fairbanks Daily News-Miner*, April 9 and 5, 1994.
30. *Anchorage Daily News*, April 14, 1994.
31. *Fairbanks Daily News-Miner*, February 6, 1994.
32. Ibid.
33. Ibid., April 14, 1994.
34. Ibid., April 14, August, 17, 1994.
35. McBeath, "Alaska," 1995, 4.
36. Ibid., 5.
37. Ibid.
38. Ibid.
39. Ibid., 6.

Chapter 25. *The Knowles Years, 1994–2002*

1. "Tony Knowles (politician)," Wikipedia Web site, available at http://en.wikipedia.org/wiki/Tony_Knowles_(politician) (accessed June 2, 2009).
2. Jerry McBeath, "Alaska," in *Proceedings, Roundtable State Budgeting in 13 Western States,* ed. Robert Huefner, F. Ted Hebert, and Carl Mott (Salt Lake City, UT: Center For Public Policy and Administration, University of Utah, 1995), 6, 10, 11.
3. "An Endorsement for Alaska's Future: The State Long-Range Financial Planning Commission Report," October 1995, Anchorage, Alaska, author Naske's files.

4. Ibid.

5. Ibid.

6. Ibid.

7. Ibid.

8. Ibid.

9. *Anchorage Daily News*, December 5, 1995.

10. *Fairbanks Daily News-Miner*, March 1, 1996.

11. McBeath, "Alaska," October 1997, 2.

12. *Fairbanks Daily News-Miner*, March 21, 1997.

13. McBeath, "Alaska," 1997, 15.

14. *Alaska v. Native Village of Venetie Tribal Government,* 522 U.S. 520 (1998), decided by a 9–0 vote, February 25, 1998. Metlakatla is the site of the model community established in 1887 when the Rev. William Duncan led one thousand Tsimshian Indians from Fort Simpson, British Columbia, to Anne Island in Alaska.

15. McBeath, "Alaska," 1997, 15; McBeath, "Alaska,"1998, 16.

16. Ibid., 1998, 16–17.

17. Ibid., 1997, 16–17.

18. Ibid., 17–18.

19. Ibid., March 2000, 16.

20. Ibid., 14.

21. Ibid.

22. Ibid.

23. Ibid., 15.

24. Ibid.

25. Ibid.

26. Ibid., 15–16.

27. Ibid., 11.

28. Ibid., 17.

29. Ibid.

30. Ibid.

31. Ibid., 12.

32. Alaska Division of Community Advocacy, Southeast Regional Timber Task Force, Kathleen Morse, lead staff and author, "Southeast Timber Task Force Report," October 1997, available at www.dced.state.ak.us/oed/forest_products/forest_products1.htm

33. McBeath, "Alaska," 2000, 13.

34. Ibid., 12–13.

35. Ibid., 13.

36. Scott Goldsmith, "From Oil to Assets: Managing Alaska's New Wealth," Fiscal Policy Paper no. 10 (June 1998), Institute of Social and Economic Research, University of Alaska Anchorage.

37. McBeath, "Alaska," 2000, 17.

38. Ibid., 17–18.

39. Ibid., 19–20.

40. Ibid., 26–27.

41. Ibid., March 2001, 10.

42. Ibid., 10–11.

43. Ibid., March 2002, 22.

44. Ibid., 14–15.

45. Ibid., 15.

46. Ibid., 16.

47. Ibid.

48. Ibid., 22–23.

49. Ibid., 23–24.

50. Ibid., 24.

51. Ibid.

52. Ibid., 25.

53. Ibid., 31, 30.

54."Frank Murkowski," Wikipedia Web site, available at www.wikipedia.org/wiki/Frank_Murkowski (accessed June 30, 2009).

55. *Anchorage Daily News*, October 27, 2002.

56. Ibid., November 13 and September 22, 2002.

57. Ibid.

58. Ibid., November 3, 2002.

59. *Fairbanks Daily News-Miner*, November 6, 2002.

60. *Anchorage Daily News*, December 3, 2002.

61. Ibid., December 1, 2002.

62. Ibid.

Chapter 26. Into the Twenty-first Century

1. Gerald A. McBeath, "Alaska," in *Proceedings*, Round-table State Budgeting in the 13 Western States, ed. Robert Huefner, F. Ted Hebert, and Carl Mott (Salt Lake City, UT: Center for Public Policy and Administration, University of Utah, 2003), 2.

2. Jerry McBeath, "Alaska's FY 08 Budget Plan, in press, 1–2; *Anchorage Daily News*, March 8, 2006.

3. Front cover of *Alaska* 71, no. 9 (November 2005); *Anchorage Daily News,* August 8, 1994.

4. *Anchorage Daily News,* August 8, 1994.

5. Ibid.

6. Ibid.; Author Naske's interview with C. W. Snedden, Fairbanks, Alaska, March 25, 1970.

7. *Anchorage Daily News,* August 10, 1994.

8. Claus-M. Naske, *Ernest Gruening: Alaska's Greatest Governor* (Fairbanks: University of Alaska Press, 2004), 215.

9. *Anchorage Daily News*, August 11, 1994.

10. Claus-M. Naske, *Ernest Gruening: Alaska's Greatest Governor* (Fairbanks: University of Alaska Press, 2004).

11. *Fairbanks Daily News-Miner*, April 13, 2007.

12. *Anchorage Daily News,* November 28, 1999.
13. Ibid.
14. Ibid.
15. Ibid.
16. Ibid.
17. Web page of Don Young, "Congressman for All Alaska," March 15, 2006, available at www.donyoung.house.gov/ (accessed June 30, 2009).
18. Ibid.
19. Ibid.
20. Rebecca Clarren, "A Bridge to Nowhere," Salon Web site, August 9, 2005, available at www.salon.com/news/feature/2005/08/09/bridges/index.html (accessed July 6, 2009).
21. Ibid.
22. Ibid.
23. *St. Petersburg Times,* April 1, 2007.
24. Ibid.
25. Ibid.
26. Ibid.
27. Ibid.
28. Ibid.
29. Ibid.
30. Michael Carey to author Naske, copy of his article that ran in the *Houston Chronicle,* August 13, 1007; *Fairbanks Daily News-Miner,* July 31, 2007.
31. *Los Angeles Times,* December 17, 2003.
32. Ibid.
33. Ibid.
34. *Fairbanks Daily News-Miner,* August 31, 2007.
35. *Anchorage Daily News,* August 10, 2007.
36. *Fairbanks Daily New-Miner,* April 2, 2009.
37. Ibid., April 3 and 5, 2009.
38. Jerry McBeath, "Alaska's FY 2004 Budget Process," in *Proceedings, Roundtable: State Budgeting in the 13 Western States,* ed. Robert Huefner, F. Ted Hebert, and Carl Mott (Salt Lake City, UT: Center for Public Policy and Administration, University of Utah, May 2004), 11.
39. Ibid.
40. Ibid., 12.
41. Ibid., 14.
42. Ibid., 14–16.
43. Ibid., 16.
44. *Anchorage Daily News,* June 12, 2003, and June 17–19, 2003.
45. McBeath, "Alaska's FY-2006 Budget Process," 2006, 4–5.
46. Gayle W. Harbo to Representative Bruce Weyhrauch, June 19, 2005, memo re: "Committee seeking information regarding PERS?TRS funding ration," in author's files.
47. *Fairbanks Daily News-Miner*, March 3, 2005.
48. Ibid., April 12, 2005, and May 6, 2006; *Anchorage Daily News,* April 30, May 5, 2005.
49. *Anchorage Daily News*, May 9, 2005; *Fairbanks Daily News-Miner*, May 9, 2005.
50. McBeath, "Alaska's FY-2006 Budget Process," 11.
51. Ibid., 12–14.
52. *Fairbanks Daily News-Miner,* March 5, 2006.
53. *Fairbanks Daily News-Miner*, February 16, 2006; *Anchorage Daily News*, February 23, 2006.
54. *Fairbanks Daily News-Miner,* February 22, 2006.
55. *Fairbanks Daily News-Miner*, March 29, 2006.
56. Ibid.
57. *Anchorage Daily News*, April 15, 2006.
58. Ibid., April 26, 2006.
59. Ibid., May 21, 2006.
60. Ibid., August 11, 2006.
61. *Anchorage Daily News*, May 6, 2006.
62. Ibid.
63. "Governors: Murkowski Fading Fast," *Capitol Journal,* http://statenet.com/capitol_journal/08-21-2006 (accessed June 3, 2009).
64. *Fairbanks Daily News-Miner,* November 8, 2006.
65. Ibid., September 21, 2008.
66. Ibid., September 6, 2008.
67. *Fairbanks Daily News-Miner*, May 5 and 8, 2007.
68. *Anchorage Daily News*, December 8, 2007; *Fairbanks Daily News-Miner*, June 2, 2008.
69. *Fairbanks Daily News-Miner,* September 3, 2007.
70. *Anchorage Daily News,* December 2, 2007.
71. *Sarah Palin: A Woman For All Seasons* (New York: Patricia Ann Publishing, Inc., 2008), 16.
72. *Fairbanks Daily News-Miner,* April 22, 2007.
73. Ibid.
74. Ibid.
75. *Newsweek*, November 17, 2008, 93.
76. Ibid., 94.
77. Ibid., 107.
78. *Fairbanks Daily News-Miner,* November 13, 2008.
79. Leonard Pitts, "Ugliness Disguised as Politics, *The Spokesman Review*, October 12, 2008.
80. *Fairbanks Daily News-Miner,* November 13, 2008.
81. Ibid., November 15, 2008.
82. Ibid., July 6, 2009.
83. Ibid., July 4, 2009
84. Ibid., July 6, 2009.

Bibliographical Essay

THE SOURCES OF ALASKA'S HISTORY

Anthropologists have long been fascinated with the Native cultures of Alaska, and bookshelves are heavy with the many studies produced over the years. In *Eskimo Prehistory* (1969), Hans-Georg Bandi, a Swiss scholar, discussed the various theories of the origin of the Eskimos and the sites, artifacts, and prehistoric cultures in the Eskimo area, extending from Alaska across Canada to Greenland. Wendell H. Oswalt, a prolific academician, has ably summarized the state of knowledge about Eskimos in his *Alaskan Eskimos* (1967), and he has traced the contacts explorers made with these northern peoples from Viking settlements in Greenland through the long history of Arctic exploration to modern times in his *Eskimos and Explorers* (1979).

In the mid-twentieth century, Norwegian Arctic expert Helge Ingstad lived for a year with the sixty-five Nunamiut Eskimos who lived in Anaktuvuk Pass in the Brooks Range and relied on the caribou as the basis of their economy. Ingstad lived with a people "whose way of life was not essentially different from the way of life in the Stone Age." His *Nunamiut: Among Alaska's Inland Eskimos* (1954) has become a classic. While in Anaktuvuk Pass, Ingstad collected Nunamiut stories that Elijah Kakinya and Simon Paneak told him in Iñupiaq and English. Michael S. Cline, who taught school for two years at Anaktuvuk Pass, wrote *Tannik School: The Impact of Education on the Eskimos of Anaktuvuk Pass* (1975). Using standard anthropological fieldwork approaches, he examined the impact of the American school upon the Nunamiut villagers. Nicholas Gubser spent time among the

Anaktuvuk Pass Eskimos, and *The Nunamiut Eskimos: Hunters of Caribou* (1965) is the outgrowth of his studies among these people.

Ann Fienup-Riordan, a cultural anthropologist, has lived, worked, and taught in Alaska since 1973. A prolific author, she has written numerous fine books. Among those are *The Real People* and the *Children of Thunder: The Yup'ik Eskimo Encounter with Moravian Missionaries John and Edith Kilbuck* (1991), *The Nelson Island Eskimo* (1986), *When Our Bad Season Comes* (1986), *Eskimo Essays: Yup'ik Lives and How We See Them* (1990), and *Freeze Frame: Alaska Eskimos in the Movies* (1995). The late James W. VanStone conducted much fieldwork in Alaska and wrote an outstanding volume on the Eskimos of the Nushagak River region of southwestern Alaska, using the research methods of history and anthropology, titled *Eskimos of the Nushagak River: An Ethnographic History* (1967). Don E. Dumond presents the prehistory of the Eskaleut peoples in the area between the Bering Strait on the north and the Aleutian Islands and the Alaska Peninsula on the south in *The Eskimos and Aleuts* (1977). Charles Campbell Hughes has written a fine study of the Siberian Eskimos of Gambell, or Sivokak, on Saint Lawrence Island based on fieldwork he conducted there in 1954–55. The title of his work is *An Eskimo Village in the Modern World* (1960). Charles C. Hughes' *Eskimo Boyhood: An Autobiography in Psychosocial Perspective* (1974) is the autobiography of an Eskimo youth in his early twenties. Hughes related the details of his life, recalling the feelings accompanying his experiences on

Saint Lawrence Island. His descriptions of life there in the 1930s and 1940s are very significant because this period saw the undercutting of the traditional Eskimo lifeways by the influences of the industrialized world.

Robert F. Spencer has written a volume titled *The North Alaskan Eskimo: A Study in Ecology and Society,* based on fieldwork he conducted in 1952 and 1953. Originally published in 1959, it was reprinted in 1969 and has become a classic in its field, offering a very full and detailed account of the culture of the North Alaskan Eskimo. Spencer analyzed the way in which two different modes of earning a livelihood, caribou hunting by the inland peoples and whaling by coastal Eskimos, represent ecological adaptations within the framework of a common Eskimo culture.

Ernest S. Burch, Jr., known as "Tiger" to his friends, was a social anthropologist and social historian who specialized in the study of northern North America, particularly the Eskimos. An independent scholar after 1974, he made research trips to the Arctic over the years. His masterful *The Iñupiaq Eskimo Nations of Northwest Alaska* (1998) is based on research he carried out from time to time between 1960 and 1969, particularly work undertaken during the fall and winter of 1969–70. In all, he was engaged in this project for almost thirty-five years. Burch wrote that anthropologists have characterized the socioterritorial organization of the early historic Iñupiat with two contrasting models. One is a binary model in which the entire Iñupiat population is conceived of as being divided between the Nunamiut, or "inland people," and the Tagiugmiut, or coastal people. The second model is a cellular one, which Burch developed in this volume, in which the Iñupiat are conceived of as having been divided into a fairly large number of territorially circumscribed "tribes" or "societies," each of which was an autonomous political unit.

Dorothy Jean Ray has produced *Aleut and Eskimo Art: Tradition and Innovation in South Alaska* (1981). The author summarized the history of traditional indigenous art in southern Alaska, tracing the innovations in style from Bering's discovery of Alaska in 1741 to 1980. An encyclopedic reference work, it is essential for art historians, critics, and collectors. Ray's other books are *Artists of the Tundra and the Sea* (1961), *Eskimo Masks* (1967), and *The Eskimos of Bering Strait, 1650–1898* (1976).

The late Diamond Jenness, a Canadian anthropologist, wrote a series of studies on the way in which governments have dealt with Eskimo populations: *Eskimo Administration: Alaska* (1962), *Eskimo Administration: Canada* (1964), *Eskimo Administration: Labrador* (1965), *Eskimo Administration: Greenland* (1967), and *Eskimo Administration: Analysis and Reflections* (1968).

J. Louis Giddings died prematurely at age fifty-five in 1964. In the period 1958 to 1961 he found, at Cape Krusenstern near Bering Strait, a series of 114 parallel ridges extending inland from the present shoreline, each representing an earlier beach, a kind of guest book recording the various peoples who once inhabited the coast and their cultures. Once coordinated with his other finds, it may yield an orderly prehistory of the frozen top of the globe and fill gaps in knowledge of the human past. His *Ancient Men of the Arctic* (1967) has rightly become a classic. His other books are *The Archeology of Cape Denbigh* (1964), *Kobuk River People* (1961), and *Forest Eskimos* (1956).

Edwin S. Hall, Jr., an anthropologist, published *The Eskimo Storyteller: Folktales from Noatak, Alaska* (1975), which was republished in paperback in 1998. The author collected the materials for this study during three summers and one winter of fieldwork, and an entire whole year when he and his wife lived in Noatak. Norman Chance gives readers an overview of the richness and complexity of Eskimo culture in *The Eskimo of North Alaska* (1966). James H. Barker, a fine photographer, is responsible for *Always Getting Ready: Yup'ik Eskimo Subsistence in Southwest Alaska* (1993), richly illustrated with black and white photographs. Wendell H. Oswalt, already mentioned, has a long list of distinguished books. His *Bashful No Longer: An Alaskan Eskimo Ethnohistory, 1778–1988* (1990) is a valuable addition to his life's work. In it he brings together the results of his many years of studying the Kuskokwim River Eskimos.

Stephen H. Braund, a consulting anthropologist, is the author of *The Skin Boats of Saint Lawrence Island, Alaska* (1988), and Molly Lee and Gregory A. Reinhardt have written an interesting and richly illustrated volume titled *Eskimo Architecture: Dwelling and Structure in the Early Historic Period* (2003). William W. Fitzhugh and Aron Crowell created the beautifully illustrated *Crossroads of Continents: Cultures of Siberia and Alaska* (1988) to accompany the Smithsonian traveling exhibition by the same name.

There is much more in the literature on Eskimos in Alaska, and this brief overview barely scratches the surface. The bibliographies in any of the books mentioned will lead the interested reader to a wealth of additional information. For readers who wish to peruse a compilation of the literature dealing with the Eskimos up to 1977, Arthur E. Hippler and John R. Wood, both former members of the Institute of Social and Economic Research of the University of Alaska Anchorage, compiled *The Alaska Eskimos: A Selected Annotated Bibliography* (1977). In conclusion, Charles D. Brower, called the "King of the Arctic," lived for more than half a century near Point Barrow, Alaska. He was a legendary figure among explorers. He was a shrewd trader and for many years the only non-Native to live year-round with the Iñupiats on the Arctic coast of Alaska. He became the patriarch of a very large Eskimo family. His *Fifty Years below Zero* was first published in 1942 and recollects his life in the Arctic. It is a fascinating tale, republished in 1994.

Considerable effort has gone into the study of the educational system for Alaska's Natives, and a vast literature has developed. A few titles will give an indication of the scope of the work. Judith S. Kleinfeld, a professor of psychology at the University of Alaska Fairbanks authored a number of these. Her *A Long Way from Home: Effects of Public High Schools on Village Children Away from Home* (1973) examined the boarding school system then in use. Her *Eskimo School of the Andreafsky: A Study of Effective Bicultural Education* (1979) examined Saint Mary's, a Catholic boarding school on the Yukon River that enrolled Eskimo adolescents from remote villages that were undergoing rapid cultural change. The school was highly effective in cross-cultural education and produced graduates with the skills necessary to access opportunities of the majority culture.

Charles K. Ray, professor of education at the University of Alaska for many years until his retirement, conducted a study of Native education in the 1950s titled *A Program of Education for Alaska Natives* (1958). It gives a convenient summary of educational history in Alaska and deals at length with the curriculum and educational objectives of Native elementary schools and secondary and post-high school education of Alaska Native youths. Although many of the ideas in this volume may seem outdated in the twenty-first century, they represented the best thinking on the subject in the 1950s. Frank Darnell, formerly a professor of education at the University of Alaska Fairbanks, has written much on Alaska education and educational issues in remote regions, including Australia. He completed a lengthy doctoral dissertation at Wayne State University in 1970 called

"Alaska's Dual Federal-State School System: A History And Descriptive Analysis." In 1972, Darnell edited the volume *Education in the North: The First International Conference on Cross-cultural Education in the Circumpolar Nations*. His *Taken to Extremes: Education in the Far North* (1996) was coauthored with Anton Hoëm and published by the Scandinavian University.

Ray J. Barnhardt is an education professor at the University of Alaska Fairbanks. Many of his papers and pamphlets have been published by the university's Center for Cross-Cultural Studies. An example is his *Culture, Community and the Curriculum* (1980). Barnhardt is also the lead author in the volume *Anthropology and Educational Administration* (1979). These are just a few examples of the extensive literature dealing with education in Alaska.

Alaskan Natives are also publishing their own oral history accounts. A good example is *Puiguitkaat* (1981), a transcription and translation of the 1978 North Slope Borough Elders' Conference. The North Slope Borough Commission on History and Culture funded the conference and the preparation of the volume, transcribed and translated by Leona Okakok, and Gary Kean edited the volume and furnished the photographs. The sponsors of the conference intended to talk about and record on tape and in books things that the Iñupiat people know before they become lost. This knowledge is deemed essential if the young are to subsist on the land that their ancestors have occupied since time immemorial, since successful survival depends on a knowledge of the land and its history as well as that of its people.

Another volume by the North Slope Borough Commission on History and Culture, *The Traditional Land Use Inventory for the Mid-Beaufort Sea*, volume 1 (1980), is based on interviews with North Slope residents and is richly illustrated with historical photographs. Helen Slwooko Carius wrote and illustrated a slender volume titled *Sevukakmet: Ways of Life on St. Lawrence Island* (1979). After living successfully in the contiguous states, she realized that she wanted to remember and record her heritage as a Saint Lawrence Islander. The volume is evidence of her acknowledgment of that heritage and her recognition that it continues to play an important part in her life and that of her family.

Yupiktak Bista commissioned Art Davidson to edit a pamphlet dealing with subsistence and conservation of the Yupik lifestyle: *Does One Way of Life Have to Die So Another Can Live?* (1974). Ticasuk, or Emily

Ivanoff Brown, an Eskimo woman who graduated from the University of Alaska Fairbanks, wrote *The Roots of Ticasuk: An Eskimo Woman's Family Story* (1981), a revision of an earlier work titled *Grandfather of Unalakleet: The Lineage of Alluyagnak* (1974). Ann Vick edited *The Cama-i Book: Kayaks, Dogsleds, Bear Hunting, Bush Pilots, Smoked Fish, Mukluks, and Other Traditions of Southwestern Alaska* (1983), a volume in the Foxfire tradition made popular by Eliot Wigginton. High school students in southwestern Alaska interviewed and photographed the older members of their communities, documenting their folklore, legends, crafts, and skills, and published the material they collected in their school magazines. *The Cama-i Book* brings together the best of this material.

Margaret Lantis, an anthropologist, has ably summarized existing knowledge about the Aleuts in "The Aleut Social System, 1750–1810, from Early Historical Sources," in *Ethnohistory in Southwestern Alaska and the Southern Yukon: Method and Content* (1970). William Laughlin, an archaeologist, has performed considerable fieldwork in the Aleutian Islands; one result of that work is his *Aleuts: Survivors of the Bering Land Bridge* (1980). Dorothy Jones, a sociologist, has written *Aleuts in Transition: A Comparison of Two Villages* (1976), a study of Aleut adaptations to white contact, and *A Century of Servitude: Pribilof Aleuts under U.S. Rule* (1980), an indictment of federal administration of the Pribilof Islands.

Recent years have seen much additional scholarship on the Alutiiq/Sugpiaq people. Good examples are Lydia T. Black's *The History and Ethnohistory of the Aleutians East Borough* (1999) and Patricia H. Partnow's *Making History: Alutiiq/Sugpiaq Life on the Alaska Peninsula* (2001). Aron L. Crowell, Amy F. Steffian, and Gordon L. Pullar are the editors of the richly illustrated catalog of a community-based exhibition from the Alutiiq people of southern Alaska, titled *Looking Both Ways: Heritage and Identity of the Alutiiq People* (2001).

Two outstanding volumes should be mentioned: *Anthropology of the North Pacific Rim,* edited by William W. Fitzhugh and Valérie Chaussonnet (1994), investigates the anthropology, history, and art of the North Pacific rim from a comparative, trans-Beringian perspective. And in *Arctic Adaptations: Native Whalers and Reindeer Herders of Northern Eurasia* (1993), Russian scholar Igor Krupnik dismisses the widely accepted notion of traditional societies as static and instead demonstrates that these societies are charac-

terized by significant evolutionary breaks. Their apparent state of ecological harmony is a conscious survival strategy resulting from a prolonged and therefore successful process of human adaptation in one of the most extreme inhabited environments in the world.

The late Richard A. Pierce has earned the gratitude of historians, social scientists, and laypeople alike for his series of translations and original works, published through his Limestone Press of Kingston, Ontario, and Fairbanks, Alaska. After a distinguished career at Queens College in Kingston, Ontario, Pierce joined the Department of History at the University of Alaska Fairbanks, where he taught, wrote, and translated for more than a decade. His series, now numbering more than fifty volumes, is called Materials for the Study of Alaska History. Included are works by contemporary Russian scholars, such as Raisa V. Makarova, *Russians on the Pacific, 1743–1799* (1975), and Svetlana G. Fedorava, *The Russian Population in Alaska and California: Late 18th Century–1868* (1973), Nikolai N. Bolkhovitnov, *Russian-American Relations and the Sale of Alaska, 1834–1867* (1996), and such classic accounts as Georg Heinrich von Langsdorff, *A Voyage around the World, 1803–1807,* translated by Victoria Joan Moessner and Ferdinand Petrovich von Wrangell; and *Russian America: Statistical and Ethnographic Information,* translated from the German edition of 1839 by Mary Sadousky and edited by Richard A. Pierce (1980). Pierce authored *Russia's Hawaiian Adventure, 1815–1817* (1976) and his *Russian America: A Biographical Dictionary* (1990), an absolutely essential volume for every student of Russian America and a labor of love.

There are many others in the series, such as Vasilie Nikolaevich Berhk's *Chronological History of the Discovery of the Aleutian Islands* (1974), translated by Dmitri Krenov and edited by Pierce. This classic was first published in Saint Petersburg in 1823. Berkh visited Russian America during the colonial period and talked to veteran seafarers, hunters, and merchants. His account acquainted the public of his day with the exploration and early exploitation of the Aleutian Island's resources. Another volume in the series is Grigorii I. Shelikhov's *A Voyage to America, 1783–1786* (1981), which Marina Ramsay translated. Pierce edited and introduced the volume. Shelikhov established the first permanent Russian settlement at Three Saints Bay on Kodiak Island in 1784. Other volumes are *The Russian Orthodox Religious Mission in America, 1794–1837, with Materials Concerning the*

Life and Works of the Monk German, and Ethnographic Notes by the Hieromonk Gedeon (1978), translated by Colin Bearne and edited by Pierce; and the *Journals of Iakov Netsvetov: The Atkha Years, 1828–1844* (1980), translated with an introduction and supplementary material by Lydia T. Black.

Also important are Kiril Timofeevich Khlebnikov's two volumes. The first is *Notes on Russian America: Part I: Novo-Arkhangel'sk,* compiled with an introduction and commentaries by Svetlana G. Fedorova, translated by Serge Le Comte and Richard Pierce, and edited by Pierce (1994). Khlebnikov served with the Russian-American Company, starting in 1801, for many years and spent 1818–1832 in Russian America. This is his collection of historical, ethnographical, and commercial information, focusing on New Archangel, the administrative center of Russian America. His *Notes on Russian America, Parts II–V: Kad'iak, Unalashka, Athka, the Pribylovs* (1994) was compiled by R. G. Liapunova and S. G. Fedorova and includes an introduction and commentaries by them. Marina Ramsay translated and Richard Pierce edited the volume. It contains essential information on various regions of Russian America.

Richard A. Pierce and Alton S. Donnelly translated and edited P.A. Tikhmenev's *A History of The Russian-American Company* (1978), first published in Saint Petersburg in two volumes in 1861–63. It is an indispensable source concerning this long and colorful period. Tikhmenev wrote the account at the request of the Russian-American Company a few years before the sale of Russian America to the United States. He glorified its activities in the mistaken hope of winning a renewal of its monopoly charter. He based his account on documentary materials, many of which subsequently were lost in the destruction of the company archives in the 1870s. A unique work, the book consists of an introduction and old letters, journals, and agreements. Katherine L. Arndt and Pierce also translated and prepared a calendar and index to the company governors' correspondence in *Russian Governors of Alaska, 1817–1867.*

Also in the Limestone Press series are *Fort Ross: California Outpost of Russian Alaska, 1812–1841* (1991) by E. O. Essig, Adele Ogden, and Clarence John Du Four. Late in the eighteenth century, the Russians began to extend southward, seeking new hunting grounds for furs and a more reliable food supply. The settlement at Fort Ross in northern California was the spearhead of the effort. Only inadequate means and

Russia's preoccupation with Europe, Asia, and its own Asian frontiers led in 1841 to the abandonment of this California extension. The material in this volume was first published in 1933 as a special issue of the *Quarterly of the California Historical Society* (vol. 12, no. 3, September 1933). Pierce also authored *Russia's Hawaiian Adventure, 1815–1817* (1965), a scholarly and careful account of Russia's attempt to secure Hawaii. The University of California Press published this volume, and Pierce republished it in his Limestone Press series in 1976. Also in the series is *The Romance of Nikolai Rezanov and Concepcion Argüello: A Literary Legend and Its Effect on California History* by Eve Iversen, and *Concha Argüello: Memory Visits with Old Vinnie* by Father Maurice M. O'Moore, O.P. (1998), edited, with historical notes by Richard Pierce. This volume has a very extensive bibliography. And there is Pierce's *Builders of Alaska: The Russian Governors, 1818–1867* (1986), a series of articles he wrote for the *Alaska Journal* from 1971 through 1973 and published together in one volume.

The Elmer E. Rasmuson Library at the University of Alaska Fairbanks sponsors a historical translation series under the capable editorship of Marvin W. Falk. The first volume in the series was *Holmberg's Ethnographic Sketches* (1985), by Heinrich Johan Holmberg and translated by Fritz Jaensch from the German. Holmberg wrote these sketches for the edification of his fellow Finns. These he first presented verbally, and then the *Finnish Academy of Sciences Journal* published them in German. As of 2003 twelve of these translations have appeared, published by the University of Alaska Press in attractive paperback format. Number eight in the series is *To The Chukchi Peninsula and to the Tlingit Indians 1881/1882: Journals and Letters by Aurel and Arthur Krause* (1993), which Margot Krause McCaffrey translated. Interested Krause family members made these travel journals and letters available over several generations. These show the human side of an expedition undertaken by two trained scientists. Volume 11 is Constantine Caspar Andreas Grewingk's *Geology of Alaska and the Northwest Coast of America: Contributions toward Knowledge of the Orographic and Geognostic Condition of the Northwest Coast of America, with the Adjacent Islands* (2002), which Fritz Jaensch translated and Marvin W. Falk edited. Constantine Caspar Andreas Grewingk was a leading geologist and mineralogist in Russia during the middle of the nineteenth century. This work represents the first documented compilation of all the geologic information about Alaska and adjoining territory available during the Russian-American era.

Volume twelve is Georg Wilhelm Steller's *History of Kamchatka: Collected Information Concerning the History of Kamchatka, Its Peoples, Their Manners, Names, Lifestyle, and Various Customary Practices* (2003). Steller (1709–1746) produced a vast body of scientific observations during more than a decade of travel through Siberia and Kamchatka and on his voyage with Vitus Bering to America. Only a part of his work has been published, none of it during his lifetime, and little has been translated into English. His influence has been substantial through the publications of others. This translation is based on J. B. Scherer's printed version of 1774 because the translators, Margritt Engel and Karen Willmore, began their work long before the opening of the Soviet Union made the original manuscripts in Russian archives available to Western scholars. The translators first became aware of a 1996 German reprint of the 1774 edition at the Steller Symposium held in November 1996 in Halle, Germany, in observance of the 250th anniversary of the author's death. The two had already completed their translation. There they first saw Steller's original manuscript about Kamchatka at the simultaneously held exhibition, "The Great Northern Expedition: Georg Wilhelm Steller (1709–1746); a Lutheran Explores Siberia and Alaska." The translators obtained answers to some questions from Russian and German scholars who attended the symposium. Unfortunately, it was too late for an extensive comparison of the 1774 text with the 1996 reprint to search for solutions to other mysteries. Scherer's edition apparently contained quite a few errors that crept into the new edition. Despite some problems, this is a fine piece of work. Also worth mentioning are Dean Littlepage's *Steller's Island,* published by The Mountaineers Books of Seattle in 2006; and *Under Vitus Bering's Command: New Perspectives on the Russian Kamchatka Expedition,* edited by Peter Ulf Moller and Natasha Okhofina Lind and published by Aarhus University Press in 2004.

Volume 13 of the Elmer E. Rasmuson translation series, published in 2003, is titled *Through Orthodox Eyes: Russian Missionary Narratives of Travels to the Kena'ina and Ahtna, 1850s–1930s,* translated and with an introduction by Andrei A. Znamenski. It brings into English an important collection of Russian missionary records that cast new light on the spread of Orthodox Christianity among the Athapaskan-speaking peoples of the Cook Inlet, Iliamna, Lake Clark, Stony River, and Copper River areas. These records provide insights into Russian perceptions of Native societies in Alaska. They also include new ethnographic information on Athapaskan seasonal hunting and fishing cycles, settlement patterns, migration, demography, shamanism, marriage practices, relationships between Natives and miners, and alcohol abuse. Znamenski, the translator of this collection, has included a new interpretive chapter that places these events into a historical perspective.

The most useful and important single book on northern Athapaskans is *Subarctic* (1981), volume 6 in the Smithsonian Institution's Handbook of North American Indians series, under the general editorship of William C. Sturtevant. *Subarctic* contains many excellent articles on the environment, prehistory, and modern conditions of the Athapaskans and on the history of research on them. The volume also contains hundreds of photographs, illustrations, and maps, many published for the first time. Each article contains references for further reading.

The Alaska Historical Commission sponsored a volume by William E. Simeone titled *A History of Alaskan Athapaskans* (1982), a summary of written materials, divided into sections on the culture of various subgroups, and including for each group a history of the contact period from 1785 to 1971. James VanStone has summarized existing knowledge about the Northern Athapaskans in his readable volume *Athapaskan Adaptations: Hunters and Fishermen of the Subarctic Forests* (1974), and Richard K. Nelson's *Hunters of the Northern Forest: Designs for Survival among the Alaska Kutchin* (1973) is a well-written account based on fieldwork Nelson conducted among the Kutchin and Koyukon Indians of interior subarctic Alaska in the villages of Chalkystat, Huslia, and Hughes from August 1969 to July 1970 and from April to June, 1971. He followed that book with another volume titled *Make Prayers to the Raven* (1983). A gifted observer and writer, Nelson will undoubtedly continue his contributions to the understanding of Alaska's complex and rich cultures.

Poldine Carlo, a Fairbanks resident and Athapaskan Indian, has written a fine autobiographical volume titled *Nulato: An Indian Life on the Yukon* (1978). In *Shandaa: In My Lifetime* (1982), Belle Herbert, a resident of Chalkyitsik and Alaska's oldest resident at the time, probably born about 1861, near the dawn of white exploration of interior Alaska, tells of her own and her people's lives and customs, recorded and edited by Bill Pfisterer with the assistance of Katherine Peter.

The Yukon-Koyukuk School District sponsored a series of biographies of Athapaskans who live in the eleven villages the district services. These books are designed for upper-elementary students living in rural Alaska, but they make good reading for anyone interested in Athapaskan lifestyles. Hancock House Publishers of Vancouver, British Columbia, and Spirit Mountain Press of Fairbanks have published the series. Included are *A Biography: Allakaket,* by Moses Henzie (1979); *Minto: A Biography,* by Al Wright (1986); *Hughes: A Biography*, by Joe Beetus (1980); *Nulato: A Biography,* by Henry Eka (1986); and *Koyukuk: A Biography,* by Madeline Solomon (1981), among many others.

Adeline Peter Raboff authored *Iñuksuk: Northern Koyukon, Gwich'in and Lower Tanana, 1800–1901* (2001), which the Alaska Native Knowledge Network of Fairbanks published. Jan Harper-Haines wrote *Cold River Spirits: The Legacy of an Athabascan-Irish Family from Alaska's Lower Yukon River* (2000). The author explores her family's powerful conflicts and contrasts with help from her grandmother, who well knew the ancient spirit world, and from her mother, the first Alaska Native to graduate from the University of Alaska.

Epicenter Press is a regional press that Kent Sturgis, the former editor of the *Fairbanks Daily News-Miner,* and several of his associates founded and then moved to the state of Washington. The press is interested in the arts, history, nature, and diverse cultures and lifestyles of the North Pacific and high latitudes. The press has created an impressive backlist and continues it active publication program. Among its bestsellers are two volumes by Velma Wallace, a Gwich'in author who grew up in Fort Yukon and lives in Fairbanks. Her books *Two Old Women: An Alaska Legend of Betrayal, Courage and Survival* (1993) and *Raising Ourselves: A Gwich-in Coming of Age Story from the Yukon River* (2002) have remained bestsellers. Wallace was born the sixth of thirteen children in a two-room log cabin in Fort Yukon. Her first book deals with the survival of two old women abandoned by their group. The latter is her autobiography. In it Velma Wallace follows her own path, a journey of persistence, recovery, reconciliation, and ultimately finding her own strength. Kafe C. Duncan with Eunice Carney wrote *A Special Gift: The Kutchin Beadwork Tradition* (1997), originally published in 1988. Among the subarctic

Athapaskans, beadwork continues a tradition that has been important for well over a century. Scholars Craig Mishler and William E. Simeone researched and wrote *Han: People of the River* (2004). The upper Yukon River basin is wild, beautiful and very cold in the winters. The indigenous Han Indians, whose homeland straddles the U.S.-Canadian border, traveled this country as hunters and gatherers and found a way to survive in it that testifies to their intelligence and tenacity.

James Kari, James A. Fall, and principal contributor Shem Pete wrote *Shem Pete's Alaska: The Territory of the Upper Cook Inlet-Dena'ina* (2nd ed., 2003). Shem Pete (1896–1989) was a colorful and brilliant storyteller from Susitna Station, Alaska. He left a rich legacy of knowledge about his people. His lifetime travel map of about 13,500 square miles is one of the largest ever documented to this degree of detail anywhere in the world. The volume is richly illustrated with black-and-white photos, some color photos, and many maps. James Huntington's autobiography *On the Edge of Nowhere* (1966) and Sydney Huntington's *Autobiography Shadows on the Koyukuk: An Alaskan Native's Life along the River* (1993) are stories rich in diverse experiences. Bill Vaudrin, a Chippewa Indian, collected legends and stories in the *Tanaina Tales from Alaska* (1969).

Historian Debra Lindsay wrote *Science in the Subarctic: Trappers, Traders, and the Smithsonian Institution* (1993), a history of the early scientific work in the North, and the history of the Smithsonian's northern science. Lindsay provides a picture of the conduct of northern science, which the Smithsonian Institution practiced in the nineteenth century. Marie-Francoise Guédon produced *People of Tetlin, Why Are You Singing?* (1974) for the National Museum of Man in Ottawa, Canada. The book deals with the Upper Tanana Indians, seminomadic hunters in central Alaska. Their subsistence was based primarily on moose and caribou hunting, while their social life was, and still is, organized on the basis of matrilineal kin groups (sibs), grouped into moieties. The kinship system is based upon consanguineal and affinal ties, as well as on sib membership. The apparent discrepancies between moieties and exogenous groups and between consanguineal, affinal, and sib relationships are found to be a normal aspect of the social system, which allows a certain freedom to the individual. Social life, on different occasions, emphasizes and strengthens different aspects of the social system. The family, the sibs, and village constitute three levels of organization. Daily life is organized around close relatives, but the potlatch expresses the sib organization and the identity of each village.

Michael E. Krauss, the founder and longtime director of the Alaska Native Language Center at the University of Alaska Fairbanks and now professor emeritus, has spent a lifetime studying Alaska's Native languages. Among his many scholarly works, *Alaska Native Languages: Past, Present, and Future* (1980) is essential to an understanding of how imperiled these languages are. He concluded that Alaska Native languages are entering a period of final crisis for their future as living languages and that "most of them are about to die."

Finally, for anyone interested in the Athapaskans, Arthur E. Hippler and John R. Wood, former members of the Institute of Social and Economic Research at the University of Alaska, have prepared an excellent volume, *The Subarctic Athapascans: A Selected Annotated Bibliography* (1974).

The Aleuts, like the Eskimos, have also begun publishing historical materials. The Aleutian/Pribilof Islands Association prepared a study called *The Aleut Relocation and Internment during World War II: A Preliminary Examination* (1981) and sponsored a handsome volume by Lydia T. Black titled *Aleut Art* (1982). Briton Cooper Bush is the author of *The War against the Seals: A History of the North American Seal Fishery* (1985), and Dean Kohlhoff wrote a scholarly examination of Aleut relocation in World War II titled *When the Wind Was a River* (1995), which was published with the financial assistance of the Aleutian/Pribilof Islands Association. Dorothy Jones, at one time associated with the Institute of Social and Economic Research of the University of Alaska, authored two volumes. *Aleuts in Transition: A Comparison of Two Villages* (1976), is a case study that compares two villages with fictitious names, New Harbor and Iliaka, to show great differences in social organization and lifestyles. New Harbor represents the ultimate of adaptive success among Aleuts under American political and economic hegemony, while Iliaka is characteristic of a number of Aleut villages and of a vastly greater number of North American Native economic, social, and cultural failures. Her second book, *A Century of Servitude: Pribilof Aleuts under U. S. Rule* (1980), is an indictment of U.S. federal government abuse of the Pribilof Islanders that began in the nineteenth century and did not end until the 1970s. For those wishing to

read more about the Aleuts, Dorothy M. Jones and John R. Wood, formerly of the Institute of Social and Economic Research of the University of Alaska, have prepared *An Aleut Bibliography* (1975), an excellent guide.

Philip Drucker wrote the standard introduction to the Northwest Coast Indians, titled *Indians of the Northwest Coast* (1963). Anthropologist Frederica de Laguna wrote the three-volume *Under Mount Saint Elias: The History and Culture of the Yakutat Tlingit* (1972), which has become a classic. Aurel Krause and his brother Arthur were geographers sent by the Geographical Society of Bremen to follow up the work done by Nordenskiold on the Chukchi Peninsula in 1878 and 1879. This was the third Arctic expedition undertaken by the society. After the completion of their Siberian research, Arthur departed for Europe, while Aurel settled at Klukwan, in southeastern Alaska, and worked intensively with the Tlingits. Subsequently he wrote an excellent ethnographic study, translated by Erna Gunther, titled *The Tlingit Indians: Results of a Trip to the Northwest Coast of America and the Bering Straits* (1956). In 1933, Kalervo Oberg completed a study of Tlingit economic and social life, published in 1973 under the title *The Social Economy of the Tlingit Indians.* Wendell Oswalt, a noted anthropologist, observed that, "Oberg's discussion of the social system and economy are outstanding for their clarity and breadth; and it is little short of amazing that this work has never been published." That has now been remedied. Wilson Duff, who wrote the foreword to Oberg's book, predicts that the period of university-initiated field research is ending and that there will be a shift in the locus of field research from the universities to the people themselves. "The topics, phrasings, and interpretations will increasingly be their own," he states, and "along with this will come an examination and testing of the previous work of anthropologist; not just of their ethnographic descriptions, but also the concepts which they, as expert witnesses in court cases, have helped harden into law."

A Tlingit scholar and her husband, equally dedicated to scholarship, have translated and edited a two-volume work. *Haa Shuká, Our Ancestors: Tlingit Oral Narratives* (1987) and *Haa Tuwunáagu Yis for Healing Our Spirit: Tlingit Oratory* (1990). Nora Marks Dauenhauer and Richard Dauenhauer received support for their labors from a variety of sources, including the Sealaska Heritage Foundation, the Alaska State Legislature, Sealaska Corporation, Rainier Bank,

Rasmuson Foundation, Kootznoowoo Inc., Huna Totem Corporation, the Alaska Humanities Forum, and the National Endowment for the Humanities. This shows a trend—that various organizations are willing to financially support Native studies by Natives.

George Thornton Emmons wrote *The Tlingit Indians,* edited and with additions by Frederica de Laguna and a biography by Jean Low (1991). Lieutenant Emmons, U.S. Navy, was stationed in Alaska, arriving on the USS *Adams* in 1882. He became a friend of the Natives in southeastern Alaska and started to collect artifacts. For the next several decades he traveled among the Native villages, collecting items and making notes and sketches in the hopes of someday writing a book. He collected thousands of Native items, some of which he sold to the American Museum of Natural History in New York. He returned to the states, but by the time he died in 1945 he had not finished his book. He left several drafts in the American Museum and also in the British Columbia Provincial Archives in Victoria. It took Frederica de Laguna some thirty-odd years to prepare Emmon's drafts for publication. He had amassed such a wealth of ethnographic data and left so many notes, drawings, sketches, and manuscripts, de Laguna wrote, that to sort them out and organize them into a coherent form proved to be a Herculean task. The result is a spectacular, illustrated book which has become a classic.

Sergei Kan, a professor of anthropology and Native American studies at Dartmouth College, has authored a comprehensive study, *Memory Eternal: Tlingit Culture and Russian Orthodox Christianity through Two Centuries* (1999). A more general study that evaluates most aspects of historical and contemporary Native life can be found in a magnificent volume titled *Alaska Natives and the Land* (1969), written by the Federal Field Committee for Development Planning in Alaska to provide Congress with information in its efforts to draft a Native land claims settlement measure.

For a number of years until the early 1980s the federal government maintained the Anthropology and Historic Preservation Cooperative Park Studies Unit at the University of Alaska Fairbanks. Headed by the energetic and enthusiastic Zorro A. Bradley, the unit produced an enormous number of highly informative and interesting studies. A few titles will give an idea of the breadth of the studies undertaken: William R. and Carrie K. Uhl, *Tagiumsinaaqmiit: Ocean Beach Dwellers of the Cape Krusenstern Area, Subsistence Patterns* (1977); Gary C. Stein, *Cultural Resources of*

the Aleutian Region, volumes 1 and 2 (1977); Russell Sackett, *The Chilkat Tlingit: A General Overview* (1979); Grant Spearman, *Anaktuvuk Pass: Land Use Values through Time* (1980); William S. Schneider and Peter M. Bowers, *Assessment of the Known Cultural Resources in the National Petroleum Reserve in Alaska* (1977), and Richard K. Nelson, Kathleen H. Mautner, and G. Ray Bane, *Tracks in the Wildland: A Portrayal of Koyukon and Nunamiut Subsistence* (1982). Unfortunately, political squabbles resulted in the disbanding of the unit.

In 1966 the *Anchorage Daily News* ran a series of articles titled "The Village People." The public reaction was favorable. To meet the demand for copies, the newspaper republished the eleven-part series, together with comments by Philleo Nash, commissioner of the Bureau of Indian Affairs, and comments by Governor William A. Egan. In 1981 the same newspaper published a five-part series of articles titled "The Village People Revisited" (1981), discussing the changes that had swept through Alaska in the 1970s, changes that often stemmed directly from the Alaska Native Claims Settlement Act of 1971, the impact of the Prudhoe Bay discovery, the construction of the Trans-Alaska Pipeline, the arrival of television in the bush, and urbanization and growth.

Joseph E. Senungetuk, an artist who was born in the village of Wales, northwest of Cape Prince of Wales, has written an interesting book titled *Give or Take a Century: An Eskimo Chronicle* (1971). The author maintains that the Eskimo people had a complex, satisfying, technologically developed culture before white contact, a culture that rapidly deteriorated after contact.

For those readers who want to pursue Native studies, the Canadian Museum of Civilization, in Gatineau, Quebec, has both ethnology and archaeology divisions and publishes scholarly monographs. Journals dealing with peoples and cultures of the north include *Arctic Anthropology* (University of Wisconsin), *Anthropological Papers of the University of Alaska* (Fairbanks), and the *Canadian Journal of Archaeology* (Canadian Archaeological Association).

Much remains to be done on the history of Alaska's Russian period, but much excellent work has been accomplished in recent years. The Russian L. A. Zagoskin wrote a unique and interesting account of his travels in the Yukon and Kuskokwim valleys in 1842–44, which the Arctic Institute of North America published in 1967 under the title *Lieutenant Zagoskin's*

Travels in Russian America, 1842–1844 (1967). With some modifications, a translation of the 1956 Soviet edition was published in 1967, edited by Henry N. Michael. It is an excellent early account of riverine Eskimos of the Yukon and Kuskokwim rivers. Frank Golder, an American historian, worked extensively in Russian archives. One result was his volume *Russian Expansion to the Pacific, 1641–1850,* reprinted in 1960. Hector Chevigny produced three fast-paced accounts of Russian America, *Lost Empire: The Life and Adventures of Nikolai Rezanov* (1937, 1958), *Lord of Alaska: The Story of Baranov and the Russian Adventure* (1965), and *Russian America: The Great Alaskan Venture, 1741–1867* (1965). In *The Russian-American Company* (1951), S. B Okun, a Soviet scholar, furnishes a Marxist interpretation of the formation and activities of that organization.

James R. Gibson has written an important volume titled *Imperial Russia in Frontier America: The Changing Geography of Supply of Russian America, 1784–1867* (1976), in which he maintains that Russia's occupancy of Alaska from the late eighteenth century was neither sudden nor novel; it was simply the latest and farthest phase of a protracted and extensive process of eastward expansion that had been launched by Muscovy in the mid-sixteenth century.

In 1972 the Oregon Historical Society inaugurated a publishing venture titled North Pacific Studies. Its purpose is to make available in English little-known or hitherto unpublished works on the early history of the North Pacific Ocean and littorals. The first volume in the series, *Explorations of Kamchatka, 1735–1741* (1972), was written by a young Russian explorer-scientist, Stepan P. Krasheninnikov, of the famous Bering expedition to Kamchatka and the shores of northwest America. It was translated with introduction and notes by E. A. P. Crownhart-Vaughan. The second volume is by Kirill Timofeevich Khlebnikov, also a Russian, who in his service as an official of the Russian-American Company left a rich account of the North Pacific. The volume's title is *Colonial Russian America: Kyrill T. Khlebnikov's Reports, 1817–1832* (1976), translated with introduction and notes by Basil Dmytryshyn and Crownhart-Vaughan. Three other, very handsome volumes, followed: *Russia's Conquest of Siberia: 1558–1700*; *Russian Penetration of the North Pacific Ocean, 1700–1797;* and *The Russian American Colonies, 1798–1867*. All three are documentary records, edited and translated by Basil Dmytryshyn, E. A. P. Crownhart-Vaughan, and Thomas Vaughan.

Mention should also be made of the University of British Columbia Press's Pacific Maritime Studies. Representative volumes include Barry M. Gough, *The Royal Navy and the Northwest Coast of North America, 1810–1914* (1971); J. Arthur Lower, *Ocean of Destiny: A Concise History of the North Pacific, 1500–1978* (1978); Barry M. Gough, *Distant Dominion: Britain and the Northwest Coast of North America 1579–1809* (1980); Glynn Barratt, *Russia in Pacific Waters, 1715–1825: A Survey of the Origins of Russia's Naval Presence in the North and South Pacific* (1981); Glynn Barratt, *Russian Shadows on the British Northwest Coast of North America, 1810–1890* (1983); and Barry M. Gough, *The Northwest Coast: British Navigation, Trade, and Discoveries to 1812* (1992).

The Hawaiian Historical Society, in collaboration with the University Press of Hawaii, has published V. M. Golovnin's *Around the World on the Kamchatka, 1817–1819* (1974), translated with an introduction and notes by Ella Lury Wiswell. Between 1803 and 1833 thirty voyages embarked from the Baltic port of Kronshtadt to the Pacific, an average of one voyage each year. Sixteen of these were naval expeditions, while the remainder had a mixed character, involving Russian-American Company vessels manned by naval personnel. Commanders such as Kruzenshtern, Lisiansky, Golovnin, Lazarev, Kotzebue, and Luteke wrote accounts that won international recognition. Notwithstanding their historical and scientific value, some of these works have escaped translation. Until Wiswell translated Golovnin's account, this was true of his report.

Victoria Joan Moessner, a careful scholar and skilled translator, added to these translations with *The First Russian Voyage around the World: The Journal of Hermann Ludwig von Löwenstern, 1803–1806* (2003). Two-hundred years after the voyage began, Moessner made the first English translation of the uncensored diary of fourth officer Hermann Ludwig von Löwenstern. Because the diary was never published and thus was not subject to the censorship of tsarist Russia, it contains frank descriptions of historical events and conflicts, most of which were removed from other accounts. Moessner provides a historical and methodological introduction, as well as color reproductions of rare paintings and sketches from the expedition, many of them never published before.

Peter Lauridsen, a Dane, wrote a biography of his famous countryman, Vitus Bering. Titled *Vitus Bering: The Discoverer of Bering Strait* (1889), it was translated by Julius E. Olson. There also is the account by Sven Waxell, Bering's second-in-command, titled *The Russian Expedition to America* (1962). Waxell had probably finished writing his report by 1756. He wrote it in German, but when his vocabulary failed him, he had recourse to Swedish or English words and phrases or Germanized versions of them. He doubtless wrote for publication, but it was almost two hundred years before the book was published. After years of residence in the czar's private library, Waxell's manuscript disappeared in the upheavals of the Bolshevik revolution. In 1938 someone discovered it displayed for sale in a bookshop; the State Library in Leningrad bought it. A few years later the Danish publishing house Rosenkilde and Bagger acquired a photostatic copy of the manuscript, together with what was once thought to be the only known portrait of Vitus Bering (now believed to be his great-uncle). Johan Skalberg translated the manuscript into Danish. Later translated into English, it is a valuable document that sketches Bering's second expedition, and it is particularly good in describing the voyage of Bering's vessel, the packet boat *Saint Peter*, and its wreck on Bering Island in 1741. Waxell describes the winter on the island; the construction of a second, smaller ship from the wreck; and the return of the survivors to Russia in 1742.

The late Corey Ford, a talented and versatile writer with thirty books to his credit, authored *Where the Sea Breaks Its Back*, first published in 1966 and republished in 1992. It is the story of naturalist Georg Wilhelm Steller, based primarily on Steller's journal and other relevant materials. Leonhard Stejneger wrote *Georg Wilhelm Steller* (1936), and Margitt A. Engel and Orcutt W. Frost rendered a modern translation of Steller's journal, which Frost edited and introduced, *Georg Wilhelm Steller, Journal of a Voyage with Bering, 1741–1742* (1988).

The Franckenschen Stiftungen zu Halle supported, among other volumes, the publication of a catalog to accompany a 1997 exhibition, called *Die Grosse Nordische Expedition: Georg Wilhelm Steller (1709–1746), Ein Lutheraner Erforscht Sibirien und Alaska* [The Great Nordic Expedition: Georg Wilhelm Steller (1709–1746), a Lutheran Explores Siberia and Alaska] (1996). The Franckesche Stiftungen zu Halle and the Archive of the Russian Academy of Sciences, Saint Petersburg, supported the publication of *Georg Wilhelm Steller: Briefe und Dokumente 1740,* volume 1 (2000).

Raymond H. Fischer, late professor emeritus of history in the University of California at Los Angeles,

has written two books dealing with Russian voyages of discovery. In *The Voyage of Semen Dezhnev in 1648: Bering's Precursor* (1981), he describes Dezhnev's voyage in the summer of 1648 around the eastern tip of Asia, from the Kolyma River, which empties into the Arctic Ocean, to a point south of the mouth of the Anadyr River, which empties into the Pacific Ocean. Dezhnev thereby anticipated by eighty years the voyage of Bering through the strait separating Asia and America. In *Bering's Voyages: Whither and Why* (1977), Fischer presents an examination of the purposes of the voyages.

Eugenii G. Kushnarev, who was the longtime academic secretary at the Central Naval Museum in Leningrad, wrote *Bering's Search for the Strait: The First Kamchatka Expedition, 1725–1730*, published in the Soviet Union in 1976. E. A. P. Crownhart-Vaughn, then the executive director of the North Pacific Studies Center at the Oregon Historical Society, translated and edited the book, published in 1990. The editor wrote that much has been written about Bering's Second Kamchatka Expedition, but that this book is the first major work devoted wholly to the First Kamchatka Expedition. Orcutt W. Frost of Anchorage, who has spent years researching and writing about Steller, Bering and Chirikov, organized a set of interdisciplinary essays with contrasting views and much new information made available in English for the first time concerning the Bering-Chirikov voyages in *Bering and Chirikov: The American Voyages and Their Impact* (1992). One of the most interesting essays concerns the excavation of Bering's grave, which a group of Danish archaeologists, responding to a Russian invitation, undertook in 1991 (see chapter 4). Frost's crowning achievement is the publication of *Bering: The Russian Discovery of America* (2003), in which he brought together much new material in a scholarly and well-written synthesis. This is a page-turner, a wonderful adventure story. Valerian Lada-Mocarski, the adviser to the Russian Collection, Yale University, compiled a useful publication titled *Bibliography of Books on Alaska Published before 1868* (1969).

One of the earliest works in English on the Russian activities in North America was that of a young British clergyman, William Coxe, who toured Russia and in 1780 published his *Account of the Russian Discoveries between Asia and America,* reprinted in 1966. Coxe described the movement of the Russian fur hunters along the Aleutian Islands, which commenced during the 1740s. After the publication of Coxe's work, the various explorers who were sent to investigate the Russian efforts wrote accounts of their own. There are, for example, volumes by the famous British explorer Captain James Cook and his colleagues George A. Vancouver, W. R. Broughton, G. Dixon, Nathaniel Portlock, and J. Meares.

Numerous scholarly journals contain articles dealing with Russian activities in North America. Alaska historian Clarence L. Andrews published a number of articles in the *Washington Historical Quarterly*, the predecessor of the *Pacific Northwest Quarterly*, including "Alaska Under the Russians: Baranof the Builder" (*Washington Historical Quarterly* 7, 1916). A look at the index yields many other useful contributions. "The Condition of the Orthodox Church in Russian America: Innokentii Veniaminov's History of the Russian Church in Alaska," translated and edited by Robert Nichols and Robert Croskey, appeared in *Pacific Northwest Quarterly* 63 (April, 1972). The index to that journal also lists many fine articles on Russian America. Other journals that have published material on Russian America and Alaska include *North American Review, Mississippi Valley Historical Review, Pacific Historical Review, National Geographic, British Columbia Historical Quarterly, American Heritage, Quarterly of the California Historical Society, Journal of American History, Journal of the West, American Scholar, Pacific Historian, Beaver, Alaska Journal, Alaska Review,* and *Orthodox Alaska*.

The National Archives holds seventy-seven microfilm reels of the records of the Russian-American Company (1802–1867) and sixty-six rolls of dispatches addressed to the Department of State by U.S. diplomatic representatives to Russia between September 1808 and August 1906. The Library of Congress houses the Alaska Russian Orthodox church files, consisting of approximately one thousand boxes.

During the early 1970s officials of the Alaska Diocese of the Orthodox Church in America discovered a large number of old documents, rare books, and periodicals in the basements and attics of several churches in their vast domain. Most of the findings came from the Kvikhpak (Yukon) River Mission, dating from its beginnings in 1845 through 1966. A search on the island of Unalaska, in the Aleutian chain; on Kodiak Island, at Saint George Church, in the Pribilof Islands; and at Nushagak, on Bristol Bay, also turned up a number of documents. Subsequently, Barbara S. Smith, of the history department of the University of Alaska Anchorage, began inventorying,

arranging, and describing these records and published a useful finding aid titled *Russian Orthodoxy in Alaska: A History Inventory and Analysis of the Church Archives in Alaska with an Annotated Bibliography* (1980). The Alaska State Library in Juneau possesses an important collection of Russian books, as does the Elmer E. Rasmuson Library at the University of Alaska Fairbanks.

Lydia T. Black, professor emerita of the University of Alaska Fairbanks, has published much on Russian and Alaskan history and anthropology, including a biography of Saint Innocent titled *A Good and Faithful Servant: The Year of Saint Innocent* (1997) and *Aleut Art*, 2nd ed. (2003). Her *Russians in Alaska, 1732–1867* (2004) is a beautifully produced volume with both color and black-and-white illustrations. Her interpretation of the Russian period differs substantially from the traditional view that it was a period of unbridled exploitation, and indeed, enslavement of the Native peoples, a wanton rape and robbery of Alaska's natural resources. In reality, she points out, there seldom were more than five hundred Russians on the ground, vastly outnumbered by the Natives. This volume is certain to spark debate and become a classic.

Peter Litke, a German citizen, management consultant, turnaround manager, and company owner in Europe and the U.S., now devotes his time to his interest in the history of the American Northwest Coast. His *Russian-American Bibliography* (2003) is a useful English guide to the literature about the history of Russian-America, 1741–1867, and related subjects. Litke also is the author of *Vom-Zarenadler zum Sternenbanner* [From the Czar's Eagle to the Stars and Stripes] (2003).

Helpful general works on Russian history include Janet Martin, "From Kiev to Muscovy: The Beginnings to 1450," in *Russia: A History*, ed. Gregory L. Freeze (New York: Oxford University Press, 1997); Neil M. Heyman, *Russian History* (McGraw-Hill, Inc., 1993); John Lawrence, *A History of Russia*, 7th rev. ed. (New York: Penguin Books, 1993); George Vernadsky, *A History of Russia*, 5th rev. ed. (New Haven, Conn.: Yale University Press, 1964); Jesse D. Clarkson, *A History of Russia* (New York: Random House, 1964); Geoffrey Hosking, *Russia and the Russians: A History* (Cambridge, Mass.: 2002); Benson Bobrick, *East of the Sun: The Epic Conquest and Tragic History of Siberia* (New York: An Owl Book, Henry Holt and Company, 1993); Geoffrey Hosking, *Russia: People and Empire, 1552–1917* (Cambridge, Mass.: Harvard University

Press, 1997); and W. Bruce Lincoln, *The Romanovs: Autocrats of all the Russians* (New York: The Dial Press, 1981).

The members of the Western Union Telegraph Expedition, 1865–67, published accounts of their labors. Among them was Frederick Whymper, an English artist whose *Travel and Adventure in the Territory of Alaska* first appeared in London in 1868. Still a useful volume for the Russian as well as early American period is Hubert Howe Bancroft's *History of Alaska, 1730–1885* (1886), reprinted by Arno Press.

A wide variety of government publications and documents on the American period fill libraries and archives. They include reports on hearings before various congressional committees and specific research studies. In short, Alaska has been discussed, debated, agonized over, and studied for a long time.

Congressional hearings have served as a means of investigating conditions in Alaska and provide the forum in which interested groups and individuals have been heard. What to do with Alaska's coal lands, as well as questions concerning oil and gas leases on public lands, prompted hearings in 1910, 1912 (two volumes), 1913, 1915, and 1917 (three volumes). The subject of fisheries—their exploitation, conservation, and regulation—fills many volumes; between 1906 and the 1950s and since, hearings on this concern alone have filled thousands of pages. Between 1947 and 1956 hearings on Alaska statehood were conducted on seven different occasions in Washington and three times in Alaska. The printed record of these investigations amounts to approximately four thousand pages. Although congressional concern over Alaska's natural resources has exceeded its interest in health, education, and various other social problems in the territory and later state, the latter have also attracted attention.

Alaska, first as a district and later as a territory, had a long, close relationship with the federal government. Over the years, an enormous amount of documentation of federal activities in Alaska developed. Much of this material is housed in the National Archives in College Park, Maryland, and the National Archives, Alaska Region, Anchorage, Alaska, as well as various federal records centers, particularly the one in Seattle, Washington. Working in this goldmine of information is difficult and time consuming, at best, but fortunately there are always dedicated staff members of the National Archives and the federal records centers to help researchers find their way to the Alaska-related holdings. Finally, researchers enjoy the luxury of being able to use a published guide for a comprehensive description of the major record groups, series, and subseries of records pertaining to Alaska. Although the manuscript was in preparation for many years, George S. Ulibarri, formerly of the National Archives staff, compiled the final form; it is titled *Documenting Alaskan History: Guide to Federal Archives Relating to Alaska* (1982).

There are other research aids as well. James Wickersham, Federal District Court judge and territorial delegate to Congress, prepared an excellent volume, *A Bibliography of Alaskan Literature, 1724–1924* (1927). The volume, according to its author, "is supposed to contain a complete list of the titles of all printed books of history, travels, voyages, newspapers, periodicals, and public documents, in English, Russian, German, French, Spanish, etc., relating to, descriptive of, or published in Russian-America, now called Alaska, from 1724 to and including 1924." Wickersham may have missed a few printed accounts, but he was thorough, and this is a helpful volume even today. Over a number of years the Arctic Institute of North America prepared and published the multivolume work *The Arctic Bibliography,* which primarily lists scientific entries but also has many important historical items. Also useful is Elsie Tourville's *Alaska: A Bibliography, 1570–1970* (1975).

For more than twenty-five years Melvin B. Ricks gathered references to books, articles, pamphlets, and other written records on Alaska's history. For years investigators used typescripts of his material in several forms; it was a useful reference tool. In 1977 the Alaska Historical Commission issued Ricks's *Alaska Bibliography: An Introductory Guide to Alaskan Historical Literature,* edited by Stephen W. and Betty J. Haycox. Although the published version is updated, it is abbreviated, and the typescript manuscript is a much more valuable reference tool. Last but not least, the Smithsonian Institution issued its *Guide to the Smithsonian Archives* (1978), valuable because many of its collections pertain to Alaska. One example is the papers of William Healy Dall, a scientist who went to Russian America as a member of the Western Union Telegraph Expedition in 1865. Since 1867, the year of purchase, the federal government has commissioned scientific studies of Alaska. Obviously since that time a vast amount of such scientific work has accumulated, representing a valuable source of information for the historian.

Other government sources of historical interest

include the innumerable annual and special reports and studies by federal executive departments operating in Alaska. It is a long list, and a few examples must suffice: the National Census of 1880, in which Alaska was included for the first time; annual reports of the governor of Alaska, 1884 to 1958; annual reports of the Alaska Road Commission, 1905 to 1956; U.S. Geological Survey bulletins and professional papers, such as the indispensable *Dictionary of Alaska Place Names,* U.S. Geological Survey Professional Paper 567 (1967), by Donald J. Orth; and commercial statistics and weather reports. Much of the material is related to the development of one or another natural resource.

Obviously there is an abundance of material for political, social, and economic historians; but there are other resources as well. The personal-narrative literature about the North is rich and varied. Explorers, missionaries, traders, trappers, miners, tourists, and others have felt compelled to describe their experiences. The men and women who rushed north during the gold rushes probably produced a disproportionate share of these narratives, partly because the world at large was fascinated by the gold rushes and because adventurous accounts, especially those that promised quick and easy riches, were well received.

The Klondike, in Canada's Yukon Territory, drew the largest number of argonauts, and many narratives deal with that spectacular strike; but many miners went on to other stampedes in Alaska. One of the best accounts by a journalist is *The Klondike Stampede of 1897–98* (1900), by Tappan Adney, a sharp observer. Those who participated in the Gold Rush as teamsters or miners rather than observers and recorders gave their narratives a distinctive flavor. A good example of such a book is Arthur T. Walden's *A Dog Puncher on the Yukon* (1928), which fully expresses the excitement and adventure the participants felt.

Many authors, however, exaggerated, boasted, and even told outright lies because of forgetfulness or prompting from ghostwriters who wanted to spice up the tales. Edward C. Trelawny-Ansell's *I Followed Gold* (1939) abounds with exaggerated descriptions of actual events at Saint Michael, Skagway, and Nome and of impossible sled journeys. A colorful fantasy attributed to Jan Welzl, *Thirty Years in the Golden North* (1932), became a best seller.

Basil Austin, a stampeder, kept a diary that fully conveys the joys and hardships the stampeders experienced. Published in 1968, it is titled *The Diary of a Ninety-eighter.* Herbert L. Heller gathered firsthand accounts of life in Alaska and the Klondike from those who participated in these events in *Sourdough Sagas: Pioneering and Gold in Alaska, 1883–1923* (1967).

It was not until a quarter of a century after the Klondike and Nome rushes, however, that a trained historian examined the documents and wrote a monograph about pioneer Alaska. In the mid-1920s Jeannette Paddock Nichols, working on her doctoral dissertation under William Dunning, completed *Alaska: A History of Its Administration, Exploitation and Industrial Development during Its First Half Century under the Rule of the United States* (1924). Republished in 1963, the book remains an indispensable source for Alaska's territorial political development. Since most of Alaska's population lived in the territory's southeastern section, the Panhandle, Nichols dealt with that area. During her work she received much help and encouragement from James Wickersham. Nichols's central assumption, that Alaska received unnecessarily shoddy treatment from Uncle Sam, has been questioned by a number of contemporary historians.

In 1938, Clarence L. Andrews's *The Story of Alaska* appeared; it was reprinted eight times. Andrews knew the pioneer period from experience because during its heyday he had served in the U.S. Customs Service at Sitka, Skagway, and Eagle. Originally from the Midwest, Andrews became fond of the territory and spent the rest of his life telling its story. He was more versatile than most other historians, for he mastered the Russian language, which allowed him to explore and write about the period before 1867. A prolific researcher and writer, he produced a steady stream of articles and books, both popular and scholarly. Although his work lacks critical perspective, it has retained its value.

In the years immediately after World War II, three textbooks appeared. Stuart Ramsay Tompkins's *Alaska: Promyshlennik and Sourdough* (1945) long remained the recommended general survey. He carefully researched his book and compiled a useful bibliography. In 1953 the University of Alaska Press published posthumously Alfred Hulse Brooks's *Blazing Alaska's Trails.* Brooks, one-time head of the U.S. Geological Survey in Alaska, always had a strong interest in the territory. Edited by Burton L. Fryxell, the volume retains its value today. It is wide ranging, dealing with Alaska's geography and climate, Natives, the Russians and the Americans, and resource development. Particularly useful are his chapters on the history of mining. The University of Alaska Press reprinted the book in 1973.

Early in the century, James Wickersham adopted Alaska and became its foremost politician, and he used pen as well as the political forum to advance the territory's interests. Late in his life appeared his delightful *Old Yukon: Tale—Trails—and Trials* (1939). Based in part on his diaries, the volume contains much social history. The late Evangeline Atwood wrote a noncritical biography of Wickersham titled *Frontier Politics: Alaska's James Wickersham* (1979).

Ernest Gruening, after a distinguished career as a journalist, entered federal service and became the first director of the Interior Department's Office of Territories and Island Possessions. In 1939, President Franklin D. Roosevelt appointed him governor of Alaska, a position he occupied until 1953. Actively involved in Alaska's struggle for statehood, Gruening eventually was elected to one of the two U.S. Senate seats from the new state. He served as U.S. senator from 1959 until 1968 and then continued his career, championing birth control and advocating U.S. withdrawal from Vietnam. Throughout a long and eventful life, he, like Wickersham, used the pen as well as the political forum to advocate his ideas. Gruening, a Democrat, left the governorship after Dwight D. Eisenhower became president in 1953. With admirable single-mindedness he spent the year 1953–54 researching and writing *The State of Alaska* (1954), in which he told his fellow Americans how the United States had neglected the territory. He concentrated his narrative on the twentieth century but outlined earlier events. Gruening stated his ideas forcefully, and his footnotes are valuable for the researcher.

For Alaska's centennial celebration in 1967, Gruening wrote a legislative account of the Alaska statehood struggle, *The Battle for Alaska Statehood,* and in the same year appeared *An Alaskan Reader,* a selection of articles he had edited. In 1973, one year before he died at age eighty-seven, Liveright of New York published his *Many Battles: The Autobiography of Ernest Gruening.* In that description of his long, rich life, Alaska occupies approximately 115 of a total of 543 pages. To write the section on Alaska, Gruening relied heavily on a diary he had kept intermittently. It is a useful book, though the reader should be aware of the author's strong opinions on a variety of Alaska topics.

In 1998, Robert David Johnson published a fine, balanced biography, *Ernest Gruening and the American Dissenting Tradition.* Claus-M. Naske's *Ernest Gruening: Alaska's Greatest Governor* (2004) concentrates on Gruening's years as a territorial governor.

Scholars have spent a disproportionate amount of time on the questions surrounding the purchase and annexation of Russian America. They have written many articles on the question, including William A. Dunning, "Paying for Alaska: Some Unfamiliar Incidents in the Process," *Political Science Quarterly* 27 (September 1912); and Richard E. Welch, Jr., "American Public Opinion and the Purchase of Russian America," *American Slavic and East European Review* 17 (December 1958). In the early 1940s, David Hunter Miller, a diplomat and specialist on international law, summed up the Alaska purchase for the Department of State's series Treaties and Other International Acts of the United States of America, of which he was editor. *The Alaska Treaty* was completed in 1944, intended as volume 9 in the series, but the series was discontinued because of budget problems before it could be published. In 1981 the Limestone Press published Miller's book. It is an authoritative and thorough work.

Ronald J. Jensen wrote a doctoral dissertation on the purchase titled "The Alaska Purchase and Russian-American Relations," which appeared in 1975. In the same year, a broader work, Howard I. Kushner's *Conflict on the Northwest Coast: American-Russian Rivalry in the Pacific Northwest, 1790–1867,* was published. Kushner argued that American expansion of fishing, whaling, and commerce led to conflict and that Russia ceded the territory to avoid its seizure by the United States.

Over the years many graduate students in American universities have completed master's theses and doctoral dissertations on Alaska topics. The titles of some of the dissertations demonstrate the range of subjects: Franklin Ward Burch, "Alaska's Railroad Frontier: Railroads and Federal Development Policy, 1898–1915" (Catholic University of America, 1965); Stanley Ray Remsberg, "United States Administration of Alaska: The Army Phase, 1867–1877" (University of Wisconsin, Madison, 1975); Bobby Dave Lain, "North of Fifty-three: Army, Treasury Department, and Navy Administration of Alaska, 1867–1884" (University of Texas, 1974); Marilyn Jody, "Alaska Literary History of Frontier Alaska with a Bibliographical Guide to the Study of Alaskan Literature" (Indiana University, 1969); and Terrence Michael Cole, "A History of the Nome Gold Rush: The Poor Man's Paradise" (University of Washington, 1983).

There has also been an increase in both the number of authors and the diversity of subjects of journal articles dealing with Alaska in the postwar period. Beginning in the 1950s–60s, there has been a veritable explosion of journal literature about Alaska. We all have to be thankful to the late Ted C. Hinckley and Morgan B. Sherwood, who pioneered in this field. A few examples are Ted C. Hinckley, "The Presbyterian Leadership in Pioneer Alaska," *Journal of American History* 52 (March 1966); John Sherman Long, "Webb's Frontier and Alaska," *Southwest Review* 56 (October 1971); Thomas G. Smith, "The Treatment of the Mentally Ill in Alaska, 1884–1912," *Pacific Northwest Quarterly* 65 (January 1974); Claus-M. Naske, "Jewish Immigration and Alaskan Economic Development: A Study in Futility," *Western States Jewish Historical Quarterly* 8 (January 1976); Claus-M. Naske, "The Relocation of Alaska's Japanese Residents," *Pacific Northwest Quarterly* 74 (July 1983); Herman Slotnick, "The Ballinger-Pinchot Affair in Alaska," *Journal of the West* 10 (April 1971); William R. Hunt, "A Soldier on the Yukon," *Journal of the West* 10 (April 1971); Charles Hendricks, "The Eskimos and the Defense of Alaska," *Pacific Historical Review* (1985); David J. Mitchell, "Continental Stalemate: How the Alaska Purchase Treaty Led to Canadian Confederation," *New Pacific* (Fall 1990); Terrence M. Cole, "Ernest Walker Sawyer and Alaska: The Dilemma of Northern Economic Development," *Pacific Northwest Quarterly* 82 (April 1991); Matthew J. Eisenberg, "The Last Frontier: Jewish Pioneers in Alaska," part 2, *Western State Jewish History* (January 1992); Ted C. Hinckley, "Glimpses of Societal Change among Nineteenth-Century Tlingit Women," *Journal of the West* (July 1993); Terrence M. Cole, "Wally Hickel's Big Garden Hose: The Alaska Water Pipeline to California," *Pacific Northwest Quarterly* 86 (Spring 1995); Stephen Haycox "William Paul, Sr., and the Alaska Voters' Literacy Act of 1925," *Alaska History* 2 (Winter 1986–87); Frank Norris, "Showing Off Alaska: The Northern Tourist Trade, 1878–1941," *Alaska History* 3 (Spring 1988); Stephen Haycox and Claus-M. Naske, "A New Face: Implementing Law in the New State of Alaska, 1958–1960," *Western Legal History* 11 (Winter/Spring 1998); Katherine L. Arndt, "Russian Relations with the Stikine Tlingit, 1833–1867," *Alaska History* 3 (Spring 1988); Claus-M. Naske, "The Shaky Beginnings of Alaska's Judicial System," *Western Legal History* 1 (Summer/Fall 1988); Elizabeth A. Tower, "Anthony J. Dimond: Statehood Pioneer," *Alaska History* 13 (Spring/Fall 1998); Claus-M. Naske, "Some Attention, Little Action: Vacillating Federal Efforts to Provide Territorial

Alaska with an Economic Base," *Western Historical Quarterly* 26 (Spring 1995); James H. Ducker, "An Auto in the Wilderness: Dr. Percival's 1911 Alaska-Yukon Drive, *Pacific Northwest Quarterly* (Spring 1999); Allison Bate, "Who Do You Believe? Has Prince William Sound Largely Recovered from the *Exxon Valdez* Oil Spill or Is the Science Itself Contaminated," *Marine Digest* (April 1999); Frank W. Anderson, "The Presidential Cruise of the U.S.S. *Henderson*," *Sea Chest* (September 2000); Orlando W. Miller, "Jewish Refugees for Alaska, 1933–1945," *Western States Jewish History* (Fall 2003); Rhoda M-Love, "The Final Cruise: Depression Era Teachers Journey North of the Arctic Circle," *Pacific Northwest Quarterly* (Fall 2005); Joshua Ashenmiller, "The Alaska Oil Pipeline as an Internal Improvement, 1969–1973," *Pacific Historical Review* (August 2006); and Steven L. Danver, "Metlakatla: Native Leadership and White Resistance in an Alaskan Mission Community," *Journal of the West* (Fall 2007).

The Spring 2008 issue of the *Journal of the West* featured five articles on Alaska: Sandra K. Mathews, "An Introduction to Colonial Russian America"; Steven L. Danver, "Innocent Veniaminow and the Growth of Russian Orthodoxy in Russian America"; Rick S. Kurtz, "Cross-Culture Relationships on the Southeast Alaskan Frontier: The Glacier Bay Case"; and Ron McGee, "Ernest Gruening: Alaska, the West, and Vietnam"; and A. V. Grinev, "Germans in the History of Russian America."

In 1967, during Alaska's Centennial year, Robert N. DeArmond's *The Founding of Juneau* appeared. Well written, it opened up a variety of topics, including mining, politics, and town building in the North. Also worthy of mention is William H. Wilson's splendid book *Railroad in the Clouds: The Alaska Railroad in the Age of Steam, 1914–1945* (1977).

Since statehood, events in Alaska have confirmed that history will increasingly find its strongest support in the state itself. In 1966, Robert A. Frederick, of Alaska Methodist University; George Hall, of the National Park Service; Robert N. DeArmond, of Juneau; and other interested citizens formed the Alaska Historical Society. Conferences, preservation projects, and various historical undertakings followed. In 1984 the society launched its own history journal, *Alaska History*. In 1985 the Alaska Historical Commission published a useful list of projects it had supported: *Publications, Research Reports and Other Projects Supported by the Alaska Historical Commission, 1973–1985*. In 1971, Robert A. Henning, owner of Alaska Northwest Publishing Company, and Robert N. DeArmond launched Alaska's first state historical magazine, the *Alaska Journal*. A very handsome publication, it combined some of the best features of *National Geographic* with those of traditional, scholarly, well-researched historical quarterlies. Unfortunately, it ceased publication with the Autumn 1985 issue.

Alaska's historical fraternity has steadily increased since statehood. The late historian Orlando Miller of the University of Alaska Fairbanks has analyzed Alaska agricultural failures in *The Frontier in Alaska and the Matanuska Colony* (1975). His conclusions destroyed cherished myths and upset many local boosters. Claus-M. Naske has analyzed and recounted Alaska's struggle for self-determination in *A History of Alaskan Statehood* (1985) and has written a biography of Alaska's last territorial delegate and the state's first senior U.S. senator in *Edward Lewis "Bob" Bartlett of Alaska: A Life in Politics* (1979).

There has been a growing literature on World War II in Alaska. Brian Garfield's *The Thousand Mile War*, first published in 1969 with a revised edition appearing in 1995, well describes the only military campaign fought on American soil during the conflict, namely, in the remote Aleutian Islands. Otis Hays, Jr., served as a senior member of the Alaska Defense Command's military intelligence staff. He supervised the staff of the command's foreign liaison operation in 1943–44. He also served as a foreign-service officer for the U.S. Information Agency. He wrote three books. The first, *Home from Siberia: The Secret Odysseys of Interned American Airmen in World War II* (1990). This is the long-secret story of how the Soviet commissariat for internal affairs interned 291 young American flyers who had crashed or made emergency landings in Soviet territory. The Soviet Union, at the risk of a second front, eventually smuggled four groups of them to south central Asia and finally across the Iranian border. There, American officials swore the airmen to secrecy and confiscated any items that would indicate they had been in the Soviet Union. This is a good read. Hays's second volume, *The Alaska-Siberia Connection: The World War II Air Route* (1996), is the story of how the American Lend-Lease program transferred almost eight thousand planes of all types to the Russians via the Alaska-Siberia Lend Lease Route from Great Falls, Montana, via Ladd Field in Fairbanks to Nome and Siberia and eventually to the European front. The third volume, *Alaska's Hidden Wars: Secret Campaigns on the North Pacific Rim* (2004), chronicles the role of Japanese-American intelligence specialists in the Aleutian theater, and details a Japanese eyewitness account of the defense of Attu. It also describes the brutal North Pacific weather and the internment of American airmen in Kamchatka.

Heath Twichell has written a wonderful book on the construction of the Alaska Highway, *Northwest Epic: The Building of the Alaska Highway* (1992). Other volumes dealing with the project are Ken Coates's *North to Alaska: Fifty Years on the World's Most Remarkable Highway* (1992). Also notable are K. A. Coates and W. R. Morrison, *The Alaska Highway in World War II: The U.S. Army of Occupation in Canada's Northwest* (1992); and William A. Morrison and Kenneth A. Coates, *Working the North: Labor and the Northwest Defense Projects 1942–1946* (1994).

Other books dealing with wartime Alaska are Howard Handleman, *Bridge to Victory: The Story of the Reconquest of the Aleutians* (1943): Lt. Robert J. Mitchell with Sewell T. Tyng and Capt. Nelson L. Drummond, Jr., *The Capture of Attu: A World War II Battle as Told by the Men Who Fought There* (2000); Jean Potter, *Alaska Under Arms* (1943); Jim Rearden, *Koga's Zero: The Fighter that Changed World War II* (1995); and William Gilman, *Our Hidden Front* (1944). Muktuk Marston wrote *Men of the Tundra: Alaska Eskimos at War* (1969), the story of the Eskimo scouts he organized. Jonathan M. Nielson's *Armed Forces on a Northern Frontier: The Military in Alaska's History, 1867–1987* (1988) is useful but marred by too many mistakes. A useful guide to materials on the war in the North is *World War II in Alaska: A Resource Guide for Teachers and Students* (2000), published cooperatively by the History Day in Alaska program and the National Park Service Alaska Support Office.

The late Ted C. Hinckley, professor emeritus at San Jose State University, has done much to advance the cause of Alaska's history. He gave presentations at conferences about Alaskan topics when that was not fashionable. He contributed to scholarly journals many articles on Alaska history, and among his books are, *The Americanization of Alaska, 1867–1897* (1973), a colorful biography, *Alaskan John G. Brady: Missionary, Businessman, Judge, and Governor, 1878–1918* (1982), and *Canoe Rocks: Alaska's Tlingit and the Euramerican Frontier, 1800–1912* (1995). The late Morgan Sherwood was another pioneer in bringing Alaska history to the scholarly community. Among his books are *Exploration of Alaska, 1865–1900* (1965), a milestone in Alaska historical literature. The natural beauty that so captivated the nineteenth-century explorers whose adventures fill the pages of this book is conveyed with a vividness and talent that is as spectacular as its subject matter. Another is *Big Game in Alaska: A History of Wildlife and People* (1981).

William H. Hanable, executive director of the Alaska Historical Commission, created by the legislature in the early 1970s to foster historical research, writing, and publication, has produced a valuable regional history titled *Alaska's Cooper River: The 18th and 19th Centuries* (1982).

Patricia Roppel, a former high school teacher who turned to history in her second career, has distinguished herself through her prolific and scholarly work. She wrote many articles on the Panhandle's mining history, which appeared with regularity in the *Alaska Journal*. She has authored several books, among them *Salmon from Kodiak Island, Alaska* (1986) and *Land of Mists: Revillagegedo and Gravina Islands Misty Fjords National Monument* (1998).

The late Richard A. Cooley's *Politics and Conservation: The Decline of the Alaska Salmon* (1963) has become a standard reference work on that topic. In his *Alaska, A Challenge in Conservation* (1966), he discussed Alaska's unparalleled opportunity to conceive and carry out an imaginative land policy with the 103-million-acre statehood land grant. It was an opportunity to show this nation new paths in land and resource policy; to highlight Alaska's achievements since statehood; to exemplify the principles by which the state government has acted; and to reveal the hopes and warnings of the future. Cooley set out to answer these and many other questions in this pioneering study of Alaska land policy.

Terrence Michael Cole, a professor at the University of Alaska Fairbanks, produced *Crooked Past: The History of a Mining Camp: Fairbanks, Alaska* (1991), first published as *E. T. Barnette: The Strange Story of the Man Who Founded Fairbanks* (1981). Cole's *Nome: City of the Golden Beaches* appeared in 1984. His monumental *Banking on Alaska: The Story of the National Bank of Alaska* (2001), volume 1, is more than the history of the NBA—it is an economic history of Alaska. Volume 2, with the same title, has the subtitle *Elmer's Memoirs: Anecdotes and Vignettes of My 90 Years,* by Elmer E. Rasmuson, who built the bank into the state's largest financial institution. Before he died, Rasmuson established a foundation in his name with an endowment of approximately half a billion dollars, designed to support Alaskan initiatives in the arts and social sciences.

Terrence Cole's twin brother, Dermot Cole, a longtime columnist for the *Fairbanks Daily News-miner,* has also written several fine books. Among them are *Frank Barr, Bush Pilot in Alaska and the Yukon* (1986), *Hard Driving: The 1908 Auto Race from New York to Paris* (1991), *Amazing Pipeline Stories: How Building the Trans-Alaska Pipeline Transformed Life in America's Last Frontier* (1997), and *Fairbanks: A Gold Rush Town That Beat the Odds* (1999). I am certain that the Cole twins will continue to research and write about Alaska. One of Terrence Cole's graduate students in Northern Studies, Timothy Rawson, now a member of the history department at Alaska Pacific University, rewrote his thesis into a fine book: *Changing Tracks: Predators and Politics in Mt. McKinley National Park* (2001).

William R. Hunt, formerly of the Department of History at the University of Alaska Fairbanks, produced a number of highly readable books. *His North of 53 Degrees: The Wild Days of the Alaska-Yukon Mining Frontier, 1870–1874* (1974) emphasized colorful personalities and episodes but also provided a much-needed overview of the far-flung region that attracted Alaskans and North Americans alike for almost half a century. His highly readable *Arctic Passage: The Turbulent History of the Land and People of the Bering Sea, 1697–1975* (1975) is a fine regional history. In 1976, his book *Alaska: A Bicentennial History* appeared in The States and Nation Series, which W.W. Norton of New York published for the American Association for State and Local History. *To Stand at the Pole: The Dr. Cook-Admiral Peary North Pole Controversy* followed in 1981. *Stef: A Biography of Vihjalmur Stefansson, Canadian Arctic Explorer* was published in 1986. In 1987, the University of Oklahoma Press published Hunt's *Distant Justice: Policing the Alaska Frontier,* a history of the territory's unique judicial system, highlighting colorful personalities and court cases. *Passage to the North: A Traveler's Companion to the Historic Sites and Frontier Legends along the Alaska Highway* (1992) illuminates the long road for the traveler.

After Hunt left the University of Alaska Fairbanks, he worked for the National Park Service in Anchorage for a few years. The agency published his *Mountain Wilderness: Historic Resource Study for Wrangell-St. Elias National Park and Preserve* in 1991. Professor Emeritus Hunt, after a long and productive career, has given up writing and turned his talents to painting. The jury is still out on that phase of his career.

George W. Rogers, Alaska's senior economist and cofounder of the University's Institute of Social and

Economic Research (ISER), located at the University of Alaska Anchorage, authored a valuable regional study, *Alaska in Transition: The Southeast Region* (1960), which he followed with a thoughtful volume titled *The Future of Alaska: Economic Consequences of Statehood* (1962).

Researchers at ISER have produced many useful studies over the years. Economist Oliver Scott Goldsmith published the first of a series called Fiscal Policy Papers in 1989. In this and the following fourteen publications, Goldsmith and associates examined Alaska's fiscal gap, namely, how shrinking oil production and revenues translate into big fiscal problems for Alaska. Despite their excellent advice, the state legislature has so far, in 2010, refused to fix that gap.

Canada and Alaska are closely linked in many ways, and their historians have been attracted to northern history. The late Pierre Berton, author, journalist, television personality, and son of a stampeder who spent his childhood in Dawson, the Yukon Territory, has written many volumes about Canadian topics. His *The Klondike Fever*, first published in 1958 and republished numerous times since then, has become a classic. His *Drifting Home* (1974) is a charming account of the author's trip in a raft down the Yukon River from Lake Bennett to Dawson, the famous Gold Rush town where he grew up. His mother, Laura Beatrice Berton, wrote her memoir, *I Married the Klondike* (1954).

Other women went to the Klondike and left accounts of their experiences. Two of the most eccentric women to travel to the Klondike and publish their experiences were Mary E. Hitchcock and Edith May Van Buren. Their *Two Women in the Klondike* is one of the most unusual memoirs of the nineteenth century. It includes travel literature and a unique first-hand account of the Klondike Gold Rush. The memoir was published in New York in 1899. Martha Louise Black left Chicago in 1898, where she managed a sawmill and eventually won election to the Canadian Parliament. Her story, *My Ninety Years* (1976), recounts her myriad adventures.

The American actress and novelist Elizabeth Robbins wrote an account of her Alaskan experiences in the 1930s. She had a close relationship with one of her brothers, Raymond, who gave up promising prospects as a lawyer to go to Nome and seek his fortune in the Gold Rush. Eventually, he became the spirited leader of the Nome pioneering community. In this book, Robbins gives an account of her visit to Nome in 1900, including a difficult voyage from Seattle on an overcrowded ship, her first impressions of the tent city of thousands on the tundra, and her discovery that her brother had become a cross between a saint and a dictator. She gained insight into a strange, enclosed little world of heroism and racketeering, claim jumping, and militant Christianity. University of Alaska Fairbanks Professor of German Victoria Joan Moessna and her collaborator, JoAnne E. Gates, edited *The Alaska-Klondike Diary of Elizabeth Robbins, 1900* (1999), one of the most engaging, witty, and readable accounts surviving from the turn of the century.

Ella Lung related her experiences of the Alaska-Klondike Gold Rush in *Trail to North Star Gold* (1969). Frances Ella Fitz told of her experiences in Nome, where she arrived in the late spring of 1900, to Jerome Odlum, who wrote *Lady Sourdough* (1941). Fitz was a New York stenographer who had been lured north by tales of Alaskan gold. She arrived armed with only her typewriter. Melanie J. Mayer and Robert N. DeArmond, Alaska's senior historians, produced the meticulously researched volume *Staking Her Claim: The Life of Belinda Mulrooney, Klondike and Alaska Entrepreneur* (2000). Historian Charlene Porsild wrote the scholarly and readable *Gamblers and Dreamers: Women, Men, and Community in the Klondike* (1998). Fairbanks author Jan A. Murray researched and assembled *Music of the Alaska-Klondike Gold Rush: Songs and History* (1999), no doubt the definitive work on the subject. Melanie J. Mayer, an academician with a specialty in psychology and psychobiology, wrote the beautifully illustrated *Klondike Women: True Tales of the 1897–1898 Gold Rush* (1989). She assembled a group of remarkable women and used many of their own words in chronicling their experiences in the Klondike Gold Rush.

The University of Alaska Press published William B. Haskell's *Two Years in the Klondike and Alaskan Gold Fields, 1896–1898* (1998) in its classic Reprint Series, which Professor Terrence M. Cole edits and for which he writes introductions. It is a remarkable story, a literary and historical gem. The late Canadian historian William Rodney wrote *Joe Boyle: King of the Klondike* (1974), the fascinating story of a many-sided and adventurous man. The late historian Murray Morgan wrote *One Man's Gold Rush: A Klondike Album* (1967) about the photographer E. A. Hegg. It is richly illustrated with Hegg's wonderful photographs. Robert N. DeArmond compiled and annotated the writings of Elmer J. "Stroller" White in *'Stroller' White: Tales of a Klondike Newsman* (1969). Lewis Greene wrote *The Gold Hustlers* (1977), a seventy-year history of placer mining in the Klondike, from the discovery of gold on Rabbit Creek in 1896 to the closure of the last gold dredge in 1966. The author interweaves two stories, that of the last money-men, the promoters and hucksters, and the stock manipulators, who scrambled after the riches found on the Klondike creeks, and that of the engineers who tried to build a profitable mining operation from the wreckage left by the promoters. Randall M. Dodd edited dispatched letters and journals of E. Hazard Wells, long lost, who was a correspondent for the *Cincinnati Post* and the Scripps-McRae Syndicate. It is titled *Magnificence and Misery: A Firsthand Account of the 1897 Klondike Gold Rush* (1984).

Basil Austin left an account of his northern adventures in *The Diary of a Ninety-Eighter* (1968). James Albert Johnson wrote *George Carmack: Man of Mystery Who Set Off the Klondike Gold Rush* (2001). W. R. Hamilton, who died in 1964 at the age of ninety-two, had been one of the 1,500 men who left Ashcroft in 1898 to take the incredibly difficult overland route to the Klondike goldfields. He worked in placer mining in both Atlin and the Klondike. After the great excitement subsided, he continued to live for about ten years in Dawson and Whitehorse in the Yukon Territory. Half-a-century later, Hamilton concluded that the Klondike story had never been gathered in one good historical account. He undertook the job and spent years researching and writing. Unsuccessful in getting his early efforts published, he persisted in collecting and writing. Finally, in 1963, he saw the corrected galley proofs of his *The Yukon Story*, printed by the Mitchell Press, but he died before it was published (1964).

Richard O'Connor wrote *High Jinks on the Klondike* (1954), the story of the colorful people who came to the Klondike at the end of the nineteenth century. Allen A. Wright had a varied career, working on surveys and construction projects in the month after his discharge from the Royal Canadian Engineers after World War II. He settled in the Yukon in 1958 and worked on highway location and design. His *Prelude to Bonanza: The Discovery and Exploration of the Yukon* (1976) explores the subject to the end of the nineteenth century. Ken S. Coates and William R. Morrison, two Canadian historians, in their *Land of the Midnight Sun: A History of the Yukon* (1988), have gone beyond the Klondike Gold Rush and rendered a very readable account of the territory's colorful

and varied history. Here, as in their other volumes, they bring to life the neglected history of that part of Canada. Ken Coates also wrote, among others, *Best Left as Indians* (1991), in which he examines the interaction between Native people and whites in the Yukon Territory, from the arrival of the fur traders through the fundamental changes following World War II. Coates examines social contact, economic relations, and church and government policies, among other topics.

Historian Keith A. Murray wrote about a little-known aspect of the turbulent 1890s. In 1898, sixty-eight men and their families came from Lapland to Alaska as employees of the U.S. Army. They were hired to carry freight and mail by reindeer to the remote outposts of Alaska. Some of these men, who were expert reindeer herders, came to teach the Eskimo people how to care for the deer. Not long after they reached the northern Pacific coast, the government transferred them to the Reindeer Service under the Department of the Interior. Soon after they arrived at the Unalakleet River, one of them discovered gold on the Seward Peninsula, not far from where Nome is now located. He became a millionaire, and some of the other herders became moderately wealthy. The gold discoveries led to a gold rush on the Seward Peninsula. The thousands who came soon mined enough gold to repay Alaska's purchase price many times over. Murray recounts these colorful events in *Reindeer and Gold* (1988).

Kathryn Morse turned her doctoral dissertation into a very interesting book. The University of Washington published *The Nature of Gold: An Environmental History of the Klondike Gold Rush* (2003) in its series of Weyerhaeuser Environmental Books. These volumes explore human relationships with natural environments in all their variety and complexity. They attempt to cast new light on the ways that natural systems affect human communities, the ways that people affect the environments of which they are a part, and how different cultural conceptions of nature change our sense of the world around us. Kathryn Morse looks at the Klondike Gold Rush through these lenses.

Robert L. Spude of the U.S. National Park Service produced *Chilkoot Trail: From Dyea to Summit with the '98 Stampeders* (1980). Since the 1960s, climbing the Chilkoot Pass has become a tourist adventure. Allan Ingelson, Michael Mahony, and Robert Scace produced *Chilkoot: An Adventure in Ecotourism* (2001) to help fill the need for a guide. Finally, Roy Minter wrote *The White Pass: Gateway to the Klondike* (1987), the story of the White Pass and Route railway.

For years, travel writers have scribbled away in their attempts to portray Alaska. The results have been as varied as the people who steamed up the Inland Passage or to Saint Michael and up the Yukon River. Many tall tales and trivia have filled notebooks, and Alaskans reading the results have often been pained by the exaggerations and outright falsehoods. It must be remembered that it is difficult to encounter the vastness and variety of Alaska and describe them accurately. Yet some have managed to do so. T. A. Rickard, geologist, mining engineer, and editor, visited Alaska's important mining areas in the summer of 1908. His description of Alaska miners and their difficulties in *Through the Yukon and Alaska* (1909) is sympathetic and perceptive; he understood the appeal the country had for those who wrested a living from its soil. The charm of the land lay in its vastness, its freedom from restraints, and its uncomplicated life.

Alaska's visitors have written extensively about their perception of and experiences in the North, often also including some history. The late Sally Carrighar wrote radio dramas and feature articles and edited a financial monthly before, in 1937, she embarked on a career as chronicler of wildlife. Her *Icebound Summer* (1953) is an account of the struggle for survival by animals, birds, and humans on Alaska's northwest coast. She followed that with *Moonlight at Midday* (1958), in which she deals with Alaska's flora, fauna, majestic scenery, and fascinating people and their way of life. Carrighar deals with Eskimo settlements well off the tourist track and other things casual travelers do not see, such as the winter life of the inhabitants of the two gold rush cities of Nome and Fairbanks.

Joe McGinnis, who produced a best seller in *The Selling of the President* (1968), visited Alaska in 1975, and Alfred A. Knopf published the result of his visit, *Going to Extremes* (1980). During much of two years, McGinnis lived in Anchorage, "a city that had got a late start; now it was trying to catch up all at once, skipping about two hundred years." He repeatedly ventured into the boondocks, hiking across tundra and glaciers. He stopped at tiny settlements, looked around, talked, watched, and listened. His is a funny and personal perspective book about the 49th State as a place in the throes of fundamental change, caused by the oil boom.

Writer John McPhee was a staff writer for the *New Yorker* and the author of many perceptive and lucidly written books, and his Alaska book *Coming into the Country* (1976) is no exception. It is about contemporary Alaskans, with occasional forays into the state's past. He blends vivid character sketches, observed landscape, and descriptive narrative in the three principal segments of the book that deal, respectively, with a total wilderness, with urban Alaska, and with life in the remote bush.

Philip L. Fradkin, author of acclaimed books on the American West, wrote a wonderful volume, *Wildest Alaska: Journeys of Great Peril in Lituya Bay* (2001). He had read a book about remote Lituya Bay, on the Gulf of Alaska coast. Attracted by the threads of violence woven through the natural and human histories of Lituya Bay, he asked himself if these histories could be related, and if so, how? Attempting to define the power of this wild place led him on a dangerous quest. His memoir tells the reader of his odyssey through recorded history and eventually to the bay itself, where he explores the dark and unyielding side of nature. This is a very good read.

As a field editor for *Audubon* magazine, George Laycock wrote many articles on natural history and related subjects. In his book, *Alaska: The Embattled Frontier* (1971), the first volume in the Audubon Library, he studied the protection and exploitation of natural resources in the wake of the 1968 Prudhoe Bay oil discovery.

Peter Jenkins is best known for his book *A Walk Across America* (1979), which was the result of his experiences as a disillusioned college graduate who set out with his dog, Cooper, to look for himself and his nation. His *Looking for Alaska* (2001) is his account of eighteen months he spent traveling in Alaska. He covered more than twenty thousand miles in small bush planes, on snow machines and snowshoes, in fishing boats and kayaks, on the Alaska Marine Highway, and traveling the Haul Road, searching for what defines Alaska. He told the stories of many Alaskans from Barrow to Craig, Seward to Deering, and everywhere in between. His family settled in Seward on the Kenai Peninsula, coming and going from there. He also writes about how his family lived, made Alaska their home, and participated in some of the author's explorations.

Hudson Stuck (1863–1920) immigrated to America from England in quest of excitement. He found it, first in Texas and later in Alaska, where he went as a missionary for the Anglican Church and became the archdeacon of the Yukon. A good writer, he appealed to an age that enjoyed travel literature, built up the National Geographic Society, admired Teddy Roosevelt, and revered "the strenuous life." Stuck organized the first successful ascent of Mount McKinley (Denali) and wrote a lively account of the expedition titled *The Ascent of Denali (Mt. McKinley)* (1914). *Ten Thousand Miles with a Dog Sled* describes his arduous travels around the entire arctic coast of Alaska. Equally captivating is his *Voyages on the Yukon and Its Tributaries* (1917). Historian David M. Dean wrote an excellent biography of Hudson Stuck, *Breaking Trail: Hudson Stuck of Texas and Alaska* (1988). Dean wrote that Stuck "was the progressive era's intrepid explorer in the far north, and his twenty-eight year labor to bring physical and spiritual solace to the isolated Indian, Eskimo, and White settlers of the Yukon made Stuck perhaps the Episcopal church's most famous missionary."

William Healy Dall, the second director of the Western Union Telegraph Expedition, which, in the 1860s, planned to connect North America via Russian Alaska and Siberia with Europe, penned the first summary of what he called *Alaska and Its Resources* (1870). The Arno Press republished it in 1970. Dall summarized "the most valuable part of the present knowledge of Alaska," including much information on the region's Natives, its history, and its resources. It is a valuable work, even today. Henry W. Elliott, who had been a member of the Western Union Telegraph Expedition and subsequently spent much time in Alaska, particularly the Aleutian Islands, wrote *Our Arctic Province: Alaska and the Seal Islands*, which Charles Scribner's Sons published in 1906 in its Library of Contemporary Exploration and Adventure. It is illustrated with many sketches and remains a valuable reference work even today.

Constance Helmericks, then the wife of Harmon "Bud" Helmericks, penned *We Live in Alaska* (1945). The two came to Alaska from Arizona in 1941. They first lived in Anchorage, next moved to Seward, and then drifted the Yukon River in a homemade canoe. They lived off the country. Their sharp observations provide lively, entertaining reading and give a vivid picture of the country and the life of its people. They followed it with *We Live in the Arctic* (1949), written jointly, describing their journey on the Yukon, Koyukuk, and Alatna rivers in a hand-built canoe, building a cabin, and living off the land. They also cowrote *Our Alaskan Winter: Adventures in Eskimo Country* (1949) and *The Flight of the Arctic Tern* (1952). Their previ-

ous books described their journeys in Alaska by foot and canoe. In this latter book, they realized a longstanding dream and purchased a Cessna 140, which they named the *Arctic Tern*. They flew the plane from Boston, Massachusetts, to Alaska's Brooks Range. They visited the Arctic coast to Point Barrow, where Bud Helmericks got lost in his plane with famed explorer Margaret Oldenbourg aboard. The search party had to comb 49,062 square miles. The couple's *Arctic Hunter* (1955) continues their story of life in Alaska. The Helmericks eventually divorced and Bud remarried. In 1969 Alfred A. Knopf published his *The Last of the Bush Pilots*, the first book about bush pilots by a bush pilot.

Grant Pearson, with the aid of Philip Newell, authored *My Life of High Adventure* (1962). In it he retells life as a U.S. National Park Ranger in Mount McKinley National Park and about how he scaled Mount McKinley's south peak, the highest peak on the North American continent in 1932. May Wynne Lamb recounted her life as a teacher in *Life in Alaska: The Reminiscences of a Kansas Woman, 1916–1919* (1988), which Dorothy Wynne Zimmerman edited. It depicts life in the Kuskokwim River region in the village of Akiak. The book provides a picture of government educational policy and of Eskimo life at a time of transition. Besides teaching, she also distributed supplies for the men in charge of the government reindeer herds, grew a demonstration vegetable garden, and maintained a first aid station. She married Frank Lamb, a young physician. He died on December 23, 1918, at Old Hamilton, Alaska, of influenza, which ravaged the world in 1918. His death hastened his widow's return to the contiguous states.

Dr. Hall Young spent fifty years in Alaska as a Presbyterian missionary. His autobiography, *Hall Young of Alaska: "The Mushing Parson"* (1927), recounts his eventful life. He wrote three other books, *Adventures in Alaska* (1919), *The Klondike Clan*, and *Alaska Days with John Muir* (1915).

Claire Fejes, a well-known Alaska painter, wrote *Cold Starry Night: An Alaskan Memoir* (1996) before she died in the late 1990s. In it she describes her Alaskan life. She had left New York, where she was a painter and a sculptor and was exhibiting her artworks, to follow her husband to Fairbanks, Alaska—the last stop on the Alaska Railroad, where her husband intended to mine for gold. Fejes described life in isolated Fairbanks. She sketched a host of wonderful Fairbanks characters and existence in a "remote outpost where a hardy breed of Alaskans transforms loneliness into powerful bonds." She also wrote *People of the Noatak* (1966), in which she describes her life among the Eskimos along that river. Her experiences informed her artwork throughout her life.

Eva Greenslit Anderson wrote *Dog-team Doctor: The Story of Dr. Romig* (1940) about the life and activities of J. S. Romig, the dean of Alaskan physicians. Journalist Nancy Jordan wrote *Frontier Physician: The Life and Legacy of D. C. Earl Albrecht* (1996). Both are interesting accounts of physicians who performed pioneering work in Alaska, but neither one gives any sources consulted, nor do the volumes have any footnotes. The reader is left with having to take the authors at their word, for there is no way to check any of the facts.

The great Yukon River has had an enduring attraction for adventurer-writers. Frederick Schwatka, an American army officer and physician, wrote a number of fast-paced books, among them *Along Alaska's Great River* (1885), his account of a trip down the Yukon. Eugene Cantin penned *Yukon* (1973), an account of his trip down the Yukon River in 1972 in a one-man collapsible kayak, with one-hundred pounds of food and the determination to travel 1,200 miles from Carcross to Tanana. Rainer Höh, a German visitor, left us with his account of a raft trip down the great river, *Flossfahrt Nach Alaska* [A Raft Trip to Alaska] (1987). He and a friend built a raft in Carmacks in the Yukon Territory and drifted to Circle, Alaska. It is a good read. Larry Rice traversed Alaska by boat, foot, ski, and Cessna plane and wrote about his adventures in the ten essays that make up *Gathering Paradise: Alaska Wilderness Journeys* (1990).

John Hildebrand's *Reading the River: A Voyage Down the Yukon* is as much about navigating the Yukon as navigating through life. Hildebrand had moved to Alaska in the early 1970s with his wife. They built a cabin on a tributary stream connected to the Yukon. After the death of a child and the breakup of the marriage, Hildebrand abandoned the North and his dream of living off the land. A decade later he returned to canoe the length of the Yukon River, seeking "the path not taken, the people I had not become . . . I like to think someone had kept faith with their dreams even if I hadn't." He journeyed two thousand miles in three months, from Whitehorse to Andreasky. He met ordinary people leading extraordinary lives: aging pioneers, subsistence fishermen of his own generation, dog mushers, trappers, missionaries, politicians,

whites, Athapaskans, and Eskimos. He shared meals, set salmon nets, slept in tents, cabins, and fish camps. It is a beautifully written book about making choices and the hard realities of one's life.

Richard Leo quit an office job in New York City, took his girlfriend, Melissa, by the hand, and with nine dollars to his name and no survival skills, headed north to Alaska. Ten years later, three trackless miles to the nearest neighbor and forty-five from the nearest town (with a population of five hundred), Leo had a team of ten sled dogs and was living with his son Janus in a log house he built in the shadow of Denali. Melissa, unable to bear the isolation, had left years earlier, moved to Talkeetna, married there, and built a new life. This book is Leo's account of homesteading, muddling through, much hard work, and a great deal of help from his neighbors—loners and eccentrics all. It is a very well-written book, titled *Edges of the Earth: A Man, a Woman, A Child in the Alaskan Wilderness* (1991).

Leo wrote another book, *Way Out Here: Modern Life in Ice Age Alaska* (1996), in which he described where he lives, Alaska's Susitna Valley, bordering Denali National Park, "the last place left on earth were people still live in a Pleistocene Ice Age environment." Then there is Grant Sims, a journalist, who wrote *Leaving Alaska* (1994), an unsentimental, detailed, well-written, and one hopes truthful account of what it is like to live in Alaska, a portrait of a land under siege. In the mind's eye it is a vast, majestic, boundlessly rich region, a symbol of America's wilderness heritage, the last remaining frontier. But Sims points out that it is also our Amazon basin. If the United States, an environmentally aware nation, cannot save our own wild lands, how can we expect others to save theirs? This is a great read.

The late and beloved Margaret E. Murie, grand old dame of the American wilderness movement, wrote a very beautiful account of her adventures on the Alaskan frontier. *Two in the Far North* (1970) has become a classic. It tells of her growing up in Fairbanks in the gold mining, dog-team era, her graduation as the first woman from the Alaska Agricultural College and School of Mines in 1923, her experiences as a young bride and then trail mate and fellow explorer of Alaska's wilderness of her distinguished biologist husband, Olaus H. Murie.

Aviation came to Alaska in the early part of the twentieth century, and soon bush pilots tied the far-flung territory together. Following are a few of the books dealing with the topic. Ira Harkey, a Pulitzer Prize winner in 1963 for distinguished editorial writing, produced *Noel Wien: Alaska Bush Pilot*, which the University of Washington originally published under a slightly different title in 1974. The University of Alaska Press republished the volume in 1999 in its Classic Reprints Series, which Professor Terrence Cole of the University of Alaska Fairbanks edits and to which he writes individual introductions. Noel Wien founded Wien Alaska Airways in 1927, and the company continued, under various names, until it went out of business in 1984. Noel Wien died in July 1977, so he did not witness the demise of the airline he had built.

Violet Bjerke conceived and researched the story of aviator Carl Ben Eielson, Dorothy G. Page wrote it, and Ada M. and Hiram M. Drache edited *Polar Pilot: The Carl Ben Eielson Story* (1962). Eielson was a famous pioneer aviator who crashed and died on a flight to Siberia while trying to resupply and help remove a load of furs from the *Nanuk*, a trading vessel ice-bound off the North Cape, Siberia. *Wing It!* (1981) is the autobiography of pioneer Alaskan aviator Jack Jefford. The late James Greiner wrote *Wager with the Wind: The Don Sheldon Story* (1974). Sheldon, who died of cancer years ago, made high-risk mountain flying a full-time job. He became a legend in his lifetime among this special group of pilots.

Stan Cohen of Missoula, Montana, owns Pictorial Histories Publishing Company. He has compiled numerous pictorial histories dealing with World War II and planes in Alaska, including *The Forgotten War: A Pictorial History of North Western Canada* (1981). All are richly illustrated with black-and-white photos and feature a minimum of text. It is a useful series.

John Hail Cloe, together with Mitchell F. Monaghan, produced the informative and profusely illustrated *Top Cover for America: The Air Force in Alaska 1920–1983* (1984). Another illustrated history is Stephen E. Mills, *Arctic War Planes: Alaska Aviation in WWII* (1978). Bruce McAllister and Peter Corley Smith wrote and assembled *Wings Over the Alaska Highway: A Photographic History of Aviation on the Alaska Highway* (2001), illustrated with color and black-and-white photos. These books continue to roll off the presses.

The use of Alaska's resources and the affect on Alaska of America's conservation movement have attracted a number of writers. The late Lawrence W. Rakestraw wrote a useful article, "Conservation Historiography: An Assessment," published in the *Pacific Historical Review* 41 (August 1972); Ted C.

Hinckley followed with a fine piece "Alaska and the Emergence of America's Conservation Consciousness" in *Prairie Scout* 2 (1974). Rakestraw also wrote *A History of the United States Forest Service in Alaska* (1981). Hugh A. Johnson and Harold T. Jorgenson produced a fine, though now outdated, reference work, *The Land Resources of Alaska* (1963). Robert B. Weeden, formerly professor of resource management at the University of Alaska Fairbanks, wrote a fascinating volume, *Alaska: Promises to Keep* (1978), in which he stated that Alaska confronted the United States with a last chance to create new and viable relationships between people and nature. Thomas A. Morehouse, professor emeritus of political science in the Institute of Social and Economic Research at the University of Alaska Anchorage, edited and contributed to a highly useful volume, *Alaska Resources Development: Issues of the 1980s* (1984). Neil Davis, professor emeritus of geophysics at the Geophysical Institute of the University of Alaska Fairbanks, provided a summary and inventory of Alaska's energy resources in *Energy/ Alaska* (1984). Ken Ross has provided a summary of environmental issues in his *Environmental Conflict in Alaska* (2000).

Claus-M. Naske and Don M. Triplehorn have addressed the topic of federal policies and the development of Alaskan coal in "The Federal Government and Alaska's Coal," *Northern Engineer* 12 (Fall 1980); and Claus-M. Naske dealt with "The Navy's Coal Investigating Expedition in Alaska," *Northern Engineer* 14 (Spring 1982). Julia Triplehorn compiled *Alaska Coal: A Bibliography* (1982), an exhaustive guide to one of the state's major resources. Through the years, the Alaska Historical Library, part of the Division of Sate Libraries and Museums, formerly led by it energetic and personable director, Richard B. Engen, has been publishing useful inventories of its collections. A sampling of these inventories gives readers some idea of the treasures in the Alaska Historical Library: *An Inventory of the Papers and Personal Correspondence, 1933–1939, of Governor John W. Troy* (1982), *An Inventory of the Lyman Brewster Papers and Photographs Concerning the Reindeer Industry and Life in Nome, Alaska* (1932–1934), *The Southeast Alaska Salmon Fisheries: A Guide to Interviews with Men and Women Engaged in Commercial Fishing, 1913–1978* (1979), *A Guide to Alaska Native Corporation Publications* (1976), and *A Guide to the Alaska Packer' Association Records and to the APA Library* (1972).

Robert N. DeArmond, Alaska's best-known

historian, has compiled the excellent *Subject Index to the* Alaskan, *1885–1907, A Sitka Newspaper* (1974). The Elmer E. Rasmuson Library of the University of Alaska Fairbanks issues occasional papers; three examples must suffice: "An Index to the Early History of Alaska as Reported in the 1903–1907 Fairbanks Newspapers" (1980), "Alaskan Environmental Impact Statements: A Bibliography" (1980), and "Alaska Newspaper Tree" (1975), all frequently revised and updated. Other good sources for the historian are the old gold-town newspapers and the back files of journals edited by men and women who knew the North and tolerated no nonsense. Among these are *Alaska Sportsman, Alaska Weekly, Alaska-Yukon Magazine, Alaska Life,* and the *Alaska Journal.*

The Seattle Federal Records Service files contain vitally important Alaska manuscript materials that contain vitally important Alaska manuscript materials, such as those of the U.S. Forest Service, the U.S. district courts, the Bureau of Land Management, the Alaska Road Commission, the Bureau of Indian Affairs, and the Bureau of Commercial Statistics. Archivists there eventually determine which records are of historical value and will be retained. During the 1960s, Elmer W. Lindgard, archivist of the National Archives and Records, inventoried a number of collections, among them the Sir Henry Wellcome Papers and the records of the Alaska territorial government. The former include written and pictorial evidence both on the missionary leader William Duncan and on the socioeconomic changes occurring among his Tsimshian parishioners.

The records of the Alaska territorial government, spanning the period from 1884 to 1958, document Alaska's major government activities during the territorial period. These rich papers include the executive office central files, which reflect the varied roles Alaska's governors have played in their formal relations with other states and territories and the federal government. The General Correspondence file, from 1909 to 1958, comprises 176 feet, and it includes the annual reports of the governor; letters received and letters sent by the secretary of Alaska, 1900–12; the Territorial Legislative file, 1913–1939; and reports of surveys and studies, 1910–58. The National Archives Trust Fund Board and the National Archives and Records microfilmed the "General Correspondence of Alaskan Territorial Governors, 1909–1958" on 378 rolls of microfilm and, in 1980, published a pamphlet describing the series.

Congress established the Regional Archives of the National Archives and Records Administration in 1969 to preserve and make available for research records generated by the U.S. Courts and offices of federal agencies located outside of the Washington, D.C., metropolitan area. The National Archives, Pacific Region (Alaska) opened for business in 1990. The records held document the impact of the federal government and its various programs at the local, state, and regional level and provide a wide variety of research opportunities. Undoubtedly the National Archives, Pacific Region (Alaska), located at 645 West 3rd Avenue, Anchorage, has acquired many, if not most of the Alaska records that the National Archives, Pacific Region (Seattle) once held. It also has acquired copies of some of the National Archives and Records Administration microfilm publications found at the archives' home in College Park, Maryland.

A number of other manuscript depositories in the United State contain Alaska materials. Among the useful guides is *Guide to the Archives and the Manuscripts in the United States* (1961), edited by Philip Hamer. This work, continued with the *National Union Catalog on Manuscript Collections*, enables the researcher to spot recently accessioned papers dealing with Alaska, while *America: History and Life* makes it possible to keep track of current journal scholarship on the North. Connie Malcolm Bradbury and David Albert Hales (the latter formerly served as a librarian at the Elmer E. Rasmuson Library at the University of Alaska Fairbanks) compiled the very useful *Alaska Sources: A Guide to Historical Records and Information Services* (2001).

Patricia L. Davis has provided a useful introduction to the rich missionary records titled "The Alaska Papers, 1884–1939," *Historical Magazine of the Protestant Episcopal Church*, June 1971; and Harrison A. Brann has compiled "A Bibliography of the Sheldon Jackson Collection in the Presbyterian Historical Society," *Journal of Presbyterian History* 30 (September 1952).

Much work remains to be done to chronicle Alaska's maritime history. An important work is *Lewis and Dryden's Marine History of the Pacific Northwest* (1985), edited by Lewis Wright. Louis H. Sloss, a retired San Francisco attorney and descendent of one of the founders of the Alaska Commercial Company, has written two fine articles on that organization, which was important in the latter part of the nineteenth century in helping keep Alaska "tied together." His first article, with coauthor Richard A. Pierce, titled

"The Hutchison, Kohl Story: A Fresh Look," is found in the January 1971 issue of the *Pacific Northwest Quarterly*; a later piece by Sloss, "Who Owned the Alaska Commercial Company?" appeared in the same journal in its July 1977 issue. Truman R. Strobridge, archivist and historian, and Dennis L. Noble, a former member of the U.S. Coast Guard, penned the highly interesting *Alaska and the U.S. Revenue Cutter Service, 1867–1915* (1999).

The discovery, in 1968, of the giant Prudhoe Bay oil field on Alaska's North Slope moved Alaska, once again, into the American consciousness, just as the gold discoveries had in the late nineteenth and early twentieth centuries and the Japanese invasions of Kiska and Attu had in 1942. Once again, national magazines paid attention to the North, and one can expect that national and international needs for raw materials will keep Alaska at center stage for years to come. *National Geographic* well reflects the nation's intermittent interest in Alaska. Between 1888 and 1940, it published 111 articles dealing with Alaska, most of them between 1890 and 1910. From 1940 to 1945, a mere 9 articles appeared, but the number increased to 36 between 1945 and 1968. From 1968 to January 1984, the magazine published 31 articles on Alaska.

The sheer bulk of modern historical materials is overwhelming. Hearings on Alaska's problems are voluminous. They provide insight into the views of witnesses and committee members and often expose conflicts between Alaskans and the federal government, between different interest groups, and between competing federal agencies. Long draft environmental statements, concerning the use of millions of acres of land, furnish excellent examples.

In the wake of the Alaska Native Claims Settlement Act of 1971 and the subsequent need to classify 80 million acres for primary and secondary uses, several federal agencies struggled over the control of land. The disposition and use of lands was settled, for the time being, by the 1980 passage of the Alaska National Interest Lands Conservation Act (94 Stat. 2371). The voluminous draft environment statements concerning the use of those 80 million acres contain much information. The U.S. Forest Service proposed to put most of the area into national forests; the Bureau of Outdoor Recreation wanted to include most areas in the national system of wild and scenic rivers; and the National Park Service had expansive plans for national wilderness parks as well as national wild lands.

Environmental statements and studies produced by federal, state, and local government bodies, Native groups, and private industry fill whole shelves. The reports reflect Alaska's growing economic development in the wake of oil discoveries and state and Native land selection. These bulky studies employ a small army of consulting firms, university research institutes, environmentalists, planners, anthropologists, archaeologist, engineers, scientists, drafters, and writers. And since the history of a region is related to its environment, they offer at least sketchy historical assessments. The impact statements must also evaluate the environmental changes that a particular development will produce and offer alternative methods of reducing environmental disruption. The statements are designed to inform the public and to enable governments to act wisely.

The final six-volume environmental impact statement on the then proposed Trans-Alaska Pipeline furnishes a good example of these fast-accumulating studies. Prepared by a special interagency task force for the Federal Task Force on Alaskan Oil Development under the auspices of the U.S. Department of the Interior, it was published in 1972. The pipeline involved other studies, hearings, and comments, as well, among them two volumes of Hearings on Proposed Pipeline Legislation, March 6–10, 1972, State of Alaska, and Comments on the Proposed Trans-Alaska Pipeline (1971), prepared under the direction of the Alaska Department of Law.

On March 26, 1964, before Alaska became an oil state, it experienced a devastating earthquake that left much of south-central Alaska in shambles. In response, the federal government created the Federal Field Committee for Development Planning in Alaska, designed to help the state get back on its feet. It also prepared studies designed to facilitate the settlement of Native claims. Over the period of several years, the committee staff released more than forty studies, ranging from "An Approach to Marine Resource Development in Alaska" (1969) to the comprehensive, magnificent "Alaska Natives and the Land" (1968).

In the wake of the Alaska Native Claims Settlement Act of 1971, the State of Alaska and the federal government established the Joint Federal-State Land Use Planning Commission for Alaska in 1972. The commission was to serve during a decade of major change in land ownership and land management in Alaska. Its goal was to create a framework for the use and protection of the state's lands and resources in the years to come. On May 30, 1979, the commission delivered its final report. During its existence, it had published dozens of valuable studies, compiled a long list of recommendations and inquiries, made formal presentations, and conducted symposia. The commission issued much valuable historical material.

An energetic group of political scientists, economists, and historians at the University of Alaska Fairbanks has addressed political developments in the state. George W. Rogers, a perceptive student of Alaska, has written much on the 49th State. His "Party Politics or Protest Politics: Current Political Trends in Alaska," *Polar Record* 14, no. 91 (1969) examines political developments in Native and non-Native Alaska. The late Herman E. Slotnick wrote on "The 1960 Election in Alaska," *Western Political Quarterly*, March 1961; "The 1964 Election in Alaska," *Western Political Quarterly*, June 1965; and "The 1966 Election in Alaska," *Western Political Quarterly*, June 1967. The late Ronald E. Chinn covered "The 1968 Election in Alaska," *Western Political Quarterly*, June 1971. Thomas A. Morehouse, Gerald A. McBeath, and Linda Leask have written a fine study titled *Alaska's Urban and Rural Governments* (1984), and Gerald A. McBeath and Thomas A. Morehouse have addressed *The Dynamics of Alaska Native Self-Government* (1980). Victor Fischer has written a useful study on *Alaska's Constitutional Convention* (1975).

Economic development has been uppermost in the minds of most politicians, and many citizens as well. Gordon Scott Harrison edited a very useful volume titled *Alaska Public Policy: Current Problems and Issues* (1971, 1973). Divided into five parts, it gives the reader an overview and then deals with land, petroleum development, environmental quality, and rural development. At the end of each section are suggestions for further reading. Harrison is also the author of the useful volume titled *A Citizen's Guide to the Constitution of the State of Alaska* (1982). David T. Kresge, Thomas A. Morehouse, and George W. Rogers pooled their talents in *Issues in Alaska Development* (1977), which contains both basic and applied policy research on current social and economic problems of northern development. Peter G. Cornwall and Gerald McBeath edited *Alaska's Rural Development* (1982), which examines the social, economic, political, and cultural concerns surrounding the development of rural Alaska.

Numerous scholars have turned their attention on Alaska's struggle to obtain statehood. Ronald Beresford Bailey wrote a PhD dissertation for the University

of Illinois, "The Admission of Alaska into the United States: Adjustments in the Federal System" (1965). Bert Woodland Marley submitted "Alaska: Its Transition to Statehood" (1970) as his PhD dissertation to the University of Utah; and Richard Henry Bloedel wrote "The Alaska Statehood Movement" (1974) for his PhD dissertation at the University of Washington. Claus-M. Naske wrote "A History of the Alaska Statehood Movement" (1971) for his Ph.D. dissertation at Washington State University. It was subsequently published as *An Interpretative History of Alaskan Statehood* (1973); in 1985, the University Press of America published his revised and expanded *A History of Alaska Statehood*.

Gerald E. Bowkett, a newspaperman who once headed the University of Alaska Fairbanks public relations office, wrote *Reaching for A Star: The Final Campaign for Alaska Statehood* (1989). Finally, John S. Whitehead, a member of the history department at the University of Alaska Fairbanks for twenty years, weighed in with *Completing the Union: Alaska, Hawai'i, and the Battle for Statehood* (2004). Roger Bell in *Last Among Equals: Hawai'ian Statehood and American Politics* (1984) and Claus-M. Naske in *A History of Alaska Statehood* (1985) performed the archival research documenting the statehood battle for both territories. Whitehead contributed the recollections of participants in this epic struggle, which he gathered over a number of years.

The Alaska Native Claims Settlement Act of 1971 has generated many scholarly volumes. Mary Clay Berry's *The Alaska Pipeline: The Politics of Oil and Native Land Claims* (1975) is an excellent introduction to the subject. Robert D. Arnold and several collaborators wrote *Alaska Native Land Claims* (1976), a good historical summary of the Native struggle for a settlement of their claims. Donald Craig Mitchell, a lawyer, former vice president, and general counsel of the Alaskan Federation of Natives, wrote *Sold American: The Story of Alaska Natives and Their Land, 1867–1959* (1997 and 2003) and *Take My Land Take My Life: The Story of Congress's Historic Settlement of Alaska Native Land Claims, 1960–1971* (2001). These comprehensive volumes are indispensable for an understanding of Alaska Native history and the struggle for the 1971 settlement. The volumes are marred, however, by the inadequate method of citation the author used for his voluminous references to archival collections. An interested reader has no way to check the accuracy of any of those citations. David Stanway Case, another lawyer, wrote *Alaska Natives and American Laws* (1984), an indispensable reference work. David S. Case and David A. Voluck prepared a second revised edition of this classic work, published in 2002.

Alaska officially became a petroleum province when Richfield Oil Corporation discovered oil at the Swanson River in July 1957. Jack Roderick has written *Crude Dreams: A Personal History of Oil and Politics in Alaska* (1997). It is an informative and entertaining volume, but it has no footnotes; the reader has to take the author's account at face value. British historian Peter A. Coates did much of his research and writing for his PhD dissertation in Fairbanks at the University of Alaska. Lehigh University Press and Associated University Presses published this excellent volume in 1991 under the title *The Trans-Alaska Pipeline Controversy: Technology, Conservation, and the Frontier.* The University of Alaska Press republished it in 1993 under the same title. Coates succeeded in skillfully weaving together the conflicts between those interests intent on developing Alaska's resources and those desiring to conserve as well as regulate development from 1867 until after the completion of the Trans-Alaska Pipeline in 1976.

In 1968 Atlantic Richfield discovered the gigantic Prudhoe Bay oilfield on Alaska's North Slope. From then until about 1980, reporters and writers came to Alaska to witness, research, and write about the momentous changes oil development brought to Alaska. In August 1969, the Twentieth Alaska Science Conference was held on the campus of the University of Alaska Fairbanks. George W. Rogers edited the conference volume, titled *Change in Alaska: People, Petroleum, and Politics* (1970) in which he extracted the key economic, social, and political issues facing Alaska on the threshold of the oil boom. It is a very informative volume, featuring papers by key social scientists attempting to figure out what the future held. It makes for good reading.

Booton Herndon of Charlottesville, Virginia, had written extensively for American magazines and had published more than twenty books, some of them bestsellers. After the Prudhoe Bay discovery, he wrote *The Great Land* (1971). Herndon was a skillful interviewer, with an ability to get relevant details. His book is authoritative on the Prudhoe Bay discovery and its immediate aftermath. It is based almost exclusively on the personal experiences of individuals he interviewed, mostly officers in oil companies. He was not concerned with environmental consciousness,

which had begun to emerge in the 1960s. Nor was he familiar with Alaska's history, geography, popular culture, politics, and wildlife, among other things. He made mistakes, but it is a good read because of the key oil players who confided in him.

John Hanrahan, a former editor and local investigative and political reporter for the *Washington Post* and the *Washington Star,* and Peter Gruenstein, the former bureau chief of Capitol Hill News Service and also an investigative reporter, collaborated in producing *Lost Frontier: The Marketing of Alaska* (1977). Public advocate Ralph Nader wrote the introduction. The authors skillfully portray the dramatic conflicts between boomers and environmentalists, proponents of traditional Native subsistence culture versus the new breed of corporate Natives which the Alaska Native Claims Settlement Act of 1971 created; and how the entry of the multinational energy giants has swallowed up the old Alaska. This is a good book, well written and researched.

Bryan Cooper's *Alaska, The Last Frontier* (1973) is a credible account. Cooper, a British citizen, lived in London and enjoyed personal contacts with key executives and personnel inside British Petroleum, one of the three major operators on Alaska's North Slope along with Exxon and Atlantic Richfield. Again, despite numerous factual errors, this volume gives the reader a good insight into BP's corporate policies and mentality. Bradford Holly Tuck, who worked as an economist within the University of Alaska system's Institute of Social and Economic Research, wrote his PhD dissertation in 1973, "The Economic Impact of the Petroleum Sector on the State of Alaska," a useful, if densely written, analysis. Tom Brown wrote the first Sierra Club Battlebook, *Oil on Ice: Alaskan Wilderness at the Crossroads* (1971). Brown deals with the extraction of "an estimated 100 billion barrels of oil" from beneath the frozen North Slope, raising the question: "What effect will the extraction of that treasure have on Alaska's fragile environment, and what effect will it have on the landscape being transported to market through an equally fragile trans-Alaska pipeline?" Kenneth Andrasco, a photographer, and Marcus Halevi published *Alaska Crude: Visions of the Last Frontier* (1977). It is a photo album of striking black-and-white images, mostly of pipeline-related scenes. The text is insignificant.

James P. Roscow, a former reporter for *Business Week,* wrote *800 Miles to Valdez* (1977), an authoritative and accurate account of the planning, design, and construction of the Trans-Alaska Pipeline and various other peripheral activities on the North Slope oilfields. Roscow had unfettered access to the pipeline project personnel, from presidents to construction workers. The author viewed the project mostly through the eyes of the owners, and he ignored many complex issues the owners encountered during the construction. Only some of these were successfully resolved. Although rich with insider information, the book mentions but few negative facets of the project.

Robert Douglas Mead is the author of *Journeys Down the Line: Building the Trans Alaska Pipeline* (1978). It is a detailed and meticulously researched, thorough, and multifaceted account of the Trans-Alaska Pipeline project. It includes useful annotated source notes. Friends of the Earth published *Cry Crisis! Rehearsal in Alaska* (1974) by Harvey Manning, with chapters by Kenneth Brower and edited by Hugh Nash. This volume is an antidote to so much of the industry-friendly writing that loads down the bookshelves. The subtitle of the volume tells the reader about the author's viewpoint: *A Case Study of What Government by Oil Did to Alaska and Does to the Earth.*

Working stiffs have written some entertaining accounts of their experiences on the pipeline. Allen Chesterfield, who worked there for two years, wrote *The Alaskan Kangaroo: An Odyssey of the Alaskan Pipeline* (1980). He wrote about the Fairbanks union halls, where humanity from all walks of life stood in line for a job; the strong, the weak, alcoholics, hippies, professionals, welfare recipients, journeymen, gamblers, fly-by-nighters, and even a few get-rich-quickly camp call girls. They all signed on the dotted line. New hiring practices gave women a major breakthrough in the construction business. Ten percent of all pipeliners were women, including office workers, bull-cooks, laborers, and some welders. In short, this is a very good and educational read. Potter Wickware's *Crazy Money: Nine Months on the Trans-Alaska Pipeline* (1979) is a personal account of life, work, booze, brawling, gambling, sex, drugs, four-letter expletives, and heroic achievements at the southern terminus of the pipeline project in Valdez. The author is a University of California-Los Angeles graduate who studied classical literature, dropped out of the university, learned welding, and became a pipeline worker.

Pulitzer Prize winner and retired Pennsylvania newspaperman John Strohmeyer applied for and received two-year tenure for a journalism chair that Robert B. Atwood, editor and publisher of the *Anchorage Daily Times,* had endowed at the University of Alaska Anchorage. After the expiration of the two years, Strohmeyer remained in Alaska. He immersed himself in Alaska's public and political affairs for a couple of years and decided to write *Extreme Conditions: Big Oil and the Transformation of Alaska* (1993), a story that he felt needed to be told. His is a tale of epic greed, corruption, avarice, and criminality often more bizarre than fiction. It is well worth reading.

H. M. "Ike" Stemmer, editor and publisher of *Pipeline Digest* of Houston, Texas, wrote an uncritical account of the pipeline construction, *South from Prudhoe: A Story of the Trans Alaska Pipeline* (1977). Dermot Cole, a longtime reporter and editorial writer for the *Fairbanks Daily News-Miner* and the author of several other books, penned *Amazing Pipeline Stories: How Building the Trans Alaska Pipeline Transformed Life in America's Last Frontier* (1997). An affectionate glimpse at a defining period in Alaska' history, Cole's account uncovers many odd pipeline stories, and many others as well. Cole recounts the many trivial but transforming events that affected the lives of tens of thousands of mostly ordinary folks associated with the pipeline project.

Finally, there is Joe E. LaRocca's *Alaska Agonistes: The Age of Petroleum, How Big Money Bought Alaska* (2003). LaRocca hails from Pennsylvania. After service in the U.S. Army and jobs as a reporter and investigative writer for various Pennsylvania enterprises, he came to Fairbanks, where he became assistant news editor of the local paper. He also covered the annual sessions of the Alaska state legislature. After a stint as resources editor for the same paper, LaRocca became a news reporter, commentator, and legislative correspondent for KFAR Radio and TV in Fairbanks. He worked until his retirement in 1986 as an independent freelance reporter and correspondent in Alaska. His articles appeared in the *Anchorage Daily Times*, the *Daily Alaska Empire (Juneau)*, the *All-Alaska Weekly*, and other publications. In 1981–82 he completed an MPA at Harvard's John F. Kennedy School of Government.

LaRocca worked undercover as a laborer on the pipeline, where he observed firsthand the "wasteful, unsafe and inefficient construction practices" along the pipeline. The author stated that the cost of the construction of the pipeline was 10 billion dollars, not 8 billion dollars, as the pipeline consortium claimed. The author asserted that Alaska's state government had long been subservient to the oil industry, and it is true that Alaska has still not developed the expertise to deal with the industry on an equal basis. A good example of this is the legislature's failure to regularly examine the state's oil tax policies. LaRocca is correct in his assertion that Alaska's news media have failed in their mission to critically examine state-oil companies relations and inform the public. In short, the author attacked the performance of elected officials, bureaucrats, the oil industry, and the media. Despite its many flaws (such as misspellings and the absence of an index), the volume is a worthwhile addition to the libraries of interested Alaskans.

At four minutes past midnight on March 24, 1989, the supertanker *Exxon Valdez* ran aground on Bligh Reef, a rock shelf on the edge of the shipping channel outside Valdez Narrows in Prince William Sound. Exxon Corporation announced that the tanker had spilled 11.2 million gallons of crude oil into Prince William Sound. Later calculations by the state and independent investigators pegged the amount in excess of 20 million gallons. Numerous books have described, and some have analyzed, the spill. The best of these are Art Davidson's *In the Wake of the* Exxon Valdez (1990), a Sierra Club Book, and John Keeble, *Out of the Channel: The* Exxon Valdez *Oil Spill in Prince William Sound* (1991). Jeff Wheelwright, in his *Degrees of Disaster, Prince William Sound: How Nature Reels and Rebounds* (1994), described how a catastrophic assault on nature affects the environment. Scientists try to measure the changes and nature reels and adopts.

Riki Ott, who received a doctorate in marine biology and toxicology, gave up academia when she visited Cordova in the mid-1980s and decided to become a commercial fisher. She witnessed the oil spill and thereafter spent more than a decade writing *Sound Truth and Corporate Myth$: The Legacy of the* Exxon Valdez *Oil Spill* (2005). In this wonderful volume she challenged Exxon to account for its lies and evasions and urged the corporation to compensate its victims and revise its safety standards. She pointed out the deadly dangers from petroleum to living organisms. For humans these have been increased asthma, allergies, and increased cancer rates. In short, hers is a book that warns that the *Exxon Valdez* spill was not an isolated incident but was caused by our dependence on oil, and that offers a premonition that it will happen time and again.

Finally, the University of Oklahoma Press published the second edition of *Alaska: A History of the 49th State* (1987) by Claus-M. Naske and Herman E. Slotnick, a modern general history of Alaska. The University of Washington Press published *Alaska: An American Colony* (2002), by Stephen Haycox, also a general history of Alaska. In 2003, HarperCollins Publishers brought out Walter R. Borneman's *Alaska: Saga of a Bold Land*, another general history. Borneman is a lawyer and author, residing in Colorado, who has written extensively on Western history.

Obviously, there is much more. This essay is designed not to be exhaustive but to whet the reader's appetite for further inquiries. Historians will have to wade through all these materials, make sense of them, and then interpret Alaska's history. If they do their job well, they will discard the persistent romantic notions about Alaska. As historian Jeannette P. Nicols has recognized, these notions are a barrier, making it difficult to make use of the historical experience as a guide to solving present problems. But they also can, and should, entertain and instruct all of us in numerous ways. Perhaps in the years ahead, history will also be used as a basis for fictional creations. Jack London and Rex Beach focused on the Gold Rush era. Edna Ferber dealt with modern-day Alaska. The material exists, and Alaska's spectacular scenery and varied cultures undoubtedly will challenge writers in the future. On the other hand, it may just be that Americans will respond to Alaska solely in economic terms—as a supplier of needed resources—as they have in the past with our gold rushes, foreign invasions, or the construction of history's largest project, the nearly eight-hundred-mile-long oil pipeline. Only the future will tell.

Index

Institute of Social and Economic Research (U. of Alaska), 354
Interior Alaska, 16, 18, 25
International Arctic Research Center, 386
Inuits, 84. *See also* Eskimos
Inupiat Paitot, formation of, 286, 287
Iñupiats, 79, 320, 432n2
Itelmen (Kamchadals), 38, 50
Ivan IV (Ivan the Terrible), 33

Jackson, Henry M. ("Scoop"), 230, 234, 292, 295, 296, 313
Jackson, Sheldon ("Apostle of Alaska"), 5, 105, 116, 117, 118, 119, 139, 141
Jackson College, Sheldon, 106, 438n33
Jamestown, USS, 116
Japan, 65, 262, 263; Aleutians invasion by, 176, 177, 178–81, 184–86, 196; fisheries market, 7, 8; passage to, 39, 40–41, 49
Japanese, 262; in Alaska, 193–94; invasion and occupation of Aleutians, 5, 178–81, 184–86; oil and gas industry, 331–32; World War II evacuation and relocation of, 189–90, 194–96
Japanese Americans, World War II evacuation and relocation of, 189–90, 193, 194–96
Johnson, Andrew, 92, 93, 94, 99, 101
Johnson, Lyndon, 233, 265, 266
Joint Federal-State Land Use Planning Commission for Alaska, 299, 301, 310, 312, 313–14
Jones Act, 154
Judicial districts, judges, 131–32, 407
Juneau, Alaska, 4, 16, 19, 193, 257, 407; as capital, 141, 268; gold mines at, 113–14, 115;

population, 225, 411; proposed movement of capital from, 267–68
Juneau, Joe, 113

Kamchadals (Itelmen), 38, 50
Kamchatka, Kuril Islands, Aleutians Diocese, 85
Kamehameha the Great, King, 68, 70
Kashevarov, Aleksandr F., 91–92
Katmai National Monument, 17, 19
Kaumualii, King, 70
Kenai, Alaska, 148, 332, 411
Kenai Bay, Alaska, 60, 71
Kenai Fjords National Park, Alaska, 349
Kenai National Moose Range, Alaska, oil on, 5, 326, 328, 329, 332–33
Kenai Peninsula, Alaska, 17, 257, 347; oil and gas leases, 326, 329, 332; Russian settlements, 53, 54; Swanson River oil field, 239, 250
Kenay, Military District of, Alaska, 403
Kennewick Man, 1, 20
Ketchikan, Alaska, 7, 16, 163, 167, 225, 257, 258; Gravina Island bridge, 387–88; pulp mills in, 249–50, 376; secession movement, 220, 221
Khitrovo, Safron, 43, 46
Khlebnikov, Kyrill T., 69, 71
Kiksadi clan, 110–11
Killisnoo, Alaska, 164, 192, 193
Kinkead, John Henry, 118
Kiska Island, Alaska, 178, 184, 185–86, 191
Klondike Gold Rush, 4, 126–28; Alaska-Canada boundary dispute, 141–42; Alaskan Natives, 142–47; impacts of, 139–41
Klondike (Thron-diuck) River, Yukon, 125, 126

Klukwan, Inc., 299
Klukwan Reserve, 299
Knowles, Anthony Carroll ("Tony"), 276, 361, 362, 369, 373, 375, 376, 393, 398; as governor, 371–72, 374, 377–78, 380, 381, 382
Kodiak, Alaska, 19, 60, 86, 148, 160, 178, 191, 265
Kodiak Island, Alaska, 17, 56, 57, 60, 82, 112, 257, 260; Russian settlements on, 53, 54; U.S. military on, 5, 95, 101, 187; World War II base on, 180, 184
Koniag Inc., 307, 424
Koniags, 53, 63
Konstantin Nikolaevich, Grand Duke, and sale of Russian America, 88, 92–93
Korean War, 229
Koyukuk River, Alaska, 79, 104, 139
Kozlov, Mr. (shipbuilder), 37
Krug, Julius A., 224
Kuparuk oil field, Alaska, 271, 320, 322, 335, 338, 395
Kuril Islands, Russia, 2, 40, 49, 56, 79, 85, 184
Kuskowim Corporation, 306
Kuskokwim River, Alaska, 18, 26, 79, 139

Labor, 82; Aleuts as forced, 60, 83; New Archangel, 68–69; RAC recruitment of, 80–81
Ladue, Joseph, 124, 125, 439n10
Lamb, Jack, 345
Land, 268, 374, 447n59; Alaskan Natives and, 144–47, 171–72, 289–93, 294–300, 303, 454n14; coal, 150–51; conservation and, 314–15; distribution of, 11, 260–61; federal, 312–13; federal agencies and, 310–12; grants of, 229, 230, 234; oil and gas leases, 164, 238–41, 293–94, 329, 330; Project Chariot and, 284–86;

RCA. *See* Radio Corporation of
America

Reagan, Ronald, 196; land issues,
314–15; military spending,
212–13, 216

Real estate business, 1980s, 277–78

Recession, 1980s, 277–79

Redoubt Saint Dionysius, Russian
America, 75, 76, 77

Refineries, Nikiski, 329, 333

Reid, Frank, 127

Reindeer, introduction of, 119,
139–40

Reparations, to Japanese and
Aleuts, 196, 443n31

Republican Party: and "bridge
to nowhere," 388–89; and
Hawaii and Alaska statehood,
225–26, 228, 229; state elections,
252–53, 368–69, 375–76; state
government, 264, 373–74

Reservations: Alaskan Natives,
171–72, 298–99, 441n34;
fisheries, 160

Reserves, Native, 289

Retirement system, reform of,
393–94

Revenue Marine Service, 109, 110

Revenues: oil industry, 6–7, 244–46,
254, 342, 364, 371, 394–96; state,
279–82, 349–57, 376, 379

Rezanov, Anna, 61, 64, 65

Rezanov, Nikolay P., 61, 67;
Russian-American Company
and, 61, 62, 65–66

Richardson Road (Richardson
Highway), 146, 148, 161

Richfield Oil Corporation, 235,
250, 326, 327–29, 331. *See also*
Atlantic Richfield

Rivers, Ralph J., 231, 253, 255, 290

Roads, road system, 5, 104, 203,
206; ALCAN, 182–83; funding
for, 148, 254, 255, 262

Rock, Howard, 283, 288

Roosevelt, Franklin Delano, 5, 169,
173, 189, 222, 223, 323

Roosevelt, Theodore, 5, 135, 149,
151; Alaska-Canada boundary
dispute, 141–42

Ruedrich, Randy, 391, 396, 397

Russia: Crimean War, 73, 78, 83,
184; in Siberia, 33–34; factory
ships, 262–63; fur trade, 49–51;
North American Territory,
74–75; under Peter the Great,
34–35; sale of Russian America,
87–95; settlements, 53–54. *See
also* Soviet Union

Russian America, 2, 437n39;
Alexander Baranov and, 67, 70;
British and Americans in, 63,
64; Chistiakov's administration,
78–79; Hudson's Bay Company
trade in, 77–78; labor shortages,
80–81; mutiny against, 68–69;
Rezanov and, 65–66; Russian
navy and, 73–74; Russian
Orthodox Church in, 84–86;
sale of, 87–89, 92–94; settlement
of, 59–60; telegraph line,
90–91; territory of, 74–75; trade
agreements, 75–77; United
States in, 94–95; Wrangel's
administration of, 79–80

Russian-American Company
(RAC), 2–3, 8, 51, 53, 62, 64,
70, 71, 73, 74, 80, 85, 123;
government review of, 89–92;
and Hudson's Bay Company,
75–78, 87; and Fort Ross, 67,
68; liquidation of, 99–100;
management changes in, 78–79;
and Native Alaskans, 81–84;
opposition to, 91–92; Rezanov
and, 65–66; and sale of Russian
America, 88–89

Russian Orthodox Church, 3, 28,
57, 60, 80; Bishop Innokentii's
work, 84–86; at Sitka, 107–108

Russians, 2–3, 81; and Aleuts,
27, 28, 52; fur hunters,
49–50; influence of, 119, 121;
settlements, 53–54; and Tlingits,
23, 24, 64–65

Sadlerochit field, Alaska, 322, 338

Saint Elias, Mount, Alaska and
Yukon, 16, 42, 56

Saint George Island, Alaska, 51,
191, 193, 404, 405

Saint Julian Island. *See* Bering
Island

Saint Lawrence Island, Alaska, 37,
106

Saint Lawrence Island Reserve, 298

Saint Michael Cathedral (Sitka),
theft from, 107–108

Saint Paul (ship), voyage of, 41–42

Saint Paul Island, Alaska, 51, 191,
404, 405

Saint Peter (ship), 41; voyage of,
42–43, 46; winter stranding of,
46–47

Salmon farms, 7, 376

Salmon fisheries, 4, 7, 8, 11, 100,
107, 111, 119, 163, 249, 261, 262,
289, 347, 376; protection and
management of, 157–60, 167–68,
259–60

Salmon processing, 17, 111–12,
155, 159

Samoilov, Konstantin A., 57;
settlements, 53–54

San Francisco, Calif., 66, 112, 126,
157

Santa Rosa Mission, Calif., and Fort
Ross, 67–68

Satellite earth stations, 209–10

Savings and loan crisis, 1980s,
278–79

Sawmills, 80, 163

Schaeffer, Georg Anton, 70

Schools, 119, 153; church-federal
system, 105–106; Russian, 3, 80,
83, 86

Science and Technology
Foundation, 356

Scientists, 80; on Second
Kamchatka Expedition, 39, 41;
U.S. Army, 102–104

Scurvy, 42, 43, 46, 54, 56, 62, 66, 67

Seafood processing, 8, 17